CONTENTS

Scheme of Examination

Section-I

S.No.	Subject	Questions	Marks
1.	Mental Ability and Reasoning Ability	20	20
2.	General Awareness	20	20
3.	English Language & Comprehension	20	20
4.	Hindi Language & Comprehension	20	20
5.	Numerical Aptitude & Data Interpretation	20	20
	Total	**100**	**100**

Section-II

S.No.	Subject	Questions	Marks
1.	MCQs pertaining to Post-Graduation qualification and teaching methodology required for the post.	**200**	**200**

Previous Years' Paper

Delhi Subordinate Services Selection Board

DSSSB-PGT (Economics) Recruitment Exam-2024

(Exam held on 21-07-2024)

Subject Knowledge – Economics & Teaching Methodology

1. Geographical Indications fall under which type of intellectual property rights?

A. Artistic and Literary Property
B. Industrial Property
C. Database Protection
D. Sui Generis Systems

2. Which of the following countries has the highest public education expenditure as a share of GDP?

A. Bhutan
B. Marshall Islands
C. Iceland
D. Kiribati

3. Wage rigidity — the observation that wages ______ — has important implications for labour markets and macroeconomic performance. Empirical evidence on the extent, causes and consequences of wage rigidity on the individual level is relatively scant, however.

A. cannot be adjusted upwards
B. cannot be adjusted downwards
C. remain at the same level
D. can be adjusted downwards

4. Which of the following is NOT a risk related to agriculture in India?

A. Yield Risk
B. Price Risk
C. Weather Risk
D. Technology Risk

5. Which of the following comes under human capital?

A. Talent, skills and abilities only
B. Health status of the population, stock of knowledge, talent, skills and abilities
C. Stock of knowledge only
D. Health status of the population only

6. ______ means the ability of the environment to absorb degradation.

A. Absorptive capacity
B. Extensive extraction capacity
C. Carrying capacity
D. Development capacity

7. The common measure of income inequality is the ratio of incomes received by the top ______ and bottom ______ of the population.

A. 10%, 80%
B. 30%, 50%
C. 20%, 40%
D. 05%, 10%

8. The concept of effective demand is associated with the name of ______.

A. Krugman
B. Marshall
C. Keynes
D. Say

1. B	2. D	3. B	4. D	5. B	6. A	7. C	8. C

9. Which of the following assumptions is NOT correct with respect to trade and development?

A. Openness to trade helps countries utilise their resources better in several ways.
B. Human and economic development often move in concert.
C. International trade shows a strong positive correlation with investment.
D. One of the principle characteristics of technological knowledge is that it cannot be transferred across countries.

10. ______ occurs when individuals do not possess the same level of material wealth or overall living economic conditions.

A. Inequality of outcomes
B. Inequality of community relationships
C. Inequality of opportunity
D. Inequality of contingent circumstances

11. Which of the following statements are NOT correct?

1. Income inequality is much more serious than health inequality.
2. Income inequality can be reduced by imposing tax or by other measures but health inequality is structural in nature.
3. It requires longer time to bring down health inequality as compared to income inequality.
4. Income inequality can be reduced even in short term by transferring income from rich to poor.
5. Health inequality may create negative externality.
6. Health and health seeking behaviour of the individuals depends on physical status.

A. 1 and 2 B. 1 and 4
C. 1 and 6 D. 1 and 5

12. Which of the following statements is NC correct?

A. Gender development plays an importa role in the context of inclusive growt
B. Gender development plays an importa role in the context of social justice.
C. Human development index is gend insensitive.
D. Gender development index is gend insensitive.

13. The concept of industrial reserve army introduced by ______.

A. Joan Robinson
B. Karl Marx
C. Turgot
D. JS Mill

14. In the Indian context, agricultural economi is NOT related to which of the following

A. Farm mechanisation
B. Yield gap analysis
C. Subsidy issues
D. Rural credit needs

15. Which of the following is NOT included i the factors determining rural-urban mark linkages in India?

A. Raw materials
B. Sourcing inputs
C. Access to public services
D. Catering to rural consumers

16. Who propounded various rules related marginal utility?

A. Walrus B. Carl Menger
C. Jevens D. Gossen

17. Who tried to give a new and scientific for to Bentham's Utilitarianism?

A. Adam Smith B. Keynes
C. Ricardo D. JS Mill

9. D	10. A	11. C	12. D	13. B	14. C	15. A	16. D	17. D

R. Gupta's®

POPULAR MASTER GUIDE

DSSSB–TEACHERS

PGT

ECONOMICS

Recruitment Exam

by

RPH Editorial Board

2027
EDITION

RAMESH PUBLISHING HOUSE, NEW DELHI

Published by

O.P. Gupta *for* Ramesh Publishing House

Admin. Office

12-H, New Daryaganj Road, Opp. Officers' Mess,
New Delhi-110002 ✆ 23275224, 23245124

E-mail: info@rameshpublishinghouse.com

For Online Shopping: www.rameshpublishinghouse.com

Showroom

• Balaji Market, Nai Sarak, Delhi-110006 ✆ 23282525 📱 9354373464
• 4457, Nai Sarak, Delhi-110006

Book Code: R-1310

ISBN: 978-93-5012-009-5

Price: ₹ 470

Printed at: Deepak Offset, Delhi

18. In classical theory, the equality between saving and investment is brought about by ______.

A. income B. rate of interest
C. multiplier D. consumption

19. Who is known as the father of agricultural economics?

A. John Wynn Baker
B. Anne van den Ban
C. Allan Buckwell
D. Henry Charles Taylor

20. Assured a high family income through higher support prices for their crops and through hardworking and cheap labourers; they should be able to settle their children abroad. The Developmental Goal given above relates to which of the following categories of individuals?

A. Farmers who depend only on rain for growing crops
B. An adivasi from Narmada valley
C. A rural woman from a land owning family
D. Prosperous farmers from Punjab

21. If a constant 60 is subtracted from each of the values of X and Y, then regression coefficient is:

A. reduced by 60
B. not changed
C. 1/60th of the original regression coefficient
D. increased by 60

22. Time series forecasting is one of the most applied data science techniques, which is used in which of the following?

1. Business
2. Finance
3. Skill development
4. Supply chain management
5. Neuro stimulations
6. Production
7. Schedule of rates
8. Inventory planning

A. 1, 2, 3, 4 and 5
B. 3, 4, 5, 6 and 7
C. 2, 3, 4, 5 and 8
D. 1, 2, 4, 6 and 8

23. 'MPI' developed by Niti Aayog is based on ______ indicators.

A. 8 B. 9
C. 10 D. 12

24. Which of the following is/are correct about the environmental economics?

1. It studies the impact of environmental policies and devises solutions to problems resulting from them.
2. It can either be prescriptive-based or incentive-based.
3. Externalities, the additional costs of doing business that are not paid by the business or its consumers, is a major subject.
4. Another major subject of environmental economics is placing a value on public goods, such as clean air, and calculating the costs of losing those goods.
5. Since environmental goods are for a country, environmental economics often requires a national approach.

A. 1, 2, 4 and 5 B. 1, 2, 3 and 4
C. 1, 3, 4 and 5 D. 1, 2, 3 and 5

25. Find the INCORRECT statement with reference to the National Food Security Act, 2013.

A. Implemented in all the States/UTs
B. Rights to welfare based approach
C. Life-cycle approach
D. Food security is characterised by availability, access, utilisation and stability of food.

18. B	**19.** D	**20.** D	**21.** B	**22.** D	**23.** D	**24.** B	**25.** B

26. Data arranged in chronological order or two variable data where one of the variables is time.

The above statement is related to which of the following?

A. Spatial Classification
B. Univariate Distribution
C. Variable
D. Time Series

27. Small enterprises are defined with turnover limit up to ______.

A. ₹ 5 Crore
B. ₹ 1 Crore
C. ₹ 10 Crore
D. ₹ 50 Crore

28. Who among the following defined rent as 'that portion of the produce of the earth which is paid to the landlord for the use of the original and indestructible powers of the soil'?

A. David Ricardo
B. James Mill
C. Adam Smith
D. Thomas Malthus

29. Which of the following statements is NOT appropriate regarding deadweight loss?

A. Price ceilings, such as price controls and rent controls can all potentially create deadweight losses.
B. Taxation can all potentially create deadweight losses.
C. Price floors, such as minimum wage and living wage laws cannot create deadweight losses.
D. Deadweight loss occurs when supply and demand are not in equilibrium.

30. An approach to forecasting using time-series data is:

A. only vector autoregression
B. only simultaneous equation regression model
C. single equation regression model, simultaneous equation regression model and vector autoregression
D. only single equation regression model

31. A purely random process is a stationary series with:

A. only zero mean
B. positive mean
C. only zero variance
D. zero mean and zero variance

32. Which of the following statements regarding economic reforms in India is INCORRECT?

A. Poor agricultural productivity growth, inadequate infrastructure and labour market rigidities are the reasons for poor industrial growth.
B. India's labour laws are the most protective of the organised labour
C. In the 1990s, the manufacturing sector underwent restructuring.
D. After 1991, public sector provided much of the infrastructure.

33. After independence, the economic policies in India were ______ looking with massive involvement of the government in the secondary sector.

A. inward B. backward
C. forward D. outward

34. Externalities are indirect costs or benefits that a third party incurs. Which of the following is NOT a type of Externality?

A. Positive Consumption
B. Negative Consumption
C. Negative Production
D. Private Production

26. D	27. D	28. A	29. C	30. D	31. A	32. D	33. A	34. D

35. In utilitarian social welfare functions, individual utilities are considered in aggregate. For two individuals x and y, it will be denoted as which of the following, where W is the social welfare function?

A. $W = \frac{u(x)}{u(y)}$

B. $W = u(x) + u(y)$

C. $W = u(x) - u(y)$

D. $W = u(x) \times u(y)$

36. The first known use of the term 'econometrics' was given by:

A. Walter Eucken B. Paweł Ciompa

C. John Maynard D. Adolph Wagner

37. In which year, the GATT was expanded to form the WTO?

A. 1985 B. 1947

C. 1990 D. 1995

38. The response of the dependent variable in the VAR system to shocks in the error terms is traced by:

A. volatility clustering

B. volatility

C. impulse response function

D. partial autocorrelation function

39. A collection of random variables ordered in time is known as ________.

A. stochastic process

B. spurious variable

C. non-stationary series

D. stationary series

40. When the government tries to, meet the gap of public expenditure and public revenue through borrowing from the banking system, it is called:

A. deficit financing

B. public financing

C. credit financing

D. debt financing

41. Political economy is an interdisciplinary branch of the social sciences. It focuses on the interrelationships of:

A. public policy only

B. governments only

C. individuals only

D. individuals, governments and public policy

42. In the context of corporate finance, what is the full form of CAPM?

A. Capital Asset Pricing Model

B. Capital Average Pricing Model

C. Cumulative Average Pricing Management

D. Capital Asset Pricing Management

43. 'Formal contracts and monetary compensation are absent in many kinds of institutional settings, but agents may nevertheless try to influence each other through verbal or written communication, or by producing data or evidence to support their case.'

The above statement indicates which issue in the economic systems?

A. Communication issue

B. Information Aggregation issue

C. Reputation issue

D. Norms, Expectations and Coordination issue

44. Real estate is a name given to land, buildings and legal rights over immovable property, especially when they can be priced for possible sale in an actual or potential market. Usually such a price reflects ________.

A. Anticipated Demand

B. Discounted Demand

C. Forced Demand

D. Derived Demand

35. B	36. B	37. D	38. C	39. A	40. A	41. C	42. A	43. A	44. D

45. Political economy is an interdisciplinary branch of the social sciences. It focuses on the interrelationships of ______.

A. governments B. individuals
C. public policy D. political parties

46. Which of the following is NOT one of the main functions of the financial market?

A. It provides pricing information resulting from the interaction between buyers and sellers in the market when they trade the financial assets.
B. It provides facilities for interaction between the investors and the borrowers.
C. It ensures liquidity by providing a mechanism for an investor to sell the financial assets.
D. It ensures low cost of transactions and high cost of information.

47. Which of the statements given below is NOT correct?

A. Ranade opposed the laissez-faire policy by the government in economic matters.
B. Kautilya regarded economics as a continuous process.
C. The Drain Theory is the greatest contributions of Deshbandhu Chittaranjan Das.
D. Mahatma Jyotiba Phule called farmers as the cloth of the world.

48. Face value is the value stated on the face of the bond and is known as:

A. redemption value
B. per value
C. intrinsic value
D. market value

49. The cash balance equation M = KPT was given by:

A. Keynes B. Pigou
C. Robertson D. Marshall

50. Labour economics involves the study of all that affects workers before, during, and after their working lives. Which of the following DOES NOT come under the scope of labour economics?

A. Non-work time B. Fertility
C. Suffrage D. Discrimination

51. The size of a country's labour force, within a given total population, depends on two factors: the proportion of the total population that is of ______ and the proportion of these who are ______.

A. working age; unemployed
B. non-working age; underemployed
C. non-working age; work for gain
D. working age; work for gain

52. Which of the following is/are correct?

1. Fundamental principle of double-entry accounting says that the company's assets and resources must be exactly equal
2. When an item is purchased, it is either capitalised or expensed
3. Assets and resources always carry the same sign, so the equilibrium of the balance sheet is always maintained
4. Inventories, receivables, marketable securities and cash represent the current assets

A. 1, 2 and 3 B. 2, 3 and 4
C. 1, 2 and 4 D. 1, 3 and 4

53. A '______' is usually a group of persons who normally live together and take their meals from a common kitchen unless the exigencies of work prevent any of them from doing so.

A. serviceable temporary house
B. census house
C. permanent house
D. household

45. D	46. D	47. C	48. B	49. C	50. C	51. D	52. C	53. D

54. The labour force comprises all those who work for gain within the labour market, whether as:

A. employees and employers
B. employees, employers, self-employed, and the unemployed who are seeking work
C. self-employed
D. unemployed, who are seeking work

55. _______ is responsible for financing the firm and acts as an intermediary between the financial system's institutions and markets, on the one hand, and the company, on the other.

A. Business Manager
B. Chief Managing Director
C. Financial Investor
D. Chief Financial Officer

56. Bulk finance for developing various large scale housing projects by state housing boards and development authorities is made available at reasonable rates by the HUDCO.

In the above context, which of the following is the full form of HUDCO?

A. Housing and Urban Development Corporation
B. Home and Utility Development Corporation
C. Housing and Union Development Company
D. Household and Urban Development Corporation

57. The main reason for India's third world country status is the poverty that prevailed after independence, which was a result of the British economic legacy. Which of the following statements is inconsistent with regard to British economic exploitation of India?

1. Introduction of Zamindari system
2. Introduction of rail network
3. Evil result of transfer of land
4. Promotion of small scale of industries
5. Imposition of heavy duty on the Indian export goods
6. Drain of India's wealth

A. 3 and 4 B. 2 and 5
C. 2 and 4 D. 1 and 4

58. The welfare definition of economics was introduced by _______.

A. Adam Smith B. Alfred Marshall
C. Lionel Robbins D. JR Hicks

59. Behavioural economics combines elements of _______ to understand how and why people behave the way they do in the real world.

A. Economics and Sociology
B. Economics and Entrepreneurship
C. Economics and Psychology
D. Economics and Anthropology

60. Health Economics is an applied field of study that allows for the systematic and rigorous examination of the problems faced in promoting _______ for all.

A. health B. medical insurance
C. wealth D. healthcare services

61. Most commonly observed managerial compensation practices greatly facilitate collusive behaviour in long-run _______.

A. duopolies B. oligopolies
C. perfect markets D. monopolies

62. Which of the following is NOT included in the stages of the ARIMA model?

A. Model application
B. Model estimation and validation
C. Model identification
D. Model classification

54. B	**55.** D	**56.** A	**57.** C	**58.** B	**59.** C	**60.** A	**61.** D	**62.** D

63. Which of the following steps is NOT recommended for a successful 'make-or-buy' decision?

A. Selecting providers
B. Creating negativity for outsourcing
C. Exploring strategic implications
D. Cost/Performance analysis

64. Which of the following is NOT the primary objective of a firm?

A. To maximise the output
B. To achieve the life goal
C. To maximise the sales
D. To maximise the growth of the organisation

65. These people are rarely leaders, but they do adopt new ideas before the average person. That said, they typically need to see evidence that the innovation works before they are willing to adopt it.

Which of the following categories of persons is referred to in the above statement?

A. Late Majority B. Early Adopters
C. Early Majority D. Laggards

66. Which state topped the Indian innovation index in major states category in 2023?

A. Tamilnadu B. Telangana
C. Karnataka D. Maharashtra

67. The analysis of variance is carried out by using _______.

A. Z-Test B. t-Test
C. X^2-Test D. F-Test

68. 'Innovative products' refer to products introduced to the market in the last _______ and _______ products are defined as 'new to the firm'.

A. two years, very good
B. three years, innovative
C. one year, incompetent
D. four years, complete

69. Which of the following statements is NC correct?

1. Comparative analysis of differe countries suggests that industrialisation India has no standard model of industr capitalism.
2. In developed countries, the majori of people are in the services secto followed by agriculture and less th 10% are in industries.
3. In India, over 90% of the work, wheth it is in agriculture, industry or servic is in the organised or formal sector.
4. Government employment in India h played a major role in overcomi boundaries of caste, religion and regic
5. The government has laws to moni conditions in the unorganised secto but in practice they are left to t whims and fancies of the employer contractor.

A. 1 and 5 B. 3 and 4
C. 1 and 3 D. 2 and 3

70. Which of the following is NOT characteristic of modern manufacturing?

A. Huge capital
B. Very small organisations
C. A complex machine technology
D. Executive bureaucracy

71. Investing in activities aimed at discoveri new knowledge and developing ne technologies is known as:

A. commercialisation
B. research and development (R&D)
C. open innovation
D. technology management

63. B	**64.** B	**65.** C	**66.** C	**67.** D	**68.** B	**69.** D	**70.** B	**71.** B

72. Which of the following is NOT a major element of the political environment?

A. The prevailing economic system.
B. The degree of politicisation of business and economic issues.
C. The dominant ideologies and values of the major political parties.
D. The nature and profile of political leadership and the thinking of political personalities.

73. Which theory of profit states that profit will be higher in industries characterised by a high degree of variability in their revenues of their cost?

A. Frictional theory
B. Innovation theory
C. Monopoly theory
D. Risk bearing theory

74. There are several limitations of the Diffusion of Innovation Theory. Which of the following is NOT one of the limitations?

A. It works better with the adoption of behaviours rather than cessation or prevention of behaviours.
B. It does not foster a participatory approach to the adoption of a public health programme.
C. It did not originate in public relations and it was not developed to explicitly apply to the adoption of new behaviours or health innovations.
D. It doesn't take into account an individual's resources or social support to adopt new behaviour (or innovation).

75. Which test is known as 'test of goodness of fit'?

A. t-test B. X^2-test
C. F-test D. Z-test

76. If two events, A and B, are mutually exclusive then which option will be true?

A. $P(A+B) = P(A) + P(B)$
B. $P(AB) = P(A) \times P(B)$
C. $P(A/B) = P(A) - P(B)$
D. $P(AB) = P(A)/P(B)$

77. Which of the following is/are the factor(s)/ resource(s) influencing the location of a proposed iron and steel plant on a developed island?

A. Iron ore only
B. Limestone, iron ore, coal and water
C. Coal and water only
D. Limestone only

78. Different license options that a party may request from NETL do NOT include:

(*i*) Exclusive - Licensor grants all rights to the licensee; licensor cannot grant rights to another.
(*ii*) Co-exclusive - Licensor grants all rights or rights to specific fields of use to a limited number of licensees (two or more).
(*iii*) Partially exclusive - Licensor grants all rights to the licensee in a particular field of use; licensor can grant rights to another in a different field of use
(*iv*) Expensive - For multiple worlds, licensor can grant rights to another world.

A. (*i*) B. (*iv*)
C. (*iii*) D. (*ii*)

79. If innovation is to be subsidized, a natural place to start is to increase the quantity and quality of _______.

A. human capital
B. reserve capital
C. surplus capital
D. ecological capital

72. A	73. D	74. C	75. B	76. A	77. B	78. B	79. A

80. Which of the following industries is known as the sunrise industry?

A. Cotton textile industry
B. Iron and steel industry
C. Cottage industry
D. IT industry

81. Which of the statements given below is NOT correct?

A. The initial allocation determines the range of possible outcomes given the initial allocation.
B. There is nothing within the barter economy that addresses or acts as a corrective for inequality.
C. Through barter, the individuals never reach a Pareto-efficient outcome, but this outcome is not dependent on the initial allocation.
D. An unequal initial allocation will lead to outcomes that are also relatively unequal.

82. The short run average cost (SAC) incurred by a firm is defined as the total cost per unit of output. We calculate it as:

A. $SAC = \frac{TFC}{q}$ B. $SAC = \frac{TC}{q}$

C. $SAC = \frac{TVC}{q}$ D. $SAC = \frac{AFC}{q}$

83. What are games that have only two players called, where the gain of one is the loss of the other?

A. Zero-sum game
B. Infinite-sum game
C. Two-sum game
D. Matrix game

84. Consider a production function $q = x_1^{\alpha} x_2^{\beta}$ where α and β are constants. The firm produces q amount of output using x_1 amount of factor 1 and x_2 amount of factor 2. What production function is this?

A. CES (Constant Elasticity of Substitution) function
B. Linear function
C. Leontief function
D. Cobb-Douglas production function

85. For profits to be maximum, some conditions must hold at q_0. Which of the following is NOT one of them?

A. For the firm to continue to produce, in the short run, price must be greater than the average variable cost ($p >$ AVC).
B. The price, p, must equal MC.
C. Marginal cost must be non-decreasing at q_0.
D. In the long run, the price must be greater than the average cost ($p >$ AC).

86. Which of the following is NOT a determinant of the supply curve of a firm?

A. Input prices
B. Output prices
C. Technological progress
D. Number of sellers

87. Which of the following statements is correct?

A. In the short run, all of the factors of production cannot be varied, and therefore, remain fixed.
B. In the short run, all of the factors of cost cannot be varied, and therefore, remain fixed.
C. In the short run, some of the factors of production cannot be varied, and therefore, remain fixed.
D. In the short run, some of the factors of cost cannot be varied, and therefore, remain fixed.

80. D	81. C	82. B	83. A	84. D	85. B	86. B	87. C

88. With respect to the theorem of welfare economics, which of the following statements is NOT correct?

A. Any Pareto-efficient competitive equilibrium is achievable through the reallocation of resources.

B. Competitive equilibrium lies on the indifference curve.

C. Any competitive equilibrium is Pareto efficient.

D. Competitive equilibrium lies on the contract curve.

89. The cost that a firm incurs to employ fixed inputs is called the total fixed cost (TFC). The cost that a firm incurs to employ variable inputs is called the total variable cost (TVC). How can we get the total cost (TC) of a firm?

A. TC = (TVC − TFC)

B. TC = (TVC + TFC)

C. TC = (TVC/TFC)

D. TC = (TVC × TFC)

90. Which of the following is change in total utility due to consumption of one additional unit of a commodity?

A. Total Utility

B. Marginal Utility × Total Utility

C. Marginal Utility/Total Utility

D. Marginal Utility

91. The presence of market power is a kind of market failure because of which of the following?

A. Additional cost is incurred by producers.

B. An increase in production is impossible.

C. It usually leads to lower production volume being sold at a higher price.

D. Agents would not possess the ability to influence prices.

92. Which of the following is NOT a feature of the principle of Pareto optimality?

A. No individual can be made better off without making someone else worse off.

B. It maximises overall welfare by allocating resources in the most efficient manner while also considering fairness.

C. It requires unanimous consent or agreement among individuals. It focuses on individual preferences rather than overall outcomes.

D. Pareto optimality does not take into account the specific preferences or desires of individuals but rather focuses on the overall improvement in welfare.

93. Select the statements which are appropriate and then select your answer from the options given below.

1. The First Fundamental Welfare Theorem asserts that market equilibria are Pareto inefficient.
2. In a pure exchange economy, a sufficient condition for the first welfare theorem to hold is that preferences be locally nonsatiated.
3. The first welfare theorem also holds for economies with production regardless of the properties of the production function.
4. Implicitly, the theorem assumes complete markets and perfect information. In an economy with externalities, for example, it is possible for equilibria to arise that are not efficient.

A. 1, 2 and 3

B. 2, 3 and 4

C. 1, 2 and 4

D. 1, 3 and 4

88. B	**89.** B	**90.** D	**91.** C	**92.** C	**93.** B

94. Which of the following points are related to the sources of market failure?

1. Market power or non-competitive markets
2. Externalities and missing markets
3. Private goods
4. Common property resources
5. Non-convexities in either production or consumption set
6. Asymmetries in market information

A. 1, 3, 4, 5, 6 B. 1, 2, 3, 4, 6
C. 1, 2, 3, 5, 6 D. 1, 2, 4, 5, 6

95. Axiomatic approach is useful for:

A. modelling of costs
B. modelling of incentives
C. modelling of consumer behaviour
D. modelling of scarcity

96. The players in each game depend on each other's rationality to make the optimal choices in every situation, thereby maximising their own utility. Which of the following is indicated in this statement?

A. Noneconomic equilibrium
B. Nash equilibrium
C. General equilibrium
D. Partial equilibrium

97. Below are some statements about general equilibrium analysis. Select the statements which are appropriate and then select your answer from the options given below.

1. It considers the economic system as a whole.
2. Goods are either competitive or substitutes.
3. Resources also face competitive demand from producers.
4. Change in the demand or supply of any commodity or factor of production sets in motion a chain reaction.

A. 2, 3 and 4 B. 1, 2 and 4
C. 1, 2, 3 and 4 D. 1, 3 and 4

98. The short run marginal cost (SMC) is defined according to which of the following equations (where Δ represents the change in the value of the variable)?

A. $SMC = \dfrac{\text{change in output}}{\text{change in total input}} = \dfrac{\Delta TC}{\Delta q}$

B. $SMC = \dfrac{\text{change in total input}}{\text{change in output}} = \dfrac{\Delta TC}{\Delta q}$

C. $SMC = \dfrac{\text{change in output}}{\text{change in total cost}} = \dfrac{\Delta TC}{\Delta q}$

D. $SMC = \dfrac{\text{change in total cost}}{\text{change in output}} = \dfrac{\Delta TC}{\Delta q}$

99. Voters are asked to vote for only one candidate, and the candidate who receives the highest number of votes is declared elected (irrespective of whether or not the winning candidate receives 50% or more votes). If there are more than two candidates, there is every likelihood that the highest scorer may not get 50% votes. Which type of voting system is referred to here?

A. Alternative Voting System
B. First Past the Post System
C. Majority Voting
D. Borda Counting Voting System

100. According to the Slutsky equation, when the price of a good changes, as it becomes relatively cheaper, if hypothetically the consumer's consumption remains the same, income would be freed up which could be spent on a combination of each or more of the goods.

What kind of effect is this?

A. Substitution effect
B. Income effect
C. Slutsky effect
D. Hicksian demand effect

94. D	**95.** C	**96.** B	**97.** C	**98.** D	**99.** B	**100.** A

136. For any firm, the change in total revenue per unit increase in _____ is the marginal revenue; and the change in total cost per unit increase in ______ is the marginal cost.

A. output; output B. input; input
C. input; output D. output; input

137. Which of the following statements is correct?

A. In economics, it is generally assumed that the consumer is a desire-driven individual.
B. In economics, it is generally assumed that the consumer is an imitator.
C. In economics, it is generally assumed that the consumer is a rational individual.
D. In economics, it is generally assumed that the consumer is an irrational individual.

138. Including relevant lagged values of the dependent variable on the right hand side of a regression equation could lead to which of the following?

A. Biased and inconsistent coefficient estimate
B. Unbiased and consistent coefficient estimate
C. Unbiased but inconsistent coefficient estimate
D. Biased but consistent coefficient estimate

139. If all other things remain constant, except an increase in the price of an input used in the production of a commodity, there will be an increase in the marginal cost of production of the firms using this input. In such a situation, which of the following statements is correct?

A. At each price, the market supply will be more than before. Hence, the supply curve shifts leftward.
B. At each price, the market supply will be less than before. Hence, the supply curve shifts leftward.
C. At each price, the market supply will be more than before. Hence, the supply curve shifts rightward.
D. At each price, the market supply will be less than before. Hence, the supply curve shifts rightward.

140. The marxist theory of dialectical materialism theoretically follows which sequence?

A. synthesis, antithesis, thesis
B. synthesis, thesis, antithesis
C. antithesis, synthesis, thesis
D. thesis, antithesis, synthesis

141. _________ is NOT a method of sampling.

A. Systematic sampling
B. Snowball sampling
C. Large sampling
D. Quota sampling

142. Endogenous growth theory predicts that countries will achieve higher economic growth rates if they manage to:

A. increase their savings rates
B. shield their industries from foreign competition
C. increase their tax rates
D. lower their population growth

143. Which of the following statements regarding phase diagrams is correct?

A. We can use Phase diagrams to determine the type of equilibration process and the equilibrium solution.
B. In a phase diagram, we graph $y(t)$ as a function of $y(t+1)$.
C. Phase lines cannot answer all questions about the equilibration process.
D. We use a line of slope $+(t+2)$, which passes through the origin to help us see how the time path will evolve.

136. A	137. C	138. D	139. B	140. D	141. C	142. A	143. A

144. If a sample survey of the same 100 households is conducted in a particular village annually for five years, the data collected will be described as:

A. pooled time series
B. panel data
C. pooled series
D. cross-section data

145. Which of the following ways can be adopted by the monopolist to create entry barrier so that rivals cannot enter the industry, in the long run?

A. Sharing exclusive rights to few products
B. Product patent or process patent
C. Maximising use of raw material
D. Charging high prices

146. In a simple regression model, assumptions of constant variance is related to which of the following?

A. Non-linearity
B. Homoscedasticity
C. Linearity
D. Non-autocorrelation

147. Identify the correct statements regarding the classical macroeconomics concept.

1. The economy is, in general, a self-correcting entity.
2. Classical concept assumes potential output at full employment levels in the economy.
3. In good times, prices and wages rise, while in bad times, prices and wages fall.

A. Only 1 and 2
B. Only 1 and 3
C. 1, 2 and 3
D. Only 2 and 3

148. Richardson's model of arms race is an example of which of the following?

A. Economic agent
B. The steady state
C. Dynamic system
D. Discounted utility

149. In a closed economy, aggregate demand is the sum of:

A. consumer expenditure, actual investment spending, government spending and net exports
B. consumer expenditure, planned investment spending and government spending
C. consumer expenditure, actual investment spending and government spending
D. consumer expenditure, planned investment spending, government spending and net exports

150. What is NOT a component of the GDP?

A. Consumption goods
B. Public sector's own demand for goods
C. Investment spending by firms on capital goods
D. Employment rate

151. The degree of freedom, v, is equal to _____ in t distribution.

A. $n*k$ B. $n-k$
C. n/k D. $n+k$

152. The Neyman-Pearson lemma provides the best critical region for testing _____ null hypothesis against _____ alternative hypothesis.

A. composite; composite
B. composite; simple
C. simple; simple
D. simple; composite

144. B	145. B	146. B	147. C	148. C	149. B	150. D	151. B	152. B

153. DSGE is a macroeconomic method that is often employed by monetary and fiscal authorities for policy analysis, explaining historical time-series data, as well as future forecasting purposes. Keeping this context in mind, which of the following is the full form of DSGE?

A. Dynamic stochastic general economics modelling
B. Dynamic stochastic general equilibrium modelling
C. Deterministic stochastic general economics modelling
D. Deterministic stochastic general equilibrium modelling

154. The best method to estimate Koyck model is ______ .

A. MLE method
B. Instrumental variable method
C. OLS technique
D. GLS method

155. In a simple regression model, OLS estimators are ______.

A. non-linear and unbiased
B. linear and biased
C. linear and unbiased
D. non-linear and biased

156. If a sample of 100 is to be taken from a population of 1000 farmers consisting of marginal, small and large farmers, which is the most appropriate sampling method?

A. Simple Random Sampling
B. Systematic Sampling
C. Cluster Sampling
D. Stratified Random Sampling

157. A sure way of removing multicollinearity from the model is to ______.

A. transform the variables by first differencing them
B. obtain additional sample data
C. work with panel data
D. drop variables that cause multicollinearity in the first place

158. During recession, the unemployment rate ______ and output ______.

A. rises; falls
B. falls; falls
C. rises, rises
D. falls; rises

159. GDP deflator is used to ______.

A. estimate the purchasing power of the citizen of a country
B. measure the inflation in a country
C. measure the relative reduction in GDP growth rate of a country
D. compare the GDP of a country vis-a-vis other countries of the world

160. Which of the following statements about differential equations is INCORRECT?

A. There are four types of solutions of differential equations, namely, the general solution, variable solution, separable solution and the particular solution
B. A differential equation is an equation that contains one or more functions with its derivatives.
C. The solution of the differential equation is the relationship between the variables included, which satisfies the given differential equation.
D. The differential equation's primary purpose is to study solutions that satisfy the equations.

153. B	154. B	155. C	156. D	157. D	158. A	159. B	160. A

161. In the following phase diagram, which is the phase line?

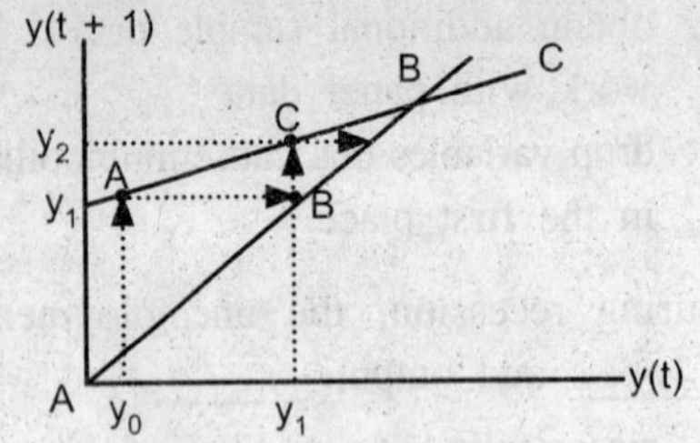

A. A – B
B. A – $y_{(t+1)}$
C. y_1 – C
D. A – $y_{(t)}$

162. According to ________, trade cycles occur due to onset of innovations.

A. JM Keynes
B. Adam Smith
C. Schumpeter
D. Hawtrey

163. The procedure where macro-behaviour of a model is based on micro-behaviour is related to the concept of:

A. micro foundations
B. rational expectations
C. exogenous variable
D. endogenous variable

164. In a new classical macroeconomic model, the demand management policies affect aggregate output:

A. only after a long time lag when the policy is anticipated
B. when the macro policy change is anticipated
C. when the macro policy change is unanticipated
D. only after a short time lag when the policy is anticipated

165. Assume an endogenous growth model with labour augmenting technology and a production function of the form Y = F(K, AN), with A = 2(K/N) such that $y = 2k$. If the rate of population growth is $n = 0.03$, the rate of depreciation is $d = 0.04$ and the savings rate is $s = 0.08$, the growth rate of output per capita is:

A. 15% B. 1%
C. 9% D. 7%

166. It is the ________ interest rate that matters for spending decisions and the ________ interest rate that is relevant when we look at monetary questions.

A. exchange; interbank
B. nominal; real
C. real; nominal
D. interbank; exchange

167. Consider the following graph of a dynamic market equilibrium model habit formation and select the correct statement from the given options.

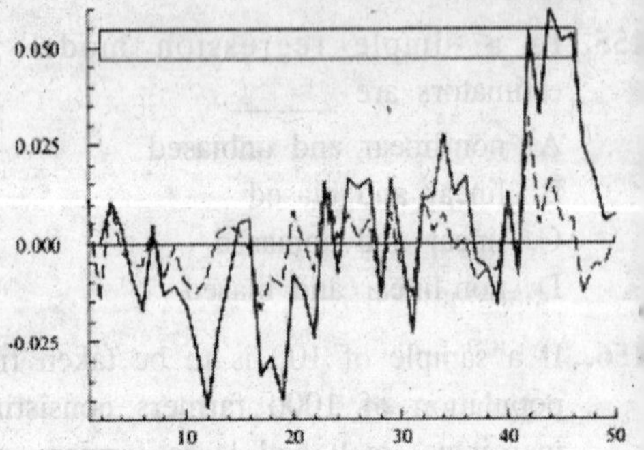

A. The continuous line indicates the net demand shock.
B. The continuous line indicates the market price.
C. The fragmented line indicates the market price.
D. The fragmented line indicates the average position.

161. C	162. C	163. A	164. C	165. C	166. C	167. B

168. The equation given below belongs to which rule of expectation formation?

$X_t^e = X_{t-1}$

A. Adaptive Expectation
B. Static Expectations
C. Perfect Foresight
D. Rational Expectation

169. Which of the following statement(s) is./are correct?

I. '1 + 1 = 2; 1 + 3 = 4; 1 + 5 = 6; 3 + 5 = 8 ...' here 1, 3, 5 are odd numbers and the result of their asddition i.e., 2, 4, 6, 8 are even numbers'. This statement represents Inductive Method.

II. 'While teaching about profit and loss in the class, a teacher announced the formula of profit percentage i.e., {P per cent = [P/C] × 100}'. This statement represents Deductive Method.

A. Only II
B. Only I
C. Neither I nor II
D. Both I and II

170. According to Bertrand model of duopoly, if a firm B sets its price as P_B and firm A sets it price as P_A and C represents the marginal cost of each firm, then under which condition firm A will be losing the market to firm B?

A. When P_A is smaller than P_B and both are greater than C.
B. When P_A is equal to P_B and both are smaller than C.
C. When P_A is greater than P_B and both are smaller than C.
D. When P_A is greater then P_B and both are greater than C.

171. Which of the following is true?

A. Cash Reserve Ratio (CRR) = Percentage of deposits which a bank must keep as cash reserves with the RBI.
B. Cash Reserve Ratio (CRR) = Percentage of deposits which government must keep as cash reserves with the RBI.
C. Cash Reserve Ratio (CRR) = Percentage of equity which government must keep as cash reserves with the RBI.
D. Cash Reserve Ratio (CRR) = Percentage of revenue which a bank must kèep as cash reserves with the RBI.

172. The Philips curve illustrates a trade-off between which of the following pairs of macroeconomics objectives?

A. Inflation and the balance of payments
B. Unemployment and inflation
C. Growth and unemployment
D. Growth and balance of payments

173. Which of the following was NOT included in Solow's key assumptions?

A. Complete information
B. Externalities
C. Constant returns to scale
D. Perfect competition

174. According to Keynesian theory:

Statement 1: Prices are sticky.

Statement 2: After full employment, changes in aggregate demands lead to statement 1.

A. Only Statement 2 is correct
B. Both Statements 1 and 2 are correct
C. Both Statements 1 and 2 are incorrect
D. Only Statement 1 is correct

175. New classical macroeconomics was initially promoted by:

A. Parato
B. Pigou
C. Keynes
D. Lucas and Rapping

168. B	169. D	170. D	171. A	172. B	173. B	174. B	175. D

176. In the context of the fundamental balance of payments identity, which of the following is INCORRECT about the breakdown of the current account?

A. Income Balance = Net Investment Income + Net International Compensation to Employees
B. Merchandise Trade Balance = Trade Balance + Income Balance + Services Balance
C. Trade Balance = Merchandise Trade Balance + Services Balance
D. Current Account Balance = Trade Balance + Income Balance + Net Unilateral Transfers

177. Which of the following macroeconomics schools DOES NOT fall under macroeconomics with microeconomics backgrounds?

A. Monetarist
B. New Classical
C. Neoclassical Synthesis
D. Post Keynesians

178. The neoclassical growth model predicts conditional convergence for countries with the same population growth and access to the same technology if one of these countries has:

(*i*) a higher savings rate
(*ii*) a lower savings rate
(*iii*) the same savings rate

A. (*i*), (*ii*) and (*iii*)
B. Only (*ii*)
C. Only (*i*)
D. Only (*i*) and (*ii*)

179. Which of the following is NOT a postulate of the dynamic general equilibrium approach?

A. Economic agents are continuously optimising/re-optimising subject to their constraints and subject to their information setup.
B. Economic agents optimise not only over their current choice variables, but also the choices that would be realised in the future.
C. The optimal choice of all agents are mediated through the markets to produce an outcome for the macro-economy.
D. All agents have irrational expectations.

180. The four phases of the business cycle are _______ .

A. peak, depression, bust, and boom
B. peak, depression, trough, and boom
C. peak, recession, trough, and boom
D. peak, recession, trough, and recovery

181. Which of the following is NOT a discipline?

A. Economics B. Psychology
C. Sociology D. History

182. Which of the following is NOT a guiding principle of inclusive education practices?

A. Inclusive education is a commitment to honour and respect each student's religious and ethnic identities and belief systems.
B. Every student, including those with special needs, should receive full-day instruction everyday, with flexibility based on the student's individual strengths and challenges.
C. Every student should be taught within a common learning environment (a classroom, and if applicable practical ability) with students of similar age within the community, with flexibility that is based on, and responsive to, the student's individual strengths and challenges.
D. Inclusive education values, draws upon, and includes student voices and choices to assist students in achieving their goals.

176. B	177. D	178. A	179. D	180. D	181. D	182. A

183. Education not only conserves the past experiences of humanity, but also helps an individual to develop his innate potentialities. The given statement is related to which of the following principles of curriculum construction?

A. Principle of integration and correlation
B. Principle of forward-looking
C. Principles of creativeness
D. Principle of individual difference

184. In the context of learning economics, which of the following statements is NOT correct with reference to the meaning of read widely and critically?

A. Contrasting your learning with other perspectives and approaches.
B. Comparing the arguments, assumptions, evidence, and implications of what you read.
C. Exposing yourself to similar sources of economic knowledge.
D. Evaluating the arguments, assumptions, evidence, and implications of what you read.

185. In a typical lesson plan of Economics, which of the following would be the correct order?

A. Introduction, Procedure, Methodology, Knowledge, Understanding, Teaching Aids, Recapitulation, Subject Linkage, Assignment, Learning outcomes.
B. Introduction, Procedure, Methodology, Knowledge, Understanding, Teaching Aids, Assignment, Recapitulation Subject, Linkage, Learning outcomes.
C. Introduction, Procedure, Methodology, Knowledge, Understanding, Teaching Aids, Recapitulation, Assignment, Subject Linkage, Learning outcomes.
D. Introduction, Methodology, Procedure, Knowledge, Understanding, Teaching Aids, Recapitulation, Assignment, Subject Linkage, Learning outcomes.

186. Economics is a science. Which of the following options DOES NOT support this statement?

A. Ascertainment or Establishment of Universal truth
B. Creation of Principles
C. Different views of Economists
D. Power of Prediction

187. The good ideas, concept and principles from various schools of thought have been chosen, picked up and blended together to make a complete philosophy.

The above statement is related to which approach of curriculum development?

A. Functional approach
B. Ecological approach
C. Holistic approach
D. Eclectic curriculum development

188. With reference to economics teaching, which of the following is NOT a disadvantage of the questioning approach?

A. Proactive and interactive communication.
B. Students will become mundane.
C. Students are passive.
D. Time consuming to be implemented effectively

189. From a constructivist perspective, learning is the process through which people construct, meaning that is adaptive in the context in which it was built. This is donc by experiencing the world and building on our prior knowledge. In this sense, they learn best when:

A. they are socially interacting within an authentic situation that is relevant to their prior knowledge and goals, and that fosters autonomous and self-directed functioning.

183. C	184. C	185. C	186. C	187. D	188. A	189. A

B. they are socially interacting within an authentic situation that is relevant to their prior knowledge and goals, and that fosters subservient and multi-directed functioning.

C. they are socially interacting within an authentic situation that is not pertaining to their prior knowledge and goals, and that fosters autonomous and self-directed functioning.

D. they are socially interacting within an authentic situation that is relevant to their new knowledge and goals, and that fosters subservient and society-directed functioning.

190. 'Skill of keen observation, skill of sensing a problem and skill of developing self-motivation are the specific objectives.'

In the above sentence, which category of Psycho-motor Domain is being talked about?

A. Precision B. Perception
C. Imitation D. Manipulation

191. Which of the following is NOT a principle of curriculum construction?

A. Principle of totality of experiences
B. Principle of backward-looking
C. Principle of utility
D. Principle of flexibility

192. Which of the following is NOT a basis of distinction between School Subjects and Academic Discipline?

A. Curriculum Construction
B. Development of Skills
C. Nature of Content
D. Language

193. Which of the statements given below is NOT correct?

A. The results of growth in terms of quantitative changes are very specific, fairly easy to observe and measure.

B. Growth is a sub-system of the development.

C. Growth implies the overall changes occurring in both the quantitative as well as qualitative aspects.

D. Growth does not continue throughout one's life.

194. The relationship between language and education can be divided into three heuristic categories. Which of the following is NOT one of them?

A. Learning about language
B. Learning through language
C. Learning language
D. Learning across language

195. The problem solving ability of the learner is dependent on the acqusition of ______.

A. cultural B. social
C. mathematical D. historical

196. Which of the following is the advantages of Expository approach of teaching?

A. Students depend on teacher all the time
B. There is no scope for the creativity of the students
C. Rote memorization is encouraged
D. Gestalitic view of the subject is spresented to the students resulting into meaningful verbal learning

197. Which of the following is/are the broad objective(s) of early childhood care and education programme?

I. Imbibe good nutrition routines, health habits, hygiene practices and self help skills.
II. Enable children for effective communication and foster both receptive and expressive language.

A. Only II B. Neither I nor II
C. Both I and II D. Only I

190. B	**191.** B	**192.** D	**193.** C	**194.** D	**195.** C	**196.** D	**197.** C

198. 'The sets of behaviours, roles and responsibilities attributed to women and men, respectively, by society which are reinforced at the various levels of the society through its political and educational institutions and systems, employment patterns, norms and values, and through the family'.

The above statement is related to which of the following concepts?

A. Gender Mainstreaming
B. Gender Roles
C. Gender Balance
D. Gender Focal Point

199. Which of the following statements is NOT correct?

A. Literary imagination is an emotional aesthetic experience. It opens doors to experience others and creates opportunities for personal transformation.
B. Emotional response to the other brings aesthetic experience to one's own self.
C. Nurturing aesthetic imagination among students and teachers would enable us to understand people's life histories and struggles.
D. The global market private interests encroached into imagination and redefined beauty and aesthetics as per the market standards. Consequently, everything associated with schooling and education is becoming more aesthetic.

200. What is NOT expected of teachers in the context of Inclusive Education Practice?

A. Work with parents/guardians to help them feel welcome in the school community and to empower them as essential decision-makers regarding programming and/or supports for their child, including, but not limited to, participating on Student Planning Teams.
B. Value student voice and choice and provide opportunities for them to speak to their strengths, challenges, and preferred ways of learning.
C. Serve as Chairman of the Planning Team for their students; work with the Planning Team through the Programme Planning Process as needed, and be responsive to students and parents/guardians.
D. Work with parents/guardians to understand their preferred ways of working with teachers, principals, and other staff, and make efforts to accommodate it. Promote students' well-being and achievement in collaboration with other staff.

EXPLANATORY ANSWERS

1. (B): Geographical Indications (GIs) are classified under Industrial Property, which includes inventions (patents), trademarks, industrial designs, and geographical indications. GIs are signifiers used on products that have a specific geographic origin and possess qualities or a reputation due to that origin. They help to distinguish the goods from others based on regional characteristics, aiding in the prevention of misuse and ensuring that only those within the designated geographic area can use the title.

2. (D): Kiribati has a high public education expenditure as a percentage of GDP compared to many countries. This reflects

198. B	**199.** D	**200.** C

the country's investment in education relative to its economic size, emphasizing the importance it places on education despite its limited economic resources. Data from various international databases typically show small island nations like Kiribati allocating a significant portion of their GDP to education, underlining their commitment to improving educational outcomes.

3. **(B):** Wage rigidity refers to the difficulty in adjusting wages downward even when market conditions might warrant such an adjustment. This rigidity can be due to various factors, including contracts, worker morale concerns, or minimum wage laws, leading to potential unemployment or inefficient labour markets since wages do not decrease easily during economic downturns, preventing market clearing.

4. **(D):** In the context of agriculture in India, Technology Risk is not typically classified as a major direct risk. Primary risks include Yield Risk, Price Risk, and Weather Risk, all directly affecting production and profitability. Technology in agriculture generally represents a potential for improvement rather than a direct risk factor; issues would more likely stem from adaptation or access rather than the technology itself posing a risk.

5. **(B):** Human capital encompasses the attributes that contribute to the workforce's productivity, including the health status of the population, which affects labour productivity and economic output; the stock of knowledge, which includes educational achievements; and the talent, skills, and abilities of the workforce. These elements combined enhance economic performance and competitiveness.

6. **(A):** Absorptive capacity refers to the environment's ability to absorb degradation without suffering long-term detrimental effects. This capacity is critical for sustainable development, as it pertains to the environmental limits within which human activity can occur without causing irreversible damage.

7. **(C):** The commonly used measure of income inequality, such as the income share ratio, compares the incomes of different segments of the population, often the top 20% and the bottom 40%. This ratio illustrates the disparity in income distribution, highlighting the concentration of wealth and how it is skewed towards the wealthier part of the population.

8. **(C):** The concept of effective demand is most closely associated with John Maynard Keynes, who introduced it as a fundamental determinant of the overall economic activity in his Keynesian economic theory. Effective demand refers to the total demand for goods and services in the economy at different price levels, underpinning his argument that demand drives supply and, by extension, employment and output levels.

9. **(D):** This assumption is incorrect as technological knowledge transfer across countries is indeed a principle characteristic of globalization and economic development. Technology transfer occurs through various means such as trade, foreign direct investment, and international collaboration, playing a critical role in the diffusion of innovation and industrial development worldwide.

10. **(A):** Inequality of outcomes occurs when there are differences in material wealth, income, and economic conditions among individuals in a society. This form of inequality is observable in the differing living standards, access to resources, and economic opportunities available to people, often influenced by factors such as education, family background, and social networks.

11. (C): The statements that are not correct include: "Income inequality is much more serious than health inequality," and "Health and health seeking behaviour of the individuals depends on physical status." The assertion that income inequality is uniformly more serious overlooks the profound impact of health inequality on individuals' lives and economic opportunities. Additionally, health and health-seeking behaviour are influenced by a broader range of factors including socio-economic status, cultural beliefs, and access to healthcare services, not just physical status.

12. (D): The Gender Development Index (GDI) is designed to be gender-sensitive. It aims to show the disparities in human development achievements between men and women in three basic dimensions of human development—health, knowledge, and living standards. This makes it explicitly sensitive to gender differences, unlike the Human Development Index (HDI), which does not specifically account for gender disparities.

13. (B): Karl Marx introduced the concept of the "industrial reserve army," referring to the pool of unemployed and underemployed workers in capitalist systems. Marx theorized that this reserve army plays a crucial role in the dynamics of the labor market, as it helps to keep wages down and maintain a supply of labor that can be used to meet fluctuating demands in the economy.

15. (A): The factors determining rural-urban market linkages in India generally include elements that facilitate or hinder the flow of goods, services, and labor between these areas. Raw materials, typically more relevant to manufacturing and industrial contexts, are less directly involved in defining rural-urban market linkages, which are more influenced by factors like sourcing inputs, access to public services, and catering to consumer bases.

16. (D): Hermann Heinrich Gossen, a German economist, propounded the laws of marginal utility, which later influenced the development of marginalism in economic theory. His work outlined the principle that the satisfaction derived from consuming additional units of a good decreases as the quantity consumed increases.

17. (D): John Stuart Mill sought to refine and expand on Jeremy Bentham's utilitarianism, giving it a more sophisticated and nuanced form. Mill introduced considerations such as the qualitative differences between pleasures, arguing that intellectual and moral pleasures hold greater value than mere physical pleasure.

18. (B): In classical economic theory, the equality between savings and investment is primarily brought about by variations in the rate of interest. Classical economists argue that the rate of interest adjusts to balance savings and investment, thereby ensuring that all saved money is invested.

19. (D): Henry Charles Taylor is often regarded as the father of agricultural economics. His work significantly shaped the field, focusing on agricultural policy, farm management, and the economic issues affecting farmers.

20. (D): The development goal described fits best with prosperous farmers from Punjab, known for their higher incomes facilitated by advanced farming techniques and support prices for crops. This economic advantage enables them to consider opportunities such as settling their children abroad, a common aspiration among affluent farming families in this region.

21. (B): The regression coefficient in a linear regression model is not affected by the subtraction of a constant from each value of the variables X and Y. This operation shifts the data points but does not change the slope of the regression line, which is what the regression coefficient represents.

22. (D): Time series forecasting is extensively used in fields like business, finance, supply chain management, production, and inventory planning. These areas often require the analysis of data over time to predict future trends, optimize operations, and make informed decisions.

23. (D): The 'Multidimensional Poverty Index' (MPI) developed by Niti Aayog is based on 12 indicators. These indicators encompass various dimensions such as health, education, and standard of living, providing a comprehensive view of multiple aspects of poverty beyond income measurements.

24. (B): Environmental economics focuses on studying the impact of environmental policies, devises solutions to environmental problems, explores prescriptive and incentive-based approaches, and deals extensively with externalities and the valuation of public goods like clean air. These are crucial for understanding how economic activities affect the environment and for developing effective strategies to mitigate negative impacts.

25. (B): The National Food Security Act, 2013, is primarily rights-based, focusing on entitlements to food for those eligible under the Act. It aims to ensure access to adequate quantities of quality food at affordable prices, securing food to people to live a life with dignity. It does not explicitly adopt a "welfare-based approach," which would imply discretionary welfare measures rather than enforceable rights.

26. (D): Time series data refers to data points arranged in chronological order, typically used to analyze trends over time. This type of data is crucial for various analytical purposes including statistical analysis and forecasting in fields like economics, business, and meteorology.

27. (D): Small enterprises in various contexts, particularly in Indian statutory definitions, have been defined with a turnover limit of up to ₹ 50 Crore, recognizing the scale of operations typical to small businesses in the country's economic structure.

28. (A): David Ricardo defined rent as "that portion of the produce of the earth which is paid to the landlord for the use of the original and indestructible powers of the soil." This definition emphasizes the economic rent concept, which is income derived from the inherent productive capabilities of land.

29. (C): This statement is incorrect as price floors, including minimum wage laws, can indeed create deadweight losses. These losses occur when the price floor disrupts the market equilibrium, potentially leading to decreased employment or surplus labor supply at the imposed wage rate.

31. (A): A purely random process, or white noise, is characterized by having a zero mean. This indicates that the values of the series, on average, fluctuate around zero without any predictable pattern or trend. The variance of the series is not necessarily zero; it can be any positive number, as the requirement is only that the mean remains constant over time.

32. (D): This statement is incorrect regarding the economic reforms in India post-1991. Post-liberalization, there was a significant shift towards inviting and increasing private sector participation in infrastructure, which previously had been predominantly in the domain of the public sector. The reforms aimed at reducing the monopolistic role of the state and fostering public-private partnerships to improve infrastructure quality and expand its reach.

54. (B): The labour force comprises all those who work for gain within the labour market, including employees, employers, the self-employed, and the unemployed who are actively seeking work. This comprehensive definition captures all individuals engaged in or seeking engagement in productive activities.

55. (D): The Chief Financial Officer (CFO) is responsible for managing a company's finances, including financial planning, management of financial risks, record-keeping, and financial reporting. The CFO acts as the intermediary between the company and the financial markets, ensuring adequate financing for the firm's operations and strategic goals.

56. (A): HUDCO stands for Housing and Urban Development Corporation. It is a governmental agency involved in financing urban and housing development projects at reasonable rates to support large-scale housing projects initiated by state housing boards and development authorities.

57. (C): The introduction of the rail network and the promotion of small scale industries are inconsistent with the historical context of British economic exploitation of India. While railroads facilitated the movement of goods, including those extracted from India, they also contributed positively by improving transportation. The promotion of small scale industries contradicts the historical fact that British policies often stifled local industries to favor British manufactured imports.

58. (B): Alfred Marshall introduced the welfare definition of economics, which focuses on material welfare as influenced by economic actions. This approach emphasizes the efficiency of resource allocation and the welfare implications of economic decisions, aligning with the concept of economics as a study of mankind in the ordinary business of life.

59. (C): Behavioural economics integrates principles from both economics and psychology to examine why people sometimes make irrational decisions and how their behaviour does not always follow the predictions of economic models. This field studies how various cognitive, emotional, and social factors influence decision-making processes.

60. (A): Health Economics is a branch of economics concerned with issues related to efficiency, effectiveness, value, and behaviour in the production and consumption of health and healthcare. Its primary focus is on promoting health for all, examining how health resources are allocated and utilized.

61. (B): Managerial compensation practices that facilitate collusive behaviour are most commonly observed in oligopolies. In such market structures, a few firms dominate, and managers might be incentivized in ways that encourage them to tacitly or explicitly collude to set prices or output levels, stabilizing their market positions at potentially higher profits.

62. (D): Model classification is not a stage in the development of an ARIMA model. The ARIMA modeling process typically involves model identification, where the form and order of the model are selected; model estimation, where the model parameters are quantitatively determined; and model validation, where the model is tested to ensure it adequately captures the data's structure.

63. (B): Creating negativity for outsourcing is not recommended when making a 'make-or-buy' decision. Successful decision-making in this context should be based on objective analysis including cost, quality, and strategic implications rather than on biases against outsourcing.

64. (B): Achieving the life goal is not a primary objective of a firm. Typical objectives of a firm include maximizing output, sales, profits, and growth, rather than focusing on personal life goals of individuals within the organization.

65. (C): The Early Majority category in the adoption curve consists of individuals who adopt new ideas before the average person but require evidence that the innovation works before adopting. These individuals are more cautious than early adopters and are not typically leaders, but they do accept innovations sooner than the late majority and laggards.

66. (C): Karnataka topped the Indian innovation index in the major states category in 2023. This recognition reflects the state's strong ecosystem supporting innovation, particularly in technology sectors, with Bangalore being a significant hub for IT and biotechnology firms.

67. (D): The analysis of variance (ANOVA) is carried out using the F-Test. This statistical test is used to determine if there are significant differences between the means of three or more groups, which helps in identifying whether any of the group differences are statistically significant.

68. (B): Innovative products are those introduced to the market in the last three years. "Innovative" products, in this context, are defined as new to the firm, indicating that they represent a novelty within the firm's product line, regardless of their existence in the broader market.

69. (D): "In developed countries, the majority of people are in the services sector, followed by agriculture and less than 10% are in industries" and "In India, over 90% of the work, whether it is in agriculture, industry or services is in the organised or formal sector." In reality, a significant portion of India's workforce is employed in the unorganised sector, and in developed countries, industrial employment typically exceeds 10%. So, statement 2 & 3 is incorrect.

70. (B): Modern manufacturing is not characterized by very small organisations. Instead, it is typically associated with large-scale operations that involve significant capital investments, complex machinery, and often an extensive bureaucratic structure.

71. (B): Investing in activities aimed at discovering new knowledge and developing new technologies is known as research and development (R&D). This term encompasses a variety of innovative activities undertaken by corporations or governments in developing new services or products, or improving existing ones.

72. (A): The major elements of the political environment include the degree of politicisation of business and economic issues, the ideologies and values of the political parties, and the nature and profile of political leadership. The prevailing economic system is not directly a political element but more so an economic framework within which political actions take place.

73. (D): The risk-bearing theory of profit states that profit will be higher in industries characterized by a high degree of variability in their revenues or their costs. This theory posits that firms that undertake greater risks are likely to earn higher profits as compensation for their risk-taking.

74. (C): This is not a limitation of the Diffusion of Innovation Theory. The theory is flexible and has been applied across various fields including technology, healthcare, and social behaviour. Its origins outside of public relations do not constitute a limitation to its application in understanding how innovations are adopted.

75. (B): The chi-square (X^2) test is known as the 'test of goodness of fit'. It is used to determine how well data fit a specific distribution or how likely observations are to occur according to an expected distribution. It is widely used in statistical analysis for categorical data to assess discrepancies between observed and expected outcomes.

76. (A): If two events, A and B, are mutually exclusive, it means they cannot happen at the same time. Therefore, the probability of either A or B occurring is the sum of the probabilities of each event occurring separately, expressed as P(A+B) = P(A) + P(B).

77. (B): The location of an iron and steel plant is heavily influenced by the availability of key resources required in the steel-making process. These include limestone, iron ore, coal, and water. Each of these materials plays a critical role in the production process, from acting as a flux to smelting iron.

78. (B): The licensing options typically offered do not include an "Expensive" license described as for multiple worlds, which sounds more fictional and not applicable in real-world licensing terms. Common license types are exclusive, co-exclusive, and partially exclusive.

79. (A): Subsidizing innovation effectively starts with increasing the quantity and quality of human capital. This includes investing in education, training, and development to enhance the skills and knowledge that drive innovation and creative solutions in various fields.

80. (D): The IT industry is referred to as the sunrise industry because it is in a phase of rapid growth and development. It symbolizes new beginnings in the economy, marked by innovations and advancements in technology that promise potential for significant economic contributions and transformation.

81. (C): This statement is incorrect. In a barter economy, individuals can indeed reach a Pareto-efficient outcome, where it's impossible to make one party better off without making another worse off, and this efficiency can be influenced by the initial allocation of resources.

82. (B): The short run average cost (SAC) incurred by a firm is calculated as the total cost (TC) per unit of output. This is obtained by dividing the total cost by the quantity of output (q), which we calculate as

$$AC = \frac{Tc}{q}$$

SAC represents the average cost per unit of output in the short run, incorporating both fixed and variable costs. This calculation is crucial for firms to understand their cost behaviour and to make efficient production and pricing decisions.

83. (A): Games that involve only two players where the gain of one player is exactly equal to the loss of the other are called zero-sum games. In such games, the total amount of benefit and loss among all players sums up to zero, meaning one player's advantage is precisely balanced by the other's loss. This concept is fundamental in game theory, reflecting situations where one party's gain is inherently dependent on another party's equivalent loss.

84. (D): The production function described, $q = x_1^{\alpha} x_2^{\beta}$, where α and β are constants, is known as the Cobb-Douglas production function. This type of function is widely used in economic modeling to represent the relationship between two or more inputs and the output produced. It is characterized by constant returns to scale if $\alpha + \beta = 1$ and exhibits diminishing marginal returns to each input factor individually.

85. (B): For profits to be maximum, it is necessary that marginal cost (MC) equals marginal revenue (MR), not necessarily the price (p), unless it is in a perfectly competitive market where p = MR. The condition that the price must equal MC is specific to perfect competition, and does not universally apply as a condition for maximum profits across all market structures.

86. (B): Output prices are a determinant of the demand curve, not the supply curve. The supply curve is influenced by factors like input prices, technological progress, and the number of sellers, which affect the cost of production and the quantity supplied at a given price.

87. (C): This statement correctly defines the conditions of production in the short run, where certain factors like capital (machinery, buildings) are fixed, while others like labour can be adjusted.

88. (B): This statement is incorrect as it confuses concepts from consumer theory with those of market equilibrium. In consumer theory, indifference curves represent levels of utility for a consumer; they do not relate directly to market supply and demand conditions or competitive equilibrium, which concerns the interactions of multiple consumers and producers.

89. (B): The total cost (TC) of a firm is calculated by adding the total variable cost (TVC), which varies with the level of output, to the total fixed cost (TFC), which remains constant regardless of output. This sum gives the complete cost of production at any level of output.

90. (D): Marginal utility is defined as the change in total utility that results from the consumption of one additional unit of a commodity. It quantifies the additional satisfaction or utility a consumer derives from consuming an additional unit of goods or services.

91. (C): The presence of market power is considered a kind of market failure primarily because it allows firms to manipulate prices and production levels. Firms with market power can restrict production to raise prices, which leads to allocative inefficiency and a deadweight loss in the economy, resulting in lower consumer surplus and overall welfare.

92. (C): This statement is not a feature of the principle of Pareto optimality. Pareto optimality focuses on the condition where no individual can be made better off without making someone else worse off. It does not necessarily require unanimous consent nor does it focus solely on individual preferences; instead, it emphasizes the overall efficiency in resource allocation.

94. (D): The sources of market failure include market power or non-competitive markets, externalities and missing markets, common property resources, non-convexities in production or consumption, and asymmetries in market information. Private goods, mentioned in option 3, do not inherently cause market failure; rather, it's the lack of public goods and presence of externalities that lead to failures.

95. (C): The axiomatic approach in economics is useful for modeling consumer behaviour. This approach uses sets of axioms or basic assumptions that underlie consumer preferences and choices. These axioms help in constructing models that predict how changes in prices and income affect consumer decisions.

96. (B): The statement describes the Nash equilibrium, where each player in a game or economic model is assumed to know the equilibrium strategies of the other players and no player can gain by unilaterally changing their own strategy. This concept is fundamental in game theory and is crucial for understanding strategic decision-making in competitive environments.

97. **(C):** All statements are appropriate in describing general equilibrium analysis. It considers the economic system as a whole, addressing how changes in one market affect other markets (statement 1), acknowledges the competitive or substitutive relationships between goods (statement 2), recognizes competitive demand for resources among producers (statement 3), and understands that any change in supply or demand can lead to widespread impacts across various markets (statement 4).

98. **(D):** The short run marginal cost (SMC) is defined as the increase in total cost that results from producing one additional unit of output. It is calculated by dividing the change in total cost (ΔTC) by the change in the quantity of output (Δq). This calculation is crucial for understanding how costs evolve as production levels change and is a key factor in production and pricing decisions.

99. **(B):** The voting system described, where voters select one candidate and the one with the most votes wins regardless of whether they achieve a majority, is known as the First Past the Post system (FPTP). This system is common in many countries and is characterized by its simplicity and potential to produce winners who do not receive an absolute majority of the votes.

100. **(A):** According to the Slutsky equation, the substitution effect occurs when a change in the price of a good alters the consumption pattern due to the good becoming relatively cheaper or more expensive, holding real income (purchasing power) constant. If the price decreases and the consumer hypothetically maintains the same level of consumption for this good, the freed-up income could be used to purchase more of this good or others, demonstrating the substitution effect where consumers substitute towards the now cheaper good.

102. **(C):** In a moral hazard situation, an economic agent has the incentive to increase its risk exposure because it does not bear the full consequences of that risk. This typically happens when one party in a transaction has information that the other party does not, or when one party acts on behalf of another but has different interests and does not fully share the consequences of their actions.

103. **(A):** If A and B are two sets, then $A \cap B = A$ if and only if A is a subset of B ($A \subseteq B$). This means all elements of set A are also elements of set B, making the intersection of A and B just A itself.

104. **(B):** Primary deficit refers to the borrowing requirements of the government excluding interest payments on debt. It represents how much the government needs to borrow to meet its expenditures other than those for interest, giving an idea of the government's fiscal health excluding the cost of its existing debt.

105. **(D):** The "broader obligations principle" is not a recognized fundamental principle of public procurement. Public procurement principles typically include transparency, integrity, value for money, fairness, and competition. These principles are designed to ensure that procurement processes are conducted in a legal and ethical manner, ensuring the best outcome for the public.

106. **(D):** The Pallavas were not part of the Sangam chiefdoms. The Sangam literature, which dates from around the first few centuries CE, primarily references the three prominent Tamil kingdoms or chiefdoms of that era: the Chera, Chola, and Pandya. The Pallavas rose to prominence later in South

India and are not mentioned in Sangam texts as one of the chiefdoms. They established a significant kingdom with a different cultural and political lineage compared to the Sangam era chiefdoms.

107. (C): In the diagram of Determination of Equilibrium in Land Markets, the horizontal axis labeled "X" representing the "Quantity of Land" correlates with the Derived demand of Land. This demand reflects the requirement for land based on its utilization for production or other economic activities, rather than for direct consumption, establishing a demand that stems from the demand for other goods or services produced using the land.

108. (C): According to Arrow, a social state involves many factors, including the allocation of commodities, money, and productive resources. However, the comprehensive detailing of every individual's commodity holdings is not typically included in the definition of a social state as Arrow theorized. Arrow's concept of social state generally revolves more around societal-level allocations and distributions, rather than granular details at the individual level.

109. (A): This statement is not correct as it oversimplifies and misrepresents the nature of energy flow in the environment. Energy sourced from the environment is converted into various forms usable by humans and is not simply "lost" in the upper atmosphere. Energy transformations adhere to the laws of thermodynamics, where it is neither created nor destroyed but changes from one form to another, and while some energy is radiated into space, it is not merely "lost."

111. (C): The three primary frameworks of contract theory include moral hazard, adverse selection, and signalling. These frameworks help explain how information asymmetry affects the behaviour of parties within a contract, how hidden actions or information can lead to suboptimal outcomes, and how signalling can mitigate issues of information asymmetry.

113. (A): Minerals are considered actual resources because they are currently being used, have been identified, and their quantity and quality are known. They are resources that have been surveyed and can be exploited with existing technology under present economic conditions.

114. (B): Union taxes are described in the Seventh Schedule of the Indian Constitution. This schedule lists the areas of legislation for the Union, the States, and the concurrent list where both can make laws. Taxes that the Union government is authorized to levy are detailed within this schedule.

115. (A): Linear programming methods are appropriate for determining the value of a game, especially when the payoff matrix is not a square (i.e., when the number of strategies for the players differs). The size 3×4 of the payoff matrix is suitable for using linear programming to solve for the value of the game as it involves more complex calculations that linear programming can efficiently handle.

117. (B): Hyper-regulation is not an advantage of the public sector in India; rather, it is often cited as a disadvantage. Excessive regulation can lead to inefficiencies, slower decision-making processes, and increased bureaucratic hurdles that may stifle innovation and responsiveness in the public sector.

118. (B): The expression $A \times (B \cup C)$ represents the set of all ordered pairs where the first element is from set A and the second element is from the union of sets B and C. This can be expressed as the union of two Cartesian products: $(A \times B) \cup (A \times C)$, where each pair consists of an element from A combined with an element from either B or C.

119. (D): In the rules specified for public procurement, preference is often given to micro and small enterprises (MSEs) to support these businesses and promote economic inclusivity. This policy helps to ensure that small businesses have fair access to public contracting opportunities, which can be crucial for their growth and sustainability.

120. (C): This statement is incorrect. Natural resources exist independently of human actions; they are not dependent on them. While human actions can impact the availability and quality of natural resources, the resources themselves exist as part of the Earth's natural endowment.

121. (A): This is the correct definition of an asymptotic distribution. It refers to the distribution toward which a sequence of distributions converges as some parameter (often sample size) approaches infinity. This concept is fundamental in statistics for understanding the behaviour of estimators as the sample size becomes very large.

122. (D): Private goods and symmetry of information are not sources of market failure. Market failures typically arise from situations like non-optimality of competitive outcomes, externalities, missing markets, non-convexities, and information asymmetries (lack of symmetry). Private goods are efficiently managed through the market as they are excludable and rivalrous, and symmetric information (if it existed) would actually prevent market failure.

123. (D): The power of a statistical test is defined as the probability of correctly rejecting the null hypothesis when it is false, which is calculated as $1-\beta$.

Here, β represents the Type II error rate, which is the probability of failing to reject the null hypothesis when it is false. Thus, the power of the test, often denoted as $1 - \beta$, measures the test's effectiveness in detecting an effect if there is one, ensuring that the test minimizes the chance of a Type II error.

124. (D): The market supply curve represents the total quantity of a good that all firms are willing and able to sell at different price levels. It is derived by horizontally summing the individual supply curves of all firms in the market. This horizontal summation means adding the quantities supplied by each firm at every price level to get the total market supply at that price.

125. (B): In classical theory, the level of employment is primarily determined by the real wage rate, which is the wage rate adjusted for inflation. Classical economists argue that employment levels adjust to bring supply and demand into equilibrium in the labor market, where the real wage clears the market, equating the quantity of labor supplied by workers with the quantity demanded by employers.

126. (C): Monopolistic competition is characterized by a market structure where many firms sell products that are similar but not perfect substitutes. Each firm has some market power to set prices due to product differentiation, which distinguishes it from perfect competition where products are uniform and sellers are price takers.

128. (C): For the Ordinary Least Squares (OLS) estimator to be consistent, unbiased, and efficient, several key assumptions are necessary:

- (*a*) E(Ui) = 0 ensures no systematic error in the error terms.
- (*b*) Var(Ui) = σ^2 implies homoscedasticity, or constant variance of the error terms.
- (*c*) E(UiUj) = 0 for i $\neq$ j ensures no autocorrelation between the error terms. These assumptions collectively help in fulfilling the Gauss-Markov theorem requirements for the best linear unbiased estimator (BLUE).

129. (C): A rickshaw puller produces rickshaw rides. This is the service that is directly offered to customers, distinguishing it from the production of labour or rickshaws themselves, which are the means to provide the service.

131. (D): In a simple regression model, the expectation of the error term Ui, denoted as E(Ui), is zero. This assumption is crucial for ensuring that the OLS estimator is unbiased. It implies that on average, the model errors do not systematically deviate from zero, helping prevent model bias.

132. (C): This statement is aligned with the economic principle of marginal analysis, where profit maximization occurs when the marginal cost (MC) of employing an additional unit of labor equals the marginal revenue product (MRP) of that labour. This equality ensures that the cost of adding one more unit of labour does not exceed the revenue it generates.

134. (A): In equilibrium, the aggregate quantity that all firms wish to sell equals the quantity that all the consumers in the market wish to buy. This is the basic principle of market equilibrium in economics, where the supply equals the demand. This equality ensures that the market is cleared, and there are no shortages or surpluses at the equilibrium price.

135. (C): In a perfectly competitive market, the demand curve of any individual firm is a horizontal straight line at the market price. This reflects the fact that each firm is a price taker, meaning it can sell as much as it wants at the prevailing market price without affecting the price itself.

136. (A): For any firm, the change in total revenue per unit increase in output is the marginal revenue, and the change in total cost per unit increase in output is the marginal cost. This definition underscores the relationship between output changes and revenue or cost changes, essential for pricing and production decisions.

137. (C): This assumption underpins much of economic theory, positing that consumers make decisions that maximize their utility based on their preferences and the constraints they face, such as budget constraints.

138. (D): Including relevant lagged values of the dependent variable in a regression equation can lead to biased but consistent estimates under certain conditions. This means while the estimator may initially be biased due to the inclusion of lagged dependent variables, it can still converge to the true value as the sample size increases, assuming there is no correlation between the lagged dependent variable and the error term.

139. (B): An increase in the price of an input increases the marginal cost of production, leading to a decrease in the quantity supplied at each price level. This results in a leftward shift of the supply curve, indicating that less is supplied at every price than before the increase in input costs.

140. (D): The Marxist theory of dialectical materialism follows the sequence of thesis, antithesis, and synthesis. This dialectic process involves an initial state (thesis) that generates its opposite (antithesis) and the interaction between these leads to a new state (synthesis), which becomes the thesis for a new cycle. This progression illustrates how contradictions are resolved through their interactions over time, leading to the development of new conditions or stages in societal evolution.

141. (C): "Large sampling" is not a recognized method of sampling in statistics. Common sampling methods include systematic sampling, where a fixed interval is used

to select samples; snowball sampling, often used in qualitative research where existing study subjects recruit future subjects from among their acquaintances; and quota sampling, which involves segmenting the population into mutually exclusive sub-groups and then selecting subjects in a way that these quotas are met proportionally.

142. (A): Endogenous growth theory highlights the importance of investment in human capital, innovation, and knowledge in sustaining economic growth. By increasing their savings rates, countries can fund more investments in these areas, which are critical drivers of productivity and growth within the framework of endogenous growth theory.

143. (A): Phase diagrams are useful tools in system dynamics and physics for visualizing the stability and behaviour of different states of a system over time. They help determine how a system moves towards equilibrium, or how it behaves in various dynamic conditions, by plotting the states against time or other variables.

144. (B): If a sample survey is conducted annually on the same 100 households for five years, the data collected is referred to as panel data. Panel data, or longitudinal data, captures multiple observations of the same subjects over a period of time, allowing for analysis of dynamic changes and time effects within the sample.

146. (B): In regression models, the assumption of constant variance, or homoscedasticity, means that the variance of the error terms is the same across all levels of the independent variables. This is crucial for reliable statistical inference, as heteroscedasticity (non-constant variance) can lead to inefficient estimates and incorrect conclusions.

147. (C): The classical macroeconomics concept posits that the economy is generally self-correcting due to flexible prices and wages, assumes that the economy operates at full employment or potential output under normal conditions, and observes that in good times, prices and wages tend to rise, whereas in bad times, they fall. This self-correcting nature is central to classical economics, emphasizing minimal government intervention.

148. (C): Richardson's model of the arms race exemplifies a dynamic system, characterized by the interplay and mutual escalation of arms between competing states. The model uses differential equations to describe how the armament levels of one state are influenced by the armament levels of the adversary, reflecting a continuous and dynamic interaction.

149. (B): In a closed economy, aggregate demand is composed of consumer expenditure, planned investment spending by firms, and government spending. Since there are no foreign transactions, net exports are excluded from this calculation.

150. (D): The employment rate is not a component of GDP. GDP is composed of consumption, investment, government spending, and net exports. It measures the total economic output of a country and does not directly include employment statistics, which are instead part of labor market indicators.

151. (B): In the context of *t*-distribution, the degrees of freedom, often denoted as n typically calculated as $n-k$, where n is the sample size and k represents the number of parameters estimated (including the intercept). This calculation reflects the number of independent pieces of information left after estimating the parameters.

152. (B): The Neyman-Pearson lemma provides a methodology for determining the most powerful test for a given size when testing a composite null hypothesis against a simple alternative hypothesis. It identifies the critical region that maximizes the probability of correctly rejecting the null when it is false, under the constraint of a fixed type I error rate.

153. (B): DSGE stands for Dynamic Stochastic General Equilibrium Modelling. This approach to macroeconomic analysis incorporates microeconomic foundations with macroeconomic applications, allowing for the analysis of how shocks to the economy can affect macroeconomic variables over time under the assumption of general equilibrium.

154. (B): The Koyck model, which typically involves lagged dependent variables, is best estimated using the Instrumental Variable method. This approach helps address the endogeneity that might be introduced by the inclusion of lagged dependent variables, providing more reliable and consistent estimates than standard OLS in such contexts.

155. (C): In a simple regression model, the Ordinary Least Squares (OLS) estimators are linear and unbiased. This assertion is based on the Gauss-Markov theorem, which states that under the classical linear regression model assumptions, OLS estimators are the Best Linear Unbiased Estimators (BLUE).

156. (D): When sampling a diverse population of 1000 farmers consisting of marginal, small, and large farmers, Stratified Random Sampling is the most appropriate. This method divides the population into homogenous subgroups (strata) based on the type of farmers and then randomly selects samples from each stratum, ensuring representation across all farmer types.

157. (D): A sure way to remove multicollinearity from a regression model is to eliminate the variables that cause it. This approach directly addresses the issue by reducing redundancy among the predictors, ensuring that the remaining variables provide unique and independent information about the dependent variable.

158. (A): During a recession, it is typical for the unemployment rate to rise as companies cut back on hiring or lay off workers due to decreased demand and lower production levels, and output falls as overall economic activity diminishes.

160. (A): There are four types of solutions of differential equations, namely, the general solution, variable solution, separable solution and the particular solution: This statement is incorrect as it improperly classifies the types of solutions. The common categorization of solutions for differential equations includes the general solution, particular solution, and singular solution. The terms "variable solution" and "separable solution" do not represent types of solutions; rather, "separable" refers to a method of solving differential equations where variables can be separated on different sides of the equation.

161. (C): In the given phase diagram, the phase line is represented by the black line labeled as 'C'. This line depicts the relationship between $y(t)$ and $y(t + 1)$ across different values. The notation y_1 – C suggests that the phase line is described in terms of the value y_1 on the horizontal axis corresponding to $y(t)$ and how it relates to $y(t + 1)$ as indicated by the vertical movement from y_1 to reach the line C. The phase line helps determine the equilibrium states and the dynamic trajectory of the system as it evolves from one period to the next. In this diagram, the line C shows the equilibrium solution where the future value $y(t + 1)$ depends on the current value $y(t)$, highlighting how values move from one period to the next within this system.

62. **(C):** According to Joseph Schumpeter, trade cycles occur due to the onset of innovations. Schumpeter's theory of economic development and business cycles emphasizes the role of the entrepreneur and technological innovations as central to economic growth and cycles. He argued that innovations lead to gales of "creative destruction" as new technologies and processes disrupt old ones, thereby driving the cyclical nature of economic activity.

63. **(A):** The procedure where macro-behaviour of a model is based on micro-behaviour is related to the concept of micro foundations. This approach integrates individual actions and interactions into the construction of macroeconomic models, ensuring that aggregate predictions reflect the behaviour of agents operating within the economy, such as households and firms.

64. **(C):** In a new classical macroeconomic models, the demand management policies affect aggregate output primarily when the macro policy change is unanticipated. These models hold that rational agents form expectations about the future, and only unexpected policy shifts can have real effects on the economy, as agents adjust their behaviour in response to new information that was not previously factored into their decisions.

5. **(C):** To calculate the growth rate of output per capita, we use the formula for the steady state growth rate in endogenous growth models where $g = sy - (n + d)$. Given $y = 2k$, and $s = 0.08$, $n = 0.03$, and $d = 0.04$, the growth rate g can be calculated as follows: $g = 0.08 \times 2\ (0.03 + 0.04) = 0.16 - 0.07 = 0.09$ or 9%. This reflects the growth rate of output per capita under these parameters.

6. **(C):** It is the real interest rate that matters for spending decisions and the nominal interest rate that is relevant when looking at monetary questions. The real interest rate, which is the nominal rate adjusted for inflation, influences individual and business spending decisions because it reflects the actual cost of borrowing money. The nominal rate is important in the context of monetary policy as it is the observed rate set by central banks and serves as a tool to influence economic activity and inflation.

167. **(B):** In the provided graph, the continuous line typically represents a more stable and consistent data trend, which is common for depicting key variables such as market prices in economic models. Market prices often follow a more smoothed or continuous trajectory in model representations, especially in dynamic market equilibrium models where habit formation might influence the consistency and smoothing of prices over time due to the persistence of consumer behaviour patterns. The line's continuity suggests it reflects an underlying value that does not abruptly change, characteristic of market prices that integrate all available information and participant behaviours in a market setting.

168. **(B):** The equation $X_t^e = X_{t-1}$ belongs to the rule of static expectations. Under static expectations, individuals form their expectations about future values based purely on the most recent available information, without attempting to predict changes due to new information or trends. Here, the expected value for the next period X_t^e is assumed to be the same as the last observed value X_{t-1}, reflecting no anticipation of change.

171. **(A):** Cash Reserve Ratio (CRR) is a regulatory mandate implemented by central banks where banks are required to keep a certain percentage of their deposits as reserves either in cash or as deposits with

the central bank, in this context, the Reserve Bank of India (RBI). This is to ensure that banks do not run out of cash to meet their depositors' demands.

172. **(B):** The Phillips Curve illustrates the trade-off between unemployment and inflation, depicting an inverse relationship where lower unemployment rates correlate with higher inflation, and vice versa. This relationship has been a fundamental part of macroeconomic policy debates, especially concerning monetary policy's role in managing economic activity.

173. **(B):** Robert Solow's growth model did not include externalities in its key assumptions. The model primarily focuses on long-term economic growth driven by capital accumulation, labour growth, and technological progress, assuming a closed economy without external influences like technological spillovers or environmental impacts.

174. **(B):** According to Keynesian theory, prices are indeed sticky, meaning they do not adjust instantly to changes in economic conditions, leading to short-term imbalances in demand and supply. Furthermore, after reaching full employment, any changes in aggregate demand lead primarily to changes in price levels rather than output, confirming both statements as correct within the Keynesian framework.

175. **(D):** New classical macroeconomics, which emphasizes rational expectations and market clearing, was initially promoted by Robert Lucas and Leonard Rapping. Their work laid the foundational principles for new classical economics, shifting the focus towards microeconomic foundations of macroeconomic analysis.

176. **(B):** This statement is incorrect because the merchandise trade balance should not include the income balance or services balance. The correct breakdown should be: Trade Balance = Merchandise Trade Balance + Services Balance, where the trade balance encompasses all trade transactions including goods and services but not primary income or transfers.

177. **(D):** Post Keynesians do not fall under the umbrella of macroeconomics with microeconomic foundations. This school of thought generally criticizes the neoclassical synthesis and emphasizes the importance of institutional, historical, and political factors in economic behaviour, which are often overlooked in models strictly focused on microeconomic foundations.

178. **(A):** The neoclassical growth model predicts conditional convergence for countries with similar savings rates, technological levels, and population growth rates. Whether a country has a higher, lower, or the same savings rate, as long as other factors like technology and population growth are the same, convergence can occur, albeit at different rates and paths.

179. **(D):** This statement is NOT a postulate of the dynamic general equilibrium approach. In contrast, dynamic general equilibrium models typically assume that economic agents are rational and have rational expectations, optimizing based on available information and anticipating future conditions accurately.

180. **(D):** The four phases of the business cycle are typically identified as peak, recession, trough, and recovery. This cyclical pattern describes the upward and downward movements of GDP and other economic indicators over time, where a peak is followed by a downturn (recession), which bottoms out at a trough, and then moves into a recovery phase leading back to a peak.

182. (A): While inclusive education emphasizes accommodating diverse learning needs and providing equal educational opportunities, it typically does not specifically mandate honoring and respecting each student's religious and ethnic identities as part of its guiding principles. The main focus of inclusive education is on ensuring that all students, regardless of their physical, intellectual, social, emotional, linguistic, or other conditions, have equal access to education within a common learning environment.

183. (C): The statement that education not only conserves past experiences of humanity but also helps an individual to develop his innate potentialities relates to the Principles of Creativeness. This principle emphasizes encouraging creative and critical thinking skills in students, allowing them to innovate and think beyond the traditional knowledge imparted, thus fostering individual potential and innovative thinking.

184. (C): The statement that one should read widely and critically in the context of learning economics implies engaging with diverse perspectives and challenging one's understanding and assumptions. Thus, exposing oneself to similar sources contradicts this directive, as it would limit exposure to a range of viewpoints and critical assessment of different economic theories and practices.

185. (C): This order correctly follows the logical flow of a typical lesson plan in economics, starting with an introduction to the topic, detailing the procedure and methodology, presenting the core knowledge and understanding, utilizing teaching aids, summarizing the key points (recapitulation), setting an assignment, linking the subject matter to broader concepts, and finally stating the expected learning outcomes.

186. (C): The statement that economics is a science is supported by its use of principles, prediction power, and efforts to establish universal truths. However, the fact that economists often have different views does not negate its status as a science; rather, it reflects the complexity and evolving nature of economic inquiry where multiple perspectives contribute to a deeper understanding of economic phenomena.

187. (D): The approach of picking and blending good ideas, concepts, and principles from various schools of thought to make a complete philosophy is best described by eclectic curriculum development. This approach involves selectively adopting the best features of various theories or styles to develop a curriculum that is robust and comprehensive.

188. (A): The questioning approach in economics teaching is designed to encourage proactive and interactive communication. This method actively involves students in the learning process by prompting them to think critically and engage in discussions, which enhances understanding and retention of economic concepts. The use of questioning is generally seen as a benefit rather than a disadvantage, as it fosters deeper learning and student engagement. Therefore, stating that it leads to "proactive and interactive communication" as a disadvantage is incorrect, making option A not a valid disadvantage of the questioning approach.

189. (A): According to the constructivist perspective, individuals construct knowledge best when they can connect new learning experiences to their existing knowledge framework in situations that encourage autonomy and self-directed activity, often through social interactions that make the learning relevant and meaningful.

190. (B): The skills of keen observation, sensing a problem, and developing self-motivation relate to the Perception category of the Psycho-motor Domain. This category involves using sensory cues to guide motor activity and encompasses skills where the response is based on sensing the characteristics of stimuli, such as detecting features of the environment necessary for guiding motor activity.

191. (B): The Principle of backward-looking is not recognized as a principle of curriculum construction. The principles of curriculum construction typically include ensuring the curriculum is comprehensive (principle of totality of experiences), useful (principle of utility), and adaptable to changing needs (principle of flexibility). A backward-looking approach would imply a focus on traditional or past practices without accommodating for current or future educational needs, which is not advocated in modern educational theory.

192. (D): Language is not typically considered a basis of distinction between school subjects and academic disciplines. Distinctions are usually made based on the nature of content, the specific skills developed through the subject, and how the curriculum is constructed, rather than the language used.

193. (C): This statement is incorrect because growth is generally understood to refer specifically to quantitative changes, such as increases in size or number. Development, in contrast, includes both quantitative and qualitative changes, encompassing improvements in complexity, understanding, or functionality.

194. (D): Learning about language, learning through language, and learning language are recognized heuristic categories in the relationship between language and education. Learning across language is not typically categorized as a separate educational approach in discussions about the integration of language and learning.

198. (B): The statement describes gender roles, which are the behaviours, responsibilities, and roles attributed to women and men by society. These roles are reinforced through various societal institutions, including political, educational, and familial systems, shaping expectations and interactions based on gender.

199. (D): This statement is not correct as it incorrectly conflates market influences on cultural perceptions of beauty and aesthetics with the fundamental nature of schooling and education. While market forces can impact cultural values and norms, they do not inherently dictate educational content or the aesthetic appreciation taught in schools.

200. (C): It is not typically expected of teachers to serve as the Chairman of the Planning Team for their students. This role often involves more administrative responsibilities that fall outside the typical duties of classroom teachers who are expected to collaborate with, but not necessarily lead, such teams.

Previous Paper (Solved)

Delhi Subordinate Services Selection Board

DSSSB–PGT (Economics) Recruitment Exam, 2023*

SUBJECT KNOWLEDGE – ECONOMICS & TEACHING METHODOLOGY

1. The public policies which are meant for specific segments of the society are known as:
A. Redistributive B. Distributive
C. Capitalization D. Regulatory

2. A perfectly competitive firm would shut down if:
A. AVC < MC B. AVC < AR
C. AVC > AR D. AVC = MC

3. Karve committee of 1955 was associated with:
A. Privatisation
B. Small scale industries
C. Large scale industries
D. Abolishing Licensing

4. A large part of fiscal deficit in India is financed by:
A. Market Borrowings
B. Securities against Small Savings
C. External Debt
D. State Provident Funds

5. In which of the following situation is the elasticity less than unity?
A. If the outlay increases with decrease in price
B. If the outlay increases with increase in price
C. If the outlay decreases with increase in price
D. If the outlay remains same with decrease in price

6. If an economy wants to increase aggregate income by ₹ 500 crore, what increase in investment will be required if the MPC is 0.4:
A. 200 crore B. 1250 crore
C. 833.3 crore D. 300 crore

7. A good which is characterized by both rivalry and excludability is called as:
A. Private good B. Normal good
C. Merit good D. Public good

8. In case of mortgage financing, the concept of Base Rate was introduced by RBI in:
A. 2009 B. 2001
C. 2010 D. 2002

9. Which plan recognized the importance of human capital in economic growth?
A. Seventh B. Eighth
C. Tenth D. Fifth

10. What may cause a leftward shift of the supply curve?
A. The imposition of an excise duty on a commodity
B. An increase in the number of sellers in the industry
C. A decrease in the cost of production for the firm
D. An improvement in technology

11. At time of liberalization, pre requisite of removing budget deficit was:
A. Increase in foreign debt
B. Decrease in development expenditure
C. Surrendering of revenue
D. Decisive reduction of non-development expenditure

12. The most popular pricing strategy at the introduction stage of a products life-cycle is:
A. Price skimming
B. Perceived value pricing
C. Loss leader pricing
D. Value pricing

* Online exam held on 21/06/2023.

13. Industrial Production was highest in which of the following plans:
A. Eighth five-year plan at 7.2%
B. Tenth five-year plan at 8.2%
C. Ninth five-year plan at 12.6%
D. Eleventh five-year plan at 6.3%

14. The assumptions behind production possibility curve include:
A. Variable supply of factors of production
B. Continuous up gradation of technology
C. Allocation of factor inputs to a single use
D. Full employment of economy

15. The skill endorsement aspect was covered under which employment scheme:
A. IRDP B. TRYSEM
C. JRY D. MNREGA

16. A monopsony is a market with:
A. few sellers B. one buyer
C. few buyers D. one seller

17. The discount rate of the RBI acts upon:
A. The interest rate that the RBI charges commercial banks and other depository institutions
B. Stabilizes prices in the economy
C. Stabilizes the exchange rate in the country
D. Stabilizes business cycle of the economy

18. The short run aggregate supply curve will shift to the right when:
A. Prices of input decrease
B. Energy prices increase
C. Investment spending decreases
D. Productivity rate decreases

19. Which of the following statements is incorrect?
A. The most important factor affecting consumption in household is disposable income
B. MPC + MPS = 1
C. MPC is the relationship between change in consumption and change in income
D. Consumption is zero when income is zero

20. Which event/s led to enforcement of Environment (Protection) Act, 1986?
A. None of these
B. Ozone layer depletion
C. Environmental degradation
D. Bhopal Gas tragedy

21. Tendulkar Committee Report (2004-05) gave report on:
A. Banking sector
B. Poverty line estimates
C. unemployment
D. Technological backwardness

22. What are transfers recorded in the current account of the BOP statement that include pension, remittances, gifts, etc. for which no specific services are rendered, called?
A. Barter
B. Bilateral transfers
C. Unilateral transfers
D. Invisible trade

23. The Annual Financial Statement or the main budget document consist of the following except:
A. Deposit and Advance Fund
B. Consolidated Fund of India
C. Contingency Fund of India
D. Public Account

24. .... arises because a single firm can supply a good or service to an entire market at a smaller cost than could two or more firms.
A. Perfect competition
B. Duopoly
C. Natural monopoly
D. Oligopoly

25. Which of the following statements is always correct about Nash equilibrium
A. It is suboptimal collective strategy
B. There can be two equilibriums when both the firms simultaneously play the same strategy
C. No player has anything to gain by changing its strategy given the strategy of the other player
D. Any player has the incentive to change its action unilaterally

26. When there are negative externalities:
A. Marginal social cost is higher than the marginal cost.
B. Marginal social cost is less than the marginal cost.

C. Marginal social benefit is equal to the marginal cost
D. Marginal social cost is equal to the marginal cost

27. The three main major macroeconomic goals of any society are:
A. Maintaining stable prices, high levels of employment and achieving high rate of economic growth
B. Maintaining high levels of employment, increasing the supply of money, and achieving high rate of economic growth
C. Achieving high rate of economic growth, reducing unemployment and reducing rate of interest
D. Maintaining stable prices, reducing interest rates and achieving high rate of economic growth

28. National Sample Surveys came into existence in:
A. 1952 B. 1950
C. 1949 D. 1951

29. By the "invisible hand of the market," Adam Smith was referring to:
A. monopoly B. scarcity
C. competition D. greed

30. Law of demand was graphical illustrated by:
A. Pigou B. Fisher
C. Marshall D. Adam Smith

31. Demand deposits of banks include:
A. Current Account Deposits
B. Government Deposits
C. Recurring Deposits
D. Fixed Deposits

32. The nominal GDP is ₹ 36,000 and real GDP is ₹ 34,000. GDP deflator therefore is:
A. 36000*34000 B. 34000/36000
C. 36000-34000 D. 36000/34000

33. Consumption spending is likely to increase with:
A. A rise in interest rates
B. a fall in wealth
C. a rise in taxes
D. a rise in investment

34. As a percentage of GDP .... has the largest share in the revenue expenditure of Union government in 2021-22.
A. Subsidies
B. Defence expenditure
C. Pensions
D. Interest Payment

35. Integrated Child Development Services, a program started by Indian Government to tackle the problem of:
A. Education B. Child labour
C. Mid-day meals D. Malnutrition

36. Read the following statements and choose the correct option:
Statement 1: In order to improve agriculture marketing, the government regulated agriculture markets to create orderly and transparent marketing conditions.
Statement 2: Cooperative marketing helps in realizing fair prices for farmers' products
A. Both statements are false
B. Both statements are true
C. Statement 1 is true, but statement 2 is false
D. Statement 2 is true, but statement 1 is false

37. In a Game Theory, the set of outcomes for a game is determined by:
A. Pay off
B. Shifting the steel firm
C. Equilibrium
D. Pay off matrix

38. These shareholders are also known as residual owners:
A. Convertible Shareholders
B. Equity Shareholders
C. Preference Shareholders
D. Debentures Holders

39. What is the main objective of Kasturba Gandhi Balika Vidyalaya?
A. Setting up residential schools at upper primary level for girls
B. Focus on elementary education of girl students

C. Providing mid-day meals to girl child
D. Increasing enrollment ratio of girl students in secondary level

40. Problems of Informalization of labour does not include:
A. Lower wages
B. Increased productivity
C. Lack of social security measures
D. Reduces the tax base based on incomes of the employees

41. What do 'a' and 'b' represent in the demand function Qd = a-bP?
A. Income and Taste
B. Elasticity of demand and supply
C. Constant Intercept and gradient
D. Quantity and price

42. Which of the following is not a function of money:
A. Medium of exchange
B. Index of prices
C. Unit of account
D. Standard of deferred payments

43. A perfectly competitive firm can sell all the output it wants to:
A. By cutting down supply of output
B. By lowering the price, it charges for each additional unit produced
C. By lowering its costs of production
D. Without lowering the price

44. If the demand equation is given by D = 1000 – P and the supply equation is given by S = 100 + 4P, equilibrium price would be:
A. 200 B. 170
C. 160 D. 180

45. Branch of economics which examines the factors that influence individual economic choices and how markets coordinate the choices of various decision makers is:
A. Macroeconomics
B. Microeconomics
C. Economics of development
D. Public economics

46. Sweezy's model fails to explain:
A. Interdependent decision making
B. Indeterminate demand curve and price rigidity
C. How price is determined
D. Non price competition

47. Which of the following was not a part of Liberalization policy?
A. Disinvestment
B. Trade and Investment Policy Reforms
C. Tax Reforms
D. Deregulation of Industrial Sector

48. What happens to Average Propensity to Save, when disposable income increases?
A. decreases B. Is unity
C. Remains constant D. increases

49. Which of the following events was not responsible for the New Industrial Policy of 1991?
A. Recommendations of WTO and IMF
B. economic crisis relating to its external debt
C. Fiscal Imbalance
D. Efficient management of the Indian economy

50. Prisoner's Dilemma is a:
A. Non-zero-sum game
B. sequential game
C. zero-sum game
D. repeated game

51. As per Periodic Labour Force Survey 2021-22, Unemployment Rate in usual status for youth persons of age 15-29 years in India was:
A. 15.8% B. 12.4%
C. 4.1% D. 8.6%

52. In case of a homogeneous production function, the expansion path is:
A. Curvilinear B. Convex
C. Linear D. Concave

53. In the standard form of the Constant Elasticity of Substitution (CES) production function with two inputs. $Q = A\,[aC^{-\theta}+(1-\alpha)\,L^{-\theta}]^{-1/\theta}$, "A" is the:
A. Scale parameter
B. Substitution parameter

C. Efficiency parameter
D. Distribution parameter

54. The best strategy in Prisoner's Dilemma is to cheat when:
A. Yon play the game several times with different opponent
B. You play the game once
C. You play the game several times with the same opponent
D. Never, cheating is wrong

55. One of the major aims of financial sector reforms is to:
A. Free entry of foreign banks.
B. Widening of tax base.
C. Transform the role of RBI from regulator to facilitator of financial sector.
D. Reduction of import tariff rates.

56. In a two-sector model, circular flow of income takes place between:
A. Government, households
B. Firms, households
C. Firms, Government
D. Foreign sectors, households

57. The levying of taxes is which function of the budget?
A. Redistribution B. Stability
C. Stabilization D. Growth

58. Who gave the Absolute Cost Advantage model of international trade?
A. Alfred Marshall B. Adam Smith
C. David Ricardo D. Bertil Ohlin

59. Monetization of an economy is measured by the ratio of GDP and:
A. M2 B. M4
C. M1 D. M3

60. Which of the following can be a reason for an exception to the law of demand?
A. Expectation about future prices
B. Greater proportion of expenditure on commodity in the consumption basket
C. Increasing marginal utility
D. Large number of substitutes

61. According to Keynes the short run aggregate supply curve is:
A. Horizontal B. Vertical
C. Upward sloping D. Indeterminate

62. Which of the following short-run cost curves is a rectangular hyperbola?
A. Average fixed cost curve
B. Average variable cost curve
C. Marginal cost curve
D. Average cost curve

63. How can a firm estimate market demand curve for its product?
A. By multiplying price by quantity demanded
B. By combining price elasticity of individual demands
C. By adding consumer surplus to total expenditure
D. By combining individual demand curves horizontally

64. Which of the following cannot be classified as a revenue receipt of the government?
A. Interest received on loan
B. Tax receipts
C. Disinvestment
D. 8 Profits of PSU

65. The immediate objective of National Population Policy, 2000 was:
A. Lower down fertility rate
B. To address the unmet needs for contraception
C. Provide integrated service for reproductive and child care
D. To achieve a stable population by 2045

66. According to Pigou, the pollution level by a steel industry affecting fisheries in the area can be brought to efficient level by:
A. Shifting the steel firm
B. Taxing the steel firm
C. Shifting the steel firm
D. Closing the steel firm

67. Where was the term Sustainable Development came into prominence:
A. Bali convention
B. Montreal Protocol
C. Vienna Convention
D. World Conservation Strategy (1980)

68. Which of the following is not a function of SEBI?
A. Registration of brokers of securities market
B. Training of intermediaries of securities market
C. Issuing debentures at stock market
D. Promotion of fair practices at securities market

69. Price discrimination on personal basis can be done through all of the following EXCEPT:
A. Need B. Paying capacity
C. Geographical D. Demographical

70. The production of a good results in positive externalities. The government should:
A. Impose a tax on the producer which reflects marginal cost of the externality
B. Give the producer subsidy which reflects marginal benefit from consumption of the good
C. Give the producer subsidy which reflects marginal cost of the externality
D. Impose a tax on the producer which reflects marginal benefit from consumption

71. Kamal Nayan Kabra emphasized that failure of Liberalisation policies was because:
A. Inefficient private sector
B. Weak policies to bring foreign capital
C. Liberalisation policies seek to accelerate growth ignoring disequalization
D. More strategic importance to cottage industries

72. According to mercantilists, trade is a:
A. Positive sum game
B. Zero sum game
C. Infinite sum game
D. Negative sum game

73. If actual output is to the right of intersection of 45-degree line and the AD curve, then which of the following is true?
A. There is excess supply of goods
B. There is fall in firms' inventories
C. There is inflation in the economy
D. There is a situation of equilibrium

74. In short run, a monopoly firm can make:
A. Losses
B. Normal profits
C. Super normal profits
D. Losses or Normal profits or Super normal profits

75. General agreement on tariff and trade was replaced by:
A. Cross Regional Trade Group
B. World Trade Organization (WTO)
C. Multilateral trade agreement
D. North American free trade agreement

76. The mercantilist propagates to:
A. Discourage exports and imports
B. Encourage exports and imports
C. Encourage exports and discourage imports
D. Discourage exports and encourage imports

77. Pareto Product Mix Efficiency equation is:
A. $MRTS^X\ KL = MRTS^Y\ KL$
B. $MRS^A\ XY = MRTS^X\ KL$
C. $MRS^A\ XY = MRPT_{XY}$
D. $MRS^A{}_{XY} = MRS^B\ XY$

78. Hypothesis can be stated in all ways except as:
A. Directional statement
B. Relation between variables
C. General statements
D. Declarative statements

79. Who suggested imposition of a tax, known today as corrective tax to tackle negative externalities?
A. Arthur Pigou B. Vilfredo Pareto
C. George Akerlof D. Ronal Coase

80. Economies of scale emanate from:
A. Production of two complementary products separately
B. Production bulk
C. Production of two different products jointly
D. Learning by doing

81. All of the following facts hold good for consumers' equilibrium except:
A. The indifference curve is the highest possible curve attainable by the consumer
B. The point of equilibrium may lie within the feasible area

C. Utility is maximized at the tangency of budget line to an indifference curve
D. At the optimum bundle slope of the indifference curve is equal to the slope of the budget line

82. Nash equilibrium is:
A. Where each player chooses his best (optimal) strategy given the strategy of the other players.
B. There is no interdependence of the players
C. at least one player is not maximizing
D. all players earn the same payoff

83. Which of the following is a non-tariff barrier in international trade?
A. Export ban B. Export control
C. Import Quota D. Import duty

84. A true indicator of economic growth is:
A. Inflation B. Per capita income
C. Employment D. Real GDP

85. Narrow money does Not include:
A. Demand deposits of banks
B. Notes in hands of public
C. Coins in hands of public
D. Term deposits

86. Which one of the following is a barrier to entry to a new firm trying to enter in a market?
A. Patents
B. Consumer sovereignty
C. Low fixed cost of production
D. Perfect knowledge

87. Which of the following is also known as Bretton Wood twins?
A. IMF and IBRD B. IBRD and IDA
C. IBRD and ADB D. IMF and IFC

88. The elasticity of supply for a good will be less if:
A. In case of long run
B. Close substitutes are available to the consumers
C. It is easy for firms to enter the industry
D. There is little spare capacity hi the industry

89. Which of the following will shift demand curve of alcohol to the left?
A. An increase in real income
B. Health research linking alcohol with heart disease
C. A decrease in indirect tax on alcohol
D. A successful advertising campaign encouraging alcohol consumption

90. In a two-sector model, an increase in investment of ₹ 100 crores, leads to an increase in consumption of ₹ 300 crore. The marginal propensity to consume will be:
A. 3/4 B. 1/3
C. 1/5 D. 1/4

91. In real estate financing, the pledging of property as security of loan without giving up the possession is known as:
A. Hypothecation B. Deed of trust
C. Mortgage D. Promissory note

92. Product homogeneity means:
A. Minor changes in the same generic product
B. Different prices for different products
C. Physically identical products
D. consumers to prefer one product over another

93. Which of the following is not a reason for excess demand?
A. Increase in disposable income
B. Increase in import demand
C. Increase in investment expenditure
D. Increase in money supply due to deficit financing

94. If APS = 0.25, this implies that the:
A. There is no relationship between saving and consumption
B. economy will save 25 per cent of its disposable income
C. economy will save 75 per cent of its disposable income
D. economy will consume 25 per cent of its disposable income

95. All revenues received by Government, loans raised by it, and also its receipts from recoveries of loans granted are part of:
A. Consolidated Fund of India
B. Public Account
C. Contingency Fund
D. Deposit and Advance Fund

96. In case of inputs being perfect substitutes, elasticity of substitution of such production functions is equal to:
A. Zero B. One
C. Constant D. Infinity

97. A monopoly is:
A. One of the many producers of a differentiated product
B. One of the few producers of a homogenous product
C. A single producer of a single product
D. One of the many producers of a homogenous product

98. Elasticity of Average Revenue Curve under monopolistic competition is:
A. More than one B. Less than one
C. Equal to zero D. Equal to one

99. All of the following are in the purview of microeconomics except:
A. Is the economy growing?
B. What to produce?
C. How to produce?
D. For whom to produce?

100. As per RBI's Working Group on Money Supply, postal deposits are a part of which of the following:
A. M1 B. M2
C. L1 D. M3

101. The advantage of On-the-job training is:
A. Saves cost
B. Saves time
C. Faster and more efficient
D. All of the given options

102. Normative economics' statements:
A. Are subjective and prescribe what should be done
B. Attempt to describe how and why it happens
C. Are objective
D. Are testable

103. In order to improve efficiency, infuse professionalism, Government started:
A. Miniratnas, major ratanas and dashratanas
B. Navratnas, Ashtratnas and rajyaratnas
C. Maharatnas, navratnas and miniratnas
D. Maharatnas, navratnas and dashratans

104. Risk refers to a situation in which:
A. The outcome is known, but hazardous
B. Exact outcome is not known, but the likelihood of each possible outcome is known.
C. Exact outcome is unknown and the likelihood of any given possible outcome is also unknown.
D. Exact outcome can be predicted

105. Average Variable Cost (AVC) maybe expressed as the ratio of:
A. TVC and Average Variable Price (AVP)
B. Total Variable Cost (TVC) and total output produced (Q)
C. W and AVP
D. Unit Price (W) and Average Fixed Cost

106. Which of the following called for a direct assault upon India's population problem?
A. 1st Five Year Plan, 1952
B. Target Free Approach, 1996
C. National Population Policy, 2000
D. Population Policy, 1976

107. A monopolistically competitive firm earns supernormal profit in the short run because of:
A. Imperfect knowledge
B. Control over the prices to be fixed of the product
C. Product differentiation
D. Freedom of entry and exit of firms

108. Regional rural Banks are sponsored by:
A. Public Sector Banks
B. Commercial banks, State Government
C. Commercial banks and Central Government
D. Commercial banks, State Government and Central Government

109. Which of the following is not a feature of monopolistic competition?
A. Perfectly inelastic demand curve
B. Marginal revenue below average revenue
C. Many buyers and sellers
D. Excess capacity

110. A monopolist's profit-maximizing level of output is:
A. Below the level that minimizes the sum of consumer and producer surplus
B. Below the level that maximizes the sum of consumer and producer surplus
C. Equal to the level that maximizes the sum of consumer and producer surplus
D. Above the level that maximizes the sum of consumer and producer surplus

111. A collusion is tacit when:
A. Member firms cheat each other
B. Firms engage in price war
C. Firms do not document their agreement and collude
D. Demand curve of a firm is kinked

112. What is the relationship between Price (P), Marginal Revenue (MR), and Marginal Cost (MC) for a profit-maximizing monopoly that charges the same price to all consumers?
A. P = MR and MR > MC
B. P = MR and MR = MC
C. P > MR and MR > MC
D. P > MR and MR = MC

113. Which of the following will not cause a shift of demand curve form its original position?
A. Increase in population
B. Change in price of the product itself
C. Increase in per capita income
D. Change in price of substitute

114. The Agricultural Price Commission was set up in:
A. 1965 B. 1985
C. 1975 D. 1955

115. National Agriculture policy was announced in:
A. 2003 B. 2001
C. 2000 D. 2002

116. If Total Revenue (TR) = $110Q - 5Q^2$, Average Revenue (AR) will be:
A. 110 – 25Q B. 5Q
C. 110 – 10Q D. 110 – 5Q

117. Which of the following is NOT the examples of commodity money?
A. Gold B. Tobacco
C. ₹ 10 note D. Cattle

118. An economy produces two goods: guns and wheat and the economy's Production possibility frontier is curved outward. What can be the reason for this?
A. There are economies of scale in production of both the goods
B. An increase in resources devoted to the production of guns requires reduction in resources devoted to the production of wheat with given the resources and technology.
C. The resources available to the economy are not in fixed supply
D. Some resources are better suited for production of guns and others to wheat as the economic resources are not completely suited to alternative uses.

119. GNP and NNP are equal if:
A. Net indirect taxes are zero
B. Subsidies are zero
C. Indirect taxes are zero
D. Capital consumption allowance is zero

120. Revenue deficit is estimated to be ₹ 20000 crore and the borrowing is estimated to be ₹ 15000 crore. If the expenditure on interest payments is estimated to be 25% of the revenue deficit, what is the primary deficit?
A. 5000 crore B. 20000 crore
C. 10000 crore D. 15000 crore

121. Long run average cost increases due to:
A. Managerial efficiency
B. Division and specialization of labour
C. Access to improved technology
D. Labour discontent

122. A kinked demand curve can be explained by:
A. Other firms follow a price rise but not a reduction
B. Monopoly power enjoyed by oligopolists
C. Firms will form a cartel to fix price
D. Other firms follow a price reduction but not a rise

123. If a monopoly's fixed costs increase, its price will .... and its profit will ....
A. increase, decrease
B. increase, stay the same

C. stay the same, decrease
D. decrease, increase

124. The marginal condition for a Pareto optimal resource allocation requires that:
A. MRS between two commodities should not be equal for both consumers
B. MRS of Consumer A for both commodities should be greater than consumer B
C. MRS of Consumer A for both commodities should be lesser than consumer B
D. MRS between two commodities be equal for both consumers

125. One necessary condition for price discrimination is:
A. A single homogenous market
B. Identical taste among buyers
C. A difference in price elasticity of demand
D. Two or more markets with easy resale of products between them

126. Perfect competition is a market condition with:
A. Very large number of sellers
B. Single buyer
C. Restricted entry and exit of players
D. One seller

127. Which of the following is/are correct with respect to PM Gati Shakti mission:
1. It mainly targets to cut logistic costs.
2. It can spur trade competitiveness, promote exports and generate employment.

It is based on 6 pillar strategy that aims to lend more power and speed to projects by connecting all departments on one platform
A. 2 and 3 B. 1, 2 and 3
C. 1 and 3 D. 1 and 2

128. Keynes theory of employment is based on which of the following concept?
A. Effective demand
B. Money supply
C. Production efficiency
D. Propensity to save

129. Gain in utility due to increased consumption of a good is equal to which of the following?
A. Product of the marginal utility of the good and increase in its consumption
B. Ratio of the marginal utility of the good and increase in its consumption
C. Difference of the marginal utility of the good and increase in its consumption
D. Sum of the marginal utility of the good and increase in its consumption

130. Following is an example of capital receipt of India's budget:
A. Interest received on loan
B. Income tax
C. Sale of assets
D. GST

131. When the short-run equilibrium exists below full employment level of output then:
A. Price level will rise
B. SRAS can be to the right of the full employment level
C. Wages will rise
D. Aggregate output will rise

132. If average product of labour is positive but declining, marginal product of labour could be:
A. Zero
B. Declining, but positive
C. Negative
D. All of the given option

133. Aggregate demand curve slopes downwards due to all of the following except:
A. Wealth effect
B. Utility effect
C. Exchange rate effect
D. Interest rate effect

134. What happens to elasticity of demand for a commodity, if the time involved is long?
A. None of these B. No change
C. Decreases D. Increases

135. Which of the following is not a feature of public policy?
A. Static
B. Positive or Negative
C. Goal oriented
D. General

136. Which of the following is not a determinant of the supply of good 'A'?
A. Price of input
B. Price of other goods

C. Improvement in technology
D. Consumer income

137. A monopoly firm face
A. A vertical demand curve
B. A backward bending demand curve
C. A horizontal demand curve
D. A downward-sloping market demand curve

138. The private marginal benefit to consumers plus any costs associated with the consumption of the good that are imposed on others is known as:
A. Marginal private benefit
B. Social marginal cost
C. Private marginal cost
D. Social marginal benefit

139. Private income is equal to:
A. Personal income – Corporate tax – Retained earnings
B. Personal income + Corporate tax + Retained earnings
C. Personal income – Corporate tax + Retained earnings
D. Personal income – Corporate tax – Retained earnings

140. Which of the following indicates that the government cannot meet its current expenditure form current revenue?
A. Primary deficit B. Current Deficit
C. Fiscal deficit C. Revenue deficit

141. PC Mahalanobis believed in:
A. Collective planning
B. None of the above
C. Financial planning
D. Physical planning

142. The intervention of the government either to expand demand or reduce it, is the .... function of government budget.
A. Allocation B. Price management
C. Redistribution D. Stabilization

143. The statement "Government should impose higher tax on rich to reduce inequality" is:
A. Subjective, prescriptive and normative
B. Objective and testable
C. A fact and very important for inclusive growth
D. A positive statement

144. New Education Policy is an example of which type of public policy?
A. Regulatory B. Redistributive
C. Distributive D. Substantive

145. From the following it can be interpreted that:

Country	Hours required for Commodity	
	X	Y
A	120	100
B	80	90

A. A has a comparative advantage in production of X while B has a comparative advantage in production of Y
B.. B has a comparative advantage in production of X while A has a comparative advantage in production of Y
C. No country has a clear comparative advantage in production of X and Y
D. A has an absolute advantage in production of Y while B has a comparative advantage in production of X

146. If the price of a product increases from ₹ 50 to ₹ 60 and as a result the quantity supplied rises from 1000 units to 1200 units, then the elasticity of supply is:
A. 2 B. 1
C. 0 D. 0.2

147. Budgetary deficit of the government is equal to:
A. Total expenditure minus market borrowings
B. Total capital expenditure minus capital receipts
C. Total plan a non plan expenditure minus revenue receipts
D. Total expenditure minus revenue receipts plus capital receipts

148. The membership of cooperative banking union is open to:
A. Commercial banks
B. Individuals
C. Cooperative societies
D. Both Individuals and Cooperative societies

149. Beehives of honey producers is an example of:
A. Negative production externality

B. Negative consumption externality
C. Positive consumption externality
D. Positive production externality

150. The opportunity cost to society for construction of a new highway would be:
A. The goods and services that otherwise would have been produced had the new highway not been constructed
B. The increased cost of taxation to pay for the new highway
C. The money spent of construction of the new highway
D. The cost of government borrowing to finance construction of highway

151. From the given diagram, which of the following represents value of investment multiplier

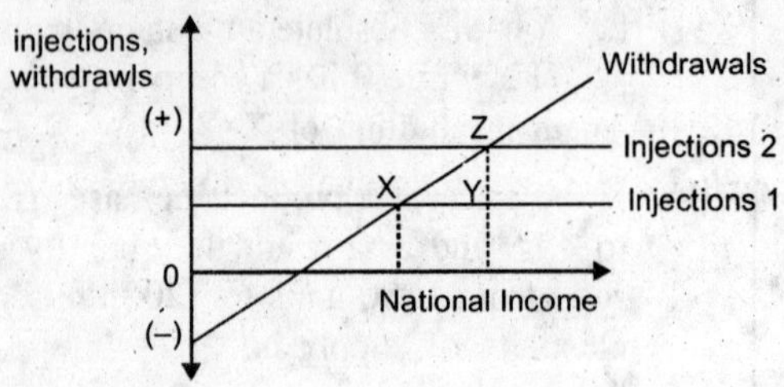

A. XZ/XY B. XY/YZ
C. XY/XZ D. YZ/XY

152. In a four-sector economy, national income is measures as:
A. Y = C + I + G – X + M
B. Y = C + I + T + X – M
C. Y = C + I + G + X – M
D. Y = C + I + G + T

153. According to Keynes, which of the following leads to establishment of equilibrium level of output:
A. AD = AS B. AD > AS
C. AD < AS D. S > I

154. What is Badla system?
A. Another word for stock market
B. Trading in multiples of 100 stock or less
C. Carry forward system of settlement
D. A period of pessimism on stock exchange

155. A shift of the AD curve to the right can be due to:
A. An increase in consumer confidence
B. Widespread fear of recession
C. An increase in income tax rate
D. A decrease in government spending

156. Statistics as data does not include:
A. Tools of analysis
B. Descriptive statistics
C. Quantitative data
D. Raw data

157. Elasticity of demand is determined by all of the following factors EXCEPT:
A. Government policies
B. Proximity of substitutes
C. Nature of commodity
D. Time

158. A monopoly maximizes profit by choosing the quantity at which marginal revenue is .... marginal cost.
A. Greater B. Less
C. Greater or lesser D. Equal

159. Formulation of hypothesis is based on:
A. Observations B. Interviews
C. Inferences D. Conclusion

160. The quantity that a consumer plans to buy depends upon all of the following except:
A. Price of the product
B. Technology
C. Income of the consumer
D. Future expectation of price

161. Negative externality is also known as:
A. Marginal damage
B. External diseconomies
C. Public goods
D. Resource curse

162. The ratio of output and input is known as:
A. Costing B. Productivity
C. Efficiency D. Production

163. **Statement 1:** Surplus budget is not desired during periods of depression
Statement 2: Deficit budget is not desired during periods of inflation

A. Statement 1 is correct, but Statement 2 is false
B. Both Statements are false
C. Both Statements are true
D. Statement 2 is correct, but Statement 1 is false

164. If GDP is ₹ 34,000 crore and net income from abroad is ₹ (–) 4200 crore, then GNP is equal to:
A. 34000 – (–4200) B. 34000 + (–4200)
C. 34000/(–4200) D. 34000 × (–4200)

165. Which of the following can be derived from the law of equi-marginal utilities?
A. Marginal utility of the first commodity purchased should be equal to marginal utility of income
B. Marginal utility of all commodities should be equal to each other
C. Marginal utility of the cheapest commodity should be equal to marginal utility of income
D. Marginal utility of the most expensive commodity should be equal to marginal utility of income

166. Match the pair:

(*a*) Collection of data	(*i*) Business Statistic
(*b*) Aggregate of facts	(*ii*) No Statistics
(*c*) Analysis of time series	(*iii*) Statistics
(*d*) One single data	(*iv*) Statistical method

	(*a*)	(*b*)	(*c*)	(*d*)
A.	(*iv*)	(*iii*)	(*i*)	(*ii*)
B.	(*i*)	(*iii*)	(*iv*)	(*ii*)
C.	(*ii*)	(*i*)	(*iv*)	(*iii*)
D.	(*iv*)	(*ii*)	(*iii*)	(*i*)

167. The extreme case of non-price competition in an oligopoly is:
A. Inter dependent decision making
B. Formation of duopoly
C. Formation of cartels
D. Attaining of economies of scale

168. Which Article of the Indian Constitution requires a statement of estimated receipts and expenditure to be laid in the Parliament every year?
A. 114 B. 112
C. 113 D. 115

169. Which of the following facts provide Central bank the power to conduct monetary policy?
A. supervision on financial institutions
B. sole source of primary money in the economy
C. financial liberalization
D. Acts as a Banker to banks

170. A monopolist's marginal revenue is .... the price of its good.
A. Equal to B. Not related to
C. More than D. Less than

171. What is true for a deductive method?
A. Economic conditions are assumed to be changed.
B. Historical
C. Realistic
D. Abstract

172. If Marginal Product of Labour (MP_L is greater than Average Product of Labour AP_L, then AP_L is:
A. Constant B. Increasing
C. Zero D. Decreasing

173. Using a car and emitting carbon contributing to global warming is an example of:
A. Positive production externality
B. Negative production externality
C. Positive consumption externality
D. Negative consumption externality

174. In the circular flow of income and output, savings is:
A. Injection of money
B. Leakage of money
C. Additions to capital stock
D. Addition to government expenditure

175. Net factor income from abroad is:
A. GDP-NNP B. GNP-GDP
C. GNP-NNP D. GDP-NDP

176. According to Pigou a necessary condition for a maximum welfare is that the marginal social net product (MSNP) of each resource employed in any use or place be:
A. Greater than zero

B. Exactly equal to one
C. Exactly equal to zero
D. Lesser than zero

177. Disposable income is equal to:
A. Personal income – direct taxes
B. Private income – direct taxes
C. Private income – indirect taxes
D. Personal income – indirect taxes

178. Which of the following is related to positive economics?
A. Women unemployment must be reduced
B. We should give pensions to old age people
C. If rent controls are imposed, vacancy rates will fall
D. New subsidies are required to help the poor

179. Marginal Rate of Technical Substitution (MRTS) in case of neutral technical progress is:
A. Zero B. Constant
C. Decreasing D. Increasing

180. Which industry saw a boost due to Outsourcing?
A. All of the given option
B. Agriculture sector
C. Cottage industry
D. IT sector

181. When student makes mistakes in spellings, especially omits letter in words or changes their place e.g. 'pat' instead of 'tap', or 'felt', as 'left' or writes numbers wrong e.g., '12' as '21', the child is having:
A. Mental disability
B. Speech disability
C. Physical disability
D. Learning disability

182. Which of the following does not comes under major discourse?
A. Diary writing B. Interview
C. Narration D. Biographical sketch

183. When we speedily dart through a text to find particular information such as a name, a date etc. it is called as:
A. Skimming B. Speed reading
C. Skipping D. Scanning

184. Lesson planning follows certain steps, select the correct sequence of steps in lesson planning:
A. 1. Introduction 2. Presentation
3. Association 4. Generalization
5. Application 6. Recapitulation
7. Home assignment
B. 1. Introduction 2. Association
3. Presentation 4. Application
5. Generalization 6. Recapitulation
7. Home assignment
C. 1. Introduction 2. Presentation
3. Recapitulation 4. Association
5. Application 6. Generalization
7. Home assignment
D. 1. Recapitulation 2. Introduction
3. Presentation 4. Association
5. Application 6. Generalization
7. Home assignment

185. Preparing and motivating children to the lesson content by linking it to the previous knowledge of the student, by arousing the curiosity of the children is associated with aspect of lesson plan:
A. Introduction B. Association
C. Evaluation D. Presentation

186. Which theory has been propounded by the Howard Gardner?
A. Multi factor theory
B. Theory of multiple intelligences
C. Two factor theory
D. Theory of social learning

187. Which does not fall under the category of advantages of learning resources?
A. It is based on the maxims of teaching
B. It encourages rote learning
C. It meets individual differences
D. It makes maximum use of senses

188. A set of linguistic forms used in given social circumstances is known as:
A. Slang B. Jargon
C. Register D. Language

189. Read the statement:
"Whether or not this more broadly defined group of children is in need of additional support, depends on the extent to which

schools need to adapt their curriculum, teaching, and organization and/or to provide additional resources so as to stimulate effective learning for these pupils."

Which type of children are being addressed in this statement?

A. Children of 21st century classroom
B. Children who perform well in academics
C. Children with special education needs
D. Children with high intellectual abilities

190. Formal operation stage in Piaget's Stages of Intellectual Development ranges from:

A. 12 to 15 years B. 2 to 7 years
C. Birth to 2 years D. 7 to 11 years

191. If the hearing loss ranges from 60-75 decibels, it is categorized as:

A. Severe hear loss
B. Mild hear loss
C. Marginal hear loss
D. Moderate hear loss

192. Which among the following categories does not falls under the Psycho-motor domain?

A. Precision B. Comprehension
C. Imitation D. Manipulation

193. Read the following statements and choose the appropriate response from the options given below:

Statement-1: Societies wherein generations of families are linked through the father's line are said to be patriarchal in nature.

Statement-2: Patriarchy as a way of life has affected men as much as it has affected women, across the world.

A. Statement-1 is false, but statement-2 is true
B. Both the statements are false
C. Children with high intellectual abilities
D. Both the statements are true

194. Read the following statements and choose the appropriate response from the options given below:

Statement-1: In learning context, the children need to feel that each one of them, their homes, communities, languages, and cultures are valuable resources for experience to be analyzed and enquired into at school.

Statement-2: Teaching should be oriented towards construction of knowledge by learners and schools must provide opportunities to question, enquire, debate, reflect and arrive at concepts or create new ideas.

A. Statement-1 is true, but statement-2 is false
B. Statement-1 is false, but statement-2 is true
C. Both the statements are false
D. Both the statements are true

195. "A learner's consistent way of responding to and using stimuli in the context of learning'. In other words, it is 'the way in which each learner begins to concentrate, processes, and retains new and complex information'." This is the definition of:

A. Learning ability B. Learning disability
C. Learning method D. Learning style

196. CCE stands for:

A. Cycle of Continuous Evaluation
B. Clear and Comprehensive Evaluation
C. Continuous and Comprehensive Evaluation
D. Cohesion and Coherence in Evaluation

197. Continuous and Comprehensive Evaluation is introduced as school-based system of evaluation as per Right of Children to Free and Compulsory Education Act in the year:

A. 2008 B. 2006
C. 2007 D. 2009

198. Which of the following does not comes under the criteria for "Content Selection" while developing the curriculum?

A. Self-sufficiency B. Significance
C. Utility D. Sequencing

199. What is considered as the average IQ range in persons?

A. Between 45 and 60
B. Between 85 and 115
C. Between 35 and 45
D. Between 60 and 70

200. Socio Cultural Theory of cognitive development was given by:

A. Jean Piaget C. Lev Vygotsky
B. Ivan Pavlov D. Sigmund Freud

ANSWERS

1. (B)	2. (C)	3. (B)
4. (A)	5. (B)	6. (D)
7. (A)	8. (C)	9. (A)
10. (A)	11. (A)	12. (A)
13. (B)	14. (D)	15. (B)
16. (B)	17. (A)	18. (A)
19. (D)	20. (D)	21. (B)
22. (C)	23. (A)	24. (C)
25. (D)	26. (A)	27. (A)
28. (B)	29. (C)	30. (C)
31. (A)	32. (D)	33. (D)
34. (D)	35. (D)	36. (B)
37. (D)	38. (B)	39. (A)
40. (B)	41. (C)	42. (B)
43. (D)	44. (D)	45. (B)
46. (C)	47. (A)	48. (D)
49. (D)	50. (A)	51. (B)
52. (C)	53. (C)	54. (B)
55. (C)	56. (B)	57. (A)
58. (B)	59. (A)	60. (A)
61. (A)	62. (A)	63. (D)
64. (C)	65. (B)	66. (B)
67. (D)	68. (C)	69. (C)
70. (B)	71. (C)	72. (B)
73. (A)	74. (D)	75. (B)
76. (C)	77. (A)	78. (C)
79. (A)	80. (B)	81. (B)
82. (A)	83. (C)	84. (B)
85. (D)	86. (A)	87. (A)
88. (D)	89. (B)	90. (A)
91. (A)	92. (C)	93. (B)
94. (B)	95. (A)	96. (D)
97. (C)	98. (A)	99. (A)
100. (B)	101. (D)	102. (A)

103. (D)	104. (B)	105. (B)
106. (D)	107. (B)	108. (A)
109. (A)	110. (B)	111. (C)
112. (D)	113. (B)	114. (A)
115. (C)	116. (D)	117. (C)
118. (D)	119. (D)	120. (C)
121. (D)	122. (D)	123. (C)
124. (D)	125. (C)	126. (A)
127. (B)	128. (A)	129. (D)
130. (C)	131. (B)	132. (D)
133. (B)	134. (D)	135. (A)
136. (D)	137. (D)	138. (D)
139. (B)	140. (D)	141. (D)
142. (D)	143. (A)	144. (D)
145. (B)	146. (B)	147. (D)
148. (C)	149. (D)	150. (A)
151. (B)	152. (C)	153. (A)
154. (C)	155. (A)	156. (A)
157. (A)	158. (D)	159. (A)
160. (B)	161. (B)	162. (B)
163. (C)	164. (B)	165. (B)
166. (A)	167. (C)	168. (B)
169. (B)	170. (D)	171. (D)
172. (B)	173. (D)	174. (B)
175. (B)	176. (C)	177. (A)
178. (C)	179. (B)	180. (D)
181. (D)	182. (A)	183. (D)
184. (A)	185. (A)	186. (B)
187. (B)	188. (C)	189. (C)
190. (A)	191. (A)	192. (B)
193. (D)	194. (D)	195. (D)
196. (C)	197. (D)	198. (D)
199. (B)	200. (B)	

Previous Paper (Solved)

Delhi Subordinate Services Selection Board

DSSSB–PGT (Economics) Recruitment Exam, 2021*

Subject Knowledge – Economics & Teaching Methodology

1. Which of the following is considered to be a better measure of economic well-being?
   A. Base GDP B. Real GDP
   C. Potential GDP D. Nominal GDP

2. A family has an income of ₹ 8000 and spends ₹ 4000 on consumption. What will be the value of Average propensity consumption?
   A. 2 B. 0.5
   C. 0.025 D. 1.5

3. Which of the following is NOT one of the components of GDP?
   A. Expenditure
   B. Net exports
   C. Government purchases
   D. Consumption

4. Technically, national income is also called ______.
   A. NNP at factor cost
   B. NDP at factor cost
   C. GDP at market price
   D. GNP at market price

5. According to New Keynesian economists, which of the following factors does NOT cause sticky prices?
   A. Aggregate demand externalities
   B. Consumption expenditure
   C. Coördination failure
   D. Menu costs

6. Which of the following statements is/are correct regarding personal income?
   I. It is the income that households and non-corporate businesses receive.
   II. It does not include sales tax and other corporate income taxes in the evaluation.
   III. Personal income includes the interest income that households receive from their holdings of government debt.
   A. Only III B. I, II and III
   C. II and III D. I and II

7. When an Indian citizen works temporarily in Canada, his production will be part of ______.
   A. India's GDP B. Canada's GNP
   C. India's GNP D. Canada's NNP

8. Which of the following statements regarding LM curve is NOT correct?
   A. The LM curve shifts to the left when the money supply increases.
   B. The LM curve is drawn for a fixed real supply of money.
   C. An increase in the price level will shift the LM curve to the left.
   D. On the LM curve the demand for money equals the supply of money.

9. For a particular year, the nominal GDP of India is 14,500 and real GDP is 5,000. What will be the value of GDP deflator?
   A. 290 B. 190
   C. 185 D. 195

10. In the national income accounts, depreciation is called the:
    A. Consumption of fixed capital
    B. Injection of real income
    C. Variable component of commerce
    D. Leakages in capital investment

* Online exam held on 17/07/2021.

11. Net value added at factor cost (NVA_{fc}) equals to:
A. Gross value added at market price (GVA_{mp}) + Subsidies – Indirect taxes
B. Net value added at market price (NVA_{mp}) – Indirect taxes + Subsidies
C. Gross value added at market price (GVA_{mp}) – Subsidies + Indirect taxes
D. Net value added at market price (NVA_{mp}) – Subsidies + Indirect taxes

12. The total personal income that households receive consists of the income created from production and ______.
A. transfer payments from the government
B. total expenditure on final product
C. consumption expenditures
D. private domestic investment

13. In which of the following conditions, inflation rate remains constant?
A. When actual real GDP is less than natural real GDP.
B. When natural real GDP is less than actual real GDP.
C. When GDP is more than GNP.
D. When natural real GDP is equal to actual real GDP.

14. Net Domestic Product (NDP) is calculated using which of the following formulas?
A. GDP + Depreciation
B. GDP – Depreciation
C. GNP + Depreciation
D. GNP – Depreciation

15. Which treasury bill replaced the 91-day tap treasury bill in 1997?
A. 270-day ITB
B. 182-day ITB
C. 14-day ITB
D. 31-day ITB

16. Which of the following results due to the decrease in Marginal Propensity to save?
A. Decrease in tax value
B. Increase in tax value
C. Lower multiplier value
D. Higher multiplier value

17. Given below are two statements. One is labelled as Assertion (A) and the other is labelled as Reason (R).
Assertion (A): Child care provided in day-care centre is part of GDP.
Reason (R) : GDP uses market prices to value goods and services and excludes the value of almost everything that takes place outside markets.

In the context of the above two statements, which of the following option is correct?
A. Both (A) and (R) are incorrect.
B. (A) is incorrect, but (R) is correct.
C. Both (A) and (R) are correct and (R) explains (A).
D. (A) is correct, but (R) is incorrect.

18. When Marginal Propensity to consume and Marginal Propensity to save are added, then it gives ______.
A. value equal to 1
B. a negative value
C. value more than 1
D. zero value

19. Who generates the mixed income?
A. Government owned companies
B. Social entrepreneurs
C. Quasi-corporate group of enterprises
D. Non-corporate enterprises

20. Which of the following purposes is served by the income method of national income estimation?
A. It is useful in planning allocation of resources.
B. It indicates the potential of raising the standard of living in the future.
C. It is useful in planning the reduction of inequalities.
D. It predicts total remuneration available to an employee.

21. The given expression represents the 'National output (Y) of a country'. What does 'M' represent in this expression?

$$Y = C + I + E + X - M$$

A. Government expenditure
B. Imports
C. Domestic investment
D. Exports

22. Which of the following correctly expresses 'Nominal Interest Rate'?
A. Real Interest Rate – Expected Inflation Rate
B. Real Interest Rate + Expected Inflation Rate
C. Expected Inflation Rate × Real Interest Rate
D. Expected Inflation Rate ÷ Real Interest Rate

23. Which of the following is NOT one of the functions of SEBI?
A. To review national trade policies.
B. To prohibit insider trading in securities.
C. To protect the interest of investors in securities.
D. To regulate the business in stock exchanges.

24. The opportunity cost theory of international trade was given by ______.
A. Gottfried Haberler
B. David Ricardo
C. Adam Smith
D. Jacob Viner

25. Intra-industry trade is dominant in ______.
A. North-north trade
B. East-west trade
C. South-north trade
D. South-south trade

26. In which year, the GATT was expanded to form the WTO?
A. 1985 B. 1947
C. 1990 D. 1995

27. Which of the following correctly expresses the valuation ratio 'Yield'?
A. (Dividend/price change) + Initial price
B. (Dividend – price change)/Initial price
C. (Dividend/price change) – Initial price
D. (Dividend + price change)/Initial price

28. Which of the following formulas is used to calculate return on assets?
A. Operating profit/total assets
B. Net profit/total asset ratio
C. Interest paid on deposit/total asset ratio
D. Interest income/total assets

29. Which of the following was the first stock exchange in India to introduce screen-based automated ring less trading system?
A. National Stock Exchange of India
B. Ahmedabad Stock Exchange Limited
C. Bombay Stock Exchange
D. Over-the-Counter Exchange of India

30. Which of the following implies that the bond is valued at discount?
A. coupon rate > discount rate
B. coupon rate < discount rate
C. value of the bond > par value
D. value of the bond = par value

31. Which of the following categories of stocks and their capitalisation is/are correctly matched?
I. Large Cap Stocks - More than ₹ 1000 crore
II. Mid Cap Stocks - ₹ 500 crore to ₹ 1000 crore
III. Small Cap Stocks - Less than ₹ 20 crore
A. I, II and III B. I and II
C. II and III D. Only I

32. Which of the following currencies is NOT used to set the (Special Drawing Right) SDR value?
A. Japanese Yen B. Pound Sterling
C. Russian Ruble D. US Dollar

33. Minimum reserves each bank must hold to customer deposits is called as ______.
A. Reverse Repo Rate
B. Liquidity Adjustment Facility
C. Statutory Liquidity Ratio
D. Cash Reserve Ratio

34. If the tariff on a product in a country is 10 per cent, it means that the government charges customs duty at the:
A. rate less than 10 per cent of the price
B. rate of 10 per cent of the price
C. rate of 5 per cent of the price
D. rate more than 10 per cent of the price

35. Payment of interest on loans and dividend payments are recorded in which of the following components of balance of payments?
A. Official reserves account
B. Unilateral transfers account
C. Current account
D. Capital account

36. Moral suasion is one of the techniques of ________.
A. monetary control
B. controlling inflation
C. regulating banks
D. reserving cash

37. Suppose XYZ Ltd. paid a dividend of ₹ 4.00 per share for the last year. The dividend is expected to grow at the rate of 5 per cent per year thereafter. If the required rate is 15 per cent, then what will be the value per share?
A. ₹ 47.11 B. ₹ 21
C. ₹ 38 D. ₹ 42

38. In which year, IMF began its financial operations?
A. 1950 B. 1944
C. 1947 D. 1945

39. In which of the following condition a country has a comparative advantage in producing a good 'A'?
A. If the opportunity cost of producing good 'A' is lower at home than in the other country.
B. If the overall cost of production of other competitive product is lower at home.
C. If the overall cost of producing good 'A' is higher at home than another country.
D. If the opportunity cost of competitive product 'B' is higher at home than in the other country.

40. Which of the following statements is/are correct regarding Financial leverage?
I. Financial leverage reduces earnings per share (EPS) and return on equity (ROE) when the return on assets is less than the cost of debt.
II. Financial leverage raises the variability or volatility of both EPS and ROE.
III. Financial leverage can have both positive and negative effects.
A. II and III B. I, II and III
C. Only III D. I and II

41. Which of the following is correct regarding the Interval estimation?
I. α – confidence coefficient
II. (1 – α) – level of significance
A. Only I B. Both I and II
C. Only II D. Neither I nor II

42. Confirmation or refutation of economic theories on the basis of sample evidence is based on a branch of statistical theory known as ________.
A. statistical proofs
B. statistical interpretation
C. statistical inference
D. statistical postulates

43. Which of the following is NOT a data adjusting method?
A. Variable respecification
B. Scale Transformation
C. Field editing
D. Weight-assigning

44. Which of the following methods is an orderly arrangement of data in columns and rows?
A. Classification B. Editing
C. Tabulation D. Coding

45. Which of the following is/are correct regarding the linear regression model?
I. The regression model is linear in the parameters, though it may or may not be linear in the variables.
II. The variance of the error, or disturbance term is the same regardless of the value of X.
A. Only II B. Both I and II
C. Neither I nor II D. Only I

46. Which of the following formula was suggested by H.A. Sturges to determine the size of class interval while preparing data?
A. $i = R/(1 + 3.3 \log N)$
B. $i = R \times (1 - 3.3 \log N)$
C. $i = R \times (1 + 3.3 \log N)$
D. $i = R/(1 - 3.3 \log N)$

47. Which of the following is NOT one of the demerits of data collection through questionnaires?

A. The cost increases as the number of respondent increases.

B. There is a possibility of ambiguous replies.

C. This method is slower in comparison to the other available methods.

D. It can only be used for educated and cooperative respondents.

48. Cobb-Dougles production function is given by $Y_i = \beta_1 X_{2i}^{\beta_2} X_{3i}^{\beta_3} e^{ui}$. Which of the following is correct?

I. X_2 = Labour input

II. X_3 = Capital inpur

A. Only I B. Only II

C. Both I and II D. Neither I nor II

49. Which of the following is a property of OLS estimator under the normality assumption (*ui* follows the normal distribution)?

I. OLS estimators are unbiased.

II. OLS estimators have minimum variance.

A. Only II B. Neither I nor II

C. Both I and II D. Only I

50. Which of the following is correct regarding model specification errors?

I. Underfitting a model – omitting relevant variables

II. Overfitting a model – including unnecessary variables

A. Neither I nor II B. Both I and II

C. Only II D. Only I

51. How many printed cards of inkblots are used in the Rorschach test?

A. 45 B. 32

C. 20 D. 10

52. Which of the following is correct about the standard error of regression?

A. $\sqrt{\dfrac{\Sigma\hat{u}_i^2}{n-1}}$ B. $\sqrt{\dfrac{\Sigma\hat{u}_i^2}{n-2}}$

C. $\sqrt{\dfrac{\Sigma\hat{u}_i}{n-1}}$ D. $\sqrt{\dfrac{\Sigma\hat{u}_i}{n-2}}$

53. 10 units of labour is used to produce one unit of good A in country X and 20 units of labour is used to produce one unit of good A in country Y. The unit of labour is reversed for both country X and Y to produce one unit of good B. Which of the following statement(s) is/are definitely correct?

I. Country Y has an absolute advantage in producing good A.

II. Country X has an absolute advantage in producing good A.

III. Either Country X or Country Y has an absolute advantage in producing both products

A. Only II B. I and II

C. II and III D. Only III

54. Which of the following scenarios does NOT violate the basic principles in the area of trade in goods in the WTO?

A. A member can ask for a particular packaging for an imported product even if it does not ask for similar packaging for a like domestic product.

B. A member can give lower tariff on a product to a country as a reward for receiving some aid or investment from that country.

C. Two countries or a group of countries cannot form regional trading arrangement among themselves and extend lower tariffs to one another.

D. Developing countries may get special benefits from other countries and they may have special arrangements among themselves without others getting the benefits.

55. In country A, supply of labour and supply of capital is 25 units and 20 units respectively. In country B, it is 12 units and 15 units respectively. Considering the H-O model of international trade, which country is richly endowed with capital and what is its capital-labour ratio?

A. Country B, 1.25

B. Country B, 0.8

C. Country A, 0.8

D. Country A, 1.25

56. Which of the following pictorial techniques uses a cartoon format?
A. Holtzman inkblot test
B. Rosenzweig test
C. Tomkins-Horn picture arrangement test
D. Thematic apperception test

57. Which of the following is a test to detect heteroscedasticity?
I. Park Test
II. Glejser Test
III. Goldfeld–Quandt Test
A. II and III B. I and II
C. I, II and III D. I and III

58. Which of the following is a factor of multicollinearity?
I. Data collection method employed
II. Constraint on the model
A. Neither I nor II B. Only I
C. Only II D. Both I and II

59. Which of the following is correct regarding classical linear regression model?
I. Regressors are assumed to be non random.
II. Regression coefficients are assumed to be fixed numbers.
A. Only I B. Both I and II
C. Neither I nor II D. Only II

60. Which of the following statements states the correct assumption of H-O model?
A. Factors of production are immobile within each country.
B. Factor supply is not fixed for each country.
C. There are artificial barriers to trade.
D. There is no transport cost.

61. Which of the following is correct regarding VNM expected utility theory?
I. 'u' represents the von Neumann-Morgenstern utility function.
II. 'U' represents the Bernoulli utility function.
A. Neither I nor II
B. Only II
C. Only I
D. Both I and II

62. Which of the following is the correct representation of Arrow-Pratt coefficient of risk aversion?
A. $r_A(x; u) = u^x(x) + u^1(x)$
B. $r_A(x;u) = \dfrac{u^x(x)}{u^1(x)}$
C. $r_A(x;u) = \dfrac{u^1(x)}{u^x(x)}$
D. $r_A(x; u) = u^x(x) - u^1(x)$

63. In the presence of uncertain situations, people tend to show some behavioural traits. Which of the following is correct?
I. People often do not want to play actuarially fair games.
II. People won't necessarily play actuarially favourable games.
A. Both I and II B. Neither I nor II
C. Only II D. Only I

64. A natural monopoly occurs in a market where the:
A. average cost curve is decreasing over the entire relevant range of outputs
B. capital cost is more than the average cost
C. marginal cost curve is constant for all the given outputs
D. single company is not able to supply the entire market

65. Which of the following gives the correct example of common property resource type of externality?
A. An individual planting an attractive garden in front of her house may benefit others living in the area.
B. A property tycoon buying up a large number of houses in a town, causing prices to rise.
C. The harvesting by one fishing company in the open sea depletes the stock of available fish for the other companies.
D. A child buying a mobile phone for the first time and increasing its usefulness among other children.

66. Which of the following statements is/are correct regarding the collection of secondary data?
I. Secondary data may either be published data or unpublished data.

II. Public records and historical documents act as a secondary data.

III. Secondary data can never be unsuitable or inadequate for a given problem.

A. I and III B. I, II and III
C. II and III D. Only III

67. Which of the following is an economic factor hindering the industralisation in developing countries?

I. Scarcity of capital

II. Absence of industries to use the byproducts of existing industries

III. Adequate infrastructure facilities

A. I and III B. I, II and III
C. I and II D. II and III

68. Which of the following is a type of lottery?

I. Simple

II. Compound

A. Only I B. Neither I nor II
C. Only II D. Both I and II

69. Which of the following pair of goods – type is correct?

I. Bicycle – Durable consumer goods

II. Beverages – Non durable consumer goods

A. Only I B. Neither I nor II
C. Both I and II D. Only II

70. Which of the following pair is correct?

I. Cooperative games – joint action agreements are enforceable.

II. Non-cooperative games – joint action agreements are not enforceable.

A. Both I and II B. Neither I nor II
C. Only II D. Only I

71. In zero sum games ______.

A. one's loss is another's loss
B. one's loss is another's gain
C. one's gain is another's gain
D. all players are at loss

72. If rate of return is r, then ______ is the discount factor.

A. $(1 + r)$ B. $(1 - r)$
C. $\frac{1}{(1-r)}$ D. $\frac{1}{(1+r)}$

73. In monopsony, there is ______.

A. Many seller B. Many buyer
C. One buyer D. One seller

74. Which criterion has used the loser's point of view for measuring the changes in social welfare?

A. Scitovsky double criteria
B. Samuelson's Criteria
C. Max-min Criterion
D. Hicks Criterion

75. Pollution by a firm in the course of its production which causes nuisance or harm to others is an example of ______.

A. Tragedy of the commons
B. Positive Externalities
C. Technological externalities
D. Negative Externality

76. Which of the following is NOT a reason for higher productivity in industrial sector?

A. No specialisation and no division of labour
B. Less dependence on natural factors
C. Continuity of production
D. Existence of greater capital intensity

77. A curve depicting all maximum output possibilities of two or more goods given a set of inputs is called ______.

A. Product possibility frontier
B. Laffer curve
C. Contract curve
D. Community indifference curve

78. In a repeat game the initial game which is repeated in every time period is called the ______ game.

A. zero B. primary
C. origin D. stage

79. Which of the following is an essential element of a game?

I. Players II. Strategies
III. Pay offs

A. I, II and III B. I and III
C. II and III D. I and II

80. Which of the following can be denoted as 'Benthamite welfare function'?

(W denotes social welfare and U_1, U_2 etc. represent the cardinal utilities)

A. $W = U_1 * U_2 * U_3 \ldots U_n$
B. $W = U_1 - U_2 + U_3 - \ldots U_n$
C. $W = U_1 + U_2 + U_3 \ldots U_n$
D. $W = U_1 + U_2 - U_3 + \ldots U_n$

81. Why are indifference curves convex to the origin?
I. Two goods are perfect complementary goods.
II. Two goods are imperfect substitutes.
A. Only I B. Only II
C. Both I and II D. Neither I nor II

82. When the income of consumer rises, then the demand curve for an inferior good ______.
A. becomes a horizontal straight line
B. shifts to the right
C. shifts to the left
D. does not change

83. If supply curve is Perfectly Inelastic, the supply curve is ______.
A. vertical
B. at an angle of 45 degrees from Y axis
C. horizontal
D. at an angle of 45 degrees from X axis

84. Which one of the following is required for a person to make a rational decision?
A. Logical choices without error
B. Choices that don't have trade-offs
C. Choices that never change
D. Choices that are consistent with a similar goal every time

85. Which of the following statements is correct?
I. In perfect competition, firms produce identical goods.
II. In monopolistic competition, firms produce slightly different goods.
A. Only I B. Only II
C. Both I and II D. Neither I nor II

86. If we want to have more of one of the goods, we will have less of the other good. Thus, there is always a cost of having a little more of one goods in terms of the amount of the other goods that has to be forgone. This is known as the ______.
A. Marginal cost B. Actual cost
C. Financing cost D. Opportunity cost

87. Which one of the following is a disadvantage for allocating resources utilizing a market system?
I. Profits will be less.
II. Uneven distribution of income may take place.
A. Both I and II B. Only II
C. Only I D. Neither I nor II

88. Which branch of economic theory is associated with the difficulty of resources allocation?
I. Microeconomic theory
II. Macroeconomic theory
A. Both I and II B. Only I
C. Only II D. Neither I nor II

89. If the supply of a commodity is perfectly elastic, an increase in demand will result in ______.
I. Equilibrium price remaining constant.
II. Increase in equilibrium quantity.
A. Both I and II B. Neither I nor II
C. Only II D. Only I

90. Which of the following is the property of indifference curve?
I. Two indifference curves can intersect each other.
II. Indifference curve is concave to origin.
A. Neither I nor II B. Only I
C. Both I and II D. Only II

91. Which of the following is an example of a perfectly competitive firm's short-run decision?
I. The profit-maximizing level of output.
II. How much to spend on advertising and sales promotion.
A. Only I B. Only II
C. Neither I nor II D. Both I and II

92. Which of the following statement is correct?
I. In positive economics we deal with scientific issues and questions.
II. In normative economics, disagreements among economists can never be resolved.
A. Only I B. Both I and II
C. Neither I nor II D. Only II

93. Due to which of the following reasons the change in the supply of a good along with same supply curve may occur?

I. change in the price of the goods.
II. change in the prices of related goods
A. Neither I nor II B. Only II
C. Only I D. Both I and II

94. The creation of choice is done by ______.
I. scarcity of resources.
II. the urgency of needs.
A. Neither I nor II B. Both I and II
C. Only I D. Only II

95. Which law defines that the demand curve to slope downward?
A. total utility maximisation
B. total utility minimisation
C. diminishing total utility
D. diminishing marginal utility

96. When the total utility is maximum, then the marginal utility is ______.
A. 0 B. minimum
C. 1 D. Infinite

97. Elasticity of demand is a ______.
I. Qualitative statement.
II. Quantitative statement.
A. Only II B. Neither I nor II
C. Both I and II D. Only I

98. Production function shows ______ of a good.
A. the economic relationship between inputs and cost
B. a technological relationship between inputs and price
C. a technological relationship between inputs and output
D. a technological relationship between inputs and cost

99. For Giffin goods, price elasticity of demand is ______.
A. positive B. negative
C. not known D. zero

100. Expansion in supply refers to a situation when the producers are willing to supply a ______ quantity of a good at an ______ price.
A. larger, same
B. larger, increased
C. smaller, increase
D. larger, decreased

101. What does monopolistic competition have in common with monopoly?
I. A large number of firms.
II. A downward sloping demand curve.
A. Neither I nor II B. Both I and II
C. Only I D. Only II

102. Which of the following is required by the First Fundamental Theorem of Welfare Economics?
I. Producers and consumers to be price takers.
II. That there be an efficient market for every commodity.
III. That the economy operates at some point on the utility possibility curve.
A. I and III B. I and II
C. I, II and III D. II and III

103. Which of the following is correct regarding perfectly competitive market?
I. It consists of large number of buyers and sellers.
II. There are no barriers to entry.
A. Only II B. Neither I nor II
C. Both I and II D. Only I

104. Firms in monopolistic competition have demand curves that are ______.
I. U shaped
II. Downward slopping
A. Both I and II B. Only II
C. Neither I nor II D. Only I

105. Which of the following is correct regarding money supply?
I. Exogenous - Money supply is determined outside the system.
II. Endogenous - Banking sector along with firms and households play an important role in influencing the money supply.
A. Neither I nor II B. Only I
C. Both I and II D. Only II

106. An important mechanism through which sellers and buyers deal with the problem of asymmetric information is ______.
A. Insurance Markets
B. Market signaling

C. Principal-Agent Problem
D. Moral Hazard

107. A single-price monopoly must ______ if it wants to increase its sales.
A. increase the price for all customers
B. lower the price for all customers
C. lower its price for only a few selected consumers
D. do price discrimination

108. Which of the following is correct regarding Pigouvian subsidy?
I. It is the same thing as a Pigouvian tax.
II. It moves production to the socially optimal level of output.
A. Both I and II B. Only II
C. Only I D. Neither I nor II

109. The concept of market signaling was first developed by ______.
A. Michael Spence B. Garrett Hardin
C. Pareto D. Kaldor

110. A spray prevents mosquitos from biting. This spray is produced by competitive firms. Which of the following will be the outcome of the market?
A. The market will demonstrate second welfare theorem
B. Due to the uncaptured positive externality very small number of sprays are produced
C. Due to the uncaptured negative externality very large number of sprays are produced
D. Due to the uncaptured positive externality very large number of sprays are produced

111. Which of the following statements is NOT correct regarding the changes in the price of a product in free market?
I. The change in the price is governed by the government.
II. The change can provide an incentive to reallocate resources.
A. Both I and II B. Only II
C. Neither I nor II D. Only I

112. When firms in monopolistic competition are making an economic profit then ______.
I. Firms will enter the industry.
II. Demand will decrease for the original firms.
A. Neither I nor II B. Both I and II
C. Only I D. Only II

113. A cartel is designed to ______ output and ______ prices.
A. expand; raise
B. restrict; lower
C. expand; lower
D. restrict; raise

114. Which of the following statements is correct?
I. If a given quantity of a good is to be produced and supplied, the supply curve would indicate the minimum price of the good expected by each seller.
II. The demand function which expresses the functional relationship between the quantity demanded of a good and its own price is based on ceteris paribus assumptions.
A. Neither I nor II B. Only I
C. Both I and II D. Only II

115. In which of the following conditions does a positive consumption externality occur?
I. The social marginal cost is greater than the private marginal cost
II. The social marginal benefit is greater than the private marginal benefit
A. Only I B. Only II
C. Both I and II D. Neither I nor II

116. Which of the following is a firm's over-riding objective?
I. Maximise economic profit.
II. Avoid an economic loss.
A. Neither I nor II B. Only I
C. Only II D. Both I and II

117. Due to which of the following reasons externalities can be positive?
I. Utility can be impacted positively as well as negatively.
II. Subsidies are positive externalities.
A. Neither I nor II B. Only I
C. Both I and II D. Only II

118. Which method can help in obtaining a welfare improvement if externalities exist?

I. Regulation.
II. Assigning property rights and permitting bargaining.
A. Only I B. Both I and II
C. Neither I nor II D. Only II

119. Which of the following is correct regarding public goods?
I. They are non-rival in consumption.
II. Consumers cannot be excluded altogether from them.
A. Only II B. Only I
C. Neither I nor II D. Both I and II

120. According to Keynes, which of the following is a component of demand for money?
I. Transactions demand
II. Precautionary demand
III. Speculative demand
A. II and III B. I and III
C. I and II D. I, II and III

121. Which of the following is correct regarding the revision of the base year of National accounts from 2004-05 to 2011-12?
I. Headline growth rate will now be measured by GDP at constant market prices.
II. Earlier, growth was measured in terms of growth rate in GDP at factor cost at constant prices.
A. Only I B. Neither I nor II
C. Both I and II D. Only II

122. What is the meaning of 'Evergreening of Loans'?
A. Loan approvals within 24 hours
B. Waiving off the interest by the banks
C. Banks give additional loans to its existing borrowers
D. Government providing loans to banks to meet their losses

123. Which of the following would lead a country to its ratings downgrade by the Rating Agencies?
I. High Fiscal Deficit and debt burden.
II. High Current Account Deficit and low FOREX reserve.
III. Weak and volatile Stock Market.
A. I and III B. I and II
C. I, II and III D. II and III

124. What is Effective Revenue Deficit?
A. It is obtained by adding Revenue Deficit with Capital Deficit
B. It is the total grant to the creation of capital asset and revenue expenditure
C. It is equal to difference of revenue receipt and revenue expenditure
D. It is the difference of revenue deficit and grant for the creation of capital assets

125. Which of the following is correct regarding the Outcome budget?
I. It reflects the itemised allocation of resources reflected under the last General Budget and prepared by ministries of the Government.
II. It was started in 2005.
A. Neither I nor II B. Only II
C. Only I D. Both I and II

126. Which of the following is an example of adverse selection?
A. High car insurance premiums resulting from the poor maintenance of the cars by people who buy these policies
B. To purchase a low-priced item even though its quality is inferior
C. Purchasing a new air conditioner on basis of a friend's recommendation without seeing it
D. Pricing a high-quality wine more than the low-quality wine

127. Which of the following is correct regarding monopoly power in a market?
I. It leads to higher producer surplus.
II. It leads to lower prices.
A. Only I B. Neither I nor II
C. Only II D. Both I and II

128. Which of the following is correct?
A. Real Interest Rate = Nominal Interest Rate – Expected Inflation Rate
B. Nominal Interest Rate = Real Interest Rate – Expected Inflation Rate
C. Real Interest Rate/Nominal Interest Rate = Expected Inflation Rate
D. Real Interest Rate = Nominal Interest Rate

129. Who has written 'The Tragedy of Commons'?
A. E.F. Schumacher
B. Irving Fisher
C. Thomas Robert Malthus
D. Garrett Hardin

130. Which of the following does not provide an incentive to reduce a negative externality?
I. A merger with affected firms.
II. Bargaining among firms.
A. Only II B. Only I
C. Neither I nor II D. Both I and II

131. Ronald Coase asserted that under perfect competition private and social cost will be equal and addressed a well-known problem of market externalities, known as the ______ effect.
A. Pareto B. Spillover
C. Overflow D. Razor

132. Which of the following is correct regarding community surplus?
A. Total utility + profit
B. Producer surplus + profit
C. Producer surplus + consumer surplus
D. Producer surplus – consumer surplus

133. The difference between Gross Value of Output (GVO) and Gross Value Added (GVA) is called as ______.
A. final consumption
B. original consumption
C. marginal consumption
D. intermediate consumption

134. Which of the following is correct regarding externality?
I. The existence of externality prevents the achievement of Pareto optimality even when perfect competition prevails.
II. An externality occurs when a decision causes benefits to individuals or groups other than the person making the decision.
A. Neither I nor II B. Only I
C. Only II D. Both I and II

135. Which of the following statement is correct regarding Capital Output Ratio?
I. The Capital Output ratio shows the relationship between the Investment rates and GDP Growth in a country.
II. The higher capital output ratio denotes higher efficiency of the capital.
A. Both I and II B. Only I
C. Only II D. Neither I nor II

136. Which of the following is correct regarding the MCA21 initiative launched by the Ministry of corporate affairs?
I. Easy and secure access to MCA services in an assisted manner for corporate entities, professionals, and general public.
II. It is designed to fully automate all processes related to enforcement and compliance of the legal requirements under the Companies Act, 1956.
A. Only II B. Neither I nor II
C. Both I and II D. Only I

137. The difference principle of justice requires that all economic inequalities be arranged so that they are ______.
I. beneficial to the least advantaged
II. attached to offices and positions open to all members under conditions of fair equality of opportunity
A. Neither I nor II B. Both I and II
C. Only II D. Only I

138. Which of the following is correct regarding Beti Bachao Beti Padhao (BBBP)?
I. The programme was launched on 22nd January, 2015 at Panipat, Haryana for promoting survival, protection and education of girl child.
II. It aims to address the issue of declining Child Sex Ratio (CSR) through a mass campaign targeted at changing social mind set and creating awareness about the criticality of the issue.
III. The overall goal of the BBBP programme is to prevent gender biased sex selective elimination, ensure survival and protection of the girl child and to ensure education and participation of the girl child.
A. I and III B. I, II and III
C. I and II D. II and III

139. A firm generating a negative externality has to reach an economically efficient output level. Which of the following condition is necessary?

A. Excise tax imposed on firm = social marginal cost + firm's marginal cost

B. Excise tax imposed on firm = firm's marginal cost

C. Excise tax imposed on firm = social marginal cost

D. Excise tax imposed on firm = social marginal cost – firm's marginal cost

140. Who gave the impossibility theorem?

A. Friedrich Hayek B. Ludwig von Mises

C. David Ricardo D. Kenneth Arrow

141. Which of the following will contribute to a higher current account deficit?

I. Increased exports of rice

II. Rise in import of mobile phones

A. Only II B. Only I

C. Both I and II D. Neither I nor II

142. Which of following is correct about the Primary deficit?

A. Fiscal Deficit – Interest Payment

B. Capital Receipts – Interest Payment

C. Fiscal Deficit + Interest Payment

D. Capital Receipts + Interest Payment

143. Which of the following statement is correct regarding the GST Compensation Mechanism?

I. The GST Compensation cess is used to compensate the states for any loss they incur within the first five years of GST implementation.

II. According to the GST Act, States are guaranteed compensation if the GST revenue growth is less than 14 per cent.

A. Both I and II B. Only I

C. Only II D. Neither I nor II

144. Which among the following International agencies publishes the Global Investment Trend Monitor Report?

A. World Economic Forum

B. United Nations Conference on Trade and Development

C. International Monetary Fund

D. World Bank

145. Which of the following are components of internal debt in India?

I. Compensation and Other Bonds.

II. 14 Day Intermediate Treasury Bills.

III. Securities issued to International Financial Institutions.

A. I and III B. I, II and III

C. II and III D. I and II

146. Which of the following reasons account for lower rural income in India?

I. Lower investment in agriculture.

II. Lower prices of primary products.

A. Both I and II B. Only I

C. Only II D. Neither I nor II

147. Which of the following statements regarding Small Finance Banks (SFBs) is correct?

I. The Small Finance Banks can accept deposits and lend loans only up to ₹ 1 lakh.

II. They are required to extend 75 per cent of their loans towards the priority sectors.

A. Only II B. Only I

C. Neither I nor II D. Both I and II

148. In India, deficit financing is used for raising resources for ______.

I. reducing the foreign debt.

II. economic development.

A. Both I and II B. Only I

C. Only II D. Neither I nor II

149. Which of the following are correct regarding the austerity measures taken by a country going through adverse economy conditions?

I. These measures include an increase in tax.

II. These measures include reduction in budget deficit.

A. Only II B. Only I

C. Both I and II D. Neither I nor II

150. Which of the following can be the likely reason for slowdown in the economy?

I. Rise in investment rates.

II. Decrease in consumption expenditure.

III. High policy rates.

A. I and III B. II and III

C. I, II and III D. I and II

151. Which of the following is part of Human Development Index?

I. Literacy rates.
II. Life expectancy at birth.
III. GNI per head at real purchasing power.

A. I and II B. II and III
C. I, II and III D. I and III

152. Which among the following is/are the initiatives started by NITI Aayog?

I. Sustainable Action for Transforming Human Capital (SATH)
II. Ek Bharat Shreshtha Bharat
III. Composite Water Management Index

A. I and III B. I and II
C. II and III D. I, II and III

153. Which among the following are instruments of the RBI's Monetary policy?

I. Open market operations
II. Cash reserve ratio
III. Bank rate
IV. Reverse Repo rate

A. I, III and IV B. II, III and IV
C. I, II and III D. I, II, III, IV

154. Which of the following statement is correct regarding Pradhan Mantri Garib Kalyan Yojana?

I. Insurance scheme for healthcare workers.
II. Cash transfers to poor and vulnerable sections.
III. Benefits for the workers employed in organised sector.

A. I and II B. I, II and III
C. I and III D. II and III

155. What does the term Free Market means?

I. It is a market where pricing is driven by the laws of supply and demand.
II. In free market things are available without restraints of the government.

A. Neither I nor II B. Only I
C. Both I and II D. Only II

156. Who has written the book 'Fault Lines'?

A. Guru Charan Das
B. Satish Y. Deodhar
C. Raghuram G. Rajan
D. Bimal Jalan

157. Which of the following is correct regarding the Kisan Credit Card scheme?

I. It was launched in 1988.
II. Only commercial banks can implement it.

A. Neither I nor II B. Only I
C. Both I and II D. Only II

158. What is disinvestment?

I. Offloading of shares of private companies to government.
II. Offloading of government shares to private companies.

A. Neither I nor II B. Only I
C. Both I and II D. Only II

159. A 'closed economy' is an economy in which ______.

A. the money supply is fully controlled
B. deficit financing takes place
C. only exports take place
D. neither exports nor imports take places

160. For the horizontal distribution of taxes among the states, which among the following criteria has been adopted by the 15th Finance Commission?

I. Income Distance
II. Population (2011 Census)

A. Only I B. Only II
C. Neither I nor II D. Both I and II

161. Which of the following statements is true?

I. Higher growth in GDP and population can occur together.
II. Per capita income always decreases with high population growth.

A. Only I B. Both I and II
C. Only II D. Neither I nor II

162. Price discrimination is said to be personal under which condition?

A. When different prices are charged for different uses for a commodity
B. When same prices are charged to different persons
C. When different prices are charged for the same person
D. When different prices are charged to different persons

163. According to Bertrand model of duopoly, if a firm B sets its price as P_B and firm A sets its price as P_A and C represents the marginal cost of each firm, then under which condition firm A will be losing the market to firm B?

A. When P_A is smaller than P_B and both are greater than C.
B. When P_A is equal to P_B and both are smaller than C.
C. When P_A is greater than P_B and both are smaller than C.
D. When P_A is greater than P_B and both are greater than C.

164. Which of the following best explains the Cascading Effect of taxation?

I. When tax imposition leads to a disproportionate increase in prices by an extent more than the rise in the tax.
II. When tax imposition leads to a disproportionate decrease in prices by an extent more than the rise in the tax.

A. Both I and II B. Only II
C. Only I D. Neither I nor II

165. Which of the following ways can be adopted by the monopolist to create entry barrier so that rivals cannot enter the industry, in the long run?

A. Sharing exclusive rights to few products
B. Product patent or process patent
C. Maximising use of raw material
D. Charging high prices

166. Which of the following is correct regarding poverty measurement?

I. Head count ratio measures incidence of poverty.
II. Poverty gap index measures both incidence as well as severity of poverty.

A. Only II B. Both I and II
C. Neither I nor II D. Only I

167. In a monopolistic competition market structure ______.

A. there is free entry and exit
B. there is a single buyer
C. the size of the market is very small
D. the products are not different at all

168. GDP deflator is used to ______.

A. estimate the purchasing power of the citizen of a country
B. measure the inflation in a country
C. measure the relative reduction in GDP growth rate of a country
D. compare the GDP of a country vis-a-vis other countries of the world

169. Which of the following statements is correct?

I. According to the unanimity rule, only those public goods on which there is complete agreement should be produced.
II. A voter externality cost, refers to the cost incurred by a voter who has voted against a fiscal choice which has been approved.

A. Both I and II B. Only I
C. Only II D. Neither I nor II

170. Given below are two statements, one labelled as Assertion (A) and the other labelled as Reason (R).

Assertion (A): The long-run equilibrium for the perfectly competitive firm occurs at the minimum point of LAC.

Reason (R) : In perfect competition, any new firm is free to set up production in the market if it wishes to, and any existing firm can leave the industry.

In the context of the above two statements, which of the following is correct?

A. (A) is correct, but (R) is incorrect.
B. Both (A) and (R) are incorrect.
C. (A) is incorrect, but (R) is correct.
D. Both (A) and (R) are correct and (R) explains (A).

171. Which of the following is a principle of public debt management?

I. The cost of servicing public debt should be the minimum.
II. If the debt is redeemed by issuing new currency, it may create inflation.

A. Only I B. Neither I nor II
C. Only II D. Both I and II

172. Which of the following is correct regarding the voluntary exchange theory?

I. Resources should be allocated to the public sector in a manner analogous to that of the market and its pricing system.

II. Every individual should get the public good for free.

A. Neither I nor II B. Only II
C. Only I D. Both I and II

173. Direct and Indirect taxes may be compared with each other in respect of ______.

I. Allocation of resources.

II. Distributional effects.

A. Neither I nor II B. Only II
C. Both I and II D. Only I

174. According to Musgrave, the total social benefit is maximum, where the net social benefit is ______.

A. One B. Minimum
C. Zero D. Maximum

175. In which of the following non-collusive oligopolistic model, one firm acts as the leader and the other as follower?

A. Bertrand mode B. Stackelberg model
C. Cournot model D. Sticky price model

176. In the Cournot Duopoly model, Conjectural Variation (CV) of each firm is ______.

A. one B. more than one
C. zero D. less than zero

177. What is a benefit of implementing Goods and Services Tax (GST) in India?

I. GST is expected to bring buoyancy to the Government Revenue by widening the tax base and improving the taxpayer compliance.

II. The removal of cascading of taxes and increased transparency will make the citizens more informed about the taxes they pay while purchasing goods or services.

A. Both I and II B. Only II
C. Neither I nor II D. Only I

178. Which of the following statement is correct regarding bilateral monopoly?

I. The market structure where there is a single seller and a single buyer for a product.

II. With bilateral monopoly the market price and output are indeterminate.

III. The price and quantity of the product is decided by negotiation.

A. I, II and III B. I and III
C. I and II D. Only II

179. What does the term 'Green shoots' represent in an Economy?

I. Signs of economic recovery during an economy downturn.

II. Signs of growth of agriculture sector in a declining economy.

A. Only II B. Both I and II
C. Only I D. Neither I nor II

180. Which of the following tax is levied by a municipal corporation?

I. Property tax.

II. Octroi and terminal tax.

A. Neither I nor II B. Only II
C. Both I and II D. Only I

181. How can a school modify the physical environment for the students?

I. The student who has difficulty seeing in bright light should be seated in a place where direct light is not falling on the face.

II. A student getting distracted easily must be given a place away from the corridor, window or door.

A. Both I and II B. Only II
C. Neither I nor II D. Only I

182. Education should be ______ and ______.

A. continuous; comprehensive
B. discontinuous; restricted
C. continuous; restricted
D. comprehensive; discontinuous

183. When children start learning English, by which of the following ways a teacher can present a new language orally to the children?

I. Through the children

II. Using a mascot

III. Puppets

A. I, II and III B. Only II
C. II and III D. Only I

184. Which of the following is/are the similarity(es) between social sciences and social studies?
I. Both are studied through pragmatic approach.
II. Both seeks social utility.
A. Only II B. Neither I nor II
C. Only I D. Both I and II

185. Learning of which of the following helps the child to perform different activities in their real life?
I. Mathematics
II. Science
III. Social Science
A. I and III B. II and III
C. I, II and III D. I and II

186. The problem solving ability of the learner is dependent on the acquisition of ______ knowledge.
A. cultural B. social
C. mathematical D. historical

187. Which of the following is not correct about Inclusive Education?
A. It is about mounting the confidence among the children
B. It is about building external strength
C. It is all about effective learning by all the children
D. It is based on social model of equality of opportunity

188. Which of the following subject(s) comes under the semi social sciences branch of social sciences?
I. Philosophy
II. Psychology
III. Ethics
A. I and III B. Only III
C. Only II D. I, II and III

189. The defining feature(s) of inclusion that can be used to identify high quality early childhood programs and services is/are ______.
I. Access
II. Participation
III. Supports
A. Only I B. I, II and III
C. Only II D. Only III

190. Which of the following statement(s) is/are correct?
I. '1 + 1 = 2; 1 + 3 = 4; 1 + 5 = 6; 3 + 5 = 8 ... here 1, 3, 5 are odd numbers and the result of their addition i.e 2, 4, 6, 8 are even numbers'. This statement represents Inductive Method.
II. 'While teaching about profit and loss in the class, a teacher announced the formula of profit percentage i.e {P per cent = [P/CP] × 100}'. This statement represents Deductive Method.
A. Only II B. Only I
C. Neither I nor II D. Both I and II

191. Which of the following statement(s) is/are not correct about Reading?
I. Reading is to be able to understand the text, follow its logic and its premises.
II. Reading is to be absorb meaning from the written information or symbols.
A. Both I and II B. Only II
C. Only I D. Neither I nor II

192. Which of the following is the advantages of Expository approach of teaching?
A. Students depend on teacher all the time
B. There is no scope for the creativity of the students
C. Rote memorization is encouraged
D. Gestaltic view of the subject is presented to the students resulting into meaningful verbal learning

193. If variety of materials are used, then any child would fully participate in the learning process. To satisfy the above statement which of the following material(s) a teacher can use to support learning?
I. Visual materials in the form of pictures or photographs.
II. Tactual materials in the form of real objects. For example, using a real mango to explain its qualities.
A. Both I and II B. Neither I nor II
C. Only II D. Only I

194. Which of the following is/are the major language abilities that a teacher may asses of the students?

I. Listening and speaking
II. Reading with comprehension
III. Writing
IV. Expression

A. II and IV B. II, III and IV
C. I, II, III and IV D. I and III

195. Which of the following is/are the broad objective(s) of early childhood care and education programme?

I. Imbibe good nutrition routines, health habits, hygiene practices and self help skills.
II. Enable children for effective communication and foster both receptive and expressive language.

A. Only II B. Neither I nor II
C. Both I and II D. Only I

196. By using different art materials as a means of expression, children should be encouraged to develop a sense of proportion, depth, light, shade and tactile feeling. Which of the following is/are those art material(s)?

I. Pencil
II. Colour
III. Adhesive

A. I and III B. I, II and III
C. Only II D. II and III

197. Which of the following dominant approach(es) is/are followed by the theories and practices of teaching–learning processes?

I. Behaviour Modification
II. Problem Solving

A. Both I and II B. Only I
C. Only II D. Neither I nor II

198. Which of the following statement(s) is/are not correct about environment studies?

I. It helps children develop a holistic understanding of their environment including socio-cultural environment.
II. It helps children in maintaining a multidisciplinary perspective to understanding of our environmental issues.

A. Both I and II
B. Neither I nor II
C. Only I
D. Only II

199. Which of the following is/are the fundamental principle(s) of the visual art?

I. Perspective
II. Balance
III. Harmony
IV. Rhythm

A. I, III and IV B. I, II, III and IV
C. I, II and III D. I, II and IV

200. Which of the following statement(s) shows the relation of mathematics with science?

I. Trigonometry helps in finding the height of a mountain.
II. With the increase in air pressure, the boiling point of water also increases.

A. Only I
B. Only II
C. Neither I nor II
D. Both I and II

ANSWERS

1	2	3	4	5	6	7	8	9	10
B	B	A	A	B	B	C	A	A	A
11	**12**	**13**	**14**	**15**	**16**	**17**	**18**	**19**	**20**
B	A	D	B	C	D	C	A	D	C
21	**22**	**23**	**24**	**25**	**26**	**27**	**28**	**29**	**30**
B	B	A	A	A	D	D	B	D	B
31	**32**	**33**	**34**	**35**	**36**	**37**	**38**	**39**	**40**
D	C	D	B	C	A	D	C	A	B

41	42	43	44	45	46	47	48	49	50
D	C	C	C	B	A	A	C	C	B
51	**52**	**53**	**54**	**55**	**56**	**57**	**58**	**59**	**60**
D	B	A	D	A	B	C	D	B	D
61	**62**	**63**	**64**	**65**	**66**	**67**	**68**	**69**	**70**
A	B	A	A	C	A	C	D	C	A
71	**72**	**73**	**74**	**75**	**76**	**77**	**78**	**79**	**80**
B	D	C	D	D	A	A	D	A	C
81	**82**	**83**	**84**	**85**	**86**	**87**	**88**	**89**	**90**
B	C	A	D	C	D	B	B	A	A
91	**92**	**93**	**94**	**95**	**96**	**97**	**98**	**99**	**100**
A	B	C	C	D	A	A	C	A	B
101	**102**	**103**	**104**	**105**	**106**	**107**	**108**	**109**	**110**
D	C	C	B	C	B	B	B	A	B
111	**112**	**113**	**114**	**115**	**116**	**117**	**118**	**119**	**120**
D	B	D	C	B	B	B	B	D	D
121	**122**	**123**	**124**	**125**	**126**	**127**	**128**	**129**	**130**
C	C	B	D	D	A	A	A	D	C
131	**132**	**133**	**134**	**135**	**136**	**137**	**138**	**139**	**140**
B	C	D	D	B	C	B	B	D	D
141	**142**	**143**	**144**	**145**	**146**	**147**	**148**	**149**	**150**
A	A	A	B	B	A	A	C	C	B
151	**152**	**153**	**154**	**155**	**156**	**157**	**158**	**159**	**160**
C	D	D	B	C	C	A	D	D	D
161	**162**	**163**	**164**	**165**	**166**	**167**	**168**	**169**	**170**
B	D	D	C	B	B	A	B	A	D
171	**172**	**173**	**174**	**175**	**176**	**177**	**178**	**179**	**180**
D	C	C	C	B	C	A	A	C	C
181	**182**	**183**	**184**	**185**	**186**	**187**	**188**	**189**	**190**
A	A	A	B	C	C	B	D	B	D
191	**192**	**193**	**194**	**195**	**196**	**197**	**198**	**199**	**200**
D	D	A	C	C	B	A	B	B	B

R.Gupta's® Highly Useful Books for DSSSB Exams

- DSSSB—Primary Teachers Exam Guide *(R-1911)* 390
- DSSSB—प्राइमरी शिक्षक परीक्षा गाइड *(R-1912)* 390
- DSSSB—Assistant Teachers Exam Guide *(R-540)* 360
- DSSSB—सहायक शिक्षक परीक्षा गाइड *(R-539)* 360
- DSSSB TGT/PGT Recruitment Exam Guide *(R-922)* 395
- DSSSB TGT/PGT भर्ती परीक्षा गाइड *(R-923)* 330
- DSSSB—संगीत शिक्षक भर्ती परीक्षा गाइड *(R-860)* 210
- DSSSB—Librarian (Tier-I) Exam Guide *(R-1578)* 360
- DSSSB शारीरिक शिक्षा शिक्षक भर्ती परीक्षा गाइड *(R-1089)* 365
- DSSSB—लाईब्रेरियन (Tier-I) परीक्षा गाइड *(R-1579)* 360

R-1911

R-1912

R-540

R-539

R-922

R-923

R-860

R-1578

R-1089

R-1579

Ramesh Publishing House 2201

4457, Nai Sarak, Delhi-110006

For Online Shopping: www.rameshpublishinghouse.com

Previous Paper (Solved)

Delhi Subordinate Services Selection Board

DSSSB–PGT (Economics) Recruitment Exam, 2018*

Subject Knowledge – Economics & Teaching Methodology

1. The concept of Marginal Rate of Substitution is an important tool in analysing:
   A. Supply
   B. Demand
   C. Both Demand and Supply
   D. Neither Demand nor Supply

2. A graphical presentation of alternative production possibilities facing an economy is called as:
   A. Production possibility curve
   B. Marginal cost curve
   C. Lorenz curve
   D. Average cost curve

3. The Arc method is used to measure:
   A. Total utility of a consumer
   B. Consumer's equilibrium
   C. Elasticity between two points on a demand curve
   D. Marginal utility of a consumer

4. If income effect is negative and X is an inferior good and Y is a normal good, then the income-consumption curve (ICC) will slope:
   A. Backward bending to the left
   B. Slope downwards to the right
   C. Straight line
   D. Constant

5. The condition of consumer's equilibrium in case of two goods under proportionality rule:
   A. $MU_A = MU_B$
   B. $\frac{MU_A}{P_A} = \frac{MU_B}{P_B}$
   C. $\frac{\Delta P_B}{\Delta Q_A} \times \frac{Q_A}{P_B}$
   D. $\frac{\Delta Q_A}{\Delta Q_B} \times \frac{P_B}{P_A}$

6. The curve that connects the various tangency points of indifference curves and wage lines is:
   A. Iso-revenue curve
   B. Wage offer curve
   C. Budget line
   D. Iso-cost curve

7. In a capitalist economy, the resource allocation is done by the:
   A. Total industry
   B. Monopolies
   C. Free market mechanism
   D. Government

8. The principle of increasing opportunity cost makes the production possibility curve as:
   A. Vertical B. Concave to origin
   C. Horizontal D. Convex to origin

9. When the price consumption curve (PCC) is horizontal then the elasticity is:
   A. $E_p < 1$ B. $E_p = \infty$
   C. $E_p > 1$ D. $E_p = 1$

10. If the consumer is affected by the principle of Demonstration effect, then the shape of the demand curve is:
    A. Vertical towards OY - axis
    B. Negative slope from left to right

* Online exam held on 03/07/2018.

C. Horizontal to OX - axis
D. Positive slope from left to right

11. Match the following.

1. Liquidity trap	(*a*) H.H. Gossen
2. Law of Diminishing Marginal Utility	(*b*) J.M. Keynes
3. Diamond-Water paradox	(*c*) Robert Giffen
4. Substitution effect	(*d*) Adam Smith
5. Demand for inferior goods	(*e*) Eugen Slutsky

	1	2	3	4	5
A.	(*b*)	(*a*)	(*d*)	(*e*)	(*c*)
B.	(*b*)	(*d*)	(*e*)	(*c*)	(*a*)
C.	(*a*)	(*c*)	(*e*)	(*b*)	(*d*)
D.	(*a*)	(*b*)	(*e*)	(*c*)	(*d*)

12. In a free market economy, the point at which the production possibility curve will operate depends upon the:
A. Consumer demand for different goods
B. Pattern of allocation of resources
C. Supply of different goods by the producers
D. Government decisions

13. The amount of a next best commodity foregone for producing an extra unit of a commodity is known as:
A. Total variable cost
B. Opportunity cost
C. Total average cost
D. Total fixed cost

14. In the case of inferior goods, the income effect is:
A. Equal to zero B. Negative
C. Positive D. Equal to one

15. If the price of good '*x*' declines, the number of its quantities purchased rises proportionately; however, the purchased quantity of good '*y*' remains same. What is the shape of the price consumption curve?
A. Horizontal B. Vertical
C. Convex D. Concave

16. Rightward movement of the economy from one production possibility curve to another indicates:
A. Increase in number of firms
B. Increase in output of goods and services
C. Increase in consumption
D. Increase in cost of production

17. Utilisation of its available resources fully and most effectively and thereby production of maximum possible output with the given amount of resources by a firm, industry or and entire economy is known as:
A. Allocation efficiency
B. Economic efficiency
C. Market efficiency
D. Technical efficiency

18. Find the incorrect statement.
A. The slope of the Indifference curve is convex to the origin.
B. Higher indifference curve represents a higher level of satisfaction.
C. The shape of the indifference curve is 'U' shaped in the case of perfect complementary goods.
D. Indifference curves neither touch nor intersect with each other.

19. Compensated demand curve includes only the:
A. Both price and income effect
B. Substitution effect
C. Income effect
D. Price effect

20. In a socialist economy, the functions of the market are performed by the:
A. Consumers
B. Managers
C. Central planning authority
D. Producers

21. Which among following is not correct assumption of perfect competition?
A. Perfect mobilisation of inputs
B. Differentiated product
C. Perfect market knowledge
D. Absence of selling costs

22. The price of a perishable commodity is influenced by:
A. No change in supply
B. Changes in the prices of substitutes

C. Changes in supply
D. Changes in demand

23. The concept of social welfare function was first introduced by:
A. Bergson B. Scitovsky
C. Hicks and Kaldor D. Arrow

24. Income derived from machines and other appliances made by man during short run is known as:
A. Interest B. Quasi-rent
C. Profits D. Rent

25. If the monopolist sells his product at a higher price in internal market and at a lower price in external market, it is known as:
A. Tariff
B. Countervailing duty
C. Export duty
D. Dumping

26. The demand curve (Average Revenue Curve) under perfect competition is:
A. Perfect elastic B. Perfect inelastic
C. Relative inelastic D. Relative elastic

27. Match the following.

1. Marginal products of factors of production becomes zero	(*a*) Budget line
2. Represents the prices of the goods and consumer's money income	(*b*) Price consumption curve
3. Locus of different equilibrium points of a consumer at different prices, given the money income	(*c*) Iso-cost curve
4. Combinations of two factors that the firm can buy with a given outlay	(*d*) Ridgelines

	1	2	3	4
A.	(*a*)	(*d*)	(*c*)	(*b*)
B.	(*d*)	(*c*)	(*b*)	(*a*)
C.	(*c*)	(*d*)	(*a*)	(*b*)
D.	(*d*)	(*a*)	(*b*)	(*c*)

28. What is the shape of the MFC and AFC if the factor market is monopsony and the product market is perfect competition?
A. Both are same and horizontal
B. An upward sloping where AFC lies above the MFC
C. Negatively sloping from left to right
D. Positively rising from left to right

29. Who introduced the concept of externalities to explain welfare?
A. Marshall B. Pareto
C. Hicks D. Pigou

30. Match the following.

1. Differential rent theory	(*a*) Wickstead
2. Marginal productivity theory	(*b*) Karl Marx
3. Surplus value principle	(*c*) Kalecki
4. Degree of monopoly theory of profit	(*d*) Alfred Marshall
5. Adding-up problem	(*e*) David Ricardo

	1	2	3	4	5
A.	(*e*)	(*b*)	(*a*)	(*c*)	(*d*)
B.	(*d*)	(*b*)	(*a*)	(*e*)	(*c*)
C.	(*e*)	(*d*)	(*b*)	(*c*)	(*a*)
D.	(*d*)	(*e*)	(*b*)	(*c*)	(*a*)

31. When labour is on x-axis, the shape of the iso-quant that combines more labour with the same quantity of capital is:
A. Convex B. Vertical
C. Horizontal D. Concave

32. The important property of the Cobb-Douglas production is that the production function is subject to:
A. Negative returns to scale
B. Constant returns to scale
C. Increasing returns to scale
D. Decreasing returns to scale

33. Constrained bliss point is the point where the:
A. Indifference curve is tangent to the budget line
B. Iso-quant is tangent to the iso-cost curve
C. There is equality between iso-cost curve and iso-project curve
D. Social indifference curve of the society is tangent to the grand utility possibility curve

34. In a competitive factor market, a firm is said to be in equilibrium in the long run when which of the following conditions is satisfied?
A. MRP = MFC
B. MRP > MFC
C. Both MRP = MFC and MRP curve must cut MFC curve from above
D. MRP curve must cut MFC curve from above

35. Under which condition price discrimination is profitable?
A. Different elasticities of demand
B. Same elasticities of demand
C. Relative inelastic demand
D. Perfect elastic demand

36. Technical substitution measures the degree of substitutability between:
A. Two firms B. Two goods
C. Two individuals D. Two factors

37. Match the following.

1. Increasing returns to scale	(*a*) Long-run period
2. All inputs are changeable	(*b*) Existence of external economies
3. Decreasing returns to scale	(*c*) Short-run period
4. Labour is the only variable input	(*d*) Existence of external diseconomies

	1	2	3	4
A.	(*b*)	(*d*)	(*c*)	(*a*)
B.	(*a*)	(*d*)	(*b*)	(*c*)
C.	(*a*)	(*b*)	(*d*)	(*c*)
D.	(*b*)	(*a*)	(*d*)	(*c*)

38. Imputed value of an entrepreneur's own resources and services is known as:
A. Selling cost B. Opportunity cost
C. Total cost D. Implicit cost

39. Which factors the modern economist took into consideration to determine interest?
A. Liquidity preference schedules
B. Savings and investment on one hand and liquidity preference and supply of money on another
C. Demand and supply of loanable funds
D. Savings and investment

40. The line that joins all the tangency points of iso-quant and iso-cost line is:
A. Production possibility curve
B. Opportunity cost
C. Output-factor curve
D. Iso-project curve

41. At zero level of income, average propensity to consume is:
A. Infinite B. Between 0 and ∞
C. Zero D. Between 0 and 1

42. Personal income includes all except ....
A. Personal Tax
B. Personal Savings
C. Transfer Payment
D. Undistributed corporate profits

43. The degrees of price discrimination has been distinguished by:
A. Marshall B. Cournot
C. Chamberlin D. Pigou

44. The best indicator of economic development is:
A. Real national income
B. Per capita real national income
C. GNP at current prices
D. National income at factor cost

45. Payments accruing to factors of production is equal to:
A. Transfer payments
B. Corporate profits
C. Net value added
D. Personal income

46. In which model each producer believes that his rival will keep the prices of his products constant at the present level, whatever price the producer night himself set?
A. Bertrand model
B. Edgeworth model
C. Chamberlin's model
D. Cournot's model

47. In a straight line demand curve meeting the two axis, the marginal revenue (MR) at the mid-point of the curve is:

A. Greater that one B. One
C. Less than one D. Zero

48. The Total Cost (TC) in monopolistic competition is a sum of:
A. Average Fixed Cost and Quantity of Output
B. Total Fixed Cost and Total Variable Cost
C. Production Cost and Selling Cost
D. Total Fixed Cost and Marginal Cost

49. Income elasticity of a luxury good is:
A. Less than one B. Greater than one
C. Zero D. Equal to one

50. Cross elasticity of demand for product of pure monopoly is:
A. $E_C = 0$ B. $E_C < 1$
C. $E_C = 1$ D. $E_C > 1$

51. The industry demand curve and the average revenue curve are same in the case of:
A. Monopolistic competition
B. Monopoly
C. Oligopoly
D. Duopoly

52. A.P. Lerner's index of monopoly power is given by:
A. $\frac{P-MC}{MC}$ B. $\frac{MC-P}{MC}$
C. $\frac{P-MC}{P}$ D. $\frac{MC-P}{AC}$

53. If GDP (at market price) = ₹ 500 crore, depreciation = ₹ 50 crore, indirect taxes = ₹ 30 crore, subsidies = ₹ 10 crore, net factor income from abroad = ₹ 20 crore, then national income is:
A. ₹ 500 crore B. ₹ 540 crore
C. ₹ 540 crore D. ₹ 450 crore

54. An expansionary monetary and fiscal policy shifts:
A. Aggregate supply curve to the right
B. Aggregate demand curve to the right
C. Aggregate supply curve to the left
D. Aggregate demand curve to the left

55. Marginal revenue of a firm under perfect competition is:
A. Equal to the price
B. Less than the price
C. Greater than the price
D. Greater than marginal cost

56. Wages and salaries + dividends paid at home + factor income received from abroad + transfers from government – personal income tax =
A. Personal disposable income
B. GDP
C. Per capita income
D. National income

57. Which is created under monopolistic competition due to entry of too many firms in long run and absence of price competition each firm produces much less than its full capacity?
A. Excess output
B. Excess capacity
C. Optimum firm size
D. Optimum output

58. Match the following.

1. Kinked demand curve	(*a*) Monopolistic competition
2. Monopolistic competition	(*b*) Oligopoly
3. Price leadership	(*c*) Price rigidity
4. Group equilibrium	(*d*) Excess capacity

	1	2	3	4
A.	(*a*)	(*d*)	(*b*)	(*c*)
B.	(*b*)	(*d*)	(*a*)	(*c*)
C.	(*b*)	(*d*)	(*c*)	(*a*)
D.	(*c*)	(*d*)	(*b*)	(*a*)

59. The slope of consumption function represents:
A. Marginal propensity to save
B. Average propensity to consume
C. Average propensity to save
D. Marginal propensity to consume

60. GDP at market price exceeds GDP at factor cost by the amount of revenue raised through:
A. Indirect taxes B. Direct taxes
C. Sales tax D. Income tax

61. Which of the following is not a classical assumption?

A. Perfect competition
B. Existence of full employment
C. Laissez-faire
D. Rigid wages and prices

62. "Ratchet effect" is the situation where households find:
A. Difficult to adjust to both raising income as well as falling income
B. Easy to adjust to rising income than falling income
C. Easy to adjust to falling income than rising income
D. Difficult to adjust to rising incomes than falling income

63. The flexible acceleration theory of investment was developed by:
A. H.B. Chenery B. J.B. Clark
C. J. R Hicks D. Nicholas Kaldor

64. Which among the following relates to macroeconomics?
A. Revenue from cement industry
B. Output of coal industry
C. Capita-output ratio in the steel industry
D. Disposable income of a country

65. Keynesian transactionary demand for money is:
A. Interest inelastic and income elastic
B. Interest inelastic and income inelastic
C. Interest elastic and income inelastic
D. Interest elastic and income elastic

64. The vertical difference between aggregate demand curve and consumption function curve is equal to:
A. Autonomous consumption
B. Autonomous investment
C. Induced investment
D. Induced consumption

67. Which is the flow variable among the following?
A. Consumption S
B. Unemployment
C. Money supply
D. Foreign exchange reserves

68. Increase in the value of multiplier will not depend on:
A. Increase in marginal propensity to save
B. Increase in average propensity to consume
C. Increase in marginal propensity to consume
D. Decrease in tax rate

69. Investment is determined by:
A. Marginal efficiency of capital and rate of consumption
B. Marginal efficiency of capital and rate of interest
C. Marginal propensity to import and rate of interest
D. Marginal propensity to consume and rate of consumption

70. If the net national product is increased by 8.8%, the population is increased by 2.0%, then the per capita income will increase by:
A. 4.4% B. 10.8%
C. 16.8% D. 6.8%

71. International current account shows:
A. Inflows and outflows of goods and services
B. Transfers to other countries
C. Total imports
D. Total exports

72. At the minimum rate of interest, the shape of liquidity preference curve:
A. is horizontal B. Intersects on axis
C. is inelastic D. is vertical

73. In evolving a detailed system of national accounts, who made a valuable contribution?
A. Richard Stone B. A Marshall
C. AC Pigou D. JM Keynes

74. The increase in autonomous investment leads to:
A. Shifting the IS curve to the right
B. Shifting the IS curve to the left
C. Shifting the LM curve to the right
D. Shifting the LM curve to the left

75. If the marginal propensity to import increases:
A. No effect on multiplier value
B. The value of multiplier decreases
C. The value of multiplier increases
D. The marginal propensity to invest increases

76. AW Phillips curve shows the relationship between:
A. Money wage rate and unemployment
B. Real wage rate and inflation
C. Deflation and unemployment
D. Real wage rate and unemployment

77. If consumption function curve intersects aggregate expenditure curve then:
A. Savings equals to zero
B. Savings equals to one
C. Investment is equal to zero
D. Savings equal to investment

78. If MPC is 0.2, then the value of the multiplier is:
A. 1.25 B. 0.8
C. 1.0 D. 5.0

79. Identify which is not the subject of macroeconomics among the following.
A. Theory of employment
B. Theory of general prices
C. Theory of economic development
D. Theory of economic welfare

80. Keynesian theory of consumption is based on:
A. Relative income hypothesis
B. Permanent income hypothesis
C. Absolute income hypothesis
D. Past income hypothesis

81. "Taxation is not just a vehicle for raising state revenue, it is critically important for economic and political development." This was opined by:
A. Shirras and Bastable
B. J.B. Say and A.C. Pigou
C. Besley and Pearson
D. Adam Smith and Dalton

82. The relationship between required reserve ratio and money supply is:
A. Positive
B. Unrelated
C. Either negative or positive
D. Negative

83. Which committee recommended the Debt-to-GDP ratio as a medium term anchor for fiscal policy in India?
A. Taxation Enquiry Commission 1953-54
B. FRBM Review Committee 2017
C. Wanchoo Committee 1970
D. Rekhi Committee 1993

84. The percentage of Fiscal Deficit was revised for the financial year ending 2018 as:
A. 3.3% of the GDP B. 3.5% of the GDP
C. 3.0% of the GDP D. 3.2% of the GDP

85. Government sells bonds and securities to the people during:
A. Stagflation B. Recession
C. Inflation D. Deflation

86. The High power money can be calculated with:

A. $H = \frac{C_r - RR_r + ER_r}{1+C_r} \times M$

B. $H = \frac{C_r + RR_r + ER_r}{1+C_r} \times M$

C. $H = \frac{1+C_r}{C_r + RR_r + ER_r} \times M$

D. $H = \frac{C_r + RR_r - ER_r}{1+C_r} \times M$

87. The difference between M_3 and M_1 is:
A. Term deposits
B. Demand deposits
C. M_2
D. Post office saving deposits

88. Find out which type of deficit is arrived at by deducting interest paid on borrowings from the fiscal deficit.
A. Budget deficit B. Revenue deficit
C. Primary deficit D. Fiscal deficit

89. A budget based on functions, activities and projects, which was adopted in USA (1949), refers to:
A. Performance Budgeting
B. Programming Budgeting
C. Planning Budget
D. Zero-Based Budget

90. In which type of budget, outlays, outputs and outcomes in measurable terms are presented to the Parliament?

A. Balanced Budget B. Deficit Budget
C. Surplus Budget D. Outcome Budget

91. Which of the following is not a quantitative measure of RBI?
A. Bank rate
B. Open market operations
C. Variable interest rates
D. Variable reserve requirements

92. Which type of budgeting technique is considered as a powerful tool for achieving gender-mainstreaming in India?
A. Outcome Budget
B. Gender Budgeting
C. Traditional Budgeting
D. Zero-Based Budgeting

93. Which type of deficit refers to the difference between revenue deficit and Grants for creation of capital assets?
A. Fiscal Deficit
B. Revenue Deficit
C. Effective Revenue Deficit
D. Primary Deficit

94. The amount of revenue deficit of the Central Government for the period April to November during the year 2017-18:
A. ₹ 4.90 lakh Crore
B. ₹ 4.58 lakh Crore
C. ₹ 3 .45 lakh Crore
D. ₹ 5.48 lakh Crore

95. Which one of the following is not a function of the RBI?
A. Issue of notes
B. Accepting the deposits from public
C. Custodian of cash reserves of banks
D. Banker to government

96. The number of GST registrants in India, as on December 2017, was estimated at:
A. 9.8 million B. 9.0 million
C. 9.1 million D. 8.9 million

97. The target for the amount of disinvestment for the year 2018-19 was set as:
A. ₹ 72,500 Cr B. ₹ 80.000 Cr
C. ₹ 79,000 Cr D. ₹ 1,00,000 Cr

98. To which parameter was the focus laid by Government of India to reset India's fiscal policy as was recommended by N.K. Singh panel?
A. Tax Revenue-to-GDP Ratio
B. Expenditure-to-GDP Ratio
C. Debt-to-GDP Ratio
D. Borrowings-to-GDP Ratio

99. The formula for money multiplier *m* is:
A. $m = C_r + RR_r + ER_r$
B. $m = \dfrac{1+C_r}{C_r + RR_r + ER_r}$
C. $m = \dfrac{1+C_r}{C_r + RR_r + ER_r} - H$
D. $m = \dfrac{1+C_r}{C_r + RR_r + ER_r} + H$

100. The targets of fixed percentages of Debt-to-GDP Ratio for Centre and States as suggested by FRBM Review Committee 2017 are:
A. 33.0% and 23.0% respectively
B. 35.0% and 19.0% respectively
C. 40.0% and 20.0% respectively
D. 30.0% and 20% respectively

101. Fixed exchange rates may lead to:
A. Appreciation of domestic currency
B. Depreciation of domestic currency
C. Inflation
D. Drain on Foreign exchange reserves

102. Indemnity payments is a component of:
A. Merchandise account
B. Short term capital account
C. Invisible account
D. Long term Capital account

103. Agreement made at present to get foreign exchange at a future date at a specified exchange rate is known as:
A. Gentlemen agreement
B. Forward contract
C. Arbitrage
D. Spot contract

104. An Indian exporter, who was getting ₹ 65 per dollar in 2017, gets ₹ 60 in 2018. The situation is known as:

A. Revaluation of Rupee
B. Depreciation of Rupee
C. Appreciation of Rupee
D. Depreciation of Dollar

105. Which of the following pairs is not correctly matched?
A. Budget – a small leather bag
B. NABH Nirman – Expansion of Airport Capacity
C. UDAN – Ude Desh Ka Aam Nagarik
D. Gr. AMs – German Agricultural Markets

106. The system of flexible exchange rates gives rise to:
A. Deficit in balance of payments
B. Equilibrium in balance of payments
C. Surplus in balance of payments
D. Depletion of foreign exchange reserves

107. When the demand for Euro rises in India, it leads to:
A. Depreciation of Rupee
B. Revaluation of Rupee
C. Appreciation of Rupee
D. Depreciation of Euro

108. From the following, identify the intra-industry trade model.
A. Ricardo's Model
B. Neo-Heckscher-Ohlin Model
C. Adam Smith Model
D. Heckscher-Ohlin Model

109. When the forces of demand for and supply of a currency operate freely to determine its foreign exchange rate, the system is known as:
A. Fixed Exchange Rate
B. Crawling Peg
C. Managed Flexibility
D. Floating Exchange Rate

110. Find out the correct matched pair from the following.
A. Fiscal Policy – Money Supply
B. Government Budget – Economic Growth
C. Taxes on Personal Income – Indirect Taxes
D. Monetary Policy – Public Borrowings

111. Foreign exchange rate is defined as:
A. Price of one unit of foreign currency expressed in terms of domestic currency
B. Number of units of domestic currency exchanged for 100 units of foreign currency
C. Number of units of foreign currency exchanged for 100 units of domestic currency
D. Price of one unit of foreign currency expressed in terms of gold equivalent

112. Leontief empirically verified the theory of:
A. Factor Proportions
B. Opportunity Cost
C. Absolute Cost Difference
D. Comparative Cost Difference

113. The problem of Surplus in India's balance of payments could be solved through:
A. Appreciation of Rupee
B. Exporting more goods and services
C. Depreciation of Rupee
D. Cutting expenditure on imports

114. Reduction in the value of rupee against US dollar under Bretton Woods system meant:
A. Revaluation
B. Devaluation
C. Depreciation
D. Realignment of parity of the currencies

115. Which of the following is a practical, nor theoretical, importance of free international trade?
A. Extensive choice of items for consumers
B. Equalization of factor values in trading countries
C. Equalization of goods values in trading countries
D. Efficient allocation of international resources

116. Under Gold standard, the exchange rates were:
A. Fixed
B. Flexible
C. Managed
D. Floating

117. Free Trade redistributes income in favour of:
A. Scarce Factor of Production
B. Abundant Factor of Production

C. Fixed Factor of Production
D. Variable Factor of Production

118. Importers and exporters can reduce their exchange risk through:
A. Speculation
B. Hedging
C. Spot buying of foreign currency
D. Arbitrage

119. Identity the item that does not fall under current account of the balance of payments.
A. Interest payments
B. Capital payments
C. Shipping charges
D. Insurance charges

120. Which of the following is not correct regarding the year of establishment?
A. International Development Association (IDA), 1960
B. Multilateral Investment Guarantee Agency (MIGA), 1988
C. International Financial Corporation (IFC), 1950
D. International Bank of Reconstruction and Development (IBRD), 1945

121. Which of the following is not the function of Stock market?
A. Ensuring the safety of the transactions
B. Pricing of Securities
C. Contribution to Economic Growth
D. Spreading the debt culture

122. The Eleventh Ministerial Conference of the WTO was held in:
A. Doha B. Bali
C. Buenos Aires D. Nairobi

123. Bombay Stock Exchange was founded in the year:
A. June, 1870 B. June, 1949
C. July, 1875 D. July, 1936

124. SEBI was given Statutory powers in:
A. July - 1982 B. April - 1990
C. January - 1992 D. April - 1988

125. If Σfd^2 is 362, Σfd is + 128 and n is 217, then σ is:
A. 1.7 B. 1.9
C. 2.0 D. 1.149

126. Which of the following awards was not obtained by NSE in the year 2015?
A. Golden Peacock Innovative Product/ Service Award
B. Global Architecture Excellence Award
C. FOW Awards for Asia - Best New Technology Product - Market Surveillance
D. Asian Banker Achievement Awards - Stock Exchange of the Year

127. The formula for the coefficient of variation is:
A. $\frac{\sigma}{\text{Mean}} \times 100$ B. $\frac{\text{Mean}}{\sigma} \times 100$
C. $\frac{\text{Mean}}{Z} \times 100$ D. $\frac{Z}{\text{Mean}} \times 100$

128. Premchand Roychand founded:
A. Calcutta Stock Exchange
B. National Stock Exchange
C. Chennai Stock Exchange
D. Bombay Stock Exchange

129. Mode is found graphically by:
A. Ogive curve
B. Pie diagram
C. Frequency polygon
D. Histogram

130. Tariffs cannot improve the terms of trade of the tariff imposing country when the elasticity of the offer curve of the foreign country is:
A. Zero
B. Perfectly elastic
C. Equal to unity
D. Perfectly inelastic

131. Which of the following is the regulatory function of SEBI?
A. Check on price rigging
B. Prohibiting fraudulent and unfair trade practices
C. Conducting inquiries and audit of stock exchanges
D. Prohibiting insider trading

132. Which of the following is not ensured by owning a share of a company?

A. Voting Rights
B. Assured Flow of Income
C. Ownership of the company
D. Dividend

133. Which of the following organisations is called 'Soft lending institution'?
A. BRICS Bank B. IBRD
C. IMF D. IDA

134. The relationship between two variables are shown in:
A. Bar diagram B. Histogram
C. Line diagram D. Pictograph

135. Mean – Mode/σ is used to calculate:
A. Karl Pearson's coefficient of skewness
B. Karl Pearson's coefficient of correlation
C. Standard Deviation
D. Quartile deviation

136. Gini coefficient is used to measure:
A. Human Development Index (HDI)
B. Poverty Index (PI)
C. Income Inequality
D. Physical Quality Life Index (PQLI)

137. Who is the current (as of April 2018) Managing Director and CEO of NSE?
A. Vikram Limaye B. Ashok Chawla
C. Deepak Mishra D. Anurag Patil

138. The Gold Tranche of the IMF quota of a country is equal to:
A. 50 percent of the country's quota
B. 125 percent of the country's quota
C. 25 percent of the country's quota
D. 100 percent of the country's quota

139. The most common form of diagrammatic representation of a grouped frequency system is:
A. Ogive curve B. Pie diagram
C. Histogram D. Frequency polygon

140. Who is the Managing Director of IMF as of April 2018?
A. Christine Lagarde
B. Horst Kohler
C. Dominique Strauss-Kahn
D. Rodrigo de Rato *y* Figaredo

141. The cultivation of which commercial crop led to 'Uprising' among the farmers during the British rule?
A. Indigo B. Tobacco
C. Jute D. Cotton

142. The classical economist who worked for the British East India company in 1857 was:
A. John Stuart Mill B. David Ricardo
C. Adam Smith D. TR Malthus

143. Which of the following was not a problem of the 'Heavy Industry First' model of the Indian planning?
A. Strengthen the relationship between magniloquent and backwards
B. Rising unemployment
C. Increasing poverty
D. Increasing regional disparities

144. 'Removal of poverty' was the objective of which five year plan?
A. Fourth Five Year Plan
B. Third Five Year Plan
C. Fifth Five Year Plan
D. Sixth Five Year Plan

145. The Fifth Five year Plan was prepared and launched by:
A. MN Roy B. S Chakraborty
C. P R Brahmananda D. D P Dhar

146. Which of the following reform measures was NOT undertaken by India on domestic sector in 1991?
A. Cut in subsidies
B. Cut in interest rates
C. Cut in fiscal deficit
D. Cut in transfers to public sector enterprises

147. Which of the following was not the goal of the First Ten Five Year Plans in India?
A. Inclusive Growth
B. Balanced Regional Development
C. Socialistic Pattern of Society
D. Increasing the National Income

148. The sum of squares of differences of ranks, given by the judges A and B, for 8 students, is 21. The value of rank correlation coefficient is:

A. 0.7 B. 0.65
C. 0.8 D. 0.75

149. The Fiscal Responsibility and Budget Management (FRBM) Act, 2003, aims to bring down fiscal deficit to:
A. 4% of GDP B. 3% of GDP
C. 4.5% of GDP D. 5% of GDP

150. As a part of the new economic reforms in 1997, the statutory liquidity ratio (SLR) was brought down to:
A. 8.0 per cent B. 25.0 per cent
C. 20 per cent D. 11.0 per cent

151. Which of the following reform measures was NOT undertaken by India on external sector in 1991?
A. Revaluation of rupee by 23% in two stages
B. Abolition of complex system of import licensing
C. Liberalisation of FDI Policy
D. Liberalisation of trade policy

152. Which sector was given the status of 'Commanding Heights' during the Second Five-Year Plan?
A. Co-operative sector
B. Public sector
C. Joint sector
D. Private sector

153. The actual public sector outlay during the First Five Year Plan was:
A. ₹ 1,960 crore B. ₹ 1,450 crore
C. ₹ 1,650 crore D. ₹ 4,600 crore

154. Which of the following was not the priority of the First Five Year Plan?
A. Rehabilitation of the refugees
B. Correction of the disequilibrium in the economy caused by the partition of the country
C. Rapid agricultural development to achieve self-sufficiency in food grains
D. Accelerated development of the industrial sector

155. The land tenure system introduced by Sir Thomas Munro was introduced:
A. Mahalwari System
B. Ryotwari System
C. Miras System
D. Zamindari System

156. The quartile deviation of 12, 7, 15, 10, 16, 17 and 25 is:
A. 4.5 B. 9
C. 5.5 D. 3.5

157. Vakil and Brahmananda attributed the existence of mass poverty in India to the shortages of:
A. Intermediate goods
B. Wage goods
C. Raw materials
D. Capital goods

158. The World Bank supported India's economic reforms of 1991 with a Structural Adjustment Loan of:
A. US$ 600 million B. US$ 5,000 million
C. US$ 500 million D. US$ 1,000 million

159. Which of the following is not considered to be the positive effect of LPG policies?
A. Control on Fiscal Deficit
B. Increased foreign exchange reserves
C. Increased role of MNCs
D. High growth rate of the economy

160. Which of the following was not the reason for the introduction of New Economic Reforms in India in 1991?
A. Fall in India's credit rating by the international agencies
B. Rising average trade deficit
C. Rising receipts on invisible account
D. Fall in the foreign exchange reserves

161. The Sustainable Development Goals (SDGs) that came into effect in January 2016 will continue to guide UNDP policy and funding until the year:
A. 2030 B. 2025
C. 2035 D. 2020

162. Which of the following is not the economic factor determining the cropping pattern?
A. Price of the product
B. Soil
C. Procurement policy of the government
D. Insurance against risk

163. The word 'Sustainable Development' was first coined by:
A. Brundtland Commission
B. European Commission
C. Global Judicial Institute on Environment
D. The Water Commission

164. According to Human Development Report 2016:
A. Both India and Pakistan are placed in Low Human Development category countries
B. Both India and Pakistan are placed in Medium Human Development category countries
C. India is placed in Medium Human Development category while Pakistan in Low Human Development category
D. India is placed in Low Human Development category while Pakistan in Medium Human Development category

165. The Report "Our Common Future" was submitted in the year:
A. 1997 B. 1982
C. 1987 D. 1992

166. Which of the following was not one of the 8 Millennium Development Goals?
A. Eradicate Extreme Poverty and Hunger
B. Achieve Universal Primary Education
C. Achieve Sustainable Cities and Communities
D. Promote Gender Equality and Empower Women

167. Studies on poverty heavily depend upon:
A. Census Data B. NSSO Data
C. CSO Data D. NCAER Data

168. The Comprehensive Crop Insurance Scheme (CCIS) was introduced in India in the year:
A. 1980 B. 1985
C. 1975 D. 1990

169. Identify the positive Effect of the Economic Reforms of 1991.
A. Erosion of cultural values
B. Lopsided growth process
C. Widening of the 'rural urban divide'
D. Shift from monopoly to competitive market

170. According to India Brand Equity Foundation (IBEF), in April 2018, India has become the second largest market for e-learning after:
A. USA B. China
C. Canada D. Australia

171. The initial Reform process in China covering the period from 1978 to 1984 focused on:
A. Non-farm activities in rural areas
B. Land tenure system and support prices for agricultural products
C. Foreign trade and investments
D. Industrial development

172. China seemed to have outstripped India for the first time in the share of World GDP in the year around:
A. 1600 B. 1100
C. 1500 D. 1000

173. Which of the following comparisons between India and China is not true?
A. China has one party authoritarian rule while India has a multi-party system
B. Chinese people are relatively homogeneous while those of India are heterogeneous
C. The economic reforms in both the countries are crisis driven
D. Chinese economy is the second largest and the Indian economy is the fourth largest in the world in terms of PPP GDP

174. The 2009 Tendulkar Committee Report related to methodology of estimation of:
A. Inequality B. Inflation
C. Poverty D. Unemployment

175. According to World Bank study of 2016, poverty rate is the highest among:
A. Others B. OBCs
C. SCs D. STs

176. Which of the following is the least important in human capital formation?
A. Good Training B. Good Health
C. Good Friendship D. Good Education

177. India's ranking in the world production of the fruits is:
A. Tenth B. First
C. Third D. Second

178. According to Human Development Report 2016, Gender inequality in India was:
A. Lower than China but higher than Pakistan
B. Higher than China but lower than Pakistan
C. Lower than both China and Pakistan
D. Higher than both China and Pakistan

179. Which of the following does not come under globalization?
A. Permission to multinational companies
B. Reduction in excise duty
C. Liberalization of FDI
D. Reduction in tariff layers

180. According to Human Development Report 2016:
A. India is placed in Medium Human Development category while China in High Human Development category
B. India is placed in Medium Human Development category while China in Low Human Development category
C. Both India and China are placed in High Human Development category countries
D. Both India and China are placed in Medium Human Development category countries

181. Which of the following is not a two-dimensional (2D) art, method or technique used in teaching a subject?
A. Rangoli B. Installation
C. Collarge D. Corroboration

182. Indentify the correct statement on the conversational activity from the given alternatives.
A. Low level of student participation
B. Effective when addressing issues are in the dominant domain
C. All types of learners are active in conversational activities
D. Introvert enjoys conversational activities

183. When a learner performs a skill according to the instruction rather than the observation, he is known to be at the _______ level of psychomotor domain.
A. 'Naturalises' B. 'Imitates'
C. 'Articulates' D. 'Manipulates'

184. When knowledge is acquired through religious texts, it is known as ______ .
A. authority B. revelation
C. testimony D. reason

185. What should be the objective of teaching science at higher secondary school level?
A. To develop economic efficiency and capacity to earn a livelihood
B. To develop the observation skills
C. To get the knowledge about the society and natural environment
D. Develop the quantitative sense to solve the problems

186. Which of these is NOT a good aspect relating to reading a newspaper?
A. Exaggerated or underplayed news of the real situation
B. Knowledge on antisocial elements in the society
C. Increased vocabulary
D. Latest update on the current happenings

187. Which of these is NOT a correct statement on the guiding principles of constructivism?
A. The learning process focuses on isolated facts, not on primary concepts
B. The purpose of learning is for an individual to construct his or her own meaning, not just to memorise the "right" answers
C. Learning requires understanding wholes as well as parts and parts must be understood in the context of wholes
D. Learning must start with the issues around which students are actively trying to construct meaning

188. _______ is/are mandated to provide academic and technical resource support to adult and continuing education through development and production of material and training modules. In addition to this, it/they would be required to conduct motivational and environmental building, action research and evaluation and monitoring.
A. Jan Shikshan Sansthans
B. The State Resource Centre(s)

C. Rashtriya Madhyamik Shiksha Abhiyan
D. Sarva Shiksha Abhiyan

189. The assessment that expands the findings of an assessment with analysis of abilities and potentials with a further dimension is known as:
A. summative assessment
B. formative assessment
C. prognostic assessment
D. diagnostic assessment

190. In a particular Mathematics class, a student can draw geometrical figures and graphs. Which stage of cognitive domain is the student exhibiting?
A. Understanding B. Knowledge
C. Application D. Skill

191. Identify the learning style from the given description:

Somu likes to have a hands-on experience in anything he learns. He enjoys field trips to experience the physical proximity of the target knowledge. He makes his own notes on whatever he learns.
A. Tactile Learning style
B. Visual / Non-verbal Learning style
C. Visual / Verbal Learning style
D. Auditory Learning style

192. Which of these is NOT a correct statement on including inclusive education in India?
A. It is an opportunity to form friendships with other children.
B. Giving all the normal and differently abled children equal opportunities to learn and get equal treatment as others.
C. It develops the tolerance and appreciation of normal children for differently abled students.
D. Children with special needs cannot be made a part of regular school.

193. _______ is a developmental disability significantly affecting verbal and non-verbal communication and social interaction, generally evident before age three and characterised by engaging in repetitive activities and stereotyped movements.
A. Dyslexia B. Autism
C. Dysgraphia D. ADHD

194. Which of these is NOT an assessment method?
A. Presentations
B. Students watching an audiovisual
C. Homework exercises
D. Simulations

195. Which of these factors does NOT affect the emotionality of a person?
A. Child A is too much excited at the thought of an ice cream
B. Child C is happily sleeping at night undisturbed for 8 hours
C. Child D is suffering from disease due to malnutrition
D. Child B is exhausted after travelling for 4 hours in the car

196. What of the following blogs don't have a tool?
A. Blogger B. Edublog
C. Trackback D. Wordpress

197. Which of the following skills is a receptive skill?
A. Writing B. Language
C. Speaking D. Listening

198. Which of these is NOT a correct statement of the CAI?
A. It facilitates reteaching and reinforcing
B. CAI can give a human touch better than traditional teaching
C. It can help teachers to improve their role in education process
D. It can create simulations in the learner

199. What is called the ability to understand current gender difference and issues and incorporate these into strategies and actions?
A. Gender parity B. Gender sensitivity
C. Gender equality D. Gender equity

200. Which of these is NOT a part of social science?
A. Statistics B. Biology
C. Sociology D. Anthropology

ANSWERS

1	2	3	4	5	6	7	8	9	10
B	A	C	A	B	B	C	B	D	D
11	**12**	**13**	**14**	**15**	**16**	**17**	**18**	**19**	**20**
A	A	B	B	A	B	D	C	B	C
21	**22**	**23**	**24**	**25**	**26**	**27**	**28**	**29**	**30**
B	D	A	B	D	A	D	D	D	C
31	**32**	**33**	**34**	**35**	**36**	**37**	**38**	**39**	**40**
C	B	D	C	A	D	D	D	B	C
41	**42**	**43**	**44**	**45**	**46**	**47**	**48**	**49**	**50**
A	D	D	B	C	A	D	C	B	A
51	**52**	**53**	**54**	**55**	**56**	**57**	**58**	**59**	**60**
B	C	D	B	A	A	B	D	D	A
61	**62**	**63**	**64**	**65**	**66**	**67**	**68**	**69**	**70**
D	B	A	D	A	B	A	A	B	D
71	**72**	**73**	**74**	**75**	**76**	**77**	**78**	**79**	**80**
A	A	A	A	B	A	A	A	D	C
81	**82**	**83**	**84**	**85**	**86**	**87**	**88**	**89**	**90**
C	D	B	B	C	B	A	C	A	D
91	**92**	**93**	**94**	**95**	**96**	**97**	**98**	**99**	**100**
C	B	C	A	B	A	B	C	B	C
101	**102**	**103**	**104**	**105**	**106**	**107**	**108**	**109**	**110**
D	C	B	C	D	B	A	B	D	B
111	**112**	**113**	**114**	**115**	**116**	**117**	**118**	**119**	**120**
A	A	A	B	A	A	B	B	B	C
121	**122**	**123**	**124**	**125**	**126**	**127**	**128**	**129**	**130**
D	C	C	C	D	B	A	D	D	B
131	**132**	**133**	**134**	**135**	**136**	**137**	**138**	**139**	**140**
C	B	D	C	A	C	A	C	C	A
141	**142**	**143**	**144**	**145**	**146**	**147**	**148**	**149**	**150**
A	A	A	C	D	B	A	D	B	B
151	**152**	**153**	**154**	**155**	**156**	**157**	**158**	**159**	**160**
A	B	A	D	B	D	B	C	C	C
161	**162**	**163**	**164**	**165**	**166**	**167**	**168**	**169**	**170**
A	B	A	B	C	C	B	B	D	A
171	**172**	**173**	**174**	**175**	**176**	**177**	**178**	**179**	**180**
B	C	C	C	D	C	D	B	B	A
181	**182**	**183**	**184**	**185**	**186**	**187**	**188**	**189**	**190**
B	B	B	B	A	A	A	B	C	D
191	**192**	**193**	**194**	**195**	**196**	**197**	**198**	**199**	**200**
A	D	B	B	B	C	D	B	B	B

Previous Paper (Solved)

DSSSB—ECONOMICS TEACHER (PGT) Recruitment Exam, 2015

Post Specific Subject-related Questions

1. Concept of permanent consumption was introduced by:
A. Samuelson
B. Simon Kuznets
C. Milton Friedman
D. Harrod

2. Speculative demand for money is inversely related to:
A. Rate of interest B. Income
C. Money supply D. Investment

3. IS-LM curve was introduced by:
A. Keynes B. Hansen
C. J.R. Hicks D. Paul Samuelson

4. The book 'Money, Interest and Price' was written by:
A. J.R. Hicks B. D. Patinkin
C. W. Mitchell D. M. Muller

5. In Cobb-Douglas production function elasticity of factor substitution is equal to:
A. Zero B. Infinity
C. One D. Two

6. "If an oligopolist decreases his price the rivals will follow". This is the basis assumption of:
A. The Kinked Supply Curve
B. The Oligopolistic Demand Curve
C. The Kinked Demand Curve
D. The Demand Curve

7. 'Change in quantity demanded' refers to:
A. Upward shift of the demand curve
B. Downward shift of the demand curve
C. Movement on the same demand curve
D. None of these

8. 'Ceteris Paribus' clause in the Law of Demand does not mean:
A. The price of the commodity does not change
B. The price of its substitutes does not change
C. The income of the consumer does not change
D. The price of complementary goods does not change

9. Aam Admi Bima Yojana provides social security to:
A. All labours in rural areas
B. All landless labours living below poverty line in rural areas
C. All labours in urban areas
D. All labours in both rural as well as urban areas

10. SEBI was established in:
A. 1993 B. 1992
C. 1988 D. 1990

11. A major financial inclusion initiative named 'Swabhiman' was formally launched on:
A. February 2010 B. February 2011
C. February 2009 D. February 2008

12. All internationally traded services are covered under which of the following WTO agreements?
A. GATS B. TRIPS
C. TRIMS D. PTA

13. Full employment and balance of payments equilibrium will be automatically achieved in an optimum currency area:
A. if exchange rates are flexible
B. foreign capital flows into the country
C. if labour and capital move freely
D. if trade is liberalized

14. The 'Golden Age' model was developed by:
A. Nicholas Kaldor
B. Joan Robinson
C. J.R. Hicks
D. R.F. Harrod

15. Neighbour's curve means:
A. Depression of country is transferred to other
B. Boom of one country is transferred to other
C. Both (A) and (B)
D. None of the above

16. Normal profits are considered as:
A. Explicit costs B. Implicit costs
C. Social costs D. Private costs

17. Free rider problem is prominent in case of:
A. Social goods
B. Private goods
C. Semi-public goods
D. None of the above

18. Y = C + I + G + (X – M) is:
A. An equation B. A formula
C. An identity D. A function

19. If the consumption function is given by C = 20 + 3/4 Y, then the value of multiplier will be:
A. 4/3 B. 1/4
C. 4 D. 20

20. Leverage effect is associated with:
A. Multiplier
B. Accelerator
C. Consumption function
D. Super multiplier

21. Which of the following is not correct?
A. 0 < MPC < 1
B. 0 < MPS < 1
C. MPC > 1
D. MPC + MPS = 1

22. The life cycle hypothesis of consumption function is propounded by:
A. Keynes
B. Dusenberry
C. Friedman
D. Ando and Modigliani

23. 'India Brand Equity Fund' was established in:
A. 1996 B. 1997
C. 1995 D. 1992

24. The rate at which banks lend to RBI is known as:
A. Bank rate
B. Repo rate
C. Reverse Repo rate
D. Interest rate

25. The new share price index (in dollar value) of Mumbai share market is:
A. SENSEX B. FOREX
C. DOLEX D. UREX

26. Oil Refinery at Bhatinda is being established by:
A. IOC B. HPCL
C. Reliance D. BPCL

27. NABARD was established in:
A. Fourth plan B. Fifth plan
C. Sixth plan D. Eighth plan

28. Index 'Residex' is associated with:
A. Share prices
B. Mutual fund prices
C. Price inflation index
D. Land prices

29. Inside Trading is related to:
A. Share market
B. Horse racing
C. Taxation
D. Public expenditure

30. If the $MRTS_{LK}$ equals 2, then MP_K/MP_L is:
A. 2 B. 1
C. $\frac{1}{2}$ D. 4

31. The factor intensity is measured by:

A. $\frac{\alpha}{A}$ B. $\frac{\alpha}{\beta}$

C. A + B D. $\alpha + \beta$

32. Histogram is used to find:

A. Mean B. Mode

C. Median D. None of these

33. One of the measure of dispersion which is more useful in case of open-ended distribution is:

A. Range

B. Standard deviation

C. Mean deviation

D. Quartile deviation

34. Lorenz curve is a graphic method of studying:

A. Correlation B. Index numbers

C. Averages D. Dispersion

35. How many number of quartiles exist?

A. Two B. Three

C. Four D. Five

36. Which is often described as 'barometers of economic change'?

A. Average B. Correlation

C. Dispersion D. Index numbers

37. Who gave the call for 'Evergreen Revolution'?

A. M.S. Swaminathan

B. A.P.J. Abdul Kalam

C. Dr. Manmohan Singh

D. Dr. K.N. Jha

38. 'Innovation Lab' has been launched by:

A. Tata Consultancy Services

B. Infosys Tech.

C. Reliance Industries

D. Anil's Reliance Communications

39. Which Road Transport Corporation has introduced AWATAR (Any Where Any Time Advance Reservation) Scheme?

A. Andhra Pradesh

B. Karnataka

C. Tamil Nadu

D. Maharashtra

40. Which of the following corporate House is developing a port in Mundra (Gujarat)?

A. Adani B. Ambani

C. Goyanka D. Birla

41. After European Union, which another group of countries have come forward for adopting common currency?

A. OPEC B. Gulf Countries

C. SAARC D. ASEAN

42. Hutch-Essar was acquired by:

A. Bharat Airtel B. Vodafone

C. Reliance D. Tata mobile

43. 'Pratibha Kiran Yojana' is a new scheme to promote higher education among girls introduced by:

A. Karnataka B. Bihar

C. Madhya Pradesh D. Uttar Pradesh

44. From 30th June, 2011 many coins would be demonetized as per RBI instructions. What would be the minimum acceptable denomination of coins?

A. One rupee coins

B. Fifty paise coins

C. Two rupee coins

D. Twenty five paise coins

45. Videsh Sanchar Nigam Ltd. has been renamed as:

A. Reliance Sanchar Nigam Ltd.

B. Tata Sanchar Nigam Ltd.

C. Tata Communication Ltd.

D. Bharati Communication Ltd.

46. A country's offer curve will be straight line when its price elasticity of supply for exports is:

A. Infinitely large B. Unity

C. Zero D. Negative

47. OPEC is an example of the type of Producer's organisation known as a:

A. Marketing board

B. Producer's cooperative

C. Trust

D. Cartel

48. R.B.I. was nationalised in:
A. 1959 B. 1947
C. 1945 D. 1949

49. Increase in net RBI credit for Central Government represents:
A. Budgetary deficit
B. Revenue deficit
C. Monetised deficit
D. Fiscal deficit

50. To which community/organisation maximum goods are exported from India?
A. EEC
B. Commonwealth Nation
C. SAFTA
D. OPEC

51. 'Focus Product' and Focus Market' are the two schemes introduced related to:
A. Industrial diversification
B. Technology upgradation
C. Export promotion
D. Control of inflation

52. Which year was declared as customer's satisfaction year by Railways?
A. 2000-01 B. 2001-02
C. 2002-03 D. 2003-04

53. National Rural Development Institute is situated at:
A. Shimla B. Hyderabad
C. Patna D. New Delhi

54. Mobile Number Portability Service has been launched nation wide w.e.f.:
A. January 19, 2011
B. January 20, 2011
C. January 22, 2011
D. January 25, 2011

55. Box diagram was introduced by:
A. F.Y. Edgeworth B. Arrow
C. A.K. Sen D. Marshall

56. Who suggested that the price of a factor or production is determined by the demand and supply forces?
A. Marshall and Hicks
B. Clark and Allen
C. Lipsey and Samuelson
D. Jevons and Walras

57. Quasi-rent is:
A. Price – AVC
B. Price – AFC
C. Price – ATC
D. Price – MC

58. Which of the following would not be considered a near-money?
A. Time deposits
B. Saving and loan shares
C. Treasury bills
D. Demand deposits

59. An active deposit is one in which the initiative lies with:
A. The Bank
B. The Depositor
C. The Government
D. The Central Bank

60. Keynes terms 'active balances' as the money held for:
A. The speculative motive only
B. The transactions and precautionary motives
C. The transactions motive only
D. The precautionary motive only

61. The secondary securities are the financial claims issued by the:
A. Financial institutions
B. Public
C. R.B.I.
D. Stock Exchange

62. Maintaining a cash reserve ratio of 20% with primary deposits of ₹ 1,000, the total derivative deposits created by banks would be:
A. ₹ 5,000 B. ₹ 1,000
C. ₹ 4,000 D. None of these

63. The word 'budget' has been derived from:
A. Greek B. Latin
C. French D. German

64. 'The veil of money' indicate that:
A. Money is only lubricant, enabling the economic machine to function continuously and smoothly, which cannot affect the real variable
B. Money is a lubricant that helps the smooth functioning of the economy and affects real variables
C. Money is a lubricant that helps the smooth functioning of the economy which affects both the real and money variables
D. None of the above

65. In collusive oligopoly for joint profit maximisation:
A. The highest cost firm makes the highest profit
B. The lowest cost firm makes the highest profit
C. The lowest cost firm produces the largest output
D. None of the above

66. Each seller determines his price on the assumption that his rival will keep his price constant, under:
A. Bertrand's model
B. Samuelson's model
C. Edgeworth model
D. Price leadership

67. The validity of kinked demand curve was empirically tested and questioned by:
A. D.S. Watson B. Hall and Hitch
C. G.J. Stigler D. F. Macklap

68. An ethical or value Judgement must be made in order to derive the:
A. Transformation curve
B. Grand utility possibility
C. Consumption contract curve
D. Social welfare function

69. Which of the following State became the first State to introduce Public Service Guarantee Act 2010?
A. Madhya Pradesh B. Gujarat
C. Bihar D. Haryana

70. What is 'Super 301'?
A. A name of modern computer
B. A new variety of rice
C. American trade law
D. American treatment name for AIDS

71. Wages paid to Mahatma Gandhi National Rural Employment Guarantee Scheme has now been linked with:
A. Wholesale Price Index
B. Consumer Price Index for Agricultural Labour
C. Consumer Price Index for Industrial Labour
D. Food Inflation

72. Which Department of the Government has completed its 150 years in 2010?
A. Income Tax
B. Customs Excise Duty
C. Post and Telegraph
D. Television and Broadcasting

73. Which constitutes the maximum share in power generation?
A. Thermal power
B. Hydro power
C. Atomic power
D. All the above have equal

74. The Committee associated with established new stock exchange was:
A. M.J. Ferwani B. M. Narsimhan
C. S.N. Jha D. R. Janakiraman

75. Consumer Protection Act (COPRA) was implemented in:
A. 1985 B. 1986
C. 1987 D. 1988

76. The headquarters of SIDBI is in:
A. Lucknow B. New Delhi
C. Mumbai D. Bengaluru

77. Which is credit rating agency in India?
A. CRISIL B. CARE
C. ICRA D. All of these

78. ₹ 20 and above value notes are printed in:
A. Currency Note Press, Nasik Road
B. Bank Note Press, Dewas

C. Security Printing Press, Hyderabad
D. All of these

79. Which of the following is not a financial regulator?
A. IRDA B. PFRDA
C. AMFI D. SEBI

80. Which country has the maximum broadband subscribers in the world?
A. USA B. China
C. Japan D. France

81. SITTDEC—'South Investment Trade and Technology Data Exchange Centre' is a scheme of:
A. SAARC B. ASIAN
C. G-7 D. G-15

82. Indian Banks have the maximum foreign branches in:
A. Bangladesh B. U.K.
C. U.S.A. D. Sri Lanka

83. Which bank in India became the first bank to open its branch in China?
A. IDBI Bank
B. HDFC Bank
C. State Bank of India
D. Punjab National Bank

84. Which rural sector is not included in 'Bharat Nirman Yojana'?
A. Irrigation B. Water supply
C. Education D. Telephone

85. 'Golden Handshake Scheme' is associated with:
A. Inviting Foreign Companies
B. Private investment in public enterprises
C. Establishing joint enterprises
D. Voluntary retirement

86. First Export Promotion Zone (EPZ) in private sector was established at:
A. Kandla B. Vishakhapatanam
C. Noida D. Surat

87. Which one of the following measures has not been adopted in recent days by RBI for controlling credit in India?
A. Cash Deposit Ratio
B. Capital Adequacy Ratio
C. Cash Reserve Ratio
D. Statutory Liquidity Ratio

88. The maximum labour-oriented industry in India is:
A. Cement industry
B. Iron and steel industry
C. Jute industry
D. Cotton industry

89. What is the ascending order of introducing following mentioned programmes?
1. DPAP 2. JRY
3. IRDP 4. MNP
A. 1, 4, 3, 2 B. 4, 3, 2, 1
C. 1, 2, 3, 4 D. 4, 3, 1, 2

90. A 'refrigerator' operating in a chemist's shop is an example of:
A. Intermediate good
B. Final good
C. Producer's good
D. Consumer's good

91. In Harrod model:
A. If the actual growth rate is higher than the warranted growth rate, there will be inflation
B. If the actual growth rate is higher than the warranted growth rate, there will be deflation
C. The economy will be in equilibrium when actual and warranted growth rates are equal
D. Higher growth rate is consequence of economising on labour

92. A number of indivisibilities hinder the process of economic growth in the initial stages. This view was enunciated by:
A. R. Nurkse
B. H.W. Singer
C. R.N. Rosenstein Rodan
D. W.W. Rostow

93. 'SAPTA' is related to:
A. Education B. Trade
C. Security D. Environment

94. Information Technology Act in India was introduced in the year:
A. 2000 B. 2001
C. 2002 D. 2003

95. Which of the following group has brought and acquired the controlling stake in ispat Industries?
A. Tata Steels
B. Arcelor-Mittal Steels
C. J.S.W. Steels
D. None of the above

96. Demand creates its own supply is advocated by:
A. Marshall B. J.B. Say
C. Keynes D. R. Solow

97. India's first export promotion zone to be declared a free trade zone is:
A. Santacruz B. Kandla
C. Noida D. Falta

98. Hick's neutral technical change implies that:
A. the unit isoquant undergoes a parallel shift upwards
B. the unit isoquant undergoes a parallel shift downwards
C. curvature of the unit isoquant changes
D. None of the above

99. The two-gap theory as applied to development planning refers to:
A. Inflationary gap and investment gap
B. Saving gap and deflationary gap
C. Foreign exchange gap
D. Saving constraint and foreign exchange constraint

100. The inequality of income can be measured by using:
A. Mean
B. Mean deviation
C. Standard deviation
D. Lorenz curve

101. The critical minimum effort theory is due to:
A. W.A. Lewis B. D. Ricardo
C. H. Leibenstein D. A.D. Hirschman

102. The 'Absorption Approach' analysing the effects of devaluation has been developed by:
A. C.P. Kindleberger
B. B. Soderston
C. T.M. Rybezynski
D. Sidney Alexander

103. According to the accelerator principle, the extent of change in demand for capital goods depends on:
A. The capital output ratio
B. Change in the level of output
C. Investment
D. All the above

104. Pradhan Mantri Gram Sadak Yojana (PMGSY) was launched in:
A. 2004 B. 2000
C. 2005 D. 1996

105. Limit pricing is an entry condition in the theory of firm by:
A. J.S. Bain B. Curnot
C. Chamberlin D. W.J. Baumole

106. High powered money is:
A. Bank's reserves at Central Bank
B. Money held by the Banks
C. All loans and advances of Banks
D. Currency held by Public and Cash reserves of the Banks

107. Input-output technique was invented by:
A. Gunnar Myrdal
B. Wassily Leontief
C. Hollis B. Chenery
D. Robert Solow

108. Given a production function $Q = AL^{\circ} K^{3}$, $\alpha, \beta > 0$, increasing returns to scale requires that:
A. $\alpha + \beta = 1$ B. $\alpha + \beta = 0$
C. $\alpha + \beta > 0$ D. $\alpha + \beta > 1$

109. Verdoon's law is about the:
A. Positive relation between the growth of population, employment and output with the growth of production per head.

B. Negative relation between the growth of population, employment and output with growth of production per head.
C. Positive relation between population growth and employment.
D. Negative relation between population growth and employment.

110. 'Vent for surplus approach' is applicable to:
A. Rich countries
B. Underdeveloped countries
C. Oil exporting countries
D. None of the above

111. In which year Kissan Credit Card System was introduced?
A. 1978 B. 1998
C. 1988 D. 2008

112. According to monetary approach, a revaluation of a nations currency:
A. increases the nation's demand for money
B. increases the nation's supply of money
C. reduces the nation's demand for money
D. reduces the nation's supply of money

113. The value of foreign trade multiplies will be high under the condition when:
A. marginal propensity to save is high
B. marginal propensity to import is high
C. there is increase in exports
D. marginal propensity to consume domestic goods is high

114. NAFED is a:
A. Company
B. Non-Government organisation
C. Government body
D. Cooperative organisation

115. The policy which aims at compensating the economy to meet chronical situation of inflation and deflation by manipulating taxes and public, expenditures is:
A. Monetary Policy
B. Compensatory fiscal policy
C. Compensatory monetary policy
D. Fiscal policy

116. Type II error is defined as:
A. Reject null hypothesis when it is true
B. Reject null hypothesis when it is false
C. Accept null hypothesis when it is false
D. Accept null hypothesis when it is true

117. Cohin Clark has argued that for most countries of the world, the safe upper limit of taxation is:
A. 40 per cent of national income
B. 30 per cent of national income
C. 25 per cent of national income
D. 20 per cent of national income

118. Accelerated irrigation benefits programme was launched in:
A. 1996-97 B. 1997-98
C. 1998-99 D. 1999-2000

119. According to Weber's Theory of location. The important factors influencing location are:
1. Transport Cost
2. Land Cost
3. Labour Cost
4. Innovation Cost
Choose the correct code:
A. 1 and 2 B. 2 and 3
C. 1 and 3 D. 1 and 4

120. Identify the correct chronological order of the following economists:
A. Adam Smith, Malthus, Ricardo, J.S. Mill
B. Adam Smith, Ricardo, Malthus, J.S. Mill
C. Adam Smith, J.S. Mill, Ricardo, Malthus
D. Adam Smith, Malthus, J.S. Mill, Ricardo

121. The third moment around the mean is useful to measure:
A. Central tendency
B. Dispersion
C. Peakedness
D. Symmetry

122. Which of the following is an ideal index number?
A. Laspeyre
B. Bowley
C. Fisher
D. Marshall-Edgeworth

123.

List-I	List-II
(*a*) Free Trade Area	1. No restriction on trade and factor movement
(*b*) Customs Union	2. Trade is free and no custom duties
(*c*) Common Market	3. No custom duties; duties on non-member
(*d*) Economic Union	4. Advanced stage of integration

Codes:

	(*a*)	(*b*)	(*c*)	(*d*)
A.	2	1	3	4
B.	3	2	4	1
C.	2	3	1	4
D.	1	3	4	2

124.

List-I (Committee)	List-II (Subject)
(*a*) Tondon Committee	1. Capital financing
(*b*) Rakesh Mohan Committee	2. Infrastructure development
(*c*) Narasimham Committee	3. Financial Sector Reforms
(*d*) Omkar Goswamy Committee	4. Industrial Sickness

Codes:

	(*a*)	(*b*)	(*c*)	(*d*)
A.	1	3	2	4
B.	4	2	3	1
C.	1	2	3	4
D.	4	3	2	1

125. Who demonstrated the abnormal shape of demand curve for diamonds through the doctrine of conspicuous consumption?
A. Thorstein Veblen B. Robert Giffen
C. David Ricardo D. Alfred Marshall

126. A consumer's demand curve can be obtained from:
A. Income consumption curve
B. Engel's curve
C. Lorenz curve
D. Price consumption curve

127. Rural women can avail the benefit of Mahila Samriddhi Yojana if they open their account in:
A. Rural Post Offices
B. Commercial Banks
C. Rural Development Banks
D. Any of the above

128. The rate at which banks lend to RBI is known as:
A. Bank Rate
B. Repo Rate
C. Reverse Repo Rate
D. Interest Rate

129. 'India Brand Equity Fund' was established in:
A. 1996 B. 1997
C. 1995 D. 1992

130. Tobin tax is a tax on:
A. exports
B. imports
C. sales
D. transactions in foreign exchange

131. The functioning of India economy was different from that of economies of western countries was the thesis first put forward by:
A. Dadabhai Naoroji
B. V.G. Kale
C. M. Visveswarayya
D. M.G. Ranade

132. 'Smart Money' is a term used for:
A. Cash with bank
B. Cash with public
C. Internet banking
D. Credit card

133. The competition law replacing the MRTP Act, of 1969 was enacted in the year:
A. 1999 B. 2000
C. 2001 D. 2002

134. Autarky is a situation of:
A. Global recession
B. No trade

C. Free trade
D. Colonial pattern of trade

135. Symbolically the marginal propensity to import is defined as:
A. ΔM/ΔX B. ΔM/Y
C. ΔX/ΔY D. ΔM/ΔY

136. The duties which are levied as a fixed percentage of value of the commodity imported are called:
A. Specific duties
B. Fixed duties
C. Ad-valorem duties
D. Compound duties

137. Growth is a .... process in the economic sense.
A. Slow
B. Radical
C. Proportionality planned
D. Continuous

138. The theory of social marginal productivity was propounded by:
A. J. Robinson
B. R. Maslow
C. A.E. Kahn
D. Rosenstein Rodan

139. 'Bank does not create credit out of thin air' is the statement given by:
A. Hansen B. Cairn cross
C. Conlbourn D. Crowther

140. The 'Hundis' issued in unorganized money market are quite similar to:
A. Cheques
B. Commercial bills
C. Treasury bills
D. Shares

141. Which of the following is responsible for differences in gross rates of interest?
A. Shortage of money
B. Difference in risk
C. Difference in productivity
D. Different uses of money

142. Deposit multiplier (K) is defined as:
A. $K = \frac{1}{r}$ B. $K = r$
C. $r = 1 - \frac{1}{K}$ D. None of the above

143. The 'bear' speculators expect that in future the bond prices will:
A. Fall
B. Rise
C. Remain constant
D. Fluctuate

144. In examining the expansion and contraction of the banking system, which of the following is not an imporant multiple to consider?
A. Excess reserves
B. Money supply
C. Demand deposits
D. New assets of banks

145. The exchange rate is kept the same in all parts of the market by:
A. Speculation
B. Interest arbitrage
C. Exchange arbitrage
D. Hedging

146. The concept of modern economic growth is associated with which one of the following economists?
A. W.A. Lewis
B. Amartya Sen
C. Simon Kuznets
D. H. Leibenstein

147. According to Boeke, in dual society is characterised by simultaneous existence of:
A. High and low castes
B. Land lords and tenants
C. Imported and Indigenous social system
D. Rural and urban population

148. The drain theory was popularised by:
A. R.C. Dutt B. Singer
C. D.B. Naoroji D. W.A. Lewis

149. The celebrated work on the Indian economic history known as 'The Industrial Evolution of India in Recent Times' was written by:
A. R.C. Dutt
B. Dadabhai Naoroji
C. D.R. Gadgil
D. William Digby

150. The Statutory Liquidity Ratio (SLR) for commercial banks in India can be raised to a maximum level of:
A. 20% B. 25%
C. 35% D. 40%

151. Due to conflict between India-Pakistan in 1965, finalisation of Fourth Plan was delayed. The planning process during the intervening period was carried out through .... Annual plans.
A. Two B. One
C. Three D. Four

152. Which of the following resources is most crucial input in India's agriculture, responsible for Green Revolution?
A. Fertilizers
B. HYV seeds
C. Agricultural machinery
D. Irrigation

153. A subsistence agriculture is one in which the farmer?
A. Produces primarily food crops
B. Does not take any loans from institutional agencies
C. Sells all his crop to the village money lender
D. All the above

154. Goods ordinarily demanded at low level of income are termed as:
A. Wage goods
B. Consumer durable
C. Producer durable
D. Any of the above

155. Rastogi Committee is related with:
A. VAT B. Infrastructure
C. Service tax D. Telecom

156. Linear programming – mathematical device was developed by:
A. George Dantzig
B. W. Leontief
C. Karl Pearson
D. Neumann and Morgenstern

157. Targeted Public Distribution System (TPDS) was launched by Govt. in the year ....
A. 1996 B. 1997
C. 1998 D. 1995

158. First export processing zone declared as Free trade zone in India is at ....
A. Santacruz B. Noida
C. Kochin D. Kandla

159. Information Technology Act in India was introduced in the year:
A. 2001 B. 2000
C. 2002 D. 2003

160. Tata Tele Services started GPS services on mobile in:
A. April 2009 B. April 2011
C. August 2008 D. April 2008

161. The World Bank's Environmentally Sustainable Development division has developed Green Index. Which one of the following is not a constituent of this Index?
A. Produced assets B. Natural resources
C. Social assets D. Human resources

162. The Central Quality Control laboratory is located at:
A. Delhi B. Lucknow
C. Nagpur D. Mumbai

163. The head office of the Asian Development Bank (ADB) is in:
A. Manila B. Jakarta
C. Honululu D. Nairobi

164. Open Sky Policy is:
A. Free Economy Policy
B. Export Promotion Scheme
C. Export Promotion Scheme of Civil Aviation Ministry
D. Tax-free policy

165. Identify the correct sequence of establishment of the following institutions in India:
A. SIDBI, NABARD, IDBI, IFCI
B. IDBI, NABARD, IFCI, SIDBI
C. IFCI, IDBI, NABARD, SIDBI
D. IFCI, SIDBI, IDBI, NABARD

166. Black Revolution is related with self sufficiency is:
A. Crude oil B. Coal
C. Kerosene oil D. None of these

167. The Slogan 'A Tree for each child' was coined for:
A. Social forestry programme
B. Clean air programme
C. Social conservation programme
D. Environmental protection programme

168. Which of the following sources of data is not based on primary data collection?
A. Census of India
B. National sample survey
C. Statistical Abstracts of India
D. National Family Health Survey

169. Probability Sampling Implies:
A. Stratified Random Sampling
B. Systematic Random Sampling
C. Simple Random Sampling
D. All of the above

170. The 'Report on Currency and Finance' for each of the financial year in India is published by:
A. Reserve Bank of India
B. Ministry of Finance
C. Planning Commission
D. Central statistical organisation

171. Another name of Basic Education or Nai Talim is:
A. Compulsory Education
B. New Education Policy
C. Wardha Education Plan
D. Sarva Shikshya Abhiyan

172. T.W. Schultz has given the following ratios in relation to education for economic growth:
A. Education capital and labour ratio
B. Education – labour ratio
C. Education – income ratio
D. Education – labour ratio, education – income ratio and education – investment ratio

173. .... test is satisfied both by Fisher's and Kelly's formula.
A. Circular B. Factor reversal
C. Time reversal D. None of these

174. Root mean square of all deviations is:
A. Mean deviation
B. Standard deviation
C. Geometric mean
D. Quartile deviation

175. Stratified sample is preferred where:
A. The population is perfectly homogeneous
B. The population is not homogeneous
C. Random sampling is not possible
D. Small samples are required

176. A non-measurable characteristic is known as:
A. Discrete variable
B. Continuous variable
C. Attribute
D. None of these

177. Platinum Jubilee year of the Reserve Bank of India is:
A. 2008-09 B. 2009-10
C. 2010-11 D. 2011-12

178. The word NELP is associated with:
A. Discovery of oil and Natural Gas
B. National highway extension
C. Communications
D. Space research

179. On the lines of Amul in Gujarat, which of the following state has come forward to bring a 'White Revolution' in the state?
A. Himachal Pradesh
B. Punjab
C. Uttarakhand
D. Uttar Pradesh

180. Which of the following corporate house is developing a port in Mundra (Gujarat)?
A. Adani B. Ambani
C. Goyanka D. Birla

181. Which one of the following is not an assumption of Harrod-Domar model?
A. Fixed capital-output ratio
B. Variable marginal and average propensity to save
C. Closed economy
D. Capital is the only factors of production

182. Which one of the following items is included in the capital account of the balance of payments of a country?
A. Invisibles
B. Investment income
C. Commercial borrowings
D. Private transfers

183. What does the Coase's theorem deal with?
A. Internalisation of externalities
B. Pricing of public goods
C. Solution to the problem of externalities of terms of well-defined and exchangeable property rights
D. None of the above

184. Opportunity costs are also known as:
A. Spilt over costs
B. Money costs
C. Alternative costs
D. External costs

185. Growth process resulting into broad based benefits and providing equality of opportunity to all is referred to as:
A. Faster growth
B. Inclusive growth
C. Exclusive growth
D. Sustained growth

186. The Oil Refinery established at Panipat belongs to:
A. Public sector B. Private sector
C. Joint sector D. Cooperative sector

187. In the early stages of planning, industrialisation is weighted in favour of consumer goods industries rather than capital goods industries. This hypothesis was advocated by:
A. Chenery B. W.G. Hoffmann
C. Kuznets D. A. Gerschenkron

188. Who is nick named as the American Keynes?
A. Marx B. Hicks
C. Marshall D. Hansen

189. Who among of the following has dealt economy model of under-developing?
A. Harrod B. Ricardo
C. Domar D. Jorgenson

190. A capitalist economy adheres to the technique of planning by:
A. Inducement B. Direction
C. Central authority D. None of these

191. "The more nearly perfect a market is, the stronger is the tendency for the same price to be paid for the same thing in all parts of the market" is the definition of perfect competition by:
A. Prof. Benham B. J.S. Mill
C. Jevons D. Prof. Marshall

192. 'In a sense all rents are scarcity rents, and all rents are differential rents' are words of:
A. Ricardo B. Adam Smith
C. K.E. Boulding D. Marshall

193. If you offered some securities as 'security' for a loan you made, you would be:
A. Buying 'on margin'
B. Selling short
C. Providing collateral
D. None of the above

194. Which of the following economists used the kinked demand curve only to explain why oligopoly prices are 'sticky'?
A. P.M. Sweezy B. Chamberlin
C. Hall and Hitch D. Stigler

195. In the stackelberg model of duopoly the cournot behaviour assumption is applied to:
A. Leader
B. The follower

C. Both (A) and (B)
D. Neither (A) nor (B)

196. Lahiri Committee is associated with:
A. Industrial sickness
B. Minimum support prices of agricultural products
C. Price structure of edible oil
D. Handicrafts exports

197. The regulator of Micro Finance in India is:
A. Finance Ministry
B. Reserve Bank of India
C. State Bank of India
D. None of these

198. The committee associated with establishing new stock exchanges was:
A. M.J. Ferwani B. M. Narsimham
C. S.N. Jha D. R. Janakiraman

199. Narsimham Committee recommended to make banking structure of the country:
A. Two tier B. Three tier
C. Four tier D. Five tier

200. ₹ 20 and above value notes are printed in:
A. Currency Note Press, Nasik Road
B. Bank Note Press, Dewas
C. Security Printing Press, Hyderabad
D. All of these

ANSWERS

1	**2**	**3**	**4**	**5**	**6**	**7**	**8**	**9**	**10**
C	A	C	B	C	C	C	A	B	B
11	**12**	**13**	**14**	**15**	**16**	**17**	**18**	**19**	**20**
B	A	A	B	A	B	A	C	C	D
21	**22**	**23**	**24**	**25**	**26**	**27**	**28**	**29**	**30**
C	D	A	C	C	B	C	D	A	C
31	**32**	**33**	**34**	**35**	**36**	**37**	**38**	**39**	**40**
B	B	D	D	B	D	A	A	B	A
41	**42**	**43**	**44**	**45**	**46**	**47**	**48**	**49**	**50**
B	B	C	B	C	C	D	D	C	A
51	**52**	**53**	**54**	**55**	**56**	**57**	**58**	**59**	**60**
C	D	B	B	A	A	A	D	A	B
61	**62**	**63**	**64**	**65**	**66**	**67**	**68**	**69**	**70**
A	C	C	A	C	A	C	D	A	C
71	**72**	**73**	**74**	**75**	**76**	**77**	**78**	**79**	**80**
B	A	A	A	B	A	D	B	C	A
81	**82**	**83**	**84**	**85**	**86**	**87**	**88**	**89**	**90**
B	B	C	C	D	D	A	D	A	C
91	**92**	**93**	**94**	**95**	**96**	**97**	**98**	**99**	**100**
A	C	B	A	C	C	A	B	D	D
101	**102**	**103**	**104**	**105**	**106**	**107**	**108**	**109**	**110**
C	D	D	B	A	D	B	D	A	B
111	**112**	**113**	**114**	**115**	**116**	**117**	**118**	**119**	**120**
B	C	C	D	B	C	C	A	C	A

121	122	123	124	125	126	127	128	129	130
B	C	C	C	A	C	A	C	A	D
131	132	133	134	135	136	137	138	139	140
D	D	C	B	D	C	D	C	D	B
141	142	143	144	145	146	147	148	149	150
B	A	A	A	C	C	C	C	B	D
151	152	153	154	155	156	157	158	159	160
C	D	D	A	C	A	B	A	B	A
161	162	163	164	165	166	167	168	169	170
C	C	A	C	C	A	D	D	D	A
171	172	173	174	175	176	177	178	179	180
C	D	B	B	B	C	B	A	C	A
181	182	183	184	185	186	187	188	189	190
B	C	C	C	B	A	C	B	D	A
191	192	193	194	195	196	197	198	199	200
D	D	C	C	B	C	D	A	C	B

MICRO-ECONOMICS

Chapter 1

Introduction

Central Problems of An Economy

Production, exchange and consumption of goods and services are among the basic economic activities of life. In the course of these basic economic activities, every society has to face **scarcity** of resources and it is the scarcity of resources that gives rise to the problem of **choice**. The scarce resources of an economy have competing usages. In other words, every society has to decide on how to use its scarce resources. The problems of an economy are very often summarised as follows:

What is produced and in what quantities?

Every society must decide on how much of each of the many possible goods and services it will produce. Whether to produce more of food, clothing, housing or to have more of luxury goods.

Whether to have more agricultural goods or to have industrial products and services. Whether to use more resources in education and health or to use more resources in building military services. Whether to have more of basic education or more of higher education. Whether to have more of consumption goods or to have investment goods (like machine) which will boost production and consumption tomorrow.

How are these goods produced?

Every society has to decide on how much of which of the resources to use in the production of each of the different goods and services. Whether to use more labour or more machines. Which of the available technologies to adopt in the production of each of the goods?

For whom are these goods produced?

Who gets how much of the goods that are produced in the economy? How should the produce of the economy be distributed among the individuals in the economy?

Who gets more and who gets less? Whether or not to ensure a minimum amount of consumption for everyone in the economy. Whether or not elementary education and basic health services should be available freely for everyone in the economy.

Thus, every economy faces the problem of allocating the scarce resources to the production of different possible goods and services and of distributing the produced goods and services among the individuals within the economy. *The allocation of scarce resources and the distribution of the final goods and services are the central problems of any economy.*

Production Possibility Curve

We explained above the behaviour of the firm in choosing the factor combination for producing a product. We have assumed so far that the firm is a single product firm, that is, it produces only one product or goods. But the majority of firms produce more than one product. For convenience, we take a firm producing two products X and Y. To produce two products the firm has to decide the proportion in which to produce them. For this, the concept of **production possibility curve,** or the **transformation curve** is used.

The concept of production possibility curve is based on the following assumptions :

1. The firm has given quantities of an input with which it produces the two products.
2. There is no change in the production technique.
3. It can produce the two goods X and Y in different proportions.

The concept of production possibility curve can be understood from the following table. The table given below displays various production possibilities of products X and Y.

Alternative Production Possibilities

Production Possibilities	*Product X (Hundreds)*	*Product Y (Hundreds)*
A	0	15
B	1	14
C	2	12
D	3	9
E	4	5
F	5	0

If all the given resources are employed by the firm for the production of product Y and none for X, 15 hundred units of product Y are produced. On the other hand, if the firm devotes all the resources for the production of X and none for Y, then 5 hundered units of product X are produced. But these are only two extreme production possibilities. In between these two there will be many other production possibilities, such as B, C, D and E. As the firm moves from production possibility A towards F it withdraws some resources from the production of product Y and devotes them to the production of product X. In other words, the firm gives up some of product Y in order to produce some more of product X. It is thus clear that with a given amount of one product only by cutting down the production of the other product. As it moves for alternative A to B, it sacrifices one hundred units of product Y for the sake of one hundred units of product X. Again, as the firm moves further from alternative B to C, it sacrifices two hundred units of product for one hundred units of product X.

The alternative production possibilities of the table have been graphically illustrated in figure 1. The curve AF has been obtained when the data of the table are plotted. This curve AF is called the **production possibility curve** which represents the various combinations of two products that the firm can produce with a given amount of resources. The production possibility curve shows that, with given resources, an increase in the production of one good necessitates the reduction in the output of the other good.

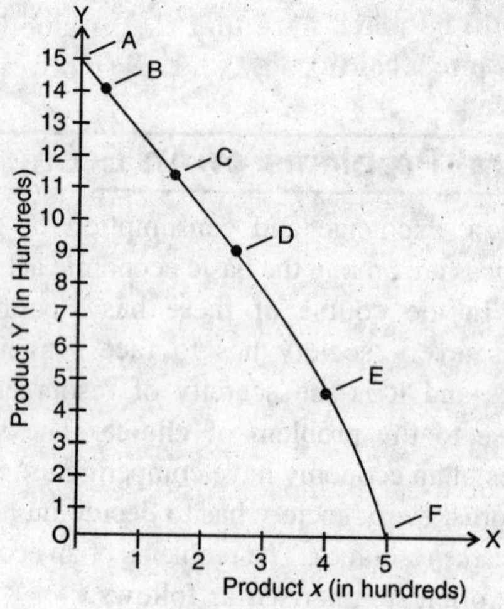

Fig. 1 : *Production Possibility Curve*

The production possibility curve is also called the **Product Transformation Curve** or simply the **Transformation Curve** because in moving from one point to another on it, one product is transformed into another, not physically but by transferring resources from one line of production to the other. With given resources being fully employed and utilized by the firm, the combination of two products produced must lie anywhere on the production possibility curve AF and not inside or outside it. The greater the amount of resources available with the firm for production, the higher the level of production possibility curve. **The rate at which one product is transformed into another, resources remaining unchanged, is called the marginal rate of transformation.** In other words, the marginal rate of transformation between X and Y is the amount of Y which is sacrificed for the production of an additional unit of X. As shown above, the sacrifice of product Y for an additional unit of X goes on increasing as the firm produces more of X and less of Y. Thus, **the marginal rate**

of transformation increases as the firm produces more of X and less of Y. The increasing marginal rate of transformation makes the production possibility curves **concave to the origin.** The marginal rate of transformation (MRT) at a point on the production possibility curve is given by the slope of the curve at that point.

It should be noted here that the production possibility curve is convex only when the increasing returns occur.

Opportunity or Alternative Cost

The concept of opportunity cost occupies a very important place in modern economic analysis. The opportunity cost of any good is the next best alternative good that is sacrificed. The factors which are used for the manufacture of a car may also be used for the production of an equipment for the military. Therefore, the opportunity cost of production of a car is the output of the military equipment foregone or sacrificed, which could have been produced with the same amount of factors that have gone into the making of a car.

Two points must be noted in the above definition of opportunity cost. **Firstly,** the opportunity cost of anything is only the **next-best alternative** foregone. That is to say, the opportunities cost of producing a good is not any other alternative good that could be produced with the same factors, it is only the most valuable other good which the same factors could produce. Second point worth nothing in the above definition is the addition of the qualification or "by an equivalent group of factors, costing the same amount of money." The need for the addition of this qualification arises because all the factors used in the production of one good may not be the same as are required for the production of the next best alternative good.

In the words of **Benham,** "The opportunity cost of anything is the next best alternative that could be produced instead by the same factors or by an equivalent group of factors, costing the same amount of money''.

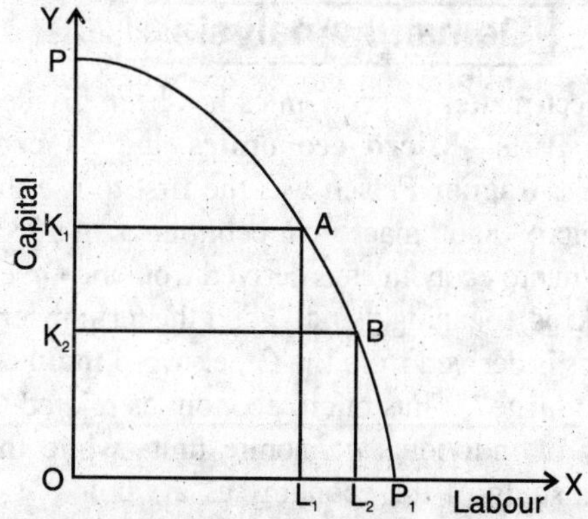

Fig. 2 : *Opportunity Cost*

The concept of opportunity cost is explained diagrammatically in figure 2 with the help of production possibility curve PP_1. At combination A on this curve, the producer uses OL_1 of labour and OK_1 of capital. If he wants to use L_1L_2 more labour, he will have to forgo K_1K_2 of capital. Thus the opportunity cost of L_1L_2 labour is K_1K_2 of capital.

The concept of opportunity cost has a wide application to economic problems. It is applicable to the determination of factor prices and in international trade. It can also be applied to consumption and public expenditure.

❑❑❑

Chapter 2

Consumer Behaviour and Demand

Demand Analysis

The Subject-matter of economics has been divided into two Parts—**Micro economics** and **Macro-economics. Ragner Frisch** was the first to use the terms "micro" and "macro" in economics in **1933.** The term micro economics is derived from the Greek word **mikros,** meaning **"small"** and the term macro economics is derived from the Greek word **makros,** meaning **"large"**. Thus micro economics related to the study of individual economic units while the latter is a study of the economy as a whole.

Micro economics

Micro economics is the study of economic actions and behaviour of individual units and small groups. In the other words, in micro economics we make a microscopic study of the economy. The determination of equilibrium output of the firm or industry, the wage of a particular type of labour, the price of a particular commodity are some of the fields of micro economics theory. Thus the theory of product pricing and the theory of factor pricing (or the theory of distribution) fall within the domain of micro economics. The whole content of micro-economic theory is presented in the following Fig.1.

MICRO ECONOMIC THEORY

- *Product Pricing*
  - Theory of Demand
  - Theory of Production and Cost
- *Factor Pricing* (Theory of Distribution)
  - Wages
  - Rent
  - Interest
  - Profits
- *Theory of* Economic Welfare

Fig. 1

Macro economics

Macro economics is the study of aggregates or averages covering the entire economy, such as total employment, the national product or income, the general price level of the economy. Therefore, macro economics is also known as **aggregative economics.** Macro economics analyses and establishes the functional relationship between these large aggregates. Thus **Professor Boulding** says, "Macro economics deals not with individuals quantities as such but with the aggregates of these quantities; not with individual incomes but with the national income; not with individual prices but with the price level; not with individual outputs but with the national output."

Macro economics is also known as the theory of income and employment, or simply income analysis. It is concerned with the problems of unemployment, economic fluctuations, inflation or deflation, international trade and economic growth.

We have now stated, in brief, all aspects of macroeconomic theory. These various aspects of macroeconomic theory are shown, in the following Fig. 1.1 :

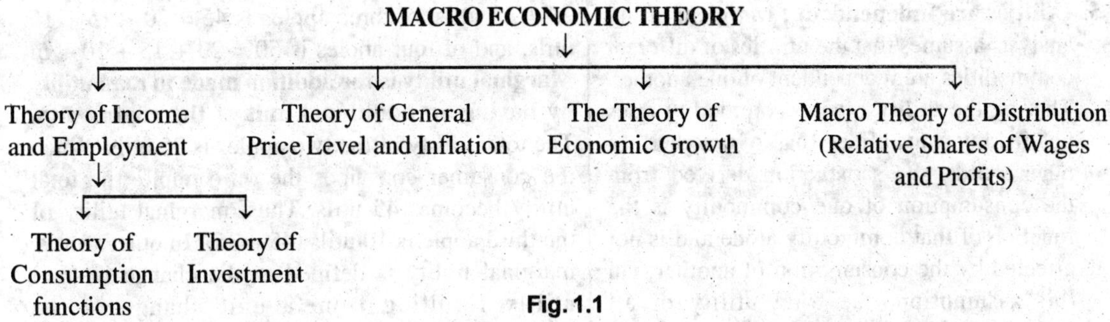

Fig. 1.1

Consumer Demand Theory

There are two basic approaches to the study of consumer demand theory. The first, or **classical approach,** involves the use of measurable marginal utility (satisfaction). It is generally called the **Cardinal utility approach.** The second, or indifference curve approach, is generally called the **ordinal approach.**

Marginal Utility Analysis

Marginal utility analysis is the oldest theory of demand which provides an explanation of Consumer's demand for a product and it derives the law of demand which establishes an inverse relationship between price and quantity demanded of the product. Though marginal utility approach to the theory of demand is very old, its final shape emerged at the hands of **Marshall.** Marginal utility analysis is based on the concept of **Cardinal approach** which assumes that utility is measurable and additive. It is expressed as a quantity measured in hypothetical units which are called **'utils'.** If a consumer imagines that one mango has 8 utils and an apple 4 utils, it implies that the utility of one mango is twice that of an apple.

Basic Assumptions of Marginal Utility Analysis

Marginal utility analysis of demand is based upon certain important assumptions. Before explaining how utility analysis explains consumer's equilibrium in regard to the demand for goods, it is essential to describe those basic assumptions on which the whole utility analysis rests. The following are the main assumptions.

1. **Rationality :** The consumer is rational. He aims at the maximisation of his utility subject to the constraint imposed by his given income.
2. **Cardinal Utility :** The utility of each commodity is measurable. Utility is a Cardinal concept. The most convenient measure is money. The utility is measured by the monetary units that the consumer is prepared to pay for another unit of the commodity.
3. **Constant Marginal Utility of Money :** Another important assumption of the marginal utility analysis is that the marginal utility of money remains constant even though the quantity of money with consumer is diminished by the successive purchases made by him. It is assumed that while marginal utility of a commodity varies with the quantity of the commodity purchased, the marginal utility of money remains throughout the same as the quantity of the goods purchased varies. This assumption becomes necessary because the marginal utility of a commodity is measured in terms of money.
4. **Diminishing Marginal Utility :** The utility gained from successive units of a commodity diminishes. In other words, the marginal utility of a commodity diminishes as the consumer acquires large quantities of it. This is the axion of **diminishing marginal utility.**

5. **Utilities are Independent :** Marginal utility analysis assumes that the utilities of different commodities are independent of one another. That is, the utility of one commodity does not in any way affect that of another. In other words, the satisfaction derived from the consumption of one commodity is the function of that commodity alone and is not affected by the consumption of another. On this assumption, the total utility of all commodity consumed by a consumer is simply the sum of total of the separate utilities of all the commodity consumed by a consumer. If there are *'n'* commodities in the bundle with quantities $x_1, x_2, ..., x_n$, the total utility is

$$U = f(x_1, x_2, ... x_n)$$

Thus, according to this assumption, the utilities of various goods are **additive.**

6. **Introspective Method :** Another important hypothesis of the marginal utility analysis is the use of introspective method in judging the behaviour of marginal utility. "Introspection is the ability of the observer to reconstruct events which go on in the mind of another person with the help of self-observation. This form of comprehension may be just guess work or intuition or the result of long-lasting experience."

Total Utility and Marginal Utility

When a consumer purchases an item, he obtains satisfaction from the possession of that item. That is, he derives utility from the possession of the item. When the consumer buys apples he receives them in units, 1, 2, 3, 4, etc. 2 apples have more utility than 1, 3 more utility than 2, and 4 more than 3. The units of apples which the consumer chooses are in a descending order of their utilities. In his estimation, the first apple is the best out of the lot available to him and thus gives him the highest satisfaction, measured as 20 utils. The second apple will naturally be the second best with lesser amount of utility than the first, and has 15 utils. The third apple has 10 utils and the fourth 5 utils. In our illustration, the total utility of two apples is 35 = 20 + 15 utils, of three apples is 45 = 20 + 15 + 10 utils, and of four apples is 50 = 20 + 15 + 10 + 5. **Marginal utility is the addition made to total utility by having an additional unit of the commodity.** The total utility of the two apples is 35 utils. When the consumer consumes the third apple, the total utility becomes 45 utils. Thus, marginal utility of the third apple is 10 utils (45 – 35). In other words, marginal utility is defined as the change in total utility resulting from a unit change in the consumption of the good in question per unit of time.

Algebraically, the marginal utility (MU) of *n* units of a commodity is the total utility (TU) of *n* units minus the total utility of (*n* – 1). Thus,

$$MU_n = TU_n - TU_{n-1}$$

The relation between the total and marginal utility is explained with the help of Table 2.1.

TABLE 2.1

Units of Apple	*TU in Utils*	*MU in Utils*
0	0	0
1	20	20
2	35	15
3	45	10
4	50	5
5	50	0
6	45	– 5
7	35	– 10

So long as total utility is increasing, marginal utility is decreasing upto the 4th unit. When total utility is maximum (at the fifth unit), marginal utility is zero. It is the point of **Satiety (Saturation)** for the consumer. When total utility is decreasing, marginal utility is negative.

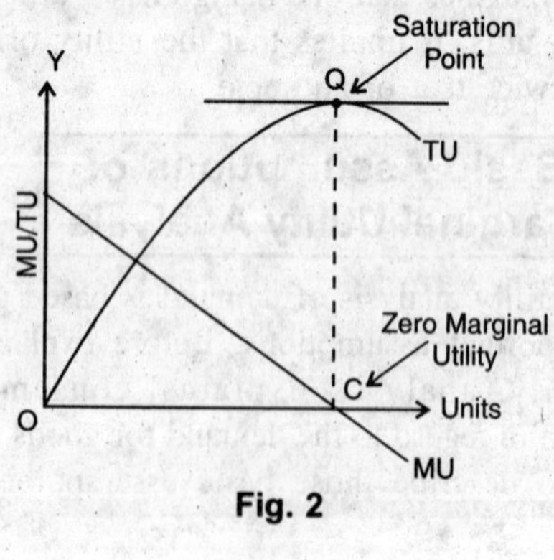

Fig. 2

In Figure 2, TU is the total utility curve and MU is the marginal utility curve. Geometrically the marginal utility curve is the slope of the total utility curve. So long as the TU curve is rising, the MU curve is falling. When the former reaches the highest point Q, the latter touches the X-axis at C where MU is zero and when the TU starts falling from Q and the MU becomes negative from C onwards.

Law of Diminishing Marginal Utility

Satisfaction of human wants follows some very importants laws and one of them is the Law of Diminishing Marginal utility. **Hermann Heinrich Gossen** was the first to formulate this law in 1854 though the name was given by Marshall. **Javons** called it **Gossen's First Law.** Gossen stated it thus, "The magnitude of one and the same satisfaction, when we continue to enjoy it without interruption, continually decreases until satisfaction is reached." According to this law the marginal utility of a good diminishes as an individual consumes more units of a good. In other words, as a consumer takes more units of a good, the extra utility or satisfaction that he derives from an extra unit of the good goes on falling. It should be carefully noted that it is the marginal utility and not the total utility that declines with the increase in the consumption of a good. The law of diminishing marginal utility means that the total utility increases but at a decreasing rate.

Marshall states the Law thus : "The additional benefits which a person derives from a given increase of his stock of a thing diminishes with every increase in the stock that he already has."

This Law is based upon two important facts. **Firstly,** while the total wants of a man are virtually unlimited, each single want is satiable. Therefore, as an individual consumes more and more units of a good, intensity of his want for the good goes on falling and a point is reached where the individual no longer wants any more units of the good. That is **when Saturation Point is reached marginal utility of a good becomes zero.** The second fact on which the law of diminishing marginal utility is based is that the different goods are not perfect substitutes for each other in the satisfaction of various particular wants. When an individual consumes more and more units of a good, the intensity of his particular want for the good diminishes but if the units of that good could be devoted to the satisfaction of other wants and yielded as much satisfaction as they did initially in the satisfaction of the first want, marginal utility of the good would not have diminished.

The significance of the diminishing marginal utility of a good for the theory of demand is that the quantity demanded of a good rises as the price falls and **vice-versa.** Thus it is because of the diminishing marginal utility that the demand curve slopes downward.

Law of diminishing marginal utility is a universal law and applies to all objects of desire including money. But, it is worth mentioning that marginal utility of money is generally never zero or negative. Money represents purchasing power over all other goods, that is, a man can satisfy all his material wants if he possesses enough money. Since man's total wants are practically unlimited, therefore the marginal utility of money to him never falls to zero.

Its Limitations

Law of diminishing marginal utility holds only under certain conditions —

(a) There should be continuity in the consumption of the commodity. Units of the commodity should be consumed in succession at one particular time.

(b) There should be no change in the taste, habit, custom, fashion and income of the consumer.

(c) All units of a commodity should be of the same weight and quality.

(d) Units of the commodity should be of a suitable size. Giving water to a thirsty person by spoons will increase utility of the subsequent spoons of water.

(e) Prices of the different units and of the substitutes of the commodity should remain the same.

Law of Equi-marginal Utility

The Law of equi-marginal utility is known by various names. It is termed as the Law of substitution, the Law of Maximum Satisfaction and **Gossen's Second Law.**

Law of equi-marginal utility occupies an important place in marginal utility analysis. It is through the principle that **Consumer's equilibrium is explained.** A consumer has a given income which he has to spend on various goods he wants. Now the question is how he would allocate his money income between various goods, that is to say, what would be his equilibrium position in respect of the purchases of the various goods.

Suppose there are only two goods A and B on which consumer has to spend a given income. The consumer's behaviour will be governed by two factors: **Firstly,** by the marginal utilities of the goods and **Secondly,** by the prices of two goods. Suppose the prices of the goods are given for the consumer. The Law of equi-marginal utility states that the consumer will distribute his money income between the goods in such a way that the utility derived from the last rupee spent on each good is equal. In other words, the consumer will spend his money income on different goods in such a way that marginal utility of each good is proportional to its price. That is, consumer is in equilibrium in respect of the purchases of two goods A and B when

$$\frac{MU_A}{P_A} = \frac{MU_B}{P_B}$$

where MU_A is the marginal utility of A, MU_B is the marginal utility of B and P_A is the price of A, P_B is the price of B.

Now, if $\frac{MU_A}{P_A}$ and $\frac{MU_B}{P_B}$ are not equal and $\frac{MU_A}{P_A}$ is greater than the $\frac{MU_B}{P_B}$, then the consumer will substitute good A for good B. As a result of this substitution, the marginal utility of good A will fall and marginal utility of good B will rise. The consumer will continue substituting good A for good B till $\frac{MU_A}{P_A}$ becomes equal to $\frac{MU_B}{P_B}$. When $\frac{MU_A}{P_A}$ becomes equal to $\frac{MU_B}{P_B}$, the consumer will be in equilibrium.

But the equality of $\frac{MU_A}{P_A}$ with $\frac{MU_B}{P_B}$ can be achieved not only at one level but at different levels of expenditure. The question is how far does a consumer go in purchasing the goods he wants. This is determined by the size of his money income.

If there are more than two goods on which the consumer is spending his income, the above equation must hold good for all of them. Thus

$$\frac{MU_A}{P_A} = \frac{MU_B}{P_B} = ... = \frac{MU_n}{P_n}$$

Law of equi-marginal utility is explained with the help of table given below –

TABLE 2.2

Number of units	MU_A	MU_B
1	20	24
2	18	21
3	16	18
4	14	15
5	12	9
6	10	3

Let the prices of goods A and B are Rs. 2 and Rs. 3 respectively. Reconstructing the above table by dividing marginal utilities of A (MU_A) by Rs. 2 and marginal utilities of B (MU_B) by Rs. 3. We get:

TABLE 2.3

Number of units	$\frac{MU_A}{P_A}$	$\frac{MU_B}{P_B}$
1	10	8
2	9	7
3	8	6
4	7	5
5	6	3
6	5	1

By looking at the table it is clear that $\frac{MU_A}{P_A}$ is equal to 6 utils when the consumer purchases 5 units of good A and 3 units of good B and will be spending (Rs. 2 × 5 + Rs. 3 × 3) = Rs. 19 on them.

Demand

Demand is a function of price, income, price of related goods and tastes and is expressed as

$$D = f(p, y, pr, t).$$

When income, prices of related goods and tastes are given, the demand function is

$$D = f(p).$$

It shows quantities of a commodity purchased at given prices. Demand is also related to a period of time. In the **Marshallian analysis,** the other determinants of demand are taken as given and constant.

Types of Demand

Three kinds of demands may be distinguished:

(*a*) Price Demand

(*b*) Income Demand

(*c*) Cross Demand

Price Demand : Price demand refers to the various quantities of a commodity or service that a consumer would purchase at a given time in a market at various hypothetical prices. It is assumed that other things, such as consumer's income, his tastes and prices of inter-related goods, remain unchanged.

The demand of the individual consumer is called **Individual Demand** and the total demand of all the consumers combined for the commodity or service is called **Industry Demand.** The total demand for the product of an individual firm at various prices is known as firm's demand or **Individual Seller's Demand.**

Income Demand : The income demand refers to the various qualities of goods and services which would be purchased by the consumers at various levels of incomes. Here we assume that the price of the commodity or service as well as the prices of inter-related goods and the tastes and desires of consumers do not change.

Cross Demand : The cross demand means the quantities of a good or service which will be purchased with reference to change in price not of this good but of other inter-related goods. These goods are either substitutes or complementary goods. A change in the price of tea, for instance, will affect the demand for coffee.

Law of Demand

This law expresses a relationship between the quantity demanded and its price. It may be defined in Marshall's words as "the amount demanded increase with a fall in price, and diminishes with a rise in price." Thus it expresses an inverse relation between price and demand. The inverse price-demand relationship is based on **other things remaining equal.** This phrase points towards certain important assumption on which this law is based.

These assumptions are :

(*i*) There is no change in the tastes and preferences of the consumer;

(*ii*) The income of the consumer remains constant;

(*iii*) There is no change in customs;

(*iv*) There should not be any change in the prices of other products;

(*v*) There should not be any change in the quality of the product;

(*vi*) The habits of the consumers should remain unchanged.

Given these conditions, the law of demand operates. If there is change even in one of these conditions, it will stop operating.

Exceptions to the Law of Demand

As we have said above, generally the demand curve slopes downward to the left. But some times, the demand curve, instead of sloping downward, will rise upwards. In other words, some time people will buy more when the price rises. This can be represented only by a rising demand curve. These were first investigated by **Sir Robert Giffen.** The **Giffen Paradox** holds that the demand is strengthened with a rise or weakened with a fall in price.

Many causes are attributed to an upward sloping demand curve :

1. War
2. Depression
3. Giffen Paradox
4. Demonstration Effect
5. Speculation

Increase and Decrease Vs. Extensive and Contraction of Demand

When the demand changes merely because the price has changed, it is a case of **extension** or **contraction.** If the change in demand is due to a factor other than the price, it is known as **increase** or **decrease** in demand.

A **movement along a demand curve** indicates that a different quantity is being demanded because the price has changed. A shift of a demand curve indicates that different quantity will be demanded at each possible price because something else, either incomes, tastes or the price of some other good, has changed.

When we refer to a movement along a curve, to a change in the quantity demanded because price has changed, we shall refer to a change in the **quantity demanded,** specifically, to an increase in the quantity demanded, indicating a movement down the curve because of a fall in price, or a decrease in the quantity demanded, indicating a movement up the curve because of a rise in price.

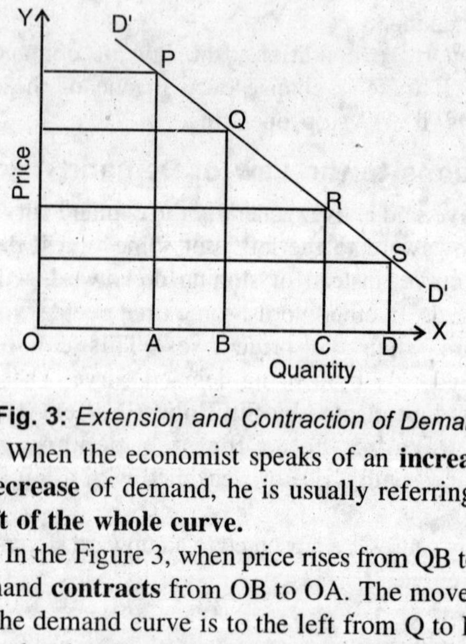

Fig. 3: *Extension and Contraction of Demand*

When the economist speaks of an **increase** or a **decrease** of demand, he is usually referring to a **shift of the whole curve.**

In the Figure 3, when price rises from QB to PA, demand **contracts** from OB to OA. The movement on the demand curve is to the left from Q to P. On the other hand, a fall in the price from RC to SD brings an **extension** in demand from OC to OD. It is a movement to the right on the same demand curve from R to S.

Figure 4 illustrates an increase and decrease in demand. Let D be the original demand curve where at price OP, quantity OB is demanded. D_1 shows an increase in demand. An increase in demand can be either of the two ways : larger quantity at the same price or the same quantity at a higher price. When the demand increases to D_1, larger quantity OC is bought at the original Price OP, or the same quantity OB is bought at the higher price OP_1. On the contrary, a decrease in demand implies same quantity at a lower price or smaller quantity at the same price, D_2 shows decrease in demand, the same quantity OB is bought at the lower price OP_2 or the smaller quantity PT is purchased at the same price OP. Demand curves are thus not stationary, rather they shift to the right or left due to a number of causes. They are changes in tastes, habits and customs of the consumers; changes in income expenditure; changes in the prices of substitutes and complements; expectations about future changes in prices and incomes; and changes in the age and composition of the population.

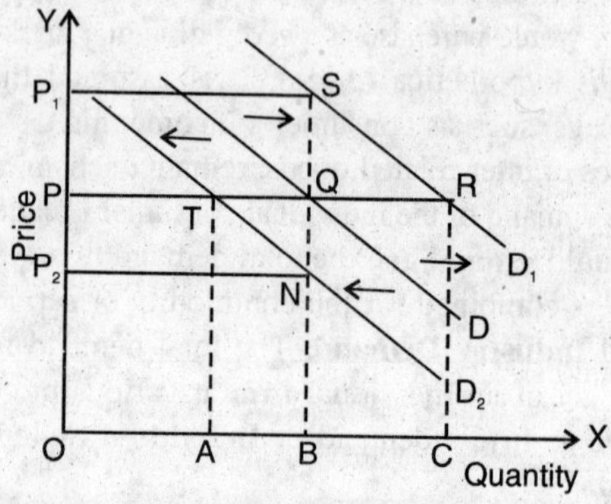

Fig. 4: *Increase and Decrease of Demand*

***A Rise (Increase) in Demand :** The demand curve shifts to the right indicating that more is demanded at each price. This can be caused by : (1) a rise in income; (2) a rise in the price of a substitute; (3) a fall in the price of a complement; (4) a change in tastes in favour of this commodity.

***A Fall (Decrease) in Demand :** The demand curve shifts to the left indicating that less is demanded at each price. This can be causes by : (1) a fall in income; (2) a fall in the price of a substitute; (3) a rise in the price of a complement; (4) a change in taste against this commodity.

Elasticity

In this section we shall consider the degree to which the quantity demanded and the quantity supplied respond to changes in price. The concept of elasticity has a very great importance in economic theory as well as in applied economics.

Various Concepts of Demand Elasticity

It is price elasticity of demand which is usually referred to as elasticity of demand. But, besides price elasticity of demand, there are various other concepts of demand elasticity. Demand for a good is determined by its price, incomes of the people, prices of related goods etc. Quantity demanded of a good will change as a result of a change in the size of any of these determinants of demand. The concept of elasticity of demand therefore refers to the **degree of responsiveness** of quantity demanded of a good to a change in its price, income or prices of related goods. Accordingly, there are three kinds of demand elasticity–

1. Price Elasticity
2. Income Elasticity
3. Cross Elasticity

Price Elasticity of Demand

Price elasticity means the degree of **responsiveness** or **sensitiveness** of quantity demanded of a good to a changes in its prices. In other words, Price elasticity of demand is a measure of the relative change in quantity purchased of a good in response to a relative change in its Price. Price elasticity can be precisely defined as "the proportional change in the quantity purchased divided by the proportional change in price." Thus

$$\text{Price Elasticity} = -\frac{\text{Percentage change in quantity}}{\text{Percentage change in price}}$$

$$= -\frac{\text{Change in quantity demanded / Quantity demanded}}{\text{Change in price / Price}}$$

or, in symbolic terms

$$e_P = -\frac{\Delta q/q}{\Delta P/P} = -\frac{\Delta q}{q} \times \frac{P}{\Delta P}$$

where,

e_P stands for price elasticity

q stands for quantity

P stands for price

Δ stands for change

Mathematically speaking, Price elasticity of demand is negative. Since demand curves slope downwards, the change in quantity will always have the opposite sign to the change in price. The minus sign in the definition of elasticity is simply designed to **'neutralize'**. This negative relation between price and quantity changes and thus to make elasticity of demand a positive number. This is a matter of convenience only; it has no more profound Justification than that.

Marshall who Introduced the Concept of Elasticity into Economic Theory remarks that the elasticity or responsiveness of demand in a market is great or small accordingly as the amount demanded increases much or little for a given fall in Price, and diminishes much or little for a given rise in price. This will be clear from figures. Figures 5 A and B represent two demanded curves.

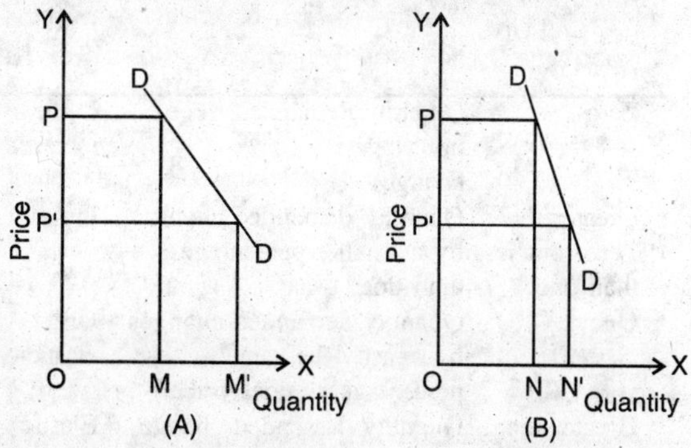

Fig.5 : *(A) More Elastic Demand, (B) Less Elastic Demand*

For a given fall in price, from OP to OP', increase in quantity demanded is much greater in Fig. 5-A than in Fig. 5-B. Therefore, demand curve in Fig. 5-A is more elastic than the demand curve of Fig. 5-B, for a given fall in price. Demand for the good represented in Fig. 5-A is generally said to be elastic and the demand for good in Fig: 5-B to be inelastic.

Interpreting Numerical Values of Elasticity of Demand

The numerical value of elasticity can vary from zero to infinity. Elasticity is zero if there is no change at all in quantity demanded when price changes, *i.e.,* when quantity demanded does not respond to a price change. The larger the elasticity, the larger the percentage change in quantity for a given percentage change in price. As long as the elasticity of demand has a value of less than one, however, the percentage change in quantity is less than the percentage change in price. When elasticity is equal to one, then the two percentage changes are equal to each other. While, when the percentage change in quantity exceeds the percentage change in price, then the value for the elasticity of demand will be greater than one.

When the percentage change in quantity is less than percentage change in price (elasticity less than one), the demand is said to be **INELASTIC.** When the percentage change in quantity is greater than the percentage change in price (elasticity greater than one), the demand is said to be **ELASTIC.**

Price Elasticity : Measures, Meaning and Nomeclature

Numerical measure of elasticity	*Verbal description*	*Terminology*
* Zero	Quantity demanded does not change as price changes	Perfectly inelastic
* Greater than Zero, but less than one	Quantity demanded changes by a smaller percentage than does price.	Inelastic
* One	Quantity demanded changes by exactly the same percentage as does price.	Unit elasticity
* Greater than one, but less than infinity	Quantity demanded changes by a larger percentage than does price	Elastic
* Infinity	Purchasers are prepared to buy all they can obtain at some price and none at all at an even slightly higher price	Perfectly elastic

We may now consider briefly the graphical representation of demand curves of various elasticity. These are summarized in Figure 6. Zero elasticity occurs when the quantity demanded does not change as the price changes. The graph of a demand curve of zero elasticity will thus be a vertical straight line indicating that the same quantity is demanded whatever the price. Unit elasticity occurs when a given percentage change in quantity at all points on the curve. The graph of a curve of unit elasticity over its whole range is shown in Figure 6 *(ii)*. A demand curve of infinite elasticity means that there exists some small price reduction which raises the demand from zero to infinity. This case occurs when, at some price, consumers will buy all that they can obtain of the commodity (an infinite amount if they could get it), while at an even slightly higher price they would buy nothing at all. In Figure 6 *(iii)*, demand is zero for all prices above OP but at price OP demand is infinite.

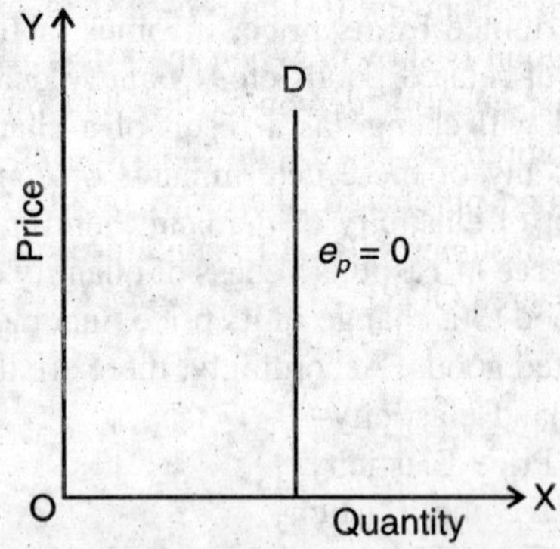

(i) A Demand Curve of Perfect Inelasticity

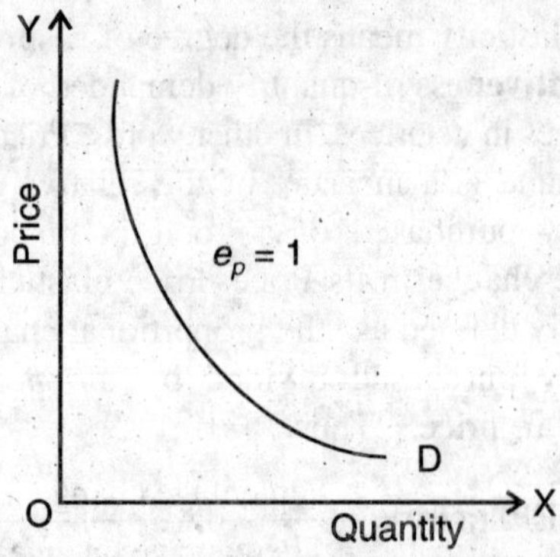

(ii) A Demand Curve of Unit Elasticity

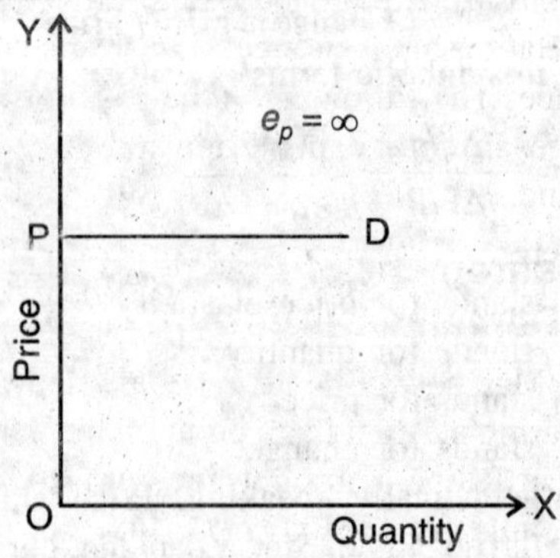

(iii) A Demand Curve of Infinite Elasticity

Fig. 6

Price Elasticity and Changes in Total Expenditure

It is often useful to know what happens to total expenditure made by the consumers on a good when its price changes. In Figure 7, a demand curve DD of a good is shown. When the price of the good is OP, its quantity demanded is OQ. Since the total expenditure is price multiplied by the quantity of the good purchased, therefore

Consumer's Total Expenditure = OP × OQ
= area OQRP

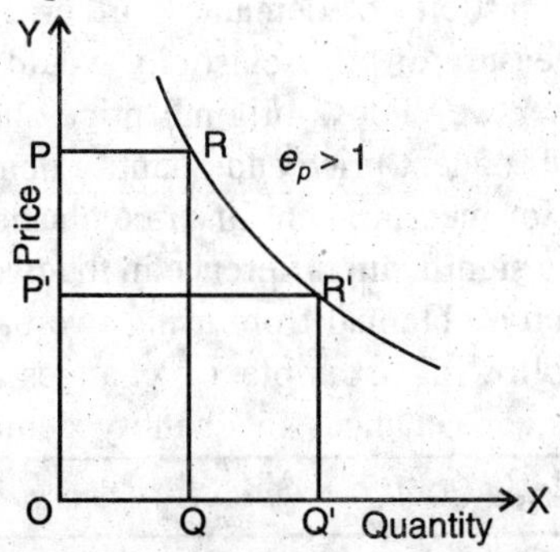

Fig. 7

Now, if the price of the good falls from OP to OP′ the quantity demanded rises from OQ to OQ′. At new Price OP′, therefore

Total Expenditure = OP′ × OQ′ = area OQ′R′P′

Now, whether the total expenditure rises or falls or remains the same with the change in the price of the good depends upon the price elasticity of demand. The total expenditure bears an important relationship with the price elasticity of demand and this relationship is of great significance in the theory of price. The following is the relationship between changes in Total expenditure and Price elasticity of demand.

Measurement of Elasticity at a Point on the Demand Curve

Prof. Marshall devised a geometrical method for measuring elasticity at a point on the demand curve.

Let RS be a straight line demand curve. If the Price falls from PB (= OA) to MD (= OC), the quantity demanded increases from OB to OD. Elasticity at point P on RS demand curve according to the formula is

$$e_P = \frac{\Delta q}{\Delta P} \cdot \frac{P}{q}$$

From Fig. 8

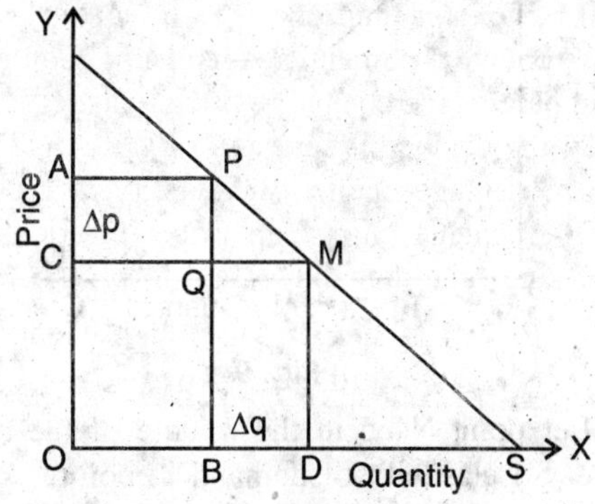

Fig. 8

$$\Delta q = BD = QM$$
$$\Delta p = PQ$$
$$p = PB$$
$$q = OB$$

Substituting these values in the elasticity formula:

$$e_P = \frac{QM}{PQ} \times \frac{PB}{OB}$$

Moreover,

$$\frac{QM}{PQ} = \frac{BS}{PB}$$

[∠PQM = ∠PBS being right angles and ΔPQM and ΔPBS are similar]

$$\therefore \quad \frac{BS}{PB} \times \frac{PB}{OB} = \frac{BS}{OB}$$

Since ΔPBS and ΔROS are similar, price elasticity of demand at point

$$P = \frac{BS}{OB} = \frac{OA}{AR}$$

$$= \frac{PS}{PR} = \frac{\text{Lower Segment}}{\text{Upper Segment}}$$

With the help of the point method it is easy to point out the elasticity at any point along a demand curve. Suppose that the straight line demand curve in Figure 9 is DC. The elasticity of demand at each point can be known with help of the above method.

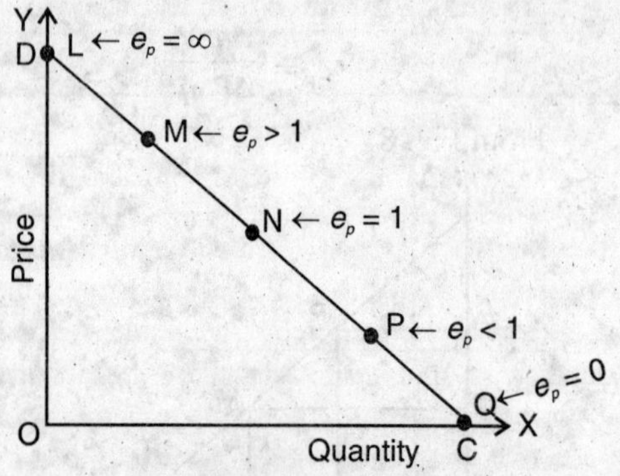

Fig. 9

Let point N be in the middle of the demand curve. So elasticity of demand at point

$$N = \frac{\text{CN (Lower Segment)}}{\text{ND (Upper Segment)}} = \text{Unity}$$

Elasticity of demand at point

$$M = \frac{CM}{MD} = \text{Greater than unity}$$

Elasticity of demand at point

$$L = \frac{CL}{O} = \infty \text{ (infinity)}$$

Elasticity of demand at point

$$P = \frac{CP}{PD} = \text{Less than Unity}$$

Elasticity of demand at point

$$Q = \frac{O}{CD} = 0 \text{ (Zero)}$$

From above it is clear that elasticity at different points on a given demand curve is different. At the mid-point in the demand curve the elasticity of demand is **Unity.** Moving up the demand curve from the mid-point, elasticity becomes greater. When the demand curve touches the Y-axis, elasticity is **infinity. Ipso facto,** any point below the mid-point towards the X-axis will show elastic demand. Elasticity becomes **zero** when the demand curve touches the X-axis.

Arc Elasticity of Demand

We have studied above the measurement of elasticity at a point on a demand curve or the concept of point elasticity of demand which refers to the price elasticity when the changes in the price and the resultant changes in quantity demanded are very small. In this case if we take the original price or the subsequent price as the basis of measurement, there will not be any significant difference in the elasticity figure. However, when the price change is somewhat large or we have to measure elasticity over an **arc of the demand curve** rather than at a specific point on it, the measure of point elasticity namely, $\frac{\Delta q}{\Delta p} \times \frac{p}{q}$, does not provide us the true and correct result of price elasticity of demand. Further, in such cases, the measure of price elasticity would depend upon whether we choose original price and quantity or the subsequent price and quantity demanded as the basis for measurement of price elasticity and there will be significant difference in the two measures of elasticity, obtained from using two basis. Consider the following example of changes in price and consequent changes in quantity demanded.

Price (Rs.)	*Quantity Demanded (units)*
15 (p_1)	100 (q_1)
10 (p_2)	200 (q_2)

If we take Rs. 15 and quantity demanded at it (100 units) as basis of measuring price elasticity with the point elasticity formula, we get the following figure for elasticity :

$$e_P = \frac{\Delta q}{\Delta p} \times \frac{p}{q}$$

$$= \frac{100}{5} \times \frac{15}{100} = 3$$

If we take Rs. 10 and quantity demanded at it (200 units) as the basis of measuring price elasticity with the point elasticity formula, we get the following figure for elasticity :

$$e_P = \frac{\Delta q}{\Delta p} \times \frac{p}{q}$$

$$= \frac{100}{5} \times \frac{10}{200} = 1$$

We thus see that when there is a somewhat large change in price, point elasticity formula will yield two significantly different elasticity measures (as 3 and 1 in our above example) depending upon whether we use the original price and quantity demanded or the subsequent price and quantity demanded as the basis for measurement.

In terms of demand curve, when we have to measure the price elasticity over an **arc of the demand curve** such as between points A and on the demand curve DD in Figure 10 the point elasticity formula will not yield the true and correct measure of price elasticity. For measuring price elasticity in such cases when the changes in price are some what large or the price elasticity over an arc of the demand curve (that is, between the two points on a demand curve which lie close together) is to be measured, the concept of arc elasticity has been evolved. In measurement of arc elasticity, we use the **average** of the two price figures (original and subsequent) and **average** of the two quantity figures (original and subsequent). Thus the formula for measuring **arc price elasticity** of demand is :

$$e_P = \frac{\Delta q}{\frac{(q_1+q_2)}{2}} \div \frac{\Delta p}{\frac{(p_1+p_2)}{2}}$$

$$= \frac{\Delta q}{\left(\frac{q_1+q_2}{2}\right)} \times \frac{\left(\frac{p_1+p_2}{2}\right)}{\Delta p}$$

$$= \frac{\Delta q}{\Delta p} \times \frac{(p_1+p_2)}{(q_1+q_2)}$$

In our above numerical example where when the price of a good falls from Rs. 15 to Rs. 10 per unit, the quantity demanded increases from 100 to 200 units the arc elasticity is :

$$e_P = \frac{\Delta q}{\Delta p} \times \frac{(p_1+p_2)}{(q_1+q_2)}$$

$$= \frac{100}{5} \times \frac{15+10}{100+200}$$

$$= \frac{100}{5} \times \frac{25}{300} = 1.66$$

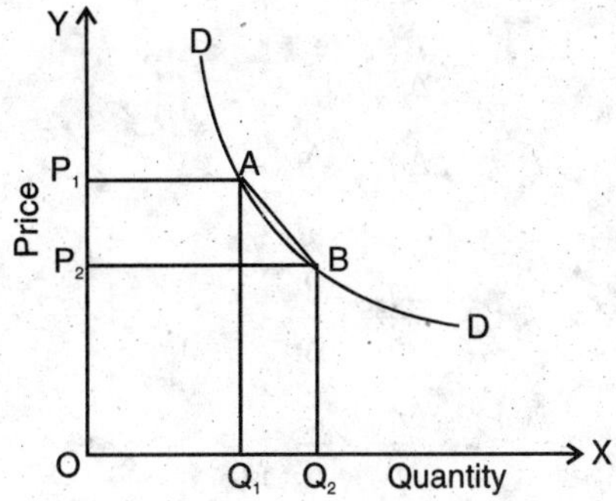

Fig. 10 : *Arc Elasticity*

In Figure 10, if the arc elasticity is to be measured between points A and B on the demand curve DD, we will have to take the average of prices OP_1 and OP_2 and average of quantities OQ_1 and OQ_2. It should be further noted that in Fig. 10, the arc elasticity formula given above measures the arc elasticity over a straight line AB which is taken to be the approximation of the arc elasticity along the **true arc** (the demand curve from point A to B). Therefore, the greater the convexity of the demand curve between A and B, the greater the divergence between the line AB and the true demand curve and therefore the poorer the approximation of arc elasticity measure (of the line AB) for the true curve between A and B.

Cross Elasticity of Demand

The change in the demand for one good in response to the change in price of the other good represents the cross elasticity of demand of one good for the other. In other words, the cross elasticity of demand is the relation between percentage change in the quantity demanded of a good to the percentage in the price of a related good.

When the quantity demanded of good x rises as a result of the fall in the price of good y, the coefficient of cross elasticity of demand of x for y will be equal to the relative change in the quantity demanded for good x in response to a given relative change in the price of good y. Therefore,

Coefficients of cross elasticity of demand of x for y

$$= \frac{\text{Percentage change in the quantity demanded of } x}{\text{Percentage change in the price of } y}$$

$$\text{or,}\quad e_c = \frac{\Delta q_x / q_x}{\Delta p_y / p_y}$$

$$= \frac{\Delta q_x}{q_x} \div \frac{\Delta p_y}{p_y}$$

$$= \frac{\Delta q_x}{q_x} \times \frac{p_y}{\Delta p_y}$$

$$= \frac{\Delta q_x}{\Delta p_y} \times \frac{p_y}{q_x}$$

where

e_c stands for cross elasticity of demand of X and Y

q_x stands for the original in quantity demanded of good X

p_y stands for the original price of good Y

Δp_y stands for a small change in the price of Y

There are two types of related goods :

(i) Substitutes *(ii)* Complementaries

Cross Elasticity of Substitutes : In case of substitutes, the cross elasticity is **positive** and large. The higher the coefficient e_c, the better substitutes the good are. If the price of butter rises, it will lead to increase in the demand for Jam, similarly a fall in the price of butter will cause a decrease in the demand for Jam.

If a change in the price of good *x* leads to more than proportionate change in the demand for good *y,* the cross elasticity is high ($e_c > 1$). In such case goods are **close substitutes.**

If cross elasticity is less than unity ($e_c < 1$), it means that goods *x* and *y* are **poor substitutes** for each other.

In case of the two goods are **perfect substitutes,** the cross elasticity of demand will be infinite ($e_c = \infty$). Hence the cross elasticity of demand for substitutes varies between zero and infinity.

Cross Elasticity of Complementary Goods

If two goods are complementary (jointly demanded), rise in the price of one leads to a fall in the demand for the other. Rise in the prices of cars will bring a fall in their demand together with the demand for petrol. Similarly, a fall in the prices of cars will raise the demand for petrol. Since the price and demand vary in the opposite direction, the cross elasticity of demand in **negative.**

Income Elasticity

The responsiveness of demand to changes in income is termed **income elasticity of demand.** It shows how the quantity demanded will change when the income of the purchaser changes, the price of the commodity remaining the same, it may be defined thus : The Income Elasticity of demand for a good is the ratio of the percentage change in the amount spent on the commodity to a percentage change in the consumer's income price of commodity remaining constant. Thus,

$$\text{Income Elasticity} = \frac{\text{Percentage change in quantity demanded}}{\text{Percentage change in income}}$$

Let *y* stand for an initial income, Δy for a small change in income, *q* for the initial quantity purchased, Δq for a change in quantity purchased as a result of a change in income and e_i for income elasticity of demand. Then $e_i = \dfrac{\Delta q / q}{\Delta y / y} = \dfrac{\Delta q}{\Delta y} \times \dfrac{y}{q}$

We can also express the income elasticity in terms of changes in expenditure made on the good rather than the change in quantity purchased of the good as a result of a change in income. It should be noted that expenditure is equal to the quantity purchased of the good multiplied by the price of the good. If *q* is the quantity purchased of the good and *p* the price of the good, then expenditure made on the good is equal to *qp*.

As defined above, $e_i = \dfrac{\Delta q}{q} \times \dfrac{y}{\Delta y}$

Multiplying the numerator and denominator by *p,* we get $e_i = \dfrac{\Delta q.p}{q.p} \times \dfrac{y}{\Delta y}$.

Now, as explained above, *qp* is the expenditure made on the good and Δqp is the change in expenditure made as a result of change in income. Let X-stand for the expenditure made on the good. Then the above equation will

$$e_i = \frac{\Delta x}{x} \times \frac{y}{\Delta y} \quad \text{or} \quad e_i = \frac{y.\Delta x}{x.\Delta y}$$

Thus, Income elasticity

$$= \frac{\text{income} \times \text{Change in expenditure}}{\text{expenditure} \times \text{Change in income}}$$

For most goods, increase in income lead to increases in demand, and income elasticity will be **positive.** For inferior goods, where a rise in income leads consumers to demand less of the commodity, income elasticity will be negative.

Income Elasticity and Proportion of Income Spent

There is a useful relationship between income elasticity for a good and proportion of income spent on it. The relationship between the two is described in the following three propositions :

1. If proportion of income spent on the good remains the same as income increases, then income elasticity for the good is equal to one ($e_i = 1$).
2. If proportion of income spent on the good increase as income increases, then the income elasticity for the good is greater than one ($e_i > 1$).
3. If proportion of income spent on the good decreases as income rises, then income elasticity for the good is less than one ($e_i < 1$).

Income Elasticity : Measures and Meaning

Numerical Value of Income Elasticity	*Verbal description*
• Negative	Demand for the commodity falls as income rises
• Zero	Demand for the commodity does not change as income changes
• Greater than Zero but less than One	Demand for the commodity rises less than in proportion to the rise in income
• Unity	Demand for the commodity rises in the same proportion as the rise in income
• Greater than Unity	Demand for the commodity rises more than in proportion to the rise in income

The Elasticity of Substitution

The elasticity of substitution is another important concept of demand elasticity. Elasticity of substitution measures the effects of the substitution of one good for another. In other words, the elasticity of substitution between two goods is a measure of the ease with which one can be substituted for the other. Just as price elasticity of demand is a relative measure of the price effect, income elasticity is a relative measure of the income effect, similarly the elasticity of substitution is a relative measure of the substitution effect.

Elasticity of substitution is defined as the proportionate change in the ratios of goods X and Y to the proportionate change in their price ratio. Its numerical coefficient is

$$e_s = \frac{\text{Proportionate change in the ratio of } x \text{ and } y}{\text{Proportionate change in their price ratios}}$$

Algebraically,

$$e_s = \frac{\Delta\left(\frac{x}{y}\right) \Big/ \frac{x}{y}}{\Delta\left(\frac{\Delta Y}{\Delta X}\right) \Big/ \frac{\Delta Y}{\Delta X}}$$

where

es stands for elasticity of substitution

$\frac{x}{y}$ stands for the ratio between the two goods x and y.

$\Delta(x/y)$ stands for the change in the ratio of x and y

$\frac{P_x}{P_y}$ stands for the price ratio between x and y

$\Delta(Px/Py)$ stands for the change in their price ratios.

There are two extremes, *i.e.,* two limiting cases: *(a)* The elasticity of substitution may be **infinite.** In this case, the goods are **perfect substitutes** for one another, *i.e.,* they are identical; *(b)* at the other extreme, there is a case of **zero** elasticity of substitution. Here there can be no substitution at all and the goods must be used in fixed proportion or not all. Between these two limits, there can be various degrees of substitution.

When it is difficult to substitute one good for another, then a small change in the proportion of the two goods will bring about a large change in the **marginal rate of substitution** between the two goods. When the substitution between the two goods is easy, then a small change in the proportion of two goods possessed by the consumer, the change in the marginal rate of substitution between the two goods will not be much. It is thus clear that from the change in the proportion of two goods and the resultant change in marginal rate of substitution we can know the elasticity of substitution. Therefore, elasticity of substitution can be expressed as follow:

$$e_s = \frac{\text{Proportionate change in the ratio of } x \text{ and } y}{\text{Proportionate change in the marginal rate of substitution of } x \text{ for } y}$$

Symbolically,

$$e_s = \frac{\Delta\left(\frac{q_x}{q_y}\right) \Big/ \frac{q_x}{q_y}}{\Delta\left(\frac{\Delta Y}{\Delta X}\right) \Big/ \frac{\Delta Y}{\Delta X}}$$

Here,

$\frac{q_x}{q_y}$ stands for the original proportion between the quantities of goods x and y

$\Delta\left(\frac{q_x}{q_y}\right)$ stands for the small change in the proportion of good x and y

$\frac{\Delta Y}{\Delta X}$ stands for the original marginal rate of substitution of good x for y

$\Delta\left(\frac{\Delta X}{\Delta Y}\right)$ stands for the change in the marginal rate of substitution of good x and y

When the two goods x and y are perfect substitutes of each other, than the proportion between them $\left(\text{that is, } \frac{q_x}{q_y}\right)$ can be increased infinitely without any change in the marginal rate of substitution between them, that is, elasticity of substitution between the **perfect substitute** is **infinite.**

When the two goods which are perfect complements to each other, they are used in a fixed proportion and no substitution between them is possible. Therefore, the goods which are perfect complements with each other, the marginal rate of substitution between them is zero, that is, elasticity of substitution between the **perfect complements** is **zero.**

Factors Affecting Price Elasticity of Demand

Elasticity of demand for any good is determined or influenced by a number of factors which are discussed as under.

1. Nature of the Commodity : The elasticity of demand for any commodity depends upon the category to which it belongs, *i.e.*, whether it is a necessity, comforts or luxury. The demand for necessaries of life or conventional necessaries is generally **less elastic.** The demand for necessaries of efficiency and for comforts is **moderately elastic** because with the rise or fall in their prices, the demand for them decreases or increases moderately. On the other hand, the demand for **luxuries** is **more elastic** because with a small change in their prices there is a large change in their demand.

2. Existence of Substitutes : For commodities having substitutes, the demand is elastic, *e.g.*, tea and coffee. If the price of any one of them falls, it will be purchased in larger quantities. If the price rise, demand for it will contract, and its substitutes will be purchased instead. There is, therefore, greater extension or contraction of demand for such commodities when their prices change. Demand for them is elastic.

3. Several Uses : The demand for a commodity having several uses is **more elastic.** With a fall in price such a commodity tends to be put to less urgent uses. Thus its demand extends, and **vice-versa.** If a commodity has only one use, a change in price of the commodity will influence its one use only. Even if its price falls considerably, it cannot be put to any other use. Hence the demand is in elastic. But it is possible to use it for a number of purposes, the demand will be obviously elastic.

4. Deferred Consumption : Commodities whose consumption can be deferred have an elastic demand. This is the case with durable consumer goods, like cloth, bicycle, fan, etc. If the price of any of these articles rises, people will postpone their consumption. As a result their demand will decrease, and **vice-versa.**

5. Habits : People who are habituated to the consumption of a particular commodity, like coffee, tea or cigarettee of a particular brand, the demand for it will be **inelastic.**

6. Income Groups : The elasticity of demand also depends on the income group to which a person belongs. Persons who belong to the higher income group, their demand for commodity is **less elastic.** On the other hand, the demand of persons in lower income groups is generally **elastic.**

7. Proportion of Income Spent : If the consumer spends a small proportion of his income on a commodity at a time, the demand for that commodity is less elastic, but commodities which entail a large proportion of the income of the consumer, the demand for them is more elastic.

8. Level of Prices : The level of prices also influences the elasticity of demand for commodities. When the price level is high, the demand for commodities is **elastic,** and when the price level is low, the demand is less elastic.

9. Time Factor : Time factor plays on important role in influencing the elasticity of demand for commodities. The shorter the time in which the consumer buys a commodity, the lesser will be the elasticity of demand for that product. On the other hand, the longer the time which the consumer takes in buying a commodity, the higher will be the elasticity of demand for that product.

Conclusion : From the above, it will be clear that there is no hard and fast rule to determine whether the demand for any commodity is elastic or inelastic. This will, in fact, depend on several factors connected with that commodity and with the consumer. However, broadly speaking, we can say that the elasticity of demand for any commodity in relation to a certain class of consumers will depend on the availability of its substitutes or the nature of the commodity whether it is a necessary or a luxury.

Elasticity of Supply

Elasticity of supply refers to the sensitiveness or **responsiveness** of the supply to changes in price. In other words, the elasticity of supply is defined as the percentage change in quantity supplied divided by the percentage change in price, and it is a measure of the degree to which the quantity supplied responds to price changes. Thus,

Elasticity of Supply

$$= \frac{\text{Percentage change in quantity supplied}}{\text{Percentage change in price}}$$

Figure 11 illustrates three cases of supply elasticity. The case of **zero supply elasticity** is one in which the quantity supplied does not change as price changes. This would be the case, for example, if suppliers persisted in producing a given quantity, q_1 in Figure 11 *(i)*, and dumping it on the market for whatever it would bring.

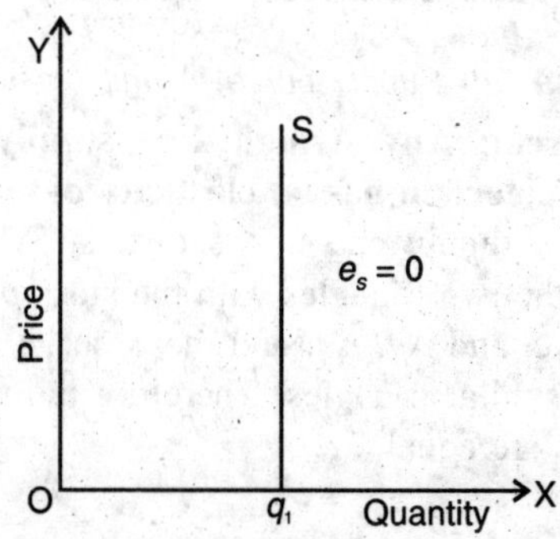

Fig. 11 *(i) Supply Curve of Zero elasticity*

Infinite supply elasticity is illustrated in Figure 11*(ii)*. The supply elasticity is infinite at the price p_1, because nothing at all is supplied at lower price, but a small increase in price to p_1 causes supply to rise from zero to an indefinitely large amount, indicating that producers would supply any amount demanded at that price.

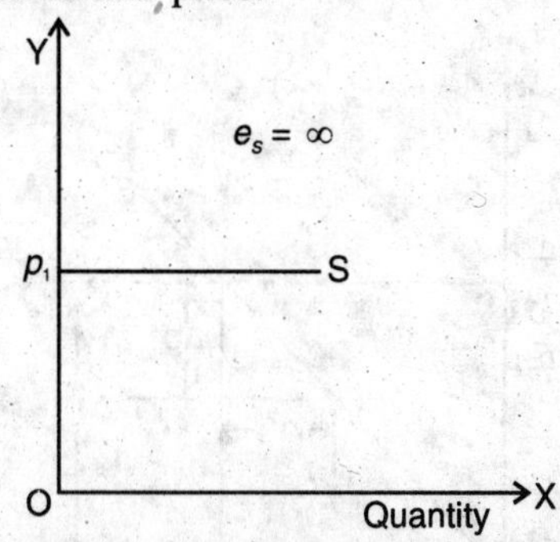

Fig. 11 *(ii) Supply curve in infinite elasticity*

The case of **unit elasticity of supply** is illustrated in Figure 11*(iii)*. Any straight-line supply curve drawn through the origin has, infact, an elasticity of unity.

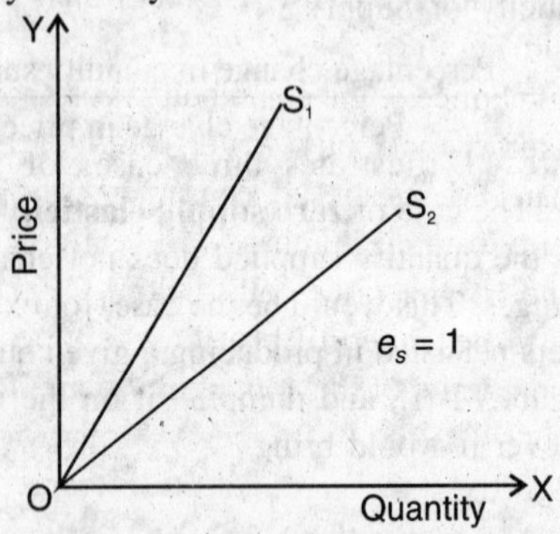

Fig. 11 *(iii) Supply curve in unit elasticity*

Theorem: Any straight-line supply curve through the origin has an elasticity of one.

Such a supply curve in shown is Figure 12. Consider the two triangles with the sides *p, q,* and the S curve, and Δp, Δq, and the S curve. Clearly these are similar triangles. Therefore the ratios of their sides are equal, *i.e.,*

$$\frac{p}{q} = \frac{\Delta p}{\Delta q} \qquad ...(1)$$

Elasticity of supply is defined as

$$e_s = \frac{\Delta q}{\Delta p} \cdot \frac{p}{q} \qquad ...(2)$$

which, by substitution from (1), gives

$$e_s = \frac{q}{p} \cdot \frac{p}{q} = 1$$

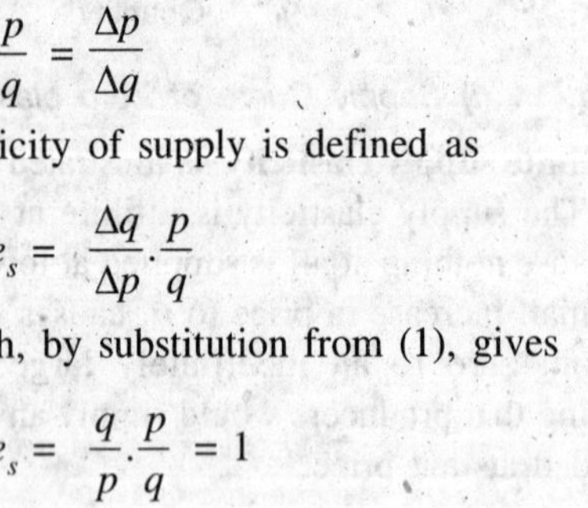

Fig. 12 : *A straight-line supply curve through the origin has an elasticity of one*

Consumer's Surplus

Concept of consumer's surplus is a very important concept in economic theory especially in welfare economics. The concept of consumer's surplus was first of all evolved by **Dr. Alfred Marshall,** who maintained that it can be measured in monetary units, and is equal to the difference between the amount of money that a consumer actually pays to buy a certain quantity of a commodity X, and the amount that he would be willing to pay for this quantity rather than do without it.

The concept of consumer surplus is important not only in economic theory but also in economic policies, such as taxation by the Government and price policy pursued by the monopolistic seller of a product. The essence of the concept of consumer's surplus is that a consumer derives extra satisfaction from the purchases he daily makes over the price he actually pays for them. **Marshall** defines the consumer's surplus in the following words :

"Excess of the price which a consumer would be willing to pay, rather than go without a thing over that which he actually does pay, is the economic measure of this surplus satisfaction ... it may be called consumer's surplus."

The amount of money which a person is prepared to pay for a good indicates the amount of utility he derives from that good, the greater the amount of money he is willing to pay, the greater the satisfaction or utility he will obtain from it. Therefore, the marginal utility of a unit of a good

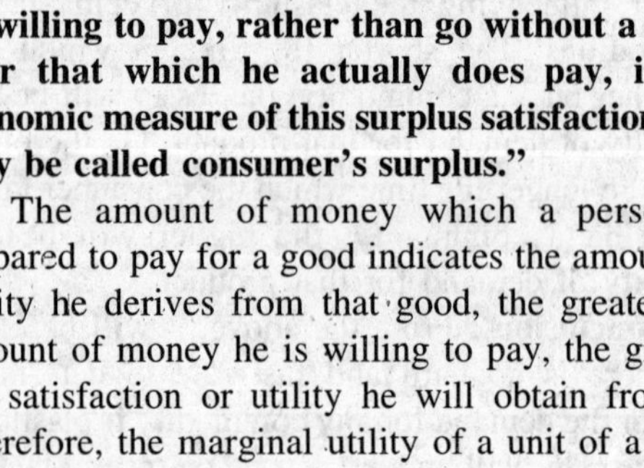

Fig. 13: *Marshall's Measure of Consumer's Surplus*

determines the price a consumer will be prepared to pay for that unit. The total utility which a person will get from a good will be given by sum of marginal utilities ($\sum$MU) of the units of the good purchased and the total price which he will actually pay is equal to the price per unit multiplied by the number of units purchased. Thus,

Consumer's Surplus = What a consumer is prepared to pay minus what he actually pays.

= $\sum$ MU – (Price × Number of units purchased)

The measurement of consumer's surplus is illustrated in Fig. 13 in which along the X-axis the amount of the commodity has been measured and on the Y-axis the marginal utility and the price of the commodity are measured. MU is the marginal utility curve which is sloping downward, indicating that as the consumer buys more units of the commodity, marginal utility of it falls. As said above, marginal utility shows the price which a person will be willing to pay for the different units rather than go without them.

If OP is the price that prevails in the market, then the consumer will be in equilibrium when he buys OM units of the commodity, since at OM units, marginal utility is equal to the given price OP. **The Mth unit of the commodity does not yield any consumer's surplus to the consumer. Since this is the last unit purchased and for this price paid is equal to the marginal utility which indicates the price he will be prepared to pay rather than go without it.** But for the intra marginal units, *i.e.*, units before Mth marginal utility is greater than the price and therefore, these units yield consumer's surplus to the consumer. The total utility of a certain quantity of a commodity to consumer can be known by summing up the marginal utilities of the various units purchased.

In Figure 13, the total utility derived by the consumer from OM units of the commodity will be equal to the area under the marginal utility curve up to point M. That is the total utility of DM units in Fig. 13 is equal to ODSM. In other words, for OM units of the good the consumer will be the prepared to pay the sum equal to Rs. ODSM. But given the price OP, the consumer will actually pay for OM units of the good the sum equal to Rs. OPSM. It is thus clear that the consumer derives extra utility equal to ODSM minus OPSM = DPS, which has been shaded in Fig. 13.

If the market price of the commodity rises above OP, the consumer will buy fewer units of the commodity than OM. As a result, consumer's surplus obtained by him from his purchase will decline. On the other hand, if the price falls below OP, the consumer will be in equilibrium when he is purchasing more units of the commodity than OM. As a result of this, the consumer's surplus will increase. Thus, given the marginal utility curve of the consumer, the higher the price, the smaller the consumer's surplus and the lower the price, the greater the consumer's surplus.

It is worth noting here that in our analysis of consumer's surplus, we have assumed that perfect competition prevails in the market so that the consumer faces a given price, whatever the amount of the commodity he purchases. But if the seller of a commodity discriminates the prices and charges different prices for the different units of the good, some units at a higher price and some at a lower price, then in this case consumer's surplus will be smaller. Thus, when the seller makes price discrimination and sells different units of a good at different prices, the consumer will obtain smaller amount of consumer's surplus than under perfect competition. If the seller indulges in **perfect price discrimination,** that is, if he changes price for each unit of the commodity equal to what any consumer will be prepared to pay for it, then in that case no consumer's surplus will accrue to the consumer.

A Note on the Diamond-Water Paradox

Classical economists were quite confused when they were asked about the low price of water, which was so necessary for life, compared with the high price of diamonds, which were so unnecessary for life.

As Figure 14 indicates, it is possible for the marginal utility of diamonds to be relatively high since diamonds are quite scarce, while the marginal utility of water is relatively low since water is quite plentiful, if we view quantities D_1 and W_1, respectively.

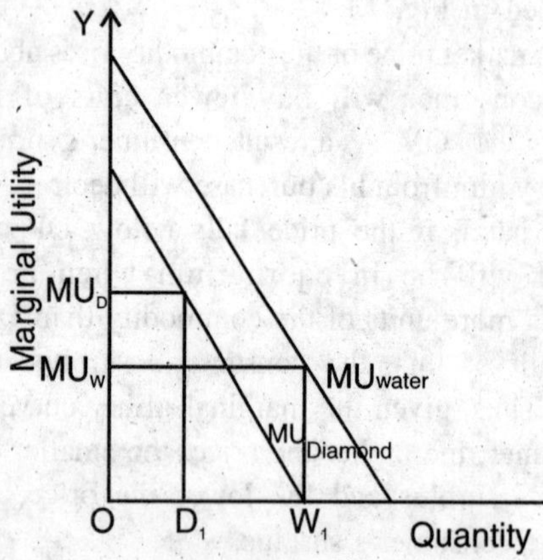

Fig. 14

As a result our marginal utility theory tells us that the price of diamonds will be quite high, while the price of water will be quite low. Nevertheless, the total utility of water can be much greater than the total utility of diamonds. The total utility of water is the area under the marginal utility curve for water upto the level of consumption W_1. That is to say, total utility is the marginal utility of the first unit plus the marginal utility of the second unit, and so on. Since the total utility of diamonds is the area under the marginal utility curve for diamonds up to consumption level D_1, it nicely follows that the total utility derived from water can be greater than the total utility derived from diamonds.

We may conclude that the more there is of a commodity, the lower is the relative desirability of the last unit despite the fact that total utility increases. Thus, a great quantity of water has a low price.

The Indifference Curve Theory

The indifference curve is a geometrical device that has been used to replace the neo-classical cardinal utility concept. **Hicks** presented its comprehensive version in his **value and capital** in 1939 and its major revision in his A Revision of Demand Theory in 1956. The fundamental approach of indifference curve analysis is that it has abandoned the concept of cardinal utility and instead has adopted the concept of **ordinal utility.** According to the supporters of the indifference curves theory, utility is a psychic entity and it cannot therefore be measured in quantitative, cardinal terms. In other words, utility being a psychological feeling is not quantifiable. The ordinal utility implies that the consumer is capable of simply 'comparing' the different levels of satisfaction. In other words, according to the ordinal utility hypothesis, while the consumer may not be able to indicate the exact amounts of utilities that he derives from commodities or any combination of them, but he is capable of judging whether the satisfaction obtained from a good or a combination of goods is equal to, lower than, or higher than another.

It is important to mention that indifference curve analysis of demand is based upon the **weak-ordering** form of preference hypothesis. The weak ordering implies that there is possibility of the consumer being indifferent between two combinations. Thus, the weak ordering recognizes the relation of preference as well as of indifference. The consumer may prefer A to B or B to A or he may be indifferent between A and B. On the contrary, **strong ordering** implies that there can be only the relation of preference, A is preferred to B, or B is preferred to A, the possibility of consumer's indifference between A and B ruled out. Thus the strong-ordering admits only the relation of preference.

Indifference Curves

An indifference curve is the locus of points-particular combinations or bundles of goods-which yields the same utility (level of satisfaction) to the consumer, so that he is indifferent as to the particular combination he consumes. In other words, all combinations of the goods lying on a consumer's indifference curve are equally desirable to or equally preferred by him. To understand indifference curves, it is better to start with indifference schedules.

TABLE 2.4 : Indifference Schedule

Combination	*Good x*	*Good y*
1	1	18
2	2	13
3	3	9
4	4	6
5	5	4
6	6	3

The indifference schedule shows the various combinations of the two commodities such that the consumer is indifferent to those combinations. In Table 2.4 indifference schedules is given. In this schedule the amount of goods x and y in each combination are so arranged that the consumer is indifferent among the combinations. In the schedule, the consumer has to start with 1 unit of x and 18 units of y. Now, the consumer is asked to tell how much of good y he will be willing to give up for the gain of additional unit of x so that his level of satisfaction remains the same. If the gain of one unit of x compensates him fully for the loss of 5 units of y, then the next combination of 2 units of x and 13 units of y $(2x + 13y)$ will give him as much satisfaction as the initial combination $(1x + 12y)$. Similarly, by asking the consumer further how much of y he will be prepared to forego for successive increments in his stock of x so that his level of satisfaction remains unaltered, we get combinations $3x + 9y$, $4x + 6y$, $5x + 4x$ and $6x + 3y$, each of which provides the same satisfaction as combination $1x + 18y$ or $2x + 13y$.

Now, we can convert the indifference schedule into indifference curve by plotting the various combinations on a graph paper. In Figure 15 an indifference curve IC is drawn by plotting the various combination in the indifference schedule. Like in an indifference schedule, combinations lying on an indifference curve will be equally desirable to the consumer, that is, will give him the same satisfaction. The smoothness and continuity of an indifference curve means that goods in question are assumed to be **perfectly divisible**.

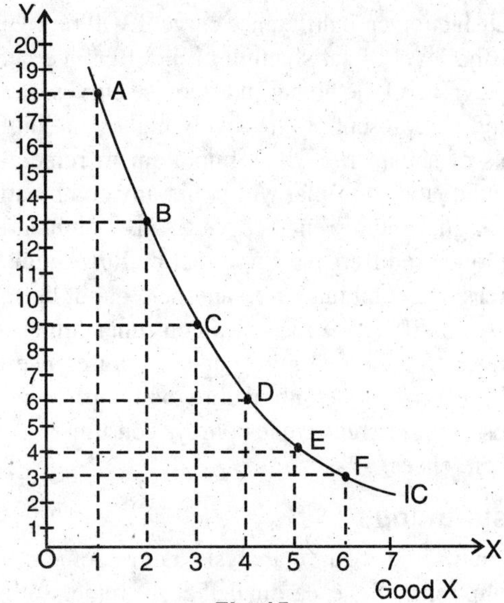

Fig. 15

An indifference map shows all the indifference curves which rank the preferences of the consumer combinations of goods situated on an indifference curve yield the same utility, Combinations of goods lying on a higher indifference curve yield higher level of satisfaction and are preferred. Combinations of goods on a lower indifference curve yield a lower utility. In Figure 16 an indifference map of a consumer is shown which consists of five indifference curves.

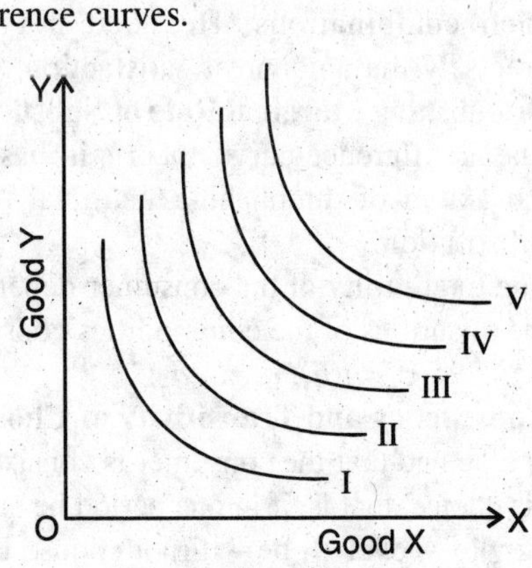

Fig. 16

The consumer regards all combinations on the indifference curve I as giving him equal satisfaction. Similarly all the combinations lying on indifference curve II provide the same satisfaction but the level of satisfaction on indifference curve II will be greater than the level of satisfaction on indifference curve I. Likewise, all the higher indifference curves, II, III, IV and V represent progressively higher and higher levels of satisfaction. It is important to remember that while the consumer will prefer any combination on a higher indifference curve to any combination on a lower indifference curve, but by **how much he prefers** one combination to another cannot be said.

An indifference map of a consumer represents his tastes for the two goods and his preferences as between different combinations of them. In other words, an indifference map portrays consumer's scale of preferences.

Assumptions

The indifference curve analysis retains some of the assumptions of the cardinal theory, rejects others and formulates its own. The assumptions of the ordinal theory are the following :

1. **Rationality :** The consumer is assumed to be rational-he aims at the maximisation of his utility, given his income and market prices. It is assumed he has full knowledge of all relevant information.
2. **Utility is Ordinal :** It is taken as axiomatically true that the consumer can rank his preferences according to the satisfaction of each combinations. He need not know precisely the amount of satisfaction.
3. **Diminishing Marginal Rate of Substitution:** The indifference-curve theory is based on the axiom of diminishing marginal rate of substitution.
4. The total utility of the consumer depends on the quantities of the commodities consumed.
$$U = f(q_1, q_2, \dots q_n)$$
5. **Consistency and Transitivity of Choice :** It is assumed that the consumer is consistent in his choice, that is, if in one period he chooses bundle A over B, he will not choose B over A in another period if both bundles are available to him. The consistency assumption may be symbolically written as follows:
If $A > B$, then $B \ngtr A$

Similarly, it is assumed that consumer's choices are characterised by transitively : If bundle A is preferred to B, and B is preferred to C, then bundle A, is preferred to C. Symbolically we may write the transitivity assumption as follows :

If A > B, and B > V, then A > C

Marginal Rate of Substitution

The concept of marginal rate of substitution is an important tool of indifference curve analysis of demand. Marginal rate of substitution of *x* for *y* (MRS_{xy}) represents the amount of *y* which the consumer has to give up for the gain of one additional unit of *x* so that his level of satisfaction remains the same.

TABLE 2.5

Combination	*Good x*	*Good y*	MRS_{xy}
A	1	12	—
B	2	8	4 : 1
C	3	5	3 : 1
D	4	3	2 : 1
E	5	2	1 : 1

In Table 2.5, when the consumer moves from combination A to combination B on his indifference schedule he forgoes 4 units of *y* for the additional one unit gain in *x*. Hence, the marginal rate of substitution of *x* for *y* is 4. Likewise, when the consumer moves from B to C, and C to D, and then from D to E in his indifference schedule, the marginal rate of substitution of *x* for *y* is 3, 2, and 1 respectively. As the consumer proceeds to have additional units of *x*, he is willing to give away less and less units of *y* so that the MRS_{xy} falls from 4 : 1 to 1 : 1 in the Eth combination.

The negative of the slope of an indifference curve at any one point is called the marginal rate of substitution of the two commodities (MRS_{xy}). In other words, the MRS_{xy} is in fact the slope of the curve at a point on the indifference curve. Thus

$$[\text{Slope of indifference curve}] = -\frac{\Delta Y}{\Delta X} = MRS_{xy}$$

It means that the MRS_{xy} is the ratio of change in good Y to given change in X. In the figure 17 there are three triangles on the IC curve. The vertical sides *ab, cd* and *ef* represents ΔY and the horizontal sides *bc, de* and *fg* signify ΔX.

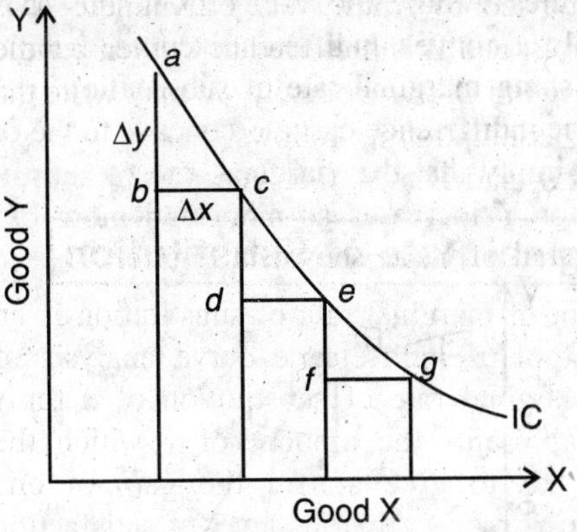

Fig. 17

At point c, $MRS_{xy} = \frac{ab}{bc}$, at e it is $\frac{cd}{de}$ and at point g, MRS_{xy} is equal to $\frac{ef}{fg}$. This also shows that as the consumer moves downwards along the curve, he possesses additional units of x, and gives up lesser and lesser units of y, *i.e.*, the MRS_{xy} diminishes.

Notes

* If the MRS_{xy} is diminishing, the indifference curve must be **convex** to the origin.
* If MRS_{xy} is constant, the indifference curve will be **straight line** sloping downwards to the right.
* If MRS_{xy} is increasing, the indifference curve will be **concave** to the origin.
* In the case of perfect complementaries the MRS_{xy} is zero and the indifference curve will be L shaped.

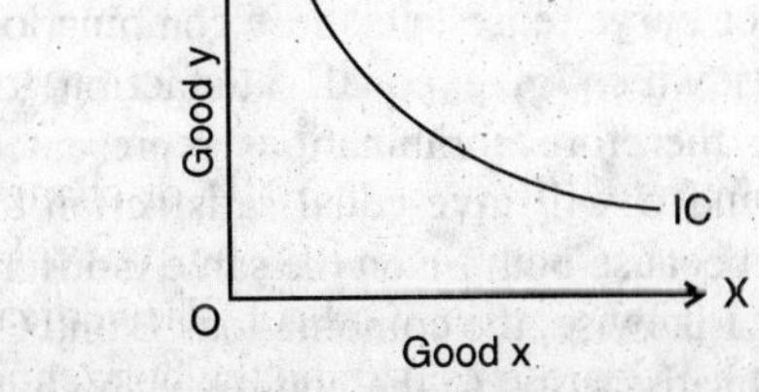

Fig. 18 (*a*) : *Convex indifference curve*

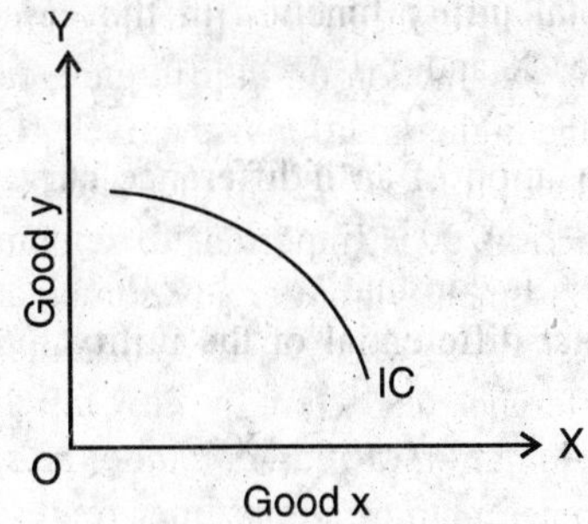

Fig. 18 (*b*) : *Concave indifferent curve*

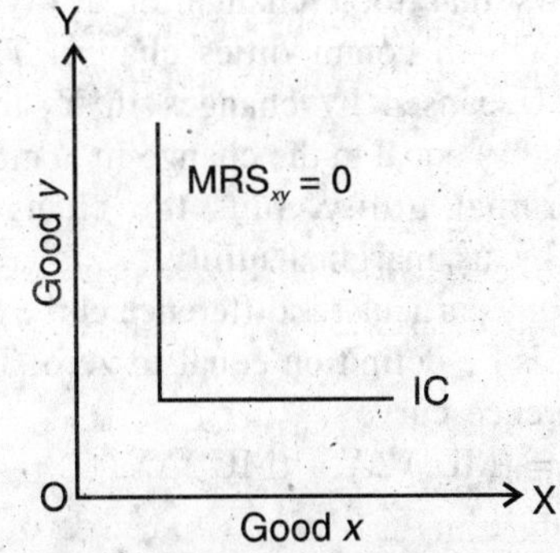

Fig. 18 (*c*) : *L-shaped indifference curve*

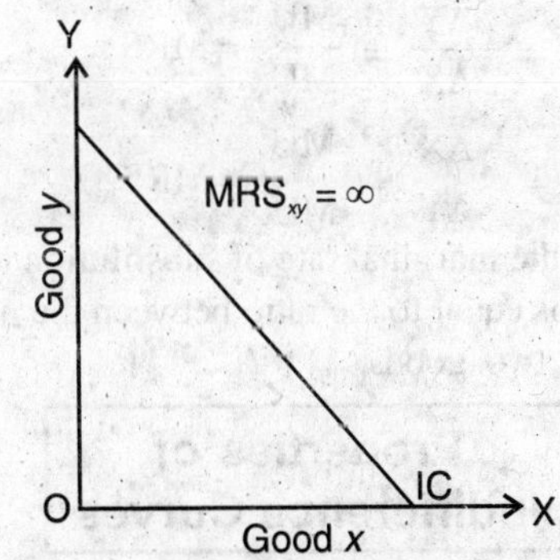

Fig. 18 (*d*) : *Straight line indifference curve*

The Relationship Between Marginal Rate of Substitution and Marginal Utilities

The slope of a indifference curve at any point is measured by the slope of the tangent at that point. The equation of a tangent is given by the total derivative or total differential, which shows the total change of the function as all its determinants change.

The total utility function in the case of two commodities X and Y is

$$U = f(X, Y)$$

The equation of an indifference curve is

$$U = f(x, y) = K$$

where K is constant.

The total differential of the utility function is

$$\Delta V = \frac{\Delta U}{\Delta Y}\Delta Y + \frac{\Delta U}{\Delta X}\Delta X$$

$$= (MU_y)\,\Delta Y + (MU_x)\,\Delta X$$

It shows that total change in utility as the quantities of both commodities change. The total change in U caused by changes in Y and X is (approximately) equal to the change in Y multiplied by its marginal utility, plus the change in X multiplied by its marginal utility.

Along any particular indifference curve the total differential is by definition equal to zero. Thus for any indifference curve

$$\Delta U = (MU_y)\,\Delta Y + (MU_x)\Delta X$$
$$= 0$$

Rearranging we obtain

$$\text{either} = -\frac{\Delta Y}{\Delta X} = \frac{MU_x}{MU_y} = MRS_{x,y}$$

$$\text{or} = -\frac{\Delta X}{\Delta Y} = \frac{MU_y}{MU_x} = MRS_{y,x}$$

Thus, the marginal rate of substitution between two goods is equal to the ratio between the marginal utilities of two goods.

Properties of Indifference Curves

From the assumptions described above the following properties of indifference curves can be deduced.

1. Indifference Curves slope downward to the right : This property implies that an indifference curve has a negative slope. This means that when the amount of one good in the combination is increased, the amount of the other good is reduced.

2. Indifference Curves are Convex to the Origin : Another important property of indifference curves is that they are usually convex to the origin. This property of indifference curves based on the marginal rate of substitution of X for Y (MRS_{xy}) diminishes as more and more of X is substituted for Y. Only a convex indifference curve can mean a diminishing marginal rate of substitution of X for Y. If the indifference curve is concave to the origin, it will imply that the marginal rate of substitution of X for Y increases as more and more of X is substituted of Y, as shown in Figure 19.

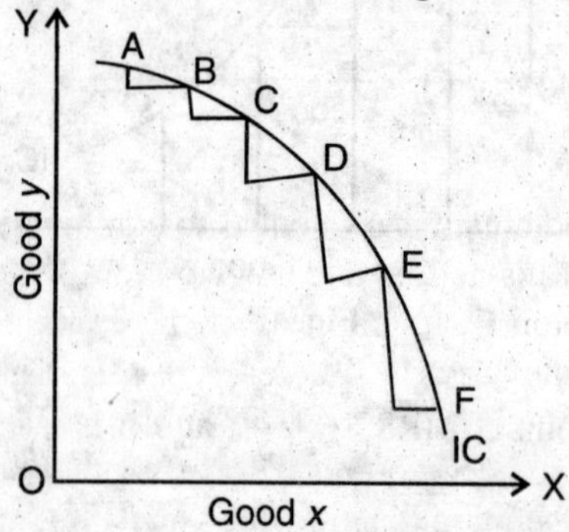

Fig. 19

It will be clear from this fig. that as more and more of x is acquired, for each extra unit of x the consumer is willing to part with more and more of y, that is, MRS_{xy} increases as more and more of x is substituted for y.

The degree of convexity of an indifference curve depends upon the rate of fall in the marginal rate of substitution of x for y.

3. Indifference Curves cannot Intersect each other : Third important property of indifference curves is that they cannot intersect each other. In other words, only one indifference curve will pass through a point in the indifference map. This property can be easily proved by first making the two indifference curves cut each other and then showing the absurdity or self-contradictory result it leads to. In Figure 20 two indifference curves are shown cutting each other at point C. Now take point A on indifference curve IC_2 and point B on indifference curve IC_1 vertically below A. Since an indifference curve represents those combinations of two goods which give equal satisfaction to the consumer, therefore combinations represented by points A and C will give equal satisfaction to the consumer because both lie on the same indifference curve IC_2. Likewise, the combinations B and C will give equal satisfaction to the consumer, both being on the same indifference curve IC_1.

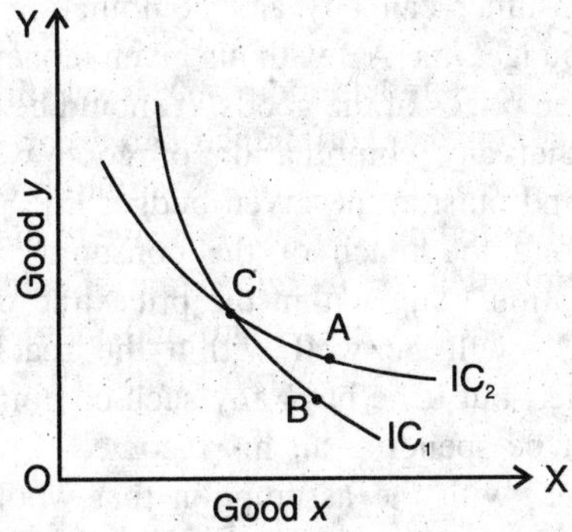

Fig. 20

If combination A is equal to combination C in terms of satisfaction, and combination B is equal to combination C, it follows that the combination A will be equivalent to B in terms of satisfaction. But a glance at Fig. 20 will show that this is absurd conclusion since combination A contains more of good Y then combination B, while the amount of good X is the same in both the combinations. Thus the consumer will definitely prefer A to B, that is A will give more satisfaction to the consumer than B. But the two indifference curves cutting each other lead us to an absurd conclusion of A being equal to B in terms of satisfaction. We therefore conclude that indifference curves cannot cut each other.

4. Indifference Curves are not necessarily parallel to each other : Though they are falling, negatively inclined to the right, yet the rate of fall will not be the same for all indifference curves. In other words, the diminishing marginal rate of substitution between the two goods is essentially not the same in the case of all indifference schedules. The two curves IC_1 and IC_2 shown in Figure 21 are not parallel to each other.

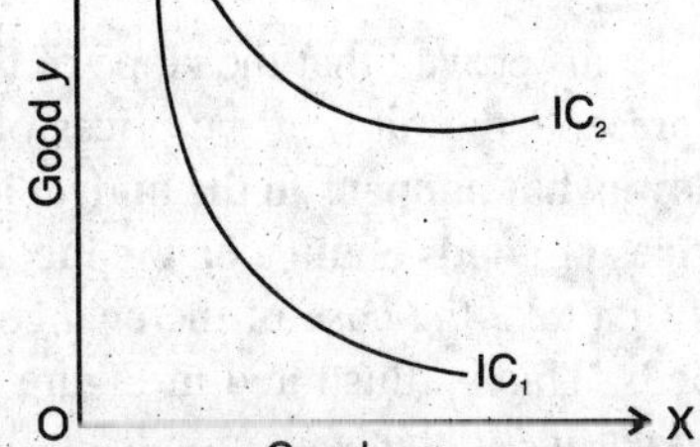

Fig. 21

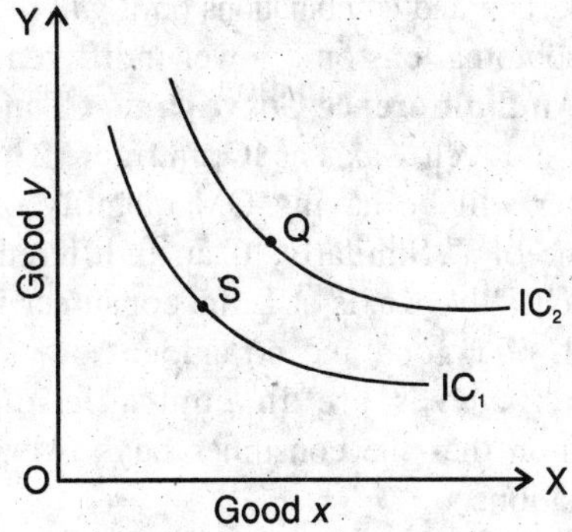

Fig. 22: *A higher indifference curve shows higher level of satisfaction*

5. A Higher Indifference Curve represents Higher Level of Satisfaction than the Lower Indifference Curve : Another property of indifference curve is that a higher indifference curve will represent a higher level of satisfaction than a lower indifference curve. Consider indifference curves IC_2 and IC_1 in Figure 22. IC_2 is a higher indifference curve than IC_1. Combination Q has been taken on a higher indifference curve IC_2 and combination S on a lower indifference curve IC_1.

Combination Q on the higher indifference curve IC_2 will give the consumer more satisfaction than combination S on the lower indifference curve IC_1 because the combination Q contains more of both goods X and Y than the combination S. Hence, the consumer must prefer Q to S. And by transitivity, he will prefer any other combination on IC_2 to any combination on IC_1. We, therefore, conclude that a higher indifference curve represents the higher level

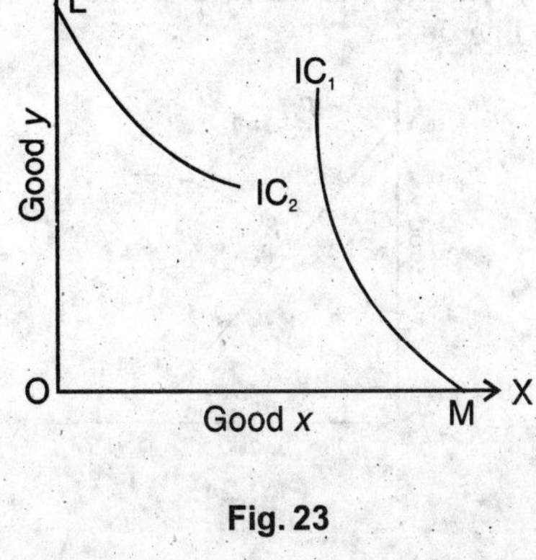

Fig. 23

of satisfaction and combinations on it will be preferred to the combinations on a lower indifference curve.

6. An Indifference Curve cannot Touch either Axis : If it touch *x*-axis as IC_1 in figure 23 at M, the consumer will be having OM quantity of good *x* and none of *y*. Similarly, If an indifference curve IC_2 touches the *y*-axis at L the consumer will have only OL of *y* good and no amount of *x*.

Such curves are in contradiction to the assumption that the consumer buys two goods in combinations.

Price Line or Budget Line

Understanding of the concept of **price line** or **budget line** is essential for understanding the theory of consumer's equilibrium. The consumer has a given income which sets limits to his maximising behaviour. Income acts as a constraint in the attempt for maximising utility. The income constraints, in the case of two commodities, may be written as

$$I = p_x q_x + p_y q_y \qquad ...(1)$$

We may present the income constraint graphically by the budget line, whose equation is derived from expression (1), by solving for q_y :

$$q_y = \frac{1}{p_y} I - \frac{p_x}{p_y} q_x$$

Assigning successive values to q_x (given the income, I and the commodity prices, p_x and p_y), we may find the corresponding values of q_y. Thus if $q_x = 0$ (that is, if the consumer spends all his income on *y*) the consumer can buy I/p_y units of Y. Similarly, if $q_y = 0$ (that is, if the consumer spends all his income an *x*) the consumer can buy I/p_x units of *x*. In figure 24 these results are shown by points A and B. If we join these points with a line we obtain the budget line.

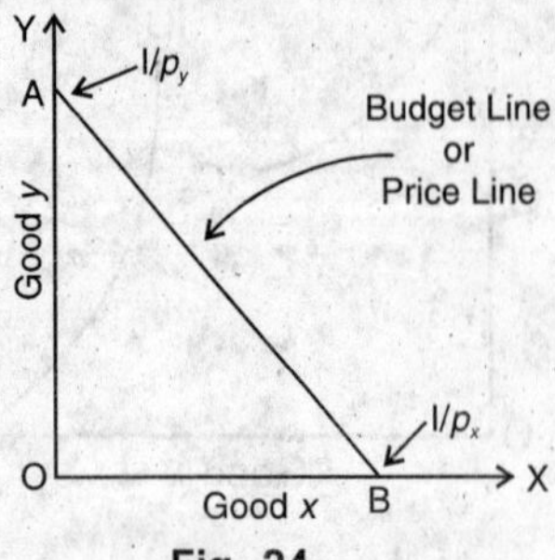

Fig. 24

Consumer can buy any combination that lies on the budget line AB with his given money income and given prices of the goods. It should be carefully noted that any combination of good which lies above and outside the given budget line, AB, will be beyond the reach of the consumer. But any combination lying within the price line or budget line, AB, will be well within the reach of the consumer, but if he buys any such combination he will not be spending all his income.

Thus, with the assumption that whole of the given income is spent on the given goods and at given prices of them, the consumer has to choose among from all those combinations which lie on the price line or budget line.

Slope of the Budget Line

The slope of the budget line is equal to the ratio of the prices of two goods. This can be proved with the aid of Fig. 24. Suppose the given income of the consumer is I, the given prices of goods *x* and *y* are p_x and p_y respectively. The slope of the price line is AB. We intend to prove that the slope is equal to the ratio of the price of goods *x* and *y*.

The quantity of good *x* purchased if whole of the given income I is spent on it is OB. Therefore

$$OB \times p_x = I$$

$$OB = I/p_x \qquad ...(1)$$

Now, the quantity of good *y* purchased if whole of the given income I is spent on it is OA. Therefore,

$$OA \times p_y = I$$

$$OA = I/p_y \qquad ...(2)$$

Dividing (2) by (1) we have :

$$\frac{OA}{OB} = \frac{I}{p_y} \div \frac{I}{p_x}$$

$$= \frac{I}{p_y} \times \frac{p_x}{I} = \frac{p_x}{p_y}$$

It is thus proved that the slope of the price line AB represents the ratio of the prices of two goods.

Now, what happens to the budget line. If either the prices of goods change or the income changes. Let us first take the case of the change in prices of the goods. This is illustrated in Figure 25. Suppose the budget line in the beginning is PL, given certain prices of the good *x* and *y* and a certain income.

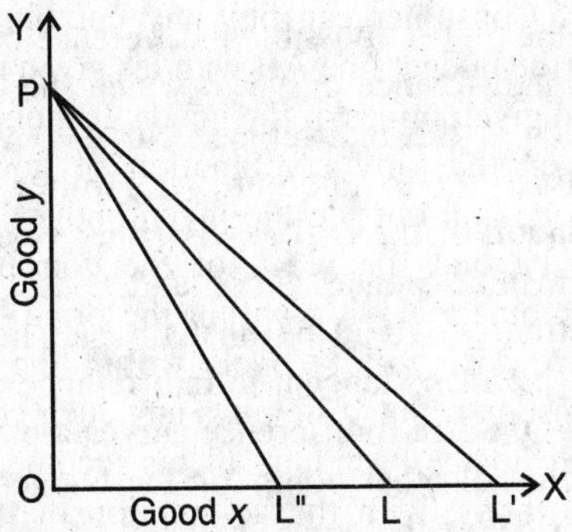

Fig. 25: *Changes in budget line as a result of changes in price of good x*

Suppose the price of *x* falls, the price of *y* and income remaining unchanged. Now with a lower price of *x* the consumer will be able to purchase more quantity of *x* than before with his given income. Let at the lower price of *x*, the given income purchases OL′ of X which of greater than OL. Since the price of Y remains the same, there can be no change in the quantity purchased of good Y with the same given income and as a result there will be no shift in the point P. Thus with the fall in the price of good *x*, the consumer's income and the price of Y remaining constant, the budget line will take the new position PL′.

Now, what will happen to the budget line as the price of good *x* rises, the price of good Y and income remaining unaltered. With higher price of good *x*, the consumer can purchase smaller quantity of X, say OL″, than before. Thus with the rise in price of X the budget line will assume the new position PL″.

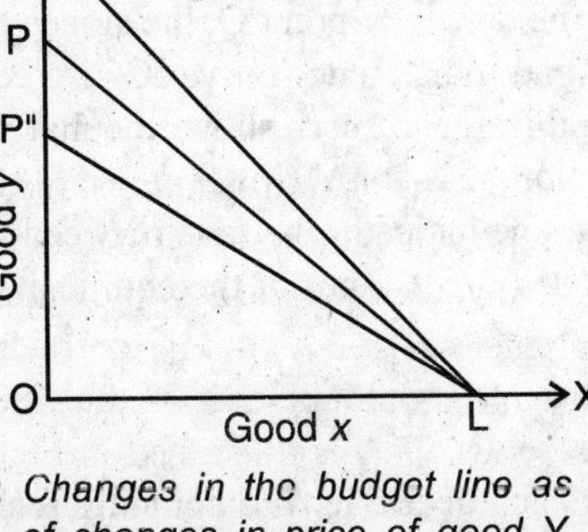

Fig. 26: *Changes in the budget line as a result of changes in price of good Y*

Figure 26 shows the changes in the budget line when the price of good Y falls or rises, with the price of X and income remaining the same.

Now, what happens to the budget line if the income changes, while the prices of goods remain the same. The effect of changes in income on the budget line is shown in Figure 27. Let PL be the initial price line, given certain prices of goods and income. If the consumer's income increases while the prices of both goods X and Y remain unaltered, the price line shifts upward (Say, to P′L′) and is parallel to the original price line PL. On the other hand, if the income of the consumer decreases, the prices of both goods X and Y remaining unchanged, the budget line shifts downward (Say, to P″L″) but remains parallel to the original price line PL.

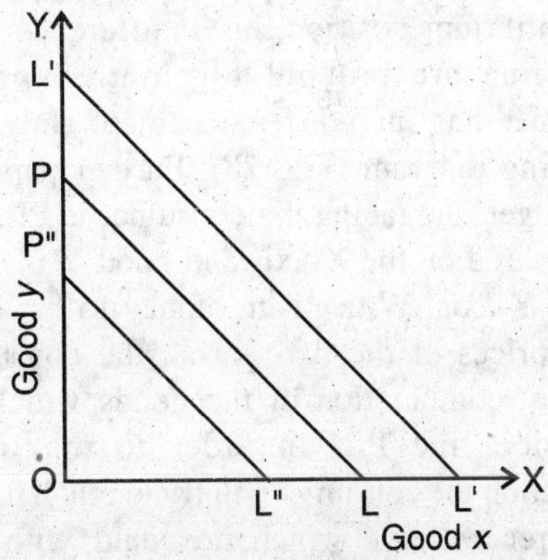

Fig. 27 : *Changes in budget line as a result of changes in income*

It is clear from above that the price line or budget line will change if either the prices of goods change or the income of the consumer changes.

Thus the two determinants of the price line or budget line are :

1. The prices of goods.
2. The consumer's income to be spent on the goods.

Consumer's Equilibrium

A consumer is in equilibrium when given his tastes, and prices of the two goods, he spends a given money income on the purchase of two goods in such a way as to get the maximum satisfaction. In the indifference curve technique the consumer's equilibrium is discussed in respect of the purchases of two goods by the consumer.

The indifference curve analysis of consumer's equilibrium is based on the following assumptions:

1. The consumer has a given indifference map exhibiting his scale of preferences for various combinations of two goods, X and Y.
2. He has a fixed amount of money to spend on the two goods. He has to spend whole of his given money on the two goods.
3. Prices of the goods are given and constant for him. He cannot influence the prices of the goods by buying more or less of them.
4. Goods are homogeneous and divisible.

To show which combination of two goods, X and Y, the consumer will decide to buy and will be in equilibrium position, his indifference map and price line are brought together. Suppose our consumer has in indifference map, shown in the following diagram (Fig. 28). Further suppose that the budget line facing the consumer is PL. Good X is measured on the X-axis and good Y is measured on the Y-axis. With given money to be spent and given prices of the two goods, the consumer can buy any combination of the goods which lies on the price line PL. In order to maximise his satisfaction the consumer will try to reach the highest indifference curve which he could with a given expenditure of money and given prices of the two goods. Budget constraint forces the consumer to remain on the given budget line, that is, to choose any combinations from among only those which lie on the given budget line.

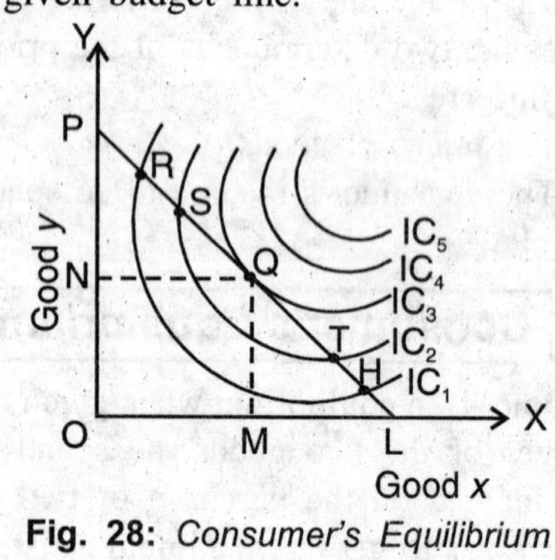

Fig. 28: *Consumer's Equilibrium*

According to the figure 28, the consumer will choose that combination on the price line PL which lies on the highest possible indifference curve. The highest indifference curve to which the consumer can reach is the indifference curve to which the price line PL is tangent. Any other possible combination of the two goods either would lie on a lower indifference curve and thus yield less satisfaction or would be unattainable. In Fig. 28, budget line PL is tangent to indifference curve IC_3 at point Q. Since indifference curves are convex to the origin, all other points on the budget line PL, above or below the point Q, would lie on the lower indifference curves. Take point R which also lies on the budget line PL and which the consumer can afford to buy. Combination of goods represented by R costs him the same as the combination Q. But, as is evident, R lies on the lower indifference curve IC_1 and will therefore yield less satisfaction than Q. Like wise, point S also lies on the price line PL, but will be rejected in favour of Q. Since S lies on the indifference curve IC_2 which is also lower than IC_3 on which Q lies. Similarly, Q will be preferred to all other points on the price line PL which lies below Q, such as T and H. It is thus clear that of all possible combinations lying on PL, combination Q lies on the highest possible indifference curve and yields maximum possible satisfaction.

It is therefore concluded that with the given money expenditure and the given prices of the goods as shown by PL the consumer will obtain maximum possible satisfaction and will therefore be in equilibrium position at point Q at which the rate budget line PL is tangent to the indifference curve IC_3. In this equilibrium position at Q the consumer will buy OM amount of good X and ON amount of good Y.

At the tangency point Q, the slopes of the price line PL and indifference curve IC_3 are equal. Slope of the indifference curve shows the marginal rate of substitution of X for Y (MRS_{xy}), while the slope of the price line indicates the ratio between the price of two goods (p_x/p_y). Thus at the equilibrium point Q,

$$MRS_{xy} = \frac{MU_x}{MU_y} = \frac{P_x}{P_y}$$

This is a necessary but not sufficient condition for equilibrium. The **second condition** is that the

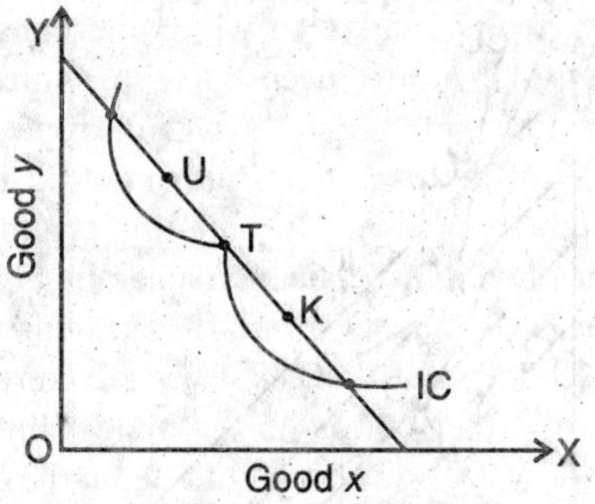

Fig. 29 : *Second order condition for consumer's equilibrium*

indifference curves be convex to the origin, or to put it in another way, the MRS_{xy} must be falling at the point of equilibrium. It will be noticed from Figure 28 that the indifference curve IC_3 is convex to the origin at Q. Thus at point Q both conditions of equilibrium are satisfied. Point Q is the optimum or best choice for the consumer and he will therefore be in stable equilibrium at Q.

But it may happen that while price line is tangent to an indifference curve at a point but the indifference curve may be concave at that point. Take, for instance, Figure 29 where indifference curve IC is concave to the origin around the point T. Price line PL is tangent to the indifference curve IC at point T and MRS_{xy} is equal to the price ratio (p_x/p_y). But T cannot be a position of stable equilibrium because satisfaction would not be maximum there. Indifference curve IC being concave at the tangency point T, there are some points on the given price line PL such as U and K, which will be on indifference curve higher than IC. Thus the consumer by moving along the given price line PL can go to points such as U and K and obtain greater satisfaction than at T. We therefore conclude that for the consumer to be in equilibrium, two conditions are required :

1. A given price line must be tangent to an indifference curve, or marginal rate of substitution of X for Y (MRS_{xy}) must be equal to the price ratio between the two goods (p_x/p_y).

$$MRS_{xy} = \frac{P_x}{P_y} = \frac{MU_x}{MU_y}$$

$$\text{or,} \quad \frac{MU_x}{MU_y} = \frac{P_x}{P_y}$$

$$\text{or,} \quad \frac{MU_x}{P_x} = \frac{MU_y}{P_y}$$

2. Indifference curve must be convex to the origin at the point of tangency. This condition is fulfilled by the axiom of diminishing MRS_{xy}, which states that the slope of the indifference curve decreases as we move along the curve from the left downwards to the right.

Income Effect

Income effect is the effect on the quantity demanded exclusively as a result of change in money income, all prices remaining constant. It has been shown above how a consumer reaches his equilibrium position with a fixed income and given market prices of the two commodities.

But the question arises what will happen to the consumer's equilibrium and the amounts of the two commodities bought if his income were to change while prices of the commodities remain the same. Obviously, as a result of a change in income, his satisfaction will either increase or diminish, for he has now a larger or smaller income to spend. The result of this type of change is described in technical language as **income effect.**

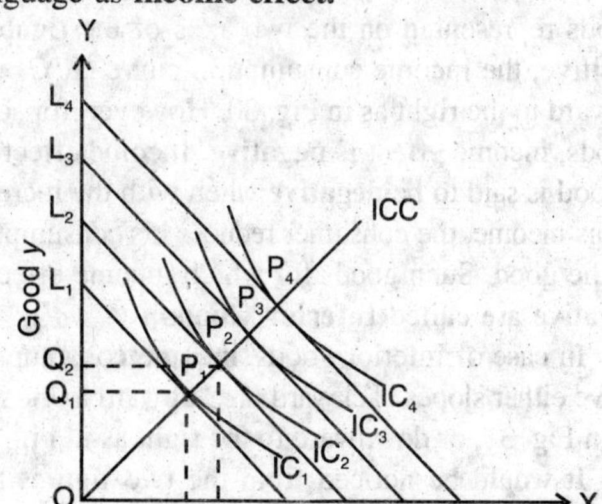

Fig. 30 : *Income Effect*

The income effect has been explained with the help of Figure 30. With Price-line L_1M_1, the consumer is in equilibrium at point P_1. Now suppose the income of the consumer increases so that his new price line is L_2M_2. As a result of this increase in income, the consumer will move to a new equilibrium position, at the point P_2, on a higher indifference curve IC_2 and will be buying OH_2 of commodity X and OQ_2 of commodity Y. Thus, the consumer will get on to a higher level of satisfaction as a result of an increase in his income.

If his income increase still further, so that the new price line becomes L_3M_3, he will be in equilibrium at the point P_3 on an indifference curve IC_3, and so on for further increases in income.

Thus, we get various points of equilibrium such as P_1, P_2, P_3, for different levels of income, prices of the commodities remaining the same. If the points P_1, P_2, P_3, P_4 etc, are joined together by a line passing from the origin, we get, what is called **Income Consumption Curve (ICC).**

Income consumption curve is thus the locus of equilibrium points at various levels of consumer's income. Income consumption curve traces out the income effect on the quantity consumed of the goods.

Income effect can either be **positive** or **negative.** Income effect for good is said to be **positive** when with the increase in income of the consumer, his consumption of the good also increases. This is the normal case. When the income effect of both the goods represented on the two axes of the figure is positive, the income consumption curve (ICC) will upward to the right as in Fig. 30. However, for some goods, income effect is **negative.** Income effect for a good is said to be **negative** when with the increase in his income, the consumer reduces his consumption of the good. Such goods for which income effect is negative are called **Inferior Goods.**

In case of inferior goods, income consumption curve either slopes backward (*i.e.*, upward to the left) as in Fig. 31, or downward to the right as in Fig. 32.

It would be noticed from the two figures that income effect becomes negative only after a point. It signifies that only at higher ranges of income, some goods become inferior goods and upto a point changes in their consumption behave like those of normal goods.

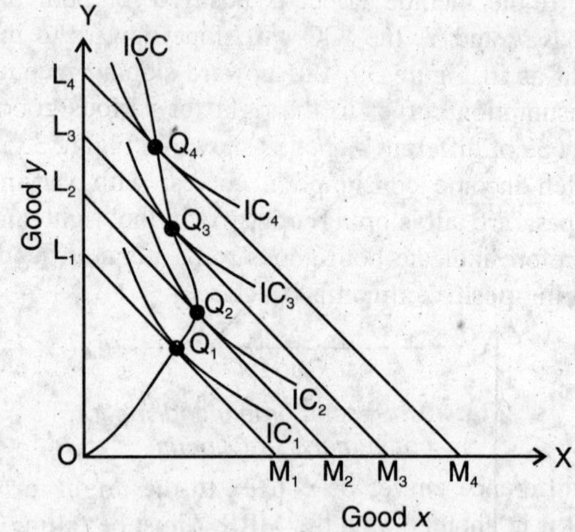

Fig. 31 : *ICC in case of Good X being inferior good*

In Figure 31, Income consumption curve (ICC) slopes backward (upward to the left) *i.e.,* bends towards the *y*-axis. This shows good *x* to be an inferior good, since beyond point Q_2, income effect is negative for good X and as a result its quantity demanded falls as income increases.

In Figure 32, ICC-curve slopes downward to the right beyond point Q_2 *i.e.,* bends towards *x*-axis. This signifies that good Y is inferior good because as beyond point Q_2, income effect is negative for good Y and as a result its quantity demanded falls as income increases.

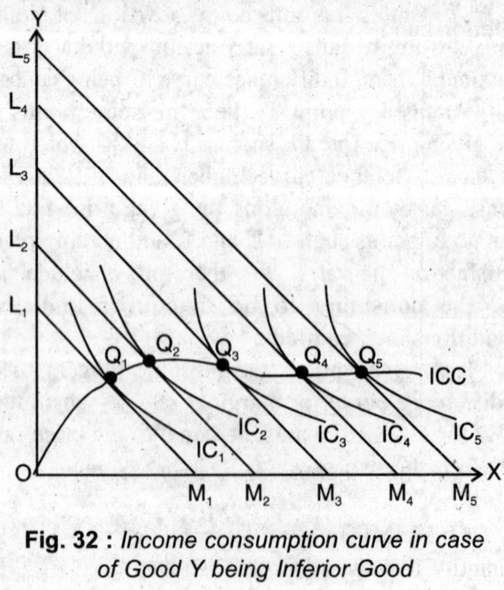

Fig. 32 : *Income consumption curve in case of Good Y being Inferior Good*

If the income effect is positive for both the goods X and Y, the ICC will slope upward to the right as in Figure 30. But upward-sloping income consumption curves to the right for various goods may be of different slopes as shown in Figure 33 in which income consumption curves, with varying slopes, are all sloping upward to the right and therefore indicate both goods to be **normal goods having positive income effect.**

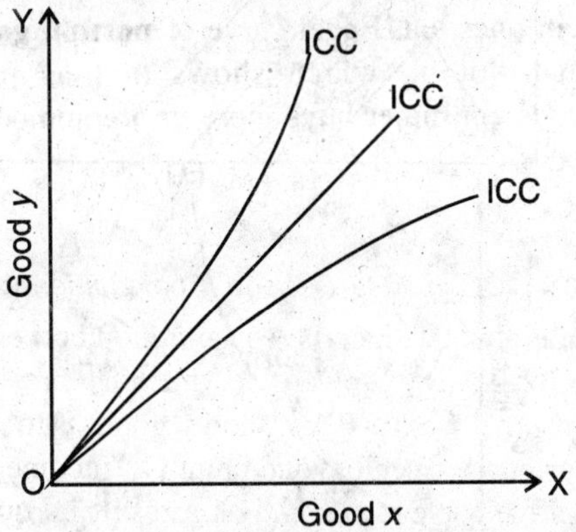

Fig. 33 : *Income consumption curves of Normal Goods*

If the income effect is negative, income consump-tion curve will slope backward to the left as ICC' in Figure 34. If good X happens to be inferior good, it will slope downward to the right as ICC" in figure 34 if good Y happens to be the inferior good.

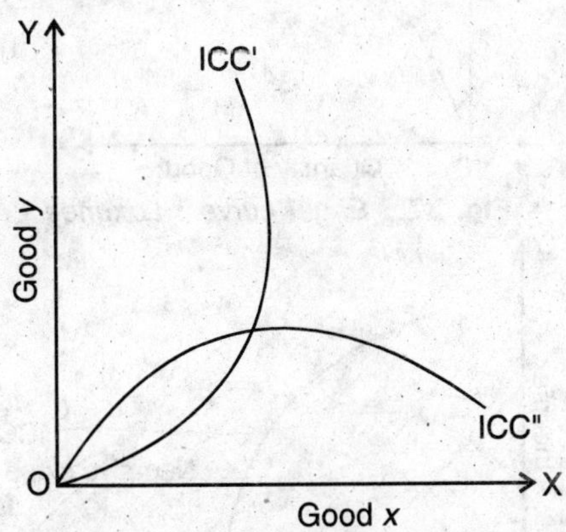

Fig. 34 : *Income consumption curves of Inferior Goods*

***Inferior Goods :** Those goods of which the quantity that the consumer would buy less, as his income rises, are called inferior goods. **Inferior goods may be defined as goods for which income effect is negative.**

Substitution Effect

We have discussed above the effect on consumer's equilibrium of a change in consumer's income, relative prices of commodities remaining the same. Now let us see the effect of a change in relative prices, consumer's income remaining the same. This leads us to the study to what is known as the **Substitution Effect.**

Substitution effect means the change in the purchases of a good as a consequence of a change in relative prices alone, real income remaining constant. When the price of a good changes, the real income or purchasing power of the consumer also changes. To keep the real income of the consumer constant so that the effect due to a change in the relative price alone may be known, price change is compensated by a simultaneous change in income.

Now, two slightly different concepts of substitution effect have been developed, one by Hicks and Allen and the other by Slutsky. These two concepts of substitution effect have been named after their authors. The two concepts differ in regard to the magnitude of the change in money income which should be effected so as to neutralize the change in real income of the consumer which results from a change in the price.

In **Hicks-Allen Substitution effect** price change is accompanied by so much change in money income that the consumer is neither better or nor worse off than before. In other words, money income of the consumer is changed by an amount which keeps the consumer on the same indifference curve on which he was before the change in the price. Thus **Hick-Allen substitution effect takes place on the same indifference curve.** The amount by which the money income of the consumer is changed so that the consumer is neither better off nor worse off than before is called **Compensating Variation in Income.**

Hicks-Allen substitution effect is illustrated in Figure 35. With a given money income and given prices of the two goods are represented by the price line PL, the consumer is in equilibrium at point Q on the indifference curve IC and is purchasing OM of the good X.

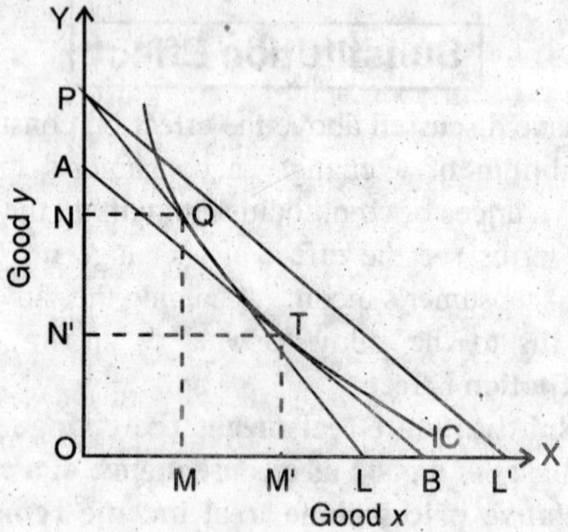

Fig. 35: *Hicks Substitution Effect*

Suppose that the price of good X falls (price of Y remaining unchanged) so that the price line now shifts to PL′. With this fall in price of X, the consumer's real income would increase. In order to find out the substitution effect, this gain in real income should be wiped out by reducing the money income of the consumer by so much amount that forces him to remain on the same indifference curve IC. On which he was before the change in price of the good X. When some money income is taken away from the consumer to cancel out the gain in real income, then the price line which shifted to position PL′ will now shift downward but will be parallel to PL′. In Fig. 35, a price line AB parallel to PL′ has been drawn as such a distance from PL′ that it touches the indifference curve. It means that reduction of consumer's income by the amount PA (in terms of Y) or L′B (in terms of X) had been made so as to keep him on the same indifference curve. PA or L′B is therefore compensating variation in income.

It will be seen from Figure 35 that with price line AB consumer is in equilibrium at point T and is now buying OM′ of X and ON′ of Y. This increase in the purchases of good X by MM′ and the decrease in the purchases of good Y by NN′ is due to the change only in the relative prices of good X and Y. Therefore, movement from Q and T represents the substitution effect. It is thus clear that as a result of substitution effect the consumer remains on the same indifference curve, he is however in equilibrium at a different point from that at which he was before the change in price of X.

Engel Curve

Engel curve shows the quantities of a good which the consumer will purchase at various income level, given his tastes, preferences and the price of the good in question. Engel curve of **normal goods** is upward sloping which shows that as income increases consumer buys more of a commodity.

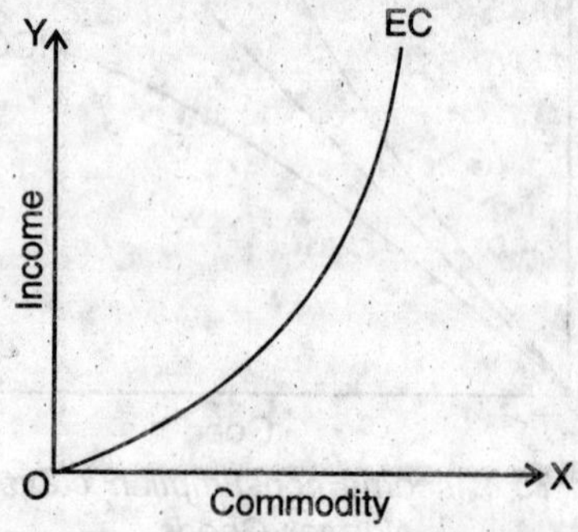

Fig. 36 : *Engel curve : Necessities*

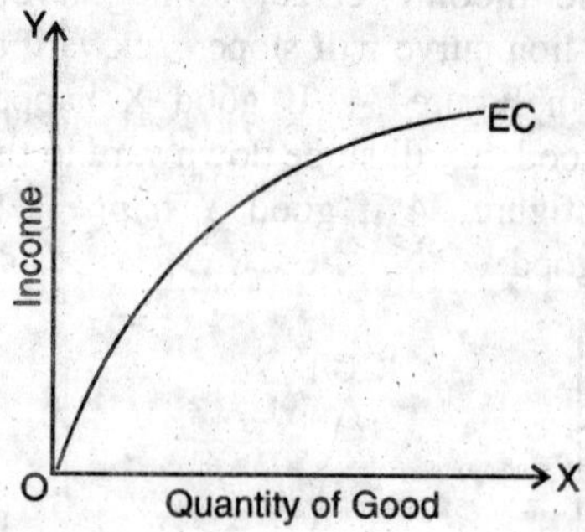

Fig. 37 : *Engel curve : Luxuries*

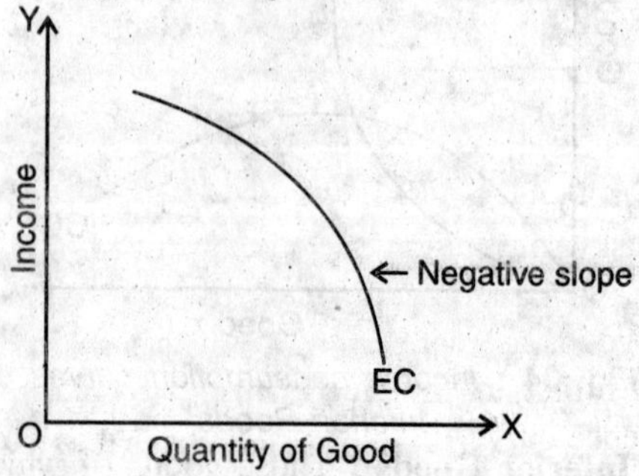

Fig. 38 : *Engel curve: Inferior goods*

Slutsky Substitution Effect

Slutsky has given a slightly different version of substitution effect. In this version when the price of a good changes and consumer's real income or purchasing power increase, the income of the consumer is changed by the amount equal to the change in its purchasing power which occurs as a result of the price change. His purchasing power changes by the amount equal to the change in the price multiplied by the number of units of the good which the individual used to buy at the old price.

In other words, in Slutsky's approach, income is reduced or increased by the amount which leaves the consumer to be just able to purchase the same combination of goods, if he so desires, which he was having at the old price. That is, the income is changed by the difference between the cost of the amount of good X purchased at the old price and the cost of the same quantity of X at the new price. Income is then said to be changed by the **Cost difference.** Thus, in Slutsky substitution effect, income is reduced or increased not by the compensating variation but by the cost difference.

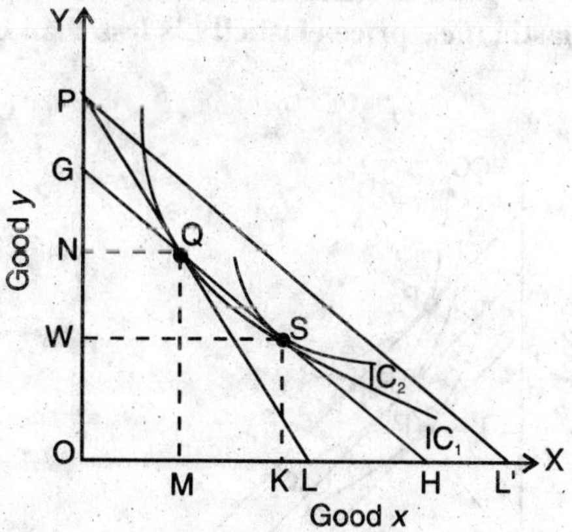

Fig. 39 : *Slutsky Substitution Effect*

Slutsky substitution effect is illustrated in Figure 39 with a given money income and the given prices of two goods as represented by the price line PL, the consumer is in equilibrium as Q on the indifference curve IC_1 buying OM of X and ON of Y. Now suppose that price of X falls, price of Y and money income of the consumer remaining unchanged. As a result of this fall in price of X, the price line will shift to PL′ and the real income or the purchasing power of the consumer will increase. Now, in order to find out the Slutsky substitution effect, consumer's money income must be reduced by the **cost-difference.** For this, a price line GH parallel to PL′ has been drawn which passes through the point Q. It means that income equal to PG in terms of Y or L'H in terms of X had been taken away from the consumer and as a result he can buy the combination Q, if he so desires. Since Q also lies on the price line GH. Actually, he will not now buy the old combination Q since X had now become relatively dearer than before.

The change in relative prices will induce the consumer to rearrange the purchases of X and Y. He will substitute X for Y. But in this Slutsky substitution case, consumer will not move along the same indifference curve IC_1, since the price line GH, on which the consumer has to remain due to the price-income circumstances, is now where tangent to the IC_2 at points S. Therefore, the consumer will now be in equilibrium at a point S on higher indifference curve IC_2. This movement from Q to S represents Slutsky substitution effect.

From the above analysis it is clear that whereas **Hicks-Allen substitution effect** takes place on the same indifference curve, Slutsky substitution effect involves the movement from one indifference curve to another curve, a higher one. The difference between the two versions of the substitution effect solely arises due to the magnitude of money income by which income is reduced or increased to compensate for the change in his real income. **Hicksian approach just restores to the consumer his initial level of satisfaction,** whereas the Slutsky approach **"Over compensates"** the consumer by putting him on a higher indifference curve.

Price Effect

We will now explain how the consumer reacts to changes in the price of a good, his money income, tastes and price of the other goods remaining the same.

When the price of a good changes, the consumer would be either better off or worse off them before, depending upon whether the price falls or rises. In other words, as a result of change in price of the good, his equilibrium position would lie at a higher indifference curve in case of the fall in price and at a lower indifference curve in case of the rise in price.

Suppose, with a certain fixed income and given market prices of the two goods X and Y represented by the Price line ML_1, the consumer is in equilibrium at point P_1 in Figure 40.

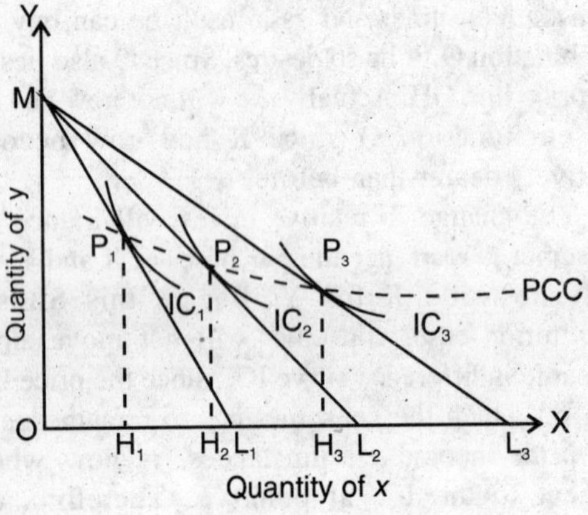

Fig. 40: *Price Effect*

Suppose the price of X falls, income and price of Y remaining unchanged, so that new price line becomes ML_2, the consumer will be in equilibrium at point P_2 on the higher indifference curve IC_2. In this position, he will be buying OH_2 of commodity X.

If the price of X falls further, so that the relevant price line is ML_3 the consumer will be in equilibrium at point P_3 and will be buying OH_3 of commodity X. In the same way, we can discover other points of equilibrium for every other price at which X-might be sold. When all the points such as P_1, P_2, P_3 are joined together we have the **price consumption curve** of the consumer for good X. This shows the **price effect. It shows how the consumption of commodity X changes, as its price changes, the consumer's income and price of Y remaining the same.**

In Fig. 40 price consumption curve (PCC) is sloping downward. Downward-sloping price consumption curve for good X means that as the price of good X falls, the consumer purchases a larger quantity of good X and smaller quantity of good Y. This is quite evident from Fig. 40. We obtain downward sloping price consumption curve for good X when demand for **it is elastic** (*i.e.*, price elasticity is greater than one).

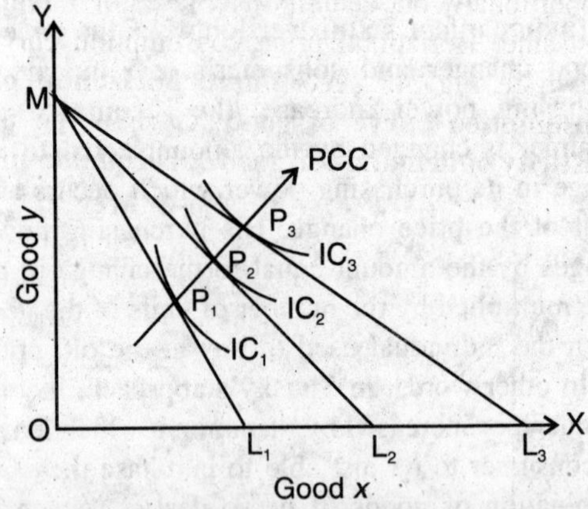

Fig. 41 : *Upward Sloping Consumption Curve*

Price consumption curve can have other shapes also. In Fig. 41 upward-sloping price consumption curve is shown. Upward-sloping price consumption curve X means that when the price of good X falls, the quantity demanded of both goods X and Y rises. **We obtain the upward sloping price consumption curve for good X when the demand for good is less elastic (*i.e.*, price elasticity is less than one).**

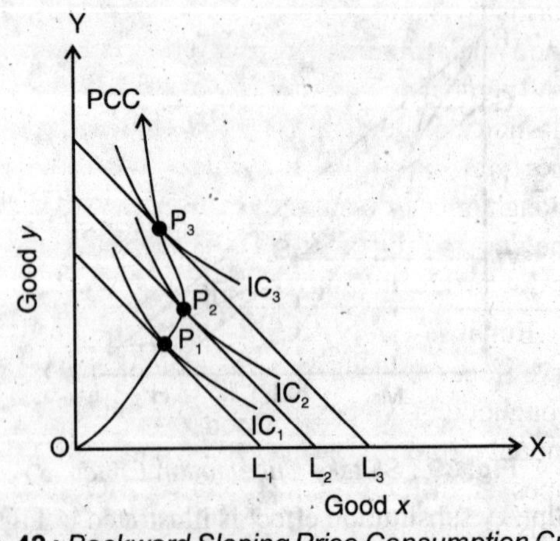

Fig. 42 : *Backward Sloping Price Consumption Curves*

Price consumption curve can also have a **backward sloping shape,** which is depicted in Fig. 42. Backward sloping price consumption curve for good X indicates that when price of X falls, smaller quantity of it is demanded or purchased. This is the case of **Giffen Goods.**

Price consumption curve for a good can take horizontal shape too. It means that when the price of the good X declines, its quantity purchased rises proportionally but quantity purchased of Y remains the same. Horizontal price consumption curve is shown in Fig. 43. **We obtain horizontal price consumption curve of good X when the price elasticity of demand for good X is equal to unity.**

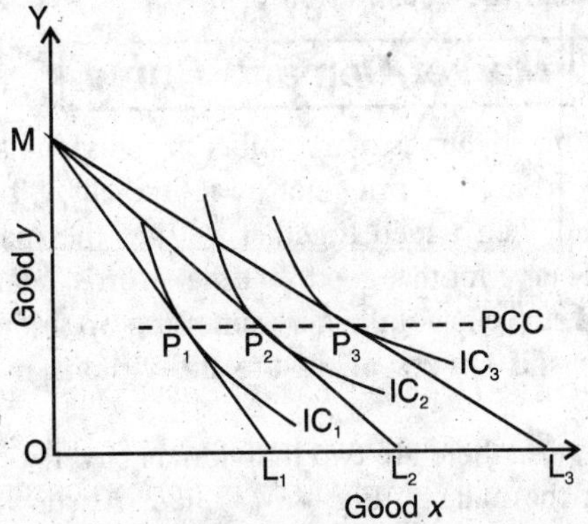

Fig. 43 : *Horizontal Price Consumption Curve*

Price Consumption Curve and Elasticity of Demand

The shape of the price consumption curve shows the degree of elasticity of demand, *i.e.,* the elasticity is unitary, greater than one or less than one. When the price consumption is horizontal, *i.e.,* parallel to X-axis (*i.e.,* has zero slope), the elasticity of demand for good X is unitary, *i.e.,* the total outlay on X remains the same even though price of X rises. If PCC is upward sloping, the demand for the good X is inelastic, and if it is downward sloping, the demand will be elastic.

But it is rarely found that price consumption curve slopes downward throughout or slopes upward throughout or slopes backward throughout. More generally, price consumption curve has different slopes at different price ranges. At higher price levels it generally slopes downward, and it may then have a horizontal shape for some price ranges but ultimately it will be sloping upward. For some price ranges it can be backward sloping as in case of **Giffen goods.**

A price consumption curve which has different shapes or slopes at different price ranges is drawn in figure 44. Such type of price consumption curve means that price elasticity of demand is different at different price ranges.

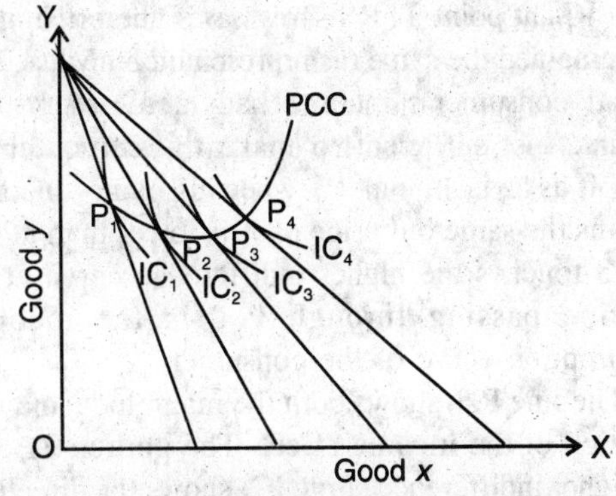

Fig. 44

Two Components of Price Effect

The movement of the consumer along the price consumption curve, such as from equilibrium point P_1 to P_2 as a result of a fall in the price of X, is in reality a resultant of two forces. The first of these components is the feeling of better-offense that a consumer experiences when the price of X falls. There is an increase in the potential purchasing power of the consumer's income following a relative fall in the price of X. It is **Income Effect.** This income effect is the first component of the price effect. The consumer is operating along the income consumption curve.

There is also the second component of the price effect viz., the **Substitution Effect.** Now that X is cheaper than before while the price of Y has remained unchanged, there will naturally be a tendency on the part of the consumer to buy more of the cheaper good and less of the relatively dearer one.

In other words, he will substitute cheaper good for the dearer one. This second components is called the **Substitution Effect** and can be viewed as operating along the price consumption curve. (Fig. 45)

These two components of the movement from P_1 to P_2 are shown in Figure 45. Initially, with the price line ML_1, the consumer is in equilibrium at point P_1. With a fall in price of X, so that the new relevant price line ML_2, he moves to a new equilibrium position P_2 on a higher indifference curve IC_2. RS is a hypothetical price line drawn parallel to ML_1 and touching the higher indifference curve IC_2 at point T. RS shows as if the price of X had remained the same (as represented by ML_1), but instead consumer's income had increased by an amount. Just sufficient to make the consumer as well-off as he is at point P_2, when his money income remains the same but price of X is lower than at P_1. As RS touches the higher indifference curve at T, the line passing through P_1T is the income consumption curve of the consumer.

The line P_1T shows both the magnitude and the direction of the **income effect.** The portion TP_2 of the higher indifference curve IC_2 shows the direction and magnitude of the **substitution effect.** The substitution effect means that the cheaper good X is substituted for the dearer good Y.

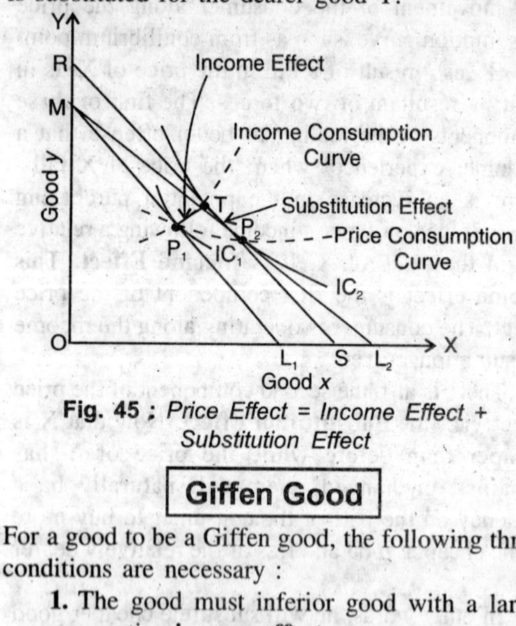

Fig. 45 : *Price Effect = Income Effect + Substitution Effect*

Giffen Good

For a good to be a Giffen good, the following three conditions are necessary :

1. The good must inferior good with a large negative **income effect.**
2. The substitution effect must be small, and
3. The proportion of income spent upon the inferior good must be very large.

Some Facts

(a) The quantity demanded of a good varies inversely with price when the income effect is positive or nil.

(b) The quantity demanded of a good varies inversely with price when the income effect is negative but is weaker than the substitution effect.

(c) The quantity demanded of a good varies directly with price when the income effect for the good is negative and this negative income effect of a change in price is larger than the substitution effect.

Market Demand Curve

If the demand curves of a number of individuals are derived from this price-consumption curve for a good and then added together we get the market demand curve for that good. **In other words, Market demand curve is obtained by summing up sideways the demand curves of all the individuals in the market.**

Suppose there are two individuals buyers of the good in the market. Fig. 46 *(a)* and *(b)* show the demand curves of the two independent individual buyers. Now, the market demand curve can be obtained by adding together the amounts of the good which individuals wish to buy at each price. Thus at price P_1, the individuals A wishes to buy Oa_1, of the good; individual B wishes to buy Ob_1 of the good. The total quantity of the good that all the two individuals plan to buy at price P_1 is therefore $Oa_1 + Ob_1$ which is equal to OQ in Fig. 46 *(c)*.

Similarly, we can plot the quantity of the good that will be demanded by all the two individuals at every other price of the good. When all the points showing the amounts demanded of the good at various prices are jointed we get a market demand curve for the good.

The market demand curve will slope downward to the right, since the individual demand curves, whose **lateral summation** gives us the market demand curve, normally slope downward to the right. Besides, as the price of the good falls, it is very likely that the new buyers will enter the market and will further raise the quantity demanded of the good. This will be another reason why the market demand curve should slope downward to the right.

Even if an individual's demand curve for a good slopes downward to the left (*i.e.*, slopes upward

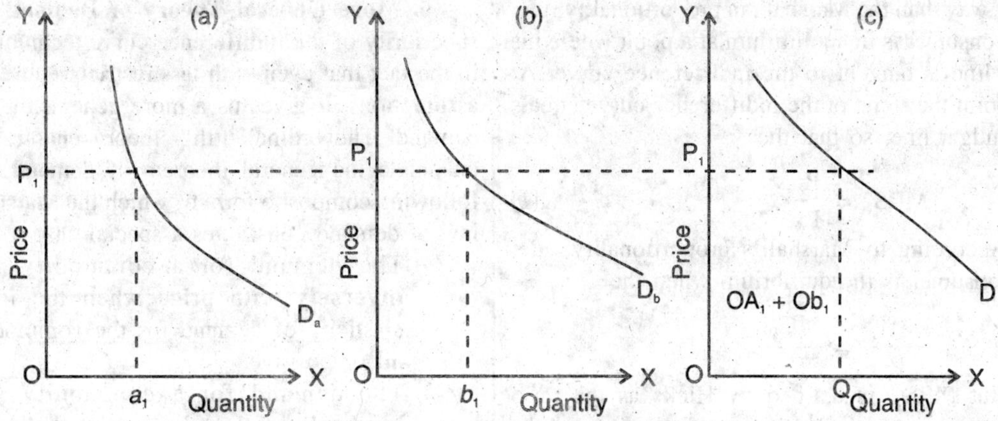

Fig. 46: *Derivation of Market Demand Curve*

to the right) because it happens to be Giffen good for him, it does not follow that the market demand curve too will slope downward to the left. This is because a good may be a Giffen good for a single consumer, but it is seldom that any good will be Giffen good for all the consumers. There will be other consumers demanding it at a lower price to whom it may not appear an inferior good. For the market as a whole a good is not likely to be inferior at all, there being always a sufficient number of buyers over the same price range. Hence **the market demand curve will always slope downward to the right.**

Superiority of Indifference Curve Technique over Utility Analysis

The indifference curve technique is superior to the Marshallian utility analysis in several respects :

1. Ordinal vs. Cardinal Measurability of Utility : The indifference curve approach is superior to the utility analysis because it measures utility **ordinally.**

The consumer arranges the various combinations of goods in a scale of preference market as first, second, third etc. He can tell whether he prefers the first to the second or the second to the first or he is indifferent between them. But he cannot tell by how much the prefers one to the other. The ordinal method and the assumption of transitivity makes this technique more realistic.

2. It is Free from the Assumption of Constant Marginal Utility of Money : Marshall in his analysis of a consumer's behaviour assumed marginal utility of money to remain constant while the consumer proceeded to make purchases. By assuming constant marginal utility of money Marshall ignored "the income effect" of a price change and thus failed to distinguish between the two components of the "price-effect". Marshallian analysis in that it does not assume constancy of marginal utility of money and is therefore able to draw a **distinction between the "income effect" and "substitution effect" of a price change,** as seen before.

3. It Studies Combinations of Two Goods Instead of One Good : The utility approach is a single-commodity analysis in which the utility of one commodity is regarded independent of the other. Marshall avoided the discussion of **substitutes** and complementary goods by grouping them together as one commodity.

This assumption is far from reality because a consumer buys not one but combinations of goods at a time. The indifference curve technique is a two commodity model which discusses consumer behaviour in the case of substitutes, complementaries and unrelated goods. It is thus superior to the utility analysis.

4. It Explains the Proportionality Rule in a Better Way : The indifference curve technique explains consumer's equilibrium in a similar and better way than the Marshallian proportionality rule. The consumer is in equilibrium at a point where his price line is tangent to the indifference curve. At this point the slope of the indifference curve equals the budget line, so that the

$$MRS_{xy} = \frac{P_x}{P_y} \qquad ...(1)$$

According to Marshall's proportionality rule, the consumer is in equilibrium when the

$$\frac{MU_x}{P_x} = \frac{MU_y}{P_y}$$

But MRS_{xy} is defined by Hicks as the ratio between the marginal utilities of the two goods. Therefore,

$$MRS_{xy} = \frac{MU_x}{MU_y} \qquad ...(2)$$

From (1) and (2), it follows that

$$\frac{MU_x}{MU_y} = \frac{P_x}{P_x}$$

which can be written as

$$\frac{MU_x}{P_x} = \frac{MU_y}{P_y} \qquad ...(3)$$

Thus, (3) is the same "proportionality rule" of equilibrium as enunciated by Marshall, and the indifference curve technique arrives at this rule with less restrictive and fewer assumptions.

5. This Analysis Explains the Dual Effect of the Price Effect : One of the main defects in the Marshallian utility analysis is that it fails to analyze the **income** and **substitution effects of a price change.**

In the indifference curve technique when the price of a good falls, the real income of the consumer increase. This is the income effect. Secondly, with the fall in price, the good becomes cheaper. The consumer substitutes it for some other good. This is the **substitution effect.** The indifference curve technique is superior to the utility analysis because it discusses the income effect when the consumer's income changes, the price effect when the price of a particular good changes and its dual effect in the form of the income and substitution effects.

6. More General Theory of Demand : The superiority of the indifference curve technique lies in the fact that even with less restrictive and fewer assumptions, it gives us a more general theory of demand. The ordinal utility theory enables us to enunciate the general theorem of demand in the following composite form of which the Marshallian law of demand constitutes a special case :

(a) The demand for a commodity varies **inversely** with price when the income elasticity of demand for the commodity is nil or positive.

(b) The demand for a commodity varies **inversely** with price when the income elasticity is negative but the income effect of the price change is smaller than the substitution effect.

(c) The demand for a commodity varies directly with price when the income elasticity is negative and the income effect of the price change is larger than the substitution effect.

In the case of *(a)* and *(b)* the Marshallian law of demand holds while in *(c)* we have a Giffen case which is exception to the Marshallian law of demand. Marshall could not account for **'Giffen Paradox'.** Marshall was not able to provide explanation for **Giffen Paradox,** because by assuming constant marginal utility of money, he ignored the income effect of the price change. The indifference curve technique by distinguishing between the income and substitution effects of the price change can explain the Giffen case. According to this, the Giffen paradox occurs in the case of an inferior good for which the negative income effect of the price change is so powerful that it outweights the substitution effect, and hence when the price of a Giffen good falls, its quantity demand, also falls instead of rising.

7. Implications of a Price change in Terms of Income and Welfare Increments : By means of indifference curve technique, welfare consequences of changes in prices can be translated into changes in income. A fall in the price of a good enables the consumer to shift from a lower to a higher level of welfare or satisfaction. That is, change in price causes a change in welfare exactly as a change in consumer's income would have done. Thus, a change in price brings about a change in consumer's welfare exactly as if his income has changed. In other words, the consumer can be thought of reaching higher (lower) level of welfare through an equivalent rise (fall) in income rather than the fall (rise) in price of a good.

In Fig. 47 with the fall in price of good X from PL_1 to PL_2 the consumer shifts from indifference curve IC_1 to IC_2 showing an increase in the level of welfare. Now, if instead to the fall in price from PL_1 to PL_2 the consumer's income is increased by the amount equal to PA and L_1B, he will reach the indifference curve IC_2.

Thus, the increase in consumer's welfare due to the rise in income by PA and L_1B is equal to that of the change in price of X from PL_1 to PL_2.

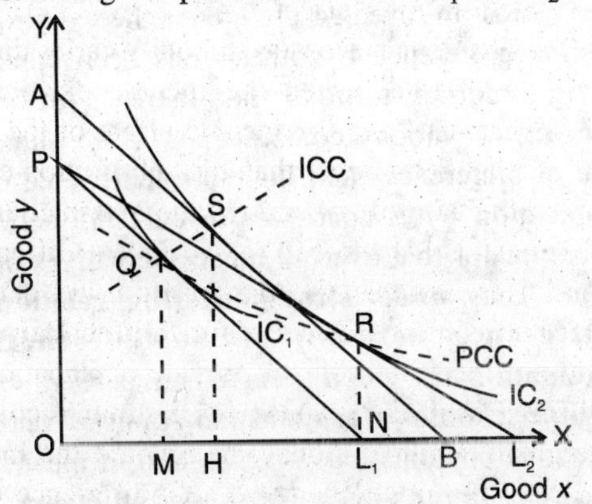

Fig. 47

"The equivalence of a given change in price to a suitable change in income is a major discovery of ordinal utility analysis." (T. Majumdar). The discovery of a suitable change in income equivalent in terms to welfare to a given change in price has enabled Hicks to extend Marshall's concept of consumer's surplus.

Revealed Preference Theory

Samuelson introduced the term **'revealed preference'** into economics in 1938. Since then the literature in this field has proliferated. Revealed preference theory is called the **behaviourist ordinal-utility theory.** Instead of the unrealistic assumption that the consumers operate with a complete and consistent scales of preferences set out in the form of indifference curves, most economists now prefer to analyse situations in which their hypothesis can be tested. Both Marshallian utility analysis and Allen-Hicksian indifference curve technique apply the **introspective method** or the subjective method. But the revealed preference theory seeks to explain consumer's demand from his actual behaviour in the market in various price-income situations. Thus, in sharp contrast to psychological or introspective explanation revealed preference theory is behaviouristic explanation of consumer's demand, besides, revealed preference theory is based upon the concept to ordinal utility.

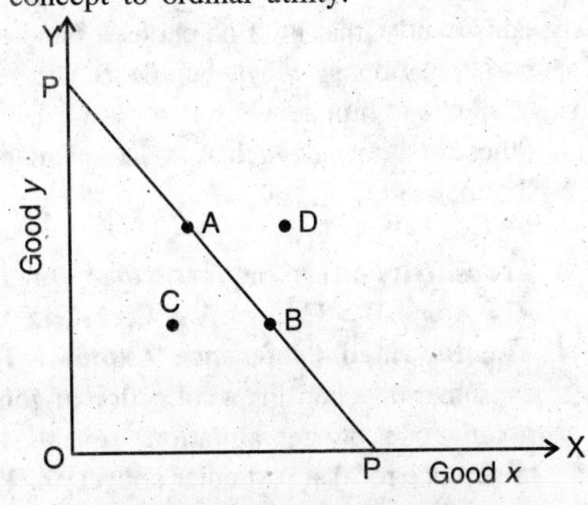

Fig. 48 : *Choice reveals preference*

This theory is based on a very simple idea. A consumer will decide to buy some particular basket of goods either because he likes it more than another basket of goods or because it is cheap when compared with other baskets of goods. Suppose a consumer buys basket of goods A rather than basket of goods B. We may not state that he prefers A to B. It is possible that he could not afford to buy B. Given price information, however, we can make a more definitive statement. If A is not less expensive than B and the consumer purchases A, he does so because he likes it better. We say in this situation that A has been **revealed** preferred to B, or B is **revealed inferior** to A.

In Figure 48 the points represents baskets of goods. Given price line PP, we see that A is just as expensive as B. If the consumer chooses A, it is revealed preferred to all other points on PP. Also, C is revealed inferior to A because every point below the price line is revealed inferior to A, for it represents a basket of goods that is less expensive than A. Clearly, any point like D lying above the price line represents basket of goods that is more expensive than A and cannot therefore be revealed inferior to A.

Assumptions

1. **Rationality :** The consumer is assumed to behave rationally, in that he prefers bundles of goods, that include more quantities of the commodities.
2. **Consistency :** The consumer behaves consistently, that is, if he chooses bundle A in a situation in which bundle B was also available to him he will not choose B in any other situation in which A is also available. Symbolically,
   If A > B, then B A
3. **Transitivity :** If in any particular situation A > B and B > C, then A > C.
4. **The Revealed Preference Axiom :** The consumer, by choosing a collection of goods in any one budget situation, reveals his preference for that particular collection. The chosen bundle is revealed to be preferred among all other alternative bundles available under the budget constraint. The chosen 'basket of goods' maximises the utility of the consumer. The revealed preference for a particular collection of goods implies (axiomatically) the maximisation of the utility of the consumer.
5. **Positive Income-Elasticity of Demand :** Another very important assumption underlying revealed preference theory is that the income-elasticity of demand of the consumer must always be positive. That is, if his income increases, his demand for the commodity must also increase, it should not remain the same and it should not also decrease as it happens in the case of inferior goods.

Strong Ordering

Prof. Samuelson's revealed preference theory is based upon the **strong form of preference hypothesis.** In other words, in revealed preference theory, strong-ordering preference hypothesis has been applied. Strong ordering implies that there is **definite ordering** of various combinations in consumer's scale of preferences and therefore the choice of a combination by a consumer reveals his definite preference for that over all other alternatives open to him. Thus, **under strong ordering, relation of indifference between various alternative combinations is ruled out.** When in Fig. 48 a consumer chooses a combination A out of various alternative combinations open to him, it means he has a definite preference for A over all others, the possibility of the chosen combination A being indifference to any other possible combination is ruled by strong ordering hypothesis.

❑❑❑

Chapter 3

Producer Behaviour & Supply

THEORY OF PRODUCTION AND COSTS

Production Function

The production function expresses a functional relationship between quantities of inputs and outputs. It shows how and to what extent output changes with variations in inputs during a specified period of time. Algebraically, it may be expressed in the form of an equation as

$$Y = f(L, K, R, S)$$

where

Y = output
L = labour input
K = capital input
R = raw materials
S = land input

Equal-Product Curves or Isoquants

Equal-Product curves are similar to the indifference curves of the theory of consumer's behaviour. An equal-product curve represents all those input combinations which are capable of producing the same level of output. These equal-product curves are also known as isoquants and iso-product curves. Since an equal-product curve represents those combinations of inputs which will be capable of producing an equal quantity of output, the producer would be indifferent between them as such. Therefore, another name which often given to the equal-product curves is **Production indifference curve.**

The production isoquant may assume various shapes depending on the degree of substitutability of factors.

Linear Isoquant

This type assumes perfect substitutability of factors of production. A given commodity may be produced by using only capital, or only labour, or by an infinite combination of K and L.

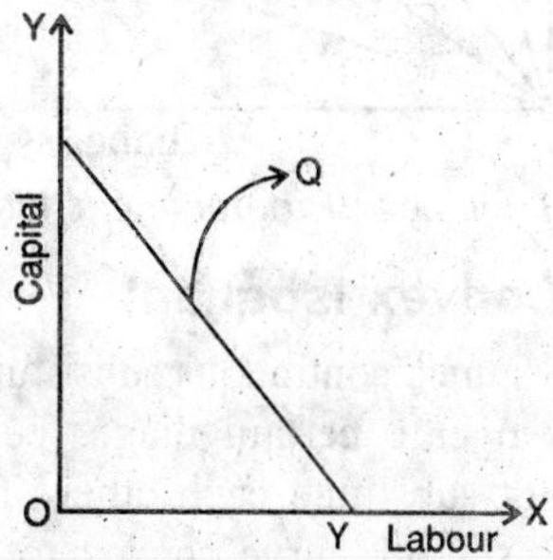

Fig. 1 : *Linear isoquant*

Input-Output Isoquant

This assumes strict complementarily (that is, zero substitutability) of the factors of production. There is only one method of production for any one commodity. The isoquant takes the shape of a **right angle.** This type of isoquant is also called **"Leontief isoquant"** after Leontief who invented the input-output analysis.

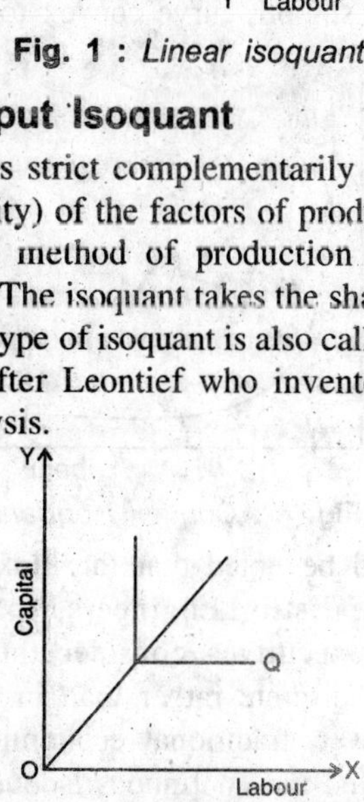

Fig. 2 : *Input-Output isoquant*

Kinked Isoquant

This assumes limited substitutability of K and L. There are only a few processes for producing any one commodity. Substitutability of the factors is possible only at the kinks. This form is also called **'activity analysis-isoquant'** or **'linear-programming isoquant',** because it is basically used in linear programming.

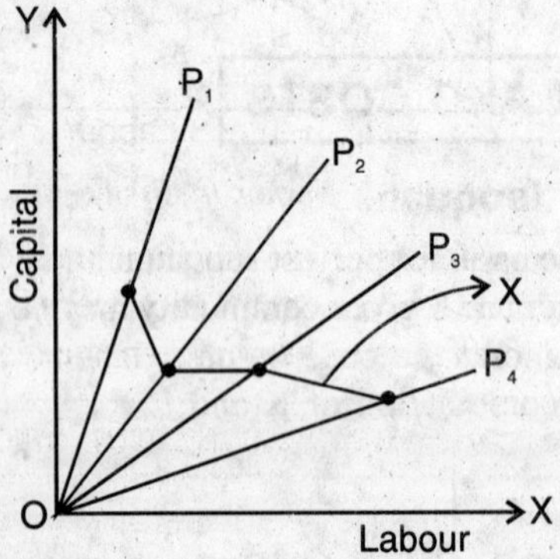

Fig. 3 : *Linear Programming Isoquant*

Smooth Convex Isoquant

This form assumes continuous substitutability of K and L only over a certain range, beyond which factors cannot substitute each other. The isoquant appears as a smooth curve convex to the origin.

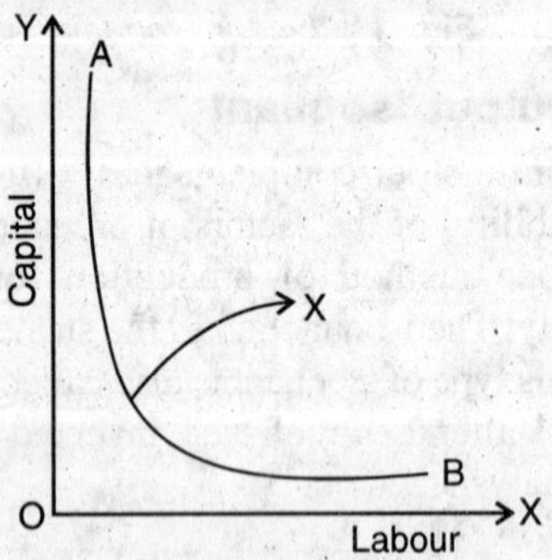

Fig. 4 : *Convex Isoquant*

It should be noted that the kinked isoquants are more realistic. Engineers, managers and production executives consider the production processes as discrete rather than in a continuous array. However, traditional economic theory has mostly adopted the continuous isoquants, because they are mathematically simpler to handle by the simple rules of calculus.

The production function describes not only a single isoquant, but the whole array of isoquant each of which shows a different level of output.

Properties of Isoquants

The following are the important properties of equal product curves.

1. Isoquants are negatively inclined.
2. An isoquant lying above and to the right of another represents a higher output level.
3. No two isoquants can intersect each other.
4. No isoquant can touch either axis.
5. Isoquants are convex to the origin.

Marginal Rate of Technical Substitution

The principle of marginal rate of technical substitution (MRTS) is based on the production function where two inputs can be substituted in variable proportions in such a way as to produce constant level of output.

Marginal rate of technical substitution indicates the rate at which factors can be substituted at the margin without altering the level of output. More precisely, marginal rate of technical substitution of factor X for factor Y may be defined as amount of factor Y which can be replaced by one unit of factor X, the level of output remaining unchanged. This can be understood with the aid of isoquant schedule.

Isoquant Schedule

Combinations	Factor X	Factor Y	$MRTS_{xy}$
A	1	12	-
B	2	8	4
C	3	5	3
D	4	3	2
E	5	2	1

Each of the input combinations A, B, C, D and E yields the same level of output. Moving down the table from combination A to combination B, 4 units of Y are replaced by 1 unit of X in the production process without any change in the level of output. Therefore, the marginal rate of technical substitution is 4 at this stage.

Switching from input combination B to input combination C involves the replacement of 3 units of factor Y by an additional unit of factor X, output remaining the same. Thus, $MRTS_{xy}$ is now 3.

The marginal rate of technical substitution at a point on the equal product curve can be known from the slope of the equal product curve at that point. Consider a small movement down the equal product curve P from G to H in figure 5 where a small amount of factor Y, say *dy* is replaced by an amount of factor X, say *dx* without any loss of output.

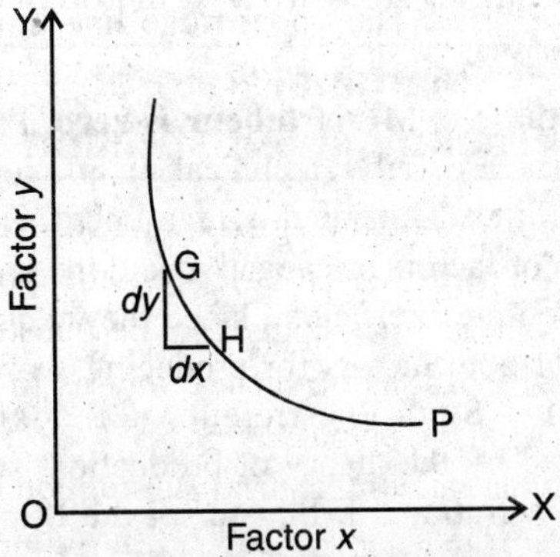

Fig. 5

The slope of the isoproduct curve P at point G is therefore equal to $\frac{dY}{dX}$. Thus, marginal rate of technical substitution

$$MRTS_{xy} = -\frac{dY}{dX}$$

An important point to be noted about the marginal rate of technical substitution is that it is equal to the ratio of the marginal products of two factors.

Factor Intensity

The factor intensity of any production process is measured by the slope of the line through the origin representing the particular process.

Thus, the factor intensity is the capital-labour ratio. In figure 6 process P_1 is more capital intensive than process P_2. Clearly

$$\frac{K_1}{L_1} > \frac{K_2}{L_2}$$

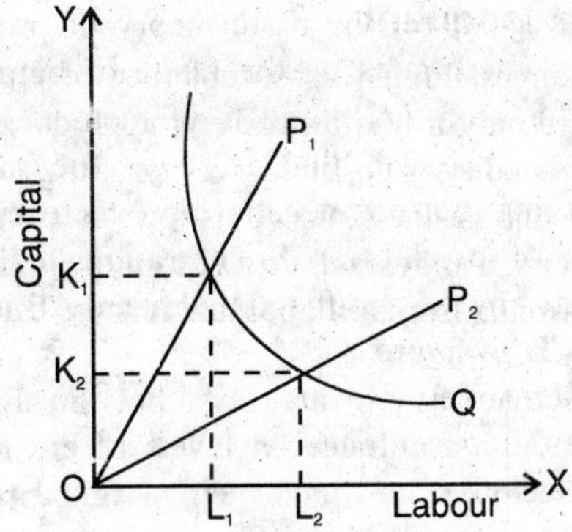

Fig. 6 : *Factor Intensity*

The upper part of the isoquant includes more capital-intensive processes. The lower part of the isoquant includes more labour-intensive techniques.

Marginal Products of the Factors

The marginal product of a factor is defined as the change in output resulting from a (very small) change of this factor, keeping all other factors constant.

Mathematically, the marginal product of each factor is the partial derivative of the production function with respect to this factor. Thus,

$$MP_L = \frac{dQ}{dL}$$

and $$MP_K = \frac{dQ}{dK}$$

where MP_L = marginal product of labour
MP_K = marginal product of capital

Graphically the marginal product is shown by the slope of the total product curve.

In principle the marginal product of a factor may assume any value, positive, zero or negative. However, basic production theory concentrates only on the efficient part of the production function, that, on the range of output over which the marginal products of the factors are positive. No rational firm would employ labour beyond OB, or capital beyond OD, since an increase in the factors beyond these levels would results in the reduction of the total output of the firm. Ranges of output over which the marginal products of the factors would be negative imply irrational behaviour of the firm, and are not considered by the theory of production.

Further more, the basic theory of production usually concentrates on the range of output over which the marginal products of factors, although positive, decrease, that is, over the range of diminishing (but non-negative) productivity of the factors of production : the ranges of output considered by the traditional theory are AB in figure 7 and CD in figure 8.

Alternatively we may say that the theory of production concentrates on levels of employment of the factors over which their marginal products are positive but decrease. Thus

$$MP_L > 0 \text{ but } \frac{d(MP_L)}{dL} < 0$$

$$\text{and } MP_K > 0 \text{ but } \frac{d(MP_K)}{dK} < 0$$

These conditions imply that **the traditional theory of production concentrates on the range of isoquants over which their slope is negative and convex to the origin.**

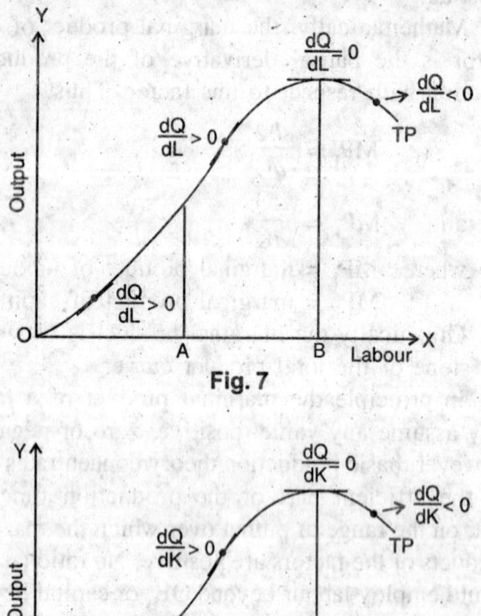

Fig. 7

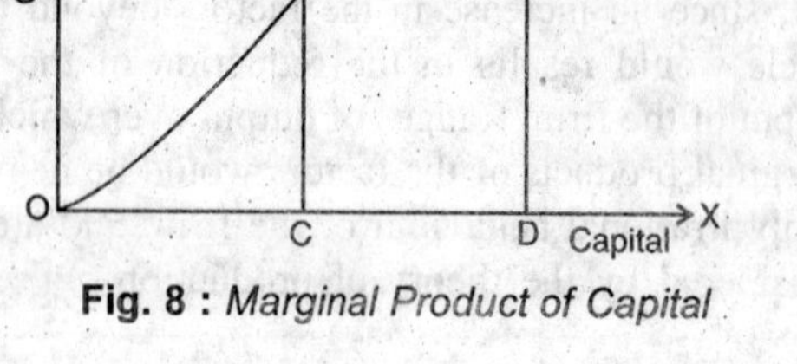

Fig. 8 : *Marginal Product of Capital*

Ridge Lines

In figure 9 the production function is depicted in the form of a set of isoquants. By construction the higher to the right an isoquants, the higher the level of output it depicts. Clearly isoquants cannot intersect, by their construction. We said that traditional economic theory concentrates on efficient ranges of output, that is, ranges over which the marginal products of factors are diminishing but positive. **The locus of points of isoquants where the marginal products of the factors are zero form the ridge lines.** The upper ridge line implies that the MP **of capital is zero.** The lower ridge line implies that the MP **of labour is zero.** Production techniques are only (technically) efficient inside the ridge lines. Outside the ridge lines the marginal products of factors are negative and the methods of production are inefficient, since they require more quality of both factors for producing a given level of output. Such inefficient methods are not considered by the theory of production, since they are imply irrational behaviour of the firm.

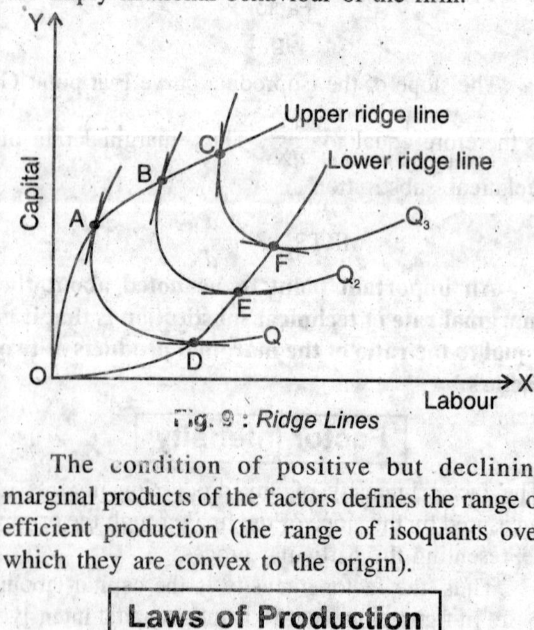

Fig. 9 : *Ridge Lines*

The condition of positive but declining marginal products of the factors defines the range of efficient production (the range of isoquants over which they are convex to the origin).

Laws of Production

The laws of production describe the technically possible ways of increasing the level of production. Output may increase in various ways.

Output can be increased by changing all factors or production. Clearly this is possible only in the long-run. Thus **the laws of returns to scale** refer to the long-run analysis of production.

In the short run output may be increased by using more of the variable factor, while capital (and possibly other factors as well) are kept constant. The marginal product of the variable factor will decline eventually as more and more quantities of this factor are combined with the other constant factors. The expansion of output with one factor constant is described by the **law of diminishing returns** of the variable factor, which is often referred to as the **law of variable proportions.**

Laws of Returns to Scale : Long-Run Analysis of Production

In the long run expansion of output may be achieved by varying all factors. In the long run all factors are variable. The laws of returns to scale refer to the effects of scale relationships.

In the long run output may be increased by changing **all factors by the same proportion,** or by different proportions. Traditional theory of production concentrates on the first case, that is, the study of output as all inputs change by the **same proportion. The term 'return to scale' refers to the changes in output as all factors change by the same proportion.**

Suppose we start from an initial level of inputs and output

$$X_0 = f(L, K)$$

and we increase all the factors by the same proportion *m*. We will clearly obtain a new level of output X^*, higher than the original level X_0,

$$X^* = f(mL, mK)$$

*If X^* increases by the same proportion *m* as the inputs, we say that there are **constant returns to scale.**

*If X^* increases less than proportionally with the increase in the factors, we have **decreasing returns to scale.**

*If X^* increases more than proportionally with the increase in the factors, we have **increasing returns to scale.**

Returns to Scale and Homogeneity of the Production Function

Suppose we increase both factors of the function

$$X_0 = f(L, K)$$

by the same proportion *m*, and we observe the resulting new level of output X^*

$$X^* = f(mL, mK)$$

If m can be factored out, then the new level of output X^* can be expressed as a function of m (to any power *a*) and the initial level of output

$$X^* = m^a f(L, K)$$

or $\quad X^* = m^a X_0$

and the production function is called **homogeneous.** If *m* cannot be factored out, the production function is non-homogeneous. The power *a* of *m* is called the **degree of homogeneity** of the function and is a measure of the returns to scale :

*If $a = 1$, we have constant returns to scale. Thus, production function is something called **linear homogeneous.**

*If $a < 1$, we have decreasing returns to scale.

*If $a > 1$, we have increasing returns to scale.

Returns to scale are measured mathematically by the coefficients of the production function. For example, in a **Cobb-Douglas function**

$$X = b_0 L^{b_2} K^{b_2}$$

the returns to scale are measured by the Sum $(b_1 + b_2) = a$.

Proof

Let L and K increase by *m*. The new level of output is

$$X^* = b_0 (mL)^{b_1} (mK)^{b_2}$$

$$= (b_0 L^{b_1} K^{b_2}) m^{b_1+b_2}$$

or $\quad X^* = m^{b_1+b_2} X.$

Thus, $\quad a = (b_1 + b_2)$

Linear Homogeneous Production Function

Production function can take several forms but a particular form of production function enjoys wide popularity among the economists. This is a linear homogeneous production, that is, production function which is homogeneous of the first degree. Homogeneous production function of the first degree implies that if all the factors of production are increased in some proportion, output also increases in the same proportion. Hence, linear homogeneous production function represents the case of **constant returns to scale.**

Product Lines

A product line shows that movement from one isoquant to another as we change both factors or a single factor. A product line is drawn independently of the prices of factors of production. The product line describes the technically possible alternative paths of expanding output. What path will actually be chosen by the firm will depend on the prices of factors.

The product line passes through the origin if all factors are variable. If only one factor is variable (the other being kept constant) the product line is a straight line parallel to the axis of the variable factor. The K/L ratio diminishes along the product line.

Among all possible product lines of particular interest are the so-called **isoclines. An isocline is the locus of points of different isoquants at which the MRS of factors is constant.**

If the production function is homogeneous the isoclines are straight lines through the origin. Along any one isocline the K/L ratio is constant. Of course the K/L ratio (and the MRS) is different for different isoclines.

If the production function is non-homogeneous the isoclines will not be straight lines, but their shape will be twiddly. The K/L ratio changes along each isocline. (Fig. 10).

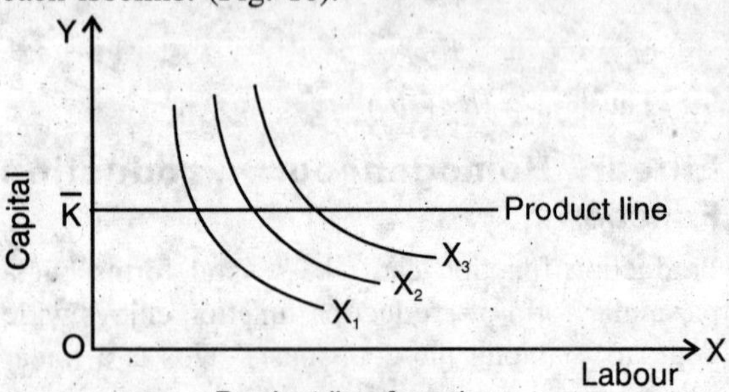

Product line for given

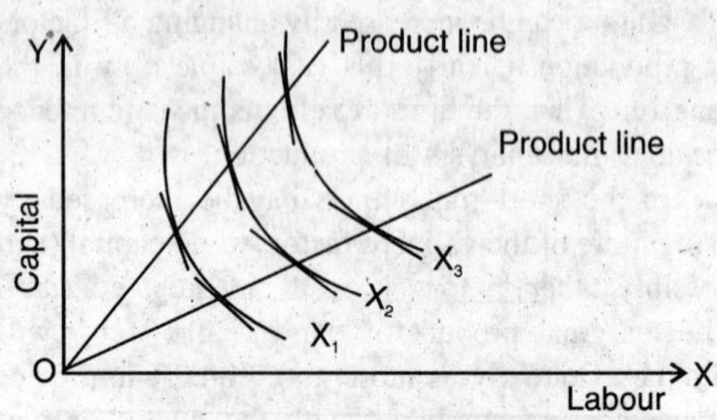

Homogeneous Production Function

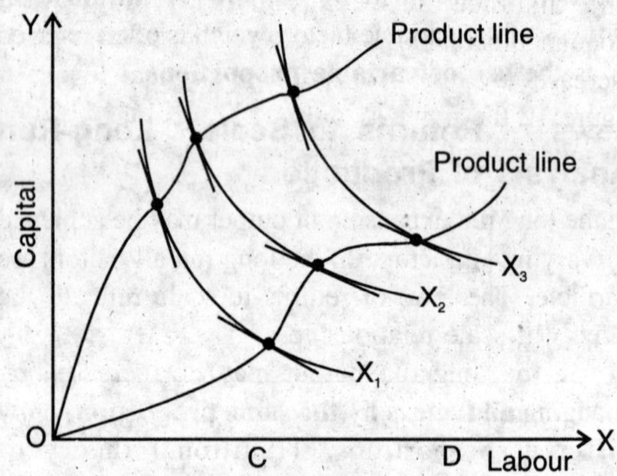

Fig. 10 : *Non-Homogeneous Production Function*

Graphical Presentation of the Returns to Scale for a Homogeneous Production Function

The returns to scale may be shown graphically by the distance (on an isocline) between successive 'multiple-level-of-output' isoquants, that is, isoquants that show levels of output which are multiples of some base level of output *e.g.,* X, 2X, 3X etc.

Constant Returns to Scale

Along any isocline the distance between successive multiple isoquants is constant. Doubling the factor inputs achieves double the level of the initial output, trebling inputs achieves treble output, and so on (Fig. 11).

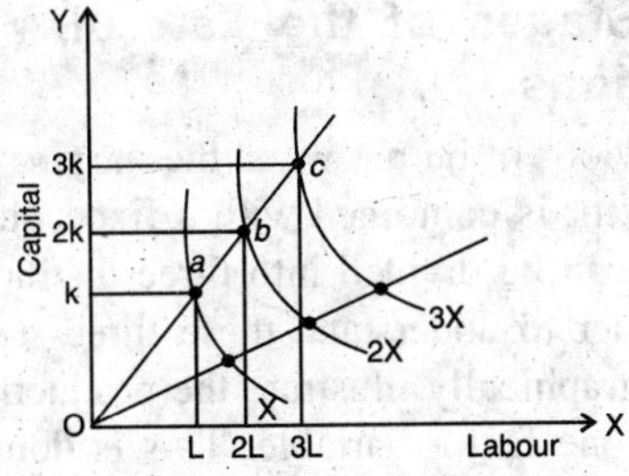

Fig. 11 : *Constant Returns to Scale : oa = ab = bc*

Decreasing Returns to Scale

The distance between consecutive multiple isoquants increases. By doubling the inputs, output increases by less than twice its original level. In figure 12 the point *a′*, defined by 2K and 2L, lies on an isoquant below the one showing 2X.

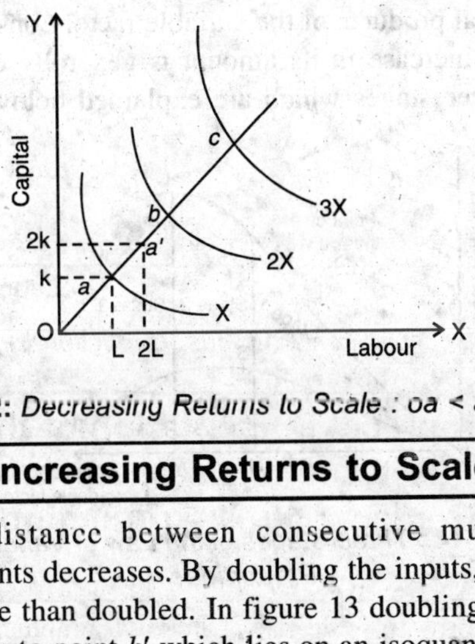

Fig. 12: *Decreasing Returns to Scale : oa < ab < bc*

Increasing Returns to Scale

The distance between consecutive multiple-isoquants decreases. By doubling the inputs, output is more than doubled. In figure 13 doubling K and L leads to point *b′* which lies on an isoquant above the one denoting 2X.

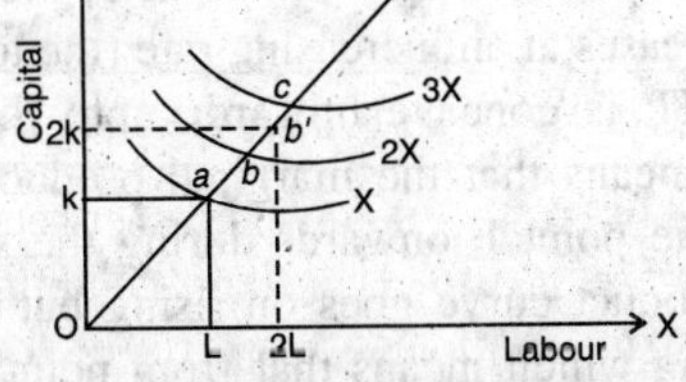

Fig. 13: *Increasing Returns to Scale : oa > ab> bc*

Returns to scale are usually assumed to be the same everywhere on the production surface, that is, the same along all the expansion-product lines. All processes are assumed to show the same returns over all ranges of output : either constant returns everywhere, decreasing returns everywhere, or increasing returns everywhere. However, the technological conditions of production may be such that returns to scale may vary over different ranges of output. Over some range we may have constant returns to scale, while over another range we may have increasing or decreasing returns to scale. Production functions with varying returns to scale are difficult to handle and economists usually ignore for the analysis of production.

Causes of Increasing Returns to Scale

The increasing returns to scale are due to **technical and/or managerial indivisibilities.** Usually most processes can be duplicated, but it may not be possible to halve them.

Causes of Decreasing Returns to Scale

The most common causes is **'diminishing returns to management.'** The management is responsible for the co-ordination of the activities of various sections of the firm. Even when authority is delegated to individual managers (production manager, sales manager, etc.) the final decision have to be taken from the final 'centre of top management.' As the output grows, top management becomes efficient overburdened and hence less difficult in its role as co-ordinator and ultimate decision-maker.

Another cause for decreasing returns may be found in the **exhaustible natural resources :** doubling the fishing fleet may not lead to a doubling of the catch of fish, or doubling the plant in mining or on an oil-extraction field may not lead to a doubling of output.

The Law of Variable Proportions : Short Run Analysis of Production

Law of variable proportions occupies an important place in economic theory. This law examines the production function with one factor variable, keeping the quantities of other factors fixed. In other words, it refers to the input-output relation when the output is increased by varying the quantity of one input. When the quantity of one factors is varied, keeping the quantity of other factors constant, the proportion between the variable factor and the fixed factor is altered, the ratio of employment of the variable factor to that of the fixed factor goes on increasing as the quantity of the variable factor is increased. **Since under this law we study the effects on output of variation in factor proportions, this is known as the law of variable proportions.** The law of variable proportions is the new name for the famous **"Law of Diminishing Returns"** of classical economics.

In general if one of the factors of production (usually capital K) is fixed, the marginal product of the variable factor (labour) will diminish after a certain range of production. We said that the traditional theory of production concentrates on the ranges of the factors are positive but diminishing. The ranges of increasing returns (to a factor) and the range of negative productivity are not equilibrium ranges of output.

Assumptions of the Law of Variable Proportions

The law of variable proportions as stated above holds good under the following conditions :

1. Firstly, the state of technology is assumed to be given and unchanged.
2. Secondly, there must be some inputs whose quantity is kept fixed. It is only in this way that we can alter the factor proportions and know its effects on output. This law does not apply in case all factors are proportionately varied.
3. Thirdly, the law is based upon the possibility of varying the proportions in which the various factors can be combined to produce a product. The law does not apply to those cases where the factors must be used in fixed proportions to yield a product. When the various factors are required to be used in rigidly fixed proportions, then the increase in one factor would not lead to any increase in output, that is, the marginal product of the factor will then be zero and not diminishing.

Three Stages of the Law of Variable Proportions

The behaviour of output when the varying quantity of one factor is combined with a fixed quantity of the other can be divided into three distinct stages.

In order to understand these three stages it is better to graphically illustrate the production function with one factor variable. This is done in Fig. 14. In this figure, on the X-axis is measured the quantity of the variable factor and on the Y-axis are measured the total product, average product and the marginal product. The total product curve TP goes on increasing to a point and after that it starts declining. Average and marginal product curves also rise and then decline, marginal product curve starts declining earlier than the average product curve. The behaviour of these total, average and marginal products of the variable factor consequent on the increase in its amount is generally divided into three stages which are explained below.

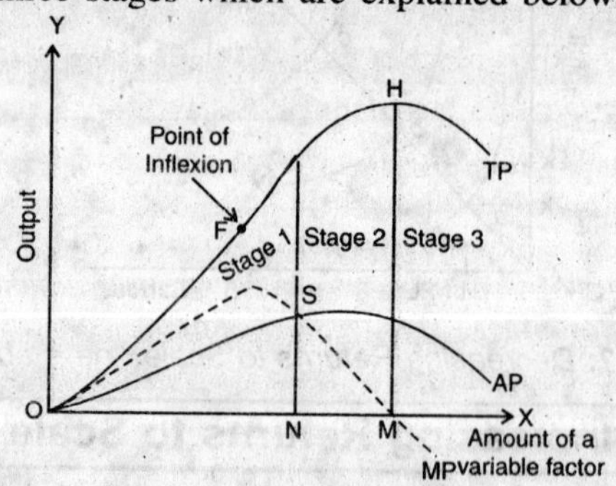

Fig. 14 : *Three Stages of the Law of Variable Proportions*

Stage 1

In this stage, total product to a point increases at an increasing rate. In figure 14 from the origin to the point F, slope of the total product curve TP is increasing, that is upto the point F, the total product increases at an increasing rate (the total product curve TP is concave upwards upto the point F), which means that the marginal product MP rises. From the point F onwards during the stage 1, the total product curve goes on rising but its slope is declining which means that from point F onwards the total product increases at a diminishing rate (total product curve is concave downwards), *i.e.*, marginal product falls but is positive. The point F where the total product stops increasing at an increasing rate and starts increasing at the diminishing rate is called the **point of inflexion.** Corresponding vertically to this point of inflexion marginal product is maximum, after which it slopes downwards.

The Stage 1 ends where the average product curve reaches its highest point. During this stage, when marginal product of the variable factor is falling, it still exceeds its average product and so continues to cause the AP-curve to rise. Thus, during the stage 1, whereas MP-curve rises in a part and then falls, the AP-curve rises throughout. In this stage, the quantity of the fixed factor is too much relative to the quantity of the variable factor so that if some of the fixed factor is withdrawn, the total product would increase. Thus, **in the first stage marginal product of the fixed factor is negative.** Stage 1 is known as **the stage of increasing returns** because average product of the variable factor increases throughout this stage.

Stage 2

This stage is also known as the stage of diminishing returns. In stage 2, the total product continues to increase at diminishing rate until it reaches its maximum point H, where the second stage ends. In this stage both the marginal product and average product of the variable factor are diminishing but are positive. At the end of the second stage, that is, at point M, marginal product of the variable factor is zero (corresponding to the highest point H of the total product curve TP). Stage 2 is very crucial and important because the firm will seek to produce in its range. This stage is known as the stage of diminishing returns as both the average and marginal products of the variable factors continuously fall during this stage.

Stage 3

In this stage total product declines and therefore the total product curve TP slopes downward. As a result, marginal product of the variable factor is negative and MP-curve goes below the X-axis. In this stage, variable factor is too much relative to the fixed factor. This stage is called the **stage of negative returns,** because the marginal product of the variable factor is negative during this stage.

It may be noted that stage 1 and stage 3 are **completely symmetrical.** In stage 1 the fixed factor is too much relative to the variable factor. Therefore, in stage 1, marginal product of the fixed factor is negative. On the other hand, in stage 3 variable factor is too much relative to the fixed factor. Therefore in, stage 3, the marginal product of the variable factor is negative.

It is clear from above that the rational producer will never be found producing in stage 1 and stage 3. Stages 1 and 3 represents non-economic region in production function. A rational producer will always seek to produce in stage 2 where both the marginal product and average product of the variable factor are diminishing. At which particular point in this stage, the producer will decide to produce depends upon the prices of factors. The stage 2 represents the range of rational production decisions.

Cobb-Douglas Production Function

The Cobb-Douglas production function is based on the empirical study of the American manufacturing industry made be Paul H. Douglas and C.W. Cobb. It is a linear homogeneous production function which takes into account only two inputs labour and capital for the entire output of the manufacturing industry. The Cobb-Douglas production function is

$$Q = A.K^{\alpha}.L^{\beta}$$

where

$Q =$ output

$K =$ capital

$L =$ labour

$A, \alpha, \beta =$ Positive constants

Properties

The Cobb-Douglas production function has some interesting mathematical properties which make them very useful for managerial decision-making. The important properties are the following :

1. The marginal product of capital and labour depends only on the quantities of capital and labour used in the production process. The equation for the marginal product of capital is given by

$$MP_K = \frac{dQ}{dK} = \alpha A.K^{\alpha-1}.L^{\beta}$$

$$= \alpha(A.K^{\alpha}.L^{\beta})K^{-1}$$

$$= \alpha.\frac{Q}{K} \qquad [\,Q = A.K^{\alpha}.L^{\beta}]$$

$$= \alpha(AP_K)$$

where AP_K = the average product of capital

Similarly, the equation for the marginal product of labour is given by

$$MP_L = \frac{dQ}{dL} = \beta A.K^{\alpha}.L^{\beta-1}$$

$$= \beta(A.K^{\alpha}.L^{\beta})L^{-1}$$

$$= \beta.\frac{Q}{L} \qquad [\,Q = A.K^{\alpha}.L^{\beta}]$$

$$= \beta(AP_L)$$

It is to be noted here that MP_K and MP_L both are positive but constantly diminishing.

2. The marginal rate of substitution

$$MRS_{LK} = \frac{dQ/dL}{dQ/dK}$$

$$= \frac{\beta(Q/L)}{\alpha(QK)} = \frac{\beta}{\alpha}.\frac{K}{L}$$

3. Thirdly α and β the exponents of K and L respectively, show the output elasticities of labour (E_L) and capital (E_K).

For $Q = A.K^{\alpha}.L^{\beta}$, the percentage rise in Q for 1% rise in L will be

$$\frac{\%\Delta Q}{\%\Delta L} = \frac{\Delta Q/Q}{\Delta L/L} = \frac{\Delta Q}{\Delta L}\times\frac{L}{Q}$$

In terms of partial derivatives, we can write

$$E_L = \frac{dQ}{dL}\times\frac{L}{Q}$$

$$= \left(\beta\times\frac{Q}{L}\right)\times\frac{L}{Q} = \beta.$$

Similarly, $E_K = \frac{dQ}{dK}\times\frac{K}{Q}$

$$= \left(\alpha\times\frac{Q}{K}\right)\times\frac{K}{Q} = \alpha.$$

Hence, if β = 0.5 then 1% rise in the amount of labour used (keeping capital constant) will raise output by 0.5%.

4. The Cobb-Douglas production function can be extended easily to more than two inputs *e.g.*, capital and labour, natural resources, non-production labour, etc.

5. The elasticity of substitution

$$\alpha = \frac{d(K/L)/(K/L)}{d(MRS)/(MRS)}$$

substitute the MRS and obtain

$$\alpha = \frac{d(K/L)/(K/L)}{d\left(\frac{\beta}{\alpha}.\frac{K}{L}\right)\Big/\left(\frac{\beta}{\alpha}.\frac{K}{L}\right)}$$

$$= \frac{d(K/L)/(\beta/\alpha)}{\left(\frac{\beta}{\alpha}\right)d(K/L)} = 1$$

Hence such a production function the elasticity of factor substitution is equal to one.

given that β/α is constant and does not affect the derivative.

6. Factor Intensity : In a Cobb-Douglas function factor intensity is measured by the ratio β/α. The higher this ratio the more labour intensive the technique. Similarly, the lower the ratio β/α the more capital intensive the technique.

7. The sum of the two exponents (α and β) shows returns to scale. In the Cobb-Douglas case the returns to scale can be predicted as follows.

(a) When (α + β) = 1 the production function exhibits constant returns to scale,

(b) When (α + β) > 1 it exhibits increasing returns to scale, and

(c) When (α + β) < 1 it exhibits decreasing returns to scale.

This property may now be explained and illustrated.

Let us take the Cobb-Douglas function *i.e.,*

$$Q_1 = A.K^{\alpha}.L^{\beta}$$

and multiple each input by the factor *m*. So, we get

$$Q_2 = A.(mK)^{\alpha}.(mL)^{\beta}$$
$$= A.m^{\alpha}.K^{\alpha}.m^{\beta}.L^{\beta}$$
$$= A.K^{\alpha}.L^{\beta}.m^{(\alpha+\beta)} = Q_1.\ m^{(\alpha+\beta)}$$

8. The Cobb-Douglas production function has an additional property. It is a homothetic production function. A homothetic production function has **straight line expansion path.**

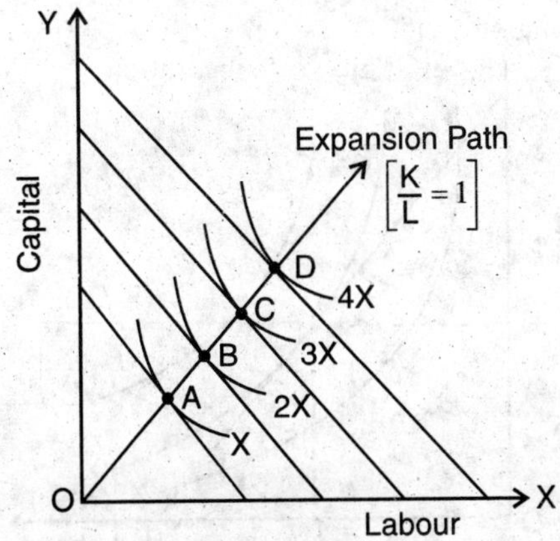

Fig. 15 : *The Expansion Path for the Cobb Douglas Function*

Equilibrium of the Firm : Choice of Optimal Combination of Factors of Production

In this section we shall show the use of the production function in the choice of the optimal combination of factors by the firm. In part A we will examine two cases in which the firm is faced with a single decision, namely maximising output for a given cost, and minimising cost subject to a given output. Both, these decisions comprise cases of constrained profit maximisation in a single period.

In part B we will consider the case of unconstrained profit maximisation, by the expansion of output over time.

In all the above cases it is assumed that the firm can choose the optimal combination of factors, that it can employ any amount of any factor in order to maximise its profits. This assumption is valid if the firm is new, or if the firm is in the long-run. However, an existing firm may be coerced, due to pressure of demand, to expand its output in the short-run, when at least one factor, usually capital, is constant.

In all cases we make the following assumptions:

1. The goal of the firm is profit maximisation-that is, the maximisation of the difference

$$\pi = R - C$$

where

π = profits
R = revenue
C = cost

2. The price of output is given, $\overline{P}x$.
3. The price of factors are **given :**

$\overline{w}$ is the given wage rate.
$\overline{r}$ is the given price of capital services.

A. Single Decision of the Firm

The problem facing the firm is that of a constrained profit maximisation, which may take one of the following forms :

(a) **Maximise Profit π, subject to a Cost Constraint.** In this case total cost and price are given and the problem may be stated as follows

$$\text{Maximum } (\pi) = R - \overline{C}$$

or $$\pi = \overline{P}x.X - \overline{C}$$

Clearly maximisation of π is achieved in this case if X (output) is maximised, since $\overline{C}$ and $\overline{P}x$ are given constants by assumption.

(b) **Maximise Profit π, for a given level of Output.** For example, a contractor wants to build a bridge (X is given) with the maximum profit. In this case we have

$$\text{Maximum } (p) = R - C$$

or $$p = \overline{P}x.\overline{X} - C$$

Clearly maximisation of π is achieved in this case if C is minimised, given that X and $\overline{P}x$ are given constants by assumption.

For a graphical presentation of the equilibrium of the firm (its profit maximising position) we will use the **isoquant map** (Figure 16) and the **isocost-line** (Figure 17).

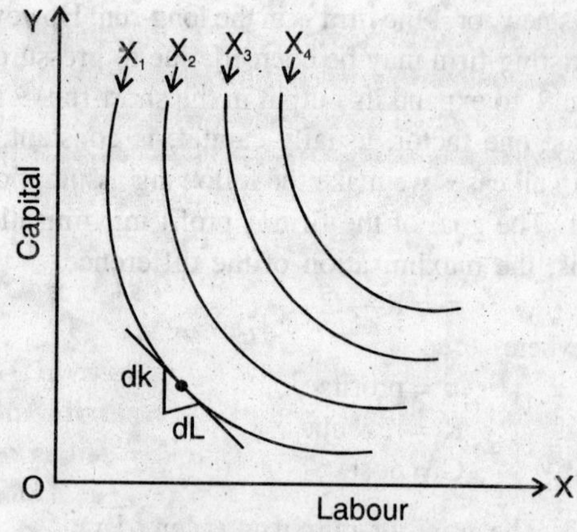

Fig. 16 : *Isoquant Map*

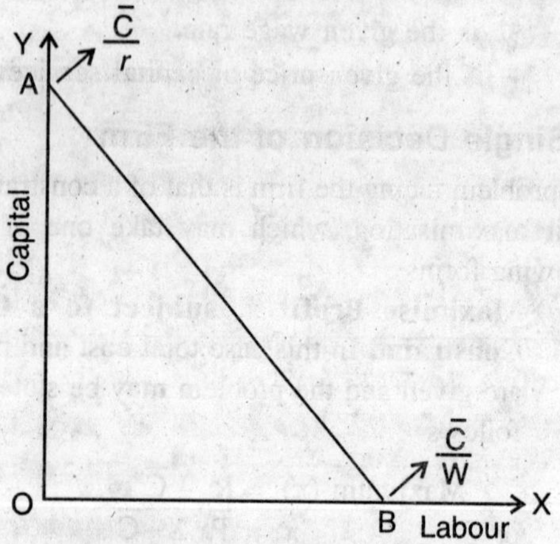

Fig. 17 : *Isocost Line*

The Slope of an isoquant is

$$-\frac{dK}{dL} = MRS_{LK} = \frac{MP_L}{MP_K} = \frac{dX / dL}{dX / dK}$$

The isocost line is defined by the cost equation

$$C = (r)\ (K) + (w)\ (L)$$

where

C = cost

w = wage rate

r = price of capital services

K = quantity of capital

L = quantity of labour

The isocost line is the locus of all combinations of factors the firm can purchase with a given monetary cost outlay. There is a close analogy between the consumer's price line and firm's isocost line.

The slope of the isocost line is equal to the ratio of the prices of the factors of production. Thus,.

$$\text{Slope of isocost line} = \frac{w}{r}$$

$$= \frac{\text{Price of Labour}}{\text{Price of Capital}}$$

Case 1 : Maximisation of output Subject to a Cost Constraint (financial constraint)

The firm is in equilibrium when it maximizes its output given its total cost outlay and the prices of the factors, w and r.

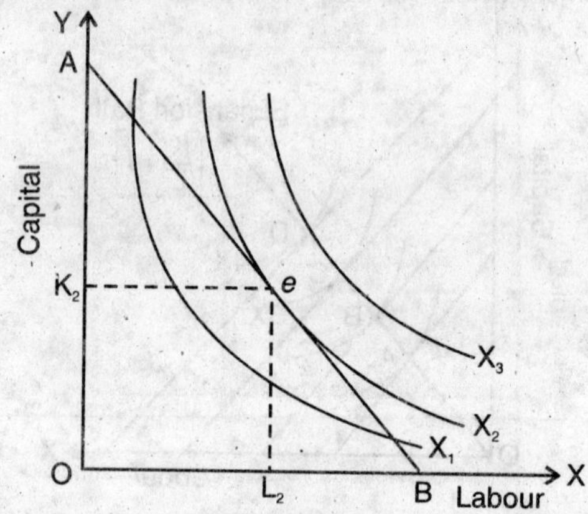

Fig. 18 : *Equilibrium of the Firm*

In Figure 18 we see that the maximum level of output the firm can produce, given the cost constraint, is X_2 defined by the tangency of the isocost line, and the highest isoquant. The optimal combination of factors of production is K_2 and L_2, for price w and r. Higher levels of output (to the right of e) are desirable but not attainable due to the cost constraint. Other points on AB or below it lie on a lower isoquant than X_2. Hence, X_2 is the maximum output possible under the above assumptions (of given cost outlay, given production function, and given factor prices). At the point of tangency (e) the slope of the isocost line (w/r) is equal to the slope of the isoquant (MP_L/MP_K). This constitutes the first condition for equilibrium. The second condition is that the isoquant be convex to the origin.

In summary : the conditions for equilibrium of the firm are :

(a) Slope of Isoquant = Slope of Isocost line

$$\text{or} \quad \frac{w}{r} = \frac{MP_L}{MP_K}$$

$$\frac{w}{r} = \frac{dX/dL}{dX/dK}$$

$$\frac{w}{r} = MRS_{LK}$$

(b) The isoquants must be convex to the origin. If the isoquant is concave the point of tangency of the isocost and the isoquant curves does not define an equilibrium position (Figure 19).

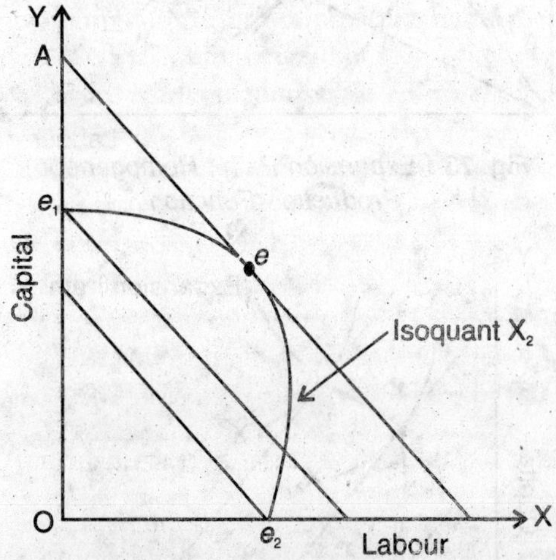

Fig. 19 : *Concave Isoquant*

Output X_2 (depicted by the concave isoquant) can be produced with lower cost at e_2 which lies on a lower isocost curve than *e* **With a concave isoquant we have *a* 'corner solution'.**

Case 2 : Minimisation of Cost for a given Level of Output

The conditions for equilibrium of the firm are formally the same as in case 1. That is, there must be tangency of the (given) isoquant and the lowest possible isocost curve, and the isoquant must be convex. However, the problem is conceptually different in case of cost minimisation. The entrepreneur wants to produce a given output (for example, a bridge, a building, or $\overline{X}$ tons of a commodity) with the minimum cost outlay.

In this case we have a single isoquant (Figure 20) which denotes the desired level of output, but we have a set of isocost curves (Figure 21). Curves closer to the origin show a lower total cost outlay. The isocost lines are parallel because they are drawn on the assumption of constant prices of factors. Since *w* and *r* do not change, all the isocost curves have the same slope *w/r*.

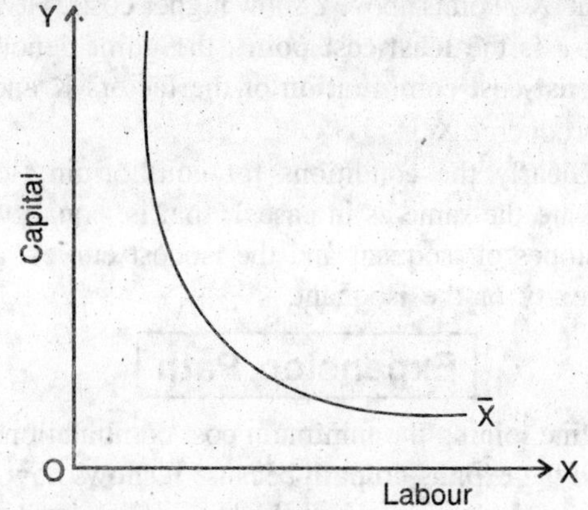

Fig. 20

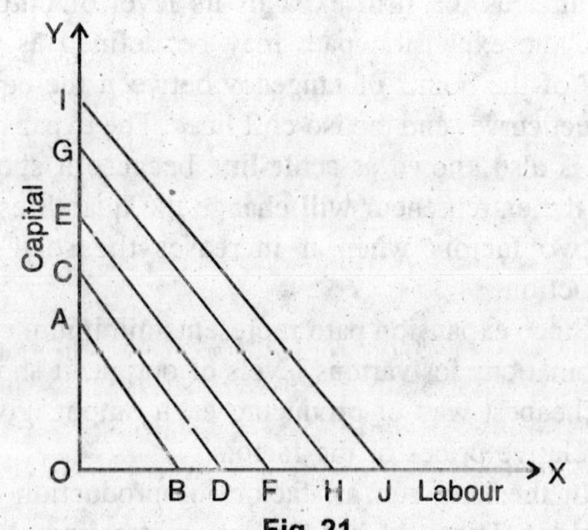

Fig. 21

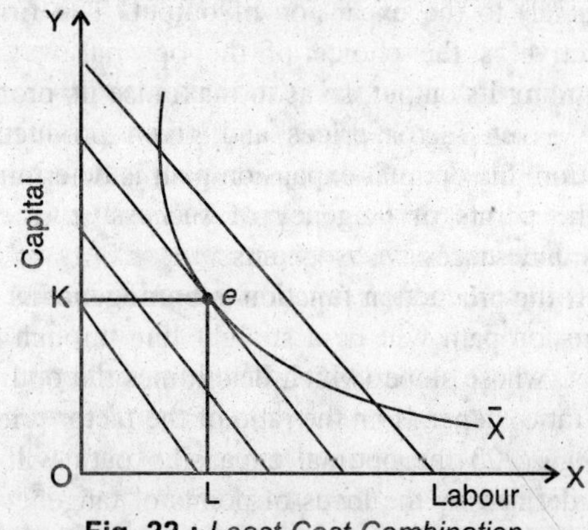

Fig. 22 : *Least-Cost Combination*

The firm minimises its costs by employing the combination of K and L determined by the point of tangency of the $\overline{X}$ isoquant with the lowest isocost line (Figure 22). Points below *e* are desirable because they show lower cost but are not attainable for output $\overline{X}$. Points above *e* show higher costs. Hence, point *e* is the **least-cost point,** the point denoting the **least-cost combination** of the factors K and L for producing $\overline{X}$.

Clearly the conditions for equilibrium (least cost) are the same as in case 1, that is, equality of the slopes of isoquant and the isocost curves, and convexity of the isoquant.

Expansion Path

The line joining the minimum cost combinations is called the **expansion path** because it shows how the factor combination with which the firm produces will alter as the firm expands its level of output. Thus, the expansion path may be defined as the locus of the points of tangency between the equal product curves and the iso-cost lines. The expansion path is also known as **scale-line** because it shows how the entrepreneur will change the quantities of the two factors when it increases the scale of production.

Since expansion path represents minimum cost combinations for various levels of output, it shows the cheapest way of producing each output, given the relative prices of the factors.

In the long run all factors of production are variable. There is no limitation (technical or financial) to the expansion of output. The firm's objective is the choice of the optimal way of expanding its output, so as to maximise its profits. With given factor prices and given production function, the optimal expansion path is determined by the points of tangency of successive isocost lines and successive isoquants.

If the production function is **homogeneous** the expansion path will be a straight line through the origin, whose slope (which determines the optimal K/L ratio) depends on the ratio of the factor prices. In Figure 23 the optimal expansion path will be OA, defined by the locus of points of tangency of the isoquants with successive parallel isocost line with s slope of *w*/*r*.

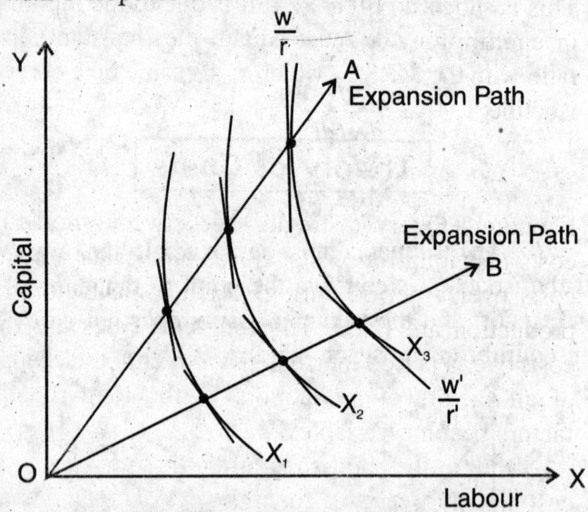

Fig. 23 : *Expansion Path : Homogeneous Production Function*

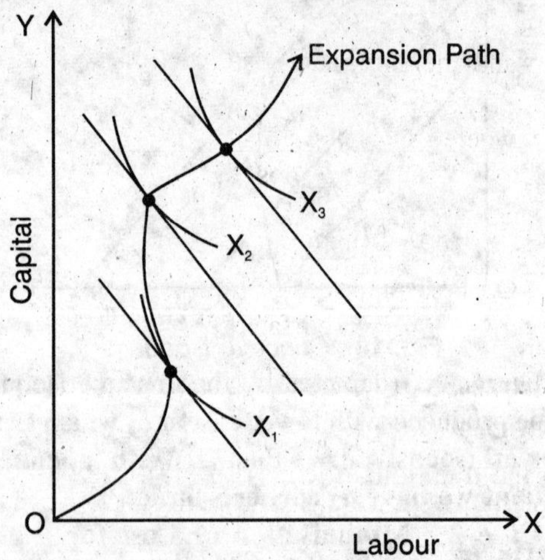

Fig. 24 : *Expansion Path : Non-Homogeneous Production Function*

If the ratio of the prices increases the isocost lines become flatter (for example, with a slope of *w'*/*r'*), and the optimal expansion path will be the straight line OB. Of course, if the ratio of prices of factors was initially *w*/*r* and subsequently changes to *w'*/*r'*, the expansion path changes : initially the firm moves along OA, but after the change in the factor prices it moves along OB.

If the production function is **non-homogeneous** the expansion path will not be a straight line, even if the ratio of prices of factors remains constant. This is shown in Figure 24. It is due to the fact that in equilibrium we must equate the (constant) w/r ratio with the MRS_{LK}, which is the same on a curved isocline.

Theory of Costs

Economic theory distinguishes between short-run costs and long-run costs. **Short-run costs** are the costs over a period during which some factors of production are fixed. The **long-run costs** are the costs over a period long enough to permit the change of all factors of production. In the long run all factors become variable.

Both in the short-run and in the long-run, total cost is a multivariable function, that is, total cost is determined by many factors. Symbolically we may write the long-run cost function as

$$C = f(X, T, P_f)$$

and the short-run cost function as

$$C = f(X, T, P_f, \bar{K})$$

where

C = total cost
X = output
T = technology
P_f = prices of factors
$\bar{K}$ = fixed factors

Short-Run Costs of the Traditional Theory

In the traditional theory of the firm total costs are split into two groups : **total fixed costs and total variable costs.**

$$TC = TFC + TVC$$

where

TC = total cost
TFC = total fixed cost
TVC = total variable cost

The **fixed costs include :**

(*a*) salaries of administrative staff
(*b*) depreciation of machinery
(*c*) expenses for building depreciation and repairs
(*d*) expenses for land maintenance

The **variable costs include :**

(*a*) the raw materials
(*b*) the cost of direct labour
(*c*) the running expenses of fixed capital, such as fuel, ordinary repairs and routine maintenance.

The total fixed cost is graphically denoted by a straight line parallel to the output axis (Figure 25).

The total variable cost in the traditional theory of the firm has broadly an inverse-S shape (figure 26) which reflects the **law of variable proportions.** According to this law, at the initial stages of production with a given plant, as more of the variable factor is employed, its productivity increases and the average variable cost falls.

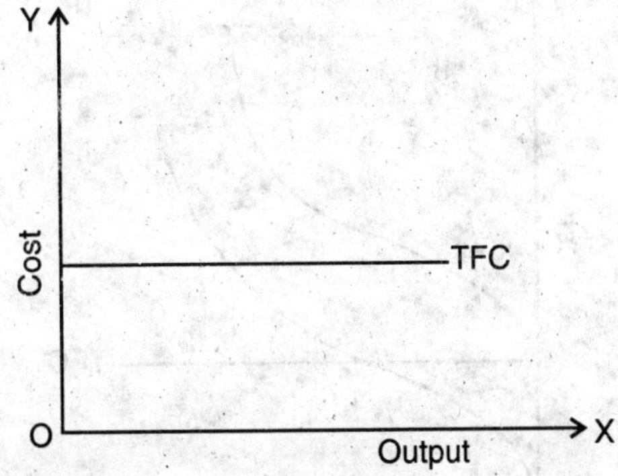

Fig. 25 : *Total Fixed Cost Curve*

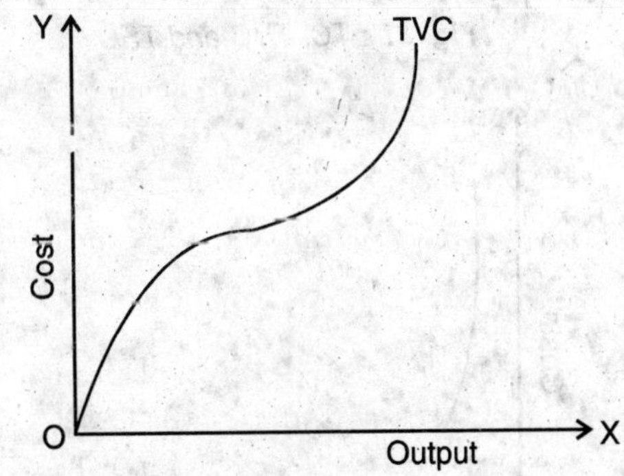

Fig. 26 : *Total Variable Cost Curve*

This continues unit the optimal combination of the fixed and variable factors is reached. Beyond this point as increased qualities of the variable factors are combined with the fixed factor the productivity of the variable factor declines (and the AVC rises). By adding the TFC and TVC we obtain the TC of the firm (Figure 27). From the total-cost curves we obtain **average-cost curves.** The average fixed cost is found by dividing TFC by the level of output. Thus

$$AFC = \frac{TFC}{X}$$

Graphically the AFC is a **rectangular hyperbola,** showing at all its points the same magnitude, that is, the level of TFC (Figure 27). The average variable cost is similarly obtained by dividing the TVC with the corresponding level of output :

$$AVC = \frac{TVC}{X}$$

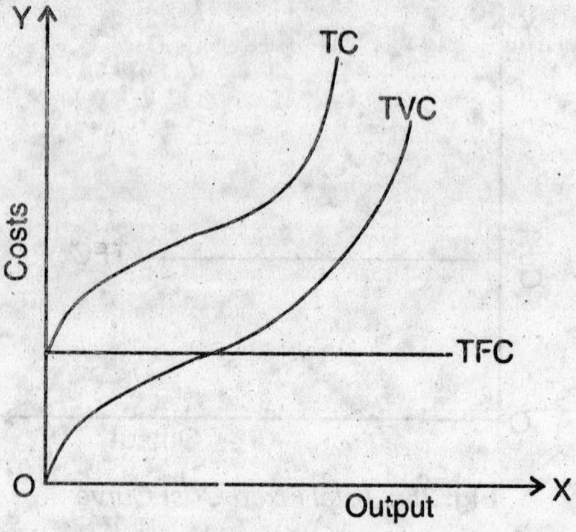

Fig. 27 : *TC, TVC and TFC*

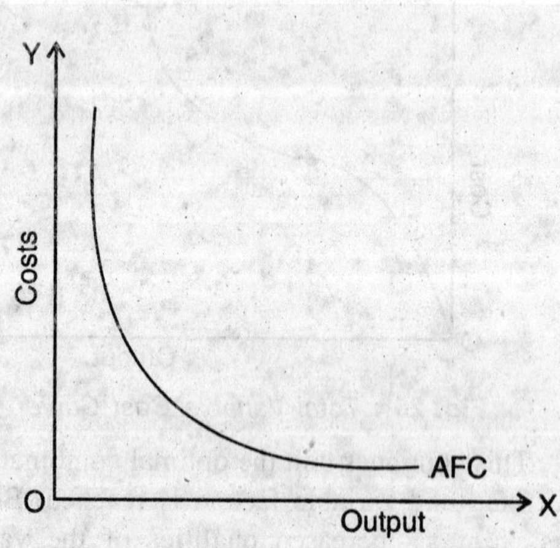

Fig. 28: *Average Fixed Cost Curve*

Graphically the AVC at each level of output is derived from the slopes of a line drawn from the origin to the point on the TVC curve corresponding to the particular level of output. For example, in figure 29 the AVC at X_1 is the slopes of the ray O*a*, the AVC at X_2 is the slope of the ray O*b*, and so on. It is clear from Figure 29 that the slope of a ray through the origin declines continuously until the ray becomes tangent to the TVC curve at C. To the right of this point the slope of rays through the origin starts increasing. Thus the SAVC curve falls initially as the productivity of the variable factor increases, reaches a minimum when the plant is operated optimally and rises beyond that point (Figure 30).

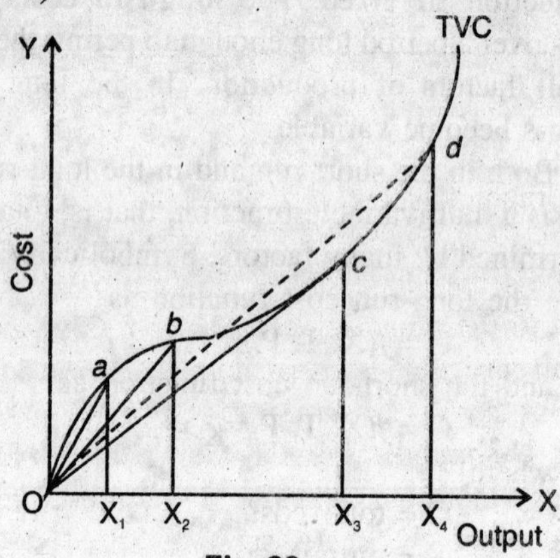

Fig. 29

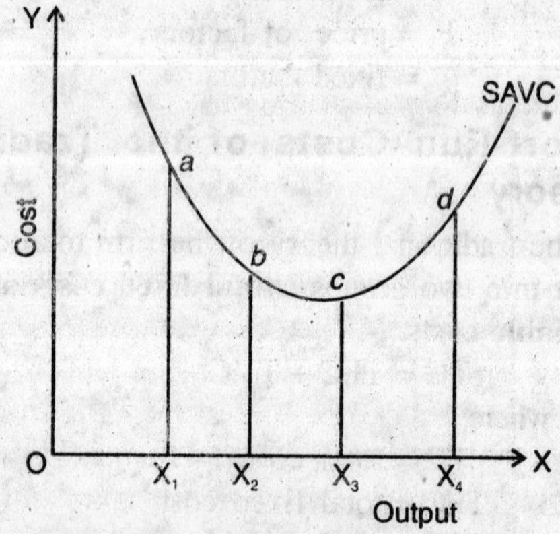

Fig. 30 : *Average Variable Cost*

The ATC is obtained by dividing the TC by the corresponding level of output.

$$ATC = \frac{TC}{X}$$

$$= \frac{TFC + TVC}{X} = AFC + AVC$$

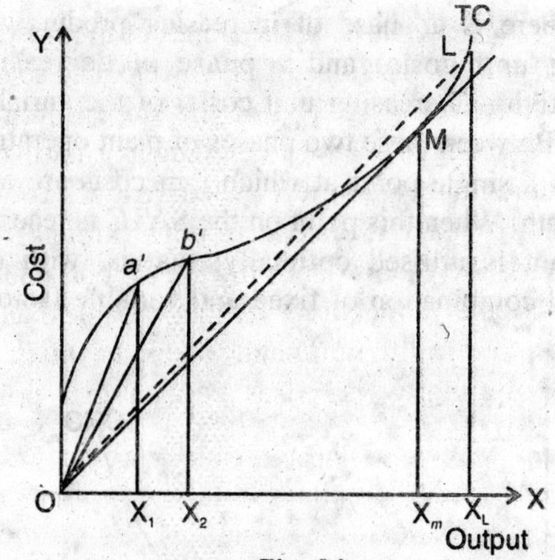

Fig. 31

Graphically the ATC curve is derived in the same way as the SAVC. The ATC at any level of output is the slope of the straight line from the origin to the point on the TC curve corresponding to that particular level of output (Figure 31). The shape of the ATC is similar to that of the AVC **(both being U-shaped).** Initially the ATC declines, it reaches a minimum at the level of optimal operation of the plant (X_m) and subsequently rises again (Figure 32). The **U-shape** of both the AVC and the ATC reflects the **law of variable proportions** or **law of eventually decreasing returns to the variable factors of production.**

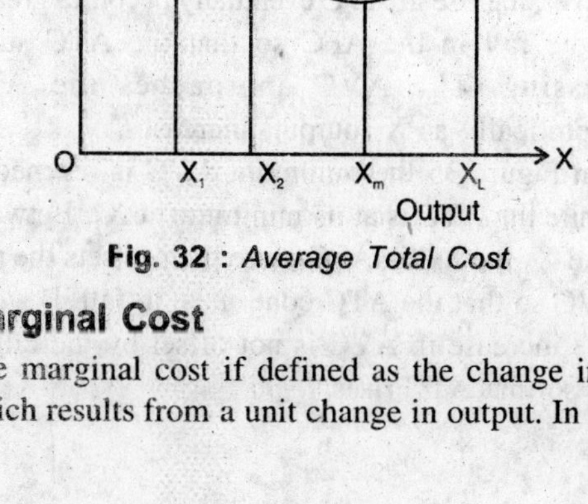

Fig. 32 : *Average Total Cost*

Marginal Cost

The marginal cost if defined as the change in TC which results from a unit change in output. In other words, marginal cost is the addition to the total cost of producing n units instead of $(n - 1)$ units where n is say any given number. In symbols :

$$MC_n = TC_n - TC_{n-1}$$

Mathematically the marginal cost is the first derivative of the TC function. Denoting total cost by TC and output by X we have

$$MC = \frac{dTC}{dX}$$

It is worth pointing out that marginal cost is independent of the fixed cost. Since fixed costs do not change with output, there are no marginal fixed costs when output is increased in the short run. It is only the variable costs that vary with output in the short run. Therefore the marginal costs are infact due to the changes in variable costs, and whatever the amount of fixed cost, the marginal cost if unaffected by it.

The independence of the marginal cost from the fixed cost can be proved algebraically as follows:

$$\begin{aligned} MC_n &= TC_n - TC_{n-1} \\ &= (TVC_n + TFC) - (TVC_{n-1} + TFC) \\ &= TVC_n + TFC - TVC_{n-1} - TFC \\ &= TVC_n - TVC_{n-1} \end{aligned}$$

Hence, **marginal cost is the addition to the total variable costs when output is increased from $n - 1$ units to n units of output.** It follows therefore that the marginal cost is independent of the amount of the fixed costs.

It should be noted that marginal cost of production is intimately related to the marginal product of the variable factor.

As noted above,

$$MC = \frac{dTC}{dX}$$

$$\text{or} \quad MC = \frac{d(TVC)}{dX}$$

Since price of the variable factor, *i.e.,* w is assumed to be constant, the change in total variable cost can occur due to the change in the amount of the variable factor.

$$\text{Therefore, } MC = \frac{wdL}{dX}$$

$$= w.\frac{dL}{dX} \quad ...(1)$$

From above discussion we know that marginal product of the variable factor is the change in total product as a result of the unit change in the variable factor. Thus

$$MP_L = \frac{dX}{dL} \quad \text{or} \quad \frac{1}{MP_L} = \frac{dL}{dX}$$

Substituting $\frac{dL}{dX}$ for $\frac{1}{MP_L}$ in equation (1), we get

$$MC = w.\frac{1}{MP_L}$$

$$\text{or} \quad MC = \frac{w}{MP_L} \quad ...(2)$$

Thus, marginal cost of production is equal to the reciprocal of the marginal product of the variable factor multiplied by the price of variable factor. Therefore, marginal cost varies inversely with the marginal product of the variable factor.

Graphically the MC is the slope of the TC curve (which of course is the same at any point as the slope of the TVC). The slope of a curve at any one of its points is the slope of the tangent at that point. With an inverse-S shape of the TC (and TVC) the MC curve will be U-shaped. In Figure 33 we observe that the slope of the tangent to the total-cost curve declines gradually, until it becomes parallel to the X-axis (with its slope being equal to zero at this point), and then starts rising. Accordingly we picture the MC curve in Figure 34 as **U-shaped.**

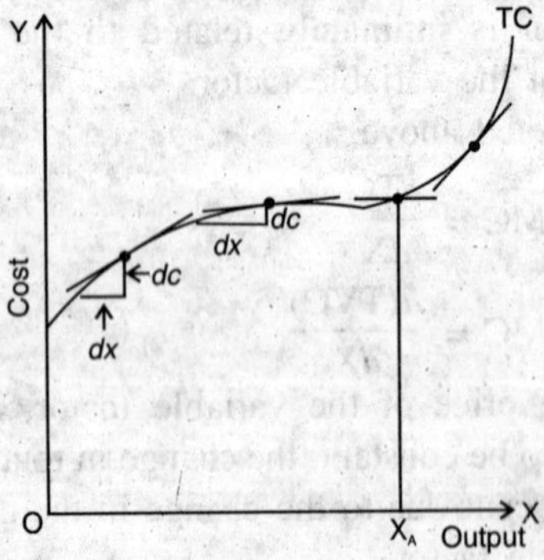

Fig. 33

In Summary : the traditional theory of costs postulates that in the short run the cost curves (AVC, ATC and MC) are **U-shaped,** reflecting the **law of variable proportions.** In the short run with a fixed plant there is a phase of increasing productivity (falling unit costs) and a phase of decreasing productivity (increasing unit costs) of the variable factor. Between these two phases of plant operation there is a single point at which unit costs are at a minimum. When this point on the SATC is reached the plant is utilised optimally, that is, with the optimal combination of fixed and variable factors.

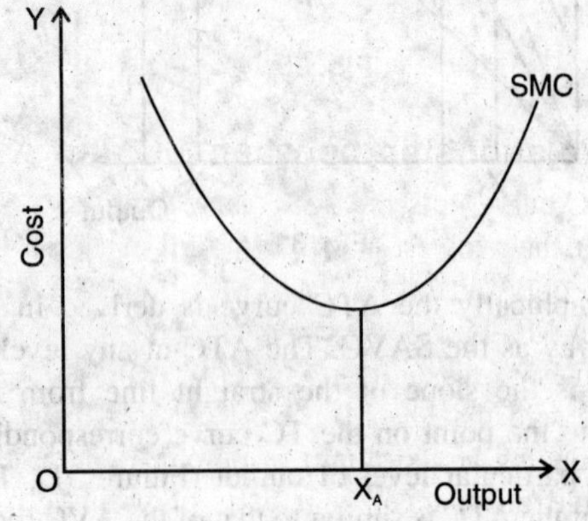

Fig. 34 : *Marginal Cost*

The Relationship Between ATC and AVC

The AVC is a part of the ATC, given ATC = AFC + AVC. Both AVC and ATC are U-shaped, reflecting the law of variable proportions. However, the minimum point of the ATC occurs to the right of the minimum point of the AVC (Figure 35). This is due to the fact that ATC includes AFC, and the latter falls continuously with increase in output. After the AVC has reached its lowest point and starts rising, its rise is over a certain range offset by the fall in the AFC, so that the ATC continues to fall (over that range) despite the increase in AVC. However, the rise in AVC eventually becomes greater than the fall in the AFC so that the ATC starts increasing. The AVC approaches the ATC asymptotically as X (output) increases.

In Figure 35 the minimum AVC is reached at X, while the ATC is at its minimum at X_2. Between X_1 and X_2 the fall in AFC more than offsets the rise in AVC so that the ATC continues to fall. Beyond X_2 the increase in AVC is not offset by the fall in AFC, so that ATC rises.

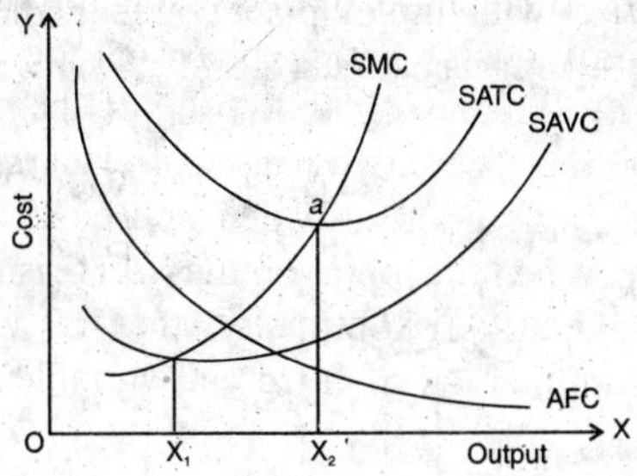

Fig. 35

The Relationship between MC and ATC

The MC-curve cuts the ATC-curve and the AVC-curve at their lowest points. We will establish this relation only for the ATC and MC, but the relation between MC and AVC can be established on the same lines of reasoning.

We said that the MC is the change in the TC for producing an extra unit of output. Assume that we start from a level of *n* units of output. If we increase the output by one unit the MC is the change in total cost resulting from the production of the (*n* + 1)th unit.

The AC at each level of output is found by dividing TC by X (output). Thus the AC at the level of X_n is

$$AC_n = \frac{TC_n}{X_n}$$

and the AC at the level X_{n+1} is

$$AC_{n+1} = \frac{TC_{n+1}}{X_{n+1}}$$

Clearly

$$TC_{n+1} = TC_n + MC$$

Thus :

(*a*) If the MC of the (*n* + 1)th unit is less than AC_n (the AC of the previous *n* units) the AC_{n+1} will be smaller than the AC_n.

(*b*) If the MC of the (*n* + 1)th unit is higher than AC_n (the AC of the previous *n* units) the AC_{n+1} will be higher than the AC_n.

So long as the MC lies below the AC-curve, it pulls the latter downwards, when the MC rises above the AC, it pulls the latter upwards. In figure 35 to the left of *a* the MC lies below the AC curve, and hence the latter falls downwards. To the right of *a* the MC-curve lie above the AC curve, so that AC rises. It follows that at point *a,* where the intersection of the MC and AC occurs, the AC has reached its minimum level.

The relationship between the MC and AC curves becomes clearer with the use of simple calculus. Given C = ZX

where C = total cost

Z = average cost

X = output

Clearly

$$Z = f(X)$$

The MC is

$$\frac{dC}{dX} = \frac{d(ZX)}{d(X)}$$

Applying the rule of differentiation of **'a function of a function'** (which states that if $y = uv$, where $u = f_1(X)$ and $v = f_2(X)$, then $\frac{dY}{dX} = \frac{dY}{dU} \cdot \frac{dU}{dX}$), we obtain

$$MC = \frac{dC}{dX} = Z\frac{dX}{dX} + X\frac{dZ}{dX}$$

or $\quad MC = AC + (X).\ (\text{Slope of AC})$

Given that AC > 0 and X > 0, the following results emerge :

(*a*) If slope of AC < 0, then MC < AC.

(*b*) If slope of AC > 0, then MC > AC.

(*c*) If slope of AC = 0, then MC = AC.

The slope of the AC becomes zero at the minimum point of this curve (given that on the theoretical grounds the AC curve is U-shaped). Hence, MC = AC at the minimum point of the average cost curve.

Long-Run Costs of the Traditional Theory : The 'Envelope' Curve

In the long run all factors are assumed to become variable. We said that the long-run cost curve is a **planning curve,** in the sense that it is a guide to the entrepreneur in his decision to plan the future expansion of his output.

The long run average-cost is derived from short-run cost curves. Each point on the LAC corresponds to a point on a short-run cost curve, which is tangent to the LAC at that point.

Long-run average cost curve depicts the least possible average cost for producing all possible levels of output. In order to understand how the long-run average cost curve is derived, consider the three short-run average cost curves as shown in Figure 36. These short-run average cost curves are also called **plant curves,** since in the short-run plant is fixed and each of the short-run average cost curve corresponds to a particular plants. In the short run, the firm can be operating on any short-run average cost curve, given the size of plant. Suppose that only these three are technically possible sizes of plants and that no other size of the plant can be built. Given the size of the plant or short run average cost curve the firm will increase or decrease its output by varying the amount of the variable inputs. But in the long-run, the firm can choose among the three possible sizes of plant as depicted by short-run average cost curves SAC_1, SAC_2 and SAC_3. In the long run the firm will examine that with which size of plant or on which short-run average cost curve it should operate to produce a given levels of output at the minimum possible cost.

It will be seen from Figure 37 that upto OB amount of output, the firm will operate on the short-run average cost curve SAC_1, though it could also produce with short-run average cost curve SAC_2, because upto OB amount of output, production on SAC_1 curve entails lower cost than on SAC_2. If the firm plans to produce an output which is larger than OB (but less than OD), then it will not be economical to produce on SAC_1. It will be seen from Figure 36 that the outputs larger than OB (but less than OD), can be produced at a lower cost per unit on SAC_2 than on SAC_1. Thus, the output OC is produced on SAC_2 costs CK per unit which is lower than CJ which is the cost incurred when produced on SAC_1. Therefore, if the firm plants to produce between outputs OB and OD, it will employ the plant corresponding to short-run average cost curve SAC_2. If the firm has to produce an output which exceeds OD, then the cost per unit will be lower on SAC_3 than on SAC_2. Therefore, for outputs larger than OD, the firm will employ plant corresponding to the short-run average cost curve SAC_3.

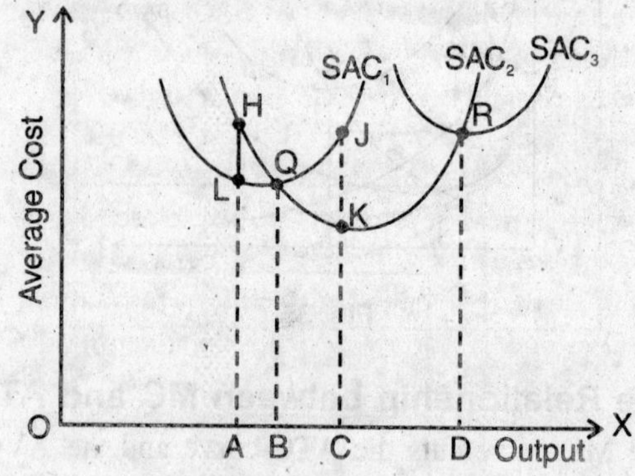

Fig. 36 : *Plant Curves*

It is thus clear that in the long-run the firm has a choice in the employment of a plant, and it will employ that plant which yields possible minimum unit cost for producing a given output. The long run average cost curve depicts the least possible average cost for producing various levels of output when all factors including the size of the plant have been adjusted.

Now if we relax the assumption of the existence of only three plants and assume that the available technology includes many plant sizes, each suitable for a certain level of output, the point of intersection of consecutive plants (which are the crucial points for the decision of whether to switch to a larger plant) are more numerous. In the limits, If we assume that there is a very large number (infinite number) of plants, we obtain a continuous curve, which is the planning LAC-curve of the firm. Each point of this curve shows the minimum (optimal) cost for producing the corresponding level of output. **The LAC-curve is the locus of points denoting the least cost of producing the corresponding output.** It is a planning curve because on the basis of this curve the firm decides what plant to set up in order to produce optimally (at minimum cost) the expected level of output. The firm chooses the short-run plant which allows it to produce the anticipated (in the long-run) output at the least possible cost. In the traditional theory of the firm the LAC-curve is U-shaped and it is often called the **'envelope curve'** because it **'envelopes'** the SAC-curve (Figure 37).

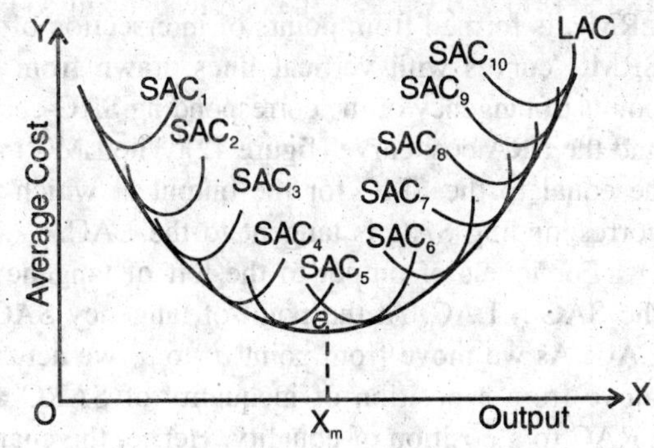

Fig. 37 : *Long-Run Average Cost Curve*

An important fact about the long-run average cost curve is worth mentioning. It is that the long-run average curve LAC is not tangent to the minimum point of the short-run average cost curves. When the long-run average cost curve is declining, that is, for output less than OX_m, it is tangent to the falling portions of the short-run average cost curves.

On the other hand, when the long-run average cost curve is rising, it will be tangent to the rising portions of the short-run average cost curves.

Long-Run Average Cost Curve in Constant Cost Case

If the production function is linear and homogeneous (that is, homogeneous of the first degree) and also the prices of inputs remain constant, then the long-run average cost will remain constant at all levels of output. Linear homogeneous production function implies **constant returns to scale** which means that when all inputs are increased in a certain proportion, the output increases in the same proportion.

Therefore, with the given prices of inputs, when returns to scale are constant, the cost per unit of output remains the same. In this case, the long-run average cost curve will be a horizontal straight line as depicted in Figure 38.

In such a case, **the optimum size of the firm is indeterminate,** since all levels of output can be produced at the same long-run average cost which represents the same minimum short-run average costs throughout.

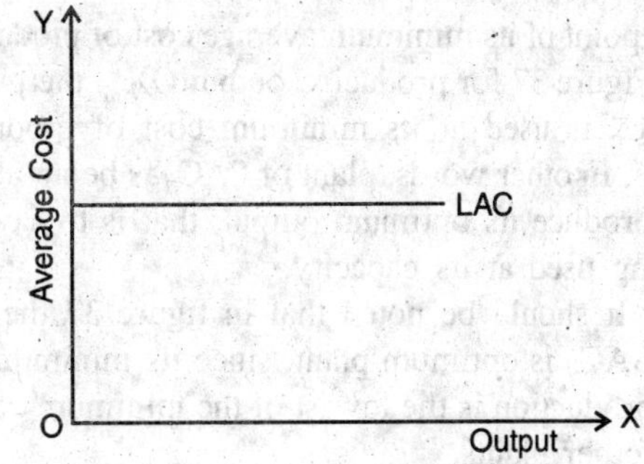

Fig. 38 : *Long-Run Average Cost Curve : Constant Costs, Constant Returns*

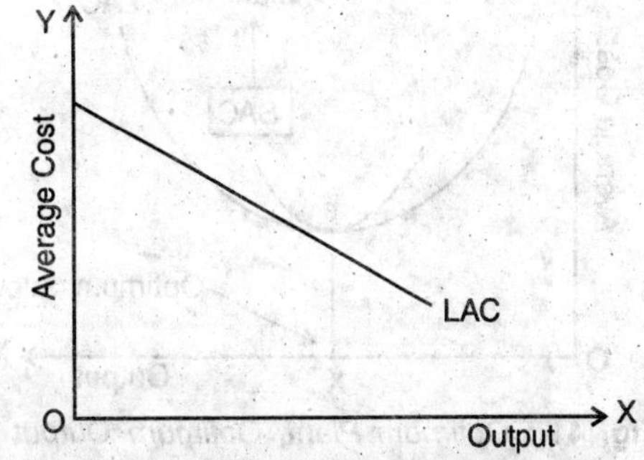

Fig. 39 : *Long-Run Average Cost Curve : Decreasing Costs, Increasing Returns*

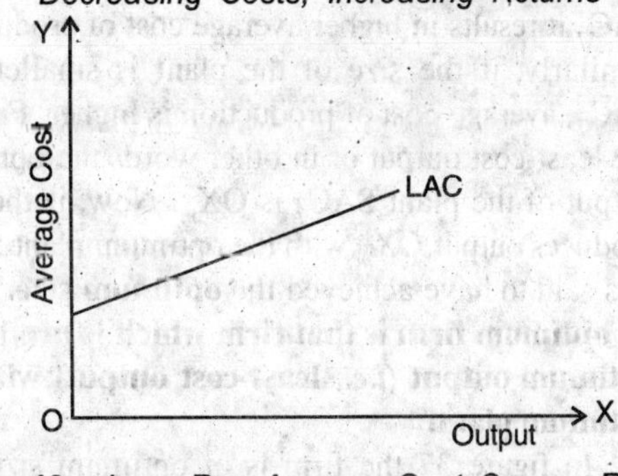

Fig. 40 : *Long-Run Average Cost Curve : Rising Costs, Decreasing Returns*

Optimum Plant, Optimum Output and Optimum Firm

It is clear from Figure 37 that in the continuous long-run average cost curve both for outputs less than OX_m and more than OX_m no plant is used at its point of minimum cost. It is only the plant, the minimum point of whose short-run average cost curve coincides with the minimum point of the long-run average cost-curve, which is operated at the point of its minimum average cost of production. In Figure 37 for producing output OX_m, the plant of SAC_7 is used at its minimum cost of production $X_m e$. In other words, plant of SAC_7 is being utilized to produce its optimum output, that is to say, it is being used at its capacity.

It should be noted that in figure 37 the plant of SAC_7 is optimum plant, since its minimum cost of production is the lowest of the minimum costs of all other plants.

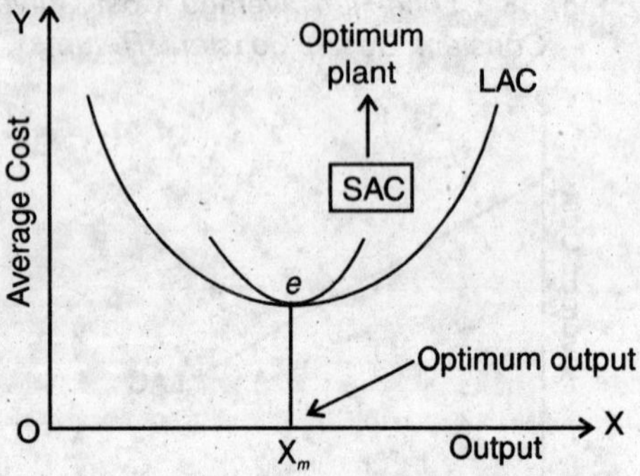

Fig. 41 : *Optimum Plant, Optimum Output And Optimum Firm*

If the size of the plant is increased beyond SAC_7 it results in higher average cost of production. Similarly, if the size of the plant is smaller than SAC_7, average cost of production is higher. Further, the least-cost output or in other words the optimum output of the plant SAC_7 is OX_m. Now, if the firm produces output OX_m with the optimum plant SAC_7, it is said to have achieved the **optimum size.** Thus, **an optimum firm is that firm which is producing optimum output *(i.e.,* least-cost output) with the optimum plant.**

In figure 37 the firm is of optimum size if it employs plant SAC_7 and uses it to produce OX_m. But the point of minimum cost of the optimum plant (SAC_7) coincides with the minimum point of the long-run average cost curve. Therefore, the optimum firm can also be defined as one which produces at the minimum point of the long-run average cost curve (LAC).

Long-Run Marginal Cost Curve

The long-run marginal cost is derived from the SRMC curves, but does not **'envelope'** them. The LRMC is formed from points of intersection of the SRMC curves with vertical lines drawn from the points of tangency of the corresponding SAC-curves and the LRA cost curve (figure 42). The LMC must be equal to the SMC for the output at which the corresponding SAC is tangent to the LAC.

For levels of output to the left of tangency *a* the SAC > LAC. At the point of tangency SAC = LAC. As we move from point *a'* to *a,* we actually move from a position of inequality of SARC and LRAC to a position of equality. Hence, the change in total cost (*i.e.,* the MC) must be smaller for the short-run curve than for the long-run curve. Thus, LMC > SMC to the left of *a*. For an increase in output beyond X_1 (*e.g.,* X_1'') the SAC > LAC. That is, we move from the position *a* of equality of the two costs to the position *b* where SAC is greater than LAC. Hence, the addition to total cost (= MC) must be larger for the short-run curve than for the long-run curve. Thus, LMC < SMC to the right of *a*.

Since to the lest of *a,* LMC > SMC, and to the right of *a,* LMC < SMC, it follows that at *a,* LMC = SMC. If we draw a vertical line from *a* to the X-axis the point at which it intersects the SMC (point A for SAC_1) is a point of the LMC.

If we repeat this procedure for all points of tangency of SRAC and LAC curves to the left of the minimum point of the LAC, we obtain points of the section of the LMC which lies below the LAC. At the minimum point M the LMC intersects the LAC. To the right of M the LMC lies above the LAC curve. At point M we have

$$SAC_m = SMC_m = LAC = LMC$$

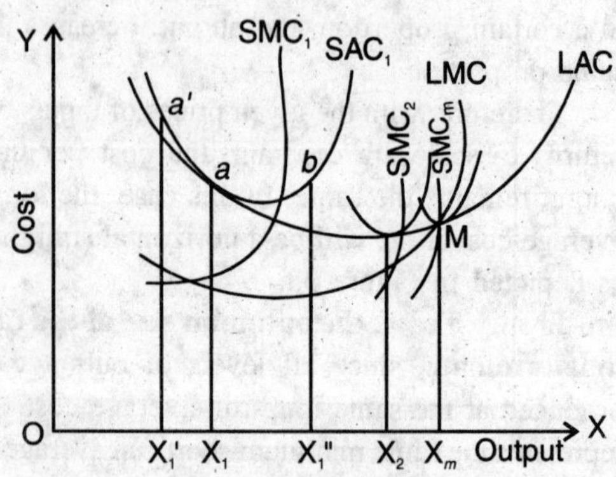

Fig. 42 : *Long-Run Marginal Cost Curve*

The TC curve is roughly S-shaped, while the ATC, the AVC and the MC are all U-shaped, the MC curve intersects the other two curves at their minimum points.

Empirical Evidence And L-Shaped Long-Run Average Cost Curve

Some economists argue on the basis of empirical evidence that the long-run average cost curve is **L-shaped,** rather than U-shaped, as in Figure 43. The L-shaped curve shows a rapid fall in the beginning but after a point "the curve remains flat, or may slope gently downwards, at its right-hand end." The difference between L-shaped LAC and the U-shaped LAC is that there is no rising portion in the former. Figure 43 shows a flat LAC curve and Figure 44 depicts a gently sloping downwards curve LAC at its right-hand end.

The following two explanations have been provided for the existence of L-shaped long-run average cost curve.

1. Technological Progress : One reason, why empirical studies do not find U-shaped long run average cost curve is that whereas economic theory assumes that technology remains unchanged or there is no technological progress, but, in the real world, technological progress does take place over time. As a result of technological progress in the real world, long-run average cost curve will shift downwards over time. The empirical investigations which are conducted at different points of time would not find the rising average cost, in view of the existence of technological progress.

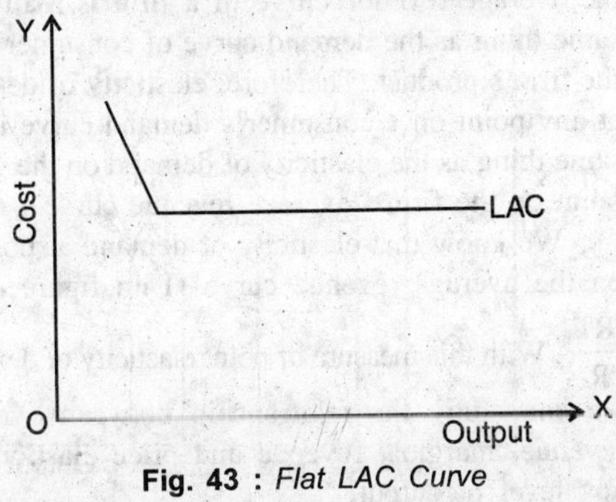

Fig. 43 : *Flat LAC Curve*

The L-shaped long-run average cost curve (LAC) is explained in Figure 44. Suppose the firm is producing OQ_1 output on LAC_1 curve at a per unit cost of OC_1. If there is an increase in demand for the firm product to OQ_2, with no change in technology, the firm will produce OQ_2 output along the LAC_1 curve at a per unit cost OC_4. If, however, there is technical progress in the firm, it will install a new plant having LAC_2 as the long-run average cost curve. On this plant, it produces OQ_2 output as a lower cost OC_2 per unit. Similarly, if the firm decides to increase its output to OQ_3 to meet further rise in demand. technical progress may have advanced to such a level that it installs the plant with the LAC_3 curve.

Now it produces OQ_3 output at still lower cost OC_3 per unit. If the minimum points L, M and N of these U-shaped long-run average cost curves LAC_1, LAC_2 and LAC_3 are joined by a line, it forms a gently sloping downwards curve LAC. Thus in a given state of technology, the long-run average cost curves are U-shaped. But when there is technical progress, the long-run average cost curve is L-shaped.

2. Learning by Doing : Learning by doing is another factor which causes the long-run average cost to slope downwards throughout. It is now common knowledge that a person learns while doing some productive work. The greater the amount of work he has done since the time he started doing a particular work, the greater the experience he attains and with the experience he learns to do thing in a better way than before. This tends to reduce the costs.

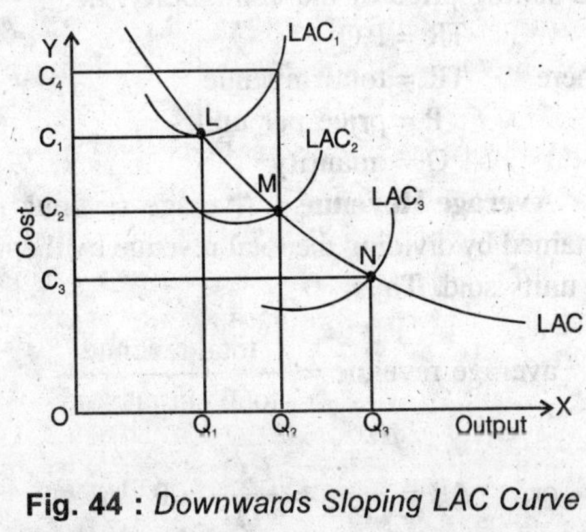

Fig. 44 : *Downwards Sloping LAC Curve*

Elasticity of Cost

If output (Q) is produced at a total cost (C), the cost function is

$$C = f(Q).$$

The elasticity of total cost is the ratio of the proportional change in total cost to the proportional change in total output. It may be written as

$$\text{Cost Elasticity (K)} = \frac{dC/C}{dQ/Q}$$

$$= \frac{dC}{C} \times \frac{Q}{dQ} = \frac{dC}{dQ} \times \frac{Q}{C} = \frac{dC}{dQ} \div \frac{C}{Q}$$

$$= \frac{MC}{AC} = \frac{\text{Marginal cost}}{\text{Average cost}}$$

Thus, cost elasticity (K) is equal to the ratio of marginal cost (*d*C/*d*Q) to average cost (C/Q). It follows from this that

(a) If MC > AC, then K > 1

(b) If MC = AC, then K = 1 and

(c) If MC < AC, then K < 1.

The Concept of Revenue

The term 'revenue' refers to the receipts obtained by a firm from the sale of certain quantities of a commodity at various prices. The revenue concept relates to total revenue, average revenue and marginal revenue.

Total Revenue : Total revenue refers to the total amount of money that the firm receives from the sale of its products. Thus, the total revenue is obviously equal to the quantity sold multiplied by the selling price of the commodity, *i.e.*,

TR = P.Q

where TR = total revenue

P = price per unit

Q = quantity

Average Revenue : Average revenue can be obtained by dividing the total revenue by the number of units sold. Thus,

$$\text{average revenue} = \frac{\text{total revenue}}{\text{total output sold}}$$

$$\text{or,} \quad AR = \frac{TR}{Q} = \frac{P.Q}{Q} = P$$

Thus, average revenue is the price of commodity. It follows from this that the curve which relates average revenue to output is identical with the demand curve that relates price to output.

Marginal Revenue : Marginal revenue is the net revenue earned by selling on additional unit of the product. In other words, marginal revenue is the addition made to the total revenue by selling one more unit of the good. Putting it in algebraic expression marginal revenue is the addition made to total revenue by selling *n* units of a product instead of (*n* – 1) where *n* is any given number. Therefore,

Marginal Revenue = difference in total revenue in increasing sales from (*n* – 1) units to *n* units

$$MR_n = TR_n - TR_{n-1}$$

If TR stands for total revenue and Q stands for output, then marginal revenue (MR) can be expressed as follows :

$$MR = \frac{d(TR)}{dQ}$$

indicates the slope of the total revenue curve. Thus, if the total revenue curve is given to us, we can find out marginal revenue at various levels of output by measuring the slopes at the corresponding points on the total revenue curve.

Average Revenue, Marginal Revenue and Elasticity of Demand

There is a very useful relationship between elasticity of demand, average revenue and marginal revenue at any level of output. We have stressed above that the average revenue curve of a firm is really the same thing as the demand curve of consumer's for the firm's product. Therefore, elasticity of demand at any point on a consumer's demand curve is the same thing as the elasticity of demand on the given point on the firm's average revenue curve.

We know that elasticity of demand at point R on the average revenue curve *t*T in figure 45 is $\frac{RT}{Rt}$. With this measure of point elasticity of demand we can study the relationship between average revenue, marginal revenue and price elasticity at any level of output.

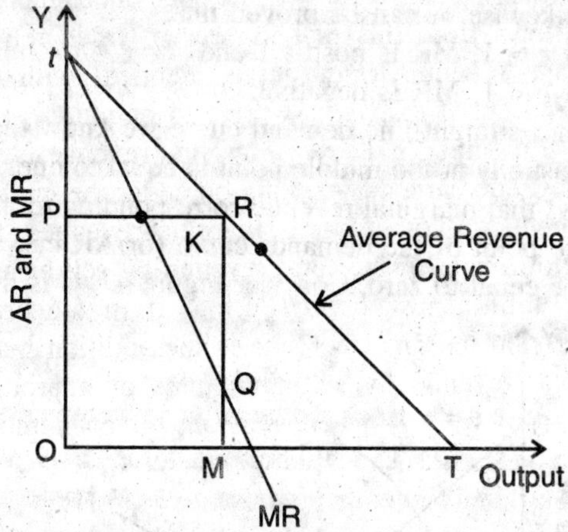

Fig. 45

In Figure 45, AR and MR are respectively average and marginal revenue curves. Elasticity of demand at point R on the average revenue curve :

$$= \frac{RT}{Tt}$$

Now in triangles P*t*R and MRT

$\angle tPR = \angle RMT$ (right angles)

$\angle tRP = \angle RTM$ (corresponding angles)

and $PtR = \angle MRT$

Therefore, triangles P*t*R and MRT are equiangular.

$$\text{Hence, } \frac{RT}{Rt} = \frac{RM}{Pt} \qquad ...(1)$$

In the triangles P*t*K and KRQ

PK = RK

$\angle PKt = \angle RKQ$ (vertically opposite)

$\angle tPK = \angle KRQ$ (right angles)

Therefore, triangles P*t*K and KRQ are congruent (*i.e.,* equal in all respects).

Hence, $Pt = RQ$ ...(2)

From (1) and (2), we get

$$\text{Elasticity at R} = \frac{RT}{Rt} = \frac{RM}{Pt} = \frac{RM}{RQ}$$

Now it is obvious from Figure 45 that

$$\frac{RM}{RQ} = \frac{RM}{RM - QM}$$

$$\text{Hence, elasticity at R} = \frac{RM}{RM-QM}$$

It will also be clear from the figure that RM is average revenue and QM is the marginal revenue at the output OM which corresponds to the point R on the average revenue curve. Therefore,

Elasticity at

$$R = \frac{\text{Average Revenue}}{\text{Average Revenue} - \text{Marginal Revenue}}$$

If, A stands for average revenue

M stands for marginal revenue

e stands for point elasticity on the average revenue curve.

$$\text{then} \quad e = \frac{A}{A-M}$$

It follows from this that

$e.A - e.M = A; \quad \Rightarrow e.A - A = e.M$

$$\Rightarrow A(e-1) = e.M; \quad \Rightarrow A = \frac{e.M}{e-1}$$

$$\text{Hence, } A = M\left(\frac{e}{e-1}\right)$$

And also,

$$M = A\left(\frac{e-1}{e}\right)$$

If the demand elasticity is equal to one then

$$MR = AR\left(\frac{e-1}{e}\right) = AR\left(\frac{1-1}{e}\right)$$

$$= AR \times 0 = 0$$

If $e > 1$, Say 2, then

$$MR = AR\left(\frac{2-1}{2}\right)$$

$$MR = \frac{1}{2}.AR$$

$$MR = AR - \frac{AR}{2}$$

MR = Positive

If $e < 1$, Say 1/2, then

$$MR = AR\left(\frac{1/2-1}{1/2}\right)$$

MR = AR − 2AR

MR = Negative

Hence, by applying the formula for various elasticities of demand at different points (or at different levels of output) on the average revenue curve it will be found that marginal revenue is always positive at any point or output where the elasticity of the average revenue curve is greater than one and marginal revenue is always negative where the elasticity of the average revenue curve is less than one.

In case the elasticity of the AR curve is unity throughout its length like a rectangular hyperbola, the MR curve will coincide with the X-axis, shown as a dotted line in figure 46.

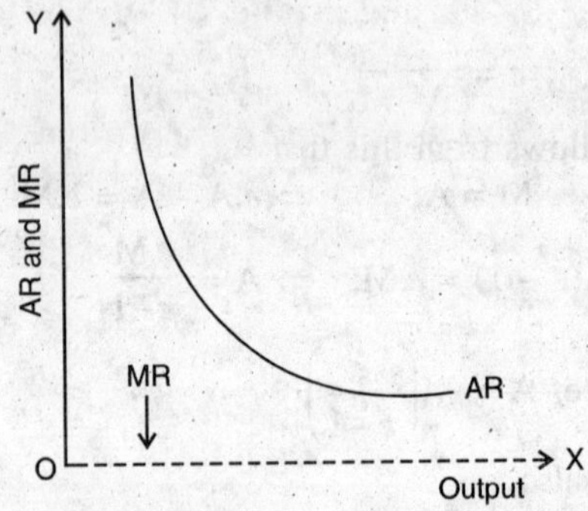

Fig. 46 : *Rectangular Hyperbola AR Curve*

Three Types of Revenue (AR, MR, TR) and Elasticity (e)

We are now in a position to describe the relationship between three types of revenue, namely, AR, MR and TR on the one side and elasticity on the other. From the formula

$$MR = AR\left(\frac{e-1}{e}\right)$$

We can know what would be the marginal revenue, if elasticity and AR are given to us. When the elasticity is equal to one, it follows from the above formula that marginal revenue will be equal to zero.

Thus, $MR = AR\left(\frac{e-1}{e}\right)$

$$MR = AR\left(\frac{1-1}{1}\right)$$

$$MR = AR \times 0$$

$$MR = 0$$

Likewise, it can be proved that,

If $e > 1$, MR is positive, and

If $e < 1$, MR is negative.

In a straight-line demand curve we know that the elasticity at the middle point is equal to one. It follows that marginal revenue corresponding to the middle point of the demand curve (or AR curve) will be equal to zero. Consider Figure 47. C is the

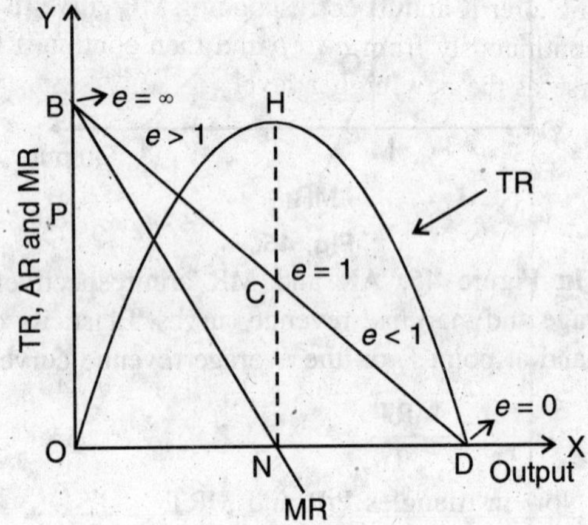

Fig. 47

middle point of the average revenue or demand curve AR. At point C elasticity is equal to one. Corresponding to C on the AR curve, marginal revenue will be zero. Thus MR curve is shown cutting the X-axis at point N which corresponds to point C on the AR curve. At a greater quantity than ON elasticity of the AR curve is less than one and the marginal revenue is negative. Marginal revenue being negative beyond ON means that total revenue will diminish if a quantity greater than ON is sold. Total revenue will be increasing upto ON output, since upto this marginal revenue remains positive. It follows therefore that **total revenue will be maximum where elasticity is equal to one.** This TR curve in this figure is shown to be at its highest level corresponding to the point C on AR curve or ON output where marginal revenue is zero and elasticity is equal to one.

Kinked Demand Curve and their Corresponding MR Curves

Under Oligopoly, the average and marginal revenue curves do not have a smooth downward slope. They possess Kinks. Since the number of sellers under Oligopoly is small, the effect of a price cut or price increase on the part of one seller will be followed by some changes in the behaviour of other firms. If a seller raises the price of his product, the other sellers will not follow him in order to earn larger profits at the old price. So the price-raising seller will experience a fall in the demand for his product. His average revenue curve in Figure 48 becomes elastic after K and its corresponding MR curve rises discontinuously from *a* to *b* and then continues its course at the new higher level.

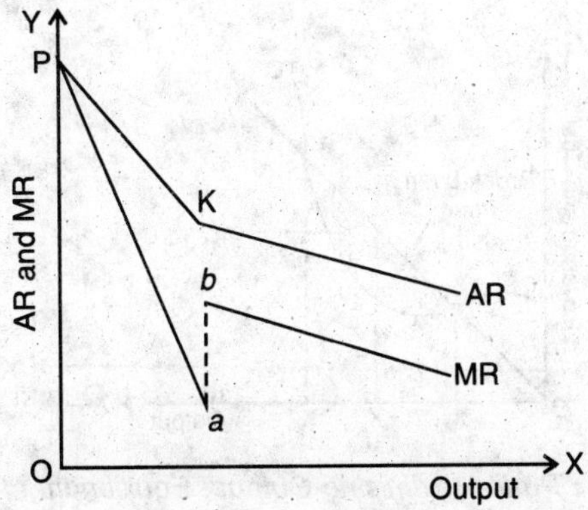

Fig. 48 : *Kinked AR Curve*

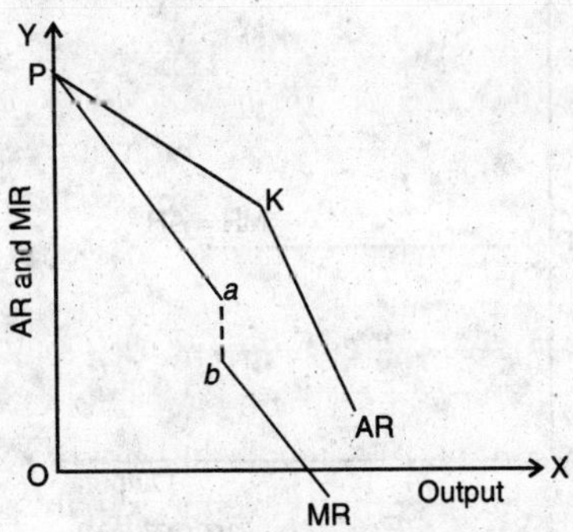

Fig. 49

On the other hand, if the Oligopolistic seller reduces the price of his product, his rivals also follow him in reducing the prices of their product so that he is not able to increase his sales. His AR curve becomes less elastic from K onwards as in Figure 49. The corresponding MR curve falls vertically from *a* to *b* and then slopes at *a* lower level.

Importance of Revenue Curves

The AR and MR curves form important tools for economic analysis. The AR curve is the price line for the producer in all market situations. By relating the AR curve to the AC curve of a firm, it can be found out whether it is earning supernormal or normal profits or incurring losses. If the AR curve is tangent to the AC curve at the point of equilibrium, the firm earns **normal profits.** If the AR curve is above the AC curve, it makes **supernormal profits.** In case the AR curve is below the AC curve at the equilibrium point, the firm incurs losses.

It can also be known from their relationship whether the firm is producing at its full capacity or under capacity. If the AR curve is tangent to the AC curve at its minimum point, (as under perfect competition) the firm produces at its **full capacity.** Where it is not so (as under imperfect competition), the firm possesses **idle capacity.**

The MR curve when intersected by the MC curve determined the equilibrium position of the firm under all market situations. Their point of intersection infact determines price, output, profit or loss of a firm.

Market Classification on the Basis of Cross Elasticity of Demand

Market Form	*Cross Elasticity of Demand*
1. Perfect Competition	Cross elasticity is infinite ($e_c = \infty$)
2. Monopolistic Competition	Cross elasticity is very high
3. Monopoly	Cross elasticity (e_c) is very low or zero

❑❑❑

Chapter 4

Forms of Market and Price Determination

PERFECT COMPETITION

Perfect competition is a market structure characterised by a complete absence of rivalry among the individual firms. In other words, perfect competition implies no rivalry among firms.

Assumptions

The model of perfect competition is based on the following assumptions.

1. There are a large number of firms producing and selling a product.
2. The product of all firms is homogeneous. The assumptions of large numbers of sellers and of product homogeneity imply that the individual firm in perfect competition is a **price-taker :** Its demand curve is infinitely elastic, indicating that the firm can sell any amount of output at the prevailing market price (Figure 1). The demand curve of the individual firm is also its average revenue curve and its marginal revenue curve.
3. Both the sellers and buyers have perfect information about the prevailing price in the market.
4. Entry into and exit from the industry is free for the firms.
5. No government regulation.
6. Perfect mobility of factors of production.

Equilibrium of the Firm in the Short Run : By Curves of Total Revenue and Total Cost

The firm is in equilibrium when it maximises its profits (π), defined as the difference between the total cost and total revenue.

$$\pi = TR - TC$$

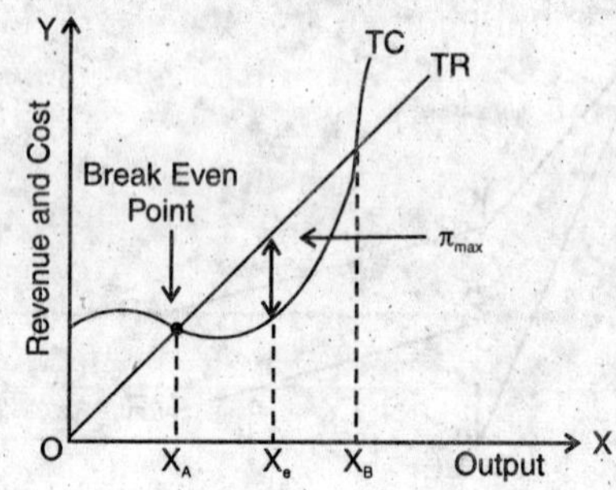

Fig. 1 : *Profit-Maximising Output : Equilibrium of the Firm*

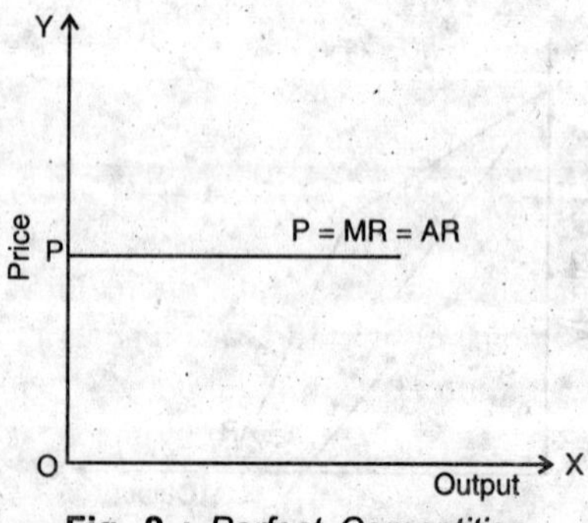

Fig. 2 : *Perfect Competition*

Given that the normal rate of profit is included in the cost items of the firm, π is the profit above the normal rate of return on capital and the remuneration for the risk-bearing function of the entrepreneur. The firm is in equilibrium when it produces the output that maximises that difference between total receipt and total costs. The equilibrium of the firm may be shown graphically in two ways, either by using the TR and TC curves, or the MR and MC curves.

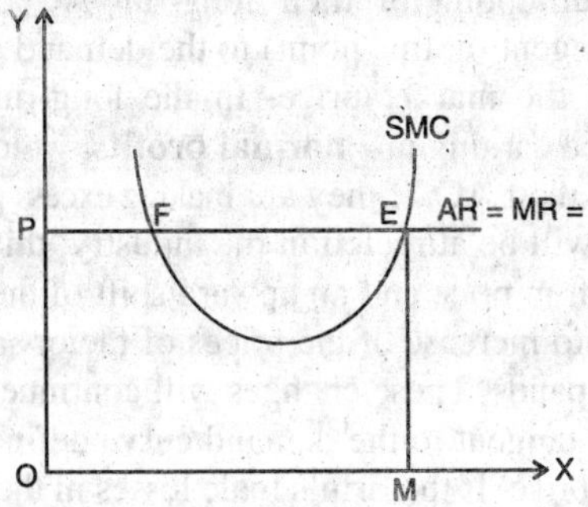

Fig. 3 : *Firm's Equilibrium Under Perfect Competition*

In figure 1 we show the total revenue and total cost curves of a firm in a perfectly competitive market. The total revenue curve is a straight line through the origin, showing that the price is constant at all levels of output. The firm is a **price-taker** and can sell any amount of output at the going market price, with its TR increasing proportionately with its sales. The slope of the TR curve is the marginal revenue. It is constant and equal to the prevailing market price, since all units are sold at the same price. Thus in pure competition MR = AR = P.

The shape of the total-cost curve reflects the U shape of the average-cost curve, that is, the law of variable proportions. The firm maximises its profit at the output, X_e, where the distance between the TR and TC curves is the greatest. At lower and higher levels of output total profits is not maximised : at levels smaller than X_A and larger than X_B the firm has losses.

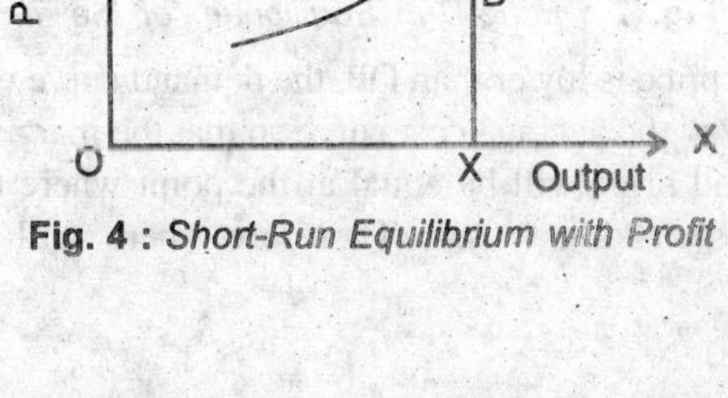

Fig. 4 : *Short-Run Equilibrium with Profit*

Equilibrium of the Firm : By Curves of Marginal Revenue and Marginal Cost (Identical Cost Conditions)

Identical cost conditions imply that all firms are facing same cost conditions, that is, their average and marginal cost curves are of the same level and shapes.

In Figure 3 we show the average and marginal-cost curves of the firm together with its demand curve.

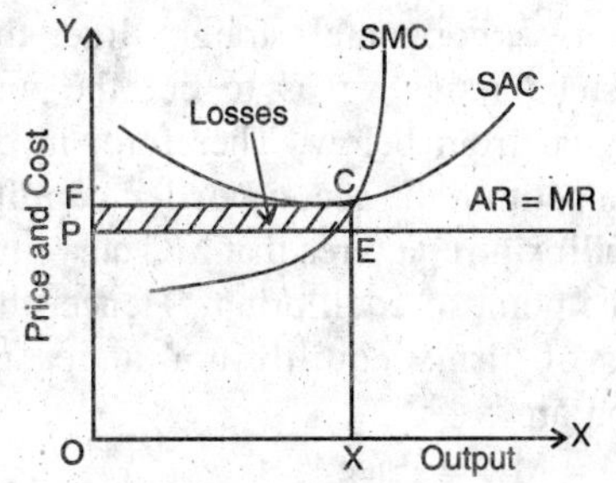

Fig. 5 : *Short-Run Equilibrium with losses*

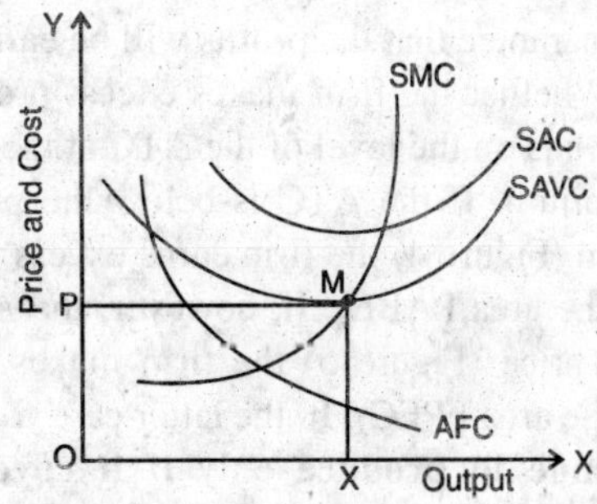

Fig. 6 : *Shut-Down Point for the Perfectly Competitive Firm*

In order to decide about its equilibrium output, the firm will compare marginal cost with marginal revenue. It will be in equilibrium at the level of output at which marginal cost equals marginal revenue and marginal cost curve is curing marginal revenue curve from below. At this level it will be maximising its profits. Consider Figure 3 in which price OP is prevailing in the market. PL would then be the demand curve or the average and marginal revenue curve of the firm. It will be seen from figure 3 that MC curve cuts average and marginal revenue curve at two different points, F and E. F can not be the position of equilibrium, since at F second order condition of firm's equilibrium, namely, that the marginal cost curve must cut marginal revenue curve from below at the point of equilibrium, is not satisfied. The firm will be increasing its profits by increasing production beyond F because marginal revenue is greater than marginal cost. The firm will be in equilibrium at point E or output OM since at E marginal cost equals marginal revenue as well as marginal cost curve is cutting marginal revenue curve from below. As under perfect competition MR curve is a horizontal straight line, the MC curve must be rising so as to cut the marginal revenue curve from below. Therefore, in case of perfect competition the **second order condition of firm's equilibrium** requires that MC curve must be rising at the point of equilibrium. Hence, the twin conditions of firms equilibrium under perfect competition are :

1. MC = MR = Price
2. (Slope of MC) > (Slope of MR)

But the fulfilment of the above two conditions does not guarantee that the profits will be earned by the firm. Whether the firm makes excess profits or losses depends on the level of the ATC at the short-run equilibrium. If the ATC is below the price at equilibrium (Figure 4) the firm earns excess profits (equal to the area PABE). If, however, the ATC is above the price (Figure 5) the firm makes a loss (equal to the area FPEC). In the latter case **the firm will continue to produce only if it covers its variable costs.** Otherwise, it will close down, since by discontinuing its operations the firm is better off: it minimises its losses. The point at which the firm covers its variable costs is called **'the closing-down point.'**

In Figure 6 the closing-down point of the firm is denoted by point M. If price falls below P the firm does not cover its **variable costs** and is better off its closes down.

Long-Rung Equilibrium of the Firm (Identical Costs)

It is assumed that all entrepreneurs are of equal efficiency. All factors are homogeneous and are available at constant and uniform prices, so that the cost curves of the firms are identical.

In the long run firms are in equilibrium when they have adjusted their plant so as to produce at the minimum point of their long-run AC curve, which is tangent (at this point) to the demand curve defined by the market price. In the long-run the firms will be earning just **normal profits,** which are included in the LAC. If they are making excess profits new firms will be attracted in the industry, this will lead to a fall in price and an upward shift of the cost curves due to increase of the prices of factors as the industry expands. These changes will continue until the LAC is tangent to the demand curve defined by the market price. If the firm's male losses in the long run they will leave the industry, price will raise and costs may fall as the industry contracts, until the remaining firms in the industry cover their total costs inclusive of the normal rate of profit.

Figure 7 represents long-run equilibrium of firm under perfect competition. The firm cannot be in the long-run equilibrium at a price greater than OP in Figure 7. Since if price is greater than OP, then the price line (demand curve) would lie somewhere above the minimum point of the average cost curve so that marginal cost and price will be equal where the firm is earning abnormal profits. Since there will be tendency for new firms to enter and compete away these abnormal profits the form cannot be in equilibrium at any price higher than OP. Likewise, the firm cannot be in long-run equilibrium at a price lower than OP in Figure 7 under perfect competition.

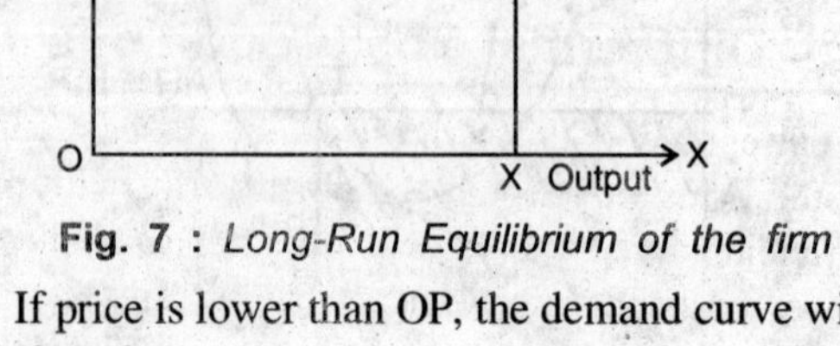

Fig. 7 : *Long-Run Equilibrium of the firm*

If price is lower than OP, the demand curve will lie below the average cost curve so that the marginal cost and price will be equal at the point where the firm is making losses. Therefore, there will be tendency for some of the firms in the industry to go out with the result that price will rise and the firms left in the field make normal profits. We therefore conclude that firm can be in long-run equilibrium under perfect competition only when price is at such a level that the horizontal demand curve is tangent to the AC curve, so the price equals average cost and firm makes only normal profits. Therefore, the condition for long-run equilibrium of firm can be written as :

SMC = SAC = LMC = LAC = MR = Price

It should be noted that a horizontal demand line can be tangent to a U-shaped average cost curve only at the latter's minimum point. Since at the minimum point of the average cost curve the marginal cost and average cost are equal, price in long-run equilibrium is equal to both MC and AC. In other words, double condition of long-run equilibrium is fulfilled at the minimum point of the average cost curve.

It is clear from above that **long-run equilibrium of the firm under perfect competition is established at the minimum point of the long-run average cost curve.** Operating at the minimum point of the long-run average cost curve signifies that the firm is of **optimum size,** that is, it is producing output at the **lowest possible cost.** The fact that the firm, working under conditions of perfect competition, tends to be of optimum size in the long run is beneficial from the social point of view in two ways. **Firstly,** working at optimum size implies that the resources of the society are being utilized in the most efficient way. **Secondly,** it signifies that the consumers are getting the goods at the lowest possible price.

Short-Run Equilibrium of the Firm : Differential Cost Conditions

If entrepreneurs differ in efficiency the cost curves of the firms vary from each other. Firms with more efficient entrepreneurs will be able to produce at lower costs than the others. Thus, different firms selling the same product at one price will be producing different quantities at different costs. More efficient firms employing better resources will have lower cost curves than others. For the sake of convenience we divide the firms having differential cost conditions into three categories A, B and C whose cost curves are shown in Figure 8. Figure 8 represents differential cost conditions.

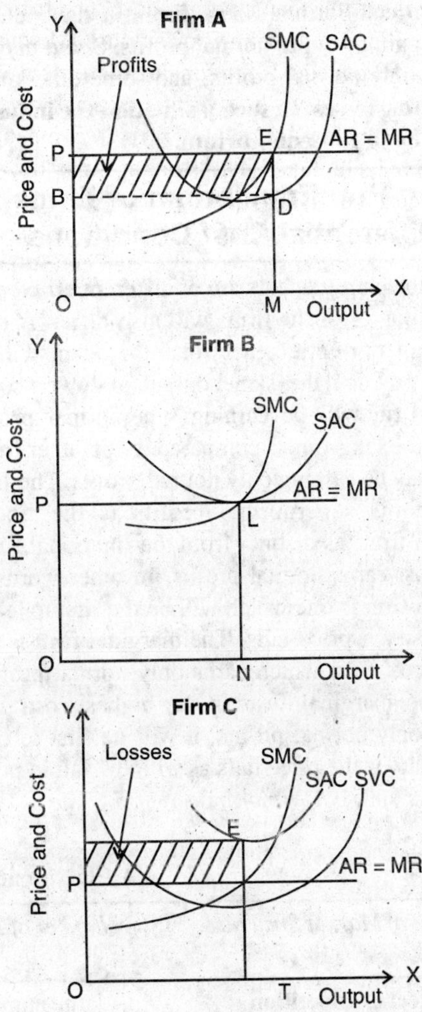

Fig. 8

If price in market is OP, then the firm of every category will adjust output where price OP equals its marginal cost. Firm A will be in equilibrium at E and will be producing OM output, firm B will be in equilibrium at L and will be producing ON, firm C will be in equilibrium at K and will be producing OT. While for all the firms, price equals their marginal cost at equilibrium output, but firm A in equilibrium is making super-normal profits, B is earning only normal profits and C is making losses. This is so because cost conditions are different for the three firms.

Thus, under conditions of different costs and in short-run equilibrium, some firms in the industry may be earning super-normal profits. Some may be making only normal profits, and some others may be incurring losses. **In such a situation the industry cannot be in full equilibrium.**

Long-Run Equilibrium of Firms : Differential Cost Conditions

In case the entrepreneurs are of different efficiency, the cost curves of the firms will also differ. A firm with a superior entrepreneur than the others will be able to produce the same output at lower costs. Such a firm will be earning supernormal profits even in the long-run as compared to the other firms which may be earning only normal profits. The firm which earns supernormal profits is the 'intra-marginal firm' as distinct from the 'marginal firm' which just earns normal profits. In other words, a marginal firm is one which will be the first to leave the industry if price falls. The marginal firm is the highest-cost firm which earns only normal profits. Since the marginal firm is the highest-cost firm making only normal profits, it will be first to quit the industry if the price falls as with the fall in price its profits sink below normal.

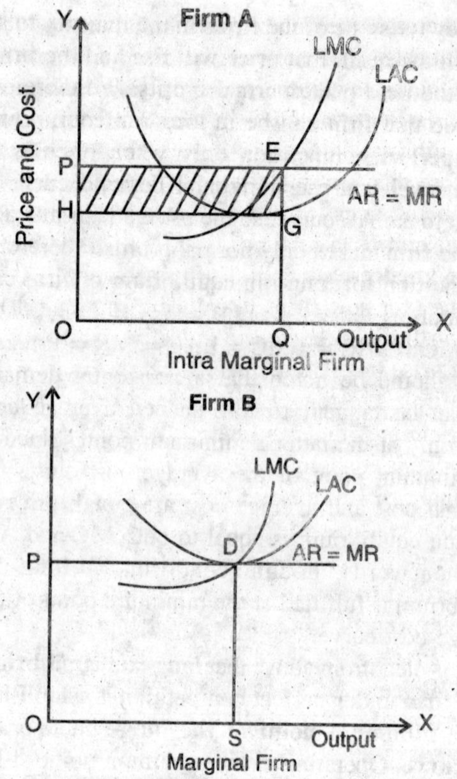

Fig. 9

Figure 9 represents long-run equilibrium of firms, which are of three categories in respect of cost conditions. The price prevailing in the long-run is OP which equals marginal cost of firm A at output OQ and marginal cost of firm B at output OS. For firms of category B price is equal to average

A Classification of Market Forms

Forms of Market Structure	*Number of Firms*	*Price Elasticity of Demand for an individual firms*	*Degree of Control over price*
(a) **Perfect Competition**	A large number of firms	Infinite	None
(b) **Imperfect Competition**	A large number of firms	Large	Some
(i) **Monopolistic Competition**	—	Large	Some
(ii) **Pure Oligopoly** (Oligopoly without Product Differentiation)	Few firms	Small	Some
(iii) **Differentiated Oligopoly** (Oligopoly with product differentiation)	Few firms	Small	Some
(c) **Monopoly**	One	Very Small	Considerable

cost, therefore they make only normal profits. Thus, firms of category B are marginal firms which will go out of the industry if the price falls below the present price OP. But price OP is greater than average cost at equilibrium output of intra-marginal firm A and therefore this firm make super-normal profits. The price being equal to average cost of the marginal firm guarantees that the marginal firm will be making only normal profits and therefore there will be no tendency for new firms to enter or for some of the existing firms to leave the industry.

If price in the long run falls below OP in Figure 9, the firms of category B will go out of the industry and some previous intra-marginal firms for which new price is equal to average cost firm will become marginal firms. We therefore conclude that in long-run competitive equilibrium under different cost conditions the output of individual firms and the number of firms in the industry is so adjusted that the following two conditions must be satisfied.

1. Price = MC of all firms,

2. Price = AC of the marginal firm.

From above it follows that **in long-run competitive equilibrium under differential cost conditions only the marginal firm will be of optimum size,** because the equilibrium of only marginal firm will be established at the minimum point of the average cost curve. The intra-marginal firms will be of more than optimum size, as is clear from Figure 9.

Thus, in the long-run where cost curves are not identical some firms may be earning supernormal profits. The industry will be in full equilibrium only by accident.

The Supply Curve of the Firm and the Industry

The supply curve of the firm may be derived by the points of intersection of its MC curve with successive demand curves. Assume that the market price increases gradually. This causes an upward shift of the demand curve of the firm. Given the positive slope of the MC curve, each higher demand curve cuts the (given) MC curve to a point which lies to the right of the previous intersection. This implies that the quantity supplied by the firm increases as price rises. The firm, given its cost structure, will not supply any quantity if the price falls below P, because at a lower price the firm does not cover its variable costs (Figure 10). If we plot the successive points of intersection of MC and the demand curves on a separate graph we observe that the supply curve of the individual firm is identical to its MC curve to the right of the closing-down point (above AVC) M. Below P the quantity supplied by the firm is zero. As price rises above P the quantity supplied increases. The supply curve of the firm is shown in Figure 11.

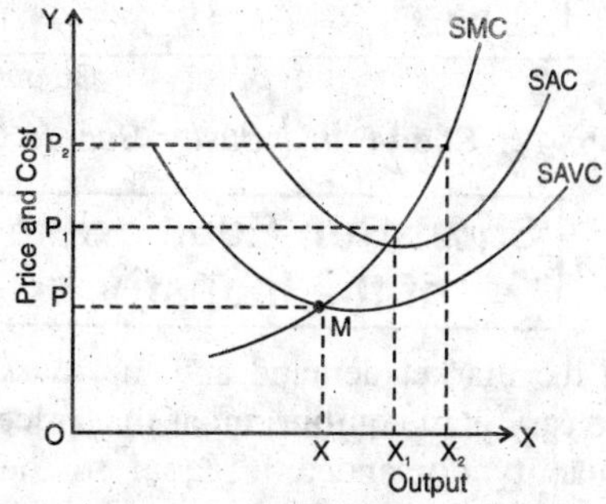

Fig. 10

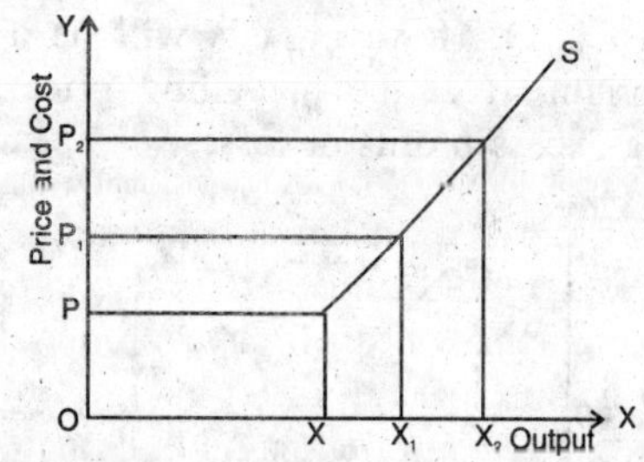

Fig. 11 : Short-Run Supply Curve of a Firm

The Industry-supply curve is the **horizontal summation** of the supply curves of the individual firms. It is assumed that the factor prices and the technology are given and that the number of firms is very large. Under these conditions the total quantity supplied in the market at each price is the sum of the quantities supplied by all firms at that price. In Figure 12 we show the industry supply as a straight line with a positive slope. It should, however, be noted that the particular shape of the market-supply curve depends on the technology and on factors prices, as well as the size distribution of the firms in the industry. All firms are not usually of the same size. The particular size of each firm in perfect competition depends on the entrepreneurial efficiency of the businessman, which is traditionally considered as a random attribute.

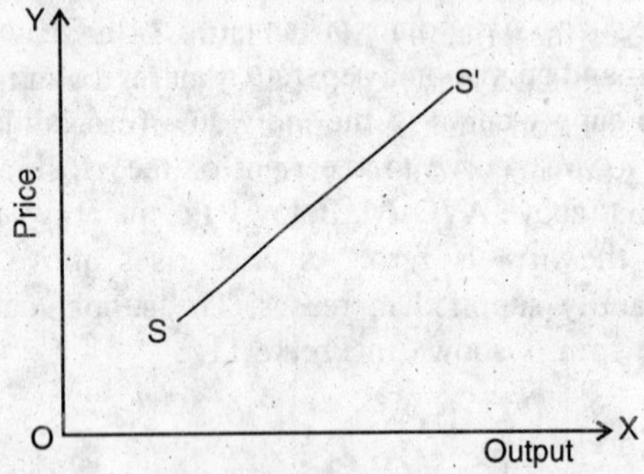

Fig. 12: *Short-Run Industry Supply Curve*

Short-Run Equilibrium of the Industry

Given the market demand and the market supply the industry is in equilibrium at that price at which the quantity demanded is equal to the quantity supplied. In Figure 13 the industry is in equilibrium at price P, at which the quantity demanded and supplied is Q. However, this will be a short-run equilibrium, if at the prevailing price firms are making excess profits or losses.

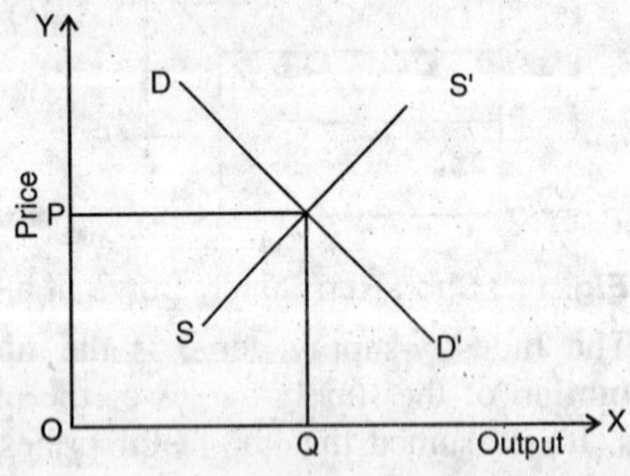

Fig. 13 : *Short-Run Industry Equilibrium*

In the long-run, firms that make losses and cannot read just their plant will close down. Those that make excess profits will expand their capacity, while excess profits will also attract new firms into the industry. Entry, exit and readjustment of the remaining firms in the industry will lead to a long run equilibrium in which firms will just be earning normal profits and there will be no entry or exit from the industry.

Optimal Resource Allocation

In perfect competition the market mechanism leads to an optimal allocation of resources. The optimality is shown by the following conditions which prevail in the long-run equilibrium of the industry :

(*a*) The output is produced at the minimum feasible cost.

(*b*) Consumers pay the minimum possible price which just covers the marginal cost of the product, that is, **price = opportunity cost.**

(*c*) Plants are used at full capacity in the long run, so that there is no waste of resources.

(*d*) Firms only earn normal profits.

In the long run these conditions prevail in all markets, so that resources are optimally allocated in the economy as a whole.

Effect of Imposition of a Tax (Perfect Competition)

We will examine the effects of the imposition by the government of a lump-sum tax, a profits tax, and a specific tax, that is, a tax per unit of output.

Imposition of a Lump-Sum Tax (Per Period)

In the short run the **lump-sum tax** will not affect the MC cost curve and the firm will continue to produce the same output as before the imposition of the tax.

However, if the firm was earning just normal profits prior to the tax, it will not be covering its ATC at the going market price and will close down in the long-run. Thus, in the long run the market-supply curve will shift to the left as firms leave the industry, the output will be lower and the price higher as compared with the pre-tax equilibrium.

Imposition of Profits Tax

This tax takes the form of a percentage on the net profit of the firm. The effects of a profits tax are the same with those of a lump-sum tax. The profits tax, while reducing the profits, will not affect its MC. Hence, in the short-run the equilibrium of the firm and the industry will not change.

However, in the long-run, exit of firms will be inevitable if in the pre-tax period firms were earning just normal profits. In the long run the supply in the market would shift to the left and a new equilibrium would be reached with a higher price, a lower quantity produced and a smaller number of firms.

Imposition of a Specific Sales Tax

This takes the form of a given amount of money (*e.g.*, Rs. 2) per unit of output produced. Such a tax clearly affects the MC of the firm. The MC curve, which is also the supply curve of the firm, will shift upwards to the left, and the amount produced at the going price will be reduced.

The market-supply curve will shift upwards to the left and price will rise. The important question here is by how much will the price increase : Will the increase in P be smaller, equal, or greater than the specific tax? This is an important question because it relates to who is going to bear the specific sales tax : the consumer-buyer, the firm, or both?

The answer to this question is that the burden of the specific tax that will be borne by the consumer (buyer) depends on the price elasticity of supply, given the market demand. In general, the most elastic the market supply the higher the proportion of the tax that the consumer will bear and the less the burden of the firm from the specific tax.

Fig. 14 : *Burden of a Sales Tax : Less Elastic Supply Curve*

So long as the market supply has a positive slope the specific tax will be paid partly by the buyer and partly by the firm. The burden to the firm will be smaller the greater the elasticity of supply. In other words, the firm will be able to pass on to the consumer more of the specific tax, the more elastic the market supply. This is illustrated in Figures 14 and 15. The demand curve is identical in both figures and the initial (pre-tax) price is the same, but the supply curve in Figure 15 is more elastic. Imposition of a specific tax equal to *ab* raises the price by ΔP in Figure 14 and by ΔP_1 in Figure 15. Clearly $\Delta P_1 > \Delta P$, that is, the tax burden to the consumer is greater in the case of a more elastic supply curve (given the market demand).

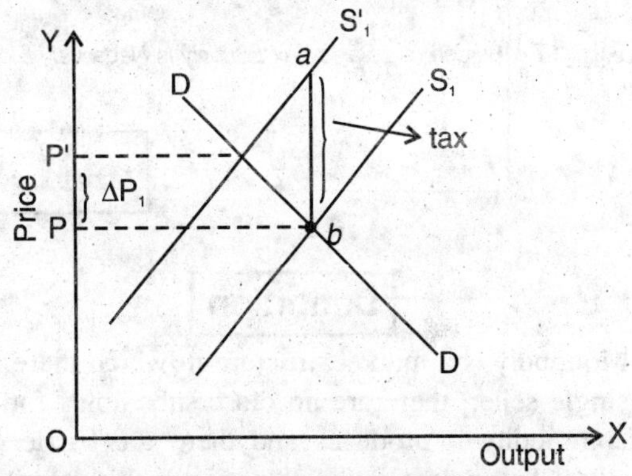

Fig. 15 : *Burden of a Sales Tax : More Elastic Supply Curve*

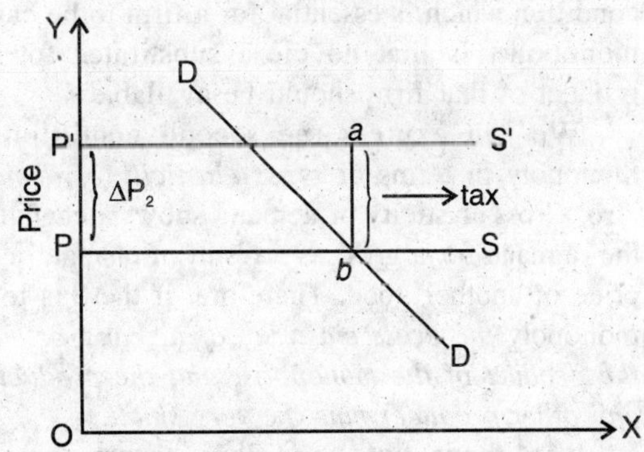

Fig. 16 : *Burden of a Sales Tax : Infinite Elastic Supply Curve*

In the limiting case of a market-supply curve with infinite elasticity the increase in price is equal to the specific tax and the whole tax burden is borne by the consumer. In Figure 16 the demand is the same as in Figures 14 and 15, but the supply curve is parallel to the horizontal axis, showing infinite price elasticity, The imposition of a specific tax equal to *ab* leads to an equal increase in the price : $\Delta P_2 = ab$.

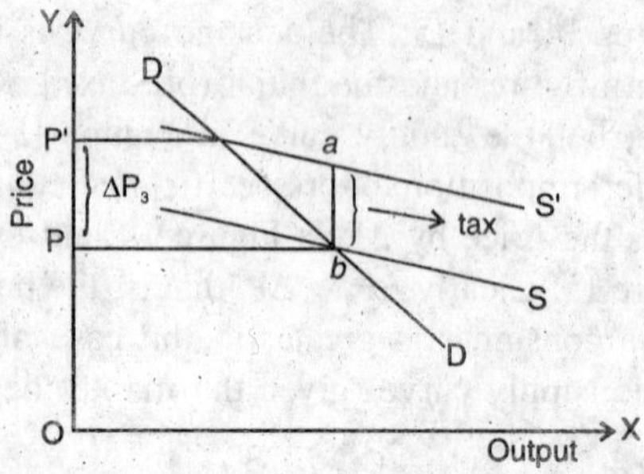

Fig. 17 : *Burden of a Sales Tax : Supply is Negatively Sloping*

If the supply curve has a negative slope (Figure 17) the imposition of a specific tax results in an increase in the price which is greater than the tax. In Figure 17 the demand is identical as in the above-examined cases but the supply curve is negatively sloping (with its slope smaller than the slope of the DD curve). Under these conditions a specific tax of *ab* leads to an increase in the market price equal to ΔP_3, which is obviously larger than the unit tax.

MONOPOLY

Definition

Monopoly is a market structure in which there is a single seller, there are no close substitutes for the commodity it produces and there are barriers to entry. Two points are worth noting in this definition. Firstly, there must be a single producer or seller of a product if there is to be monopoly. A second condition which is essential for a firm to be called monopolist is that no close substitutes for the product of that firm should be available.

We can express the second condition of monopoly in terms of *cross elasticity of demand* also. Cross elasticity of demand shows a change in the demand for a good as a result of change in the price of another good. Therefore, if there is to be monopoly *the cross elasticity of demand between the product of the monopolist and the product of any other producer must be very small.*

The above two conditions ensure that the monopolist can set the price of his product and can pursue an independent price policy. Power to influence price is very essence of monopoly. From this it must not be gathered that the monopolist is so powerful that he can dictate the price as well as the amount sold. Monopolist can do one of these things only; either he can fix the price leaving the amount sold to the consumers, or he can fix the quantity he wants to produce and sell and leave the price to be determined by the demand of the consumers.

Average and Marginal Revenue for a Monopolist

In perfect competition the price is unaffected by variations in the Firm's output, and if follows that the addition to revenue resulting from increasing the level of sales by one more unit is the market price of that unit. Thus, the marginal and average revenue curves coincide in the same horizontal straight line. In the case of monopoly, however, the average revenue curve, which is the same as the market demand curve, is *downward sloping*. Furthermore, the marginal revenue curve does not coincide with the demand curve : since the side of an extra unit forces down the price at which all units already being sold can now be sold, the sale of an extra unit results in a net addition to revenue of an amount less that its own selling price.

It is easy to prove algebraically that, if the demand curve slopes downwards, marginal revenue is always less than price. Let subscripts n and $(n + 1)$ indicate the revenue associated with the sale of nth and the $(n + 1)$th unit. So that, *e.g.*, TR_n is the total revenue associated with the sale of n units period.

$$\begin{aligned} MR_{n+1} &= TR_{n+1} - TR_n \\ &= (n+1)\,P_{n+1} - n.P_n \\ &= n.P_{n+1} + P_{n+1} - n.P_n \\ &= n\,(P_{n+1} - P_n) + P_{n+1}. \end{aligned}$$

Since the demand curve slopes downwards P_{n+1} (the price ruling when $n + 1$ units are sold) will be less than P_n (the price ruling when n units are sold). Thus, the MR of the $(n + 1)$th unit is less than P_{n+1}.

Demand and Revenue

Since there is a single Firm in the industry, the Firm's demand curve is the industry demand curve. The demand equation (linear demand function), *ceteris paribus*, is

$$X = b_0 - b_1.P$$

The clause cetris paribus implies that all the other factors (such as income, tastes, other prices which affect demand are assumed constant. Changes in these factors will shift the demand curve (Figure 18).

The slope of the demand curve (DD') is

$$\frac{dX}{dP} = \frac{d(b_0 - b_1.P)}{dX}$$
$$= -b_1$$

The price elasticity of demand is

$$e_P = \frac{dX}{dP}.\frac{P}{X}$$
$$= -b_1.\frac{P}{X}$$

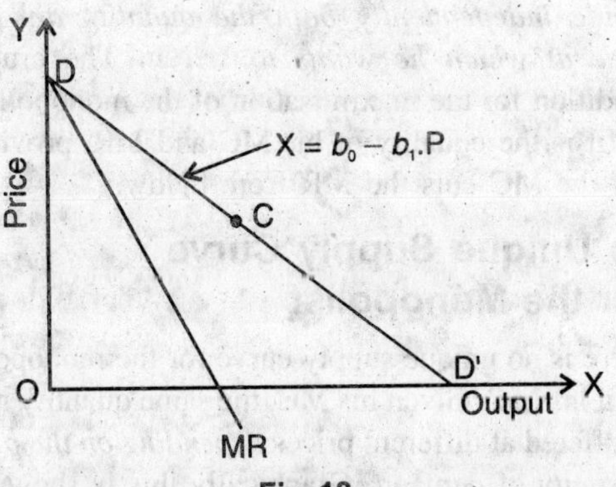

Fig. 18

That is, elasticity changes at any one point of the demand curve.

(*a*) At point D the elasticity approaches infinity.

$$e_P = -b_1.\frac{P}{X} \to \infty$$

(*b*) At point D' on the demand curve DD', the elasticity is zero.

$$e_P = -b_1.\frac{P}{X}$$
$$= -b_1.\frac{0}{X} = 0$$

(*c*) At the mid point C the price elasticity is unity.

$$e_P = -1$$

The total revenue of the monopolist is

$$TR = P.X$$

Solving the demand equation for P we find

$$P = \frac{b_0}{b_1} - \frac{1}{b_1}.X$$

Setting $\left(\frac{b_0}{b_1}\right) = a$ and $\left(\frac{1}{b_1}\right) = b$ we may rewrite the price equation as

$$P = a - b.X$$

Substituting into the revenue equation we find

$$TR = P.X$$
$$TR = (a - b.X)\ X$$
$$TR = a.X - b.X^2$$

The average revenue is equal to the price :

$$AR = \frac{TR}{X}$$
$$= \frac{P.X}{X} = P$$
$$= a - b.X$$

Thus, the demand curve is also the AR curve of the monopolist.

The marginal revenue is : $MR = \frac{dTR}{dX}$

$$= \frac{d(a.X - b.X^2)}{dX}$$
$$= a - 2b.X$$

That is, the MR is a straight line with the same intercept as the demand curve, but twice as steep.

The general relation between P and MR is found as follows. Given

$$TR = P.X$$
$$MR = \frac{dTR}{dX}$$
$$MR = \frac{d(P.X)}{dX}$$
$$MR = P.\frac{dX}{dX} + X.\frac{dP}{dX}$$
$$\therefore \quad MR = P + X.\frac{dP}{dX}$$

The marginal revenue is at all levels of output smaller than P, given that

$$P = MR - X.\frac{dP}{dX}$$

and the term $\left(X.\frac{dP}{dX}\right)$ is positive (since the slope of the demand curve, $\frac{dP}{dX} > 0$). Hence P > MR.

Costs

In the traditional theory of monopoly the shapes of the cost curves are the same as in the theory of perfect competition. The AVC, MC and ATC are U-shaped, while the AFC is a *rectangular hyperbola.* However, the particular shape of the cost curves does not make any difference to the determination of the equilibrium of the Firm, provided that the slope of the MC is greater than the slope of the MR curve.

One point should be stressed here. *The MC curve is not the supply curve of the monopolist, as is the case in perfect competition.* In monopoly there is no unique relationship between price and the quantity supplied.

Equilibrium of the Monopolist

A. Short-Run Equilibrium

The monopolist maximises his short-run profits if the following two conditions are fulfilled :

1. MC = MR
2. The slope of MC is greater than the slope of the MR at the point of the intersection.

In Figure 19 the equilibrium of the monopolist is defined by point E, at which the MC intersects the MR curve from below. Thus, both condtions for equilibrium are fulfilled. Price is P and the quantity is X. The monopolist realises excess profits equal to the shaded area APCB. Note that the price is higher than the MR.

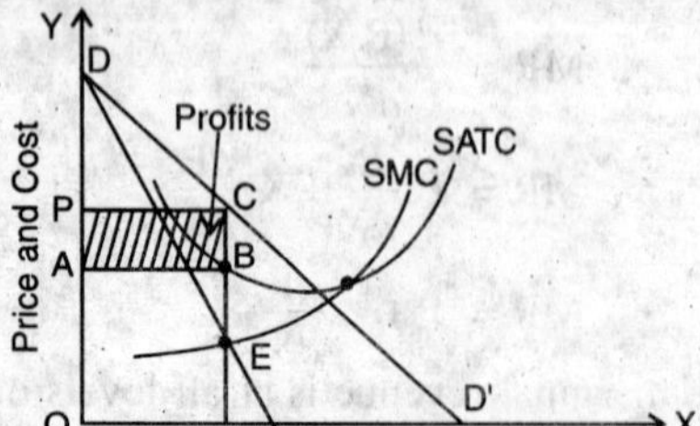

Fig. 19 : *Short-Run Equilibrium Under Monopoly*

It is generaly thought that monopolists always earn profits and therefore in layman's mind profits are generally associated with monopoly. But this is a wrong notion.

In the short-run, monopolist can make losses also. If demand is inadequate, the complete absence of competition is of little benefit to the seller. In the short-run, monopolist will continue working so long as price is above the average variable cost. If the price falls below average variable cost, the monopolist would shut down even in the short-run.

In perfect competition the Firm is a price-taker, so that its only decision is output determination. The monopolist is faced by two decisions : setting his price and his output. However, given the downward-sloping demand curve, the two decisions are interdependent. The monopolist will either set his price and sell the amount that the market will take at it, or he will produce the output defined by the intersection of MC and MR, which will be sold at the corresponding price, P. *The monopolist cannot decide independently both the quantity and the price at which he wants to sell it.* The crucial condition for the maximisation of the monopolist's profit is the equality of his MC and MR, provided that the MC cuts the MR from below.

No Unique Supply Curve For the Monopolist

There is no unique supply curve for the monopolist from his MC. Given his MC, the same quantity may be offered at different prices *depending on the price elasticity* of demand. Graphically this is shown in Figure 20. The X will be sold at price P_1 if demand is D_1, while the same quantity X will be sold at price P_2 if demand is D_2. Thus, there is no unique relationship between price and quantity.

Similary, given the MC of the monopolist, *various quantities may be supplied at any one price*, depending on the market demand and the corresponding MR curve. In Figure 21 we depict such a situation. The cost conditions are represented by the MC curve. Given the costs of the monopolist, he would supply OX_1, if the market demand is D_1, while at the same price P, he would supply only OX_2 if the market demand is D_2.

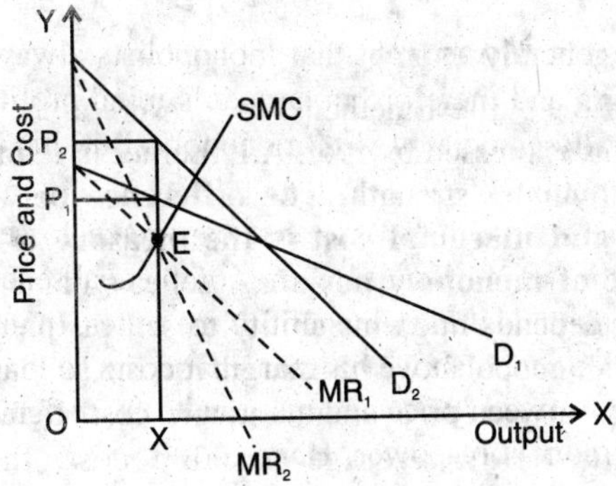

Fig. 20

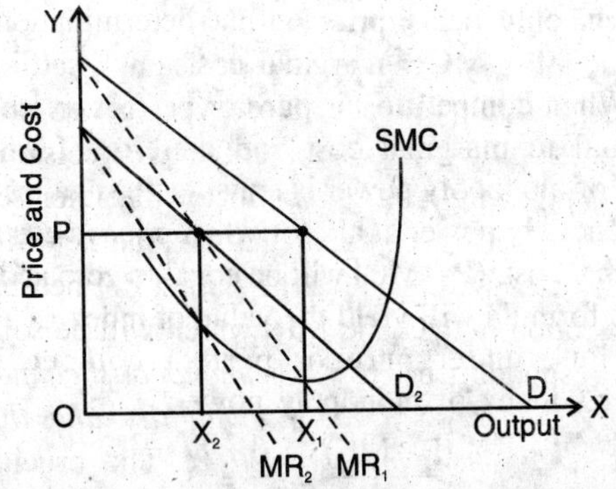

Fig. 21

B. Long-Run Equilibrium

In the long-run the monopolist has the time to expand his plant, or to use his existing plant at any level which will maximise his profit. With entry blocked, however, it is not necessary for the monopolist to reach an optimal scale (that is, to build up his plant until he reaches the minimum point of LAC). Neither is there any guarantee that he will use his existing plant at optimum capacity. What is certain is that the monopolist will not stay in business if he makes losses in the long run. He will most probably continue to earn supernormal profits even in the long-run, given that entry is barred. However, the size of his plant and the degree of utilisation of any given plant size depend entirely on the market demand. He may reach the optimal scale (minimum point of LAC) or remain at suboptimal scale (falling part of his LAC) or surpass the optimal scale (expand beyond the minimum LAC) depending on the market conditions. In Figure 22 we depict the case in which the market size does not permit the monopolist to expand to the minimum point of LAC. In this case not only is his plant of suboptimal size but also the existing plant is under utilized. This is because to the left of the minimum point of the LAC the SAC is tangent to the LAC at its falling part, and also because the short-run MC must be equal to the LMC. This occurs at E, while the minimum LAC is at *b* and the optimal use of the existing plant is at *a*. Since it is utilised at the level E′, there is excess capacity.

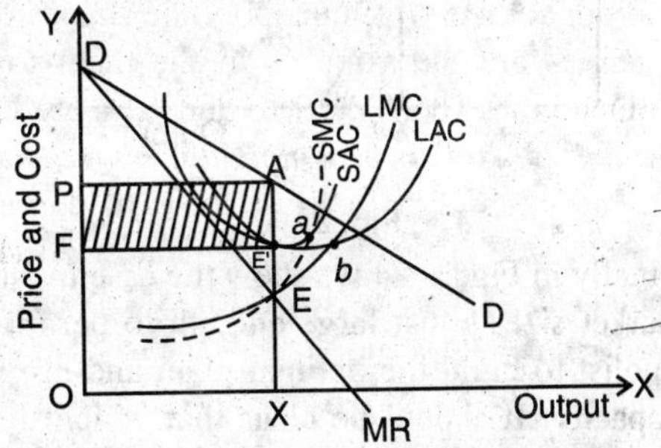

Fig. 22 : *Monopolist with Suboptimal Plant and Excess Capacity*

In Figure 23 we depict the case where the size of the market is so large that the monopolist, in order to maximise his output, must build a plant larger than the optimal and overutilise it. This is because to the right of the minimum point of the LAC the SAC and the LAC are tangent at a point of their positive slope, and also because the SMC must be equal to the LAC. Thus, the plant that maximes the monopolist's profits leads to higher costs for two reasons : Firstly because it is larger than the optimal size, and secondly because it is overutilised.

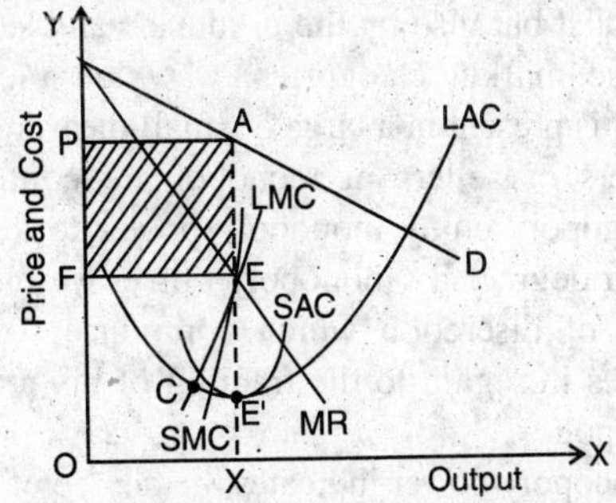

Fig. 23 : *Monopolist Operating in a Large Market: His Plant is Larger than the Optimal (C) and it is being overutilised.*

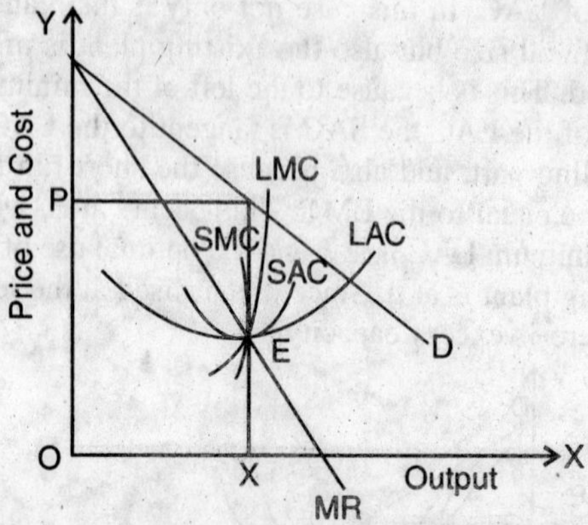

Fig. 24

Finally in Figure 24 we show the case in which the market size is just large enough to permit the monopolist to build the optimal plant and use it at full capacity. It should be clear that which of the above situations will emerge in any particular case depends on the size of the market (given the technology of the monopolist). There is no certainty that in the long-run the monopolist will reach the optimal scale, as is the case in a perfect competitive market. In monopoly there are no market forces similar to those in perfect competition which lead the firms to operate at optimum plant size in the long run.

Measurement of the Degree of Monopoly Power

Monopoly is a matter of degree. Monopoly power is not only enjoyed by the pure or ordinary monopolist but also by the producers and sellers of all those market categories in which monopoly element is present in a large or small measure. Thus, producers or sellers in monopolistic competition and oligopoly enjoy monopoly power to a greater or lesser degree. By monopoly power we mean the amount of discretion which a producer or seller possesses in regard to the framing of his price and output policy.

Monopoly power indicates the degree of control which a producer or seller wields over the price and output to his product. Various measures of monopoly power have been suggested by different economists, we shall discuss some of them below.

Lerner's Measure

One of the earliest methods' to measure monopoly power is expressed by Prof. A.P. Lerner in terms of the bargaining strength. **The difference between price and marginal cost is the measure of the degree of monopoly power.** A seller's monopoly power depends upon his ability to sell his product at a price much above his marginal cost. The larger the gap between price and marginal cost, the greater is the monopoly power. Hence,

$$\text{Degree of monopoly power} = \frac{P-MC}{P}$$

where P = price

MC = marginal cost

When competition is pure or perfect, price (P) is equal to marginal cost and therefore Lerner's index of monopoly power is equal to zero indicating no monopoly power at all, for when price is equal to marginal cost, (P – MC) will be equal to zero and the above formula will yield the value of index as zero.

Thus, under pure or perfect competition, Lerner's index of monopoly power

$$\frac{(P-MC)}{P} = \frac{0}{P} = 0.$$

On the other hand, when the monopolised product entails no cost of production, that is, when the product is a free good whose supply is controlled by one person, the marginal cost will be equal to zero and Lerner's index of monopoly power $\left(\frac{P-MC}{P}\right)$ would be equal to one or unity. Thus, when MC is equal to zero,

$$\text{Degree of monopoly} = \frac{P-MC}{P} = \frac{P-O}{P} = 1$$

It is thus clear that Lerner's index of **monopoly power can vary from zero to unity.** Within this range, the greater the value of the index $\left(\frac{P-MC}{P}\right)$, the greater the degree of monopoly power possessed by the seller.

Now it has been known that **Lerner's index of monopoly power is nothing else but the inverse of the price elasticity of demand.** We can prove this as follows :

$$\text{Lerner's degree of monopoly power} = \frac{P-MC}{P}$$

For profit maximisation, MC = MR, and this formula becomes

$$= \frac{P - MR}{P} \quad ...(1)$$

We know that MR = $P\left(\frac{e-1}{e}\right)$, where e is price elasticity of demand at the equilibrium output. Thus putting $P\left(\frac{e-1}{e}\right)$ in the place of MR in (1) above we get,

Lerner's degree of monopoly power

$$= \frac{P - P\left(\frac{e-1}{e}\right)}{P} = \frac{P - P\left(1 - \frac{1}{e}\right)}{P}$$

$$= \frac{P\left[1 - \left(1 - \frac{1}{e}\right)\right]}{P} = 1 - 1 + \frac{1}{e} = \frac{1}{e}$$

= inverse of the elasticity of demand

It therefore follows that Lerner's index of monopoly power is equal to the inverse of price elasticity of demand. This degree of monopoly power can be judged by merely knowing the elasticity of demand at the equilibrium output. **The degree of monopoly varies inversely with the elasticity of the demand for the good.**

Monopoly Equilibrium and Perfectly Competitive Equilibrium Compared

1. Under perfect competition, demand curve or the average revenue curve faced by an individual firm is perfectly elastic and is a horizontal straight line parallel to the X-axis. But under monopoly, demand curve or AR curve faced by the firm is falling downwards from left to right. Therefore, MR is less than AR at all levels of output and MR curve lies below the AR curve.

2. Both under perfect competition and monopoly, the firm is in equilibrium at that level of output where MC is equal to MR. But in perfect competition since MR is equal to AR or price, therefore, MC, when equal to MR in equilibrium condition, is also equal to price or AR. This is not true in case of a monopoly. Since under monopoly, MR is always less than AR or price, in equilibrium MC will, therefore, be equal to MR but it will be less than price.

Hence,

Under perfect competition

MC = MR = AR = Price.

But under monopoly

MC = MR < AR = Price

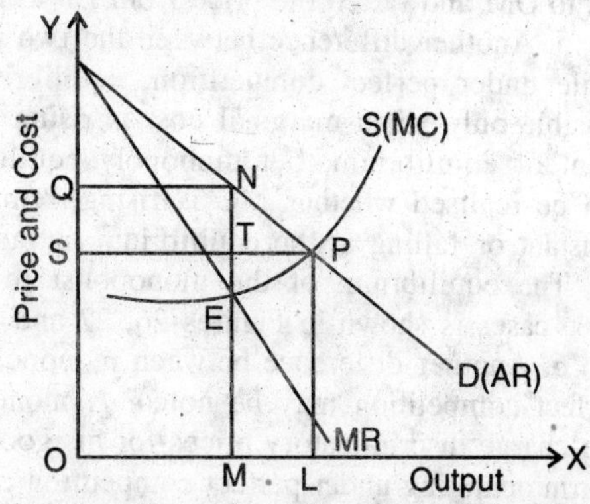

Fig. 25 : *Under Monopoly, price is higher and output smaller than under perfect competition*

3. Another significant difference between the two is that whereas a perfectly competitive firm is in long-run equilibrium at the minimum point of the long-run average cost curve, monopolistic firm is generally in equilibrium at the level of output where average cost is still declining and has yet not reached its minimum point.

4. Another important difference between monopoly equilibrium and perfectly competitive equilibrium is that under monopoly price is higher and output smaller than under perfect competition, assuming cost conditions in the two cases to be the same.

This can be explained with Figure 25. In this figure, D is the demand curve. It is also the average revenue curve. S is the supply curve of the industry. It is in fact the lateral summation of the short-run summation of the short-run marginal cost curves of the various firms constituting the industry. Now under perfect competition, the price LP (= OS) will be determined at which demand curve D and supply curve S intersect each other. The equilibrium output determined is OL.

Now suppose that all the firms combine or merge to form a cartel, that is, become monopoly. Now a monopolist will be in equilibrium at that price-output level where MC equals MR. In this figure, MC equals MR at output OM and price fixed is MN. It is quite evident from the figure that when all the firms have merged together and become a monopoly, they have reduced the total output from OL to OM and raised the price from LP to MN.

5. Another difference between the two is that while under perfect competition, equilibrium is possible only when marginal cost is rising at the point of equilibrium, but monopoly equilibrium can be realised whether MC is rising, remaining constant or falling at the equilibrium output.

The equilibrium of the monopolist in these three cases is shown in Figures 26, 27 and 28.

6. Another difference between monopoly and perfect competition may be noted. A monopolist can charge discriminatory prices for his goods but a firm operating under perfect competition cannot.

7. Another difference between the monopoly equilibrium and perfectly competitive equilibrium is that while under perfect competition in to long-run, a firm can earn only normal profits, but a monopolistic firm may be earning supernormal profits even in the long-run.

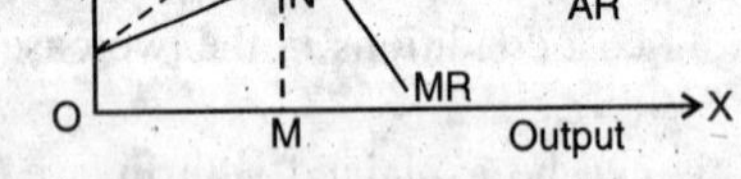

Fig. 26 : *Monopoly Equilibrium in Case of Rising Costs*

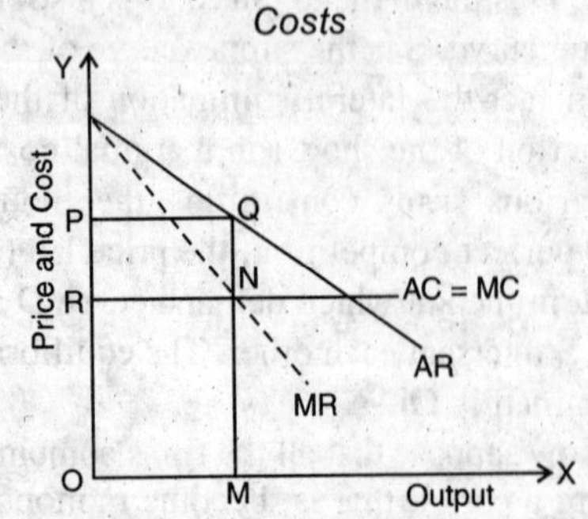

Fig. 27 : *Monopoly Equilibrium in Case of Constant Costs*

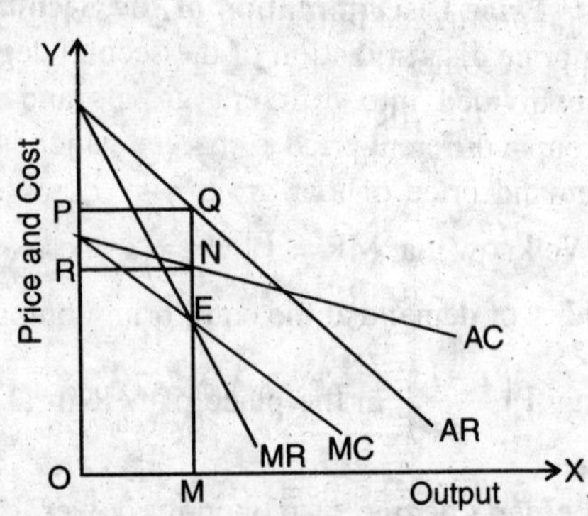

Fig. 28: *Monopoly Equilibrium in Case of Falling Cost*

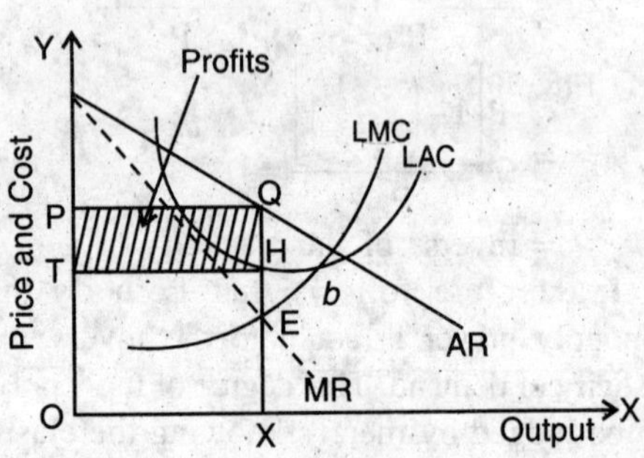

Fig. 29 : *Long-Run Equilibrium (with Profits) Under Monopoly*

Price Discrimination

Price discrimination refers to the practice of a seller of selling the same good at different prices to different buyers.

Degrees of Price Discrimination

Prof. **A.C. Pigou** has distinguished between the following three types of price discrimination on another ground :

1. Price discrimination of the first degree,
2. Price discrimination of the second degree, and
3. Price discrimination of the third degree.

Price Discrimination of the First Degree : Price discrimination of the first degree is also known as perfect price discrimination because this involves maximum possible exploitation of each buyer in the interest of a seller's profits. **Price discrimination of the first degree is said to occur when the monopolist is able to sell each separate unit of the output at a different price.**

Price Discrimination of the Second Degree : In price discrimination of the second degree buyers are divided into different groups and from each group a different price is charged which is the lowest demand price of that group.

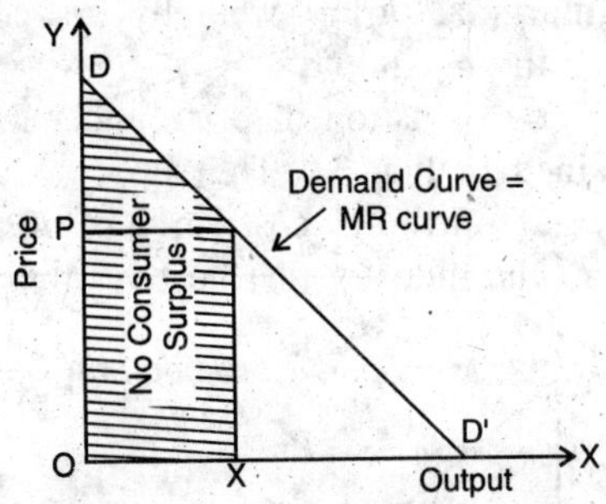

Fig. 30 : *Price Discriminating Monopolist of the First Degrees Extracts all the Consumer's Surplus from the Buyers*

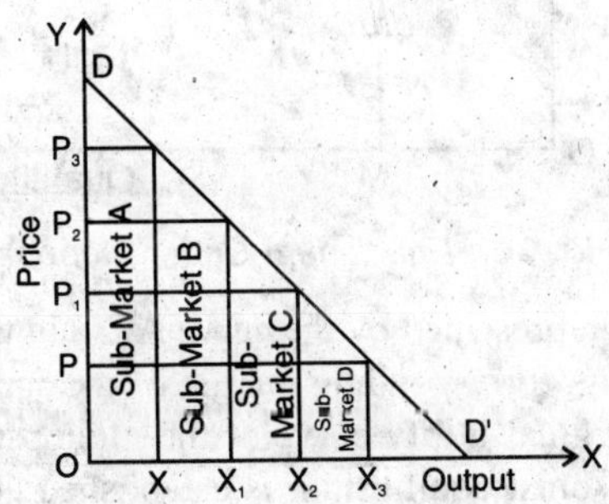

Fig. 31 : *Different Groups under Price Discrimination of the Second Degree*

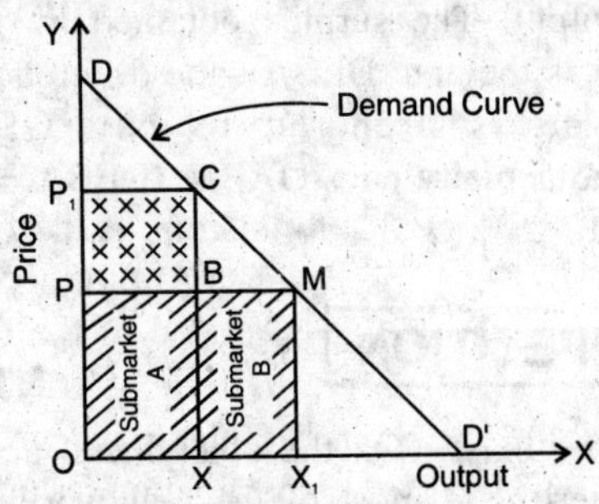

Fig. 32 : *Third-degree Price Discrimination*

Price Discrimination of the Third Degree : Price discrimination of the third degree is said to occur when the seller divides his buyers into two submarkets or groups and charges a different price in each submarket. In this case monopolist will receive the entire consumer's surplus, First-degree price discrimination is also known as **'take-it-or-leave-it'** price discrimination, because in negotiating with each buyer the monopolist charges him the maximum price he is willing to pay under threat of denying the selling of any quantity to him : he offers each buyer a 'take-it-or-leave-it' choice. **In this case the demand curve also becomes the MR curve of the monopolist.**

When is Price Discrimination Possible?

The necessary conditions, which must be fulfilled for the implementation of price discrimination are the following :

1. The market must be divided into sub-markets with different price elasticities.

2. There must be effective separation of the sub-markets, so that no reselling can take place from a low-price market to a high-price market.

Price Discrimination and the Price Elasticity of Demand

We know that $MR = P\left(1-\frac{1}{e}\right)$

In case of price discrimination we have

$$MR_1 = P_1\left(1-\frac{1}{e_1}\right)$$

$$MR_2 = P_2\left(1-\frac{1}{e_2}\right)$$

and $MR_1 = MR_2$

Therefore

$$P_1\left(1-\frac{1}{e_1}\right) = P_2\left(1-\frac{1}{e_2}\right)$$

or

$$\frac{P_1}{P_2} = \frac{\left(1-\frac{1}{e_1}\right)}{\left(1-\frac{1}{e_2}\right)}$$

Where

e_1 = elasticity of D_1

e_2 = elasticity of D_2

If $e_1 = e_2$ the ration of prices is equal to unity:

$$\frac{P_1}{P_2} = 1$$

that is,

$$\mathbf{P_1 = P_2}$$

This means that **when elasticities are the same price discrimination is not profitable.** The monopolist will charge a uniform price for his product.

If price elasticities differ price will be higher in the market whose demand is less elastic.

This is obvious from the equality of MR's

$$P_1\left(1-\frac{1}{e_1}\right) = P_2\left(1-\frac{1}{e_2}\right)$$

if $|e_1| > |e_2|$ then

$$\left(1-\frac{1}{e_1}\right) > \left(1-\frac{1}{e_2}\right)$$

Thus, for the equality of MR's to be fulfilled

$$P_1 < P_2$$

that is, the market with the higher elasticity will have the lower price.

Monopsony

Monopsony refers to a market situation when there is a single buyer of a commodity or service it applies to any situation in which there is a 'monopoly' element in buying.

The analysis of monopoly pricing is similar to that under monopoly pricing. Just as a monopolist is able to influence the price of the product by the amount he offers for sale, similarly the monopsonist is able to influence the supply price of his purchases by the amount he buys. Again, the monopolist aims at the maximisation of his surplus. The monopolist equates the marginal cost with his marginal revenue to maximise his profit. The monopsonist regulates his purchases in such a way that marginal cost equals marginal utility whereby his consumer's surplus is the maximum.

The determination of price under monopsony is explained in Fig. 34. The supply curve of the industry is the average cost curve of monopsonist. It is from the industry that he buys the product.

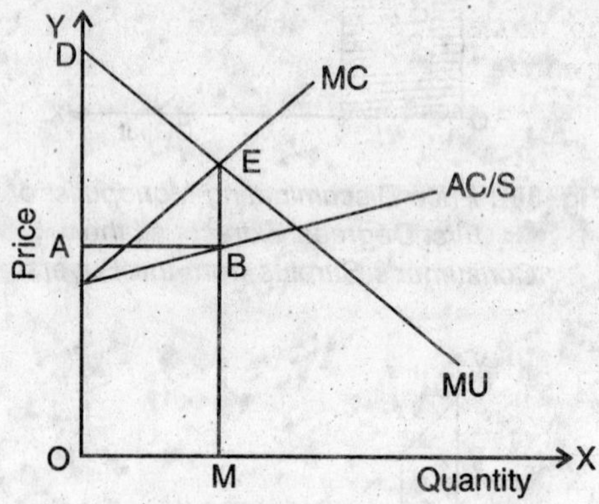

Fig. 34 : *Equilibrium Under Monopsony*

This is represented by the curve AC/S in the Figure. MC is its corresponding marginal cost curve. MU is the marginal utility curve of the monopsonist. The monopsonist equilibrium is established at E where the marginal utility of the product to the monopsonist equals the marginal cost. He buys OM quantity at MB price which is the supply price for that output. The surplus obtained by the monopsonist is the area DEBA—the difference between what he is prepared to pay ODEM and what he actually pays OABM (DEBA = ODEM – OABM).

MONOPOLISTIC COMPETITION

The concept of monopolistic competition put forth by *Prof. Chamberlin* was a true revolutionary as well as more realistic than either pure competition or pure monopoly. Before Chamberlin, monopoly and competition were regarded as two mutually exclusive alternatives; one would be absent when the other exists. On the other hand, according to Chamberlin, in most of the real world economic situations, both monopoly and competitive elements are presents. Chamberlin's concept of monopolistic competition is thus a blending of competition and monopoly. The distinguishing feature of monopolistic competition which makes it as a blending of competition and monopoly is the *differentiation of the product*. This means that the products of various firms are not homogeneous but different though they are closely related to each other. Product differentiation does not mean that the products of various firms are altogether different. They are only slightly different so that they are quite similar and serve as close substitutes of each other.

Assumptions

The basic assumptions of Chamberlin's large-group model are the same as those of pure competition with the exception of the homogeneous product we may summarise them as follows :

1. There is a large number of sellers and buyers in the 'group'.
2. The products of the sellers are differentiated, yet they are close substitutes of one another.
3. There is free entry and exist of Firms in the group.
4. The goal of the Firm is profit maximisation, both in the short run and the long run.
5. The prices of Factors and technology are given.
6. The Firm is assumed to behave as if it knew its demand and cost curves with certainty.
7. The long run consists of a number of indentical short-run periods, which are assumed to be independent of one another in the sense that decisions in one period do not affect future periods and are not affected by past actions. The optimum decision for any one period is the optimum decision for any other period. Thus, by assumption, maximisation of short-run profits implies maximisation of long-run profits.
8. Finally, Chamberlin makes the 'heroic' assumption that both demand and cost curves for all 'products' are uniform throughout the group. This requires that consumer's preferences be evenly distributed among the different sellers, and that differences between the products be such as not to give rise to differences in costs.

Cost Curves and Selling Cost

Chamberlin, in his model of monopolistic competition has assumed the traditional U-shaped cost-curves—AC, AVC and MC. In addition he has introduced a new cost, *i.e., Selling Cost*. "Selling Costs are defined as costs incurred in order to alter the position or the shape of the demand curve for a product." Selling costs include all the expenses that are intended to promote the sales, including cost of advertisement, salesman's salaries, expenses of sales department, margins granted to dealers, wholesalers and retailers, window displays and demonstration of new goods.

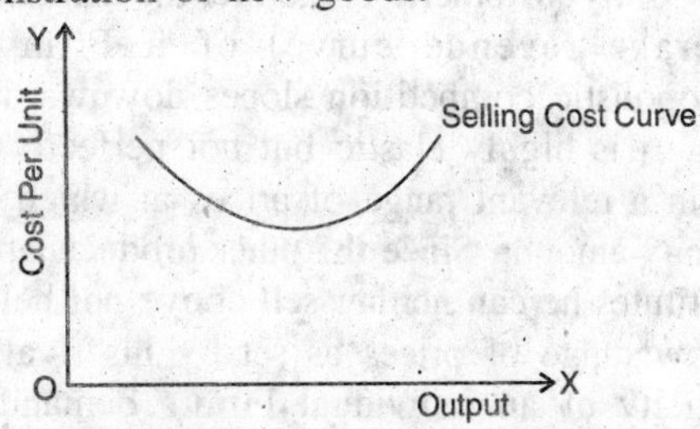

Fig. 36 : *Selling Costs Curve*

Chamberlin argues that the selling-costs curve is U-shaped, that is, there are economies and diseconomies of output will not required an equiproportional increase in selling costs, and this leads to a fall in the average selling expenditure. However, beyond a certain level of output the Firm will have to spend more per unit in order to attract customers from other Firms : as output expands the Firm has to attract customers which are well used to the product of other Firms. The U-shaped selling cost, added to the U-shaped production cost, yields a U-shaped ATC curve.

Product Differentiation and the Demand Curve

Product differentiation as the basis for establishing a downward-falling demand curve was first introduced in economic theory by *Sraffa*. Yet it was Chamberlin who elaborated the implication of product differentiation for the pricing and output decisions as well as for he selling strategy of the firm.

Under monopolistic competition no single firm controls more than a small portion of the total output of a product. No doubt there is an element of differentiation, nevertheless the products are close substitutes. As a result, a reduction in price will enable a Firm to increase its sales by attracting some customers of its competitors provided the latter do not reduce the price. Similarly, by raising its price it will be losing many of its customers to its rival Firms. A reduction in its price will no doubt increase the sales of the Firm but it will have little effect on the price-output conditions of other Firms, each will lose only a few of its customers. Likewise, an increase in its price will reduce its demand substantially but each of its rivals will attract only a few of its customers. Therefore, the demand curve (average revenue curve) of a Firm under monopolistic competition slopes downward to the right. It is highly elastic but not perfectly elastic within a relevant range of prices at which he can sell any amount. Since the other products are close substitutes he can neither sell above nor below the narrow range of prices as set by his rivals. This elasticity of an individual Firm's demand curve will, however, depend *Firstly*, upon the value of cross elasticity among the products of the rival sellers; and *Secondly*, on the number of sellers and the contribution of each of the total industry demand.

Equilibrium Under Monopolistic Competition

The demand curve for the product of an individual Firm, as noted above, is downward sloping. Since the various Firms under monopolistic competition produce products which are close substitutes of each others, the position and elasticity of the demand curve for the product of any of them depend upon the availability of the competiting substitutes and their prices. Therefore, the equilibrium adjustment of an individual Firm cannot be defined in isolation to the general field of which it is a part. However, for sake of simplicity in analysis, conditions regarding the availability of substitute products produced by the rival Firms and prices charged for them are held constant while the equilibrium adjustment of an individual Firm is considered in isolation. Since close substitutes for his products are available in the market, the demand curve for the product of an individual Firm working under conditions of monopolistic competition is fairly elastic thus, although a Firm under monopolistic competition has a monopolistic control over his variety of the product but his control is tempered by the fact that there are close substitutes available in the market and that if he sets too high a price for his product, many of his customers will shift to the rival products.

A. Short-Run Equilibrium

The short-run analysis of the Firm under monopolistic competition is based on the following assumptions :

1. that the number of sellers is large and they act independently of each other. Each is a monopolist in his own spheres;
2. that the product of each seller is differentiated from the other products;
3. that the Firm has a determinate demand curve (AR) which is elastic;
4. that the factor-services are in perfectly elastic supply for the production of the product in question;
5. that the short-run cost curves of each Firm differ from each other; and
6. no new Firms enter the industry.

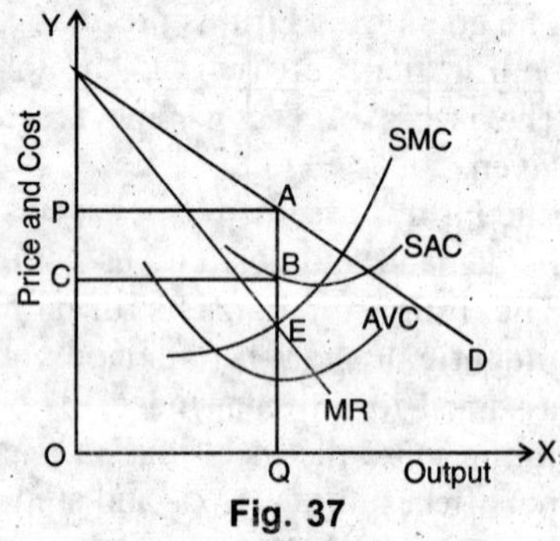

Fig. 37

Given these assumptions, each Firm fixes such price and output which maximises its profit. The equilibrium price and output is determined at a point where the short-run marginal cost equals marginal revenue.

Since costs differ in the short-run, Firm with lower units costs will be earning only normal profits.

In Figure 37 the short-run marginal cost curve (SMC) cuts the marginal revenue curve at E. This equilibrium point establishes the price QA (=OP) and output OQ. As a result the Firm earns *super normal profits* represented by the area PABC.

Figure 38 indicates the same equilibrium point, price and output. But in this case the Firm just covers the short-run average unit cost as represented by the tangency of demand curve (D) and the short-run average unit cost curve (SAC) at A. It earns just normal profits.

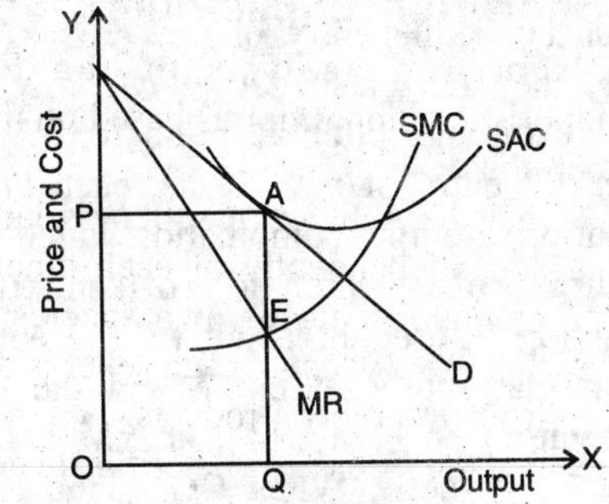

Fig. 38

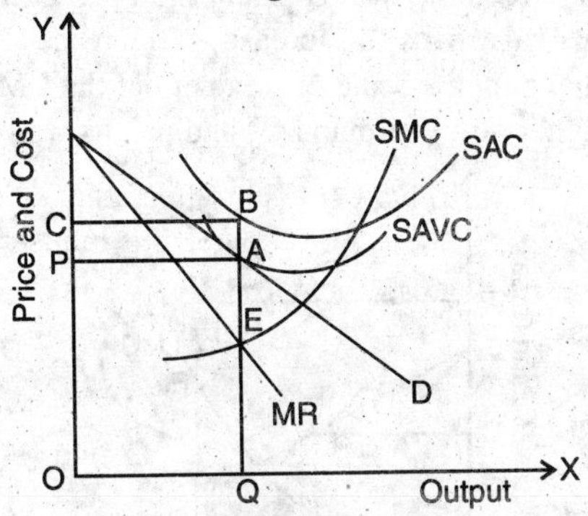

Fig. 39

Figure 39 shows a situation where the Firm is not able to cover its short-run average unit cost and therefore incurs losses. Price set by the equality of SMC and MR curvc is QA which covers only the average Variable cost. The tangency of the demand curve (D) and the average variable cost curve (AVC) at A makes it a *shutdown point*. If the Firm lowers the price below QA, it will have to stop further production. However, at this price the Firm will incur losses equal to the area CBAP during the short-run in the hope of lowering its costs in the long-run.

B. Long-Run Equilibrium

In the Long-run the adjustment process may take place in two ways :

1. With entry open, 2. With entry blocked

WIth Open Entry

Assuming entry and exit of Forms in a monopolistic competitive industry as under pure competition, the adjustment process will ultimately lead to the existence of only normal profits. This is a realistic assumption for the long-run no Firm can earn either super-normal profits or incur losses, since each produces a similar product.

If Firms in the monopolistic competitive industry are earning super-normal profits, new Firms will be attracted into group. With the entry of new Firms, the existing market is divided among more sellers so that each Firm will sell less quantities of the product than before. As a result, the demand curves faced by individual Firms shift down to the left. At the same time the entry of new Firms will increase the demand for inputs and hence the prices of factor-services which will shift the cost curves of individual Firms upward. This two-way adjustment process of lowering the demand curve and raising the cost curves will squeeze out super normal profits. Thus, each Firm will be earning only normal profits in the long-run. This situation is represented in Figure 40 vis-a-vis Figure 41.

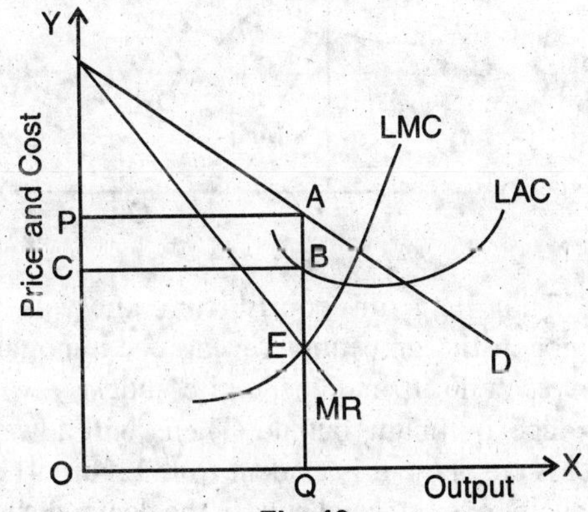

Fig. 40

Before the entry of new Firms the demand and cost conditions of the Firm are represented in Figure 40 where it sells OQ quantity of the product at QA (= OP) price and earns PABC extra profits. When new Firms enter the group, the demand curve of the Firm shifts downward to D_1 and the long-run marginal and average cost curves shift upward as LMC_1 and LAC_1 as shown in Figure 41. As a result of these two opposite forces excess profits are squeezed out. The Firm earns only normal profits at the point of tangency (A_1) between the demand curve (D_1) and the long-run average cost curve

(LAC_1). In this situation each Firm produced less than before (OQ) and also sells at a lower price (OP_1) with the result that further entry into the industry is stopped.

If firms cannot earn extra profits in monopolistic competition, they cannot incur losses either. In such a situation the losing Firms will leave the industry. Supply will be reduced and price will go up. On the other side, resources will become abundant with the exist of Firms, and they will become cheaper. Costs will fall. Ultimately, a rise in price and reduction in costs will eliminate losses. The final situation will be as shown in Figure 41 where each Firm and the industry as a whole will be in long-run equilibrium.

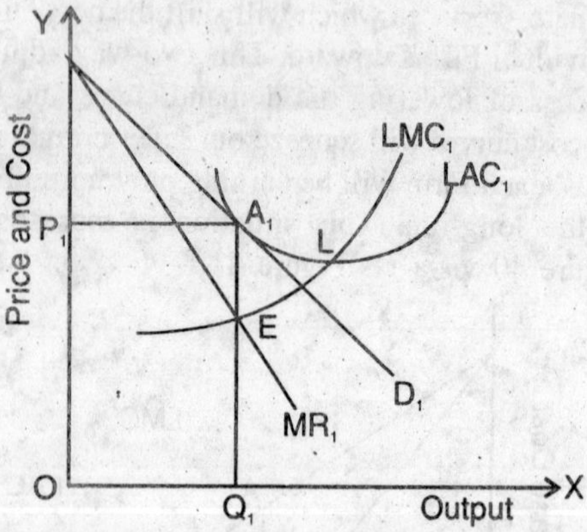

Fig. 41

This long-run equilibrium analysis under monopolistic competition reveals one important fact that each Firm and the entire industry will not produce optimum output. There will always be *excess capacity*. It is evident from Figure 41 where the point of tangency between the demand curve D_1 and the LAC_1 curve is not at the lowest level L. Rather L is to the right of the point of tangency A_1. *This is because the demand curve D_1 is not horizontal but slopes downward to the right.* This each Firm under monopolistic competition has unutilized capacity even in the long-run.

With Entry Closed

Long-run adjustments under monopolistic competition also take place with entry closed for new Firms into the industry. This may be due to deliberate collusion by the existing Firms or the result of market changes.

First, the monopolistic competitive producers may form a powerful association, assure the government of a regular supply of product at a reasonable price consistent with some extra profits and thus block the entry of new Firms. For this purpose, they may also get a law passed by the legislature through political pressure. There being no threat of entry of new Firms, each Firms will have that price-output combination which brings in maximum profits. Such a profit-maximisation combination is brought about by the equality of long-run marginal cost curve and the marginal revenue curve. In Figure 40, the LMC curve cuts the MR curve at E. When OQ quantities of the product are sold at AQ price, the Firm earns PABC profits. If it tries to increase or decrease the output by changing the scale of production, the LMC would be higher or lower than MR and profits would shrink.

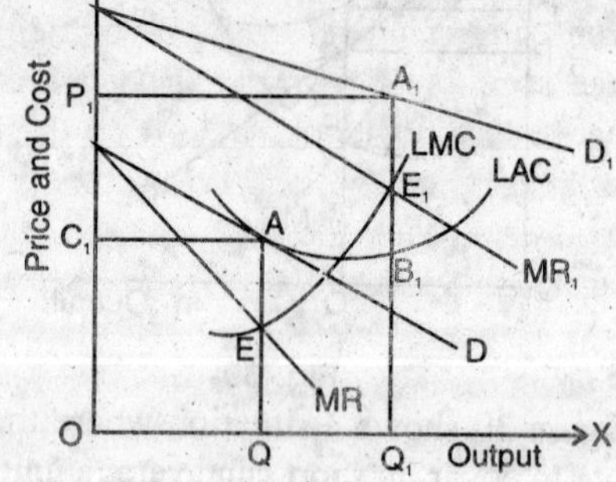

Fig. 42

Secondly, if strong consumer preferences are developed for (differentiated) products of certain Firms their demand curves may shift upward. These Firms will thus be in a position to charge higher prices than other Firms and earn extra profits. But extra profits earned by such Firms will not attract new Firms into the industry. Strong consumer preferences for their products will act as a barrier to the entrance of new Firms. Such a situation is illustrated in Figure 42.

The original demand curve and its corresponding marginal revenue curve faced by the Firm are D and MR respectively. With the increase in consumer preferences for the product, both the curves shift upward as D_1 and MR_1. The earlier output OQ and price QA were determined by the equality of the LMC curve and the MR curve at point E. This price output combination was realising only normal profits for the Firm. The change in consumer preferences towards the products brings about E_1 the new equilibrium level of OQ_1 output at a higher price Q_1A_1 which maximizes $P_1A_1B_1C_1$ profits. Strong consumer preferences for this product will deter new Firms from entering the industry.

Theory of Excess Capacity

The concept of excess capacity is not of recent origin rather it existed in the earlier works of Wicksell and Cairnes. Piero Sraffa and Mrs. Robinson also outlined it. But it was Chamberlin who expounded it in a most systematic manner followed by Kaldor, Kahn, Harrod and Cassels.

Theories of Chamberlin's monopolistic competition and Joan Robinson's imperfect competition have revealed that a Firm under monopolistic competition or imperfect competition in long-run equilibrium produces an output which is less than socially optimum or ideal output. This means that Firms operate at the point on the falling portion of long-run average cost curve, that is, they do not produce the level of output at which long-run average cost is minimum. Long-run equilibrium of a Firm under monopolistic competition is achieved when the demand curve (AR-curve) facing it becomes tangential to the long-run average cost curve so that it earns only normal profits. Under such circumstances Firms can reduce average cost (and hence price) by expanding output to the minimum level of long-run average cost, but it will not because its profits are maximised (equality of marginal revenue with marginal cost is attained) at the level of output smaller than that at which his long-run average cost is minimum.

Society's productive resources are fully utilised when they are used to produced the level of output which renders long-run average cost minimum.

This means a monopolistically competitive Firm produces less than the socially optimum or ideal output, that is, the output corresponding to the lowest point of average cost curve. This is in sharp contrast to the position of the Firm in long-run equilibrium under perfect competition, which operates at the minimum point of the long-run average cost curve. The amount by which the actual long-run output of the Firm under monopolistic competition falls short of the social ideal output is a measure of *excess capacity* which lie unutilised.

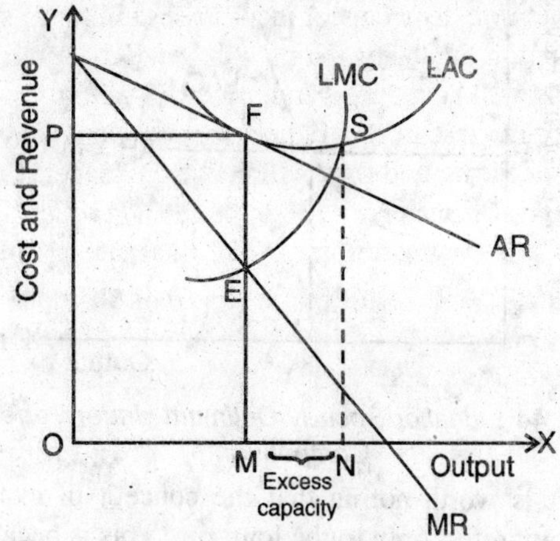

Fig. 43 : *Production of Ideal Output (Socially Optimum) Under Imperfect Competition*

The existence of excess capacity under imperfect or monopolistic competition can be understood from Figures 43 and 44. Figure 44 depicts the long-run position of a perfectly competitive Firm which is in long-run equilibrium at the level of output ON corresponding to which long-run average cost is minimum. It is at output ON that the double condition of long-run equilibrium, namely, Price = MC = AC is fulfilled. It is thus clear that Firms under perfect competition produce socially ideal output. On the other hand, a Firm under monopolistic condition depicted in Figure 43 is in long-run equilibrium at output OM at which its MR is equal to MC and price is equal to average cost (Average revenue curve AR is tangential to average cost curve AC at point F corresponding to output OM). It will be noticed that at output OM average cost is still falling and goes on falling up to output ON.

This means that the Firm can expand his production up to ON and reduce his long-run average cost to the minimum.

Ideal output is ON at which long-run average cost is minimum. Therefore, the Firm is producing

MN less than the ideal output. This MN output represents the excess capacity which emerges under monopolistic competition.

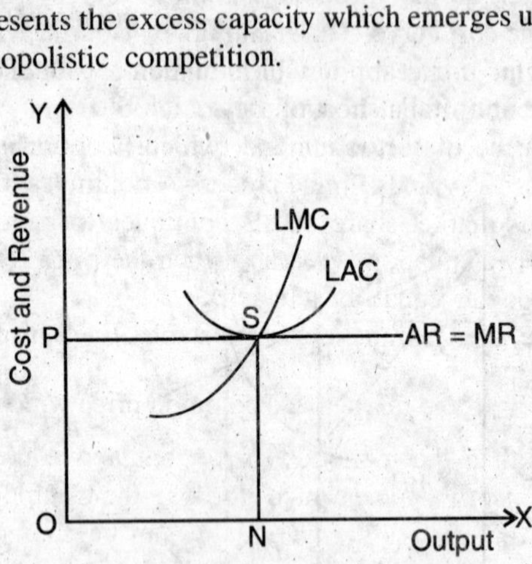

Fig. 44 : *Ideal or Socially Optimum Under Perfect Competition*

It is worth noting that the concept of excess capacity refers only to the long-run. This is because in the short-run under any type of market structure (including perfect competition) there can be all sorts of departures from the ideal reflecting in complete adjustment to existing market conditions. *Another point worth noting is that excess capacity under monopolistic competition emerges because of the downward-sloping demand curve of the Firm.* A downward sloping curve can be tangent to a U-shaped average cost curve only at the latter's falling portion. It is only the horizontal demand curve or average revenue curve (as is actually found under perfect competition) which can be tangent to a U-shaped average cost curve at the latter's minimum point. From this, it also follows that the greater the elasticity of average revenue (or demand) curve confronting a monopolistically competitive firm, the less the excess capacity and vice versa. When the demand curve facing a Firm is perfectly elastic, there is no excess capacity, as is the case under perfect competition.

OLIGOPOLY

We have studied price and output determination under three market forms, namely, perfect competition, monopoly, and monopolistic competition. However, in the real world economies we find that many of the markets or industries are oligopolistic. Oligopoly is an important form of imperfect competition. **Oligopoly is said to prevail when there are few firms or sellers in the market producing or selling a product.** In other words, when there are two or more than two, but not many, producers or sellers of a product, oligopoly is said to exist. Oligopoly is also often referred to as **"Competition among the Few."** The simplest case of oligopoly is duopoly which prevails when there are only two producers or sellers of a product.

When products of few sellers are homogeneous, we talk of **Oligopoly without Product Differentiation or Pure Oligopoly.** On the other hand, when products of the few sellers or firms instead of being homogeneous, are differentiated but close substitutes of each other, Oligopoly with Product Differentiation or Differentiated Oligopoly is said to prevail. Capacity, is as the case under perfect competition.

Cournot's Duopoly Model

The earliest duopoly model was developed in **1838** by the French economist **Augustin Cournot.**

Cournot assumed that there are two firms each owning a mineral well and operating with zero costs. They sell their output in a market with a straight line demand curve. **Each firm acts on the assumption that its competition will not change its output, and decides its own output so as to maximise profit.**

Cournot's duopoly model has been presented in Figure 45. To begin the analysis, suppose that, initially, A is the only seller of mineral water in the market. In order to maximise his profits or revenue, he sells quantity OQ where his MC = O = MR, at price OP_2. His total profit is OP_2PQ.

Now let B enter the market. The market open to him is QM which is half of the total market. That is, he can sell his product in the remaining half of the market. He assumes that A will not change his price and output because he is making the maximum profit. That is, B assumes that A will continue to sell OQ at price OP_2.

Thus, the market available to him is QM and relevant demand curve is PM. When he draws his MR curve, PN, it bisects QM at point N where QN = NM. In order to maximise his revenue, B sells QN at price OP_1. His total revenue is maximum at QRP'N.

Note that B supplies only QN = $\frac{1}{4}\left(\frac{1}{2}\cdot\frac{1}{2}\right)$ of the market.

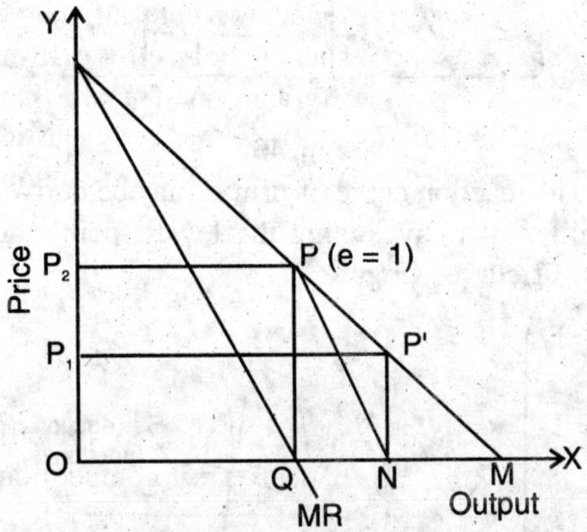

Fig. 45 : *Cournot's Model*

With the entry of B, Price falls to OP_1. Therefore, A's expected profit falls to OP_1, RQ. Faced with this situation, A attempts to adjust his output to the changed condition. He assumes that B will not change his output QN. Accordingly, A assumes that B will continue to supply ¼ of the market and he has ¾ $=\left(1-\frac{1}{4}\right)$ of the market available to him. To maximise his profit, A will therefore supply $\frac{1}{2}\cdot\frac{3}{4}=\frac{3}{8}$ of the market. A's share has fallen from ½ to ¾.

Now B turns to react. Following Cournot's assumption B assumes that A will continue to supply only $\frac{3}{8}$ of the market and the market open to him $1-\frac{3}{8}=\frac{5}{8}$. To maximise his profit under the new conditions, B will supply $\frac{1}{2}\cdot\frac{5}{8}=\frac{5}{16}$ of the market. It is new for A to reappraise the situation and adjust his price and output accordingly.

This process of action and reaction continues in successive periods. In the process A continues to loosen his market share and B continues to gain. Eventually a situation is reached when their market share becomes equal at 1/3 each.

Thus, the Cournot solution is stable. Each firm supplies $\frac{1}{3}$ of the market, at a common price which is lower than the monopoly price, but above the pure competitive price (which is zero in the Cournot example of costless production). It can be shown that if there are three firms in the industry, each will produce one-quarters of the market and all of them together will supply $\frac{3}{4}\left(=\frac{1}{4}.3\right)$ of the entire market OM. And, in general, if there are n firms in the industry each will provide $\frac{1}{(n+1)}$ of the market, and the industry output will be $\frac{n}{(n+1)}$. Clearly as more firms are assumed to exist in the industry, the higher the total quantity supplied and hence the lower the price. The larger the number of firms the closer is output and price to the competitive level.

Criticism

Cournot's model leads to a stable equilibrium. However, his model may be criticised on several accounts:

The behavioural pattern of firms is naive. Firms do not learn from past miscalculations of competitior's reactions.

Although the quantity produced by the competitors is at each stage assumed constant, a quantity competition emerges which drives P down, towards the competitive level.

The model does not say how long the adjustment period will be.

The assumption of costless production is unrealistic.

Bertrand's Duopoly Model

Bertrand developed his duopoly model in 1883. His model differs from Cournot's in that he assumes that each firm expects that the rival will keep its price Constant, irrespective of its own decision about pricing. Thus each firm is faced by the same **market demand,** and aims at the maximisation of its own profit on the assumption that the price of the competition will remain constant.

The model may be presented with the analytical tools of the reaction functions of the duopolists. In Bertrand's model the reaction curves are derived from **isoprofit maps** which are convex to the axes, on which we now measure the prices of the duopolists. Each isoprofit curve for firm A shows the same level of profit which would accrue to A from various levels of prices charged by this firm and its rival. The isoprofit curve for A is convex to its price axis (P_A). This shape shows the fact that firm A must lower its price up to a certain level (point *e* in Figure 46) to meet the cutting of price of its competitior, in order to maintain the level of its profits at A_2. However, after that price level has been reached and if B continues to cut its price, firm A will be unable to retain its profits, even if it keeps its own price unchanged (at P_3). If, for example, firm B cuts its price at B, firm A will find itself at a lower isoprofit curve A_1 which shows lower profits. The reduction of profits of A is due to the fall in price, and the increase in output beyond the optimal level of utilisation of the plant with the consequent increase in costs. Clearly the lower the isoprofit curve, the lower the level of profits.

To Summarise : For any price charged by firm B there will be a unique price of firm A which maximises the latter's profit. This unique profit—maximising price is determined at the lowest point on the highest attainable isoprofit curve of A. The minimum points of the isoprofit curves lie to the right of each other, reflecting the fact that as firm A moves to a higher level of profit, it gains some of the customers of B when the latter increases its price, even if A also raises its price. If we join the lowest points of the successive isoprofit curves we obtain the reaction curve of firm A: this is the locus of points of maximum profits that A can attain by charging a certain price, given the price of its rival.

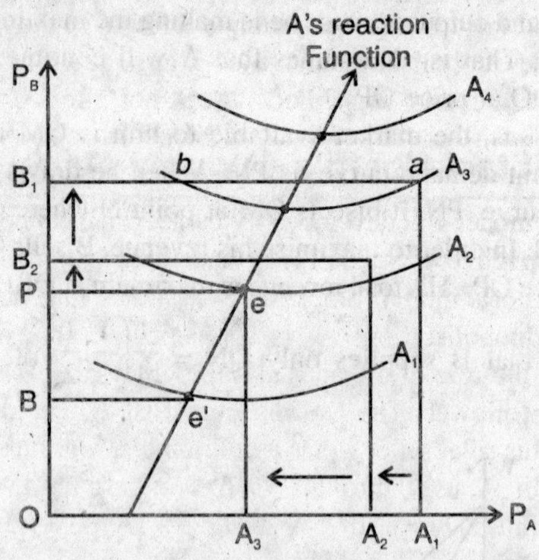

Fig. 46

The reaction curve of firm B may be derived in a similar way, by joining the lowest points of its isoprofit curves (Figure 47).

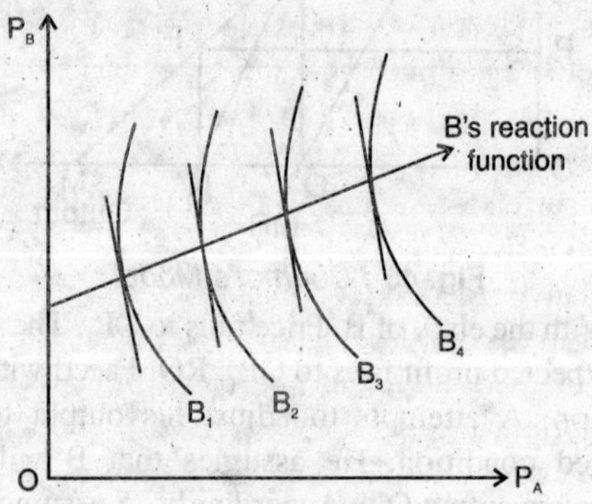

Fig. 47

Bertrand's model leads to a stable equilibrium, defined by the point of intersection of the two reaction curves.

Bertrand's model may be criticised on the same grounds as Cournot's model:

The behavioural pattern emerging from Bertrand's assumption is naive: firms never learn from past experience.

Each firm maximises its own profit, but the industry (Joint) profits are not maximised.

The equilibrium price will be the competitive price. (In the example of costless mineral-water production, the price in Bertrand's model would fall to zero. If production is not costless, then price would fall to the level which would cover the costs of the duopolists inclusive of a normal profit.)

The model is 'closed'– does not allow entry.

Stackelberg's Duopoly Model

This model was developed by the German economist **Heinrich von Stackelberg** and is an extension of Cournot's model. Stackelberg assumes that one of the duopolist (Say A) is sophisticated enough to play the role of a leader and the other (Say B) acts as a follower. The leading duopolist A recognises that his rival seller B has a definite reaction function which A uses into his own profit function and maximises his profits. In summary, if only one firm is sophisticated, it will emerge as the leader, and a stable equilibrium will emerge, since the naive firm will act as a follower.

However, if both firms are sophisticated, then both will want to act as leaders, because this action yields a greater profit to them. In this case the market situation becomes unstable. The situation is known as **Stackelberg's disequilibrium** and the effect will either be a price war until one of the firms surrenders and agrees to act as follower, or a collusion is reached, with both firms abandoning their naive reaction functions and moving to a point closer to (or on) the Edgeworth contract curve with both of them attaining higher profits. If the final equilibrium lies on the Edgeworth contract curve the industry profits (Joint profits) are maximised.

Stackelberg's model has interesting implications. It shows clearly that naive behaviour does not pay. The rivals should recognise their interdependence.

By recognising the other's reactions each duopolist can reach a higher level of profit for himself.

If both firms start recognising their mutual interdependence, each starts worrying about the rival's profits and the rival's reactions. If each ignores the other, a price war will be inevitable, as a result of which both will be worse off.

This model shows that a bargaining procedure and a collusive agreement becomes advantageous to both duopolists. With such a collusive agreement the duopolists may reach a point on the Edgeworth contract curve, thus attaining joint profit maximisation.

Non-Collusive Models of Oligopoly

The theory of non-collusive or uncoordinated oligopoly is one of the oldest theories of competition and monopoly or perhaps of all the theories of the behaviour of the individual firm. The non-collusive models of oligopoly explain the price and output determination in a market structure in which oligopolists recognise their inter-dependence. A model of oligopoly was first of all put forth by **Cournot** in 1838. Cournot's model of oligopoly was subjected to criticism in 1883 by Joseph Bertrand, a French mathematician, whose criticism of Cournot provided a substitute model of oligopoly. In 1897, Edgeworth offered another model of oligopoly in an article published in an Italian Journal.

It should be noted that in Cournot's model, it is rival's output which is assumed by an oligopolist to remain fixed at the present level, while he contemplates a certain change in his own output. On the other hand, Bertrand and Edgeworth in their models assume that the oligopolist believes that rival's price remains unchanged at the present level.

Collusive Oligopoly

There are at least three major factor which bring collusion between the oligopolistic firms. Firsts collusion reduces the degree of competition between the firms and helps them act monopolistically in their effort of profit maximisation. Second, collusion reduces the oligopolistic uncertainty surrounding the market since cartel members, are not supposed to act independently and in the manner that is detrimental to the interest of other firms. Third, collusion forms a kind of barrier to the entry of new firms.

Collusion between oligopoly firms may take many forms depending on their relative strength, their objective and whether collusion is legal or illegal. There are however two main types of collusion: *(i)* Cartels, *(ii)* Price leadership.

Cartels

A cartel is a formal organisation of the oligopoly firms in an industry. Cartels are the perfect form of collusion. A cartel is an organisation of independent firms within the same industry formed for the purpose of increasing the profits of the members of subjecting their competitive tendencies to some form of control. If follows common policies in relation to prices, outputs and sales territories. Cartels may be in the form of **open collusion** or secret collusion. Whether open or secret, cartel agreements are explicit and formal in the sense that agreements are enforceable on member firms willing to pursue an independent pricing policy. Cartels are therefore regarded as the perfect form of collusion.

A cartel performs a variety of services for its members. The two typical services of central importance are *(a)* fixing price for joint maximisation of industry profits; and *(b)* market sharing between its members. In this section, we will examine these two activities of cartels.

A. Cartels Aiming at Joint-Profit Maximisation

Cartels imply direct agreements among the competing oligopolist with the aim of reducing the uncertainty arising from their mutual interdependence. In this particular case the aim of the cartel is the maximisation of the industry profit. Let us suppose that a group of firms producing a homogeneous commodity form a cartel aiming at joint profit maximisation. The firms appoint a central management board with powers to decide *(a)* the total quantity to be produced; *(b)* the price at which it must be sold; and *(c)* share of each firm in the total output. The central management board is provided with cost figures of individual firms. Besides, it is supposed to obtain the necessary data required to formulate the market demand (AR) curve. The management board calculates the marginal cost (MC) and marginal revenue (MR) for the industry. Further, the management board holds the position of a multiplant monopoly. It determines the price and output for each firm in the manner a multiplant monopoly determines the price and output for each plant.

The model of price and output determination for each firm has been presented in Figure 48. It is assumed for the sake of convenience that there are only two firms A and B, in the cartel. Their respective cost curves are given in the first two panels of the figure. In the third panel, the AR and MR curves represent the revenue conditions of the industry. The MC curve is the summation of MC curves of the individual firms. The MC and MR intersect at point C determining the industry output at OQ. The market price is determined at PQ. The industry output OQ is so allocated between firms A and B that their individual MC = MR. The share of each firm in the industry output OQ, can be obtained by drawing a line from point C and parallel to X-axis through MC_2 and MC_1. The points of intersection C_1 and C_2 determine the level of output for firms A and B respectively. Thus, the share of each of the two firms A and B, is determined at Oq_1 and Oq_2, where $Oq_1 + Oq_2 = OQ$.

Note that the firm with the lower costs produces a larger amount of output. However, this does not

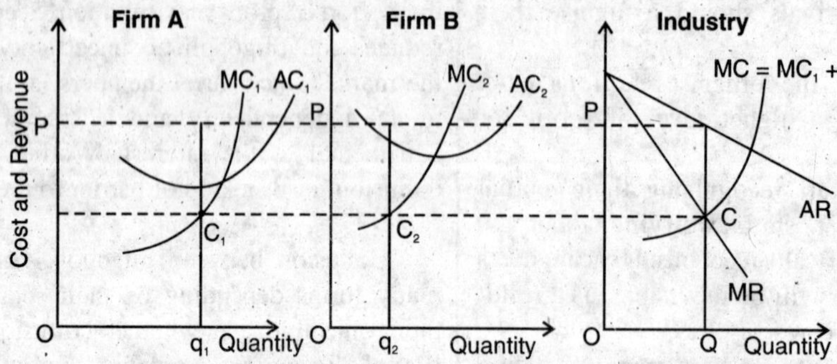

Fig. 48 : *Price and Output Determination Under Cartel*

mean that A will also take the larger share of the attained joint profit. The total industry profit is the sum of the profits from the output of the two firms, denoted by the shaded areas of figures. The distribution of profits is decided by the central agency of the cartel.

B. Market-Sharing Cartels

This form of collusion is more common in practice because it is more popular. The firms agree to share the market, but keep a considerable degree of freedom concerning the style of their output, their selling activities and other decisions. There are two basic methods for sharing the market: non-price competition and determination of quotas.

Price Leadership

Another form of collusion is price leadership. In this form of co-ordinated behaviour of oligopolists one firm sets the price and the others follow it because it is advantageous to them or because they prefer to avoid uncertainty about their competitor's reactions even if this implies departure of the followers from their profit-maximising position. Price leadership is widespread in the business world. It may be practised either by explicit agreement or informally. In nearly all cases price leadership is tacit since open collusive agreements are illegal in most countries.

Price leadership is more widespread than cartels, because it allows the members complete freedom regarding their product and selling activities and thus is more acceptable to the followers than a complete cartel, which requires the surrendering of all freedom of action to the central agency.

If the product is homogeneous and the firms are highly concentrated in a location the price will be identical. However, if the product is differentiated prices will differ, but the direction of their change will be the same, while the same price differentials will broadly be kept.

Types of Price Leadership

Price leadership is of various types. Firstly, there is a price leadership of the dominant firm. Under this one of the few firms in the industry may be producing a very large proportion of the total production of the industry and may therefore dominate the market of the product. This dominant firm wields a great influence over the market of the product, while other firms are small and are incapable of making any impact on the market. As a result, the dominant firm estimates its own demand curve and fixes a price which maximises its own profits. The other firms which are small having no individual effects on the price, follow the dominant firm and accepting the price set by him, they adjust their output accordingly.

Secondly, there is a **barometric price leadership** under which an old, experienced, largest or most respected firm assumes the role of a custodian who protects the interest of all. He assesses the change in the market conditions with regard to the demand for the product, costs of production, competition from the related products etc. and makes changes in price which are best from the viewpoint of all the firms in the industry.

Thirdly, there is **exploitative** or **aggressive price** leadership under which a very large or dominant firm establishes its leadership by following aggressive price policies and thus compel the other firms in the industry to follow him in respect of price. Such a firm will often initiate a move threatening to compete the others out of the market if they do not follow him in setting their prices.

Price-Output Determination Under Price Leadership

Economists have developed various models concerning price-output determination under price leadership taking different assumptions about the behaviour of price leader and his followers. We

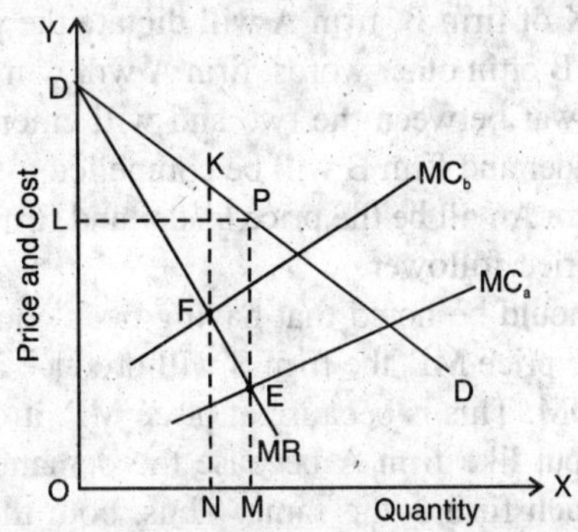

Fig. 49 : *Price-Output Equilibrium Under Price Leadership*

shall confine ourselves to price-output determination under dominant price leadership and explain a simple case. We make the following assumptions:

1. There are two firms, A and B. The firm A has a lower cost of production than B.
2. The product produced by the two firms is homogeneous so that the consumers have no preference between them.
3. Each of the two firms has equal share in the market. In other words, demand curve facing each firm will be the same and will be half of the total market demand curve of the product.

Given the above assumptions, price and output determination under price leadership is illustrated in Figure 49. Each firm is facing demand curve DD which is half of the total market demand curve for the product. MR is the marginal revenue curve of each firm. MC_a is the marginal cost curve of firm A and MC_b is the marginal cost curve of firm B. MC_a lies below MC_b because we are assuming that firm A has a lower cost of production than firm B.

The firm A will be maximizing its profits by selling output OM and setting price MP, since at output OM, its marginal cost is equal to the marginal revenue. Firm B's profits will be maximum when it fixes price NK and sells output ON. It will be seen from the figure that profit maximizing price MP of firm A is lower than the profit-maximizing price NK of firm B. Since the two firms are producing a homogeneous product, they cannot charge two different prices. Because the profit-maximizing price MP of firm A is lower than the profit-maximizing price NK of firm B, firm A will dictate the price to the firm B or in other words, firm A will win if there is price war between the two and will emerge as a price leader and firm B will be compelled to follow. Thus, firm A will be the price leader and firm B will be the price follower.

It should be noted that having been compelled to charge price MP, the firm B will produce and sell output OM. This is because at price MP, it can sell OM output like firm A because the demand curve facing each firm is the same. Thus, both the firms will charge the same price (MP) and sell the same amount (OM). But there is an important difference between the two. While firm A, the price leader, will be maximizing its profits by selling output OM and charging price MP, the firm B will not be making maximum profits with this price output combination because its profits are maximum at output ON and price NK. Profits earned by firm B by selling output OM and charging price MP will be smaller than those of firm A because its costs are greater.

When the products of the price leader and his price-followers are differentiated, then the price charged by them will be different but the prices charged by the followers will be only slightly different either way from that of the price leader and they will conform to a definite pattern of differentials.

Kinky Demand Curve

The Kinked demand curve hypothesis was put forward by **Paul M. Sweezy.** In explaining price and output especially under oligopoly with product differentiation economists often use the kinked demand curve hypothesis. This is because when under oligopoly products are differentiated, it is unlikely that when a firm raises its price, all customers would leave it because some customers are intimately attached to it due to product differentiation. As a result, demand curve facing a firm under differentiated oligopoly is not perfectly elastic.

The demand curve facing an oligopolist, according to the kinked demand curve hypothesis, has a **'Kink'** at the level of the prevailing price. The kink is formed at the prevailing price level because the segment of the demand curve above the prevailing price level is highly elastic and the segment of the demand curve below the prevailing price level is inelastic. A kinked demand curve D with a kink at point P has been shown in Figure 50. The prevailing price level is MP and the firm is producing and selling the output OM.

Now the upper segment *d*P of the demand curve *d*D is relatively elastic and the lower segment PD is relatively inelastic. This difference in elasticities is due to the particular competitive reaction pattern assumed by kinky oligopoly demand curve hypothesis.

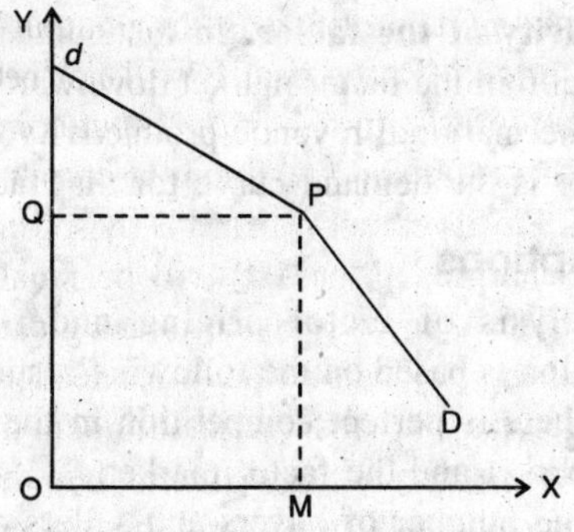

Fig. 50 : *Kinked Demand Curve Under Oligopoly.*

The competitive reaction pattern assumed by the kinky oligopoly demand curve theory is as follows:

Each oligopolist believes that if he lowers the price below the prevailing level his competitors will follow him and will accordingly lower their prices, whereas if he raises the price above the prevailing level his competitors will not follow his increase in price.

Theories of Distribution

Theory of factor pricing or the theory of distribution is concerned with analysis of how and in what manner the factors of production get remuneration for their contribution to the production process as the production of goods and services in an economy is the result of the joint efforts of factors of production.

Though like the pricing of goods, the factor pricing is also based on market demand and supply, the essential difference between these two lies in the force operating behind demand and supply of these factors. How much will be the demand for a factor depend upon the quantity of goods that it helps to produce and the extent of demand for these goods in the market. Thus, the demand for a factor of production depends upon the demand for its products in the market. This type of demand is known as derived demand.

Concepts of Productivity

Average Physical Productivity is the total production divided by the number of units of a factor employed.

Average Productivity of a factor

$$= \frac{\text{Total Output}}{\text{Total Number of units of a factor}}$$

Marginal physical productivity of a factor is the increase in total output caused by employing an additional unit of the factor, quantity of other factors remaining fixed.

$$MP_L = \frac{dX}{dL} \text{ and } MP_K = \frac{dX}{dK}$$

Where

MP_L = marginal productivity of labour
MP_K = marginal productivity of capital
dX = change in output
dL = change in labour
dK = change in capital.

Marginal Revenue Product (MRP) : Marginal Revenue Product is the increment in the total value product caused by employing an additional unit of a factor, the expenditure on other factors remaining unchanged. In other words, marginal revenue product is the marginal physical product of the factor multiplied by the marginal revenue.

$$MRP = MPP \times MR$$

Value of Marginal Product (VMP) : It means the marginal physical product of the factor multiplied by the price of the product (i.e. average revenue).

$$VMP = MPP \times \text{Price (or AR)}$$

Since under perfect competition the demand curve of the product facing an individual firm is perfectly elastic and therefore price and marginal revenue are equal, the value of marginal product and marginal revenue product are equal to each other as is shown in Figure 51. But since in monopoly or imperfect competition average revenue (or demand curve) is falling downward and MR curve lies below the average revenue curve, price is not equal to marginal revenue. Therefore, in monopoly or in others forms of imperfect competition, MRP will not be equal to the value of marginal product (VMP). Since price is higher than marginal revenue under monopoly or monopolistic competition in the product market, the value of marginal product (VMP) will be larger than the marginal revenue product (MRP) and the marginal revenue product (MRP) curve will lie below the value of marginal product (VMP) curve as is shown in Figure 52. Thus, **in perfect competition MRP and VMP have identical meanings but in imperfect competition they diverge.**

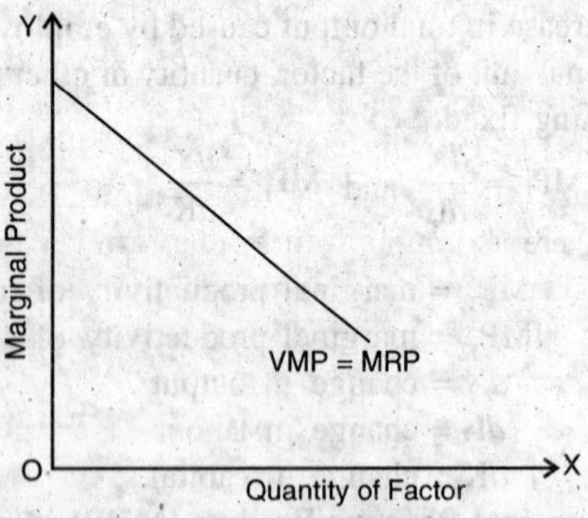

Fig. 51 : *VMP and MRP under Perfect Competition in the Product Market*

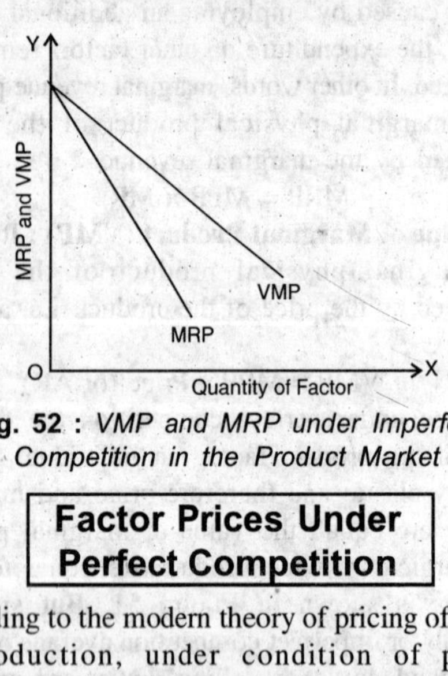

Fig. 52 : *VMP and MRP under Imperfect Competition in the Product Market*

Factor Prices Under Perfect Competition

According to the modern theory of pricing of factors of production, under condition of perfect competition it is the forces of demand for and supply of factors which determine their prices. The demand for a factor service is **derived demand** which is derived from the demand for the product that it helps to produce. Thus, the demand for a factor ultimately depends upon the demands for goods it helps to produce. The greater the demand for goods a particular type of factor helps to make, the greater the demand for that type of factor. **Just as demand for a good depends upon its utility, the demand for a factor depends upon the marginal revenue productivity of the factor.** In fact, under perfect competition in the factor market downward sloping part of the marginal revenue productivity curve of the factor is the demand curve for that factor.

Assumptions

The analysis of factor pricing under perfect competition is based on the following assumptions.

1. There is perfect competition in the product market and the factor market.
2. The number of buyers and sellers of factor services is large.
3. All units of a factor are homogeneous.
4. Factors of production are perfectly mobile.
5. There is perfect substitutability between factors and their units.
6. All factor-units are divisible.
7. Buyers and sellers of factor services have complete knowledge about market conditions.
8. Buyers and sellers of factor services have complete freedom to enter and leave the market.

The supply of a factor service means the number of units which a resource owner sells at a particular price. There is a direct relationship between price and the supply of a factor service. This is in the short-run when the supply of productive service is not perfectly elastic. More of it will be supplied at a higher price and less at a lower price. Thus, the shape of the supply curve of a factor service is upward sloping from left to right, i.e. it has a positive slope.

Under a perfectly competitive factor market there are many buyers of a productive service so that a single firm purchases only a small portion of the total factor service and in no way influences its market price. It takes the price of the factor service as given and employs as many units as it needs at that price. Thus, the supply of a factor service to the firm is **perfectly elastic** in the long-run at the given market price. As a result, for a firm working under perfect competition in the factor market, the extra cost of hiring an extra unit of the factor will be equal to the price of the factor which remains unchanged. Thus, marginal factor cost under perfect competition in the factor market is equal to the price of the factor (P_f = MFC). This is shown in figure 53. In this figure, ruling price of the factor in the market is OP, which the firm has to accept as given and constant. Supply curve of the factor (or AFC curve) is horizontal straight line and MFC curve coincides with it.

Determination of Factor Price

Given the demand and supply conditions of the factor service as enumerated above the firm will continue to employ more units of a particular factor service so long as the additional revenue obtained from an additional unit of the factor service (MRP) exceeds the extra cost of employing it (MFC). It will be earning maximum profits at the point at which the MRP equals the MFC. If the firm employs less than this, MRP would be higher than MFC and it would be to its advantage to hire more units of the factor service because they would add to revenue more than costs. In case the firm decides to hire beyond the point of equality of MRP and MFC, it would be a loser because costs would rise more than revenue. Thus, in a perfectly competitive factor market the firm will be in equilibrium when MRP ≥ MFC which implies two conditions.

1. MRP must equal MFC

2. The MRP curve must cut the MFC curve from above at the equilibrium point.

The pricing of a factor service as stated above can be explained diagrammatically. In Figure 53,

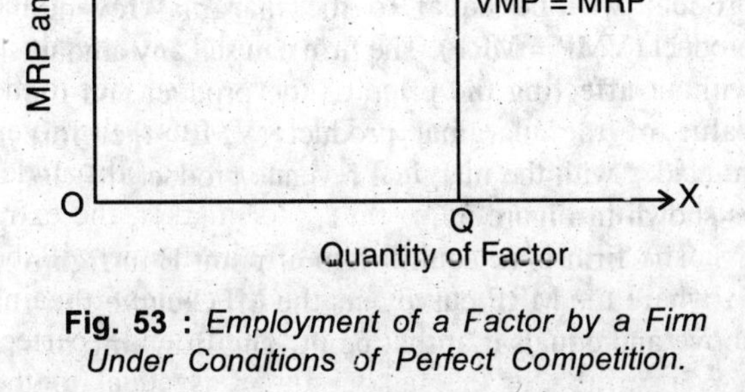

Fig. 53 : *Employment of a Factor by a Firm Under Conditions of Perfect Competition.*

VMP = MRP is the demand curve and AFC = MFC is the supply curve of the factor service. Since the price of the factor service is given and constant at OP for the firm, the MRP curve cuts the MFC curve at E from above. This is the equilibrium point for the firm at which it employees OQ units of the factor service. The MRP curve also cuts the MFC curve at R. But this cannot be the equilibrium point because MRP cuts MFC from below. It is not the point of maximum profit for the firm because MRP is higher than MFC beyond this point R. Thus, E is the point of equilibrium in a perfectly competitive factor market when

MRP = VMP = MFC = AFC = Price

Under perfect competition in both factor and product markets, a firm may be at a profit or at a loss in the short-run. But in the long-run it must earn normal profits.

Factor Pricing Under Imperfect Competition

Factor pricing under imperfect competition or monopoly is studied under three categories:

(a) When the factor market is perfectly competitive and the product market is imperfectly competitive or monopolistic.

(b) When there is monopsony in the factor market and perfect competition in the product market.

(c) When there is monopsony in the factor market and monopoly in the product market.

We discuss these variants of factor pricing under imperfect competition.

A. Factor Market Perfectly Competitive and Product Market Imperfectly Competitive or Monopolistic

In a perfectly competitive factor market, the price of the factor service is given for the firm and does not affect the volume of its purchases. The supply curve or the cost curve is horizontal to the X – axis (AFC = MFC). But because there is imperfect or monopoly in the product market, the MRP curve will lie below the VMP curve. Since we know that under imperfect competition or monopoly in the product market marginal revenue is less than the price (AR) of the product, therefore the MRP will be less than the value of marginal product (VMP). Symbolically,

$$MRP < VMP$$

$\because$ MR < P (Under imperfect competition both AR and MR curves slope downward)

The firm will be in equilibrium where MRP equals MFC, the price of the factor under perfect competition. This is shown in figure 54 by point E where the firms employs OQ units of factor service at OP price. Hence, the MRP of employing OQ units is QE which is less than QA the value of its marginal product. Thus, the factor service gets less than the value of its marginal product by EA amount. This means that when the firms have monopolistic power the factor is paid its MRP which is smaller than the VMP. This effect has been called **monopolistic exploitation** by **Joan Robinson.**

When the firm equates MRP with MFC it employs less units of the factor service because of imperfect competition in the product market than what is would have had there been perfect competition. Thus it employs OQ units of the factor, as compared with OQ_1 units (where VMP = MFC) that a competitive product seller would employ consequently. Under imperfectly competitive product market, the demand for the factor will be less by Q_1Q.

According to Joan Robinson a productive factor is exploited if it is paid a price less than the value of its marginal product (VMP). We saw that a profit maximiser will employ a factor until the point where an additional unit adds precisely the same amount to total cost and total revenue.

For a **perfectly competitive firm**

$$VMP_L = MRP_L$$

Because:

$$VMP_L = MPP_L.MR_X$$

But $P_X = MR_X$

So that

$$VMP_L = MRP_L$$

Thus, when the commodity market is perfectly competitive the profit maximising behaviour of firms leads to the payment of factor prices which are equal to the value of the marginal product (VMP) of the factors.

However, the condition of equilibrium of a monopolistic firm is

$$MRP_L = MPP_L.MR_X = w$$

and $MR_x < Px$, so that factors are paid less than the value of their marginal product. The difference AE in Figure 54 shows that profit maximising behaviour of imperfectly competitive firms causes the factor price to be less than the value of its marginal produc .

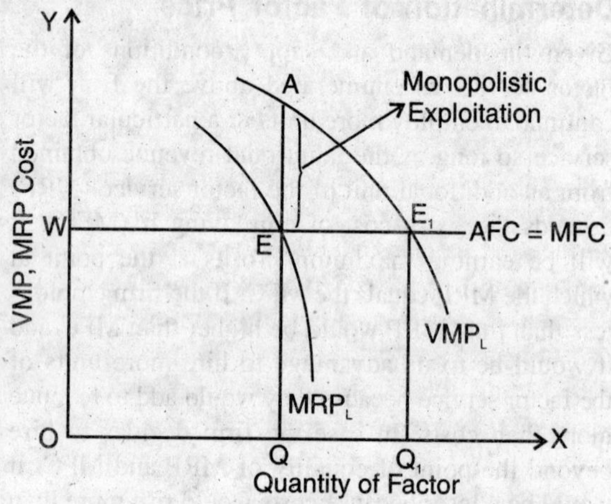

Fig. 54

B. Monopsony in the Factor Market and Perfect Competition in the Product Market

A monopsonist firm is a single buyer of a particular factor in the market. Since the firm is the market for the factor in this case, the supply of factor service to the monopsonist is identical to its supply to the market. Thus, the supply curve to the firm (AFC) is positively sloping from left to right upward. The firm can employ more units of the factor service by offering a higher price per unit. The MFC curve to this AFC curve will also be sloping upward and will be above the AFC curve throughout its length.

Since we are assuming perfect competition in the product market, the value of the marginal product will be equal to the marginal revenue product (VMP = MRP). The firm can sell any amount without affecting the price of the product and the value of the marginal product (VMP) therefore coincides with the marginal revenue product (MRP), as shown in Figure 55.

The firm is in equilibrium at point E in figure 51 where the MRP curve cuts the MFC curve from above and equals it at that point. The firm employs

OQ units of the factor service by paying OP (= QA) price for them. In this case, there is **monopsonistic exploitation** of the factor because the factor service is being paid less than its marginal revenue product. For OQ units the factor is being paid QA (= OP) price whereas its marginal revenue product is QE. The difference between the MRP and the price paid to the factor is AE (QE – QA) which measures monopsonistic exploitation per unit of the factor employed.

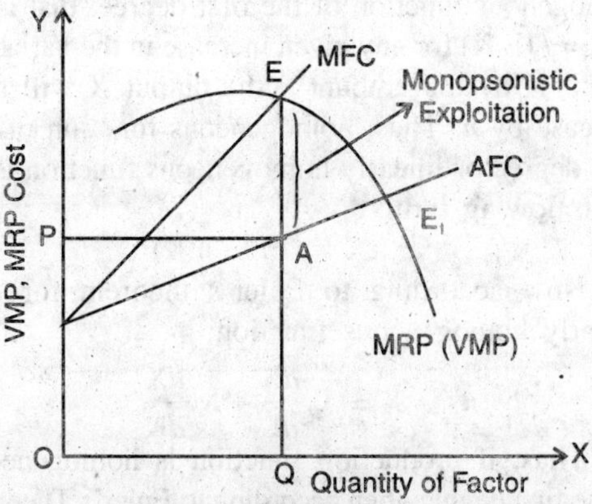

Fig. 55

C. Monopsony in the Factor Market and Monopoly in the Product Market

When there is monopsony in the factor market and monopoly in the product market, MRP < VMP and the MFC > AFC. This implies that the MRP curve will lie below the VMP curve and MFC curve will lie above the AFC curve, as shown in Figure 56.

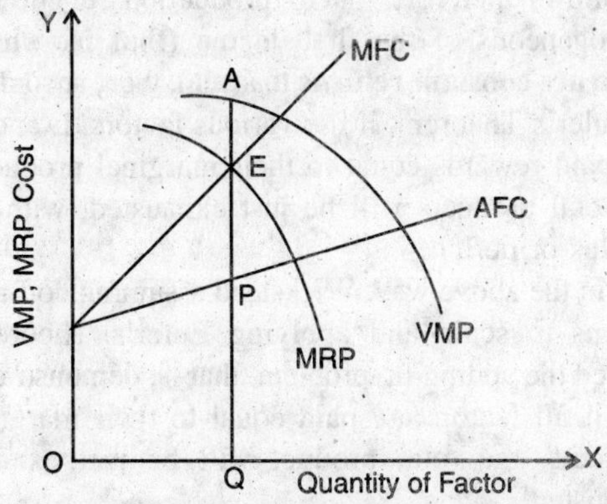

Fig. 56

As usual, the firm is in equilibrium at point E where the MRP curve cuts the MFC curve from above and equals it. The firm employs OQ units of the factors service at QP price which is less than QE the marginal revenue product of the factor. Thus due to its monopsonistic position in the factor market, the firm exploits the factor units used to the extent of PE (QE – QP). On the other hand, due to its monopolistic position in the product market, the MRP of the factor is less than its VMP and the firm exploits the factor units employed further to the extent of EA amount. We may conclude that in the case of monopsony in the factor market and monopoly in the product market, the factor used in production by the firm is doubly exploited: **first,** due to the excess of MRP over the price of the factor, and **second,** due to the excess of the VMP over the marginal revenue product of the factor.

In summary

(a) In perfectly competitive markets the factor is paid its VMP.

(b) If the firm has monopolistic power in the product market but no power in the input market, the factor is paid its MRP < VMP.

(c) If the firm has both monopolistic power in the product market and monopsonistic power in put market the factor is paid a price which is even lower than its MRP. This is the basic characteristic of monopsonistic exploitation.

Role of Collective Bargaining by Trade Unions In Raising Wages

First. If the firm-buyers have no monopsonistic power, labour unions can attain an increase in the wage rate at the expense of a lower employment. Whether this result is beneficial to all the members of the union depends on the elasticity of demand for labour and the distribution policies of the union.

Second. If the firm-buyers have monopsonistic power, the union's actions can eliminate one part of the **monopsonistic exploitation**, namely the part that is solely attributable to the monopsonistic power of the firms. However, the other portion of the monopsonistic exploitation, that which is due to the monopoly power of firms in the product market, cannot be eliminated by trade union action.

Third. If the firm-buyers have monopsonistic power, trade unions can increase the total wage bill in cases, by either increasing employment, or the wage rate, or both. Only if the demand for labour is elastic can the union harm its members, if it sets the wage rate above the maximum level for the initial (pre-union) level of employment.

The 'Adding-Up' Problem: 'Product Exhaustion' Theorems

As soon as it was propounded that the factors of production are paid equal to their marginal products, a perplexing problem cropped up over which there was a serious debate among the famous economists at that time. The perplexing problem which was posed was that if all factors were paid rewards equal to their marginal products, would the total product be just exactly exhausted? In other words, If each factor is rewarded equal to its marginal product, the total product should be disposed of without any surplus or deficit. The problem of proving that the total product will be just exhausted if all factors are paid rewards equal to their marginal products has been called **"Adding-up-Problem"** or **Product Exhaustion Problem**.

Wicksteed's Solution of Product Exhaustion Problem

Philip Wicksteed was one of the first economists who posed this problem and provided a solution for it. Wicksteed applied a mathematical proposition called **Euler's Theorem** to prove that the total product will be just exhausted if all the factors are paid equal to their marginal products. Let X stand for the total output of the product, L stand for the labour and K stand for the capital. Then, the adding-up problem implies that,

$$X = MP_L.L + MP_K.K$$

That is, the marginal product of labour (MP_L) multiplied by the amount of labour (L) plus the marginal product of capital (MP_K) multiplied by the amount of capital (K) equals the total product of the firm. Marginal products of various factors can be expressed as partial derivatives. Thus, the marginal product of labour can be expressed as $\frac{dX}{dL}$, and the marginal of capital as $\frac{dX}{dK}$, then for the adding-up problem to be fulfilled, the following equation must hold good:

$$X = L.\frac{dX}{dL} + K.\frac{dX}{dK}$$

Where $L.\frac{dX}{dL}$ represents share of the total product going to labour.

$K.\frac{dX}{dK}$ represents share of the total product going to capital.

Now, Euler's Theorem states that if X is a homogenous function of the first degree, that is, if in $X = f(L,K)$ for any given increase in the variables L and K by the amount n the output X will also increase by n. Thus, homogeneous function of the first degree or linearly homogeneous function is of the following form:

$$nX = f(n.L, n.K)$$

Now according to Euler's theorem for this linearly homogeneous function:

$$X = L.\frac{dX}{dL} + K.\frac{dX}{dK}$$

Thus, if production function is homogeneous of the first degree, then according to Euler's Theorem the total product.

$$X = L.\frac{dX}{dL} + K.\frac{dX}{dK}$$

Where $\frac{dX}{dL}, \frac{dX}{dK}$ are partial derivatives of the production function and therefore represent the marginal products of labour and capital respectively. It follows therefore that if production function is homogeneous of the first degree **(that is, where there are constant returns to scale),** then, according to Euler's Theorem, if the various factors, L and K are paid rewards equal to their marginal products, the total products will be just exhausted, with no surplus or deficit.

In the above way, Wicksteed assuming constant returns to scale and applying Euler's Theorem, proved the adding-up problem, that is, demonstrated that if all factors are paid equal to their marginal products, the total product will be just exactly exhausted.

Wicksteed's solution was criticized by Walras, Barone Edgeworth and Pareto. It has been asserted by these writers that production function is not homogeneous of the first degree, that is, returns to scale are not constant in the actual world. Critics pointed out that production function is such that it yields a U-shaped long run average cost curve. The U-shape of the long-run average cost curve implies that up to a point increasing returns to scale occur and after it diminishing returns to scale are found. In case a firm is still working under increasing returns to scale, then if all factors are paid equal to their marginal products, the total factor rewards would exceed the total product. On the other hand, if a firm is working under diminishing returns to scale, and all factors are paid equal to their marginal products the total factor rewards would not fully exhaust the total product and will therefore leave a surplus. It follows that Euler's Theorem does not apply and therefore the adding-up problem does not hold good when either there are increasing returns to scale or decreasing returns to scale.

Another drawback pointed out in Wicksteed's solution is that when there is constant returns to scale, the long run average cost curve of the firm is a horizontal straight line which is incompatible with perfect competition. (Under horizontal long-run average cost curve, the firm cannot have a determinate equilibrium position). But competition was essential to the marginal productivity theory and therefore to Wicksteed's solution. Thus, Wicksteed solution leads us to two contradictory things.

THE THEORY OF RENT

Rent as an economic surplus, as used by modern economists means the earning of a factor of production in excess of the minimum amount necessary to keep it in its present use. It is not a differential surplus, the difference between the superior and the inferior grades of lands as **Ricardo** meant by rent. Moreover, it accrues not to land alone, but to all other factor services.

Ricardian Theory of Rent

David Ricardo was a brilliant 19th century economist of England who propounded a systematic theory of rent which is in many ways the basis of the modern concept of rent.

Ricardo defined rent as follows: **"Rent is that portion of the produce of earth which is paid to the land lord for the use of the original and indestructible powers of the soil."** It should be noticed that land rent, according to Ricardian definition, is a payment for the use of only land and is different from contractual rent which includes.

- According to Ricardo, marginal land earns no rent.
- In Ricardian Theory, rent is not price determining. In fact, in this theory rent is price determined, that is, it is price which determines rent. To quote Ricardo, **"Corn is not high because a rent is paid, but a rent is paid because corn is high."**

Modern Theory of Rent

Modern theory of rent does not confine itself to the determination of the reward of only land as a factor of production. Rent according to the modern sense can arise in respect of any factor of product ion. It is a surplus payment in excess of transfer earnings of that factor. **Transfer earnings means the amount of money which any particular unit of a factor could earn in its next best alternative use.** In other words, economic rent in such a case is the difference between the present earnings and transfer earnings. **In Joan Robinson's words,** "The essence of the conception of rent is the conception of a surplus earned by a particular part of a factor of production over and above the minimum earnings necessary to induce it to its work."

How Economic Rent Arises

Now the question is how economic rent arises. Economic rent in the sense of surplus over transfer earnings will arise when the supply of the factor units is less **than perfectly elastic or not perfectly elastic.** From the point of view of elasticity of supply, there are three possibilities:

(a) When the supply is perfectly elastic
(b) When it is less than perfectly elastic, and
(c) When it is inelastic.

(a) When the supply of factor units is perfectly elastic

In this case, there will be no surplus or economic rent and the actual earnings and transfer earnings will be equal. When the supply of a factor is perfectly elastic, it means that at a given price, or remuneration, the entrepreneur can engage or employ any number of the factor units. It is obvious that, when the factor units are available at a minimum price or transfer earnings, their equilibrium price will be equal to that minimum price at which the present earnings are equal to the transfer earnings. Thus, no factor unit in such a situation will be able to earn more than its transfer earnings. That is, there will be no rent or surplus earnings.

This is shown in Figure 57 given below. In this figure, the supply curve of the factor of production SS is perfectly elastic and is, therefore, shown as a horizontal straight line. This means that all factor units are available at the given price OS or in other words, the transfer earnings of each factor unit are also equal to OS. DD is the demand curve. The two curves intersect at P. OM is the quantity of the factor used. The price determined is OS. The total earnings are OSPM. But since transfer earnings are equal to the actual earnings, they are also equal to OSPM. There is no surplus and hence no rent.

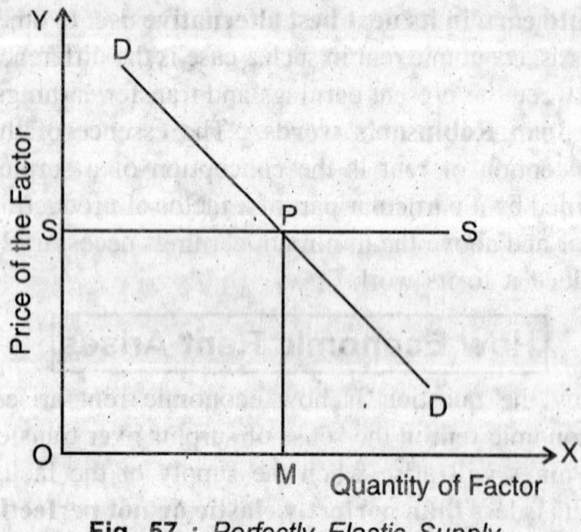

Fig. 57 : *Perfectly Elastic Supply*

If this firm does not pay the price OS, the factor units will be shifted to some other use and earn there as much, because present earnings are equal to transfer earnings.

Thus, it is clear that if the supply of factor units is perfectly elastic for a particular use or industry, then no factor unit can earn surplus or economic rent.

(b) Less than Perfectly Elastic Supply

Now let us take a case when the supply is less than perfectly elastic, *i.e.,* it is some what elastic. This means that the transfer earnings of all the factor units are not equal. As, in some industry or use, the price of the factor increases, more and more of the factor units will offer their services to this industry in use. Suppose that in a particular industry or use, a factor unit can earn Rs. 200 p.m. It is obvious that only such units of the factor will offer their services to this industry whose price in other alternative occupations is less than Rs. 200 or in other words the transfer earnings are less than the present earnings. In this manner, as the price paid for a factor in a particular industry or occupation increases, the supply of the factor will increase if the transfer earnings are less. It is clear that the supply of a factor of production depends on its transfer earnings. This is shown in the figure 58.

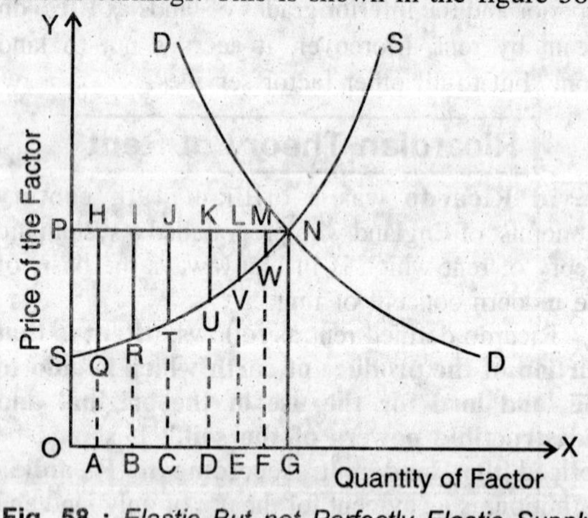

Fig. 58 : *Elastic But not Perfectly Elastic Supply*

SS is the supply curve sloping upwards to the right. It is somewhat elastic but not perfectly elastic as in the case (*a*). The supply curve SS indicates what quantity of the factor will be available at various prices. In other words, it shows the transfer earnings of different factor units. Thus, the transfer earnings of A unit of the factor, is AQ whereas the price is OP. Therefore, surplus or rent, is HQ. In the same manner, the other units earn surplus or rent. It is assumed that all factor units are equally useful for this industry. Hence, the price of all factor units in the industry will be the same. The supply curve cuts DD demand curve at N. In this case, OG is the quantity of the factor used. The rent or price per unit is OP (= GN). But the transfer earnings of each factor unit are less than the price OP. All units except the last G unit are earning more than their transfer earnings. That is they are earning economic rent. Economic rent or surplus will be different for different units because the transfer earnings are different, although the price is the same.

The total earnings are OGNP. But the transfer earnings are OGNS. Hence,

Economic Rent = OGNP – OGNS = PNS

(*c*) Absolutely Inelastic Supply

Now we come to a case when the supply of a factor is absolutely inelastic. The obvious example of this case is the supply of land for the community as a whole. We know that land for the community is fixed and it cannot be increased or decreased whatever the price offered. High price will not increase it or low price will not decrease it. That is why it is said that land has no supply price.

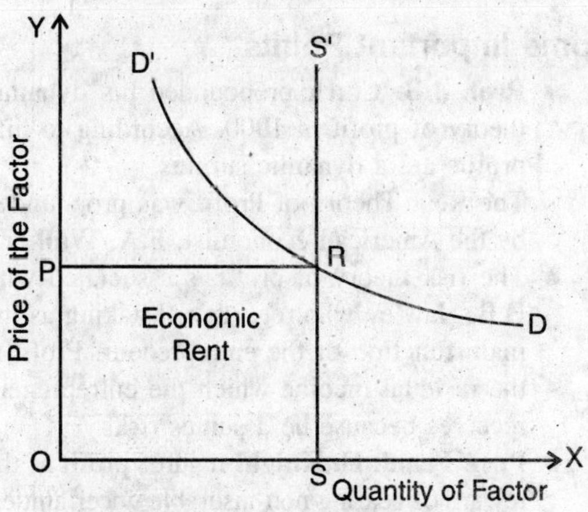

Fig. 59 : *Absolutely Inelastic Supply*

In the Figure 59, the supply curve SS shows an absolutely inelastic supply which represents the supply of land for the community as a whole. Since the supply is fixed, the supply curve SS' is a vertical straight line. This means that from the point of view of the community as a whole, the transfer earnings are zero, since the land cannot be transferred to any other place.

In this Figure DD′ is the demand curve for the whole land. The supply curve SS′ and the demand curve DD′ intersect at R. In equilibrium the price of land or rent is determined at OP and the total earnings of land are equal to OPRS area. Since in this situation the transfer earnings of land are zero, the entire earnings of land, *i.e.,* OPRS is rent.

Thus, it is clear that in case the supply of a factor is absolutely inelastic, its earnings are rent.

Conclusion: We may conclude that rent arises when the supply of a factor is less than perfectly elastic.

Quasi-Rent

The doctrine of quasi-rent was introduced in to economic literature by **Marshall** who extended Ricardo's theory of land-rent to other factors fixed in supply during the short-run.

In short run some factors are fixed, while in the long-run they become variable. The payment to an input which is in fixed supply in the short run is called **quasi-rent,** because it disappears in the long-run (as the factor becomes variable), unlike rents which persist in the long-run.

In the short-run fixed inputs cannot be with drawn from their present use and transferred to another where payments are higher, while variable inputs are free to move to alternative uses where returns are highest. Thus, firms pay the variable inputs their opportunity cost (otherwise these factors would move elsewhere), while the fixed inputs receive what is left over; quasi-rents are a residual payment. To understand this we examine the short-run equilibrium of a firm in a perfectly competitive market (figure 60). Assume the price is P. The firm maximises its profit, producing OX units of output, from which it receives a total revenue (TR) equal to the area OPEX.

The firm pays OXBA = TVC to the variable factors. (it cannot pay less and keep them in its employment). The fixed factors earn the residual ABEP, which is the quasi-rent. Thus

Quasi-Rent = TR – TVC

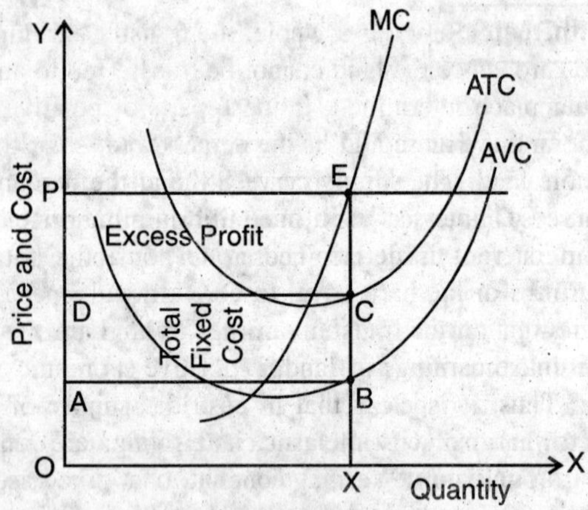

Fig. 60 : *Quasi Rent*

The quasi-rent can be divided into two parts, the total fixed cost (area ABCD in figure 60) and excess (or pure) profit (DCEP). The TFC is the opportunity cost of the fixed factors, that is, the return that would have been earned if the fixed factors were utilised in their best alternative employment (*e.g.,* by another firm in the same industry which pays higher returns on the fixed factors). The excess profit is the difference between the quasi-rent and the TFC:

Quasi-Rent = TFC + Excess Profit

or

Excess Profit = Quasi-Rent – TFC

In the long run the quasi-rent becomes zero and the firm is in equilibrium, earning just normal profits. **In summary:** The price of a factor, whose supply is fixed in the long-run, is called **rent.** The price of a factor, which is in fixed supply only in the short-run, is called **quasi-rent**. Rent persists in the long-run, whereas quasi-rent disappears in the long-run as the factor becomes variable.

Profits

In ordinary parlance, profit is the surplus of income over expenses of production according to a businessman. It is the amount left with him after he has made payments for all factor services used by him in the process of production. But he may not have been careful in calculating all such expenses of production in the economic sense. Therefore, economists regard businessman's profit as gross profit as distinct from pure or net profit because it includes the following constituents.

1. Rent on Land
2. Interest on Capital
3. Wages of Management
4. Depreciation changes
5. Insurance charges

All these elements are present in **gross profit** even in the long-run as they are relatively stable.

Net Profit : Net, true, economic or pure profit is the residue left to the entrepreneur after deducting all the items enumerated above from gross profit. Net profit, however, includes the following elements within it.

1. Reward for Uncertainty Bearing
2. Reward for Coordination
3. Rent of Ability
4. Reward of Innovation
5. Monopoly Gains
6. Windfalls

We may conclude that an economist's profit is quite distinct from a businessman's profit. The former is concerned with net profit which is arrived at by deducting from the businessman's gross profit, the remuneration for the latter's own land, labour and capital.

Some Important Points

- **Prof. J.B. Clark** propounded his dynamic theory of profit in 1900. According to him profits are a dynamic surplus.
- The Rent Theory of Profit was propounded by the American economist, **F.A. Walker.**
- The risk theory of profit is associated with H.B. Hawley who regards risk-taking as the main function of the entrepreneur. Profit is the residual income which the entrepreneur receives because he assumes risks.
- **Prof. Frank H. Knight** regards profit as the reward of bearing non-insurable uncertainties.
- The Innovation Theory of Profit is associated with **Joseph A. Schumpeter.** According to Schumpeter, the principal function of the entrepreneur is to make innovations and profits are a reward for performing this important function.

WELFARE ECONOMICS

The literature on welfare economics has grown rapidly in recent years. Vilfredo Pareto considered the question of maximising social welfare on the basis of general optimum conditions. Marshall and Pigou, the neo-classical economists, concentrated on particular sectors of the economic system in their postulates of welfare economics. It was **Prof. Robbin's** ethical neutrality view about economics that led to the development of welfare economics as an important field of economic studies. **Kaldor, Hicks** and **Scitovsky** have laid the foundations of the **New Welfare Economics** with the help of the **'compensation principle'** avoiding all value judgements. On the other hand, **Bargson, Samuelson** and others have developed the concept of the **Social Welfare Function** without sacrificing value judgements.

Welfare economics has been defined by **Scitovsky** as "Welfare economics is that branch of economic analysis which is concerned primarily with establishment of criteria that can provide a positive basis for adopting policies which are likely to maximise social welfare." In short, welfare economics is to prescribe criteria or norms with which to judge the desirability of certain economic re organisations and prescribe policies on that basis.

Positive Economics and Welfare Economics

Welfare economics is a normative study. Hence, it is important to know the difference between **positive economics** and **normative economics**. Positive economics is concerned with explaining what is, that is, it describes theories and laws to explain observed economic phenomena, whereas normative economics is concerned with what should be or what ought to be the things.

In positive macro-economics, we are broadly concerned with explaining the determination of relative prices and the allocation of resources between different commodities. In positive macro-economics we are broadly concerned with how the level of national income and employment, aggregate consumption and investment and the general level of prices are determined. In these parts of positive economics, what should be the prices, what should be the saving rate, what should be the allocation of resources, and what should be the distribution of income are not discussed. These questions of, what should be and what ought to be, fall within the purview of normative economics. Thus, given the profit maximisation assumption, positive economics states that monopolist will fix a price which will equate marginal cost with marginal revenue. The question what price should or ought to be fixed so that maximum social welfare is achieved lies outside the purview of positive economics. Similarly, given the monopsony in the labour market, positive economics explains what actual wage rate is determined. It does not go into the question how wage rate should be paid to the labourer so that they should not be exploited. Likewise, how national income between different individuals is distributed falls within the domain of positive economics. But positive economics is not concerned with the question of how income should be distributed. On the other hand, normative economics is concerned with describing what should be the things. It is therefore, also called **prescriptive economics.** What price for a product should be fixed, what wage rate should be paid, how income should be distributed, etc., fall within the purview of normative economics.

It should be noted that normative economics involves **value judgements** or what are simply known as values. By value judgements or values, it is meant the conceptions of the people about what is good or bad. These conceptions regarding values of the people are based on the ethical, political, philosophical and religious beliefs of the people and are not based upon any scientific logic or law. Because normative economics involves value judgements, eminent economist Prof. Robbins contended that economics should not become normative in character.

Value judgements of various individuals differ and their rightness or wrongness cannot be decided on the basis of scientific logic or laws. Therefore, in our view, positive economics should be kept separate and distinct from normative economics. However, because normative economics involves value judgements, it does not mean that it should be considered as useless or not meaningful and should not be the concern of economics. As a matter of fact, many vital issues concerning economic welfare of the society necessarily involve some value judgements.

From the above it seems that difference between positive and welfare economics is quite clear; in one case what a man does without considering the favourable or unfavourable effects on others while in the other it is what he should do and must consider the favourable or unfavourable effects on others.

Neo-Classical Welfare Economics

Neo-Classical economists **Marshall, Pigou, Cannon** and his followers considered economics as a normative science. Marshall formulated the concepts of **'Consumer's Surplus'** and **'National Dividend'** in his **'Principles of Economics'** published in 1890. These concepts became the basis of old welfare economics.

Pigovian Welfare Economics

A.C. Pigou is another important neo-classical economist who laid the scientific foundation of welfare economics through the publication of **'Economics of Welfare'** in 1932. Welfare is a mental phenomenon and 'the elements of welfare are the states of consciousness' which is made of utilities or satisfaction of human wants. Pigou also differentiated economic welfare from general (social) welfare. The former is a part of the latter. General welfare depends on a large number of economic and non-economic variables. Economic welfare alone is the subject matter of economics. Pigou limited the scope of welfare economics to economic welfare because general (or social) welfare is a very wide and complex term.

Pigovian welfare economics is related to the satisfaction derived from the use of exchangeable goods and services. Pigovian welfare economics is based on the following assumptions:

A. Every individual attempts to maximise his satisfaction from the use of limited monetary resources.

B. Satisfaction derived from the consumption of goods and services can be compared interpersonally and intrapersonally.

C. Marginal utility of money income decreases with every increase in it which implies that the marginal utility of a unit of money to the poor is greater than that of the rich.

Pigou's Dual Criterion of Welfare

Pigou formulated dual criterian to maximise welfare on the basis of the above assumptions. They are:

1. An increase in national income brought about either by increasing some goods without reducing the others or by transferring factors from less productive to more productive activities increases economic welfare.
2. Any reorganisation of the economy, which increases the purchasing power of the poor without reducing the national income, increases social welfare.

In this way Pigou explicitly brought the conditions of maximisation of welfare. The **first condition** states that given the tastes and income distribution, the level of social welfare increases with any increase in national income. **Second** condition states that given the constant level of national income, the transfer of purchasing power from the rich to the poor will also increase economic welfare.

A Critique of Neo-Classical Welfare Economics

Neo-classical economists particularly Marshall and Pigou made significant contribution to the development of welfare economics by giving the concept of consumer's surplus and economic surplus. Pigou also discussed the various types of externalities, which are great obstacles in the achievement of maximum welfare, in his **'Economics of Welfare'**. But neo-classical welfare economics is based on the unrealistic assumption of cardinal utilities which can be compared interpersonally and intrapersonally. Secondly, national income is not an appropriate measure of social welfare because it is the product of real outputs and their prices. Therefore, it is possible, that national income increases only due to rise in price level without any increase in the quantity and quality of goods and services. Thirdly, Dr. Graff is of the opinion that money is not an appropriate and satisfactory measure of economic welfare because the value of money changes with variation in price level and welfare does not depend only on exchangeable goods and services. Fourthly, Pigou's 'man's equal capacity for satisfaction' assumption is based on an ethical rather than an scientific principle.

Analysis of Externalities or Divergences Between Private And Social Costs And Returns

Divergences between private and social costs and returns (benefits) are known as **externalities.** Externalities are, in fact, **market imperfections** where the market offers no price for service or disservice. These externalities lead to misallocation of resources and cause production or consumption to fall short of an optimum level. Thus they do not lead to maximum social welfare, Pigou's major contribution lies in studying the main causes leading to divergences between private and social costs and returns and in suggesting measures for removing these divergences.

External Economies of Production

When some firm renders a benefit or cost of a service to other firms without appropriating to itself all the benefit or cost of the service, it is an external economy. External economies (or diseconomies) therefore reflect non-market interdependence. The act of producing a good on the part of one firm may either benefit or impose costs on other firms without passing through the market process. In other words, the benefit or cost is not market process. Hence, external economies involve non-market interdependence.

External economies of production may also arise when the expansion of a firm makes it possible for other firms in the industry to obtain their inputs at low cost. In all such cases, social marginal benefits exceed the private marginal benefits and the private costs exceed the social costs. For the expanding firm does not receive any remuneration for the costs incurred by it and the benefits which it has conferred on others.

External Diseconomies of Production

External diseconomies of production also lead to divergence between private and social costs and returns when the production of a commodity or service by a firm affects adversely other firms in the industry. Professor Pigou's example of air pollution explains these divergences. Suppose a factory is situated in a residential or populated area and it emits smoke. The smoke from the factory soils clothes, household articles, buildings and damages the health of the inhabitants of the area. As a result, the maintenance costs of the inhabitants increase in the form of increased expenses on washing clothes, cleaning of household articles and rooms, and cleaning and painting of buildings and enhanced medical expenses. These are social costs for which the factory does not compensate the inhabitants of the area and in a sense benefits itself. The private costs are thus less than the social costs, and the private benefits to the factory are higher than the social benefits because the factory-owner escapes costs incurred by the inhabitants of the area and thereby gets private benefits.

External Economies of Consumption

External economies of consumption arise from non-market interdependences of the satisfactions enjoyed by different consumers. An increase in the consumption of a good or service which affects favourably the consumption patterns and desires of other consumers is an external economy of consumption. When an individual installs a TV set, the satisfaction of his neighbours increases when they and their children view the various programmes. This is a case of external economy in consumption in which social benefit is larger and social cost is lower than private benefit and cost, because the TV-owners does not receive any money in return as the neighbours are not asked to pay anything for seeing TV programmes.

External Diseconomies of Consumption

When the consumption of a good or service by one consumer confers a **disadvantage** or effects adversely the consumption patterns and desires of other consumers, it is an external diseconomy of consumption. Diseconomies of consumption especially arise in the case of dress fashions and articles of conspicuous consumption. When a rich lady in a particular locality adopts a new style of dress, it leads to the discarding of clothes already in use not only by her but by other women who emulate her. This results in higher social costs and lower social benefits than private costs and benefits. Individuals who are not in a position to emulate the consumption patterns of their rich neighbours feel dissatisfied and jealous. As a result, their productive efficiency falls and serious divergences emerge between social and private costs and returns. Other instances are of noise nuisance from loud-speakers.

Conclusion. We may conclude the discussion in the words of **Prof. Baumol,** "External economies and diseconomies can lead to a misallocation of resources even in the world of perfect competition. Too much may be produced by industries in which external diseconomies prevail, while there may be a less than optimal output of commodities whose production involves external economies. In principle it is even possible that, where there are external diseconomies, the presence of monopolies can lead to output smaller and therefore more nearly optimal than those which would result from competition."

The Case of Public Goods

Another cause of divergences between private and social costs, and private and social benefits is the case of public goods which Pigou completely ignored. According to Samuelson, 'each individual's consumption of such a good (public good) leads to no subtractions from any other individual's consumption of that good, every individual benefits from public goods. But divergences arise when one individual arranges for a public good he confers a benefit on some other individuals and thereby creates a social benefit that is higher than his own private benefit. When a person manages a municipal street light in front of his house through his personal efforts all the residents of the locality benefit from it. The social benefit far exceeds his own benefit.

Remedial Measures

To bring about the equality of private and social costs and benefits, Pigou favoured state interference rather than self-interest. He, therefore, suggested the use of taxes, subsidies and other social control measures to close the gap between private and social costs and benefits arising from externalities in production and consumption.

Conditions of Pareto Optimality

Neo-classicals and earlier economists defined social welfare as a sum total of cardinally measurable utilities of different members of the society. An optimum allocation of resources was one which maximised the social welfare in this sense. **Pareto** was the first to part with this traditional approach to social welfare in two important respects. First, he rejected the notion of cardinal utility and its additive nature and, second, he detached welfare economies from the interpersonal comparisons of utilities. **Pareto's concept of maximum social welfare which is based upon ordinal utility and is also free from value judgements occupies a significant place in modern welfare economists. Pareto optimum may not be sufficient condition for attaining maximum social welfare but it is a necessary condition for it.** Pareto optimum (often called Economic Efficiency) is a position from which it is impossible to make anyone better off without making someone worse off by any reallocation of resources of inputs and outputs. Thus, in the Pareto optimum position the welfare of an individual of the society cannot be increased without decreasing the welfare of another member.

Pareto Criterion

This criterion refers to economic efficiency which can be objectively measured. It is called Pareto criterion after the famous Italian economist **Vilfredo Pareto.** According to this criterion any change that makes at least one individual better-off and no one worse-off is an improvement in social welfare. Conversely, a change that makes no one better-off and at least one worse-off is a decrease in social welfare.

The criterion can be stated in a some what different way: a situation in which it is impossible to make anyone better-off without making someone worse-off is said to be Pareto-optimal or Pareto efficient.

Pareto criterion can be explained with the help of **Samuelson's utility possibility** curve. **Utility possibility curve is the locus of the various combinations of utilities obtained by two persons from the consumption of a particular bundle of goods.**

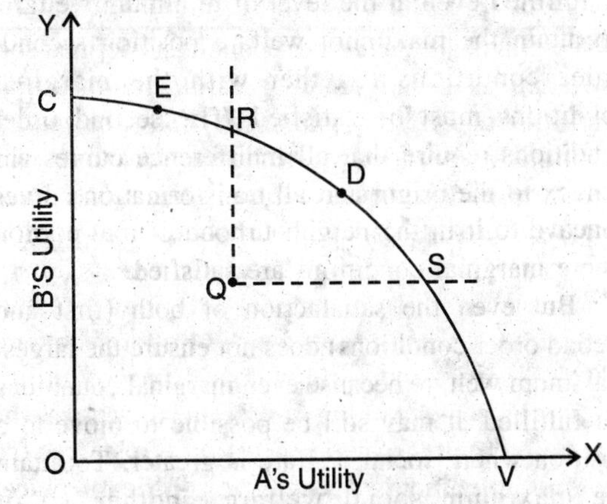

Fig. 61 : *Pareto Criterion*

In Figure 61, CV is a utility possibility curve which shows the various levels of utilities obtained by two individuals A and B of the society resulting from the redistribution of a fixed bundle of goods and its consumption by them. According to Pareto criterion, a movement from Q to R, or Q to D, or Q to S represents the increase in social welfare because in such movements the utility of either A or B or both increases. A movement from Q to R implies that the utility or welfare of B increases, while that of A remains the same. On the other hand, a movement from Q to S implies that while A has becomes better off, B is no worse off. And a movement from Q to D or any other point on the segment between R and S will mean increase in welfare or utility of both the individuals. Thus, points R, D and S are preferable to Q from point of view of social welfare. But unfortunately Pareto criterion does not help us in evaluating the changes in welfare if the movement as a result of redistribution is from the point Q to a point outside the segment RS, such as point E on the utility possibility curve CV. As a result of the movement from point Q to E, the utility of A decreases while that of B increases. In such circumstances, Pareto criterion can not tell us as to whether social welfare increases or decreases.

Marginal Conditions of Pareto Optimum

Pareto concluded from his criterion that competition leads the society to an optimum position but he had not given any mathematical proof of it, nor he derived the marginal conditions to be fulfilled to achieve the optimum position. Later on, **Lerner and Hicks** derived the marginal conditions which must be fulfilled for the attainment of Pareto optimum. These marginal conditions are based on the following important assumptions:

1. Each individual has his own ordinal utility function and possesses a definite amount of each product and factor.
2. Production function of every firm and the state of technology is given and remains constant.
3. Goods are perfectly divisible.
4. A producer tries to produce a given output with the least cost combination of factors.
5. Every individual wants to maximise his satisfaction.
6. Every individual purchases some quantity of all goods.
7. All factors of production are perfectly mobile.

Given the above assumptions various marginal conditions (first order conditions) required for the achievement of Pareto optimum or maximum social welfare are explained below:

1. The Optimum Distribution of Products among the Consumers: Efficiency in Exchange : The first condition relates to the optimum distribution of the goods among the different consumers composing a society at a particular point of time. The condition says: **"The marginal rate of substitution between any two goods must be the same for every individual who consumes them both."**

Thus,

$$MRS^A_{x,y} = MRS^B_{x,y}$$

2. The Optimum Allocation of Factors : The second condition for Pareto optimum requires that the available factors of production should be utilized in the production of different goods in such manner that it is impossible to increase the output of one good without a decrease in the output of another or to increase the output of both the goods by any reallocation of factors of production. This situation would be achieved if **"The marginal technical rate of substitution (MRTS) between any pair of factors must be the same for any two firms using both to produce the same product."** Thus

$$MRTS^{x}_{L,K} = MRTS^{y}_{L,K}$$

3. The Optimum Direction of Production : The third condition relates to the technical conditions of production and the state of consumer's preferences. The fulfilment of this condition determines the optimum quantities of different commodities to be produced with given factor endowments. This condition states that **"the marginal rate of substitution between any pair of products for any person consuming both must be the same as the marginal rate of transformation (for the community) between them."**

Thus

$$MRPT_{x,y} = MRS^{A}_{x,y} = MRS^{B}_{x,y}$$

According to this condition, for the attainment of maximum social welfare goods should be produced in accordance with consumer's preferences.

In summary. A Pareto-optimal state in the economy can be attained if the following three marginal conditions are fulfilled:

1. The $MRS_{x,y}$ between any two goods be equal for all consumers.
2. The $MRTS_{L,K}$ between any two inputs be equal in the production of all commodities.
3. The $MRPT_{x,y}$ be equal to the $MRS_{x,y}$ for any two goods.

A situation may be Pareto-optimal without maximising social welfare. However, welfare maximisation is attained only at a situation that is Pareto-optimal. In other words, Pareto optimality is a necessary but not sufficient condition for welfare maximisation. **All points on the PPC are Pareto-optimal.**

The Second-Order and Total Conditions

The marginal or the first order conditions explained above are 'necessary' but not sufficient for the attainment of maximum social welfare because the marginal conditions by themselves do not guarantee maximum welfare, for the marginal conditions can be fulfilled even at the level of minimum welfare. To attain the maximum welfare position second-order conditions together with the marginal conditions must be satisfied. The second order conditions require that all indifference curves are convex to the origin and all transformation curves concave to it in the neighbourhood of any portion where marginal conditions are satisfied.

But even the satisfaction of both (first and second order conditions) does not ensure the largest maximum welfare because even marginal conditions are fulfilled, it may still be possible to move to a position where social welfare is greater. To attain the maximum social welfare, another set of conditions which are called by **Hicks** as the **'total conditions'** must also be satisfied. The total conditions state, **"that if welfare is to be a maximum, it must be impossible to increase welfare by producing product not otherwise produced or by using a factor not otherwise used."** If it is possible to increase welfare by such activities the optimum position is not determined by marginal conditions alone.

Therefore, welfare will be really maximum if the marginal as well as total conditions are satisfied. But such a social optimum too is not a unique one. It is one of a large number of optima. The whole analysis of conditions of Pareto optimality assumes a given distribution of income. With a change in the distribution of income Pareto optimality will be achieved with different output-mix of various products and different allocation of various factors among products. Thus, a new optimum will emerge due to redistribution of income and there are no criteria to judge whether the new optimum is better or worse than the previous social optimum. For this can be known with the help of some value Judgements regarding income distribution which has been ruled out by the Pareto criterion.

Its Criticism

Pareto Criterion and the concept of Pareto optimality or maximum social welfare based on it occupies a significant place in welfare economics. To Judge the efficiency of an economic system, the notion of Pareto optimality has been used to bring out the gains of trading or exchange of goods between individuals. But even Pareto criterion which rules out comparing those changes in policies which make some worse off has been a subject of controversy and has been criticised on several grounds.

1. There can be an infinite number of Paretian optima, each with a different level of welfare.
2. The Pareto criterion is not completely free from value Judgements.
3. An important limitation of Pareto criterion is that it cannot be applied to Judge the social desirability of those policy proposals which benefit some and harm others.
4. A chief drawback of Pareto-optimality analysis is that it accepts the prevailing income distribution and no attempt is made to find an optimal distribution of income, since it is thought that there does not exist any objective, value-free and scientific way of finding optimal distribution of income. Thus, Pareto optimality analysis remains either silent or biased in favour of status quo on the issue of income distribution.

Perfect Competition And Pareto Optimality

All the marginal conditions of attaining Pareto optimality are fully satisfied under perfect competition. Now we shall show how perfect competition satisfies all the marginal conditions required for the achievement of Pareto optimum.

Perfect Competition And Optimal Distribution of Goods or Efficiency in Exchange : The condition for Pareto optimality with regard to the distribution of goods among consumers requires that the marginal rate of substitution (MRS) between any two goods, say X and Y, must be the same for any pair of consumers. Let A and B be the two consumers between whom two goods X and Y are to be distributed. Under perfect competition prices of all goods are given and same for every consumer. It is also assumed that consumers try to maximize their satisfaction subject to their budget constraint. Now, given the price of two goods, consumer A will maximize his satisfaction when he is buying the two goods X and Y in such amounts that:

$$MRS^{A}_{x,y} = \frac{P_x}{P_y} \quad ......(i)$$

Likewise, the consumer B will also be in equilibrium when he purchasing and consuming the two goods X and Y in such amounts that:

$$MRS^{B}_{x,y} = \frac{P_x}{P_y} \quad ......(ii)$$

Since this is essential condition of perfect competition that prices of goods are the same or uniform for all consumers, the price ratio of the two goods $\left(\frac{P_x}{P_y}\right)$ in equations *(i)* and *(ii)* above will be the same for consumers A and B. Thus under perfect competition.

$$MRS^{A}_{x,y} = MRS^{B}_{x,y}$$

Perfect Competition and Optimal Allocation of Factors

The second marginal condition for Pareto optimality relates to the optimal allocation of factors in the production of various goods. This condition requires that for the optimal allocation of factors marginal rate of technical substitution (MRTS) between any two factors must be the same for all producers. This condition is also satisfied by perfect competition. For a producer working under perfect competition prices of factors he employs are given and constant and he is in equilibrium at the combination of factors where the given isoquant is tangent to an iso-cost line. As is well known, the slope of the isoquant represents marginal rate of technical substitution between the two factors and the slope of the iso-cost line measures the ratio of the prices of two factors. Thus, under perfect competition, a cost minimizing producer A will equate MRTS between labour and capital with the price ratio of these two factors. Thus under perfect competition:

$$MRTS^{A}_{L,K} = \frac{P_L}{P_K} \quad ...(i)$$

Where P_L and P_K are the prices of labour and capital respectively and $MRTS^A_{L,K}$ is the marginal rate of technical substitution between labour and capital of producer A. Similarly, producer B working under perfect competition will also equate his marginal rate of technical substitution between the two factors with their price ratios. Thus

$$MRTS^B_{L,K} = \frac{P_L}{P_K} \quad ...(ii)$$

Since under perfect competition $\frac{P_L}{P_K}$ will be the same for all the producers. Therefore

$$MRTS^A_{L,K} = MRTS^B_{L,K}$$

Perfect Competition and Optimum Direction (*i.e.,* Composition) of Production: General Economic Efficiency

This condition states that marginal rate of substitution between any two commodities for any consumer should be the same as the marginal rate of transformation for the community between these two commodities.

Under conditions of perfect competition, each firm to be in equilibrium produces so much output of a commodity that its marginal cost is equal to the price of the commodity. Thus, for firms in perfect competition,

$$MC_x = P_x \text{ and } MC_y = P_y$$

Where MC_x and MC_y are marginal costs of productions of commodities X and Y respectively and P_x and P_y are prices of commodities X and Y. Therefore, it follows that firms in perfect competition will be in equilibrium when they are producing commodities in such quantities that

$$\frac{MC_x}{MC_y} = \frac{P_x}{P_y}$$

The ration of marginal costs of two commodities represents the marginal rate of transformation between them. Therefore, for each producing firm in perfect competition:

$$MRT_{xy} = \frac{MC_x}{MC_y} = \frac{P_x}{P_y} \quad ...(ii)$$

When there prevails perfect competition on the buying side, each consumer maximises his satisfaction and is in equilibrium at the point where the given price line is tangent to his indifference curve. In other words, each consumer is in equilibrium when:

$$MRS_{xy} = \frac{P_x}{P_y} \quad ...(ii)$$

Since, under perfect competition, the ratio of prices of two commodities $\left(\frac{P_x}{P_y}\right)$ is the same for a consumer and a producer it follows from *(i)* and *(ii)* above that

$$MRS_{xy} = MRT_{xy}$$

We thus see that all first order marginal conditions required for the attainment of Pareto-optimality or maximum social welfare are fulfilled under perfect competition. It is in this sense that perfect competition represents economic optimum from the viewpoint of social welfare.

Perfect Competition does not always ensure Pareto Optimality

Perfect competition does not guarantee that second order conditions required for the achievement of Pareto optimality will also be fulfilled. Besides, when externalities, that is, external economies and diseconomies in production and consumption are present, perfect competition will not lead to Pareto optimality.

Further, even if the above two factors, namely, non-fulfilment of the second order conditions and the existence of externalities are not actually found, the perfect competition will not lead to economic efficiency or Pareto optimality if the given distribution of income is not optimal from the viewpoint of social welfare.

Finally, there is another factor which prevents the achievement of Pareto-optimality or maximum social welfare even when perfect competition prevails in the economy. This factor relates to the employment or utilisation of available resources. Pareto optimality will not be attained if the available resources are not fully employed or utilised.

It follows from above that perfect competition though a necessary condition is not a sufficient condition for Pareto-optimality. Therefore, that a free enterprise economy characterised by perfect competition ensures efficient allocation of resources or maximum social welfare cannot be accepted without some qualifications. And these qualifications are:

1. the second order conditions are satisfied,
2. the externalities in production and consumption are absent,
3. prevailing distribution of income is optimal from the social point of view, and
4. available resources are fully employed.

Obstacles to the Attainment of Pareto Optimality or Maximum Social Welfare

We have explained above the conditions for the attainment of Pareto optimality or maximum social welfare. We have also briefly discussed above that with some qualifications perfect competition ensures the achievement of Pareto optimality or maximum social welfare. Now the pertinent question is what are the factors which hinder the attainment of Pareto-optimality and maximum social welfare. The main obstacles are:

1. the existence of monopoly or imperfect competition,
2. the presence of externalities, i.e. external economies and diseconomies in production and consumption:
3. the consumption of Public Goods, and
4. the lack of perfect knowledge.

The Compensation Criteria or New Welfare Economics

The compensation criteria also known as the New Welfare Economics, have been formulated by Hicks, Kaldor and Scitovsky. Accepting Pareto's ordinal measurement of utility and the impossibility of its interpersonal comparisons, they tried to show that social welfare could be increased without making **value judgements.**

Assumptions. The various compensation criteria are based on the following assumptions:

(a) Each individual's satisfactions are independent from the others so that he is the best Judge of his welfare.

(b) There is the absence of external effects in production and consumption.

(c) The tastes of the individuals remain constant.

(d) The problems of production and exchange can be separated from the problems of distribution. Compensation principle accepts the level of social welfare to be a function of the level of production. Thus, it ignores the effects of a change in distribution on social welfare.

(e) Utility can be measured ordinally and interpersonal comparisons of utilities are not possible.

Kaldor-Hicks Welfare Criterion

Nicholas Kaldor was the first economist to give a welfare criterion based on compensating payments. Kaldor's criterion helps us to measure the welfare implications of a movement in either direction on the contract curve in terms of Edgeworth box diagram. **According to Kaldor's welfare criterion, if a certain change in economic organisation or policy makes some people better off and other worse off, then that change will increase social welfare if those who gain could compensate the losers and still be better off than before.** Thus, if any policy change benefits any one section of the society to such an extent that he is better off even after the payment of compensation to the other section of the society out of the benefits received, then that change leads to increase in social welfare. **Prof. J.R. Hicks** supported Kaldor for employing compensation principle to evaluate the change in social welfare resulting from any economic reorganisation that benefits some people and harms the others. This criterion states that, "if A is made so much better by the change that he could compensate B for his loss and still have something left over, than the reorganisation is unequivocal improvement." In other words, a change is an improvement if the losers in the changed situation cannot profitably bribe the gainers not to change from the original situation.

Hicks has given his criterion from the loser's point of view, while **Kaldor** had formulated his criterion from gainer's point of view. Thus, the two criteria are really the same though they are clothed in different words.

Kaldor Hicks criterion can be explained with the help of the utility possibility curve. In Figure 62 ordinal utility of two individuals A and B is shown on X and Y axes respectively. DE is the utility possibility curve which represents the various combinations of utilities obtained by individuals A and B.

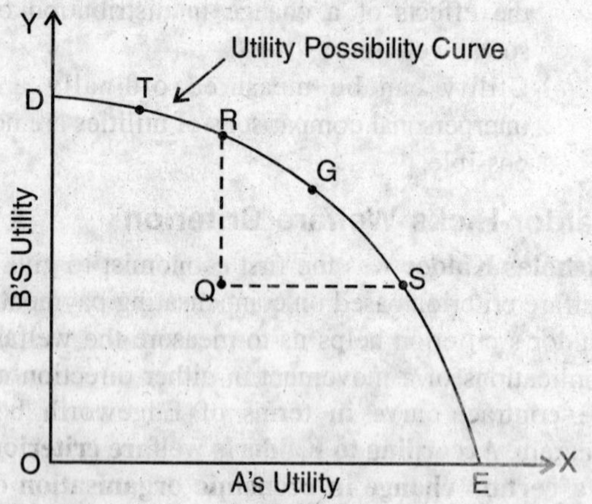

Fig. 62 : *Kaldor-Hicks Criterion Explained with Utility Possibility Curve*

As we move downward on the curve DE, utility of A increases while that of B falls. On the other hand, if we move up on the utility curve ED, utility of B increases while that of A falls.

Suppose the utilities obtained by A and B from the distribution of income or output between them are represented by point Q inside the utility possibility curve DE. Let us assume that as a result of some change in economic policy, the two individuals move from point Q to point T on the utility possibility curve DE. As a result of this movement, utility of individual B has increased while the utility of A has declined, that is, B has become better off and A has become worse off than before. Therefore, this movement from point Q to point T cannot be evaluated by means of Pareto criterion of course points such as R, G, S or any other point on the segment RS of the utility possibility curve DE are socially preferable to point Q on the basis of Pareto criterion. But since the movement from Q to T involves interpersonal comparison of utility it cannot be said whether or not social welfare increases on the basis of Pareto criterion. However, the compensation principle propounded by Kaldor-Hicks enables us to say whether or not social welfare has increased as a result of movement from Q to T. According to Kaldor-Hicks criterion, we have to see whether the individual A who gains with the movement from position Q to position T could compensate the individual A who is loser and still be better off than before. Now, it will be seen from figure 62 that utility possibility curve DE passes through points R, G and S. This means that by mere redistribution of income between the two individuals, that is, if individual B gives some compensation to individual A for the loss suffered, they can move to the position R. It is evident from the figure that at position R individual A is as well off as compared to position Q. It means due to a policy change and consequent movement from position Q to position R gainer (individual B) could compensate the loser (individual A) and still is better off than at Q. Therefore, according to Kaldor-Hicks criterion, social welfare increases with the movement from position Q to position T, far from T they could move to the position R through mere redistribution of income.

MULTIPLE CHOICE QUESTIONS

1. The law of Demand refers to
- A. Price-supply relationship
- B. Price-cost relationship
- C. Price-demand relationship
- D. Price-income relationship

2. In a typical demand schedule, quantity demanded
- A. Varies directly with price
- B. Varies proportionately with price
- C. Varies inversely with price
- D. Is independent of price

3. Normally when price per unit of a good falls, its
- A. Quantity demanded increases
- B. Quantity demanded decreases
- C. Quantity demanded remains constant
- D. None of these happens

4. A fall in the price of a commodity leads to
- A. A shift in demand
- B. A fall in demand
- C. A rise in consumers real income
- D. A fall in the consumers real income

5. Demand schedule is shown as
   A. A result of increase in the size of the family
   B. A result of change in state
   C. A function of price alone
   D. None of these
6. Market demand for any good is a function of the
   A. Price per unit of the good
   B. Price per unit of other goods
   C. Income & Tastes of consumers
   D. All of the above
7. The demand curve for a commodity is generally drawn on the assumption that
   A. The commodity has no substitutes
   B. Tastes, income and all other prices remain constant
   C. The average house hold consists of two persons
   D. Purchases of the commodity are made by a free market.
8. A typical demand curve cannot be
   A. Convex to the origin
   B. A straight line parallel to y-axis
   C. A straight line parallel to x-axis
   D. Rising upwards to the right
9. When the law of demand operates the demand curve
   A. Slopes downward from left to right
   B. Slopes upward from left to right
   C. Slopes upward from right to left
   D. Parallel to horizontal axis
10. For most consumers apples and oranges are substitutes goods. Therefore we would expect a rise in the price of apples to lead to
   A. A right ward shift in the demand curve of oranges
   B. A left ward shift in the supply curve of apples
   C. A downward change in the demand curve of oranges
   D. A fall in the price of oranges
11. 'Ceteris paribus' clause in the Law of Demand does not mean
   A. The price of the commodity does not change
   B. The price of its substitutes does not change
   C. The income of the consumer does not change
   D. The price of complementary goods does not change
12. Which of the following could provide an example of exceptional demand curves?
   I. Demand for "Giffen goods"
   II. Demand based on fears of a future rise in prices
   III. Demand for second-hand clothes
   IV. Demand for daily newspapers
   A. I only B. I and II
   C. II and III D. I, II, III and IV
13. Which one of the following is true increase of normal goods?
   A. When Price increases, demand decreases
   B. When Price increases, demand also increases
   C. When Price remains constant, demand falls down
   D. When Price falls down, demand remains constant
14. An exceptional demand curve is one that slopes:
   A. Upwards to the right
   B. Downwards to the right
   C. Upwards to the left
   D. Horizontally
15. When there is decrease in demand the demand curve–
   A. Moves downwards towards the axis
   B. Moves upwards away from the axis
   C. Remains unchanged
   D. None of the above
16. Two goods have to be consumed simultaneously are
   A. Identical
   B. Complementary
   C. Substitutes
   D. None of these
17. Which of the following pairs of commodities is an example of substitutes
   A. Coffee and milk
   B. Diamond and Cow
   C. Pen and ink
   D. Mustard oil and coconut oil
18. Bread and butter, lamb and mint sauce, illustrate the type of inter related demand known as

A. Rival demand
B. Composite demand
C. Competitive demand
D. Joint demand

19. A commodity, the price of which has fallen but is expected to fall further, will present a demand curve
A. Regressive at the lower end
B. Regressive at the upper end
C. Kinked in the middle
D. Downward sloping to right

20. When an individual's income falls (while everything else remains the same), his demand for an inferior goods:
A. Increases
B. Decreases
C. Remains unchanged
D. We cannot say without additional information

21. If two goods are complements, this means that a rise in the price of one commodity will induce
A. An upward shift in demand for the other commodity
B. A rise in the price of the other commodity
C. A downward shift in demand for the other commodity
D. No shift in demand for the other commodity

22. An income-demand curve for a "Luxury commodity" slopes:
A. Upwards to the right from the origin
B. Vertically
C. Upwards from left to right only beyond a certain level of consumer's income
D. Horizontally

23. An income demand curve for inferior commodity always slopes
A. Upwards to the right
B. Backwards to the left
C. Downwards to the right
D. Horizontally

24. 'Change in quantity demanded' refers to
A. Upward shift of the demand curve
B. Downward shift of the demand curve
C. Movement on the same demand curve
D. None of these

25. When the price of a substitute of commodity X falls, the demand for X—
A. Rises
B. Falls
C. Remains unchanged
D. Any of the above

26. An increase in demand can result from
A. A decline in market price
B. An increase in income
C. A reduction in the price of substitutes
D. An increase in the price of complements
E. All of the above

27. If the price of coffee suddenly shoots up, ceteris paribus, the demand for Tea is expected to—
A. Move rightward along the original demand curve
B. Increase
C. Remain unaffected
D. Decrease

28. In the case of Giffen good like bajra, a fall in its price tends to—
A. Make the demand remain constant
B. Reduce the demand
C. Increase the demand
D. Change demand in an abnormal way

29. Cross demand is the change in the quantity demanded to a given commodity in response to the
A. Change in the utility of another commodity
B. Change in the price of another commodity
C. Change in the nature of another commodity
D. Change in the size of another commodity

30. To calculate the elasticity of demand which of the following formula is used

A. $\dfrac{\text{Percentage change in demand}}{\text{Original demand}}$

B. $\dfrac{\text{Proportionate change in demand}}{\text{Proportionate change in price}}$

C. $\dfrac{\text{Change in demand}}{\text{Change in price}} \div \dfrac{\text{Original demand}}{\text{Original price}}$

D. $\dfrac{\text{Change in demand}}{\text{Change in price}}$

31. When the demand curve is a rectangular hyperbola, it represents

A. Unitary elastic demand
B. Perfectly elastic demand
C. Perfectly inelastic demand
D. Relatively elastic demand

32. If total consumer expenditure on a good falls as its price falls this indicates that
A. $e_P < 1$ B. $e_P > 1$
C. $e_P = 1$ D. $e_P = \infty$

33. Market demand is
A. The sum of all individual demands
B. Demand at prevailing average prices
C. Ability to pay the price asked
D. Demand in a perfectly free market

34. Extension and contraction of demand are results of
A. Change in consumer's income
B. Change in consumer's tastes
C. Change in price
D. None of these

35. 'Extension of demand' means
A. More quantity demanded at a lower price
B. More quantity demanded at a higher price
C. More quantity demanded at the same price
D. None of these

36. A negative income elasticity of demand for a commodity indicates that as income falls the amount of the commodity purchased
A. Rises
B. Falls
C. Remains unchanged
D. Any of the above

37. Giffen goods are those goods—
A. For which demand increases as price increases
B. Which have a high income elasticity of demand
C. Which are in very short supply
D. None of these

38. In measuring price-elasticity
A. Price is a dependent variable and quantity is an independent variable
B. Price is an independent variable and quantity is a dependent variable
C. Price and quantity both are independent variables
D. Price and quantity both are dependent variables

39. The demand for pepper is likely to have a low price elasticity because it—
1. Involves only a small proportion of consumers expenditure
2. It is single-use goods
3. Has no close substitutes
4. Can readily be foregone

A. 1 and 2 only B. 1 and 3 only
C. 2 and 3 only D. 2 and 4 only
E. 2, 3 and 4 only

40. Consider a demand curve which takes the form of a straight line cutting both axis. Elasticity at the mid point of the line would be
A. 0 B. 1.0
C. 1.5 D. 2.0

41. When with a change in price the total outlay of a commodity remains constant, it is a case of
A. Perfect elasticity B. Perfect inelasticity
C. Unit elasticity D. Zero elasticity

42. Income-Elasticity of demand will be zero when a given change in income brings about
A. A less than proportionate change in quantity demanded
B. A more than proportionate change in quantity demanded
C. The same proportionate change in demand
D. No change in demand

43. Cross elasticity of complementary goods is
A. Negative B. Zero
C. High D. Infinite

44. One common definition of luxury goods is goods with an income elasticity
A. Greater than one
B. Equal to one
C. Less than one but more than zero
D. None of these

45. Match the following:

1. For a given 10 percent change in price, demand changes by zero percent	*(i)* $e > 1$
2. For a given 10 percent change in price, demand changes by 5 percent	*(ii)* $e = 1$
3. For a given 10 percent change in price, demand changes by 10 percent	*(iii)* $e < 1$

4. For a given 10 percent change in price, demand changes by 20 percent — (*iv*) $e = 0$

	1	2	3	4
A.	(*iii*)	(*i*)	(*ii*)	(*iv*)
B.	(*iv*)	(*iii*)	(*ii*)	(*i*)
C.	(*i*)	(*ii*)	(*iii*)	(*iv*)
D.	(*ii*)	(*iii*)	(*i*)	(*iv*)

46. A straight line, downward-sloping demand curve implies that, as price falls, the elasticity of demand

A. Increases B. Decreases
C. Remains the same D. is zero

47. In the longer period permitting adjustment, demand is likely to be

A. Inelastic B. Elastic
C. Unit elastic D. Cannot be known

48. Elasticity of demand is equal to unity while marginal revenue is

A. Positive B. Zero
C. Negative D. Indeterminate

49. A demand curve which takes the form of a horizontal line parallel to the quantity axis illustrates elasticity which is

A. Zero B. Infinite
C. > 1 D. < 1

50. Which of the following does not have a uniform elasticity of demand at all points—

A. A downward sloping demand curve
B. A vertical demand curve
C. A rectangular hyperbola demand curve
D. A horizontal demand curve

51. If the percentage increase in the quantity of a commodity demanded is smaller than the percentage fall in its price, the coefficient of price elasticity of demand is—

A. Greater than 1 B. Equal to 1
C. Less than 1 D. Zero

52. Match the following:

1. Responsiveness of demand to change in price — (*i*) Income elasticity of demand
2. Responsiveness of demand to change in tastes — (*ii*) Price elasticity of demand
3. Responsiveness of demand to change in income — (*iii*) Cross elasticity of demand
4. Responsiveness of demand to change in price of related goods. — (*iv*) Taste elasticity of demand

	1	2	3	4
A.	(*i*)	(*ii*)	(*iii*)	(*iv*)
B.	(*iv*)	(*iii*)	(*i*)	(*ii*)
C.	(*iii*)	(*iv*)	(*ii*)	(*i*)
D.	(*ii*)	(*iv*)	(*i*)	(*iii*)

53. A monopolist charging high price operates on

A. The elastic part of a demand curve
B. The inelastic part of a demand curve
C. The constant elastic part of a demand curve
D. Ignores elasticity of demand altogether

54. Elasticity of demand in the following figure at point Q_1 is

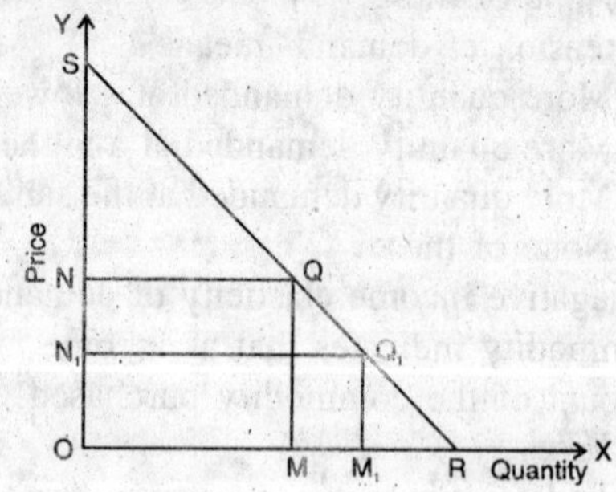

A. $\frac{RQ_1}{SQ_1}$ B. $\frac{Q_1N_1}{OS}$

C. $\frac{Q_1F}{RQ_1}$ D. $\frac{RQ}{RQ_1}$

55. Arc elasticity gives a better measure of point elasticity of a curvilinear demand curve as

A. The size of the arc becomes smaller
B. The curvature of the demand curve over the arc becomes less
C. Both of the above
D. Neither of the above

56. Ceteris paribus, a change in the price of a commodity causes the quantity purchased of its complements to move

A. In the same direction
B. In the opposite direction

C. In an insignificant manner
D. Cannot be known

57. If there were no changes in the quantity of food sold, even when its price falls, we would know that—
A. Demand was entirely inelastic
B. Demand was entirely elastic
C. Demand was more elastic than one
D. Demand was unit elastic

58. When the income elasticity of demand is greater than unity, the commodity is
A. A necessity
B. A luxury
C. An inferior good
D. A non-related good

59. Which of the following statement is correct—
A. When the slope of the demand curve is zero, demand is infinitely elastic and when the slope is infinite, elasticity is zero
B. When the slope of the demand curve is zero, elasticity is also zero and when the slope is infinite, elasticity is also infinite
C. When the slope of the demand curve is zero, elasticity is unity and also when the slope is infinite, elasticity is unity
D. None of these

60. If two commodities are substitutes a change in the price of one, ceteris paribus, causes a change in the quantity purchased of the other
A. In the same direction
B. In the opposite direction
C. In an insignificant manner
D. Cannot be known

61. Income elasticity of demand is expressed as
A. $\dfrac{\text{Percentage change in quantity demanded}}{\text{Percentage change in income}}$
B. $\dfrac{\text{Percentage change in income}}{\text{Change in quantity demanded}}$
C. Change in quantity demanded $\times \dfrac{\text{Change in marginal income}}{100}$
D. $\dfrac{\text{Change in income}}{100 \times \text{change in quantity demanded}}$

62. In the case of an inferior commodity, the income elasticity of demand is
A. Positive B. Unitary
C. Negative D. Infinity

63. Income elasticity of demand will be zero when a given change in income brings about—
A. A less than proportionate change in quantity demanded
B. A more than proportionate change in quantity demanded
C. The same proportionate change in demand
D. No change in demand

64. The degree of price elasticity of demand used for goods is influenced by whether
1. It has close substitutes
2. Its output is easily altered
3. It account for a small input
4. It is a durable use or single use goods
A. 1, 3 and 4 only B. 1 and 2 only
C. 2 and 3 only D. 2, 3 and 4 only

65. Pick out the correct formula for arc elasticity
A. $\dfrac{\Delta q}{\Delta P} \cdot \dfrac{P_1 + P_2}{q_1 + q_2}$ B. $\dfrac{\Delta P}{\Delta q} \cdot \dfrac{P_1 + P_2}{q_1 + q_2}$
C. $\dfrac{\Delta P}{\Delta q} \cdot \dfrac{100}{q_1 + P_1}$ D. $\dfrac{\Delta q \times 100}{P}$

66. A country is advised to devalue (reduce external value of) its currency only when its exports face
A. Inelastic demand in foreign markets
B. Elastic demand in foreign markets
C. Unit elastic demand in foreign markets
D. None of these

67. Consider the following demand schedule

Price per unit (Rs.)	*Quantity demanded* (000)
6	3
5	9
4	15
3	20

When price falls from Rs. 5 to Rs. 4, elasticity of demand can be expressed numerically as
A. 1.0 B. 2.5
C. 3.3 D. 3.75

68. Two commodities are considered to be perfect substitutes for each other if the elasticity of substitution is

A. Positive B. Negative
C. Zero D. Infinite

69. If a straight line demand curve is tangent to a curvilinear demand curve, the elasticity of the two demand curves at the points of tangency is—
A. The same
B. Different
C. Can be the same or different
D. Depends on the location of the point of tangency

70. Which of the following is the method of measuring elasticity of demand when changes in price of a commodity is substantial—
A. Percentage method
B. Point method
C. Arc method
D. None of these

71. In which case the elasticity shown by the different points of a curve is the same—
A. A rectangular hyperbola curve
B. A straight line curve
C. A downward sloping curve
D. None of these

72. Which of the following statements is correct?
A. Slope of a curve and its elasticity are one and the same thing
B. Slope of a curve may remain constant; elasticity still can and does change
C. With a change in the slope of a curve, its elasticity necessarily changes
D. Two parallel demand curves, each cutting the two axis, have the same elasticity at a point corresponding to the same price

73. A demand curve is a boundary concept because it shows
A. The maximum price and minimum quantity
B. The minimum price and minimum quantity
C. The maximum quantity and the minimum price
D. Both price and quantity is maximum

74. In case the two commodities are good substitutes, cross-elasticity will be
A. Positive B. Unitary
C. Negative D. Infinite

75. In case the two commodities are complements, cross elasticity will be
A. Positive B. Unitary
C. Negative D. Infinite

76. If cross-elasticity of one commodity for another turns out to be zero, it means they are
A. Close substitutes
B. Good complements
C. Completely unrelated
D. None of these

77. A high value of cross-elasticity indicates that the two commodities are
A. Very good substitutes
B. Poor substitutes
C. Good complements
D. Poor complements

78. The vertical demand curve for a commodity shows that its demand is
A. Highly elastic B. Perfectly elastic
C. Fairly elastic D. Moderately elastic

79. If more is demanded at the same price or the same quantity is demanded at a higher price, this is known as
A. Extension of demand
B. Contraction of demand
C. Increase in demand
D. Decrease in demand

80. Utility may be defined as
A. The power of a commodity to satisfy wants
B. The usefulness of a commodity
C. The level of satisfaction given by a commodity
D. The desire for a commodity

81. The economic analysis expects the consumer to behave in a manner which is
A. Rational B. Irrational
C. Emotional D. Indifferent

82. The economically relevant range of the total utility curve is the portion over which
A. The total utility is rising at a declining rate
B. The total utility is rising at an increasing rate
C. The total utility is maximum and constant
D. The total utility is declining

83. After reaching the saturation point, consumption of additional units of the commodity cause

A. Total utility to fall and marginal utility to increase
B. Total utility and marginal utility both to increase
C. Total utility to fall and marginal utility to become negative
D. Total utility to become negative and marginal utility to fall

84. Which of the following concepts are most closely associated with Alfred Marshall?
A. Marginal utility theory
B. Price mechanism under monopoly
C. Modern theory of wage
D. Interest theory

85. The law of Equi-Marginal utility states
A. $MU_x . P_x = MU_y . P_y = MU_z . P_z$
B. $\frac{MU_x}{P_x} = \frac{MU_y}{P_y} = \frac{MU_z}{P_z} = MU_m$
C. $\frac{MU_x}{P_x} > \frac{MU_y}{P_y} > \frac{MU_z}{P_z} > MU_m$
D. $\frac{MU_x}{P_x} < \frac{MU_y}{P_y} < \frac{MU_z}{P_z} < MU_m$

86. Law of diminishing Marginal utility states
A. Total utility diminishes with the consumption of every additional unit
B. Utility always diminishes whether something is consumed or not
C. Utility first increases and after that diminishes at every point
D. The additional benefit which a person derives from a given increase of his stock of a thing diminishes with every increase in stock that he already has

87. Marginal utility (MU) curve is always
A. Rising B. Falling
C. Parallel to x-axis D. Parallel to y-axis

88. The total utility is maximum when
A. M.U. is zero
B. A.U. is the highest
C. M.U. is the highest
D. M.U. is equal to A.U.

89. The falling part of a TU curve show
A. Increasing marginal utility
B. Decreasing marginal utility
C. Zero marginal utility
D. Negative marginal utility

90. MU of nth unit is found by the following formula
A. $\frac{TU}{n}$ B. TU.n
C. $TU_n - TU_{(n-1)}$ D. $TU + n$

91. Total utility curve is
A. Concave to x-axis
B. Convex to x-axis
C. Concave or convex depending on situations
D. Concave to y-axis

92. "Utils" is a term used
A. By Marshall in Demand theory
B. By Walras to measure cardinal utility
C. To mean Marginal utility
D. None of the above

93. Given below is the MU schedule for commodities x and y

MU_x	11	10	9	8	7	6
MU_y	19	17	15	13	12	10

If price is Rs. 1 permit in each case the consumer will spend his 10th rupee on
A. Commodity x
B. Commodity y
C. Commodity x and y
D. Save from both

94. A consumer's demand curve can be obtained from
A. Income-consumption curve
B. Engel's curve
C. Price-consumption curve
D. None of these

95. A consumer will be in equilibrium if he consumes three commodities when
A. $\frac{\text{Price of } x}{\text{Price of } y} = \frac{\text{Price of } y}{\text{Price of } z} = \frac{\text{Price of } y}{\text{Price of } x} = K$
B. $\frac{MU_x}{P_x} = \frac{MU_y}{P_y} = \frac{MU_z}{P_z} = K$
C. $P_x = P_y = P_z = Z$
D. $MU_z = MU_x = MU_y$

96. 'Marginal utility approach' was finalised by
A. J.R. Hicks B. Alfred Marshall
C. J.S. Mill D. A.C. Pigou

97. A consumer will be maximizing his utility if he allocated his money income so that—
A. The marginal utility of the last unit of each product consumed is equal
B. The marginal utility from the last rupee spent on each purchased product is the same
C. Elasticity of demand is the same for all purchased products
D. Total utility gained from each product consumed is the same

98. Adam Smith spoke about the famous diamond water paradox to show that
A. Utility is related to supply
B. Utility is related to demand
C. Utility could be the cause of value
D. Utility could not be the cause of value

99. The area which lies under the demand curve for a given good measures
A. Marginal utility
B. Total utility
C. Disutility
D. Marginal cost of production

100. Which of the following creates time utility?
A. Farmer B. Carpenter
C. Trader D. Driver

101. Total utility of a commodity can be found by
A. Multiplying the number of units by its marginal utility
B. Adding up the marginal utility of all units
C. Multiplying price by number of units
D. None of these

102. "The concept marginal utility is useful for explaining diamond-water paradox" this statement is
A. Absolutely correct
B. Partially correct
C. Absolutely wrong
D. None of these

103. MU curve will be below x-axis when
A. MU is positive B. MU is negative
C. MU is zero D. MU is constant

104. As a consumer increases his consumption of a commodity, the total utility he derives from its consumption increases, but at a diminishing rate. This is—
A. A statement of fact
B. An economic law
C. A hypothesis
D. None of the above

105. A consumer reaches equilibrium at the point where
A. MU = P B. MU < P
C. MU > P D. TU = P

106. At the saturation point of commodity y the MU is
A. Positive B. Zero
C. Negative D. None of the above

107. The term optimum allocation on consumer's expenditure on various goods and services is used in
A. Law of demand
B. Giffen paradox
C. Law of equi-marginal utility
D. Law of diminishing marginal utility

108. A falling MU curve illustrates
A. The principle of diminishing marginal utility
B. The principle of diminishing marginal rate of substitution
C. The principle of equi-marginal utility
D. None of these

109. Which of the following is most closely connected with Paul A. Samuelson?
A. Indifference curve analysis
B. Marginal utility analysis
C. Revealed preference theory
D. Liquidity preference theory

110. The Law of Equi-Marginal utility tells that if price of commodity falls
A. More units of it will be bought
B. Less units of it will be bought
C. Same units of it will be bought
D. Nothing of it will be bought

111. Which of the following is called as the Gossen's First Law?
A. Law of substitution
B. The Law of equi-marginal utility
C. The Law of diminishing utility
D. The Law of indifference

112. After reaching the saturation point additional unit of the commodity causes
A. Total utility to fall and marginal utility to become negative

B. Total utility and marginal utility both to increase
C. Total utility and marginal utility both to decrease
D. Total utility become negative and marginal utility to fall

113. A stable equilibrium position is one in which
A. There are never any departures from the equilibrium position
B. There are only two forces influencing equilibrium
C. Any departure from the equilibrium position calls into play forces which end to restore that position
D. There are endless oscillations

114. Marginal utility has no place in a ordinal theory because it is
A. Introspective B. Subjective
C. Not observable D. Additive

115. At the point of inflexion, the marginal utility is
A. Increasing B. Decreasing
C. Maximum D. Negative

116. Ordinal approach is based on
A. Law of maximum satisfaction
B. Utility could not be measured in cardinal numbers
C. Utility could not be measured in ordinal numbers
D. Utility can be measured

117. Put into chronological order on the basis of development
(i) Law of demand
(ii) Law of indifference
(iii) Law of diminishing marginal utility
(iv) Revealed preference curve
(v) Indifference curve

A.	*(i)*	*(ii)*	*(iii)*	*(iv)*	*(v)*
B.	*(i)*	*(v)*	*(iii)*	*(iv)*	*(ii)*
C.	*(i)*	*(iii)*	*(ii)*	*(v)*	*(iv)*
D.	*(i)*	*(iii)*	*(iv)*	*(ii)*	*(v)*

118. Match the following:

1. Principles of Economics	*(i)* Gunnar Myrdal
2. Diamond water paradox	*(ii)* J.K. Galbraith
3. Value and Capital	*(iii)* Alfred Marshall
4. Asian Drama	*(iv)* J. R. Hicks
5. Language of Economics	*(v)* Adam Smith

	1	2	3	4	5
A.	*(i)*	*(ii)*	*(iii)*	*(v)*	*(iv)*
B.	*(ii)*	*(iv)*	*(iii)*	*(v)*	*(i)*
C.	*(v)*	*(ii)*	*(iii)*	*(i)*	*(iv)*
D.	*(iii)*	*(v)*	*(iv)*	*(i)*	*(ii)*
E.	*(iv)*	*(v)*	*(iii)*	*(ii)*	*(i)*

119. The price which a consumer would be willing to pay for a commodity equals to his
A. Total utility
B. Marginal utility
C. Average utility
D. Does not have any relation to any one of these

120. Gossen's second law states that—
A. When the income increases the money value or real income will decrease
B. The consumers consume only when

$$\frac{P_x}{P_y} = MU_m$$

C. Once a person has spent his entire income he would have maximised his total pleasure from it only if the satisfaction gained from the last item of each commodity bought was the same
D. None of these

121. The concept of indifference curves analysis was given scientific touch by—
A. Irving Fisher in 1982
B. F.Y. Edgeworth in 1881
C. Slutsky in 1915
D. Alfred Marshall in 1921

122. Economists associated with the development of indifference curve analysis are
A. Hicks and Allen
B. Hicks and Robbins
C. Marshall and Hicks
D. Hicks and Walras

123. The indifference curve technique
A. has replaced utility technique altogether
B. is used as alternative to the utility technique
C. is used along with the utility approach
D. has become a part of the utility approach

124. Which of the following is one of the assumptions of the indifference curve analysis—

A. Cardinal utility
B. Ordinal utility
C. Independent utility
D. Constant marginal utility of money

125. Other things remaining the same, when a consumer's income increases, his equilibrium point moves to
A. A higher indifference curve
B. A lower indifference curve
C. Remains unchanged on the same indifference curve
D. Moves to the left-hand side on the same indifference curve

126. The general equation of the budget constraint line is
A. $P_x \cdot Q_x + P_y \cdot Q_y = M$
B. $\frac{P_x}{M} = Qx$
C. $Q_x \cdot P_x = M + P_y$
D. $P_x + P_y = O$

127. An indifference curve is always
A. Concave to the origin
B. Convex to the origin
C. A vertical straight line
D. A horizontal straight line

128. When the consumer's income increases, the budget line on an indifference map moves to
A. A parallel position to the right
B. A parallel position to the left
C. A parallel position to the origin
D. None of the above

129. Goods X and Y are perfect substitutes. A consumers's indifference curve for these commodities is represented by a
A. Upward sloping straight line
B. Upward sloping curve which is convex from below
C. Downward sloping straight line
D. Downward sloping curve which is convex to origin

130. The indifference curve which is 'L' shape represents
A. Perfect complementarity
B. Perfect substitutability
C. No substitutability
D. Non Complementarity

131. "We are much better off when drawing purely imaginary indifference curves than we are when speaking of purely imaginary utility functions." This is remarked by—
A. J. R. Hicks B. Allen
C. Schumpeter D. P. A. Samuelson

132. Indifference curve is downward sloping from left to right since more x and less y give
A. Less satisfaction
B. More satisfaction
C. Equal satisfaction
D. Maximum satisfaction

133. When the price of one commodity in a combination of commodities falls in such a way that the consumer's real income changes but he remains on the same level of satisfaction as before, it is known as
A. Income effect
B. Variation effect
C. Price effect
D. Compensating variation in income

134. If two goods are perfect substitutes for each other, it necessarily follows that
A. An indifference curve relating the two goods will be curvilinear
B. An indifference curve relating the two goods will be linear
C. An indifference curve relating the two goods will be divided into two segments which meet at a right angle
D. An indifference curve relating the two goods will be convex to the origin

135. MRS_{xy} and MRS_{yx} both will be zero where the commodity x and y are
A. Complement to each other
B. Substitutes to each other
C. Perfect complementarity
D. Imperfect complementarity

136. The amount of a commodity that the consumer would purchase per unit of time at various levels of his income is shown by
A. Contract curve B. Lorenz curve
C. Engel curve D. Indifference curve

137. All the points on a budget line represent
A. Increasing total expenditure
B. Decreasing total expenditure
C. The same total expenditure
D. None of the above

138. If the $\frac{MU_x}{MU_y}$ for individual A is greater than the $\frac{MU_x}{MU_y}$ for individual B it is possible for individual A to gain by giving up

A. Y in exchange for more X from B
B. Y in exchange for more X from A itself
C. Y in exchange for less X from B
D. X in exchange for less Y from A

139. If indifference curve has a positive slope, it means

A. Consumer preferences unpredictable
B. Consumer preferences are irrational
C. *x*-is a discommodity
D. *y*-is a discommodity

140. For perfect substitutability between *x* and *y*—

A. MRS_{xy} will be constant
B. MRS_{xy} will be decreasing
C. MRS_{xy} will be increasing
D. None of the above

141. Match the following—

1. Various combinations of two commodities that a consumer can purchase	(*i*) Indifference map
2. Various combinations of two commodities that give consumer equal satisfaction	(*ii*) Indifference curve
3. A set of indifference curves	(*iii*) Budget line
4. Point of tangency of a budget line and an indifference curve	(*iv*) Consumer's equilibrium

	1	2	3	4
A.	(*i*)	(*ii*)	(*iv*)	(*iii*)
B.	(*iv*)	(*iii*)	(*i*)	(*ii*)
C.	(*ii*)	(*iii*)	(*iv*)	(*i*)
D.	(*iii*)	(*ii*)	(*i*)	(*iv*)

142. On an indifference map higher indifference curves show

A. The same lower level of satisfaction
B. The optimum level of satisfaction
C. The higher level of satisfaction
D. Levels of satisfaction among which the consumer is indifferent

143. Match the following:

1. Cardinal approach	(*i*) Marginal utility
2. Ordinal approach	(*ii*) Alfred Marshall
3. Hicks-Allen approach	(*iii*) J.R. Hicks
4. Consumer's surplus	(*iv*) Indifference curve
	(*v*) Revealed preference theory

	1	2	3	4
A.	(*i*)	(*ii*)	(*iii*)	(*iv*)
B.	(*i*)	(*v*)	(*iv*)	(*ii*)
C.	(*i*)	(*iii*)	(*iv*)	(*ii*)
D.	(*i*)	(*iii*)	(*ii*)	(*iv*)

144. On an indifference map, if the income consumption curve slopes downwards to the right it shows that

A. X is an inferior good
B. Y is an inferior good
C. Both X and Y are superior goods
D. Both X and Y are inferior goods

145. Price effect in indifference curve analysis arises—

A. when the consumer becomes either better off or worse off because price change is not compensated income change
B. When income and price change
C. When the consumer is better off due to a change in income and price
D. None of the above

Question 146 to 147 are based on the following figure—

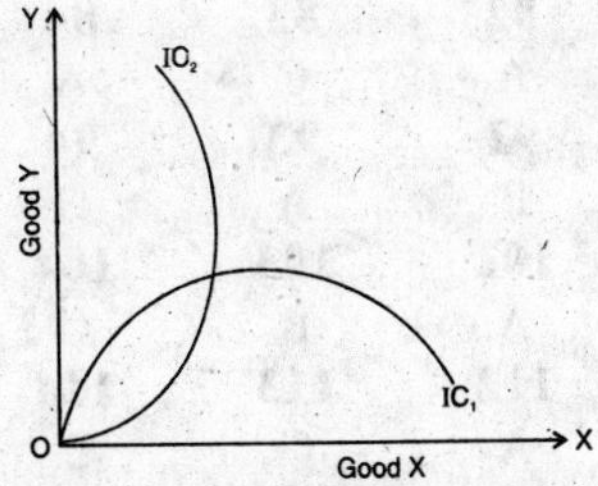

146. If curve IC_2 represents the income consumption curve, then we can conclude that—

A. X only is an inferior good
B. Y only is an inferior good
C. Both X and Y are inferior good
D. X only is a superior good

147. If we assume that curve IC_1 is the income consumption curve, it can be concluded that—
- A. Only y is an inferior good
- B. Neither y nor x is an inferior good
- C. Only x is an inferior good
- D. x is inferior but y is a superior good

148. In the case of an inferior good, the income effect
- A. Partially offsets the substitution effect
- B. Reinforces the substitution effect
- C. Is equal to the substitution effect
- D. More than offsets the substitution effect

149. The substitution effect works to encourage a consumer to purchase more of a product when the price of that goods is falling because
- A. The consumer's real income has increased
- B. The consumer's real income has decreased
- C. The product is now relatively less expensive the before
- D. Other products are now less expensive than before

150. The total effect of a price change of a commodity is
- A. Substitution effect + Price effect
- B. Substitution effect + Income effect
- C. Substitution effect + Demonstration effect
- D. Substitution effect – Income effect

ANSWERS

1	2	3	4	5	6	7	8	9	10
C	C	A	C	C	E	B	D	A	A
11	**12**	**13**	**14**	**15**	**16**	**17**	**18**	**19**	**20**
A	B	A	A	A	B	D	D	A	A
21	**22**	**23**	**24**	**25**	**26**	**27**	**28**	**29**	**30**
C	C	B	C	B	B	B	B	B	B
31	**32**	**33**	**34**	**35**	**36**	**37**	**38**	**39**	**40**
A	A	A	C	A	A	B	B	C	B
41	**42**	**43**	**44**	**45**	**46**	**47**	**48**	**49**	**50**
C	D	A	A	B	B	B	B	B	C
51	**52**	**53**	**54**	**55**	**56**	**57**	**58**	**59**	**60**
C	D	B	A	C	B	A	B	A	A
61	**62**	**63**	**64**	**65**	**66**	**67**	**68**	**69**	**70**
A	C	D	A	A	B	C	D	A	C
71	**72**	**73**	**74**	**75**	**76**	**77**	**78**	**79**	**80**
A	C	D	A	C	C	A	B	C	A
81	**82**	**83**	**84**	**85**	**86**	**87**	**88**	**89**	**90**
A	A	C	A	B	D	B	A	D	C
91	**92**	**93**	**94**	**95**	**96**	**97**	**98**	**99**	**100**
A	B	A	C	B	B	B	B	B	C
101	**102**	**103**	**104**	**105**	**106**	**107**	**108**	**109**	**110**
B	A	B	C	A	B	C	A	C	A
111	**112**	**113**	**114**	**115**	**116**	**117**	**118**	**119**	**120**
C	A	C	D	C	B	C	D	D	C
121	**122**	**123**	**124**	**125**	**126**	**127**	**128**	**129**	**130**
B	C	B	B	A	A	B	A	C	A
131	**132**	**133**	**134**	**135**	**136**	**137**	**138**	**139**	**140**
C	C	D	B	C	C	C	B	C	A
141	**142**	**143**	**144**	**145**	**146**	**147**	**148**	**149**	**150**
D	C	B	B	A	A	A	A	C	B

MACRO-ECONOMICS

Determination of Income and Employment

Classical Theory of Employment

The classical theory assumes the existence of full employment without inflation. Given wage-price flexibility, there are automatic forces in the economic system that tend to maintain full employment, and produce output at that level. Thus full employment is ragarded as a normal situation and any deviation from this level is something abnormal which automatically tends towards full employment. The classical theory of output and employment is based on the following assumptions:

1. There is the existence of full employment without inflation.
2. There is perfect competition in labour and product markets.
3. There is a closed *laissez faire* capitalist economy without foreign trade.
4. Labour is homogenous.
5. Total output of the economy is divided between consumption and investment expenditures.
6. The quantity of money is given.
7. Wages and prices are flexible.
8. Money wages and real wages are directly related and proportional.
9. Capital stock and technological knowledge are given in the short run.

Say's Law and Classical Theory

According to the classical theory propounded by Ricardo and Adam Smith, levels of income and employment are governed by fixed capital stock on the one hand and wage-goods fund on the other. In fact, the wage goods surpluses are also called by them as capital and have been given the name of circulating capital or liquid capital in contrast to the fixed capital consisting of machines, plants, factory buildings, irrigation works, etc. It may be noted in the begining that the classical theory believes in full employment or near full employment prevailing in the economy. This belief of classical theory regarding the existence of full employment in the economy is based on **Say's Law** put forward by a Frenchy economist **J. B. Say**. According to J. B. Say's law, **"Supply creates its own demand"**. This implies that every increase in production made possible by the increase in the productive capacity or the stock of fixed capital will be sold in the market and there will be no problem of lack of demand.

Thus, classical economists rule out the possibility of overproduction; there being no problem in selling the output produced. Thus, deficiency in demand being no problem, the process of capital accumulation and expansion of productive capacity will continue till all people are employed and there is no reason why the productive capacity created remains unutilized or underutilized.

According to this theory, the income which is not spent on consumer goods and thus saved will be automatically invested. Indeed, in classical theory, saving and investment are two factors of the same phenomenon *i.e.*, an act of saving is an act of investment itself. Thus, the leakage caused by the saving in the income flow is made up by the investment expenditure. In this way, a given productive capacity continue to be fully utilized and no problem of deficiency of demand arises.

Classical economists thought that if price mechanism in a capitalist economy is allowed to work freely without any interference by the Government, then there is always a tendency to full employment in it. Of course, they admitted that in an advanced capitalist economy often certain circumstances arise due to which economy is not in a full-employment equilibrium. But they firmly believed that there was always a tendency to full employment in the economy and certain economic forces automatically operate so as to move the economy towards full employment. Therefore, according to the classical economists when ever there are lapses from full employment level, then these are removed automatically by the working of **free price mechanism.**

Price Flexibility and Employment

In the classical model of employment, changes in money wages and real wages are directly related and are propoportional. When there is a cut in the money wage, the real wage is also reduced to the some extent which reduces unemployment and ultimately brings full employment in the economy. This relationship is based on the assumption that prices are proportional to the quantity of money. It is argued that in a competitive economy a reaction in the money wage reduces the cost of production and prices of products thereby raising their demand. In order to meet the increased demand for the products, more workers are employed to produce them.

As employment increases, total output also increases till full employment is reached. But when the economy is at the full employment level, total output becomes stable. Thus, given the stocks of capital, technological knowledge and resources, a precise relation exists between total output and the amount of employment. Total output is an increasing funciton of the number of workers.

$$Q = f(K, T, N)$$

where Q = total output

K = capital stock

T = technological knowledge

N = number of workers

This production function shows that in the short run the total output is an increasing function of the number of workers given the capital stock and technological knowledge.

Keynes's Criticism of Classical Theory

Keynes in his renowned book **"General Theory"** severely criticised the classical theory of employment. Keynes attacked the classical theory on the following counts.

1. Keynes rejected the fundamental classical assumption of full employment equilibrium in the economy. He considered it as unrealistic. He regarded full employment as a special situation. The general situation in a capitalist economy is one of underemployment.
2. Keynes refuted Say's law of markets that supply always created its own demand. He maintained that all income earned by the factor owners would not be spent in buying products which they helped to produce. A part of the income is saved and is not automatically invested because saving and investment are distinct functions. So when all earned income is not spent on consumption goods and a portion of it is saved, there results a deficiency of aggregate demand. This leads to general over production because all that is produced is not sold. This, in turn, leads to general unemployment.
3. The classicists believed that saving and investment were equal at the full employment level and in case of any divergence the equality was brought about by the mechanism of rate of interest. Keynes held that the level of saving depended upon the level of income and not on the rate of interest. Similarly investment is determined not only by rate of interest but by the marginal efficiency of capital. A low rate of interest cannot increase investment if business expectations are low.
4. Keynes did not agree with the classical view that the **laissez-faire** policy was essential for an automatic and self-adjusting process of full employment equilibrium. He pointed out that the capitalist system was not automatic and self-adjusting because of the non-egalitarian structure of its society. Keynes, therefore, advocated state intervention for adjusting supply and demand within the economy through fiscal and monetary measures.

5. The classical economists regarded money as neutral. Therefore they excluded the theory of output, employment and interest rate from the monetary theory. According to them, the level of output and employment, and the equilibrium rate of interest were determined by real forces. Keynes criticised the classical view that the monetary theory was separate from the value theory. He integrated monetary theory with value theory, and brought the theory of interest in the domain of monetary theory.
6. Keynes refuted the Pigovian formulation that a cut in money wage could achieve full employment in the economy. The greatest fallacy in Pigou's analysis was that he extended the argument to the economy which was applicable to a particular industry. Keynes also did not accept the classical view that there was a direct proportionate relationship between money wages and real wages. According to him, there is an inverse relation between the two. When money wages fall, real wages rise and vice versa.
7. The classicists believed in the long-run full employment equilibrium through a self-adjusting process. Keynes had no patience to wait for the long period for he believed that "In the long-run we are all dead."

Keynes's Theory of Employment

Concept of Effective Demand

The priciple of 'effective demand' is basic to Keynes analysis of income, output and employment. Prior to Keynes no satisfactory explanation was given of the factors determining the level of employment in the economy. The economists mostly assumed the prevalence of the state of full employment believing in Say's Law of Markets. **T. R. Malthus** tried hard to convince Ricardo that demand in general might fall short of supply in general and the deficiency of aggregate demand might cause general over production and hence general unemployment. But Malthus failed to explain how effective demand could be deficient or excessive. It was Keynes, who for the first time, put forward a systematic and convincing theory of employment based on the **"Principle of Effective Demand."**

Meaning of Effective Demand

Effective demand represents the money actually spent by people on the products of industry. Keynes used the term 'effective demand' to denote the total demand for goods and services at various levels of employment. Different levels of employment represent different levels of aggregate demand. But there can be a level of employment where aggregate demand equals aggregate supply. This is the point of effective demand.

Determinants of Effective Demands

For an understanding of Keynes theory of employment and how an equilibrium level of employment is established in the economy, we must know the determinants of effective demand—the aggregate demand function and the aggregate supply function and their interrelationship.

Aggregate Supply

When entrepreneurs employ some people they incur some cost of production. If the proceeds obtained from the sale of output produced by a certain number of people employed is greater than the cost of production incurred, then it will be worthwhile to employ them. This cost of production incurred on the employment of a certain number of labourers must be received by the entrepreneur, otherwise they will not produce and provide employment to labour. At any given level of employment of labour, **aggregate supply price is the total amount of money which all the entrepreneurs in the economy taken together must expect to receive from the sale of** the output produced by the given number of labourers employed. In other words, the aggregate supply price is the total cost of production incurred by employing a certain given number of labourers. It is obvious that if the cost of production incurred by the entrepreneur in employing a certain number of labourers is not covered, they will reduce the amount of employment offered. As the amount of employment of labour increases, the total cost of production will also increase. Therefore, aggregate supply price will rise as more labour is employed to produce goods and serices. Thus, we can construct a schedule and curve of aggregate supply showing aggregate supply price at different levels of employment. The curve of aggregate supply price is represented by AS in Figure 1. This curve of aggregate supply price starts from the point of origin and slopes upward to the right. In the beginning aggregate supply price curve AS rises slowly, afterwards it rises rapidly. This curve AS shows that as the number of men employed is increased, the aggregate supply price rises slowly in the beginning and rapidly afterwards. This, is because cost of production rises as more people are employed and further due to the operations of law of diminishing returns total cost of production increases at an increasing rate. Once all the men willing to get employment are employed, then we have a state of full employment. When the state of full employment is reached further increases in aggregate demand or monetary expenditure will be unable to increase employment further since output of goods and services cannot be increased further as no more labour is available for production after full employment level is reached. Therefore, aggregate supply curve assumes a vertical shape after full employment is reached. In Figure 1, ON_F is the level of full employment at which aggregate supply price assumes a vertical shape.

Aggregate Demand

It is the aggregate demand which plays a more important role in the determination of employment. Aggregate demand price at any level of employment is the amount of total money or price (proceeds) which all the firms or entrepreneurs in the economy **actually expect** to receive from the sale of output produced by a given number of men employed. In other words, aggregate demand price represents the amount of expenditure expected by the entrepreneurs when a given number of men are employed to produce goods and services. Like the aggregate supply price, aggregate demand price also varies at different levels of employment.

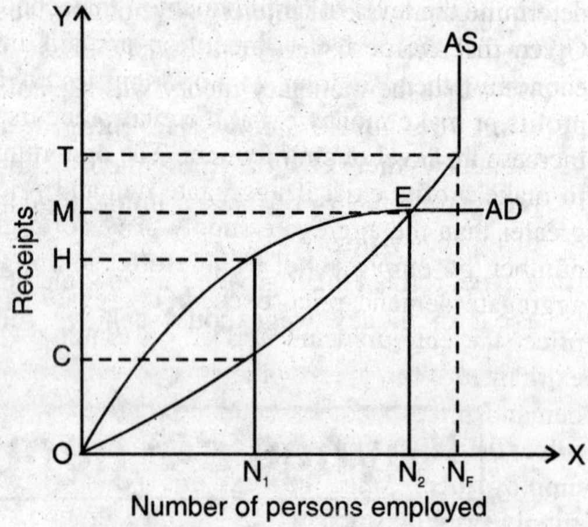

Fig. 1 : *Determination of Employment: Keynesian Theory*

This is because at different levels of employment different income levels would be generated and at different income levels, consumption demand would be different. Therefore, we can construct a schedule or curve of aggregate demand price showing different aggregate demand price at different levels of employment. The curve of aggregate demand is shown by the curve AD in Figure 1. The aggregate demand price curve also rises from left to right. It will be seen in figure 1 that when ON_1 number of men are employed, the aggregate demand price is OH and when ON_2 men are employed, agregate demand price is OM.

Determination of the Equilibrium Level of Employment by Effective Demand

In Figure 1 we have shown together aggregate suply curve and aggregate demand curve. The amount of employment is measured along the *x*-axis and the receipts or proceeds obtained at various levels of employment are measured along the *y*-axis. As said above, aggregate supply curve shows the revenue or receipts which **must be received** by the entrepreneurs so as to provide employment to a given number of men. Whereas aggregate demand curve shows proceeds or receipts which entrepreneurs actually expect to receive at different levels of employment and production. These aggregate demand and the aggregate supply curves determine the level of employment in the economy. Given that the perfect competition prevails in the economy, then so long as opportunities to earn profits or make money exist, the entrepreneurs will increase the level of employment. The opportunities to make profits exist if aggregate demand price is greater than the aggregate supply price for a given number of employment. Therefore, so long as, aggregate demand price exceeds aggregate supply price, the entrepreneurs will go on employing the extra men. When at a level of employment aggregate demand price becomes equal to aggregate supply price, then after this it will be no more profitable to employ men. Since beyond this point aggregate supply price will exceed aggregate demand price, the cost of production incurred on employing a certain number of people will not be covered. Therefore, when aggregate demand price falls short of aggregate supply price, employment of labour will fall. Equilibrium level of employment is determined by the intersection of aggregate demand curve and the aggregate supply curve, where the amount of money which the entrepreneurs actually expect to receive from employing a certain number of men is equal to the amount of money which they must receive. In other worlds, the employment of labour will be in equilibrium at the level at which aggregate demand price equals aggregate supply price. It will be seen in figure 1 that aggregate supply curve and aggregate demand curve intersect at point E and therefore ON_2 level of employment is determined.

However, it will be seen from Figure 1 that in the situation of equilibrium at the employment level ON_2, N_2N_F persons remain unemployed. Thus equilibrium at E represent an **under-employment equilibrium.** It is important to note that N_2F_2, persons are **involuntarily unemployed**: they are willing to work at the existing wages but are unable to find jobs. It is important to remember that, according to Keynes, this unemployment is due to **deficiency of aggregate demand.**

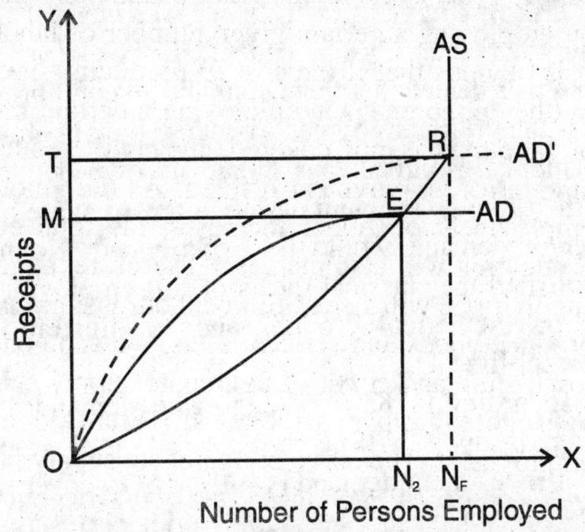

Fig. 2

This unemployment will be removed and full employment equilibrium will be reached if through increase in investment demand or increase in consumption, or increase in both aggregate demand curve shifts upward so that it intersects the aggregate supply curve at point R as depicted in Figure 2. It will be seen that with the intersection of aggregate demand and aggregate supply curves at point R, equilibrium is established at full employment level ON_F.

It is thus clear that employment in the economy in the **short run** is determined by effective demand. The higher the level of effective demand, the greater is the volume of employment and vice versa. Unemployment is due to the deficiency of effective demand and the basic remedy to remove this unemployment is to raise the level of effective demand. The classical economists believed that effective demand was always large enough to ensure full employment. But Keynes proved that it was not so and that is why the phenomenon of unemployment is common in free market capitalist economies.

Equilibrium Not Necessarily at Full Employment

It is not necessary that the equilibrium levels of employment is always at full employment. Equality between aggregate demand and aggregate supply does not necessarily indicate the full employment level. The economy can be in equilibrium at less than full employment or, in other words, an under employment equilibrium can exist. The classical economists denied that there could be an equilibrium at less than full employment, because they believed that supply would always create its own demand and therefore no problem of deficiency of aggregate effective demand would be experienced. Keynes demolished the classical thesis of full employment both on theoretical grounds and by illustrations from real life.

According to Keynes, aggregate demand and aggregate supply will be equal at full employment only if investment demand is sufficient to cover the gap between the aggregate supply price corresponding to full employment and the consumption expenditure out of income at the full employment level. The view of Keynes is that investment demand generally falls short of this gap between full-employment income and consumption. According to him, when inducement to invest in capitalist countries declines due to the fall in marginal efficiency of capital, aggregate demand falls so that equilibrium is established at less than full employment level. As a result, output and income of the community also fall.

Determination of National Income : Keynesian Theory

We explained earlier the Keynesian theory with special reference to the determination of employment. It is worth noting here that the Keynesian theory is relevant in the context of the **short run** only since the stock of capital, techniques of production, efficiency of labour, the size of population, forms of business organisation have been assumed to remain constant in this theory. Therefore, in the Keynesian theory which deals with the short run, the level of income of the country will change as a result of changes in the level of labour employment. Thus, in an advanced capitalist economy in the short-run, income is a function of employment. In fact, both income and employment go together. The higher the level of employment; the higher the level of income. As level of employment is determined by aggregate demand and aggregate supply, the level of income is also determined by aggregate demand and aggregate supply.

Aggregate Supply

Equilibrium level of national income in the short run depends upon aggregate demand and aggregate supply. The aggregate supply depends on physical or technical conditions of production which do not change in the short-run. Since Keynes assumes the aggregate supply to be stable, he concentrates his entire attention upon the aggregate demand to fight depression and unemployment.

Aggregate Demand

Aggregate demand is determined by consumption demand and investment demand. Therefore,

Aggregate Demand = Consumption Demand + Investment Demand

$$AD = C + I$$

Where, AD = aggregate demand
C = consumption demand
I = investment demand

Consumption Demand

As for consumption demand, it depends upon the propensity to consume of the community and the level of national income. Given the propensity to consume, as income will increase consumption demand will also increase. In other words, given the propensity to consume, consumption demand is a function of income. Consider Figure 3 in which income is measured along the *x*-axis and consumption demand (C) and investment (I) are shown on the *y*-axis. In this figure, a straight line OZ which makes 45° angle with the *x*-axis has been drawn. This straight line OZ with 45° angle with the *x*-axis represents the aggregate supply curve of the economy. This is also often called income line. In this figure a curve C has also been drawn which shows the propensity to consume slopes upward from left to right, which shows that as income increases the amount of consumption demand also increases. The gap between propensity to consume curve C and the income line OZ represents the saving of the community. The reason for this is that a part of the income is consumed and a part is saved, *i.e.*,

National Income = Consumption + Saving
or Y = C + S
where Y = income
C = consumption
S = saving

It will be seen from the figure that the gap between the propensity to consume curve C and the income line OZ goes on increasing as income increases. In other words, the amount of saving or saving gap increases as income increases. It is worth mentioning that in the short run propensity to consume does not change. This is because the propensity to consume, that is, the whole propensity to consume curve C depends upon the tastes, preferences, the income distribution in the society, the population level, etc. which do not undergo any change in the short-run.

Investment Demand

The other constituent of the aggregate demand is investment which is a crucial factor in the determination of equilibrium level of national income. Investment demand depends upon two factors:

1. Marginal efficiency of capital
2. Rate of interest

Of these two factors, rate of interest is comparatively stable and does not frequently change in the short-run. Therefore, the fluctuations in the level of investment demand chiefly depend upon the changes in the marginal efficiency of capital. The MEC means the expected rate of profit which the business community hopes to get from the investment in capital assets. MEC depends upon the replacement cost of the capital goods on the one hand and profit expectations of entrepreneur on the other.

In Keynesian theory of income determination, investment is not taken to be function of income. In actual practice when the level of income rises, the demand for goods will also rise and this will favourably effect the expectations of the entrepreneurs regarding making of profits. Rise in the profit expectations will raise the MEC which in turn will increase the level of investment. But it is quite clear that investment demand does not directly depend upon income; It is only effected indirectly by changes in income.

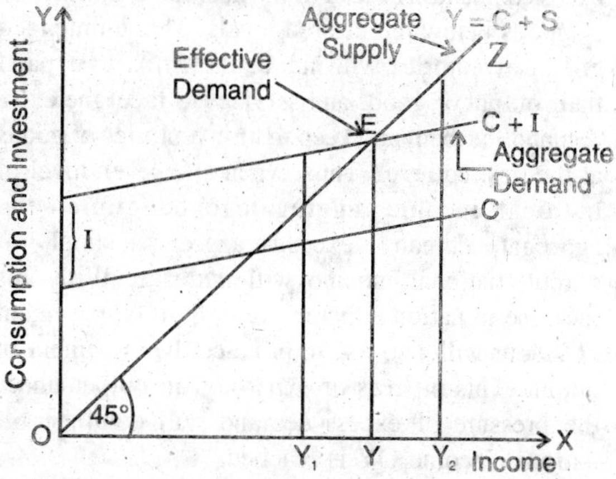

Fig. 3 : *Equilibrium Level of National Income*

Therefore, in our figure we have taken a given level of investment demand independent of the level of income. The distance between the C curve and the C + I curve is parallel to the C - curve throughout which indicates that the level of investment is constant and does not change with the change in income.

Equilibrium Level of Income : Equality of Aggregate Demand and Aggregate Supply

The equilibrium level of national income is determined at a point where the aggregate demand function intersects the aggregate supply function. The aggregate demand function is represented by C + I in the Figure 3. It is drawn by adding to the consumption function C and the investment demand I. The 45° line represents the aggregate supply function (Y = C + S). The aggregate demand function C + I intersects the aggregate supply function Y = C + S at point E and the equilibrium level of income OY is determined.

Therefore, E is the equilibrium point and OY represents the equilibrium level of national income. Now, income cannot be in equilibrium at levels smaller than OY.

This is because at any level of income smaller than OY, aggregate demand exceeds aggregate supply of output since C + I curve lie above 45° line which depicts aggregate supply of output. This excess demand will lead to the decline in inventories of goods below the desired levels. This unintended fall in inventories will induce the firms to expand their output of goods and services to meet the extra demand for them and keep their inventories of goods at the desired level. Thus, when at a given level of national income, aggregate expenditure (*i.e.* aggregate demand) exceeds aggregate supply of output, national income will increase. With this increase in national income or output, employment of labour will also rise to produce the increment in output. This process of expansion in output under the pressure of excess demand will continue till national income OY is reached.

On the contrary, the level of national income cannot be greater than OY because at any level greater than OY, aggregate expenditure or demand (C + I) falls short of aggregate supply of output. This will cause the increase in inventories of goods with the firms beyond the desired levels. To this situation of the unintended increase in inventories of goods, the firms will respond by cutting down production to keep their inventories at the desired levels. Thus, deficiency in aggregate demand relative to the aggregate supply of output will lead to the fall in national income and output until the level OY is reached where aggregate demand (C + I) is equal to the value of aggregate supply. Thus, OY is the equilibrium level of national income.

Criticism of Keynesian Theory

1. Closed Economy : The Keynesian theory is based on the assumption of a **closed economy** which excludes the impact of foreign trade on the level of employment and income. This makes Keynes's analysis unrealistic because all economies are open economies, and foreign trade has an important impact on their level of employment. Thus, Keynes's neglect of the repercussions of foreign trade on the volume of employment is a serious defect in his theory.

2. Perfect Competition : Another weakness of the Keynesian theory is that it is based on the unrealistic assumption of perfect competition. This makes his theory inapplicable to socialist or communist societies where the entire economy is regulated by the state.

3. General Theory : Keynes considered his theory as a "general theory." But as is clear from the above points, it is not a general theory but a special theory which is applicable only under static conditions in a perfectly competitive closed economy. Moreover, it fails to solve the problems of underdeveloped countries.

4. Problem of Unemployment : Keynes has been criticised for tackling only **cyclical unemployment**, and neglecting other types of unemployment to be found in capitalist economies.

5. Short-run Economics : Another criticism of the Keynisian economics is that it is applicable to the short-run. Keynes himself remarked, "**In the long-run, we are all dead.**" He, therefore, assumed a given stock of capital equipment, existing technique, tastes and habits of the people, organisation, size of population, etc. But all these factors change during the short-run. This makes Keynes's analysis unrealistic. Moreover, economics is an incomplete study without concentrating on the long-run effects of these forces on the economy.

6. Expectations : Keynes has been criticised for his over emphasis on expectations. Expectations breed uncertainty. Though Keynes gave a dominant role to expectations in influencing the marginal efficiency of capital, yet he failed to formulate a precise theory of expectations.

7. Dynamic Theory : Keynes regarded his theory dynamic and called it "the theory of shifting equilibrium." Even his foremost pupil **Roy Harrod** calls him **"the father of dynamic economics."** Keynes introduced an element of dynamism in his theory through the 'expectations'. But his analysis was concerned with the level of employment at any time. It is a log less analysis.

Government Expenditure and National Income

In our above analysis we have not taken into account the rate of Government expenditure in the determination of national income. However, in all economies today including the free market capitalist economies the Government expenditure on goods and services plays an important role in the determination of national income and therefore it should also be included in the analysis of income determination. We assume that Government spends on goods and services keeping taxes unchanged. We denote Government expenditure by G. Thus when we take into account the income generating effects of Government expenditure, we get the following equation for the equilibrium level of National Income.

$$Y = C + I + G$$

Where, Y is national income or output and C + I + G represents the level of aggregate demand including Government expenditure, G. Since consumption function is

$$C = a + bY$$

where, $b = mpc$

a = autonomous consumption expenditure

We can rewrite the equilibrium level of national income as under:

$$Y = a + by + Ia + G$$

$$Y - by = a + Ia + G$$

$$Y\,[1 - b] = a + Ia + G$$

$$Y = (a + Ia + G)$$

Thus, it is clear that the equilibrium level of income (when impact of Government expenditure is also considered) is equal to the sum of three types of fixed autonomous expenditure, namely, autonomous consumption, autonomous investment and Government expenditure (a + I + G) multiplied by the value of the multiplier $\left(\frac{1}{1-b}\right)$.

Taxes and Equilibrium Income

In our above analysis of impact of Government expenditure on national income we have ignored the effect of taxes. We assumed that increase in Government expenditure was financed by borrowing by the Government. The equilibrium level of income is

$$Y = C + Ia + G$$

$$C = a + b\,Y_d$$

where Y_d = disposable income

Since disposable personal income is less than net national income (product) by the amount of taxes. Therefore

$$Y_d = Y - T$$

The consumption function becomes

$$C = a + b\,(Y - T) \text{ [where T = tax]}$$

With this consumption function, with investment assumed to be entirely autonomous (Ia) and with fixed amounts of government purchases and tax receipts assumed per time period, the equilibrium level of income is given by

$$Y = a + b\,(Y - T) + Ia + G$$

$$Y - b.Y = a - b.T + Ia + G$$

$$Y[1 - b] = a - b.T + Ia + G$$

$$Y = \frac{1}{1-b}(a - b.T + Ia + G)$$

In this form, it may be seen that a change in any single value within the parentheses will produce a change in income equal to the change in that value times the ordinary multiplier, $\left(\frac{1}{1-b}\right)$.

If now, for example, we assume a change in G, the other values remaining unchanged, the new equilibrium level of Y is equal to the original level of Y plus the change in Y:

$$Y + \Delta y = \frac{1}{1-b}(a - b.T + Ia + G) + \frac{1}{1-b}\Delta G$$

subtracting Y from both sides, there remains

$$\Delta y = \frac{1}{1-b}\Delta G \quad \text{or,} \quad \frac{\Delta y}{\Delta G} = \frac{1}{1-b}$$

= Government Expenditure Multiplier

where b = marginal propensity to consume

In the same, we will find that

$$\Delta Y = \frac{-b}{1-b}.\Delta T$$

$$\frac{\Delta Y}{\Delta T} = \frac{-b}{1-b} = \textbf{Tax Multiplier}$$

It is clear from above that a change in T of the same size as the change in G will produce a smaller change in Y and the change will be in the opposite direction.

Foreign Trade and National Income

Foreign trade, that is, volume of exports and imports of a country also effects the level of national income of the country. We now extend the Keynesian model of determination of national income by including the effect of exports and imports of a country on the generation of income. For example, the exports of India represent the foreign demand and generates income for the Indian people. On the other hand, imports represent the demand for foreign goods by the Indians and generate incomes for the people of other countries therefore, imports tend to reduce the aggregate expenditure. It therefore follows that national income will depend on the net exports, that is, exports minus imports (X – M, where X- stands for exports and M for imports). The exports and imports of a country depend to a great extent on the level of economic activity. Thus, when the growth of industrial output in India is rapid, it will generate greater demand for imported materials. On the other hand, the higher industrial growth would also cause our exports to rise provided there is demand for our goods abroad. However, in the Keynesian model of income determination, exports and imports are considered as autonomous, that is, independent of income, being determined outside the model. Further, as mentioned above, the increase or decrease in aggregate expenditure or demand due to exports and imports depends on the net exports, that is, (X – M). If net exports are positive, there will be addition to the aggregate demand or expenditure of a country. On the other hand, if the net exports are negatives there will be decrease in aggregate expenditure.

When we include net exports in our analysis we get the following equation for the equilibrium level of income

$$Y = C + I + G + (X - M)$$

Since $C = a + b.Y$

$$Y = a + b.Y + I + G + (X - M)$$

or $Y - b.Y = a + I + G + (X - M)$

$$Y[1 - b] = a + I + G + (X - M)$$

$$Y = \frac{1}{1-b}[a + I + G + (X - M)]$$

Thus, the equilibrium level of income is the sum of all fixed autonomous expenditures [*i.e.* $a + I + G + (X - M)$] times the value of multiplier $\left(\frac{1}{1-b}\right)$.

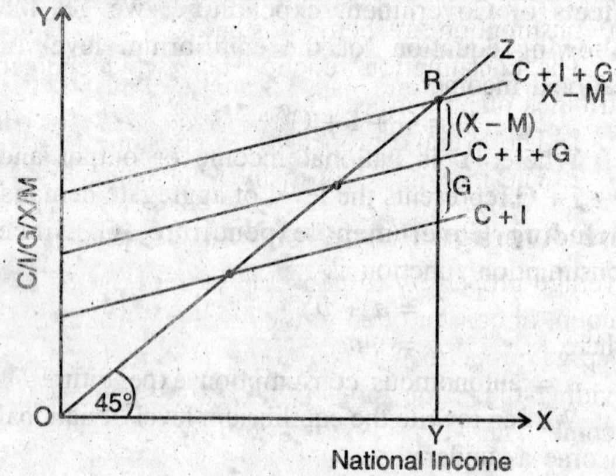

Fig. 4 : *Determination of National Income with Foreign Trade*

Graphic Illustration

In Figure 4 we have depicted the determination of national income when there are positive net exports (*i.e.*, (X – M) > O).

To obtain the aggregate demand curve incorporating the positive net exports we add the amounts of net exports to (C + I + G) to get the higher aggregate demand curve [C + I + G + (X – M)] which intersects the 45° line at point R and determines a higher level of income OY. If the net exports (X – M) were negative, that is, imports exceed exports, (X – M) < O, the aggregate demand curve incorporating net exports would lie at a lower level than C + I + G + X – M curve and determine a lower level of income than OY.

Consumption Function

Consumption function can be defined as the schedule detailing the relationship between aggregate consumption expenditures and income, Therefore,

$$C = f(Y)$$

Where C is consumption, Y is income, and *f* is

the functional relationship. Thus the consumption function indicates a functional relationship between C and Y, where C is the dependent and Y is the independent variable. This relationship is based on the ceteris paribus (other things being equal) assumption, as such only income-consumption relationship is considered and all possible influences on consumption are held constant.

The consumption function has two technical attributes or properties:

1. The average propensity to consume
2. The marginal propensity to consume

The Average Propensity to Consume

Average propensity to consume is the ratio of the amount of consumption to total income. Therefore, average propensity to consume is calculated by dividing the amount of consumption by the total income. Thus,

$$APC = \frac{C}{Y}$$

Where,

APC = average propensity to consume
C = amount of consumption
Y = level of income

Diagrammatically, the average propensity to consume is any one point on the consumption curve. In Figure 5, point R measures the APC of the CC curve which is OC'/OY'.

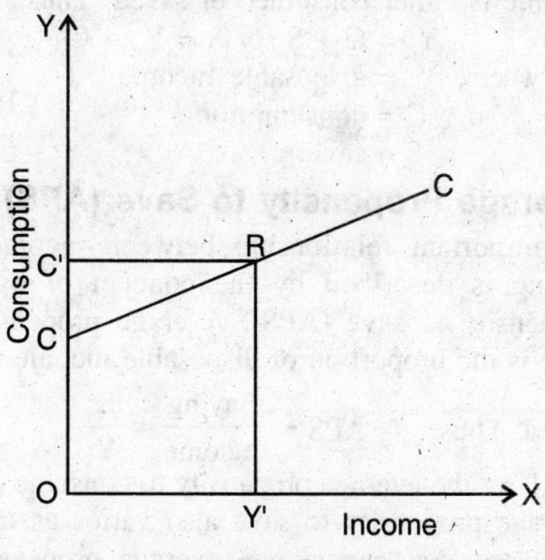

Fig. 5

If with the increase in income, average propensity to consume remains constant, the consumption function curve or propensity to consume curve will be **linear** or straight line as is shown by the curve CC in Figure 6.

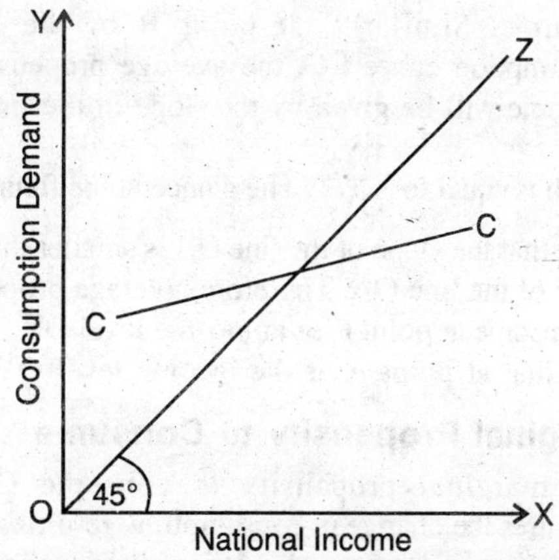

Fig. 6 : *Linear Consumption Function*

When with the increase in income, average propensity to consume declines, then the curve of consumption function is not a straight line passing through the origin and has a shape as shown in Figure 7. From any point on the propensity to consume curve CC we can find out average propensity to consume by joining that point with the point of origin by a straight line whose slope will measure the average propensity to consume. In Figure 7, if we have to find out average propensity to consume at point A on the propensity to consume curve CC, we connect point A with the origin by a

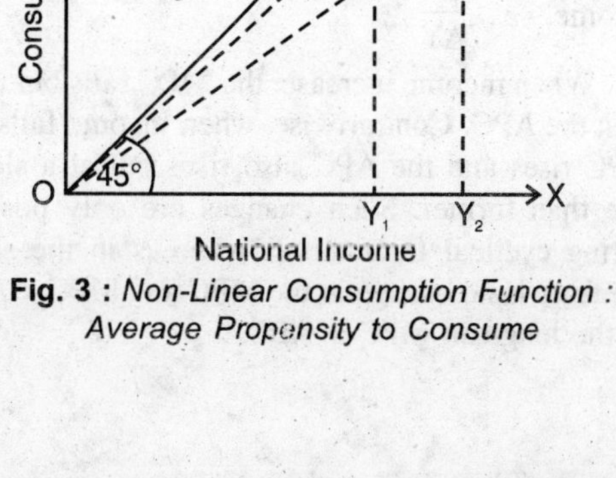

Fig. 3 : *Non-Linear Consumption Function : Average Propensity to Consume*

straight line. Now, the slope of the line OA, *i.e.*, $\frac{AY_1}{OY_1}$ will indicate the average propensity to consume. Similarly, at point B of the given consumption curve CC, the average propensity to consume will be given by the slope of the line OB which is equal to $\frac{BY_2}{OY_2}$. The glance at the figure will show that the slope of the line OB is smaller than the slope of the line OA. Therefore, average propensity to consume at point B or at income level OY_2 is less than that at point A or the income level OY_1.

Marginal Propensity to Consume

The marginal propensity to consume (MPC) measures the change in consumption resulting from a change in income. In other words, marginal propensity to consume may be defined as the ratio of the change in consumption to the change in income or as the rate of change in the average propensity to consume as income changes. Thus,

$$MPC = \frac{\Delta C}{\Delta Y}$$

Where,

MPC = marginal propensity to consume

ΔC = change in consumption

ΔY = change in income

Significance of MPC

Marginal propensity to consume needs to be carefully distinguished from average propensity to consume. Whereas average propensity to consume is the ratio of total consumption to total income, *i.e.*, $\frac{C}{Y}$, the marginal propensity to consume is the ratio of change in consumption to the change in income, *i.e.*, $\frac{\Delta C}{\Delta Y}$.

When income increase, the MPC falls but more than the APC. Contrariwise, when income falls, the MPC rises and the APC also rises but at a slower rate than former. Such changes are only possible during cyclical fluctuations whereas in the short-run there is no change in the MPC and MPC < APC. In the long-run MPC = APC.

It is worth noting that when average propensity to consume remains constant, marginal propensity to consume is equal to it. Marginal propensity to consume can be estimated by drawing the tangent at a point on the consumption function.

When marginal propensity to consume declines with the increase in income, consumption curve is non-linear whose slope declines as income rises. But if consumption curve is a straight line, *i.e.*, the slope of the consumption curve remains constant then MPC which is given by the slope of the propensity to consume curve (consumption curve) remains constant.

It is worth noting that marginal propensity to consume is neither zero nor equal to one. It has been found by empirical studies that marginal propensity to consume varies between zero and unity. If the MPC was zero, then the whole of the increment in income would have been saved and the consumption curve would have a horizontal shape. On the other hand, if the MPC was equal to unity, then the whole of the increment in income would be consumed and in that case consumption curve would have coincided with 45° line.

Propensity to Save

We will now explain what happens to saving when income increases. Saving is defined as that part of income which is not consumed because disposable income is either consumed or saved. Thus,

$$Y_d = C + S \quad \text{or} \quad S = Y_d - C$$

where, Y_d = disposable income

C = consumption

S = saving

Average Propensity to Save (APS)

An important relationship between income and saving is described by the concept of average propensity to save (APS). Average propensity to save is the proportion of disposable income that is saved. Thus, $APS = \frac{\text{Saving}}{\text{Income}} = \frac{S}{Y}$

Like the average propensity to consume (APC) average propensity to save also varies as income increases. As seen above, average propensity to consume falls as income increases. This implies that average propensity to save will increase as income rises.

Let us derive an important relationship between average propensity to consume and average propensity to save. Restating below the relation that income is either consumed or saved:

$$C + S = Y$$

Dividing both sides by disposable income Y we have

$$\frac{C}{Y} + \frac{S}{Y} = \frac{Y}{Y} \quad \text{or} \quad \frac{C}{Y} + \frac{S}{Y} = 1$$

Since $\frac{C}{Y}$ is average propensity to consume and $\frac{S}{Y}$ is average propensity to save, we have

$$APC + APS = 1 \text{ or } APS = 1 - APC$$

Marginal Propensity to Save (MPS)

Whereas average propensity to save indicates the proportion of income that is saved, marginal propensity to save represents how much of the additional disposable income is devoted to saving. The marginal propensity to save is therefore change in savings induced by a change in the disposable income. Thus, $MPS = \frac{\Delta S}{\Delta Y}$

Since the additional income is either consumed or saved, the sum of marginal propensity to consume and marginal propensity to save is equal to one.

$$MPC + MPS = 1$$

This can be mathematically proved as under.

From C+ S = Y, it follows that any change in income (ΔY) must induce either change in consumption (ΔC) or change in saving (ΔS). Thus

$$\Delta C + \Delta S = \Delta Y$$

Dividing both sides by ΔY we have

$$\frac{\Delta C}{\Delta Y} + \frac{\Delta S}{\Delta Y} = \frac{\Delta Y}{\Delta Y}$$

$$MPC + MPS = 1$$

Keynes's Psychological Law of Consumption

Keynes propounded a basic law about the consumption function. This has been described as **psychological law** of consumption by **Prof. Kurihara.** According to this law of consumption, when the aggregate income increases, consumption expenditure will increase but by a some what smaller amount. It means that out of the increment in income, a part is saved and not consumed. In other words, marginal propensity to consume is less than one.

Keynes's psychological law of consumption is based upon three assumptions—

1. The marginal propensity to consume will be less than one provided the psychological and institutional complex of the society remains constant.

2. The second assumption on which the Keynes's law of consumption is based is that the normal conditions should continue to prevail in the economy, that is, neither any war should break out nor should occur any revolution, hyper-inflation, or any other extraordinary event.

3. The third assumption underlying, the Keynesian law is that it applies to an advanced capitalist country in which the Government does not interfere in the working of free private enterprise. In other words, it applies where the Government follows a **laissez faire** policy.

The Concept of Multiplier

The concept of multiplier was first developed by **Richard F. Kahn** in 1931. Kahn's multiplier was the 'employment multiplier.' Keynes took the idea from Kahn and developed the **Investment Multiplier.** The concept of Investment Multiplier constitutes an important pillar in the whole edifice of the Keynesian theory of income and employment. The concept of multiplier is closely connected with the MPS.

The multiplier expresses a relationship between an initial investment and the final increment in aggregate income. To be more accurate, the multiplier is the ratio of the change in income to the change in investment. It shows by how many times the effect of an initial change in investment is multiplied by causing changes in consumption and finally in the aggregate income. According to Keynes, the multiplier establishes "a precise relationship between aggregate employment, income and the rate of investment given the propensity to consume. Whenever an investment is made in the economy, the effect is to increase aggregate income not only by the amount of original investment, but by something much more than that. There is, thus, a precise relationship between the initial investment and the ultimate increase in income. This relationship Keynes designates as 'K'.

In the words of Alvin H. Hansen, Keynes's investment multiplier is the coefficient relating an increment of investment to an increment in income. The multiplier is the number by which an initial change in aggregate monetary demand must be multiplied to find out the eventual change in income. It is the ratio of the change in one of the components of aggregate demand, viz. Planned investment, consumption expenditure, export receipts or governmental expenditure, to the total change in national income. The general form of the multiplier is $\frac{1}{1-MPC}$. In the multiplier theory, the important element is the multiplier coefficient 'K', which refers to the power by which an initial investment expenditure is multiplied to obtain a final increase in income. The value of the multiplier is determined by the MPS. The higher the MPC, the higher the value of the multiplier and vice versa.

Assumptions of Multiplier

The Keynesian theory of Multiplier requires specific conditions under which it operates. Some assumptions are necessary for its smooth movement. They are as follows—

1. There is a change in investment.
2. Marginal propensity to consume is constant.
3. Consumption is a function of current income.
4. There are no time lags in the multiplier process. An increase (decrease) in investment instantaneously leads to a multiple increase (decrease) in income.
5. The new level of investment is maintained steadily for the completion of the multiplier process.
6. There is net increase in investment.
7. Consumer goods are available in response to effective demand for them.
8. There is a surplus capacity in consumer goods industries to meet the increased demand for consumer goods in response to a rise in income following increased investment.
9. Other resources of production are also easily available within the economy.
10. There is an industrialised economy in which the multiplier process operates.
11. There is a closed economy unaffected by foreign influences.
12. There are no changes in prices.
13. The accelerator effect of consumption on investment is ignored.
14. There is less than full employment level in the economy.

Derivation of the Multiplier

The size of the multiplier depends upon the size of the MPC. The two are closely related. Given the MPC, the multiplier can be easily derived. Keynes has expressed it by the symbol K. 'K' can be found out from the formula

$$K = \frac{1}{1-MPC} \text{ or } K = \frac{1}{MPC}$$

The multiplier is derived as follows: $\Delta Y = K.\Delta I$

$$K = \frac{\Delta Y}{\Delta I}$$

ΔI is increased investment and ΔY is increased income. Aggregate saving S is equal to aggregate investment I. By the same argument increased saving ΔS must be equal to increased investment ΔI.

Saving is the difference between income (Y) and consumption (C) so that $S = Y - C$.

By the same reasoning, $\Delta S = \Delta Y - \Delta C$

Since $\Delta S = \Delta I$, we can substitute $\Delta Y - \Delta C$ for ΔI.

Substituting $\Delta Y - \Delta C$ for ΔI we have

$$K = \frac{\Delta Y}{\Delta Y - \Delta C}$$

Dividing both the numerator and the denominator by ΔY we get,

$$K = \frac{\frac{\Delta Y}{\Delta Y}}{\frac{\Delta Y}{\Delta Y} - \frac{\Delta C}{\Delta Y}} \text{ or } K = \frac{1}{1 - \frac{\Delta C}{\Delta Y}}$$

The denominator $\left(1-\frac{\Delta C}{\Delta Y}\right)$ is 1 – MPC which is the MPS. So, multiplier K is the reciprocal of the fraction saved, that is, $\frac{1}{MPS}$.

If MPC = $\frac{\Delta C}{\Delta Y}$ is deducted from 1 we get the MPC. So that MPS = 1 – MPC.

$$\therefore \quad K = \frac{1}{MPS}$$

MPC and Multiplier

Multiplier varies directly with the MPC and inversely with the MPS. Since the MPC is always greater than zero and less than one (*i.e.,* $0 < MPC < 1$), the multiplier is always between one and infinity (*i.e.,* $1 < K < \infty$).

1. The MPC is very rarely zero. If it is zero, the multiplier is 1. What this means is that nothing is spent by consumers out of increased income. The whole increased income is saved, with the result that the multiplier is one. Suppose there is a new investment of Rs. 10 crore in public works and the MPC is zero. It means that the whole of Rs. 10 crore is saved. The multiplier is one. The aggregate income increase by Rs. 10 crore.

2. The other limiting case is when MPC is 1. What this implies is that the consumers spend the whole of the increment of their incomes on consumption and nothing is saved; and the MPS is zero. The result in such a case is highly "explosive". Suppose Rs. 10 crore is invested in public works. The workers who receive Rs. 10 crore shall spend the whole of it on consumption. Others who receive increased incomes shall also spend the whole of them. In this way, Rs. 10 crore shall emerge and re-emerge and result in an infinite increase in income. It will soon lead to full employment in the economy and then create a limitless inflationary spiral.

Both these cases are rare. Actually the multiplier can never be 1 or infinity. It generally varies between 1 and infinity.

Leakages of Multiplier

Leakages are the potential diversions from the income stream which tend to weaken the multiplier effect of new investment. Given the marginal propensity to consume, the increase in income in each round declines due to leakages in the income stream and ultimately the process of income propagation "peters out". The following are the important leakages:

1. Saving
2. Strong Liquidity Preference
3. Purchase of old stocks and securities
4. Debt cancellation
5. Price Inflation
6. Net Imports
7. Undistributed Profits
8. Taxation
9. Excess Stocks of Consumption Goods.

The Paradox of Thrift

An interesting paradox arises when all people in a society try to save more but in fact they are unable to do so. According to this paradox of thrift, the attempt by the people as a whole to save more for hard times such as impending period of recession or unemployment may not materialise and in their bid to save more the society in fact may not only end up with the same savings (or, even lower savings) but also in the process cause their consumption or standard of living to decline. According to classical economists, savings determine investment which plays a crucial role in accelerating the rate of economic growth. However, the paradox of thrift shows that the efforts to save more, especially at times of depression, may actually deepen the economic crisis and cause output to fall and unemployment to increase. It goes to the credit of Keynes that with his multiplier theory he has been able to resolve the paradox of thrift.

According to the Keynesian theory, the saying "penny saved is penny earned" is quite inappropriate for the economy as a whole when it is working at under-employment equilibrium, that is, when there prevails recession or depression. Keynes has showed that if all people in a society decide to save more, they may actually fail to do so but nevertheless reduce their consumption. This is because according to Keynes, the effort to save more by all in a society will lower the aggregate demand for goods and services resulting in a drop in the level of national income. At the lower level of national income the savings fall to original level but consumption will be less than before which implies that the people would become worse off.

The Principle of Acceleration

The term "**acceleration principle**" was first introduced into economics by **J.M. Clark** in 1917. It was further developed by Hicks, Samuelson, and Harrod in relation to the business cycles.

The principle of acceleration is based on the fact that the demand for capital goods is derived from the demand for consumer goods which the former help to produce. The acceleration principle explains the process by which an increase (or decrease) in the demand for consumption goods leads to an increase (or decrease) in investment on capital goods.

Symbolically,

$$\beta = \frac{\Delta I}{\Delta C} \quad \text{or} \quad \Delta I = \beta\, \Delta C$$

where

β = accelerator coefficient

ΔI = net change in investment

ΔC = net change in consumption expenditure

This version of the acceleration principle has been more broadly interpreted by Hicks as the ratio of induced investment to changes in output it calls forth. Thus, $\Delta I = \gamma\, DY$

where γ = accelerator

It shows that the demand for capital goods is not derived from consumer goods alone but from any direct demand of national output.

There is little difference between $\Delta I = \gamma\, \Delta Y$, as defined by **Hicks** and $\Delta I = \beta\, \Delta C$, as defined by **Samuelson** and others. The accelerator γ and β are the same. Hicks takes the increase in final output (ΔY) while Samuelson takes the increase in the demand for consumer goods (ΔC). In Hicks's model net investment equals $I_{nt} = (Y_t - Y_{t-1})$ while in Samuelson's model $I_{nt} = \beta\,(C_t - C_{t-1})$.

Assumptions

The acceleration principle is based upon the following assumptions.

1. The acceleration principle assumes a constant capital-output ratio.
2. It assumes that resources are easily available.
3. The acceleration principle assumes that there is no excess or idle capacity in plants.
4. It is assumed that the increased demand is permanent.
5. The acceleration principle also assumes that there is elastic supply of credit and capital.
6. It further assumes that an increase in output immediately leads to a rise in net investment.

Inflation and Deflation

By inflation, in ordinary language, we mean a general rise in prices. However, when discussing inflation, we are thinking of a persistent rise in prices rather than a once–for–all rise in prices (which may be, for example, brought about by a bad weather leading to destruction of crops).

Inflationary Gap

Inflationary gap arises when consumption and investment spending together is greater than the full employment GNP level. This means that people are demanding more goods and services than can be produced. In other words, the amount by which the actual aggregate demand exceeds the level of national income corresponding to full employment is known as **inflationary gap** because this excess in aggregate demand causes inflation or rise in prices in the country.

Diagrammatically, the inflationary gap EE′ is shown in Figure 8. Y_F is the full employment level of income which is arrived at by the equality of aggregate consumption and investment expenditure line C + I + G and the 45° line representing aggregate supply of goods at point E. At the full employment level, there is excess demand because consumers, firms and government expenditure more than the available output at current prices by EE′ amount. This increased demand or expenditure shifts the C

+ I + G curve upward to C + I + G′ position. This intersects the 45° line at E_1 so that the total expenditure is E_1 Y_1 while the available output is EY_F. Thus, E_1A = EE′ is the inflationary gap.

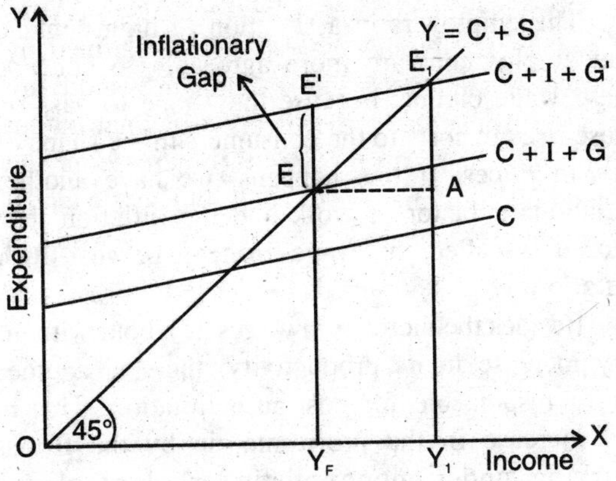

Fig. 1 : *Inflationary Gap*

The inflationary gap can be wiped out by increase in saving so that aggregate demand is reduced. Another solution is to raise the value of available output to match the disposable income. But output cannot be increased during the short run. Private investment cannot be reduced while the government expenditure is autonomous. So, both cannot be reduced during the short run. Thus, the only alternatives left to the government are to increase taxation and induce saving.

Deflationary Gap

Deflationary gap represents the difference between the acutal aggregate demand and the aggregate demand which is required to establish the equilibrium at full employment level of income.

The concept of deflationary gap is illustrated in Figure 9 in which along the *x*–axis national income is measured and along the *y*–axis expenditure is measured. Suppose national income at the equilibrium level of full employment is equal to OY_F. Now the equilibrium level of income and employment would be established at OY_F when aggregate demand (C + I +G) is equal to Y_FE (which is equal to national income OY_F). But in the real world if aggregate demand is less than the full employment level of income OY_F or it is less than Y_FE then the problem of deficiency of aggregate demand will arise. Therefore, EH in Figure 9 represents deflationary gap.

It should be carefully understood that due to deflationary gap E, the level of national income and employment will decline. The decline in national income and employment will not only be equal to the deflationary gap EH but it will be much greater than this. The decline in national income is determined by the value of the multiplier. In Figure 9 when aggregate demand is Y_F H, *i.e.*, deflationary gap is equal to EH, then the aggregate demand curve is C + I + G′ which cuts the 45° line at point Q as a result of which equilibrium is established at OY_1 level of national income. It will be seen from figure 9 that OY_1 is less than full employment level of income OY_F.

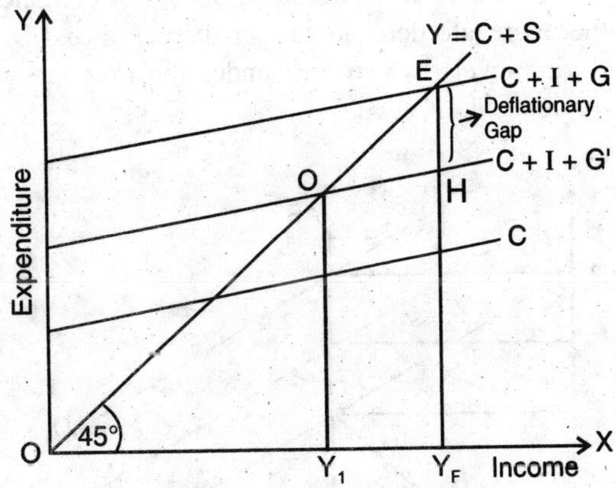

Fig. 9 : *Deflationary Gap*

Demand–Pull Inflation

Basically, inflation represents a situation where by the pressure of aggregate demand for goods and services exceeds the available supply of output. In such a situation, the rise in price level is the natural consequence. Now this excess of aggregate demand over supply may be the result of more than one force at work. As we know, aggregate demand is the sum of consumer's spending on goods and services, government spending on goods and services and net investment being contemplated by the entrepreneurs. Inflation is thus caused when aggregate demand for all purposes–consumption, investment and government expenditure, exceeds the supply of goods at current prices. Thus is demand pull inflation.

Demand-pull inflation can be illustrated with aggregate demand and aggregate supply curves. Consider Figure 10 in which aggregate demand and supply are measured along the X–axis and general price level along the Y–axis. Curve AS represents the aggregate supply which rises upward in the beginning but when at full employment level aggregate supply OY_F is reached, aggregate supply curve AS takes a vertical shape. This is because after the level of full employment, supply of output cannot be increased. When aggregate demand curve is AD_1, the equilibrium is at the full employment level where price level OP_1 is determined.

Now, if the aggregate demand increases to AD_2 and aggregate supply cannot be raised, the price level will rise to OP_2 due to the excess of demand. If the aggregate demand further increases to AD_3, the price level rises to OP_3 under the pressure of more demand.

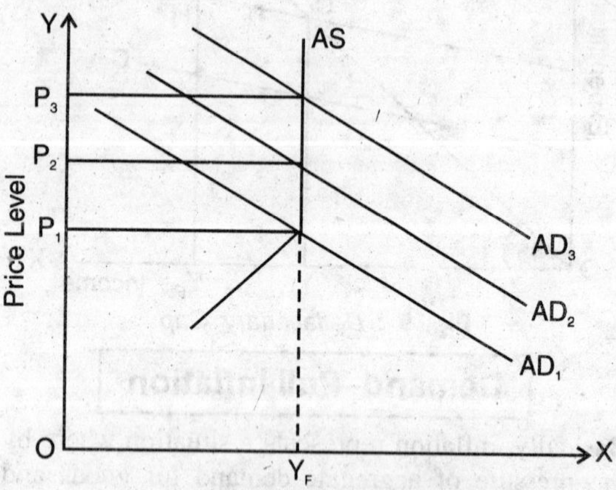

Fig. 10 : *Demand-Pull Inflation*

Cost-Push Inflation

We can visualise a situation where, even though there is no increase in aggregate demands, prices may still rise. This may happen if costs, particularly the wage costs, go on rising. Now as the level of employment rises, the demand for workers also rises so that the bargaining position of the workers becomes stronger. To exploit this situation, they may ask for an increase in wage rates which are not justifiable on grounds either of a prior rise of productivity or of cost of living.

The employers in a situation of high demand and employment are more agreeable to concede these wage claims, because they hope to pass on these rises in costs to the consumers in the shape of rise in prices. If this happens, we have another inflationary factor at work and the inflation thus caused is called the **wage-induced** or **cost-push inflation.**

Besides the increase in wages of labour without any increase in its productivity, there is another factor responsible for cost-push inflation. This is the increase in the profit margin by the firms, working under monopolistic or oligopolistic conditions and as a result charging higher prices from the consumers. In the former case when the cause of cost-push-inflation is the rise in wages, it is called **wage-push inflation** and in the latter case when the cause of cost-push inflation is the rise in profit margins, it is called **profit-push-inflation.**

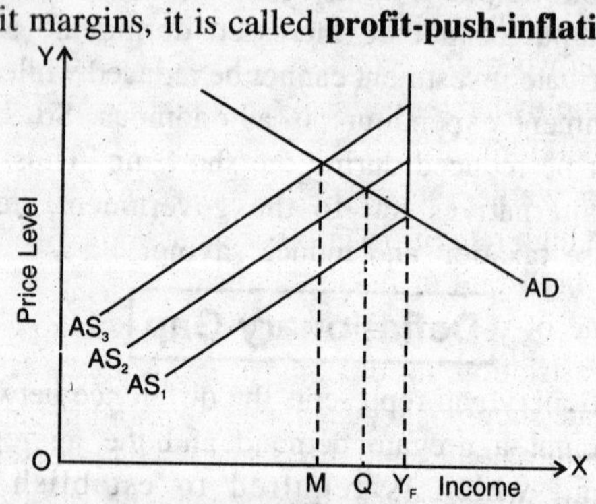

Fig. 11 : *Cost-Push Inflation*

The cost-push-inflation can also be illustrated with the aggregate demand and supply curves. Consider Figure 11 where aggregate supply and demand are measured along the X-axis and price level along the Y-axis. AD is the aggregate demand curve and AS_1 and AS_3 curves are aggregate supply curves.

Since aggregate supply curves become vertical at full employment level their vertical portions coincide.

Now, when wages increase, and as a result cost of production increases, the aggregate supply curve would shift upward. As will be seen in Figure 11, when there is an upward shift in the aggregate supply curve from AS_1 to AS_2 due to the rise in wages, price level rises from OP_1 to OP_2. It should be noted that price level OP_1 corresponds to the full employment, since aggregate demand curve AD intersects original aggregate supply curve AS at full employment level OY_F. If the wages further rise and the aggregate supply curve shifts upwards to AS_3, the equilibrium price level rises to OP_3.

We have thus seen above that cause of inflation may be that aggregate demand has become excessive in relation to supply of output (demand–pull–inflation) or it may be that costs have risen because of the increase in wages of labour or profit margins of the producers (cost–pust–inflation).

Stagflation

The word "Stagflation" is the combination of stag plus flation, taking 'stag' from stagnation and 'flation' from inflation. Thus, it is a paradoxical situation where the economy experiences stagnation or unemployment alongwith a high rate of inflation. It is, therefore, also called **inflationary recession**. In other words, the stagflation refers to a situation when a high rate of inflation occurs simultaneously with a high rate of unemployment.

Onc of thc principal causcs of stagflation has been restriction in the aggregate supply. When aggregate supply is reduced, there is a fall in output and employment, and the price level rises. A reduction in aggregate supply may be due to a restriction in labour supply. The restriction in labour supply, in turn, may be caused by a rise in money wages on account of strong unions or by a rise in the legal minimum wage rate, or by increased tax rates which reduce work effort on the part of workers.

When wages rise, firms are forced to reduce production and employment. Consequently, there is a fall in real income and consumer expenditure. Since the decline in consumption will be less than the fall in real income, there will be excess demand in the commodity market which will push up the price level.

The rise in the price level, in turn, reduces output and employment in the following three ways:

(*a*) It reduces the real quantity of money, raises interest rates and brings a fall in investment expenditure.

(*b*) The rise in the price level reduces the real value of cash balances with the government and the private sector via the pigou effect which reduces their consumption expenditure.

(*c*) The rise in prices of domestic goods makes exports dearer to foreigners and makes exports goods relatively more attractive to domestic output and employment.

Restriction on aggregate supply may also be caused by external factors such as rise in the world prices of foods grains and crude aid prices. In all these cases, the domestic price level is raised by outside forces. When international prices of food grains and crude oil rise, they lead to the outflow of purchasing power away from domestic consumers. They accentuate inflation, raise wages and prices. As a result, the real quantity of money declines, interest rates rise and investment declines, via the pigou effect, and making exports dearer and imports attractive, domestic output and employment decline. They lead to **Stagflation**.

The phenomenon of stagflation is illustrated in Figure 12, where employment is measured on the horizontal axis and the price level on the vertical axis.

The initial equilibrium is at E where aggregate demand curve AD intersects the aggregate supply curve AS and the price level is OP and the employment level is ON. When the aggregate supply is reduced due to any of the factors mentioned above, the aggregate supply curve S shifts to the left at AS_1. The new equilibrium is at E_1 where AS_1 intersects the AD curve. Now the price level rises from OP to OP_1 and the level of employment declines from ON to ON_1.

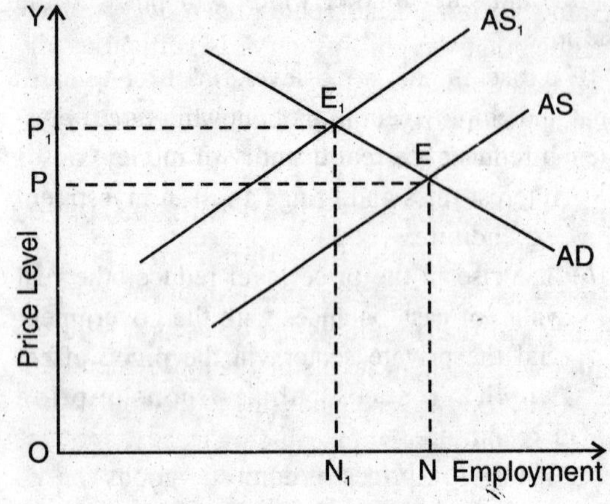

Fig. 12 : *Stagflation*

Phillips Curve

Professor Phillips urged there was a close link between the level of unemployment and the rate of wage increase. Phillips curve expresses an inverse relationship between the rate of unemployment and the rate of increase in money wages.

Prof. Phillips studied the relationship between unemployment and changes in money wages in the U.K. over the period 1862–1957. As a result of this study, he seems to have discovered a stable and inverse relationship over the whole period between the rate of wage increase and the per cent of unemployment.

The Phillips curve depicts the **trade off** betweeen unemployment and money wages. It relates percentage change in money wages on the vertical axis with percentage of labour force unemployment on the horizontal axis, as shown in Figure 13. The curve is **convex to the origin** which shows the percentage change in money wages rises with decrease in the unemployment rate.

Suppose that ON rate of unemployment (3%) is associated with OM growth rate of money wages (2%). Suppose also that the rate of labour productivity is 2 per cent, that is, equal to OM. Since the growth rate of money wages equals the rate of labour productivity, the price level remains constant. If now aggregate demand is increased, this lowers the unemployment rate to OT (2%) and raises the wages rate to OS (4%) per year. If lower productivity continues to grow at 2% per annum, the price level will also rise at the rate of 2 per cent per annum at OS in the figure.

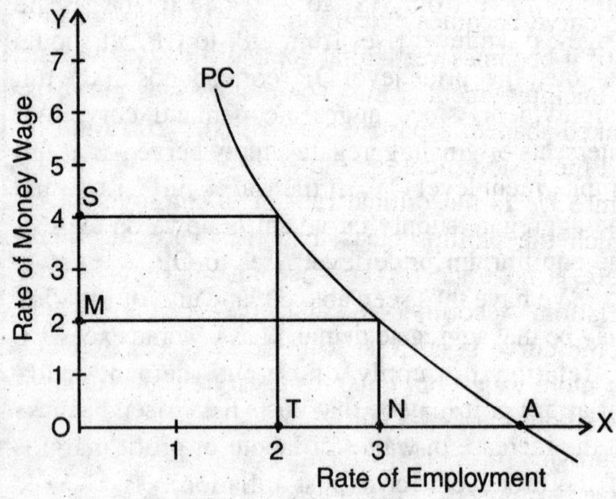

Fig. 13 : Phillips Curve

Thus, a money wage rate increases which in excess of labour productivity leads to inflation. To keep wage increase to the level of labour productivity (OM) in order to avoid inflation, ON rate of unemployment will have to be tolerated.

Samuelson and Solow extended the Phillip's analysis to the **trade off** between the level of unemployment and the rate of change in the level of prices. Thus, **the Phillips curve suggests that unemployment can always be reduced by having more inflation and that the inflation rate can also be reduced by having more unemployment.**

Its Criticism

Economists have criticised the phillips curve. They argue that the phillips curve relates to the short run and it does not remain stable. It shifts with changes in expectations of inflation. *In the long run, there is no trade off between inflation and employment.* These views have been expounded by *Friedman and Phelps* in what has come to be known as the "accelerationist" hypothesis.

According to Friedman, the long run phillips curve is vertical.

Tobin's View : James Tobin in his presidential address before the American Economic Association in 1971 proposed a compromise between the negatively sloping and vertical phillips curve. Tobin believes that there is a phillips curve within limits, but as the economy expands and employment grows, the curve becomes even more fragile and vanishes until it becomes vertical at some critically low rate of unemployment. Thus Tobin's Phillips curve is kinked-shaped, a part like a normal phillips curve and the rest vertical, as shown in Figure 14. In the figure U*c* is the critical rate of unemployment at which the phillips curve becomes vertical where there is no trade off between unemployment and inflation. According to Tobin, the vertical portion of the curve is not due to increase in the demand for more wages but emerges from imperfections of the labour market. At the U*c* level, it is not possible to provide more employment because the job seekers have wrong skills or wrong age or sex or are in the wrong place.

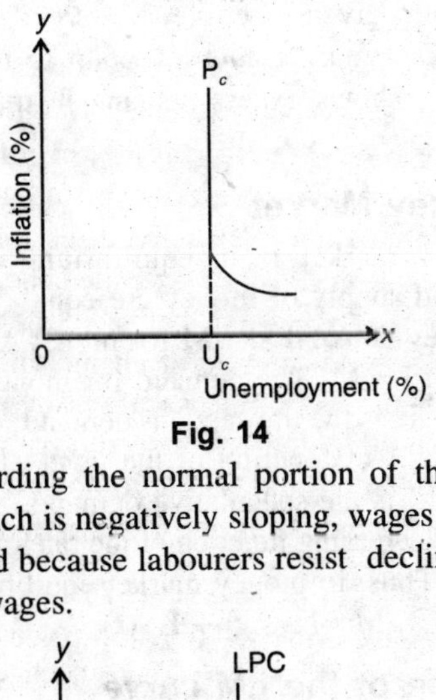

Fig. 14

Regarding the normal portion of the phillips curve which is negatively sloping, wages are sticky downward because labourers resist decline in their relative wages.

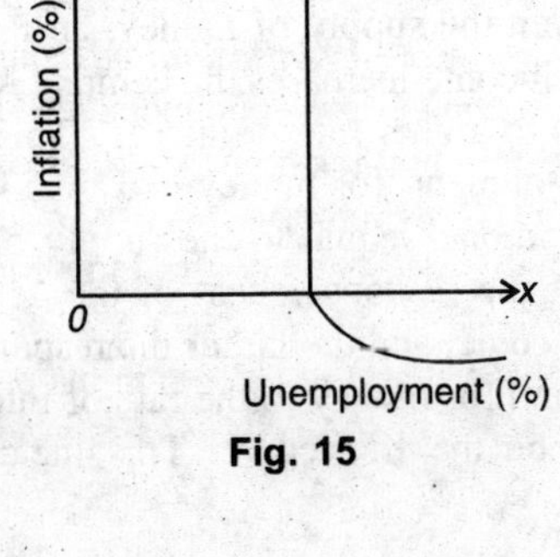

Fig. 15

Solow's View : Like Tobin *Robert Solow* does not believe that the phillips curve is vertical at all rate of inflation. According to him, the curve is vertical at positive rates of inflation and is horizontal at negative rates of inflation as shown in Figure 15.

Policy Implications of the Phillips Curve

The phillips curve has important policy implications. It suggests the extent to which monetary and fiscal policies can be used to control inflation without high levels of unemployment. In other words, it provides a guide line to the authorities about the rate of inflation which can be tolerated with a given level of unemployment. For this purpose, it is important to know the exact position of the phillips curve. If the curve is PC_1 as in Figure 16, where there labour productivity and the wage rate are equal at point E, both full employment and price stability would be possible. Again a curve to the left of point E suggests full employment and price stability as consistent policy objectives. It implies that a lower level of inflation can be traded-off for a low level of unemployment. If, on the other hand, the phillips curve is PC as in the figure. It suggests that the authorities will have to choose between price stability and more unemployment. Thus by observing the position of the phillips curve the authorities can decide about the nature of monetary and fiscal policies to be adopted. For instance if the authorities find that the inflation rate P_2 is in compatible with the unemployment rate U_1 of Figure 16, they would adopt such monetary and fiscal policies as to shift the phillips curve PC to the left in the position of PC_1 curve. This will give a better trade-off between a lower inflation rate P_1 with the same level of unemployment U_1.

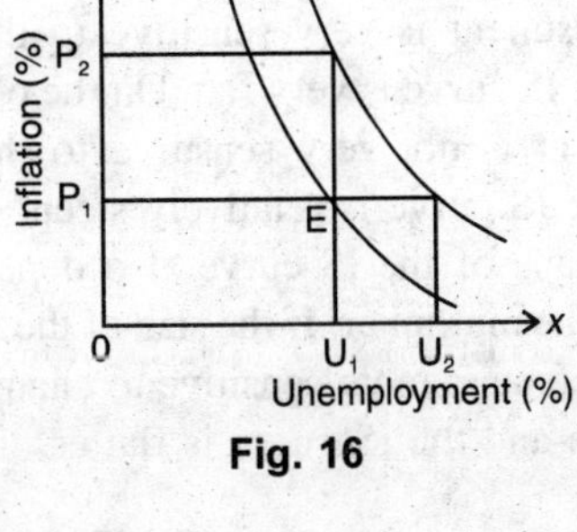

Fig. 16

IS and LM Functions

General Equilibrium of Product and Money Markets

The term IS is the shorthand expression of the equality of investment and saving which represents the product market equilibrium. On the other hand, the term LM is the shorthand expression of the equality of money demand and money supply and represents the money market equilibrium.

The Product Market

The product market is in equilibrium when saving and investment are equal. Saving is a direct function of the level of income,

$$S = f(y) \quad ....(1)$$

Investment is a decreasing function of the interest rate,

$$I = f(r) \quad ....(2)$$

In case of equilibrium, S = I

The IS Schedule reflects the equilibrium of the product market. It shows the combinations of interest rates and income levels where saving-investment equality takes place so that the product market of the economy is in equilibrium. It is also known as "real" equilibrium.

The slope of the IS curve

Figure 17 shows that the IS curve slopes downward from left to right. This negative slope reflects the increase in investment and income as the rate of interest falls. The IS curve may be Flat or steep depending on the sensitiveness of investment to changes in the rate of interest, and also on the size of the multiplier.

If investment is very sensitive to the rate of interest, the IS curve is very flat. On the other hand, if investment is not very sensitive to the rate of interest, the IS curve is relatively steep.

The shape of the IS curve also depends upon the size of the multiplier. If the size of the multiplier is large, income is more sensitive to changes in the interest rate and the IS curve is flatter.

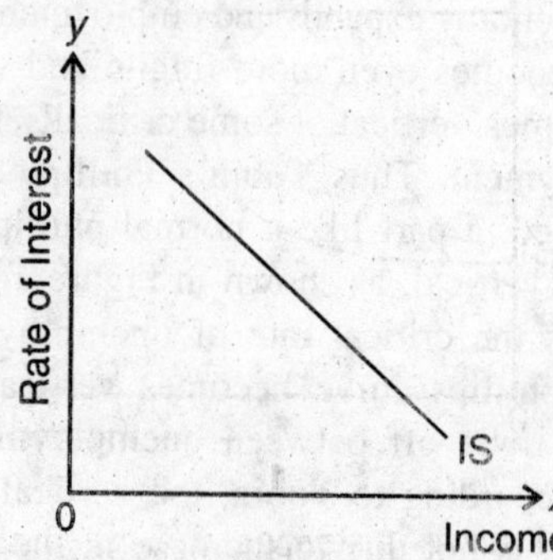

Fig. 17

A few more properties of the IS curve may be noted. *First,* the IS curve shifts to the right or left as a result of an increase or decrease in autonomous or government investment. *Second,* any point to the right of a given IS curve shows excess supply in the product market and any point to the left of an IS curve shows excess demand in the product market.

The Money Market

The money market is in equilibrium when the demand and supply of money are equal. Denoting L for money demand and M for money supply, in equilibrium L= M. The demand for money $L = L_t + L_s$, where L_t is the transactions demand for money which is a direct function of the level of income, $L_t = f(y)$. L_s is the speculative demand for money which is a decreasing function of the rate of interest, $L_s = f(r)$. Thus, in money market equilibrium,

$$M = L_t(y) + L_s(r)$$

The Slope of the LM curve

The LM curve slopes upward from left to right because given the supply of money, an increase in the level of income increases the demand for money which leads to higher rate of interest. This, in turn, reduces the demand for money and thus keeps the demand for money equal to the supply of money. The smaller the responsiveness of the demand for money to income, and the larger the responsiveness of the demand for money to the rate of interest, the flatter will be the LM curve. This means that a given change in income has a smaller effect on the interest rate.

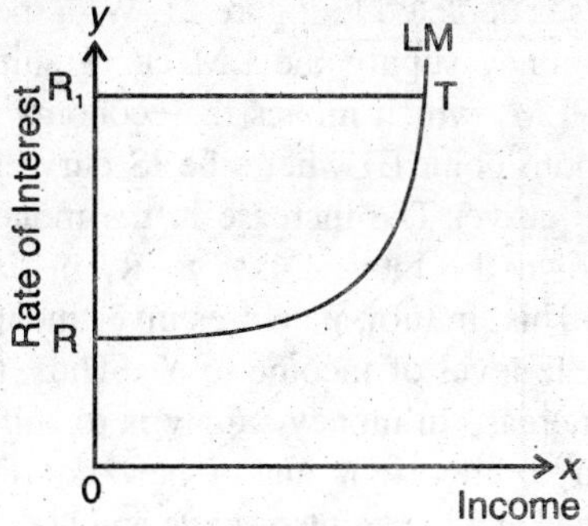

Fig. 18

The LM curve is steeper, if a given change in income has a larger effect on the rate of interest. In this situation, the responsiveness of the demand for money to income is larger and is smaller for the interest rate. If the demand for money is insensitive to the interest rate, the LM curve is *vertical* that is, it is *perfectly inelastic.* This is shown in Figure 18 as the portion from T above on the LM curve. In this case, a large change in the interest rate is accompanied by almost no change in the level of income to maintain money market equilibrium. If the demand for money is very sensitive to the rate of interest, the LM curve is *horizontal*, that is, it is a *perfectly elastic.* In this case, a small change in the interest rate is accompanied by a large change in the level of income to maintain the money market equilibrium.

Shifts in the LM curve

The LM curve shifts downward to the right when the stock of money supply is increased and it shifts upward to the left if the stock of money supply is reduced.

The LM curve shifts upward to the left if there is an increase in the money demand function which raises the quantity of money demanded at the given interest rate and income level. On the other hand, the LM curve shifts downward to the left if there is a decrease in the money demand function which lowers the amount of money demanded at given levels of interest rate and income.

Another important property of the LM curve is that on any point to the right of the LM curve, there is excess demand for money in the money market, and on any point to the left of the LM curve, there is excess supply of money in the money market.

General Equilibrium of Product and Money Market

Now we study how these markets are brought into simultaneous equilibrium. It is only when the equilibrium pairs of interest rate and income of the IS curve equal the equilibrium pairs of interest rate and income of the LM curve that the general equilibrium is established. In other words, when there is a single pair of interest rate and income level in the product and money markets that the two markets are in equilibrium.

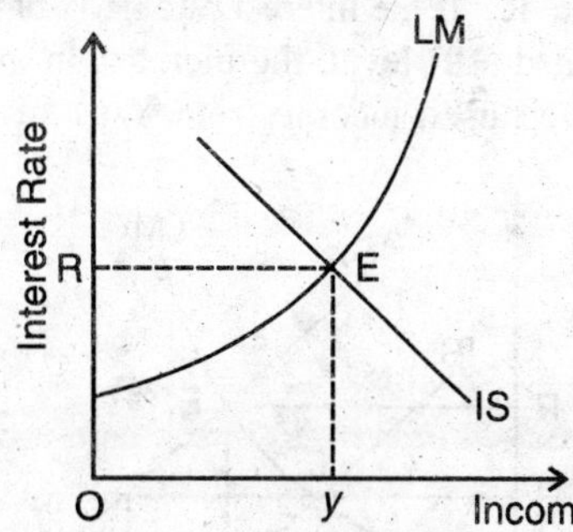

Fig. 19

Such an equilibrium position is shown in Figure 19 where the IS and LM curves intersect each other at point E relating Y level of income to R interest rate. This pair of income level and interest rate leads to simultaneous equilibrium in the real or goods (saving investment) market and the money (demand and supply of money) market.

This general equilibrium position persists at a point of time, given the price level. If there is any deviation from this equilibrium position, certain forces will act and react in such a manner that the equilibrium will be restored.

Shifts in the IS and LM Functions : Changes in General Equilibrium

The general equilibrium combination of Y income level and R rate of interest may change either due to a shift in the IS function or the LM function, or by both the functions shifting simultaneously. The

IS function may sihft due to changes in the saving function or the investment function and the shifts in the LM function may be caused by changes in the money supply or liquidity preterence.

Shifts in the IS Function. The IS function shifts to the right with a reduction in saving. The IS function also shifts to the right by an autonomous increase in investment.

The shifting of the IS curve to the right and the consequent equilibrium with the given LM curve is illustrated in Figure 20. With the increase in the outonomous investment (or reduction in saving), the IS curve moves from IS to IS_1 and the new equilibrium is established at point E_1 which indicates a higher level of income Y_1 at a higher interest rate R_1. If the interest rate had not increased but remained at R level, the increase in investment would have raised income from Y to Y_2 level.

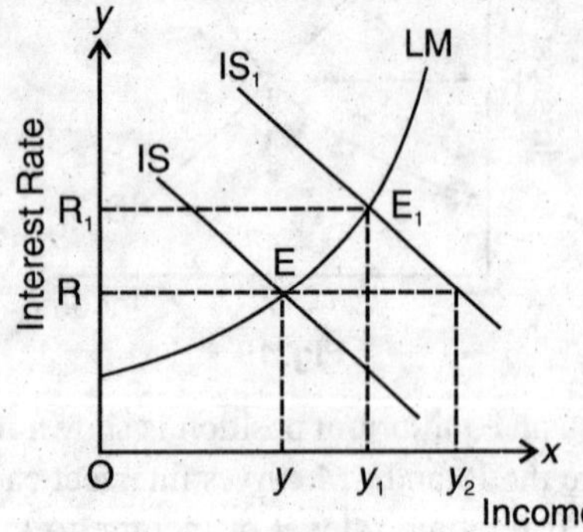

Fig. 20

But this much increase in income would not take place. This is because with the increase in income the demand for money for transactions purposes will raise the interest rate to R_1 level where the IS and LM functions intersect at point E_1. Thus the expansionary affect of increase in investment is dampened by the rise in the interest rate and the income rises by less than the full multiplier.

In the opposite case when investment falls or saving increases, the IS function will shift to the left and the equilibrium will be established at a lower level of income and interest rate.

Shifts in the LM Function. The LM function shifts to the right with the increase in the money supply, given the demand for money or due to the decrease in the demand for money, given the supply of money.

This is depicted in Figure 21. With the increase in the money supply the LM curve shifts to the right as LM_1 which moves the economy to a new equilibrium point E_1 where the IS curve intersects the LM_1 curve. The increase in the money supply bring down the interest rate to R_1 in the money market. This, in turn, increases investment there by raising the level of income to Y_1. Thus, the effect of the increase in money supply is to shift the LM function to the right and a new equilibrium is established at a lower interest rate and higher income level.

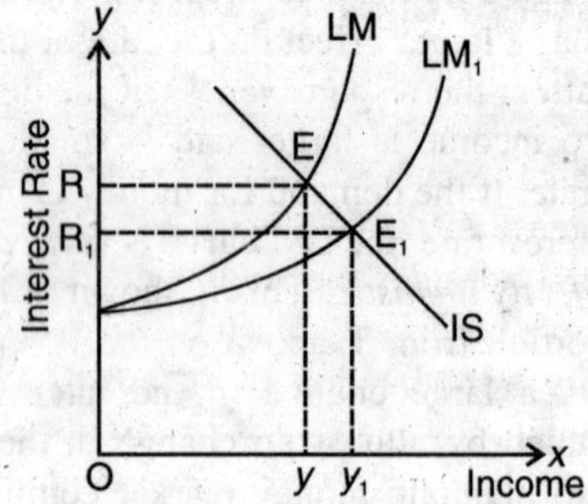

Fig. 21

Contrariwise a decrease in the money supply, or an increase in the demand for money will shift the LM function to the left such that a new equilibrium is established at a higher interest rate and lower income level.

Effectiveness of Monetary and Fiscal Policies

The relative effectiveness of monetary and fiscal policy has been the subject of controversy among economists. The monetarists regard monetary policy more effective than fiscal policy for economic stabilisation. On the other hand, the keynesians hold the opposite view. In between these two extreme views, there are the synthesists who advocate the middle path. Modern economists explain these three views in terms of the elasticities of the IS-LM curves. The IS curve represents fiscal policy and the LM curve represents monetary policy.

The IS-LM technique explains the effectiveness of monetary and fiscal policies in relation to the keynesian, monetarist and synthesist views in terms of the elasticities of the IS-LM curve. The LM curve slopes upward to the right and has three segments, as shown in Figure 22. Starting from the left it is *perfectly elastic*. This segment is known as "*the keynesian range*". At the other extreme to the right, the LM curve is *perfectly inelastic*. This segment of the curve is known as "the classical range". In between these two segments of the curve is "*the intermediate range.*" The keynesian range represents the fiscalist or Keynesian view, the classical range the monetarist view, and the intermediate range the synthesist view.

Monetary Policy

Monetary policy is explained in Figure 22 where the three-range LM curves LM_1 and L_2 are shown with three IS curves. The LM_2 curve emerges after an increase in the money supply.

First consider the *Keynesian range* where the LM curve is perfectly elastic. This is the Keynesian liquidity trap situation in which the LM curve is horizontal, and the interest rate cannot full below OR_1. An increase in the money supply shifts the LM curve from LM_1 to LM_2. This shift in the curve has no effect on the rate of interest. Consequently, investment is not affected at all so that the level of income remains unchanged at OY_1. Thus, under the Keynesian assumption of the liquidity trap, the horizontal portion of the LM curve is not affected by an increase in the money supply. This IS curve intersects the LM curve in the flat range at A with little effect on the interest rate, and consequently on investment and income. *Monetary policy is therefore, totally ineffective in the Keynesian range.*

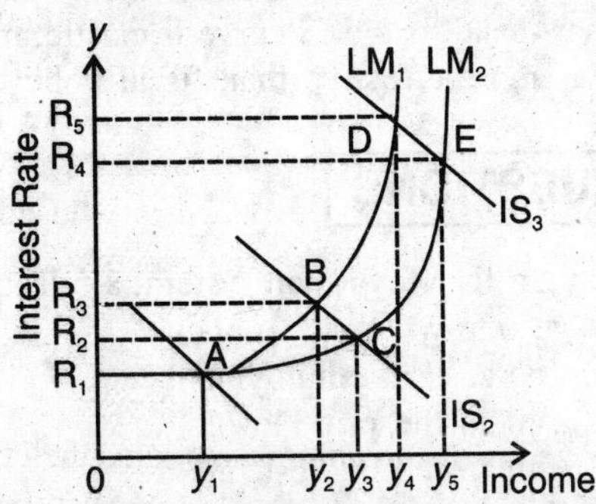

Fig. 22

In the classical range, the system is in equilibrium at D where the IS_3 curve intersects the LM_1 curve and the interest rate is OR_5 and income level OY_4. An increase in money supply shifts the LM_1 curve to the right to LM_2 position. As a result, the income level increases from OY_4 to OY_5, and the interest rate falls from OR_5 to OR_4 when the IS_3 curve crosses the LM_2 curve at E. The increase in the income level and fall in the interest rate as a result of the increase in the money supply is based on the classical assumption that money is primarily a medium of exchange. Thus, the monetary policy is highly effective in the classical range when the economy is at high levels of income and interest rate and utilises the entire increase in the money supply for transactions purposes the rely raising national income by the full increase in the money supply.

Now consider the intermediate range when the initial equilibrium is at B where the IS_2 curve intersects the LM_1 curve, and the income level is OY_2 and the interest rate is OR_3. The increase in the money supply shifts the LM_1 curve to LM_2 position. As a result, the new equilibrium is established at point C where the IS_2 curve crosses the LM_2 curve. It shows that with the increase in the money supply the rate of interest falls from OR_3 to OR_2 and the income level rises from OY_2 to OY_3. In the intermediate range the increase in income by Y_2Y_3 is less than that in the classical range Y_4 Y_5. This is because in classical case the entire increase in the money supply is absorbed for transactions purposes. But in the intermediate case, the increase money supply is partly absorbed for speculative purposes and partly for transactions purposes. That which is held for speculative purposes is not invested by wealth holders and remains with them in the turn of idle balances. This has the effect of raising the income level by less than the increase in the money supply. Thus, in the intermediate range monetary policy is less effective than in the classical range.

Fiscal Policy

Fiscal policy is explained in terms of Figure 23 in which the three range LM Curve is taken along with six IS curves that rise after increase in government expenditure in the case of the Keynesian, intermediate and classical ranges.

Consider first the keynesian range when the initial equilibrium is at A where the IS_1 curve intersects the LM curve. Suppose the government expenditure is increased. This brings about new equilibrium at B where the IS_2 curve cuts the LM curve. Consequently the income level rises from OY_1 to OY_2 with the interest rate unchanged at OR. The increase in income in the keynesian case is equal to the full multiplier times the increase in government expenditure. This *in the Keynessian range, the fiscal policy is very ettective.*

In the classical range, the LM curve is perfectly inelastic and the IS_5 curve intersects it at E so that the interest rate is OR_3 and the income level is OY_5. When the government expenditure increases for an expansionary fiscal policy, the IS_5 curve shifts upward to IS_6. As a result, the IS_6 curve crosses the LM curve at F and the interest rate rises to OR_4 with income remaining unchanged at OY_5. This is become the classical case relates to a fully employed economy where the increase in government expenditure has the effect of raising the interest rate which reduces private investment. Since the increase in government expenditure exactly equals the reduction in the private investment, there is no effect on the level of income which remaining constant at OY_5. Thus, *fiscal policy is not at all effective in the classical range.*

In the *intermediate range,* the initial equilibrium is at C where the IS_3 curve intersects the LM curve. Here OR_1 is the interest rate with OY_3 the level of income with the increase in the government expenditure, the IS_3 curve shifts upward to the right from IS_3 to IS_4 and the new equilibrium is established at point D. As a result, the increase in government expenditure raises the income level from OY_3 to OY_4 and the interest rate from OR_1 to OR_2. The increase in both the income level and the interest rate in the intermediate range is due to two reasons. First, the increase in income resulting from a rise in government expenditure occurs because additional money balances are available for transactions purposes.

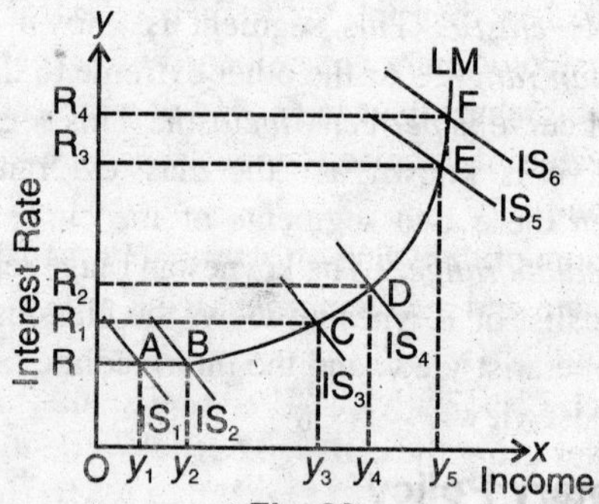

Fig. 23

Second, given a fixed money supply, a part of available transactions are held as idle balances by wealth holders which raise the interest rate. As a result of the rise in the interest rate, investment falls and the fiscal policy is not so effective as in the Keynesian range.

Conclusion

The relative effectiveness of monetary and fiscal policy depends upon the shape of the IS and LM curves and the economy's initial position. If the economy is in the Keynesian range, monetary policy is in effective and fiscal policy is highly effective. On the other hand, in the classical range, monetary policy is effective and fiscal policy is ineffective. But in the intermediate range both monetary and fiscal policies are effective. In fact, in the intermediate range, the effectiveness of monetary and fiscal policies depends largely on the elasticities of the IS curve. If the IS curve is inelastic, fiscal policy is more effective than monetary policy. On the other hand, if the IS curve is elastic, monetary policy is more effective than fiscal policy.

MULTIPLE CHOICE QUESTIONS

1. In the IS-LM model of income determination, an increase in the propensity to save leads to a—

A. right ward shift of the LM curve
B. right ward shift of the IS curve
C. left ward shift of the LM curve
D. left ward shift of the IS curve

2. Under the Keynesian system, a full in money wage rate will lead to a/am—

A. increase in employment
B. fall in the price level
C. fall in the interest rate
D. fall in the quantity of money

3. If there is to be large oscillation in the path of income through the interaction of multiplier and accelerator then the—

A. value of marginal propensity to save must be less than the value of accelerator
B. value of marginal propensity to save must be greater than the value of accelerator
C. value of accelerator must be greater than one
D. Sum of the value of marginal propensity to save and accelerator must be greater than one

4. Match List-I with List-II and select the correct answer using the codes given below the lists—

List-I	List-II
(a) C = 4 + 0.6Y	1. LM function
(b) I = 80 – 5*i*	2. IS function
(c) 0.3*y* –20*i* –150 = 0	3. Consumption function
(d) 0.3*y* + 20*i* – 150 = 0	4. Investment function

Codes :	*(a)*	*(b)*	*(c)*	*(d)*
A.	3	4	1	2
B.	4	3	1	2
C.	3	4	2	1
D.	4	1	2	3

5. Neutrality of money implies that a given increase in the money supply will—

A. increase all prices in the same proportion
B. increase all prices in different proportions
C. decrease all prices in the same proportion
D. not change prices at all

6. The theory that the transactions demand for money also depends on the rate of interests, was put forward by—

A. Keynes and Pigou
B. Baumol and Tobin
C. Hicks and Solow
D. Samuelson and Meada

7. Where M is money-supply, *i* is rate of interest and I is investment, the correct likely sequence would be—

A. M decreases, *i* goes down, I goes down, GNP goes down
B. M decreases, *i* goes up, I goes down, GNP goes down
C. M decreases, *i* goes up, I goes up, GNP goes up
D. M goes up, *i* goes up, I goes up, GNP goes up

8. The quantity theory of money implies that an increase in the price level will be associated with—

A. an increase in out put
B. an increase in money supply
C. a decrease in money supply
D. both (A) and (B)

9. High powered money is—

A. Bank's reserves at the Central Bank
B. all loans and advances of banks
C. money held by banks
D. currency held by public and reserves with the Central Bank

10. Which one of the following pair is NOT correctly matched ?

A. Inflationary Gap : Keynes
B. Cash Balance Approach : Pigou
C. Accelerator-Multiplier : Hicks Analysis
D. Equation of Exchange : Marshall

11. Given the total investment expenditure, an increase in the propensity to save will lead to a—

A. rise in income
B. rise in the rate of interest
C. fall in savings
D. fall in income

12. If the investment multiplier is 4, the relevant consumption function is given by—

A. $c = 28 + 0.75y$ B. $c = -28 + 0.78y$
C. $c = 28 + 0.70y$ D. $c = 28 + 0.40y$

13. Which of the following is consistent with the cross-sectional consumption function ?

A. APC = MPC B. MPC = O
C. APC > MPC D. APC = O

14. The speculative demand for money depends on—

A. interest rate B. income
C. profit D. out put

15. Consider the following statements—
Classical economists believed that unemployment in an economy would persist because of

1. labour-saving technical progress.
2. deficiency in demand for goods.
3. Government intervention in the free working of the economy.

Which of the above statements is/are correct?

A. 1, 2 and 3 B. 1 and 2
C. 2 and 3 D. 3 alone

16. Liquidity preference curve slopes downward to right because—
A. as rate of interest rises, the opportunity cost of holding money falls.
B. as rate of interest rises, the opportunity cost of holding money rises.
C. as rate of interest falls, the opportunity cost of holding money does not change.
D. when the rate of interest is low, the central banks reduces the supply of money.

17. Quantity theory of money should be regarded as a theory of demand for money. This view has been given by—
A. D.H. Robertson B. J.M. Keynes
C. A.C. Pigou D. M. Friedman

18. Inflation is unjust and deflation is inexpedient. Of the two, deflation is worse. Who made this statement—
A. J.M. Keynes B. G. Crowther
C. A. Marshall D. A.H. Hansen

19. The quantity theory of money was first propounded by—
A. D. Ricardo B. Davanzatti
C. D. Hume D. J. Mill

20. Money is an asset. Its demand is determined along with the demand for all the other assets. This view has been held by—
A. A. Marshall B. J. Tobin
C. M. Friedman D. H. Johnson

21. Who among the following Economists, was the first to mention effective demand as a determinant of the level of economic activity—
A. D. Ricardo B. T.R. Malthus
C. A. Marshall D. J.M. Keynes

22. In classical theory of employment what ensures the perfect clearing of the labour market—
A. flexibility of interest rate
B. flexibility of wage rate
C. flexibility of prices of the commodity
D. classical assumption of perfect competition in the product market

23. When a linear consumption function undergoes a parallel shift downwards, the investment multiplier—
A. falls B. rises
C. doubles D. does not change

24. A direct increase in initial employment leads to a multiple increase in total employment. This relationship was propounded by—
A. J.M. Keynes B. R.F. Kahn
C. A.C. Pigou D. J. Robertson

25. Who among the following Economists introduced the concept of permanent income as a determination of consumption function—
A. M. Friedman B. J.M. Keynes
C. J.S. Duesenberry D. N. Kaldor

26. An increase in money supply leads to—
A. rightward shift of IS curve
B. leftward shift of IS curve
C. leftward shift of LM curve
D. rightward shift of LM curve

27. Consider the following statements in relation to Accelerator and choose the correct answer from the code given below—
1. It depends on the rate of growth of demand.
2. It works when there is no idle capacity in the economy.
3. It increases with increase in the rate of depreciation.
4. It depends on the level of demand.

Code :
A. 1 and 2 are correct.
B. 2 and 3 are correct.
C. 3 and 4 are correct.
D. 2, 3 and 4 are corect.

28. According to the IS-LM model, given by Hicks-Hansen there is simultaneous equilibrium between—
A. income level and rate of interest
B. income level and consumption
C. inflation and unemployment
D. demand and supply of money

29. Okun's law postulates a—
A. positive relationship between unemployment and real gross domestic product.
B. negative relationship between unemployment and real gross domestic product.

C positive relationship between money supply and price level.

D. negative relationship between money supply and rate of interest.

30. Which of the curves shown in the diagram below truly represent Keynes saving function—

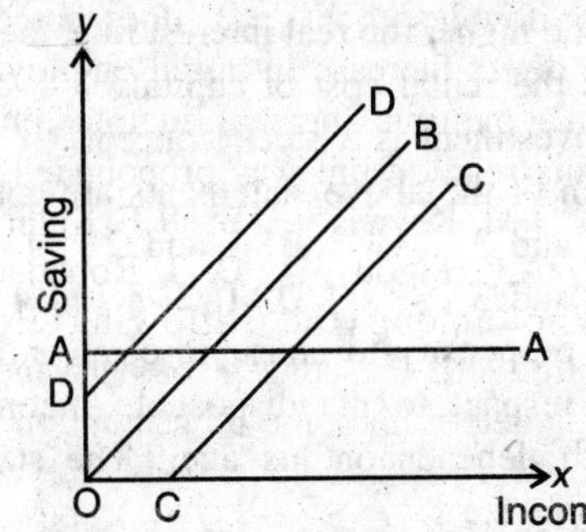

A. AA B. OB

C. DD D. CC

31. Before full employment, if price level falls, aggregate demand will increase which will lead to rise in employment and income. This relationship between price level and aggregate demand has been called—

A. real balance effect

B. income effect

C. price effect

D. employment effect

32. In which of the following situations will an increase in money supply have no effect on equilibrium effect—

A. LM is steeply sloped and IS is relatively flat.

B. LM is vertical and IS is steeply sloped.

C. LM is steeply sloped and IS is vertical.

D. LM is relatively flat as is IS.

33. **Assertion (A) :** Keynes pointed out that during depression private investment is not induced.

Reason (R) : The marginal productivity of capital is high in depression.

Choose the correct answer from the code given below—

A. Both A and R are true and R is the correct explanation of A.

B. Both A and R are true and R is *not* the correct explanation of A.

C. A is true but R is false.

D. A is false but R is true.

34. Keynes was most concerned with—

A. demand-pull inflation

B. cost-push inflation

C. structural inflation

D. stagflation

35. The speculative demand for money depends only on the expected prices of bonds. This view has been held by—

A. J.M. Keynes B. K. Wickscell

C. D.H. Robertson D. M. Friedman

36. Money multiplier is the ratio between—

A. quantity of total money and money national income

B. quantity of primany money and quantity of secondary money

C. quanity of primary money and quantity of total money

D. quantity of money and aggregate investment

37. According to the quantity theory of money, the price level rises if—

A. there is a decrease in money supply

B. the velocity of circulation of money rises

C. the aggregate volume of transactions increases

D. the real demand for money rises

38. Let $I = 5 + 0.2y$; $S = -15 + 0.3y$ and $\overline{G} = 5$ (where I = Investment, y = National Income, S = Saving and $\overline{G}$ = Government spending). What is the equilibrium level of y?

A. 200 B. 100

C. 250 D. 300

39. Consider the following statements—

1. Absolute Income Hypothesis is associated with Keynes
2. $S = -20 + 0.4y$ and $C = 20 + 0.6y$ yield the same investment multiplier
3. Investment multiplier rises when ever income tax is introduced in the system
4. Bond price and interest rates are directly related which of the above statements is/ are correct ?

A. 1 alone B. 2 and 3

C. 3 and 4 D. 1 and 2

40. Consider the following statements relating to classical theory of employment—

1. Classical theory is based on the assumption of full employment
2. Classical version of full employment is a situation where involuntary unemployment is present
3. Classical version of full employment is consistent with seasonal unemployment and frictional unemployment
4. Classical economists advocated wage cuts to reduce the unemployment level

Which of the above statements are correct?

A. 1, 2 and 3 B. 2, 3 and 4
C. 1, 3 and 4 D. 1 and 2

41. Which one of the following saving functions corresponds to the investment multiplier of 5?

A. $S = -28 + 0.25y$
B. $S = -40 + 0.75y$
C. $S = -60 + 0.20y$
D. $S = -75 + 0.60y$

42. When investment is negatively related to the rate of interest, the equilibrium output in the goods market is—

A. unrelated to the rate of interest
B. inversely related to the rate of interest
C. positively related to the rate of interest
D. indeterminate

43. Consider the following statements denoting the relationship between marginal propensity to consume and value of multiplier—

1. Higher the marginal propensity to consume, higher is the multiplier
2. Higher the marginal propensity to consume lower is the multiplier
3. When the marginal propensity to consume is one, multiplier takes the value of infinity

Which of the above statements is/are correct?

A. 1 alone B. 2 and 3
C. 1, 2 and 3 D. 1 and 3

44. An increase in fiscal spending leads to—

A. a shift of the Phillips curve to the right
B. a shift of the Phillips curve to the left
C. movement along the Phillips curve such that unemployment rises and inflation falls
D. movement along the Phillips curve such that unemployment falls and inflation rises

45. Consider the following statements—

1. According to the accelerator models, investment demand is proportional to the change in GNP
2. The real rate of interest is the nominal rate of interest plus the inflation rate
3. The higher the real interest rate, the higher is the rental cost of capital
4. Investment is a stock concept

Which of the above statements are correct?

A. 2 and 3 B. 1 and 2
C. 1 and 3 D. 1, 2, 3 and 4

46. 'The propensity to consume of an individual with respect to his disposable income and wealth depends on his age.' The statement refers to the

A. relative income hypothesis
B. permanent income hypothesis
C. life-cycle hypothesis
D. absolute income hypothesis

47. When income falls, what happens to the liquidity preference curve?

A. It does not shift
B. It shifts to the left
C. It shifts to the right
D. It becomes parallel to the vertical axis

48. Consider the following statements—

1. If Government expenditure increases the IS curve shifts to the right
2. If the taxes increase the IS curve shifts to the right
3. If the price level increases the LM curve shifts to the left
4. The more interest elastic the investment function, the more interest elastic will be the IS curve

Which of the above statements is/are correct ?

A. 2, 3 and 4 B. 1, 3 and 4
C. 1 and 2 D. 2 alone

49. Stagflation refers to situation which is characterised by—

A. deflation and rising unemployment
B. inflation and rising employment
C. inflation and rising unemployment
D. stagnant employment and deflation

50. The elasticity in respect of speculative demand for money under the liquidity trap condition is

A. zero
B. one
C. greater than one
D. infinite

51. When the intrinsic value of money and its face value are equal, it is called

A. token money
B. full-bodied money
C. quasi-money
D. fiat money

52. Which one of the following according to Miltan Friedman is NOT a key determinant of the demand for money ?

A. Aggregate wealth
B. Precautionary motive
C. Relative rates of return obtainable on different forms of assests
D. Physical non-human capital goods and human capital

53. Which one of the following factors affects velocity of circulation ?

A. Time unit of income receipts
B. Frequency of transaction
C. Liquidity preference
D. All of the above

54. Which one of the following statements is correct in respect of equation of exchange MV = PT ?

A. If M is doubled, leaving V and T unaffected, then P must double
B. If M is doubled, leaving V unaffected, then P will be halved
C. If M and T are doubled, leaving V unaffected, then P will be halved
D. If M is doubled, V is halved, leaving T unaffected, then P gets multiplied 3 times

55. Match List-I (Name of the Economist) with List-II (Concept /Theory) and select the correct answer using the codes given below the Lists;

List-I	List-II
(a) A.W. Phillips	1. Central Bank
(b) Findlay Shirras	2. Trade-off between wage and unemployment rate
(c) J.M. Keynes	3. Theory of profit
(d) R.S. Sayers	4. Taxable capacity
	5. Liquidity trap

Codes :	*(a)*	*(b)*	*(c)*	*(d)*
A.	5	4	1	2
B.	2	3	5	1
C.	5	3	1	2
D.	2	4	5	1

56. To which one of the following, does the liquidity trap correspond?

A. Consumption function
B. Production function
C. Money demand function
D. Labour demand function

57. The speculative demand for money, according to Keynes, is a function of—

A. Rate of interest B. Level of income
C. Level of savings D. Level of output

58. Anticipation of an increase in the rate of inflation will—

A. cause the short run Phillips curve to shift upward to the right
B. cause an increase in the real rate of interest
C. reduce the normal rate of unemployment in the long run
D. cause the rate of inflation to slow down, other things remaining constant

59. Fisher's quantity theory of money has mainly been criticised because—

A. it does not tell us as to how the change in the quantity of money influence the price level
B. it over emphasises the demand for money by assuming supply of money as being constant
C. it analyses short term variations in the value of money
D. it emphasises too much on the price level

60. Gresham's law explains that—

A. two grams of silver is equal to half gram gold for conversion
B. good money chases bad money out
C. velocity of circulation of money fluctuates rapidly
D. bad money drives good money out of circulation

61. Match List-I (Economists) with List-II (Concepts) and select the correct answer using the codes given below the lists—

List-I	List-II
(a) Keynes	1. Money illusion
(b) Modigliani	2. IS-curve
(c) Hicks	3. Life cycle hypothesis
(d) Pigou	4. Liquidity trap

Codes :	*(a)*	*(b)*	*(c)*	*(d)*
A.	4	1	2	3
B.	2	3	4	1
C.	4	3	2	1
D.	2	1	4	3

62. 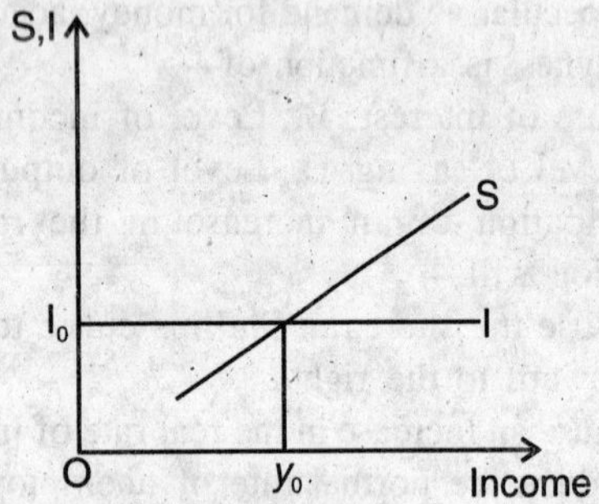

In respect of the diagram given above, consider the following statements—

1. Saving (S) is autonomous.
2. Investment (I) is autonomous.
3. Saving is determined by income (Y).
4. Investment (I) is not autonomous.

Which of these statements are correct ?

A. 2 and 3 B. 3 and 4
C. 1 and 4 D. 1 and 2

63. Assume consumption function of an economy to be C = Rs. 30 Crore + 0.8 Y. Investment is Rs. 40 Crore. Then, the equilibrium level of income is

A. Rs. 700 crore B. Rs. 350 crore
C. Rs. 560 crore D. Rs. 140 crore

64. M_2, money supply measure in India, constitutes

A. M_1 + all post-office deposits
B. M_1 + time deposits of cummercial banks
C. M_1 + post-office saving deposits
D. M_3 + all post-office deposits

65. Consider the following items—

1. Currency with the public
2. Cash with banks
3. Post-office saving bank deposits
4. Time deposits with the banks

Reserve money includes

A. 1, 2 and 3 B. 2, 3 and 4
C. 1 and 2 D. 1, 2, 3 and 4

66. According to Keynes, transaction demand for money L can be stated as (symbols have the usual meaning)

A. L = K (*y*)
B. L = I (*r*)
C. L = K (*y*) + I (*r*)
D. L = Y – I

67. Supply of money remaining the same, when there is an increase in demand for money, there will be

A. a fall in the level of prices
B. an increase in the rate of interest
C. a decreacse in the rate of interest
D. an increase in the level of income and employment

68. Fisher's equation of exchange establishes

A. direct relationship between money and prices
B. inverse relationship between money and prices
C. direct and proportionate relationship between money and prices
D. inverse and proportionate relationship between money and prices

69. Consider the following statements—

A rise in the general level of prices may be caused by

1. an increase in the money supply
2. a decrease in the aggregate level of output
3. an increase in the effective demand.

Of these statements

A. 1 alone is correct
B. 1 and 2 are correct
C. 2 and 3 are correct
D. 1, 2 and 3 are correct

70. Match List-I with List-II and select the correct answer using the codes given below the lists—

List-I	List-II
(a) A continuous increase in general price level	1. Hyper inflation

(b) Raising prices deliberately to relieve depression	2. Disinflation
(c) Fall in prices without a decline in the existing level of employment, out put and income	3. Stagflation
(d) Recession accumpanied by inflation	4. Reflation
	5. Inflation

Codes :	*(a)*	*(b)*	*(c)*	*(d)*
A.	5	1	2	4
B.	1	3	2	5
C.	1	4	5	3
D.	5	4	2	3

71. Consider the following types of assets held by a commercial bank—

1. Money at call and short notice
2. Government securites
3. Advances
4. Cash

The correct DECREASING order (highest to lowest) of liquidity of the given assents is—

A. 4, 1, 3, 2 B. 1, 4, 3, 2
C. 1, 4, 2, 3 D. 4, 1, 2, 3

72. In the given diagram, LK represents—

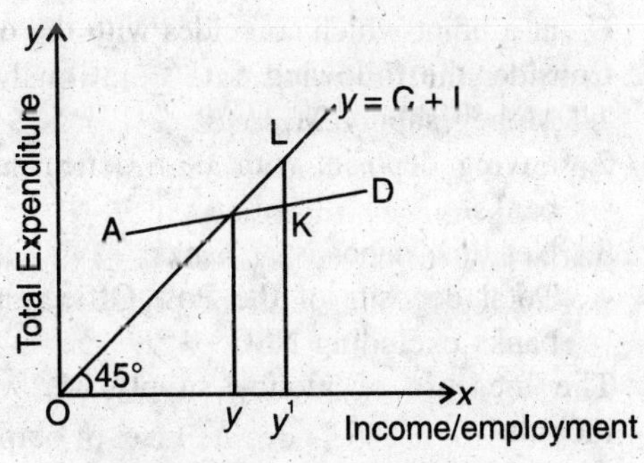

A. deficiency of demand
B. excess demand
C. deficiency of supply
D. excess supply

73. Assuming that: change in investment $\Delta I = 25$
marginal propensity to save (MPS) = 0.5
marginal propensity to investment (MPI) = 0
the change in income Δy will equal to—

A. 25 B. 50
C. 200 D. 100

74. Given the total investment expenditure an increase in the propensity to save will lead to a—

A. fall in the rate of interest
B. fall in income
C. rise in the rate of interest
D. rise in income

75. Investment multiplier can be obtained from (symbols have the usual meaning)

A. $\dfrac{1}{1-\dfrac{\Delta c}{\Delta s}}$ B. $\dfrac{1}{1-\dfrac{\Delta c}{\Delta y}}$

C. $\dfrac{1}{1+\dfrac{\Delta c}{\Delta s}}$ D. $\dfrac{1}{1+\dfrac{\Delta c}{\Delta y}}$

76. If there is an expectation of a rise in the price level, investment will be encouraged because

A. there will be an increase in the production of capital goods
B. there will be a rise in the prospective return from captial
C. people will save more and the interest rate will fall
D. the cost of production of capital goods will fall

77. The aggregate demand curves slopes downwards because an increase in price level leads to

A. reduction in real balances and increase in interest rate
B. increase in the interest rate and reduction in aggregate spending
C. reduction in real balances alone
D. reduction in real balances, increase in interest rate and reduction in aggregate spending

78. According to permanent income hypothesis, the

A. long-run aggregate Average propensity to consume (APC) equals long-run aggregate Marginal Propensity to consume (MPC)
B. long-run aggregate APC is greater than the long run aggregate MPC
C. long-run aggregate APC is less than the long-run aggregate MPC

D. APC of every individual is equal irrespective of different levels of income of families

79. Match List-I with List-II and select the correct answer using the codes given below the lists—

List-I	List-II
(a) Supply creates its own demand	1. J.B. Say
(b) Chioce reveals preference	2. Adam Smith
(c) Division of labour is limited by the extent of the market	3. Ricardo
(d) Corn is high not because rent is paid, but rent is paid because corn is high	4. Samuelson

Codes :	(a)	(b)	(c)	(d)
A.	1	4	2	3
B.	1	4	3	2
C.	4	1	3	2
D.	4	1	2	3

80. In the given diagram, speculative demand for money curve $l(r)$ has four regions R_1, R_2, R_3, and R_4. Liquidity trap is indicated by the regions.

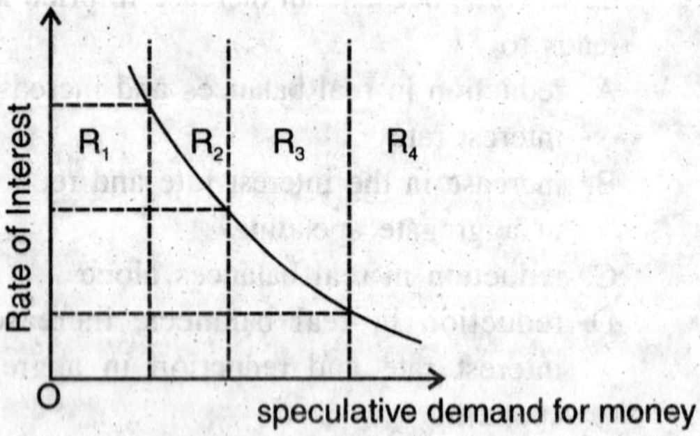

A. R_1 alone
B. R_1 and R_4
C. R_3 and R_4
D. R_4 alone

81. According to Keynes, marginal propensity to consume
A. can never exceed unity
B. may exceed unity when dissaving occurs
C. can never exceed the average propensity to consume
D. is the reciprocal of the marginal propensity to save

82. Super multiplier refers to
A. interaction of the Multiplier and the Accelerator
B. reciprocal of the marginal propensity to consume
C. capital output ratio
D. budget multiplier

83. A Production Possibility Frontier (PPF) is shown in the given diagram. A Less Developed Country (LDC) will be

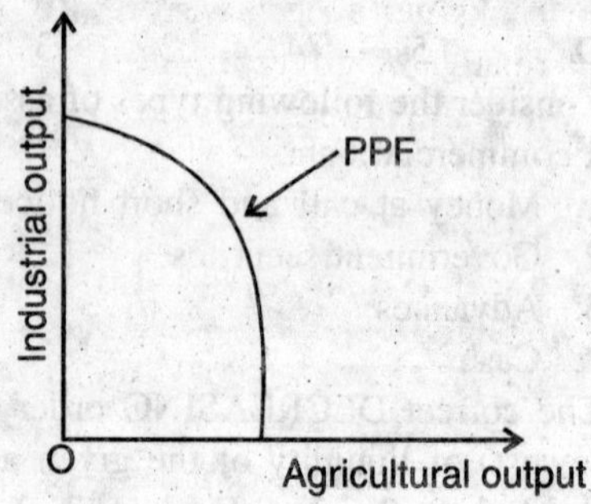

A. inside the PPF
B. on the PPF
C. above the PPF
D. at a point which coincides with the origin

84. Consider the following :
1. Money supply M_1.
2. Saving deposits with Post Office saving banks.
3. Net time deposits of banks.
4. Total deposits of the Post Office saving banks excluding NSC.

The measure of money supply M_3 would include
A. 1, 2 and 3 B. 1 and 3
C. 1 and 4 D. 3 and 4

85. The correct sequence of the stage through which a trade cycle in an economy passes is
A. Depression, Inflation, Reflation, Disinflation
B. Reflation, Disinflation, Inflation, Depression
C. Depression, Reflation, Inflation, Disinflation
D. Inflation, Depression, Disinflation, Reflation

86. The credit multiplier is based on which of the following assumptions?
1. The cash reserve ratio remains constant.

2. The banks maintain a fixed relationship between deposit liabilities and cash reserves.
3. People prefer higher cash holding.
4. People have well developed banking habits.

Select the correct answer using the codes given below—

Codes :

A. 1, 2 and 3 B. 2, 3 and 4
C. 1, 3 and 4 D. 1, 2 and 4

87. If cash reserve ratio is 40% and the commercial banks get a fresh cash of Rs. 15 crores as a result of government spending then the increase in loans advanced by the commercial banks will be

A. Rs. 37.5 crores B. Rs. 40 crores
C. Rs. 60 crores D. Rs. 30.5 crores

88. Liquidity preference refers to—

A. the extent to which investors prefer to keep their assets in money
B. RBI's share holdings in other financial institutions
C. community's preference for gold
D. community's effective demand for capital goods

89. Consider the following statements :

Intersection of the IS and LM curves corresponds to—

1. equilibrium in the real sector.
2. equilibrium in the monetary sector.
3. liquidity trap necessarily.
4. walrasian general equilibrium.

Of these statements

A. 1 and 3 are correct
B. 1 and 2 are correct
C. 2, 3 and 4 are correct
D. 1, 2, 3 and 4 are correct

90. Match List-I with List-II and select the correct answer using the codes given below the lists—

List-I	List-II
(a) $c = 9 + 0.1y$	1. IS realation
(b) $0.25y - 20i - 193 = 0$	2. Consumption relation
(c) $0.06y + 29i - 500 = 0$	3. Investment relation
(d) $I = 50 - 10\,i$	4. LM relation

Codes :	(a)	(b)	(c)	(d)
A.	4	3	2	1
B.	4	3	1	2
C.	2	4	3	1
D.	2	4	1	3

91. Excess of ex-ante savings over ex-ante investment means that—

A. income will fall
B. income will rise
C. income will remain the same
D. price will rise and inventories will accumulate

92. Which one of the following consumption functions corresponds to the income multiplier, R = 4?

A. $c = 24 + 0.5y$ B. $c = 240 + 0.25y$
C. $c = 24 + 0.55y$ D. $c = 240 + 0.75y$

93. Consider the following statements—

1. Points to the left of the IS curve indicate excess supply of goods.
2. Points to the right of the LM curve indicate excess demand for money.
3. Points to the right of the IS curve indicate excess supply of money.
4. Points to the right of the IS curve indicate excess supply of goods.

Of these statements

A. 2 and 4 are correct
B. 1 and 3 are correct
C. 2 and 3 are correct
D. 1, 2 and 3 are correct

94. Suppose, MPC falls. The IS curve shifts to the left. Then what happens ceteris paribus?

A. The level of equilibrium becomes lower
B. The level of equilibrium becomes higher
C. There is no change in equilibrium
D. Only the rate of interest becomes lower

95. Match List-I with List-II and select the correct answer using the codes given below the Lists—

List-I	List-II
(a) Life Cycle Hypothesis	1. Keynes
(b) Permanent Income Hypothesis	2. Duesen Berry
(c) Absolute Income Hypothesis	3. Friedman

(d) Relative income Hypothesis		4. Ando-Modigliani	

Codes :

	(a)	*(b)*	*(c)*	*(d)*
A.	4	3	1	2
B.	4	3	2	1
C.	3	2	1	4
D.	3	2	4	1

96. The author of employment multiplier is—
A. Lord Beveridge B. Keynes
C. R.F. Kahn D. J.R. Hicks

97. In a two sector economy, the saving and investment functions are as follows—
S = –10 + 0.2Y
I = –3 + 0.1Y
what will be the equilibrium level of income?
A. 70 B. 80
C. 90 D. 100

98. The IS-LM model has been formulated by—
A. J.R. Hicks B. F. Modigliani
C. P.A. Samuelson D. J.M. Keynes

99. The speculative demand for money is—
A. interest determining
B. interest determined
C. income determining
D. income determined

100. Which one of the following is represented by M_3 ?
A. M_1 + post office savings bank deposits
B. Currency with the public + demand deposits
C. M_1 + time deposits with bank
D. None of these

101. In an economy where people always consume half of any additional income and save the other half, an additional Govt. expenditure of Rs. 20,000 can create an additional income of—
A. Rs. 10,000 B. Rs. 40,000
C. Zero D. Rs. 20,000

102. When a linear consumption function undergoes a parallel shift downwards, the investment multiplier will—
A. fall B. rise marginally
C. remain as before D. become double

103. If the consumption function passes through the origin, then APC = MPC it must be—
A. linear without any intercept
B. non-linear without any intercept
C. linear with a negative intercept on the income axis
D. linear with a positive intercept on the consumption axis

104. Given the consumption function
$c = 205 + 0.9y$
what is the multiplier?
A. 0.09 B. 10.0
C. 0.9 D. 9.00

105. Suppose that the money supply in an economy is constant and the demand for money is a function of income and interest rate, then if the level of income increases, there will be—
A. a decrease in the quantity of money demanded and an increase in the rate of interest
B. an increase in the quantity of money demanded and an increase in the rate of interest
C. a decrease in the quantity of money demanded and a decrease in the rate of interest
D. an increase in the quantity of money demanded and a decrease in the rate of interest

106. Portfolio theory of the demand for money assumes that the individual—
A. disregards risk B. is risk neutral
C. is risk lover D. is risk averse

107. If the rate of interest increases, people holding bonds will—
A. experience a capital gain on the bonds
B. experience a capital loss on the bonds
C. not be able to find a buyer should they decide to sale
D. experience neither capital gains nor a capital loss

108. When the demand for money is infinitely interest elastic, the effectiveness of an expansionary monetary policy is—
A. the highest
B. moderate
C. verylow
D. nil

109. **Assertion (A):** Real rate of interest is better indicator of returns on savings than nominal rate of interest.

Reason (R): The real rate of interest is estimated after removing the effect of the expected rate of inflation.

A. Both A and R are true and R is the correct explanation of A
B. Both A and R are true but R is not a correct explanation of A
C. A is true but R is false
D. A is false but R is true

110. Assertion (A): If the government expenditure and taxation are increased by an equal amount, the equilibrium income of the economy will remain the same, ceteris paribus.

Reason (R): A given change in the government expenditure affects aggregate spending more than an equal amount of tax.

A. Both A and R are true and R is the correct explanation of A
B. Both A and R are true but R is not a correct explanation of A
C. A is true but R is false
D. A is false but R is true

111. Assertion (A): In India, monetary policy alone cannot eliminate inflation.

Reason (R): There are structure factors which make prices rigid in the downward direction but flexible in the upward direction.

A. Both A and R are true and R is the correct explanation of A
B. Both A and R are true but R is not a correct explanation of A
C. A is true but R is false
D. A is false but R is true

112. Assertion (A): Keynes pointed out that during depression, private investment is not induced.

Reason (R): The marginal productivity of capital is high in depression.

Choose the correct answer from the code given below:

A. Both A and R are true and R is the correct explanation of A.
B. Both A and R are true and R is not the correct explanation of A
C. A is true but R is false
D. A is false but R is true

113. Assertion (A): Money is a link between the present and the future.

Reason (R): Money is a store of value.

A. Both A and R are true and R is the correct explanation of A
B. Both A and R are true but R is not a correct explanation of A
C. A is true but R is false
D. A is false but R is true

114. Assertion (A): According to Baumol, the transactions demand for cash varies with respect to the square-root of the volume of transactions.

Reason (R): Transaction demand for money is a function of income.

A. Both A and R are true and R is the correct explanation of A
B. Both A and R are true but R is not a correct explanation of A
C. A is true but R is false
D. A is false but is true

115. Assertion (A): There would be no trade-off between inflation and unemployment even in the short run if people's expectations are rational.

Reason (R): Rational expectations imply forecasting the future correctly.

A. Both A and R are true and R is the correct explanation of A
B. Both A and R are true but R is not a correct explanation of A
C. A is true but R is false
D. A is false but R is true

116. Assertion (A): The major distinguishing feature of a commercial bank is its ability to create money.

Reason (R): It has a legal power to do so.

A. Both A and R are true and R is the correct explanation of A
B. Both A and R are true but R is not a correct explanation of A
C. A is true but R is false
D. A is false but R is true

ANSWERS

1	2	3	4	5	6	7	8	9	10
D	C	A	A	D	B	B	B	D	D
11	**12**	**13**	**14**	**15**	**16**	**17**	**18**	**19**	**20**
D	A	A	A	D	B	D	A	B	C
21	**22**	**23**	**24**	**25**	**26**	**27**	**28**	**29**	**30**
B	B	D	B	A	D	D	A	B	D
31	**32**	**33**	**34**	**35**	**36**	**37**	**38**	**39**	**40**
A	D	C	A	A	B	B	A	D	C
41	**42**	**43**	**44**	**45**	**46**	**47**	**48**	**49**	**50**
C	B	D	D	C	C	B	B	C	D
51	**52**	**53**	**54**	**55**	**56**	**57**	**58**	**59**	**60**
B	B	D	A	D	C	A	B	A	D
61	**62**	**63**	**64**	**65**	**66**	**67**	**68**	**69**	**70**
C	A	B	C	A	A	B	C	D	D
71	**72**	**73**	**74**	**75**	**76**	**77**	**78**	**79**	**80**
D	B	B	B	B	B	D	A	A	D
81	**82**	**83**	**84**	**85**	**86**	**87**	**88**	**89**	**90**
A	A	A	B	C	D	A	A	B	D
91	**92**	**93**	**94**	**95**	**96**	**97**	**98**	**99**	**100**
A	D	A	A	A	C	A	A	B	C
101	**102**	**103**	**104**	**105**	**106**	**107**	**108**	**109**	**110**
B	C	A	B	B	C	B	D	A	D
111	**112**	**113**	**114**	**115**	**116**				
A	C	A	B	A	C				

❑❑❑

NATIONAL INCOME ACCOUNTING

CONCEPT AND MEASUREMENT OF NATIONAL INCOME

INTRODUCTION

Economic well-being of society is obviously influenced by the volume of total output as well as by composition of the output and relative size of the shares received by various groups. The portion of economic theory which deals with the determination of total output is known as *National Income Analysis* or the process of National Income Accounting.

National income is an uncertain term which is used interchangeably with national dividend, national output and national expenditure. On this basis, national income has been defined in a number of ways. In common parlance, national income means the total value of goods and services produced annually in a country. In other words, the total amount of income accruing to a country from economic activities in a year's time, is known as national income. It includes payments made to all resources in the form of wages, interest, rent and profits.

Definitions of National Income

The definitions of national income can be grouped into two classes. One, the *traditional definitions* advanced by Marshall, Pigou and Fisher; and two, modern definitions. According to Marshall, "*The labour and capital of a country acting on its natural resources produce annually a certain net aggregate of commodities, material and immaterial including services of all kinds. This is the true net annual income or revenue of the country or national dividend.*" In this definition, the word 'net' refers to deductions from the gross national income in respect of depreciation and weaving out of machines. And to this must be added income from abroad.

National income, according to *Pigou*, "*is that part of the objective income of the community including, of course, income derived from abroad, which can be measured in money.*"

Fisher adopted *'Consumption'* as the criterion of national income whereas Marshall and Pigou regarded it to be production. According to Fisher, "The national dividend or income consists solely of services as received by ultimate consumers, whether from their material or human environments. Thus, a piano, or an overcoat made for me this year is not a part of this year's income, but an addition to the capital. Only the services rendered to me during this year by these things are income." Fisher's definition is considered to be better than that of Marshall or Pigou, because Fisher's definition provides an adequate concept of economic welfare which is dependent on consumption and consumption represents our standard of living.

From the modern point of view, *Simon Kuznets* has defined national income as "the net output of commodities and services flowing during the year from the country's productive system in the hands of the ultimate consumers."

Concepts of National Income

There are various concepts of national income which we shall study one by one.

1. Gross National product (GNP)

Gross National product is defined as the total market value of all final goods and services produced in a year. Two things must be noted in regard to gross national product. *First,* it measures the market value of annual output. In other words, GNP is a *monetary measure.*

Secondly, for calculating gross national product accurately, all goods and services produced in any given year must be counted once, and not more than once. Most of the goods go through a series of production stages before reaching a market. As a result, parts or components of many goods are bought and sold many times. Hence to avoid counting several times the parts of goods that are sold and resold, gross national product only includes the market value of final goods and ignores transactions involving intermediate goods.

The "gross national product at market prices" may be obtained by adding up :

A. What private persons spend on consumption, or what is called *personal consumption* expenditure.

B. What private businessmen spend on replacement, renewal and new investment. This is called *gross domestic private investment.*

C. What the rest of the world spends on the output of the national economy over and above what this economy spends on the output of the rest of the world, *i.e.*, export-import or net foreign investment; and

D. What the government spends on the purchase of goods and services, *i.e., government purchases.*

2. GNP at Factor Cost

GNP at factor cost is the sum of the money value of the income produced by and accruing to the various factors of production in one year in a country.

GNP at market prices, always includes indirect taxes levied by the government on goods which raise their prices. But GNP at factor cost is the income which the factors of production receive in return for their services alone. It is the cost of production. Thus, GNP at market prices is always higher than GNP at factor cost. Therefore, in order to arrive at GNP at factor cost, we deduct indirect taxes from GNP at market prices. Again, it often happens that the cost of production of a commodity to the producer is higher than the price of a similar commodity in the market. In order to protect such producers, the government helps them by granting monetary help in the form of subsidy equal to the difference between the market price and the cost of production of the commodity. Thus in order to arrive at GNP at factor cost, subsidies are added to GNP at market prices.

GNP at Factor Cost =
GNP at Market Prices – Indirect Taxes + Subsidies.

3. Gross Domestic Product (GDP)

GDP = GNP – Net Foreign Investment

Net Foreign Investment = Export – Import (X – M)

∴ GDP = GNP – (X– M).

4. Net National Product (NNP)

GNP includes the value of total output of consumption goods and investment goods. But the process of production uses up a certain amount of fixed capital. Some fixed equipment wears out, its other components are damaged or destroyed, and still other some rendered obsolete through technological changes. All this process is termed depreciation or capital consumption allowance. In order to arrive at NNP, we deduct depreciation from GNP. The word 'net' refers to the exclusion of that part of total output which represents depreciation.

NNP = GNP – Depreciation.

5. NNP at Market Prices

Net National Product at Market prices is the net value of final goods and services evaluated at market prices in the course of one year in a country. If we deduct depreciation from GNP at market prices, we get NNP at market prices. Thus, NNP at Market Prices = GNP at Market Prices – Depreciation.

6. NNP at Factor Cost

Net National Product at factor cost is the net output evaluated at factor prices. It includes income earned by factors of production through participation in the production process such as wages and salaries, rates, profits, etc. It is also called *National Income.* This measure differs from NNP at market prices in that indirect taxes are deducted and subsidies are added to NNP at market prices in order to arrive at NNP at factor cost. Thus,

NNP at factor cost = NNP at Market Prices – Indirect Taxes + Subsidies.

= GNP at Market Prices – Depreciation – Indirect Taxes + Subsidies.

= National Income.

7. NDP at Factor Cost

Net Domestic Product at factor cost is arrived by making adjustments for net indirect taxes *i.e.*, indirect taxes and subsidies in the Net Domestic Product at market prices. The market prices contain an element of indirect taxes which though paid out by the buyers in the form of Product Prices, do not accrue to the production units.

Hence to find out factor incomes, we deduct the indirect taxes from the Net Domestic Product at market prices. Like wise, we add subsidies to the Net Domestic Product at market prices because these subsidies form the factor incomes though they are not a part of the market prices. Thus,

Net Domestic Product at Factor Cost = Net Domestic Product at Market Prices – Indirect Taxes + Subsidies.

8. Private Income

Private income is income obtained by private individuals from any source, productive or other wise, and the retained income of corporations. It can be arrived at from NNP at factor cost by marking certain additions and deductions. The additions include transfer payments such as pensions, unemployment allowances, sickness and other social security benefits, gifts and remittances from abroad, windfall gains and from lotteries or from horse racing and interest on public debt. The deductions include income from government departments as well as surpluses from public undertakings and employee's contribution to social security schemes like provident funds, life insurance, etc. Thus,

Private Income = National Income + Transfer payments + Interest on Public Debt – Social Security, Profits and Surpluses of Public under takings.

9. Personal Income

Personal income is the total income received by the individuals of a country from all sources before direct taxes in one year. Personal income is never equal to the national income, because the former includes the transfer payments where as they are not included in national income. Personal income is derived from national income by deducting undistributed corporate profits, profit taxes, and employee's contributions to social security schemes. But business and government transfer payments, and transfer payments from abroad in the form of gifts and remittances, wind fall gains and interest on public dept which are a source of income for individuals are added to national income. Thus,

Personal Income = National income – Undistributed Corporate Profits – Profit Taxes – Social Security Contributions + Transfer Payments + Interest on Public Debt.

Personal income differs from private income in that it is less than the latter because it excludes undistributed corporate profits. Thus,

Personal Income = Private Income – Undistributed Corporate Profits – Profit Taxes.

10. Disposable Income

The concept of disposable income tells us the amount of money available to individuals and house holds in a year for the purposes of spending. After a good part of personal income is paid to government in the form of personal taxes like income tax, personal property tax etc, what remains of personal income is called disposable income. Thus,

Disposable Income = Personal Income – Direct Taxes. Disposable Income can either be consumed or saved. Therefore,

Disposable Income = Consumption + Saving.

11. Real Income

Real income is national income expressed in terms of a general level of prices of a particular year taken as base. National income is the value of goods and services produced as expressed in terms of money at current prices. But it does not indicate the real state of the economy. It is possible that the net national product of goods and services this year might have been less than that of last year, but owing to an increase in prices, the NNP might be higher this year. On the contrary, it is also possible that NNP might have increased but the price level might have fallen, as a result of which national income would appear to be less than that of the last year. In both the situations, the national income does not depict the real state of the country. To rectify such a mistake, the concept of real income has been propounded.

In order to find out the real income of a country, a particular year is taken as base year when the general price level is neither too high nor too low and the price level for that year is assumed to be 100. Now the general level of the prices of the given year for which the national income (real) is to be determined is assessed in accordance with the prices of the base year. For this purpose the following formula is employed

Real National Income = National Income for the current year × $\frac{100}{\text{Current year Index}}$

Suppose 1970 is the base year and the national income for 1980 is Rs. 20000 crores and the index number for this year is 250. Hence,

Real National Income for 1966 = 20000 × $\frac{100}{250}$

= Rs. 80000 crores.

This is also known as National Income at constant prices.

12. Per Capita Income

The average income of the people of a country in a particular year is called Per Capita Income for that year. This concept also refers to the measurement of income at current prices and at constant prices. For instance, in order to find out the per capita income for 2001, at current prices, the national income of a country is divided by the population of the country in that year.

Per Capita Income for 2001

$$= \frac{\text{National income for 2001}}{\text{Population in 2001}}$$

Similarly, for the purpose of arriving at the Real Per Capita Income, the following formula is employed.

Real Per Capita Income for 2001

$$= \frac{\text{Real National Income for 2001}}{\text{Population in 2001}}$$

This concept enables us to know the average income and the standard of living of the people. But it is not very reliable, because in every country due to unequal distribution of national income a major portion of it goes to the richer sections of the society and thus income received by the common man is lower than the per capita income.

Methods of Measuring National Income

There are four methods of measuring national income, which method is to be employed depends on the availability of data in country and the purpose in hand.

1. Product Method

Accordig to this method, the total value of final goods and services produced in a country during a year is calculated at market prices. To final out the GNP, the data of all productive activities, such as agricultural products, wood received from forests, mineral received from mines, commodities produced by industries, the contributions to production made by transport, communications, insurance companies, lawyers, doctors, teachers etc. are collected and assessed at market prices. Only the final goods and services are included and the intermediary goods and services are left out.

2. Income Method

According to this method, the net income payments received by all citizens of a country in a particular year are added up, *i.e.,* net incomes that accrue to all factors of production by way of net rents, net wages, net interest and net profits are all added together but incomes received in the form of transfer paymets are not included in it. The data pertaining to income are obtained from different sources, for instance, from income tax department in respect of high income groups and in case of workers from their wages will.

3. Expenditure Method

According to this method, the total expenditure incurred by the society in a particular year is added together and includes personal consumption expenditure, net domestic investment, government expenditure on goods and services and net foreign investment. This concept is based on the assumption that national income equals national expenditure.

4. Value Added Method

Another method of measuring national income is the value added by industries. The difference between the value of material outputs and inputs at each stage of production is the value added. If all such differences are added up for all industries in the economy, we arrive at the gross domestic product.

Problems of Measurement in a Developing Economy

In a developing economy, complete and reliable information relating to the various methods of estimating nationl income are not available due to the following problems :

1. Non-monetised sector
2. Lack of occuptional specialisation
3. Non-market Transactions
4. Illiteracy
5. Non availability of Data

Social Accounting

The term 'social accounting' was first introduced into economics by *J.R. Hicks* in 1942. In his words, it means 'nothing else but the accounting of the whole community or nation, just as private accounting is the accounting of the individual firm'. Social accounting, also known as national income accounting, is a method to present statistically the interrelationships between the different sectors of the economy for a thorough understanding of the economic conditions of the entire economy. It is a technique of presenting information about the nature of the economy of a society with a view not merely to get an idea of its prosperity, past or present, but also to get guidelines for collective (or state) policy to influence (or regulate) the economy. In other words, social accounting describes statistically the economic activities of the different sectors of the entire economy, indicates their mutual relationship and provides a frame work for analysis.

The principal forms of economic activity are production, consumption, capital accumulation, government transactions and transactions with the rest of the world. These are the components of social accounting. If the incomings and outgoings of a country relating to these five activities are shown in the form of accounts, they show a closed network of flows representing the basic structure of the economy. These flows are always expressed in money terms. We classify these flows as follows :

1. Production Account
2. Consumption Account
3. Government Account
4. Capital Account
5. Foreign Account

Input-output Accounting

The input-output analysis was first developed by W.W. Leontief in his 'The structure of the American Economy.' The input-output analysis tells us that there are industrial inter-relationships and inter-dependencies in the economic system as a whole. The inputs of one industry are the outputs of another industry and *vice versa*, so that ultimately their mutual relationships lead to equilibrium between supply and demand in the economy as a whole. Coal is an input for steel industry and steel is an input for coal industry, though both are the outputs of their respective industries. A major part of economic activity consists in producing intermediate goods (inputs) for further use in producing final goods (outputs). There are flows of goods in "whirlpools and cross currents" between different industries. The supply side consists of inter-industry flows of intermediate products and the demand side of the final goods. In essence, the input-output analysis implies that in equilibrium the money value of aggregate output of the whole economy must equal the sum of the money values of inter-industry inputs plus the sum of money values of inter-industry outputs.

The national income accounts are related to an economy's final product. They do not explicitly show the inter-industry flows of outputs and their relationships with the goods and services demanded. The input-output analysis analyses these relationships. It is, thus, an improvement over the national income accounting method.

Flow of Funds Accounts

National income accounts do not tell anything about monetary or financial transactions where by one sector places its saving at the disposal of the other sectors of the economy by means of loans, capital transfers, etc. The flow of funds accounts were developed by *Professor Morris Copeland* in 1952 to overcome this weakness of national income accounting.

The flow of funds accounts show the financial transactions among different sectors of the economy and the link between saving and investment aggregates with lending and borrowing by them. This system of accounts is concerned with the sources and uses of funds by the various sectors of the economy. "The account for each sector reveals all the sources of funds (whether from income or borrowing) and all the uses to which the funds are put (whether for spending or lending), this way of looking at transactions in their entirely has come to be known as the flow of funds approach or sources and uses of funds."

The flow of funds accounting system is presented in the form of a matrix which is divided into a number of sectors, such as households, corporate business, non-corporate business, farm business, non-farm business, commercial banks, saving institutions, insurance companies, other investors, local, state and central governments, and the rest of the world sector which includes foreign individuals, firms and government. The columns of the matrix are used for institutional sector classification and the rows for various types of transactions.

Balance of Payments Accounts

The balance of payments account of a country is a systematic record of all its economic transactions with the outside world in a given year. It is a statistical record of the character and dimensions of the country's economic relationships with the rest of the world. It shows the country's trading position, changes in its net position as foreign lender or borrower and changes in its official reserve holdings.

MULTIPLE CHOICE QUESTIONS

1. Which of the following is not, by definition, equal to National Income ?
A. National output B. National expenditure
C. National product D. National wealth

2 If GNP is 16% higher than the last year's and the rate of inflation is 9%, production in the economy has grown by
A. 4% B. 5%
C. 6% D. 7%

3. Which of the following is a transfer payment?
A. Payment made to housewife
B. Pocket allowance to children
C. Maintenance allowance to old parents
D. All of the above

4. The difference between gross domestic product and net domestic product equals
A. Transfer payments
B. Depreciation cost
C. Indirect taxes
D. Subsidies

5. The best method of computing national income is
A. Product Method
B. Income Method
C. Expenditure Method
D. Combination of income and production method

6. Which of the following will directly increase the GNP?
A. A rise in the market price
B. A surplus in budget
C. An increase in investment
D. A deficit in budget

7. "National dividend is that part of objective income of the community, including of course the income derived from abroad which can be measured in money"

This is the remark of
A. Marshall B. J.R. Hicks
C. David Ricardo D. A.C. Pigou

8. While calculating personal income, we have to deduct the following from private income :
A. Saving of private corporate sector and corporation tax
B. Consumption of fixed capital
C. Direct taxes paid by households
D. All of the above

9. The National income is equal to
A. GNP – Subsidies – Taxes
B. NNP – Indirect Taxes + Subsidies
C. NNP – Direct Taxes + Subsidies
D. GNP – Subsidies + Taxes

10. "National income as the aggregate net product of, and the sole source of, payment for all the agents of production" has been defined by
A. A.C. Pigou B. Alfred Marshall
C. Robbins D. Dusenbery

11. "The labour and capital of a country acting upon its natural resources produce annually a certain net aggregate of commodities, material and immaterial including services of all kinds." This definition of National Income is given by
A. Adam Smith B. Lionel Robbins
C. John Stuart Mill D. Alfred Marshall

12 The total income earned in any given year by the owners of productive resources is measured by
A. Personal income
B. Disposable Income
C. Gross national product
D. National income

13. In calculating a country's GNP at market prices one of the following is not included
A. Wages and salaries before tax
B. Indirect taxes
C. Bonds to the employees
D. Depreciation allowances

14. An example of double counting in national income would be
A. Wages of bus and train drivers
B. Cotton output and cotton cloth output
C. Electricity output and water output
D. Tax receipts and earnings of inland revenue officials

15. Double counting must be avoided when calculating national income. This means that there must be a deduction of the value of
A. Food subsidies
B. Personal consumption of alcoholic drinks
C. Transfer payments
D. Net interest from abroad

16. Which of the following is counted in determining GNP ?
A. A do it yourself roof repair job
B. A housewife's work at home
C. An operation performed in a hospital
D. Vegetables grown by a farmer for his own use

17. Among these statements which one clearly explains the meaning of "Subsidies"
A. Payment by Government for purchase of goods and services
B. Payment by business enterprises to factors of production
C. Payment by companies to shareholders
D. Payment by Government to business enterprises without buying any goods and services

18. The difference between Gross National Product and Gross Domestic Product is equal to
A. Gross Domestic Investment
B. Net Foreign Investment
C. Net imports
D. Net factor income from abroad

19. Net domestic product at factor cost equals net domestic product at market prices
A. Plus subsidies – indirect taxes
B. Minus subsidies + indirect taxes
C. Minus subsidies
D. Plus indirect taxes

20. When gross investment is positive, net investment
A. is the highest
B. is zero
C. is positive
D. can be either positive or negative

21. National product is not affected by which of the following?
A. Sale of a second hand automobile by A to B
B. Sale of a new car by an automobile dealer
C. Sale of a new car by an automobile company
D. Sale of a new car on hire purchase

22 Net foreign investment is equal to
A. Total amount of foreign investment in a country
B. Investment by foreigners during a particular year
C. Investment by local resident in a foreign country
D. Investment by the foreigners in this country minus investment by residents of this country in foreign countries during a given time period

23. "Disposable income" does not include
A. Business transfer payments
B. Social security benefits
C. Corporate dividends
D. Personal income taxes

24. Circular flow of income in a two sector model implies
A. Payments from households to firms and back again
B. Payments from firms to firms
C. Payments from households to households
D. Payments from households to firms

25. Which one of the following is not a Transfer Payment in National Income accounting ?
A. Interest on government bonds held by Indians
B. Drought relief payments
C. Unemployment benefits
D. Salaries of supreme court judges

26. Which one of the following is a transfer income?
A. The salary of an M.P.
B. Company dividends to share holders
C. Rents from house property
D. Unemployment allowance

27. The smallest national income accounting aggregate is usually
A. PI B. GNP
C. DPI D. NI

28. Which one of the following is not included in calculating gross national product of an economy?
A. Wages and salaries before tax
B. Depreciation allowances
C. Indirect taxes
D. Subsidies

29. For the study of the long term growth of the economy we use
A. Real GNP
B. Transfer payments
C. Per capita income
D. Disposable income

30. Interest on the national debt is included in
A. NNP B. GNP
C. Personal income D. National income

31. Double counting has the effect of
A. Underestimating national product
B. Overestimating national product
C. Distorting national product
D. Misleadig conclusions about national income

32 The Government sector's contribution to GNP is measured by
A. Government purchases of goods and services
B. Wages and salaries paid by the government
C. Inter-governmental surplus
D. The size of the government surplus

33. A certain part of corporate business income gets into the calculation of personal income. Which is that?
A. Government transfer payments
B. Social security payment made by firms
C. Dividends
D. None of the above

34. Depreciation means
A. Destruction of a plant in a fire accident
B. Loss of equipment over time due to wear and tear
C. Closure of the plant due to raw material problem
D. Closure of the plant due to lockout

35. Which of the following is not a method of estimating GNP?
A. The value added approach
B. Product approach
C. Income approach
D. The financial approach

36. Depreciation is the loss of value of
A. Capital assets
B. Stocks
C. Intermediate goods
D. Final goods

37. If value added at different stages are added, the total will
A. Equal the value of the final product
B. Underestimate the value of the final product
C. Overestimate the value of the final product
D. Misrepresent the value of the final product

38. GNP is Rs. 600 crores and NNP is Rs. 475 crores: therefore depreciation is
A. Rs. 100 B. Rs. 175
C. Rs. 50 D. Rs. 125

39. Which of the following is not true?
A. GNP – Depreciation = NNP
B. GNP = GDP + Net income from abroad
C. $NNP_{FC} = NNP_{MP}$ + Subsidies – Indirect taxes
D. GNP = NNP – Depreciation

40. NNP at market prices and NNP at factor costs will be equal when there is
A. No direct tax
B. No indirect tax
C. No subsidy
D. No indirect tax and no subsidy

41. Gross domestic product at factor cost plus net income from abroad minus capital consumption is equal to
A. Gross domestic product at market prices
B. Gross national product at factor cost
C. Net national product at market prices
D. Net national product at factor cost

42 In a closed economy model one of the sectors below is not to be considered which?
A. Households B. Firms
C. Government D. Foreign trade

43. National product at market prices is higher than national product at factor cost by the amount of
A. Subsidies
B. Indirect taxes
C. Indirect taxes plus subsidies
D. Indirect taxes minus subsidies

44. Net exports are negative when
A. Net investment is positive
B. Exports are exceeded by imports
C. Exports exceed private transfer to foreigners
D. Imports are exceeded by exports

45. The importants leakages in the circular flow of income are as follows except one which?
A. Saving
B. Imports
C. Government expenditure
D. Taxes

46. Which of the following formula could be used for calculating the per capita income of a country
A. $\frac{\text{Total family income}}{\text{Number of family members}}$
B. $\frac{\text{National Income}}{\text{Total Population}}$
C. $\frac{\text{Total income of various industries}}{\text{Total number of industrial workers}}$
D. $\frac{\text{Total government revenue}}{\text{Total population}}$

47. Per capita income increases when
A. GNP increases at the same rate as population
B. GNP increases slower than population
C. GNP increases faster than population
D. GNP does not increase and population increases slowly

48. This year, if national product at factor cost is Rs. 600 crores, indirect taxes Rs. 200 crores and subsidies Rs. 75 crores, national product at market prices is
A. Rs. 750 crores B. Rs. 725 crores
C. Rs. 500 crores D. Rs. 250 crores

49. Which one of the following measures does not include final goods and services
A. GNP
B. NNP
C. Disposable income
D. National income

50. Imports into a country generate income for
A. Domestic manufacturers
B. Government
C. Trader
D. Foreign products

51. A household in a two sector model is essentially a unit of
A. Consumption B. Production
C. Investment D. None of the above

52 When less output is consumed than produced during a given income period, national wealth
A. Increases
B. Remains unchanged as there is no relationship
C. Decreases
D. May increase or decrease

53. National product at current prices is higher than national product at constant prices during a period of
A. Rising prices B. Falling prices
C. Stable prices D. Changing costs

54. Which of the following items are not included in estimating National income or $NNP_{FC?}$
A. Salary income of artists, dancers and singers
B. Income of smugglers
C. Payments to form workers in food grains
D. Payments of bank interest for capital borrowed

55. The purchase of a new home is included in the GNP as a part of
A. Capital consumption allowance
B. Personal consumption expenditures
C. Investment
D. Personal saving

56. Expenditure on defence is an item of
A. Private investment
B. Public investment
C. Private consumption
D. Public consumption

57. GNP at market prices is Rs. 200 : net property income from abroad is Rs. 20 and indirect taxes are Rs. 20 and subsidies are Rs. 10; GDP factor cost is—
A. Rs. 160 B. Rs. 180
C. Rs. 200 D. Rs. 250

58. National income at constant prices can be found out by

A. $\dfrac{\text{Price index number}}{\text{N.I. at current prices}} \times 100$

B. $\dfrac{\text{N.I. at current prices}}{\text{Price index number}} \times 100$

C. $\dfrac{\text{N.I. at market prices}}{\text{Price index number}} \times 100$

D. $\dfrac{\text{N.I. at factor cost}}{\text{Price index number}} \times 100$

59. A ''refrigerator'' operating in a chemist's shop is an example of
A. Intermediate good
B. Final good
C. Producer's good
D. Consumer's good

60. The workers were classified as "Productive and unproductive" on the productivity context by
A. David Ricardo B. J.S. Mill
C. Adam Smith D. Karl Marx

61. Consider the following statements—
The study of national income accounts is of great importance because it
1. reveals the change in the size and composition of the national product.
2. provides us with information about the distribution of national income in the society among various groups.
3. reveals the manner in which national expenditure is divided between consumption and investment.

A. 1 and 2 are correct
B. 2 and 3 are correct
C. 1 and 3 are correct
D. 1, 2 and 3 are correct

62 Consider the following types of income :
1. Personal income
2. Private income
3. Disposable income
4. National income

The correct sequence in *descending* order of their magnitude is
A. 4, 2, 1, 3 B. 4, 2, 3, 1
C. 2, 4, 3, 1 D. 2, 4, 1, 3

63. The national income of a country for a given period is equal to the
A. total value of goods and services produced by the nationals
B. sum of total consumption and investment expenditure
C. sum of personal income of all individuals
D. money value of final goods and services produced

64. Gross National Savings measure the
A. amount of GNP not consumed
B. excess of income over consumption plus the net taxes

C. sum of retained earnings and depreciation amounts
D. excess of disposable income over consumption

65. Social accounting system in India is classified into which one of the following sets of sectors?
A. Enterprise, households and government
B. Assets, liabilities and debt position
C. Public sector, private sector and joint sector
D. Income, production and expenditure

66. For a closed economy having no foreign trade which one of the following is correct?
A. GDP = GNP B. GDP > GNP
C. GDP < GNP D. GDP $\gtrless$ GNP

67. Which of the following statements explain the difference between NNP(Net National Product) and NMP (Net Material Product)?
1. NNP includes services.
2. NNP excludes services.
3. NMP includes services.
4. NMP excludes services.

Select the correct answer using the codes given below.

Codes :
A. 1 and 4 B. 2 and 4
C. 1 and 3 D. 2 and 3

68. Assertion (A) : Y = C + I (where Y = National Income, C = Consumption, I = Investment)
Reason (R) : C and I are important determinants of national income
A. Both A and R are true and R is not correct explanation of A.
B. Both A and R are true but R is not correct explanation of A.
C. A is true but R is false.
D. A is false but R is true.

69. The GNP gap is the gap between
A. GNP and NNP
B. GNP and depreciation
C. GNP and GDP
D. Potential and actual GNP

70. Which one of the following is the most important limitation of the per capita GNP as the Measure of welfare?
A. The increase in the per capita GNP may not always raise the real standard of living of the masses
B. This measure does not take into account the increase in the population
C. This measure does not take into account the employment aspect
D. This measure does not take into consideration government expenditure

71. The 'Hindu rate of growth'
A. refers to growth of Hindu population
B. is the term used by Raj Krishna to represent the nature of the growth of the Indian economy at around 3.5 per cent per year
C. is the term used by Amartya Sen to represent the nature of the growth of the Indian economy at around 3.5 per cent per year
D. is the term used by V.K.R.V. Rao to decide the nature of the growth of the Indian economy at around 4 per cent

72 Value added means value of
A. output at market prices
B. goods and services less depreciation
C. goods and services less cost of intermediate goods and services
D. output at factor cost

73. Which one of the following statements is correct?
A. Gross national product includes depreciation
B. Value added includes transfer payments
C. Personal income includes undistributed profits
D. Disposable income includes personal taxes

74. The GNP at market prices for 1983-84 was Rs. 192866 crores and the GNP at factor cost was Rs. 171201 crores. The government paid at Rs. 5107 crores as subsidies during the year. The amount of indirect taxes in crores for the year should work out to
A. Rs. 31879 B. Rs. 26772
C. Rs. 21665 D. Rs. 16558

75. GNP exceeds NNP by
A. the amount of total taxes
B. government expenditure
C. transfer payments
D. the difference between gross investment and net investment

76. National Income total reveals :
1. Production side of the economy
2. Distribution side of the economy
3. Expenditure side of the economy

Choose your answer from

A. 1 only B. 2 only
C. 1, 2 and 3 D. 3 only

77. National Income is the—
A. Net National Product at market price
B. Net National Product at factor cost
C. Net Domestic Product at market price
D. Net Domestic Product at factor cost

78. Improvement in the standard of living in a country are best reflected by increase in—
A. GNP at constant prices
B. Per capita income at constant prices
C. Per capita income at current prices
D. GNP at current prices

79. Which one of the following statements is not correct?
A. Compensation of employees *plus* operating surplus *plus* mixed income of self employed *plus* consumption of fixed capital equals GDP at factor cost
B. GDP at factor cost *plus* indirect taxes *minus* subsidies equals GDP at market prices
C. GDP at factor cost *minus* depreciation equals net domestic product at factor cost
D. GDP at market prices *minus* net receipts from abroad *plus* indirect taxes *minus* subsidies equals net national product

80. Which one of the following constitutes government consumption expenditure?
A. Compensation to employees *plus* net purchases from business enterprises
B. Wages and salaries of government employees
C. Government expenditure on defence
D. Transfer payments to individuals and state governments

81. Which one of the following denotes net state domestic product?
A. Money value of final goods and services produced within the boundary of a state *plus* net inflow of income from outside the state
B. Money value of final goods and services produced within the boundary of a state *minus* depreciation *plus* indirect taxes of fixed assets
C. Money value of final goods and service produced with the boundary of a state *minus* depreciation *plus* indirect taxes
D. Money value of goods and services consumed within the boundary of a state *plus* net income from outside the state

82 Which one of the following equals the value of output of a factory?
A. Total value added by factors
B. Value of all non-factor inputs *plus* indirect taxes
C. Payments for factor inputs and non factor inputs
D. Payments for non-factor inputs *plus* wages

83. Which one of the following items is excluded in calculating national income?
A. Service of a rental TV set
B. Rs. 10,000/- won in a lottery
C. Rented residences
D. Paid house work

84. In which of the following sectors, is product method used in computing national income in India?
1. Agriculture and allied activities
2. Mining and quarrying
3. Registered manufacturing
4. Unregistered manufacturing

Select the correct answer using the codes given below :

Codes :

A. 2, 3 and 4 B. 1, 2 and 3
C. 1 and 3 D. 1, 3 and 4

85. Consider the following statements regarding saving different sectors of an economy :
1. Savings of private corporate sector constitute undistributed profits
2. Saving of private corporate sector constitute excess of income over expenditure
3. Saving of government sector constitute excess of revenue receipts over revenue expenditure
4. Saving of government sector constitute excess of total revenue over total expenditure

Of the above statements

A. 2 and 3 are correct
B. 3 and 4 are correct

C. 1 and 3 are correct
D. 2 and 4 are correct

86. The implicit national income deflator represents a price index number of the type known as
A. Laspeyre's index number
B. Fisher's index number
C. Paasche's index number
D. Marshall-Edgeworth's index number

87. Human Development Index (HDI) is a composite index of
A. Life expectancy, education and per capita income
B. National income, size of population and the general price level
C. National income, per capita income and per capita consumption
D. Physical resources, monetary resources and population size

88. Which one of the following agencies in India is responsible for computation of national income?
A. N.C.A.E.R. B. C.S.O.
C. N.S.S D. R.B.I

89. Which one of the following represents the saving in the private corporate sector?
A. Total profits of a company
B. Undistributed profits
C. Excess of income over expenditure
D. Dividends paid to share holders

90. An economy's Net National Income is $ 20,000 million, indirect taxes are $ 2000 million, subsidies are $ 1000 million and its population 150 million. What will be the National Income at factor cost?
A. $ 21000 million B. $ 19000 million
C. $ 23000 million D. $ 22000 million

91. Given are the following informations about an economy :
Consumption = Rs. 5000
Gross Investment = Rs. 1000
Govt. Purchases = Rs. 800
Exports = Rs. 600
Imports = Rs. 800
Depreciation = Rs. 250
What is the GNP at market prices?
A. Rs. 7100 B. Rs. 6850
C. Rs. 6600 D. Rs. 6350

92 Consider the following statements :
1. In an economy where productive capacities are increasing, gross private domestic investment exceed depreciation
2. Interest on the public debt is not a part of national income but is included in personal income
3. Disinvestment occurs when inventories expand
4. The purchase of new home is included in the GNP as a part of investment

Which of the above statements are correct?
A. 1 and 2 B. 3 and 4
C. 1, 2 and 4 D. 1, 3 and 4

93. **Assertion (A) :** Per capita income figures are poor tools of ordinal ranking of countries with respect to the real well being.
Reason (R) : A good portion of the national income in poor countries is unreported.
Codes :
A. Both A and R are true and R is the correct explanation of A
B. Both A and R are true but R is *Not* a correct explanation of A
C. A is true but R is false
D. A is false but R is true

94. Estimate gross national product from the data given below :

Value of consumer goods and services	Rs. 20000 crore
Value of capital goods and services	Rs. 10000 crore
Value of exports	Rs. 4000 crore
Value of Imports	Rs. 2600 crore
Total depreciation	Rs. 1600 crore

Which one of the following is correct—
A. Rs. 31400 crore B. Rs. 38600 crore
C. Rs. 29800 crore D. Rs. 29200 crore

95. National income at market price is equal to
A. the sum of wages, interest, rent and profits earned
B. national income at factor cost *plus* indirect taxes *minus* subsidies
C. the sum of earnings of all the factors *plus* direct tax *minus* subsidies
D. total quantity of goods and services produced

96. Which of the following prevents national income from falling to zero when gross investment falls to zero—
A. consumption B. multiplier
C. accelerator D. none of the above

97. In India, the main source of national income is
A. Primary sector B. Secondary sector
C. Tertiary sector D. Foreign sector

98. The GNP of an economy at market prices is Rs.1000. Net factor income from abroad is Rs. 1000, indirect taxes Rs. 800, subsidies Rs. 500 and depreciation Rs.1000. What is the GDP at market prices?
A. Rs. 9000 B. Rs. 7700
C. Rs. 11000 D. Rs. 13300

99. Consider the following statements—
1. At the time of rising prices, NNP at current prices is less than NNP at constant prices.
2. At the time of rising prices, NNP at current prices is higher than NNP at constant prices.
3. NNP at current prices and NNP at constant prices are always same irrespective of changes in prices.
4. NNP at current prices is equal to NNP at constant prices at the time of stable prices.

Which of these statements are correct?
A. 1and 2 B. 1 and 3
C. 2 and 3 D. 2 and 4

100. Match List-I with List-II and select the correct answer using the codes given below the lists:

List-I	**List-II**
(a) Capital consumption allowances	1. Are included in estimating National Income at factor cost
(b) Subsidies	2. Are excluded while calculating disposable income
(c) Personal taxes	3. Are excluded in calculating personal outlays
(d) Personal savings	4. Are excluded in estimating Net National Product

Codes :	*(a)*	*(b)*	*(c)*	*(d)*
A	3	1	2	4
B.	4	1	2	3
C.	3	2	1	4
D.	4	2	1	3

ANSWERS

1	**2**	**3**	**4**	**5**	**6**	**7**	**8**	**9**	**10**
D	D	D	B	D	C	D	A	B	B
11	**12**	**13**	**14**	**15**	**16**	**17**	**18**	**19**	**20**
D	D	D	B	C	C	D	D	A	D
21	**22**	**23**	**24**	**25**	**26**	**27**	**28**	**29**	**30**
A	D	D	A	D	D	C	B	A	C
31	**32**	**33**	**34**	**35**	**36**	**37**	**38**	**39**	**40**
B	A	C	B	D	A	A	D	D	D
41	**42**	**43**	**44**	**45**	**46**	**47**	**48**	**49**	**50**
D	D	D	D	C	B	C	B	C	D
51	**52**	**53**	**54**	**55**	**56**	**57**	**58**	**59**	**60**
A	A	A	B	C	D	B	B	C	C
61	**62**	**63**	**64**	**65**	**66**	**67**	**68**	**69**	**70**
D	A	D	C	D	A	A	A	D	A
71	**72**	**73**	**74**	**75**	**76**	**77**	**78**	**79**	**80**
B	C	A	D	D	C	B	B	A	A
81	**82**	**83**	**84**	**85**	**86**	**87**	**88**	**89**	**90**
C	C	B	B	D	A	A	B	B	B
91	**92**	**93**	**94**	**95**	**96**	**97**	**98**	**99**	**100**
C	A	A	A	B	A	C	A	D	B

DEVELOPMENT AND PLANNING

Growth and Development—Concepts

The term 'economy growth' refers to increase over time in a country's real output of goods and services—or more appropriately product per capita. The term 'economic development', in contrast, is more comprehensive. It implies progressive changes in the socio-economic structure of a country. Viewed in this way, economic development involves a steady decline in agriculture's share in GNP and a corresponding increase in the share of industries, trade, banking, construction and services. This transformation in economic structure is invariably accompanied by a shift in the occupational structure of the labour force and an improvement in its skill and productivity.

In fact, the terms 'development' and 'growth' have nothing to do with the type of economy. The distinction between the two relates to the nature and causes of change. *Schumpeter* makes the distinction clearer when defines development as a discontinuous and spontaneous change in the stationary state which forever alters and displaces the equilibrium state previously existing; while growth is a gradual and steady change in the long run which comes about by a gradual increase in the rate of savings and population. This view of Schumpeter has been widely accepted and elaborataed by the majority of economists. According to Kindleberger, "Economic growth means more output, while economic development implies both more output and changes in the technical and institutional arrangements by which it is produced and distributed. Growth may well invole not only more output derived from greater amounts of inputs but also greater efficiency, *i.e.*, an increase in output per unit of input. Development goes beyond this to imply changes in the composition of output and in the allocation of inputs by sectors."

Friedman defines growth as an expansion of the system in one or more dimensions without a change in its structure, and development as an innovative process leading to the structural transformation of social systems.

Thus, *economic growth* is related to a quantitative sustained increase in the country's per capita output or income accompanied by expansion in its labour force, consumption, capital and volume of trade. On the other hand, economic development is a wider term. It is related to qualitative change in economic wants, goods incentives and institutions.

Characteristics of an under Developed Country

1. General Poverty
2. Agriculture, the Main Occupation
3. A Dualistic Economy
4. Underdeveloped Natural Resources
5. Demographic Features
6. Unemployment and Disguised Unemployment
7. Economic Backwardness
8. Lack of Enterprise and Initiative
9. Insufficient capital Equipment
10. Technological Backwardness
11. Foreign Trade Orientation

Vicious Circles of Poverty

There are circular relationships known as the 'vicious circles of poverty' that tend to perpetuate the low level of development in LDCs. *Nurkse* explains the idea in these words : "It implies a circular constellation of forces tending to act and react upon one another in such a way as to keep a poor country in a state of poverty. For example, a poor man may not have enough to eat; being under fed, his health may be weak; being Physically weak, his working capacity is low, which means that he is poor, which in turn means that he will not have enough to eat; and so on. A situation of this sort relating to a country as a whole, can be summed up in the trite proposition . "A country is poor because it is poor."

The basic vicious circle stems from the fact that in LDCs total productivity is low due to deficiency of capital, market in perfections, economic backward-ness and under development. However, the vicious circles operate both on the demand side and the supply side, The *demand side* of the vicious circles is that the low level of real income leads to a low level of demand which, in turn, leads to a low rate of investment and hence back to deficiency of capital, low productivity and low income. This is shown in Figure 1. Low productivity is reflected in low real income. The low level of real income means low saving. The low level of saving leads to a low investment and to deficiency of capital. The deficiency of capital, in turn, leads to a low level of productivity and back to low income. Thus, the vicious circle is complete from the supply side. It is depicted in Figure 2. The low level of real income, reflecting low investment and capital deficiency is a common feature of both the vicious circles.

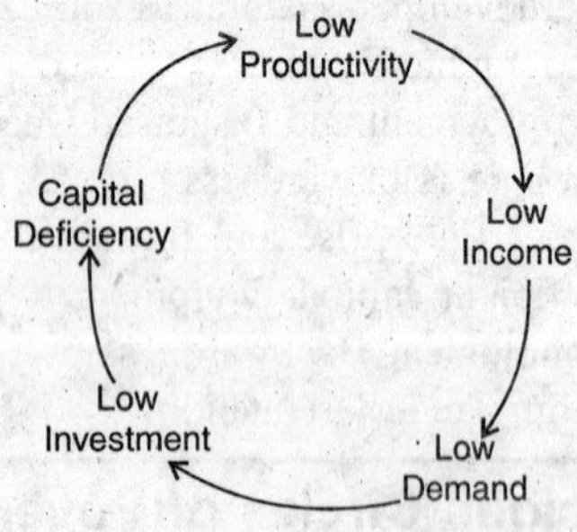

Fig. 1

A third vicious circle envelops underdeveloped human and natural resources. Development of natural resources is dependent upon the productive capacity of the people in the country. If the people are backward and illiterate, lack in technical skill, knowledge and entrepreneurial activity, the natural resources will tend to remain unutilized, underutilized or even misutilized. On the other hand, people are economically backward in a country due

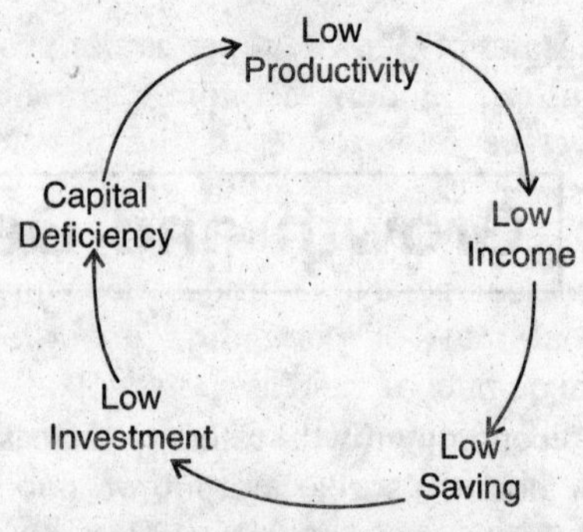

Fig. 2

to under developed natural resources. Under-developed natural resources are, therefore, both a consequence and cause of the backward people.

Modern Economic Growth

Professor Simon Kuznets defined modern economic growth "as a long-term rise in capacity to supply increasingly diverse economic goods to its population, this growing capacity based on advancing technology and the institutional and ideological adjustments that it demands." This definition has three components :

First, the economic growth of a nation is identified by the sustained increase in the supply of goods.

Second, advancing technology is the permissive factor in economic growth which determines the growth of capacity in supplying diverse goods to the population.

Third, for an efficient and wide use of technology and its development, institutional and ideological adjustments must be made to effect the proper use of innovations generated by advancing stock of human knowledge For example, modern technology is incompatible with the rural mode of life, the large and extended family pattern, family enterprise and illiteracy.

Characteristics

Professor Simon Kuznets has pointed out six characteristics of modern economic growth that have emerged in the analysis based on national product and its components, population, labour force and the like.

1. High Rates of Growth of per capita Product and Population: Modern economic growth, as revealed by the experience of the developed countries since the late eighteenth or early nineteenth century, is characterised by the high rates of increase in per capita product accompanied by substantial rates of population growth. The extremely high rate of increase are at least five times as high for population and at least ten times as high for production as observed in the post. Professor Kuznets has shown that the rates of population growth of thirteen countries, excluding France, have been high in modern times than in pre-modern times. Leaving France with a population increase of 2.5 percent per decade, the rates of population growth range from 6-7 percent for UK, Sweden, Italy and the former USSR, to 8 percent for Switzerland and Norway, to 10-14 percent for Denmark, Germany, Japan and the Netherlands and to 19-20 percent for Canada, the United States and Australia".

The decade rates of growth in per capita product of all these developed countries, except Australia with 8 percent decade rate, are above 13 percent. They range from 13.5-14.1 percent for the Netherlands and the UK, to 16-15 percent for Switzerland, the United States, France, Germany, Canada, Italy, Norway and Denmark and to above 26 percent for Japan, 28.3 percent for Sweden and 43.9 percent for the former USSR.

2. The Rise in Productivity : Modern economic growth is characterised by a rise in the rate of per capita product due to improvements in the quality of inputs which led to greater efficiency or rise in productivity per unit of input. This is traceable either to an increase in input of resources of labour and capital or to an increase in efficiency or to both. Increase in efficiency implies greater output per unit of input.

The growth of national product has been due to the enormous addition to population which led to a large increase in labour force. The increase in national product in trun led to a considerable increase in capital accumulation and hence in reproducible capital. The proportions of labour force to total population showed an upward trend for all developed countries except Switzerland, Italy and Australia.

Economic growth of developed nations has been accompanied by the long-term decline in number of man-hours per capita. This tendency reflects increase in efficiency or productivity. Leaving the exceptional case of Italy where man-hours per capita declined by 7.5 percent per decade, the overall decline in man-hours per capita per decade for all other developed countries ranged between 4.1 percent for Great Britain, 2 to 2.4 percent for Belgium. Germany, Denmark, Sweden, Norway and the United States, 2.8 to 3.5 percent for Canada, France and Australia and 4.1 percent for Switzerland and 4.5 percent for the Netherlands.

3. High Rate of Structural Transformation: Structural transformations in modern economic growth include the shift away from agriculture to non-agricultural activities and from industry to services, a change in the scale of productive unit and a related shift from personal enterprises to impersonal organization of economic firms, with a corresponding change in the occupational status of labour.

4. Urbanisation: Modern economic growth has been characterised by the movement of an increasing proportion of the population in developed countries from rural areas to urban areas. This is urbanisation. Urbanisation is largely a product of industrialisation. The economies of scale arising from non-agricultural pursuits as a result of technological changes led to the movement of a large proportion of labour and population from the rural to the urban area. As the technical means of transportation, communication and organisation grew more effective, there was the spread of increasing optimum scale units. All these processes affected the grouping of population by social and economic status and transformed the basic pattern of life. The effects of urbanisation on modern economic growth of developed nations led to the decline in birth-rate and the shift toward the small family. It brought people together from different rural areas who initiated and learnt from each other and from those already living in towns. It facilitated the development of impersonal relations of modern life and also taught cooperation. Above all, it created conditions for the intense intellectual activity associated with modern civilisation and there by created favourable conditions for the increase in knowledge.

Theories of Economic Development

A. The Classical Theory of Economic Development

The main features of classical economic theory are:

1. Laissez-Faire Policy: The classical economists believe in the existence of and automatic free market and perfectly competitive economy which is free from any government interference. It is the "invisible hand" which maximises the national income.

2. Capital Accumulation, the Key to Progress: All classicists regard capital accumulation as the key to economic progress. They, therfore, lay emphasis on larger savings. Only capitalists and landlords are capable of saving, according to them. The working class is incapable of saving because it gets wages equal to the subsistence level.

3. Profits, the Incentive to Investment: According to the classicists, profits induce investment. The larger the profits, the greater the capital accumulation and investment.

4. Tendency of Profits to Decline: Profits do not increase continuously. They tend to decline when competition increases for larger capital accumulation among capitalists. The reason, according to Smith, is increase in wages due to competition among capitalists whereas, according to Ricardo, when wages and rent rise with the increase in the price of corn, profits decline.

5. Stationary State: All classical economists visualize the stationary state as the end of the process of capital accumulation. When once profits start declining, this process continues till profits become zero, population and capital accumulation stop increasing and the wage rate reaches the subsistence level. According to Smith, it is the scarcity of natural resources that finally stops growth and leads the economy to the stationany state.

In broad outline, the classical theory of economic development may be stated thus: Suppose an expected increase in profits brings about an increase in investment which adds to the existing stock of capital and to the steady flow of improved techniques. This increase in capital accumulation raises the wage fund. As a result wages rise. Higher wages induce an accelerated population growth which causes the demand for food to rise. Food production is raised by employing additional labour and capital. But diminishing returns to land bring about a rise in labour cost. Consequently, the price of corn goes up and in turn rents increase, wages rise, there by reducing profits. Reduction in profits implies reduction in investment, retarded technological progress, diminution of wages fund and slowing down of population growth and capital accumulation. When this happens, capital accumulation ceases, population becomes constant and the stationary state sets in.

Criticisms

The classical theory of development has been criticised due to following reasons :

1. Ignores Middle Class
2. Neglects Public Sector
3. Less Importance to Technology
4. Wrong Notions about Wages and Profits
5. Unrealistic Growth Process

B. The Marxian Theory of Economic Development

Marx contributed to the theory of economic development in three respects, namely, in broad respect of providing an economic interpretation of history, in the narrower respect of specifying the motivating forces of capitalist development, and in the final respect of suggesting an alternative path of planned economic development.

Marx uses his theory of *surplus value* as the economic basis of the 'class struggle' under capitalism and it is on the basis of his theory of surplus value that he builds the superstructure of his analysis of economic development. The surplus value, believes Marx, arises because labour, which is the absolute and ultimate source of all economic or exchange value, produces more economic value than the cost of labour itself as measured by the supply price of labour or, the subsistence wage that barely maintains the labour force intact. Exploitation does exist since workers fail to receive the whole of the value of the output. The difference between the value of total output and the supply price of labour represents the surplus value which is expropriated by the capitalists, who are the owners of non-human instruments of production, capital equipment and land. It is the ownership to these instruments of production that enables the capitalists to extract surplus value from labour by forcing them to work longer hours and receive subsistence wage and thus grab a disproportionately large slice of the national cake for themselves. The theory of surplus value thus, implies that there is an antagonism between the share of wages and profits. More profits are clearly at the expense of workers since their magnitude is determined directly by the magnitude of surplus value that capitalists extract from labour.

In the Words of Peterson :

"The notion of surplus value is crucial to the Marxian theory of economic development; surplus value is the source of all profit and thus the amount of surplus value that can expropriated by the capitalistic class will determine the relative share of profit in the income total".

According to Marx, it is surplus value that leads to capital accumulation.The capitalist's main motive is to increase the surplus value which goes to swell his profits.

To explain the origin of profit and to analyse the relation between wages and profits, Marx separates capital into *Constant capital* and *Variable capital*. Capital invested in stocks or raw materials or equipment which directly assists the productivity of labour, Marx calls *constant capital* (C). Capital devoted to the purchase of labour power in the form of wages or direct subsistence, he terms *variable capital* (V). The Surplus value is denoted by (S). So the total value of product = $c+v+s$

In order to analyse the nature of capitalist accumulation, Marx establishes certain relationships between c, v and s. The ratio of constant capital to total capital $\left(\frac{c}{c+v}\right)$ is termed as the *organic composition of capital*. The ratio of surplus value (S) to the variable capital (V) has been termed the rate of exploitation by Marx.

$$\text{Rate of Exploitation} = \frac{S}{V}$$

According to Marx the rate of profit is not dependent solely on the rate of exploitation. The rate of profit can change even though the rate of exploitation remains constant, if a change occurs in the organic composition of capital. The influence of technical progress is to alter the organic composition of capital, generally in the direction of raising the ratio of constant to total capital. Hence the tendency of industrial progress is to lower the rate of profit-even though there is no decrease in the rate of exploitation.

One of the consequences of capital accumulation is the concentration of capital in gigantic enterprises. Competition among capitalists forces them to cheapen their products. This can be done by introducing labour saving machines which increase labour productivity. Those capitalists who are unable to replace labour by machines are 'squeezed out' and their enterprises are taken over by big capitalists. Capital accumulation and concentration involve increase in constant capital and decline in variable capital. The rapid growth of constant capital as compared with variable capital leads to a relative decrease in the demand for labour. This process of supplanting labour by machines creates an *industrial reserve army* which increase as capitalism develops. The larger the industrial reserve army, the worse are the conditions of the employed workers, since the capitalist can dismiss dissatisfied and troublesome workers, being able to replace them from the ranks of the reserve army. Capitalists are also able to cut down wages to a semi-starvation level and appropriate more and more surplus value. This is the law of the increasing misery of the masses under capitalism. This is shown in Figure 3 where the labour force is taken on the horizontal axis and the wage rate on the vertical axis. D is the demand curve for labour and S is the supply curve of labour.

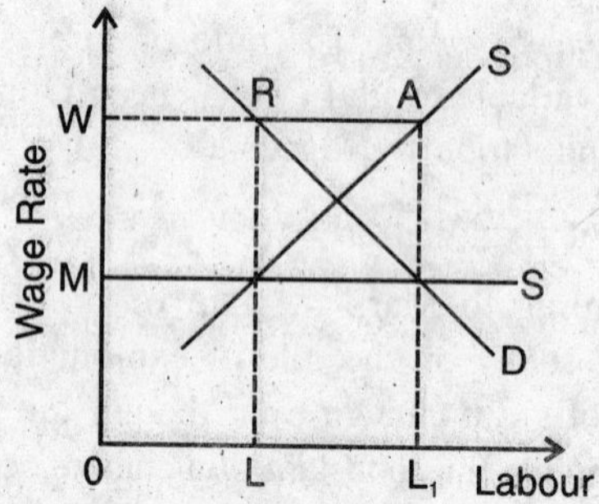

Fig. 3

At the wage rate W, there is an increase in the industrial reserve army equal to RA (LL_1). As the industrial reserve army expands, capitalists start adopting labour-saving machines and reduce the wage rate to minimum subsistence level OM in order to have more surplus value.

But when the capitalist is replacing the workers by machines, he is killing the goose that laid the golden eggs. There is a continual reduction of the surplus value. Marx believes that technological progress tends to increase the organic composition of capial. Since the rate of profit is inversely related to the organic composition of capital the former tends to decline with accumulation. Marx explained this tendency of falling rate of profit in terms of the following equation :

The rate of profit is equal to the ratio of total surplus value (S) to the total capital (C+V).

Thus, $P = \dfrac{S}{C+V}$

where P stands for the rate of profit.

Now $P = \dfrac{S}{C+V}$ ...(*i*)

Multiplying both the numerator and the denominator by V we get

$$P = \frac{S \times V}{V(C+V)}$$

$$= \frac{S}{V} \times \frac{V}{(C+V)} \quad ...(ii)$$

Here, $\dfrac{S}{V}$ is the rate of exploitation and $\dfrac{V}{C+V}$ is the ratio of variable capital to total capital. $\dfrac{V}{C+V}$ can also be expressed as :

$$\frac{V}{C+V} = \left(1 - \frac{C}{C+V}\right) \quad ...(iii)$$

Substituting (*iii*) in (*ii*)

$$P = \frac{S}{V}\left(1 - \frac{C}{C+V}\right)$$

Now given the rate of exploitation $\left(\dfrac{S}{V}\right)$, the rate of profit is related inversely with the organic composition of capital $\left(\dfrac{C}{C+V}\right)$.

The greater the $\dfrac{C}{C+V}$, the lesser will be the rate of profit and *vice versa.* As greater accumulation and technology results in a more capital-intensive productive process or as there is an increase in the capital-output ratio, the rate of profit tends to decline. From this follows the Marxian conclusion about the inevitable eventual, collapse of the capitalist economic superstructure. Summing up the Marxian views about the collapse of capitalism, *W.C. Peterson* remarks,"The process of capital accumulation and growth leads inevitably to a severe economic crisis. This crisis is the result of both the "falling rate of profit", which must sooner or later adversely affect capital accumulation itself and second, over-production because of an insufficiency of aggregate demand. The latter stems from the progressive decline in the relative share of wage income in the output total. Marx thought the capitalist system would be increasingly wrecked by crises of greater and greater severity until finally it would collapse amidst an uprising of the working class that would usher in the era of communism."

Criticisms

Marx's theory of capitalist development has been accepted by his followers as a gospel truth while it has been severely criticised by his opponents for the following reasons :

1. Surplus Value Unrealistic
2. Technological Progress Helpful in Increasing Employment.
3. Falling Tendency of Profits not Correct
4. Marx could not Understand Flexibility in Capitalism
5. Static Analysis

Conclusion

Despite these weaknesses, some to the Marxian tools pertaining to his theory of economic development have ever since become part and parcel of the theory of economic growth. Technological progress and innovations are the main stay of any theory of economic development. Similarly capital accumulation is the fundamental idea behind economic growth. Profits are still regarded as both the hallmark of capitalist development and its Achilles'heal. Marx showed that economic development does not follow a smooth course but comes about in "fit and starts." Business cycles are inevitable. He pointed output that a state of under-consumption was the main cause of depression and that for stable growth a proper balance between investment and consumption was essential. He also indicated that too low or too high wages in relation to total output can adversely affect investment and thus stifle economic growth.

C. The Schumpeterian Theory

Schumpeter assumes a perfectly competitive economy which is in stationary equilibrium. In such a stationary state, there is perfect competitive equilibrium : no profits, no interest rates, no savings, no investments and no involuntary unemployment. This equilibrium is characterised by what Schumpeter terms the "*circular flow*" which continues to repeat itself in the same manner year after year, similar to the circulation of the blood in an animal organism. In the circular flow, the same products are produced every in the same manner.

According to *Schumpeter*, "development is spontaneous and discontinuous change in the channels of the *circular flow*, disturbance of equilibrium, which for ever alters and displaces the equilibrium state previously existing". These 'spontaneous and discontinuous' changes in economic life are not forced upon it from without but arise by its own initiative from within the economy and appear in the sphere of industrial and commercial life. Development consists in the carrying out of new combinations for which possibilities exist in the stationary state. New combinations come about in the form of innovations. An innovation may consist of :

1. the introduction of a new product;
2. the introduction of a new method of production;
3. the opening up of a new market;
4. the conquest of a new source of supply of raw materials or semi-manufactured goods; and
5. the carrying out of the new organisation of any industry like the creation of a monopoly.

According to Schumpeter, it is the introduction of a new product and the continual improvements in the existing ones that lead to development. Schumpeter assigns the role of an innovator not to the capitalist but to the *entrepreneur*. The entrepreneur is not a man of ordinary managerial ability, but one who introduces something entirely new. He does not provide funds but directs their use. To perform his economic function, the entrepreneur requires two things: *First,* the existences of technical knowledge in order to produce new products, second, the power of disposal over the factors of production in the form of credit. According to Schumpeter, reservoir of untapped technical knowledge exists which he can make use of. Therefore, credit is essential for development to start.

Schumpeter's model starts with the breaking up the circular flow with an innovation in the form of a new product by an entrepreneur for the purpose of earning profits. In order to break the circular flow, the innovating entrepreneurs are financed by *bank-credit* expansion. Since investment in innovations is risky, they must pay interest on it. Once the new innovation becomes successful and profitable, other entrepreneurs follow it in ''Swarm-like clusters''. Innovations in one field may induce other innovations in related fields. The emergence of a motor car industry may, in turn stimulate a wave of new investments in the construction of highways, rubber tyres and petroleum products, etc. But the spread of an innovation is never cent percent. Since investment is assumed to be financed by creation of bank-credit, it increases money incomes and prices and helps to create a cumulative expansion throughout the economy. With the increase in the purchasing power of the consumers, the demand for the products of the old industries increases in relation to supply. Prices rise, profits increase and old industries expand by borrowing from the banks it induces a secondary wave of credit inflation which is super-imposed on the primary wave of innovation. Over-optimism and speculation add further to the boom. After a period of gestation the new products start appearing in the market displacing the old products and enforcing a process of liquidation, re-adjustment and absorption. The demand for the old products is decreased. Their prices fall. The old firms contract output and some are even forced to run into liquidation. As the innovators start repaying bank loans out of profits, the quantity of money is decreased and prices tend to fall. Profits decline. Uncertainty and risks increase, the impulse for innovatoin is reduced and eventually comes to an end. Depression ensues.

Schumpeter believes in the existence of the Kondratief long-wave of upswings and downswings in economic activity. Each long-wave upswing is brought about by an innovation in the form of a new product which leads to further innovations in the methods of production, new forms of business organisation, new sources of supply of raw materials and intermediate products and new markets. Thus, there is abundance of goods available for the masses. Once the upswing ends, the long-wave downswing begins and the painful process of readjustment to the "point of previous neighbourhood of equilibrium" starts. Ultimately the natural forces of recovery bring about a revival. Once again equilibrium is restored. Then some enterprising entrepreneurs begin with a new set of innovations, others follow and a new boom begins. Schumpeter describes this process of capitalist development as one of "creative destruction", where in the old economic structures of society are being continually destroyed and the new structures are being continually created in their place. Schumpeter's cyclical process of economic development is illustrated in Figure 4, where the secondary wave is super imposed on the primary wave of innovation with over-optimism and speculation, development proceeds more rapidly in the prosperity phase. When recession starts, the cycle continues downward below the equilibrium level to the depression phase.

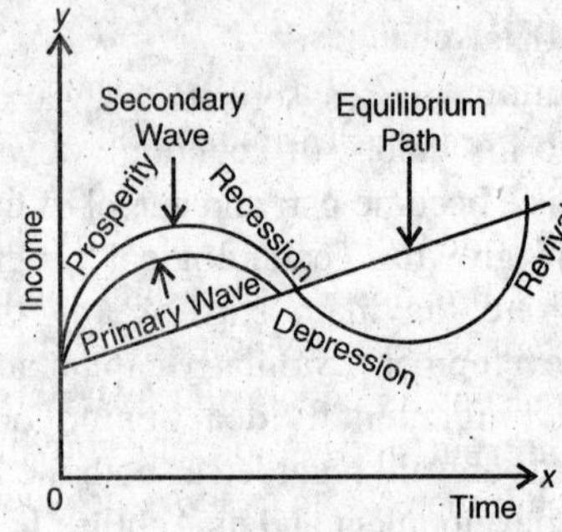

Fig. 4

Ultimately; another innovation brings about revival. Thus,, entrepreneurs are the key figures in the Schumpeterian analysis. They bring about economic development in spontaneous and discontinuous manner. "Can capitalism survive? No, I do not think it can", wrote Schumpeter, as his final appraisal of the future of capitalism. To him, the very success of capitalism "undermines the social institutions which protect it, and "inevitably"creates conditions in which it will not be able to live and which strongly point to socialism as the heir-apparent".

According to Schumpeter, capitalism can maintain itself only so long as entrepreneurs behave like knights and pioneers. But such daring innovators are being destroyed by the capitalist system itself which rests on a rational attitude. This enquiring, sceptical and rational attitude permeates the entire capitalist society. As a result, three forces are discernible, that are the beginning of the creeping death of capitalism. They are :

1. the decadence of the entrepreneurial function;
2. the disintegration of the bourgeois family;
3. the destruction of institutional framework of the capitalist society.

Criticisms of the Theory

Schumpeter's theory has certain weaknesses.

1. Schumpeter's analysis of the process of transition from capitalism to socialism is not correct.
2. Schumpeter gives too much importance to bank-credit in his theory.
3. The downswings and the upswings are not essential for economic development.
4. Economic development not only depends

on innovations but also on many economic and social changes.

5. Schumpeter's contention that cyclical changes are due to innovations is also not correct.

To conclude with *Meier and Baldwin*, "Schumpeter's broad socio-economic analysis of capitalist process is generally admired. Yet few seem prepared to accept its conclusions. His arguments are stimulating but not completely convincing..... Although Schumpeter's analysis is provocative, it seems one-sided and over-emphasized".

Schumpeter's Analysis and Underdeveloped Countries

The applicability of Schumpeter's theory to underdeveloped countries is limited for the following reasons :

1. Different Socio-Economic Order
2. Lack of Entrepreneurship
3. Not Applicable to Socialist Countries
4. Not Applicable to Mixed Economies
5. Neglects Population Growth
6. Neglects External Effects
7. Neglects Savings
8. Neglects Consumption
9. Unsatisfactory Explanation of Inflationary Forces.

Conclusion

All the same, Schumpeter's theory underlines the importance of inflationary financing and innovations as the main factors in economic development. Inflationary financing is one of the potent methods which every underdeveloped country tries to use at one time or another. His analysis is relevant to underdeveloped countries from the standpoint of long range increase in productivity and absorption of surplus labour in gainful employment as a result of innovations. Though it purports to analyse the problems of western capitalism, "it can certainly give clues to problems that may arise in underdeveloped countries, once the process of industrialisation begins, as well as provide a lesson for avoiding waste and extra hardships that attend an un-planned uncoordinated development."

Theory of Growth

A. HARROD-DOMAR MODEL

R.F. Harrod and E. Domar have made a distinct contribution in evolving dynamic models to suit the changing conditions of an economy. Both these models are very similar, and to answer the questions posed by the post-Keynesians. In fact, one can say that Domar's model is the American version of Harrod's model, or alternatively Harrod's model is the English Version of Domar's model. Both these models stress on the conditions which are very essential for achieving and maintaining steady growth.

Like classical economists, Harrod and Domar assign a crucial role to capital accumulation and investment in the process of growth. Investment plays a double role. On the one hand, investment (through the operation of multiplier) generates income and, on the other hand, it increases the productive capacity, by enlarging the capital stock. In other words, investment affects the level of income as well as production. The effect of investment on income is known as '*Multiplier Effect*' and that on production is known as '*Productivity Effect*' or '*Sigma Effect*'. In mathematics sigma is denoted by σ. Multiplier effect is the Keynesian tool and productivity effect is the classical tool. *Harrod-Domar* analysis takes into consideration both the tool. In short, Harrod-Domar model strikes a synthesis between the multiplier effect and productivity effect. The simultaneous operation of these two effects is an essential condition for dynamic equilibrium.

Assumptions : The main assumptions of Harrod-Domar model are as follow:

1. An inital full-employment level of income has already been achieved.

2. There is no government interference in the functioning of the economy, *i.e.*, the policy of *laissez-faire* prevails.

3. The model is based on the principle of "closed economy", there are no exogenous factors or forces

influencing the growth variables of the economy. In short, government restrictions on trade and the complications caused by international trade are ruled out.

4. There are no lags in adjustment, *i.e.*, the Economic Variables, such as saving, investment, income and expenditure adjust themselves in the same period of time. To make it cleaver, it can be stated that any change in saving brings about corresponding changes in the level of investment in the same period of time. All these variables relate to the same period of time.

5. The average propensity to save (APS) and the marginal propensity to save (MPS) are equal to each other. In other words, APS = MPS or $\frac{S}{Y} = \frac{\Delta S}{\Delta Y}$; *i.e.*, the absolute change in saving is equal to the relative change in saving.

6. Propensity to save and "Capital Coefficient" (*i.e.*, capital-output ratio) are constant. The law of constant returns operates in the economy because the capital-output ratio is assumed constant.

7. Income, investment and saving are all defined in the net sense, *i.e.*, they are over and above depreciation. In other words, depreciation charges are not included in these variables.

8. Saving and investment are equal in ex-ante as well as in ex-post sense, *i.e.*, there is accounting as well as functional equality between saving and investment. The equality can be expressed as

So = Io (accounting equality)

Sc = Ic (functional equality)

So and Io are observed saving and observed investments respectively.

Sc and Ic are expected saving and expected investments respectively.

Domar's Model

Domar's analysis shows that he is very emphatic about the necessity of viewing growth from the demand as well as the supply side. He is of the opinion that pre-Keynesian analysis emphasised the capacity (supply side) of the problem and the Keynesian approach concentrated on the demand side alone. But his emphasis on the dual character of the investment process makes the approach to the equilibrium rate of growth from investment (capital) point of view more promising. Investment increases the productive capacity and also generate income, thus providing us both sides of the equation, the solution of which yields the required rate of growth.

The following symbols are used in Domar's model:

Y_α = level of net national income or level of effective demand at full-employment (demand side)

Y_s = level of productive capacity or supply at full-employment level (supply side)

K = real capital

I = net investment, which results in the increase of real capital *i.e.*, Δk

α = marginal propensity to save, which is the reciprocal of multiplier *i.e.*, $\frac{1}{\text{multiplier}}$

σ = sigma or productivity of capital or of net investment

It would be interesting to explain Domar's model with the help of equations used by K.K. Kurihara and the above notations are used in the equations, given below:

$$Y_\alpha = \frac{I}{\alpha} \quad \text{...(1)}$$

This equation explains (*a*) that the level of effective demand (Y_α) is directly related to the level of investment (I). Any increase in the level of investment will directly increase the level of effective demand and *vice versa.* (b) The effective demand is inversely related to the MPS(α). Any increase in MPS(α) will decrease the level of effective demand and *vice versa.* This is the demand side.

$$Y_s = \sigma K \quad \text{...(2)}$$

This equation explains that the supply of output (Y_s) at full employment depends upon two factors, *i.e.*, productive capacity of the capital (σ) and the amount of the capital (K). Any increase or decrease in any of these two factors will raise or reduce the supply of output. If the productivity of capital (σ) increase, that will favourably affect the supply. Similar will be the effect of real capital on supply of output . This is the supply side.

For equilibrium, the demand and supply should be equal. Therefore,

$$Y_\alpha = Y_s$$

$$\frac{I}{\alpha} = \sigma K$$

or $$I = \alpha\sigma K \qquad ...(3)$$

This is the condition for "*achieving the steady growth*". Now we proceed further to explain the condition for maintaining the steady growth. For that we have to add increments to the demand as well as to the supply equations discussed above. The demand and supply equations in the incremental form can be written as follows :

$$\Delta Y_\alpha = \frac{\Delta I}{\alpha} \qquad ...(4)$$

Increments have been shown in the level of effective demand and investment, because they are variables, but increment has not been shown in 'α' because it remains constant on the basis of the assumptions employed.

$$\Delta Y_s = \sigma \Delta k \qquad ...(5)$$

Change in the supply of output (ΔY_s) can take place because of change in real capital (ΔK), as the productivity of capital (σ) remains constant. Moreover the change in real capital is equal to net investment. Therefore

$$\Delta K = I$$

substituting the value of ΔK in (S) we get

$$\Delta Y_s = \sigma I \qquad ...(6)$$

The equality between (4) and (6) will provide us the conditions for the maintenance of steady growth. Equating these two equations (4) and (6) we get,

$$\Delta Y_\alpha = \Delta Y_s \text{ or } \frac{\Delta I}{\alpha} = \sigma I \text{ or } \frac{\Delta I}{I} = \sigma\alpha$$

This shows that the rate of growth of net investment $\left(\frac{\Delta I}{I}\right)$ should be equal to the product of marginal propensity to save (α) and the productivity of capital (σ). This equality must be ensured to maintain the stable and steady growth of the economy. In Kurihara's words, "It is an increase in productive capacity (ΔY_s) due to increment of real capital (ΔK), which must be matched by an equal increase in effective demand (ΔY_α) due to an increment of investment (ΔI), if a growing economy with an expanding stock of capital is to maintain continuous full employment." So, the essential and sufficient condition for maintaining the steady growth of an expanding economy is

$$\frac{\Delta I}{I} = \sigma\alpha$$

or $$\frac{\Delta Y}{Y} = \sigma\alpha \left(\because \frac{\Delta Y}{Y} \text{ is also equal to } \frac{\Delta I}{I}\right)$$

In the words of Meier and Baldwin, "The answer to the problem of what rate of growth is necessary to maintain a continuous state of full employment is that, investment and real income must grow at a constant annual percentage rate (or compound interest rate) equal to the product of the propensity to save and the average productivity of investment (the inverse of capital coefficient or accelerator)."

Domar's equation of steady growth rate can be explained with the help of a numerical example. Suppose the productivity of capital (σ) is 25% and the marginal propensity to save 'α' is 12% then, the growth rate of investment $\left(\frac{\Delta I}{I}\right)$ would be equal to σα, *i.e.*,

$$\frac{25}{100} \times \frac{12}{100} = \frac{3}{100} = 3\%$$

Thus, income or investment must grow at the annual rate of 3% if full employment growth rate or steady growth rate is to be maintained. In brief, "Full employment requires that investment and income grow at a constant annual relative rate equal to the product of propensity to save and the average productivity of investment".

Path of Disequilibrium : If the investment grows at a constant percentage rate σα, the productive capacity, although continually growing, will be fully used. On the other hand, if investment grows at a greater or lesser rate than the σα, then the following two types of situations will arise:

(*i*) when $\frac{\Delta I}{I}$ or $\frac{\Delta Y}{Y} > \sigma\alpha$

(*ii*) when $\frac{\Delta I}{I}$ or $\frac{\Delta Y}{Y} < \sigma\alpha$

Under the first situation, inflation will appear in economy because as higher rate of income it will provide greater purchasing power to the people. This will result in the expansion of demand, leading to the emergence of inflation as the productive capacity ($\sigma\alpha$) will not cope with the increased level of income or investment. *The first situation will, therefore, create inflation in economy.*

The second situation, under which growth rate of income or investment $\left(\frac{\Delta Y}{Y} \text{ or } \frac{\Delta I}{I}\right)$, is lagging behind the productive capacity, will result in overproduction. The lesser growth rate of income will put a constraint on the purchasing power of the people, thus reducing the level of demand and resulting in the overproduction of goods,

So, under these situations, the maintenance of stable and steady growth is impossible and economy will be under the constant strain of either inflation or overproduction and unemployment.

Harrod's Model

So far, we have discussed Domar's model, which explains the conditions for achieving and maintaining the dynamic equilibrium Harrod's growth model also concentrates on these issues. Broadly speaking *R.F. Harrod*, has raised three sets of issues:

1. How can steady growth rate be achieved in the model with a fixed capital-output ratio (capital-coefficient) and the fixed saving income ratio (propensity to save)?

2. How can the steady growth rate be maintained? or What are the conditions for maintaining the stable growth?

3. How do natural factors put a ceiling on the growth rate of the economy?

In order to discuss these three sets of issues, Harrod has explained three growth rates. The growth rates are:

(a) Actual growth rate

(b) Warranted growth rate

(c) Natural growth rate

Now we discuss these growth rates sepaprately.

***(a)* Actual Growth Rate:** It is the growth rate, which is determined by the actual amount of saving and investment in the country. In other words, it can be defined as the ratio of change in income (ΔY) to the total income (Y) in the given period. If actual growth rate is denoted by G, then $G = \frac{\Delta Y}{Y}$.

According to Harrod, actual growth rate G is determined by two factors, saving-income ratio and capital-output ratio, which remain fixed in a given period. The relationship between the actual growth rate and its determinants, can be expressed in the form of an equation given below:

$$GC = S \quad \text{...(1)}$$

Where G is the actual rate of growth, C represents the capital output ratio or $\frac{\Delta K}{\Delta Y}$, S refers to the saving-income ratio (S/Y). This equation explains the simple truism that saving and investment (in the ex-post sense) are equal to each other. This simple truism is explained below:

$$\text{Since} \quad G = \frac{\Delta Y}{Y} \text{ and } C = \frac{\Delta K}{\Delta Y}$$

$$\text{or } C = \frac{I}{\Delta Y} \; [\because \Delta K = I] \text{ and } S = \frac{S}{Y}$$

Substituting the values of G, C and S in equation (1), we get

$$\frac{\Delta Y}{Y} \times \frac{I}{\Delta Y} = \frac{S}{Y}$$

$$\frac{I}{Y} = \frac{S}{Y} \text{ or } I = S$$

Thus,, equation (1) explains that the condition for achieving the steady growth rate or dynamic equilibrium is that ex-post saving must be equal to ex-post investment. In other words, there should be accounting equality between saving and investment, if dynamic equilibrium is to be achieved.

***(b)* Warranted Growth Rate:** Warranted growth rate refers to that growth rate of the economy, when it is working at full capacity by making full and optimum use of machine and manpower. It is also known as *"Full capacity growth rate" or "Full-employment growth rate"* or *"Potential growth rate"*. This growth rate is denoted by G_w and has been defined by *Meier and Baldwin* in these words, "G_w is interpreted as the rate of income growth required for the full *utilisation* of a growing stock of capital, so that entrepreneurs will be satisfied with the amount of investment actually made".

Warranted growth rate (G_w) is determined by two factors-

(*i*) capital-output ratio

(*ii*) saving-income ratio

The relationship between the warranted growth rate and its determinants can be expressed in the form of an equation $G_w C_r = S$

Where G_w refers to warranted growth rate, C_r denotes the amount of capital required to maintain the warranted growth rate or the growth rate of output. S is the saving-income ratio.

Having discussed the two rates of growth (*i.e.*, actual and warranted), we now discuss the issue, as how to achieve the steady growth. According to Harrod, the economy can achieve stable growth if $G = G_w$ and $C = C_r$, *i.e.*, actual growth rate must be equal to the warranted growth rate. In other words, growth rate of income must be equal to the growth rate of output. Secondly, the capital-output ratio needed to achieve G, must be equal to the required capital-output to maintain G_w, given the saving coefficient (S). This amounts to saying that actual investment (ex-post investment) must be equal to the expected investment (ex-ante investment), if an economy were to achieve the objectives of stable growth.

Instability of Growth: We have just discussed that the stable growth of economy requires an equality between G and G_w on the one hand, and C and C_r on the other. But the reader should bear in mind that this type of equality is rarely found in the economy, however planned and regulated it may be. Harrod analyses this situation, when these conditions are not satisfied.

(*i*) when $G > G_w$ then $C < C_r$

(*ii*) when $G < G_w$ then $C > C_r$

Proof : $GC = S$ and $G_w C_r = S$

$$\text{or} \quad GC = \frac{S}{C} \text{ or } G_w = \frac{S}{C_r}$$

if $G > G_w$

$$\frac{S}{C} > \frac{S}{C_r} \quad \text{or} \quad \frac{1}{C} > \frac{1}{C_r}$$

cross multiplying

$$C_r > C \quad \text{or} \quad C < C_r$$

Similarly it can be proved

When $G_w < G$ then $C > C_r$

We take up the discussion of the first situation when G is greater than G_w. Under this situation the growth rate of income being greater than the growth rate of output, the demand for output (because of higher level of income) will exceed the supply of output (because of lower level of output) and the economy will experience a chronic inflation. It can be explained in another way too when $C < C_r$. Under this situation the actual amount of capital falls short of the required amount of capital. This will lead to deficiency of capital, which in turn would adversely affect the volume of goods to be produced. Fall in the level of output will result in the scarcity of goods and hence inflation and the growth of economy under inflation can never be stable.

If, on the other hand, G is less than G_w, then the growth rate of income will be less than the growth rate of output. Under this situation there would be more goods for sale, but the income would not be sufficient to purchase those goods. In Keynesian terminology we can say that there would be deficiency of demand and the economy will face the problem of chronic deflation. This situation can also be explained when C is greater than C_r. Under this situation, the actual amount of capital is more than the required amount of capital for investment. When the capital amount available is more, it would dampen the marginal efficiency of capital and lead to *chronic depression* and unemployment. Thus, growth of the economy under the situation of chronic depression can never be stable.

On the basis of the above discussion, we can conclude that stable growth or steady-state growth can occur only when $G = G_w$. Any deviation of G from G_w will result in cumulative departure from the path of steady growth. In other words, the economy will be in a state of instability when G and G_w are not equal to each other. The equilibrium between G and G_w is called *steady-state equilibrium* or *knife-edge equilibrium.*

Harrod also states that deviations of G from G_w are unstable. If G departs from G_w then it will depart farther and farther from it, as departure from the path of steady growth is self-sustaining. It feeds on itself. In contrast, if G is less than G_w, then desired saving would exceed desired investment, the entreprenuers will be pessimistic about the future and they will keep the level of output below G_w, and this would further retard the growth.

(c) **Natural Growth Rate:** If it is assumed that propensity to save or capital-output ratio does not change,what will stop income from shooting up or down without limit? Harrod points out that generally there is an upper limit to the expansion of output, which is determined by natural conditions such as size of the labour force, natural resources, capital equipment and state of technical knowledge. This limit is called *"full employment ceiling"*. This upper limit may change as the factors of production grow, and technological progress takes place. Harrod calls the growth in this upper full employment ceiling the natural growth rate. In other words, it is the maximum growth rate, which an economy can achieve with its available natural resources. Natural growth rate is denoted by G_n.

Interactions of G, G_w, G_n: While discussing the interaction of three rates if growth, Harrod points out that in the years after recession G may be higher than G_n for a considerable period of time, but it will not continue to rise indefinitely. In other words, the process of expansion cannot go on indefinitely, as it is limited by the availability of natural factors. The ceiling fixed by labour and natural resources prevent further rise. This has been, shown in Figure 5. The economy cannot remain at the ceiling level; it has either to rise or fall.

When G touches G_n,G_w cannot lag behind, but will tend to catch up with it. Since the rate of rise

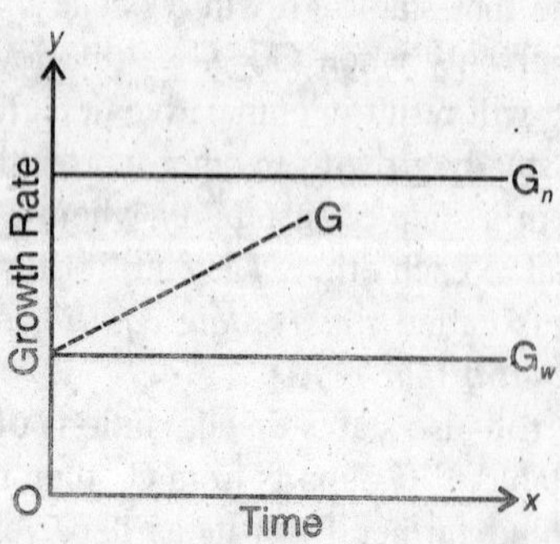

Fig. 5

of G cannot be maintained, G_n will exceed G and then the downtrend starts. The downtrend will result in over-production, which in turn will lead to a cumulative downswing. The economy will face the problem of secular stagnation and chronic unemployment. This has been shown in the diagram. But this down trend cannot continue undefinitely. The reason is that the lower limit of depression is set by the minimum consumption level. As the consumption level cannot fall below a minimum level, so the fixed capital too cannot fall though working capital may be reduced. In this way gross investment cannot be negative. This position, combined with the investor's expectation for the bright future generated by the actual resources position, will gradually set the wheels of recovery in motion. The economy will once again be in the upward phase. This has been shown in Figure 6.

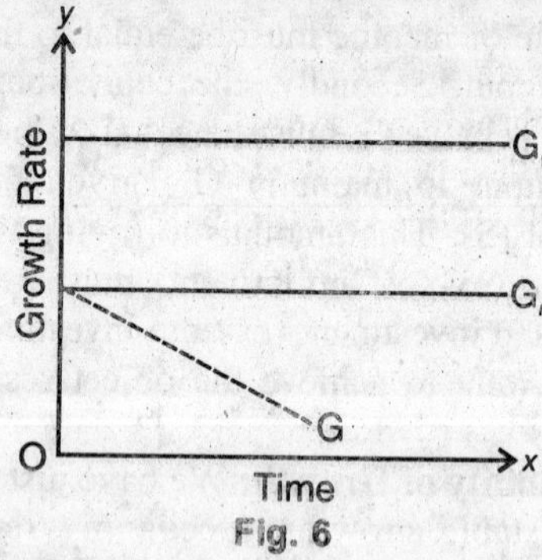

Fig. 6

Analysis of Business Cycle: From the study of this model, it is quite evident, that the process of growth of a capitalist economy is never steady because of its inherent characteristics. There cannot be a steady growth of income and output in such an economy. There will always be ups and downs in a capitalist economy. Therefore cyclical fluctuations are implicit in the phenomena of growth in such an economy.

Business cycles are not free to vary without limit. In upward direction G_n provides a limit in the form of a "full employment ceiling" beyond which real income cannot expand in short period because of the shortage of labour and capital. In the downward direction there is also a limit set by a floor of autonomous investment, because gross investments cannot be negative.

Main Point: The main points of the Harrod-Domar analysis can be summarised as below:

1. Investment is the centre of the problem of steady and stable growth, because investment plays a double role; on the one hand, it generates income and on the other, it increases the productive capacity of the economy.

2. The increased capacity can result in greater output or greater unemployment depending on the behaviour of income.

3. Conditions can be stated for the behaviour of income, that will allow full employment to be maintained over time. These conditions specify the growth rates, which can ensure full employment of labour and full utilisation of capital stock.

4. These conditions, however, designate only a steady line of growth for the economy. The actual growth rate may differ from the warranted rate of growth. If the actual growth rate is greater than the warranted rate of growth, the economy will experience chronic inflation. If the actual growth rate is less than the warranted growth rate, the economy will slide towards chronic deflation.

5. The business cycles are viewed as the deviation from the path of steady growth. These deviations become self-aggravating and self-cumulating, but are limited in the upward trend by the "full employment ceiling" and in the downward direction by the floor of autonomous investment and consumption.

B. The Solow Model (Long-run Growth Model)

Prof R.M. Solow builds his model as an alternative to the Harrod-Domar model. The latter model is at best a knife-edge balance built on three key parameters *viz*, the saving ratio, the capital-output ratio and the rate of increase of the labour force. If the magnitudes of these parameters change the consequence would be gloomy, perpetuating growing unemployment or chronic inflation. The balance itself is poised on the equality between G_w and G_n which is very delicate. If once the fixed proportions assumption of the Harrod-Domar model is abandoned, the knife-edge balance also disappears with it.

Assumptions: Solow builds his model around the following assumptions:

(a) One composite commodity is produced.

(b) Output is measured in net terms.

(c) Constant returns to scale.

(d) There are only two factors-labour and capital. They are paid according to their marginal physical productivities. They are substitutable for each other.

(e) Prices and wages are flexible.

(f) There is not only perpetual full employment of labour but also full employment of the available stock of capital.

(g) There is neutral technical progress.

On the basis of these assumptions Solow's model shows that there would be a tendency for capital-labour ratio to adjust itself through time in the direction of equilibrium ratio. If the initial ratio of capital to labour is more, capital and output would grow more slowly than labour force and *vice versa.*

Solow takes output as a whole, the only commodity, in the economy. Its annual rate of production is designated as Y_t which represents the real income of the community, part of it is consumed and the rest is saved and invested. That which is saved is a constant S, and the rate of saving is $S.Y_t$. K_t is the stock of capital. Thus, net investment is the rate of increase of this stock of capital *i.e.*, $\frac{dk}{dt}$ or K. So the basic identity is K = S.Y ...(1)

Since output is produced with capital and labour, technological possibilities are represented by the production function

$$Y = F(K, L) \qquad ...(2)$$

That shows constant returns to scale. Inserting equation (2) in (1), we have

$$K = S\,F(K, L) \qquad ...(3)$$

In equation (3), L represents total employment. Since population is growing exogenously, the labour force increases at a constant relative rate *n*. Thus,

$$L_t = Loe^{et} \qquad ...(4)$$

N = Harrod's natural rate of growth in the absence of technological change

L_t = the available supply of labour at time *(t)* the right hand side of equation (4) shows the compound rate of the growth of labour force from period O to period T. Equation (4) can be regarded as a supply curve of labour. By inserting equation (4) in (3), Solow gives the basic equation

$$K = SF(K, Loe^{nt}) \quad ...(5)$$

Solow regards this basic equation as determining the time path of capital accumulation, K, that must be followed if all available labour is to be fully employed. It also provides the time profile for capital stock. Once the time paths of capial stock and of the labour force are known, the corresponding time path of real output can be computed from the production function.

Possible Growth Patterns. In order to find out if there is always a capital accumulation path consistent with any rate of growth of the labour force towards steady state, Solow introduced his fundamental equation.

$$R = SF(r, 1) - nr \quad ...(6)$$

In this equation r is the ratio of capital to labour (K/L), n is the relative rate of change of the labour force (L/L). The function SF (r, 1) represents output per worker as a function of capital per worker. In other words, it is the total product curve as varying amounts r of capital are employed with are unit of labour. Equation (6) states that the rate of change of capital-output ratio ($\bar{r}$) is the difference of two terms, one representing the increment of capital SF (r, 1) and the other increment of labour (nr).

The possible growth patterns based on his fundamental equation (6) are illustrated in the Figure 7.

The straight line passing through the origin is the function nr. The other curve represents the function SF (r, 1). It is so drawn as to show diminishing marginal productivity of capital. At the point of intersection of the two curves nr = SF (r, 1) and $\bar{r} = 0$, then $r = \bar{r}$. When $\bar{r} = 0$ the capital-labour ratio is a constant and the capital stock must expand at the same rate as the b labour force, *i.e.*, n. Once the capital-labour ratio $\bar{r}$ is established. It will be maintained, and capital and labour will grow in proportion. Assuming constant returns to scale real output will also grow at the some relative and output per hand of labour force will be constant. At r' then will be the balanced growth equilibrium.

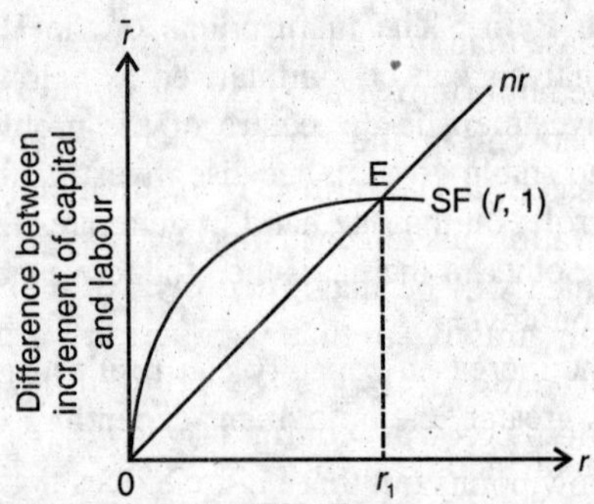

Fig. 7

What will be the behaviour of the capital-labour ratio if then is a divergence between $\bar{r}$ and R. If r lies to the right of $\bar{r}$ or $r > \bar{r}$, $nr <$ SF (r, 1), and R will decrease toward $\bar{r}$. On the contrary, if r lies to the left of $\bar{r}$ or $r < \bar{r}$, $nr <$ SF (r, 1), and r will increase toward $\bar{r}$. Thus, the equilibrium value $\bar{r}$ is stable.

But the strong stability shown in the above figure is not inevitable. It depends on the slope of the productivity curve SF (r, 1). In figure 8 the productivity curve SF (r,1) intersects the curve nr at three points r_1, r_2, r_3. But r_1 and r_3 are stable equilibrium positions because the total productivity curve SF (r, 1) is above nr but at r_2 it is below nr. Therefore, r_2 is an unstable equilibrium position.

"Depending on the initial observed capital-labour ratio, the system will develop either to balanced growth at capital-labour ratio r_1 or r_3. In either case labour supply, capital stock and real output will asymptomatically expand *at raten,* but around r_1 there is less capital than around r_3, hence the level of output per head will be lower in the

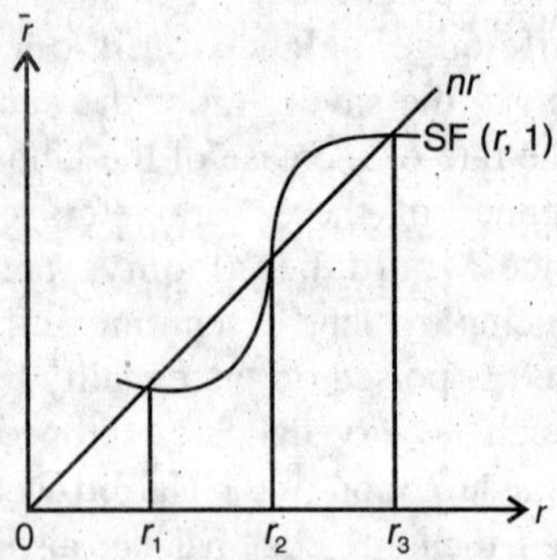

Fig. 8

former case than in the latter. The relevant balanced growth equilibrium is at r_1 for an initial ratio any where between O and r_2, it is at r_3 for any initial ratio greater r_2. The ratio r_2 is itself an equilibrium growth ratio, but an unstable one, any accidental disturbance will be magnified over time. Figure 8 has been drawn so that production is possible without capital; hence the origin is not an equilibrium 'growth' configuration."

Solow points out that Figure 8 does not exhaust all possibilities, the shows two more possibilities, as shown in Figure 9. The curve NR depicts the equilibrium growth path where the warranted and natural rates of growth are equal. The curve $S_1F'(r, 1)$ which is above nr represents a highly productive system in which capital and income increase more rapidly than the labour supply. In this system, which is of perpetual full employment, income and saving increase so much that the capital-labour ratio increases limitlessly. On the other hand, the curve $S_2F''(r, 1)$ depicts a highly unproductive system in which the full employment path leads to ever diminishing per capita income.

However, aggregate income rises in this system because net investment is always positive and the labour supply is increasing. It is to be noted that both the systems have diminishing marginal productivity throughout.

Professor Solow concludes his model thus: "When production takes place under the usual neo-classical conditions of variable proportions and constant returns to scale, no simple opposition between natural and warranted rates of growth is possible. There may not be ...... any knife ...... edge. The system can adjust to any given rate of growth

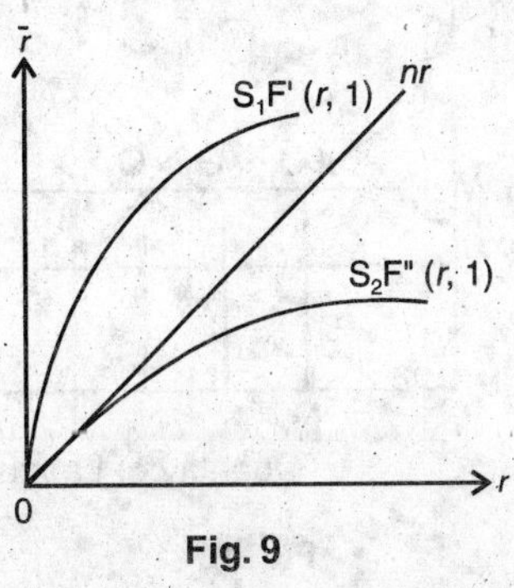

Fig. 9

of the labour force, and eventually approach a state of steady proportional expansion", *i.e.*,

$$\frac{\Delta K}{K} = \frac{\Delta L}{L} = \frac{\Delta Y}{Y}$$

Critical Appraisal

Solow is a pioneer in constructing a neo-classical model. The solow model is a major improvement over the Harrod-Domar model. This takes a continuous production function which has come to be known as the new-classical production in analysing the process of growth. The assumption of substitutability between labour and capital gives the growth process an adjustability and provides a touch of realism.

The aim of the Solow model "was to examine what might be called the fight-rope view of economic growth and to see where more flexible assumptions about production would lead to a simple model". Still the Solow model is weak in many respects.

1. The model takes up only the problem of balance between Harrod's G_w and G_n and leaves out the problem of balance between G and G_w.

2. There is the absence of an investment function in this model. If the investment function is introduced than the model would present all instabilities noticeable in the Harrodian model. *Prof. A. Sen* mentions in this connection that the assumption of substitutability between labour and capital does not seem to be a key difference between neo-classical and neo-Keynesian studies of growth and the main difference seems to lie in the investment function and the consequent failure to assign a major role to entrepreneurial expectations about the future.

3. The labour-augmenting technical progress on which the theory is based is a special case of Harrod-Domar neutral technical progress of the Cobb-Douglas production function which does not possess any empirical justification.

4. Flexibility of factor prices assumption of Solow may bring difficulties in the path towards steady growth.

5. The model is based on the unrealistic assumption of homogeneous and malleable capital. Capital goods are of aggregation.

6. The model leaves out the causative process of technical progress and treats the latter as an exgeneous factor in the growth process. Solow ignores the problem of inducing technical progress through learning, investment research and capital accumulation.

C. Lewis' Theory of Unlimited Supplies of Labour

Professor W. Arthur Lewis has developed a very systematic theory of Economic Development with Unlimited supplies of labour. Like the classical economists, he believes that in many under-developed countries an unlimited supply of labour is available at a subsistence wage. Economic development takes place when capital accumulates as a result of the withdrawal of surplus labour from the "subsistence" sector to the "capitalist" sector. Since the supply of labour is unlimited, new industries can be established or existing industries expanded without limit at the current wage by drawing upon labour from the subsistence sector. The main sources from which workers would be coming for employment at the subsistence wage as economic development proceeds are "the farmers, the casuals, the petty traders, women, in the household and population growth". But the capitalist sector also needs skilled workers. Lewis argues that skilled labour is only a "*quasi bottleneck*" a temporary bottleneck-which can be removed by providing training facilities to unskilled workers.

Capitalists aim at profit maximisation. It is they who save and automatically invest what they save. Since the marginal productivity of labour in the capitalist sector is higher than the capitalist wage, this results in capitalist surplus. This surplus is reinvested in new capital assets. Capital formation takes place and more people are employed from the subsistence sector. This process continues till the capital-labour ratio rises and the supply of labour becomes in-elastic and the surplus labour disappears. Thus, capital formation depends on the capitalist surplus. The Lewis theory can be explained with the help of the Figure 10. The horizontal axis measures the quantity of labour employed and the vertical axis, its wage and marginal product. OS represents average subsistence wage in the subsistence sector, and OW the capitalist wage. At OW wage in the capitalist sector, the supply of labour is unlimited, as shown by the horizontal supply curve of labour WW. In the beginning, when ON_1 labour is employed in the capitalist sector, its marginal productivity curve is $P_1 L_1$ and the total output of this sector is $OP_1 Q_1 N_1$. Out of this, workers are paid wages equal to the area $OW Q_1 N_1$. The remaining area $WP_1 Q_1$ shows surplus output. This is the capitalist surplus or total profit earned by the capitalist sector. When this surplus is reinvested, the curve of marginal productivity shifts upwards to P_2L_2. The capitalist surplus and employment are now larger than before being $WP_2 Q_2$ and ON_2 respectively. Further reinvestments raise the marginal productivity curve and the level of employment to $P_3 L_3$ and ON_3 and so on, till the entire surplus labour is absorbed in the capitalist sector. After this, the supply curve WW will slope from left to right upwards like an ordinary supply curve, and wages and employment will continue to rise with development.

Thus,, capital is formed out of profits earned by the capitalists. According to Lewis, if technical progress is capital-saving, it may be considered as an increment in capital, and if it is labour saving, it may be considered as an increment in the marginal productivity of labour. As such, he does not make any distinction between the growth of technical knowledge and the growth of productive capital and treats them as a "single phenomenon" with the

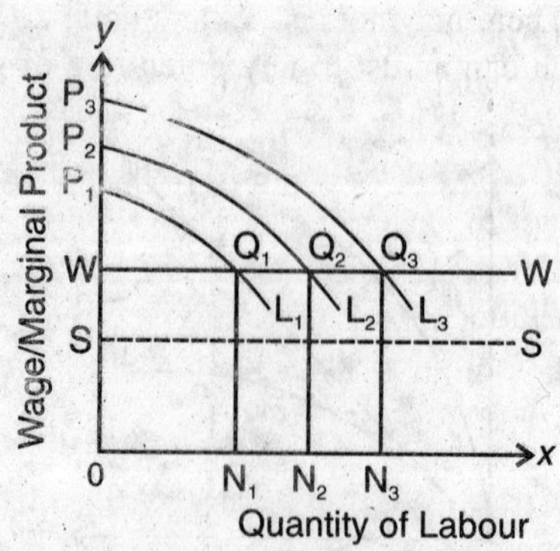

Fig. 10

result that technical progress tends to raise profits and increase employment in the capitalist sector.

"The central problem in the theory of economic development", according to Lewis, "is to understand the process by which a community which was previously saving and investing 4 or 5 percent of its national income or less converts itself into an economy where voluntary saving is running at about 12 to 15 percent of national income or more. This is the central problem because the central fact of economic development is rapid capital accumulation (including knowledge and skills with capital)". In underdeveloped countries with surplus labour, only 10 percent of the people with the largest income save who receive about 40 percent of the national income. The wage and salary classes hardly save 3 per cent of the national income. But the dominant classes consisting of landlords, traders, moneylenders, priests, princes are engaged in prodigal consumption rather than in productive investment. It is, therefore the state capitalist and indigenous private capitalist who create capital out of profits earned. "The indigenous private capitalist is bound up with the emergence of new opportunities, especially some thing that widens the market, associated with some new technique which greately increases the productivity of labour, and hence the capitalist surplus. The state capitalist, on the other hand, can accumulate capital even faster than the private capitalists, since he can use for this purpose not only the profits of the capitalist sector, but also what he can force or tax out of the subsistence sector". Thus,, once a capitalist sector has emerged it is only a matter of time before it become sizable. If the opportunities for using capital productivity increase rapidly, the surplus will also grow rapidly, and the capitalist class with it. But capital is created not only out of profits, it is also created out of *bank credit.* in an underdeveloped economy which has abundant idle resources and shortage of capital, credit creation has the same effect on capital formation as profits. It will raise output and employment. Credit financed capital formation, however, leads to inflationary rise in prices for some time. When the surplus labour is engaged in the capitalist sector and paid out of created money, prices rise because income increases while consumer-goods output remains constant. This is only a temporary phenomenon, for as soon as capital goods start producing consumption goods, prices start falling. In the words of Lewis, "Inflation for the purpose of capital formation is very different kettle of fish. It is self destructive. Prices begin to rise but are sooner or later overtaken by rising output, and may, in the last stage, end up lower than they were at the beginning".

The theory shows that "if unlimited supplies of labour are available at a constant real wage, and if any part of profits is reinvested in productive capacity, profits will grow continuously relatively to the national income". But the process of growth cannot go on indefinitely, if as a result of capital accumulation no surplus labour is left. It may also stop it, despite the existence of surplus labour, real wages rise so high as to reduce the capitalist profits to the level where they are all consumed and nothing is left for net investment.

A Critical Appraisal

The Lewis theory is applicable to overpopulated underdeveloped countries under certain set conditions. Its applicability is, therefore, circumscribed by its assumptions which are the bases of criticisms discussed below:

1. Wage Rate not constant in the capitalist sector
2. Not Applicable if Capital Accumulation is Labour Saving
3. Skilled Labour not a Temporary Bottleneck
4. Multiplier Process does not Operate in LDC
5. This is a one-sided theory because Lewis does not consider the possibility of progress in the agricultural sector.
6. Mobility of Labour not so Easy
7. *Schultz* does not agree that the marginal productivity of labour in overpopulated under-developed countries is zero or negligible. If it were so, the subsistence wage would also be zero.
8. Lewis assumes that when the surplus labour is withdrawn from the subsistence sector to the capitalist sector, the agricultural production remains unaffected in the subsistence sector. But the fact is that withdrawal of workers from the farms will reduce output.

9. It is not correct to say that only 10 per cent of the people with the largest income save. Infact, people with low incomes also save due to social reasons and even small farmers save for capital accumulation in underdeveloped countries.
10. Inflation not Self-Destructive.

Conclusion : Despite these limitations, the Lewis theory has the merit of explaining in a very clear cut way the process of development. This two sector theory has great analytical value. It explains how low capital formation takes place in underdeveloped countries which have plethora of labour and scarcity of capital. His study of the problems of credit inflation, population growth, technological progress, and international trade gives the theory a touch of realism.

D. Fei-Ranis Theory of Development

John Fei and **Gustav Ranis** in an article entitled "A Theory of Economic Development" analyse "the transition process through which an underdeveloped economy hopes to move from a condition of stagnation to one of self-sustained growth", Their theory is an improvement over Lewis's theory of Unlimited Supplies of Labour because Lewis failed to present a satisfactory analysis of the growth of the agricultural sector.

Fei-Ranis theory relates to an underdeveloped labour-surplus and resource-poor economy in which the vast majority of the population is engaged in agriculture amidst widespread unemployment and high rates of population growth. The agrarian economy is stagnant. People are engaged in traditional agricultural pursuits. Non-agricultural pursuits exist but they are characterised by a modest use of capital. There is also an active and dynamic industrial sector. Development consists of the re-allocation of surplus agricultural workers, whose contribution to output is zero or negligible, to the industrial sector where they become productive at a wage equal to the institutional wage equal to the institutional wage in agriculture.

Assumptions

In presenting their theory of economy development, Fei and Ranis make the following assumptions :

1. There is a dual economy divided into a traditional and stagnant agricultural sector and an active industrial sector.
2. The output of the agricultural sector is a function of land and labour alone.
3. There is no accumulation of capital in agriculture except in the form of land reclamation.
4. Land is fixed in supply.
5. Agricultural activity is characterised by constant returns to scale with labour as a variable factor.
6. It is assumed that the marginal productivity of labour becomes zero at some point. If population exceeds the quantity at which the marginal productivity of labour becomes zero, labour can be transferred to the industrial sector without loss in agricultural output.
7. The output of the industrial sector is a function of capital and labour alone. Land has no role as a factor of production.
8. Population growth is taken as an exogenous phenomenon.
9. The real wage in the industrial sector remains fixed and is equal to the initial level of real income in the agricultural sector. They call it the institutional wage.
10. Workers in either sector consume only agricultural products.

Given these assumptions, Fei and Ranis analyse the development of a labour-surplus economy into three phases.

In the first phase, the disguised unemployed workers, who are not adding to agricultural output, are transferred to the industrial sector at the constant institutional wage.

In the second phase, agricultural workers add to agricultural output but produce less than the institutional wage they get. Such workers are also shifted to the industrial sector. If the migration of workers to the industrial sector continues, a point is eventually reached when farm workers produce output equal to the institutional wage. This begins the third phase which marks the end to the take-off and the beginning of the self-sustained growth when farm workers produce more than the institutional wage they get. In this phase, the surplus labour is exhausted and the agricultural sector becomes commercialised.

Thus, Fei-Ranis model is an improvement over the Lewis model. The Lewis model ignores the development of the agricultural sector and concentrates exclusively on the industrial sector. The Fei-Ranis model shows the interaction between the two sectors in initiating and accelerating development. Moreover, its explanation of the Lewis turning point is more realistic. But the major merit of the theory is that it shows the importance of agricultural products in capital accumulation in underdeveloped countries.

Despite these merits, the model is not free from criticisms which are discussed below.

1. Fei and Ranis begin with the assumption that the supply of land is fixed during the development process. But in the long run, the amount of land is not fixed.

2. The model is based on the assumption of a constant institutional wage which is above the MPP during phases I and II of the development process. But there is no empirical evidence to support this assumption. In fact, in labour surplus underdeveloped countries, wages paid to the agricultural workers are much below their MPP.

3. The theory assumes that the institutional wage remains constant in the first two phases even when agricultural productivity increases. This is highly unrealistic because with a general rise in agricultural productivity, farm wages also tend to rise.

4. This model is based on the assumption of a closed economy where foreign trade does not exist. But this assumption is unrealistic because underdeveloped countries are not close but open economies which import agricultural commodities when shortages arise.

Conclusion

However, these limitations do not undermine the importance of the Fei-Ranis model for the economic development of labour surplus countries. It systematically analyses the development process from the take-off to self-sustained growth through the interaction of the agricultural and industrial sectors of an under developed economy.

E. Meade's Growth Model

Prof. J.E. Meade has presented a growth model which analysis the relationship between income growth and population growth in an economy. This model draws attention to the role of population growth, capital increase and technology in determining the increase of income per head. It also analyses the conditions necessary for stable growth of income per head, when population changes along with other determinants.

Assumptions

Meade constructs his model around the following assumptions :

1. There is a laissez-faire closed economy where there is perfect competition.
2. There are constant returns to scale.
3. Two commodities—consumption goods and capital goods—are produced in the economy.
4. Machines are the only form of capital in the economy.
5. All machines are assumed to be alike.
6. It is assumed that there is a constant money price of consumption goods.
7. There is full use of land and labour.
8. The ratio of labour to machinery can be changed both in the short and the long run. Meade calls this the assumption of perfect malleability of machinery.
9. It is further assumed that there is perfect substitutability in production between capital goods and consumption goods.

According to this model, net output produced in an economy depends upon four things :

(*i*) net stock of capital in the form of instruments of production (machines),

(*ii*) the labour force,

(*iii*) land and natural resources,

(*iv*) the state of technical knowledge,

These four factors may be expressed in the form of a production function as given below :

$$Y = F(K, L, N, T)$$

where Y = net national income or output
K = existing stock of machines
L = existing labour force
N = natural resources
T = state of technical knowledge

F. Leibenstein's Critical Minimum Effort Thesis

The Critical Minimum Effort Thesis was developed by *Harvey Leibenstein* in his book "Economic Backwardness and Economic Growth," 1957. This thesis supported the Theory of Balanced Growth and the Theory of 'Big Push'.

Prof. Harvey Leienstein has propounded his thesis of critical minimum effort, as an attempt to provide a lasting solution to the problems of development, faced by underdeveloped countries. The most pressing problem of underdeveloped countries is the vicious circle of poverty, which is an atmosphere of inertia in the economy. Because of such an atmosphere, the development variables (income, employment, saving, investment, etc,) move in the backward direction and thus reverse the process of development. Hence, a minimum effort is needed to overcome the original inertia of the underdeveloped economies. In other words, critical minimum effort is necessary to achieve a steady, secular growth, raising per capita income in the long period. Leibenstein has expressed the idea in these words, "In order to achieve the transition from the state of backwardness to the more developed state, where, we can expect steady secular growth, it is necessary, though not always a sufficient condition, that at the same point or during the same period, the economy should receive a stimulus to growth that is greater than a certain minimum size." Thus,, critical minimum effort is the only way to break the vicious circle of poverty and to release the force of growth.

Explanation of the Theory : Every economy is under the influence of two forces—"stocks" and "stimulants" stocks dampen and depress the developmental forces. They are also referred to as "income-depressing forces", which reverse the wheels of development stimulants impress and encourage the developmental forces. They are "income generating forces", which lubricate the wheels of development. Income despressing forces are evil forces and the income-generating forces are known as good factors. These two not only co-exist but interact with each other. It usually happens that evil forces triumph in the initial stages, but ultimately the good forces come out victorious; the bad forces nip the developments in the initial stages, but in the long-run the income-generating forces over-power the bad forces and the process of development starts. The question is to what extent is the minimum effort needed? Here, Leibenstein stresses a 'particular level' of investment which can ensure the steady, secular growth or which can break the vicious circle of poverty. "If the level of investment is less than a particular level then the derived goal of steady growth cannot be realised. The level of investment should be higher than a particular level."

The particular level is what Leibenstein calls the critical minimum. Hence, the crux of the theory is that any level of investment lower than the critical minimum cannot ensure the sustained growth. The term 'critical' is the indicator of the fact that the level of investment should at least be of such an order which could raise per capita income for achieving sustained growth.

According to this thesis, "a development programme must be at least of a certain size, or of a critical Minimum to reduce the indivisibilities and discontinuties in the economies, overcome the economies of scale, have an impact on values and offset certain other factors that arise to depress development."

The underdeveloped country is caught in a vicious circle as it has a low per capita income sustained growth is possible only when a certain minimum critical effort is made to raise the per capita income. In other words, the underdeveloped economy should receive the necessary stimulus to growth. According to Leibenstein, every economy is under the impact of shocks and stimuli. A shock has an adverse impact on the per capita income and a stimulus has the effect of raising it. In underdeveloped countries, the impact of shocks is greater than that of the stimuli.

According to Leibenstein, there are income-depressing factors like population growth and also income-stimulating factors in underdeveloped countries. There is a biologically determined maximum rate of population growth between 3 and 4%. The rate of population growth is relevant to the level of per capita income. It is related to the various stages of economic development. The rate of population growth is an increasing function of income up to a certain level of income and beyond that it is the decreasing function of income.

To begin with, at the subsistence equilibrium level of income, fertility and mortality rates are high. If the per capita income is to be pushed above the subsistence equilibrium level, the mortality rate follows it without any decline in the fertility rate. Consequently, there is a higher rate of growth of population. But this trend will continue only to a certain point. Beyond the point, increase in per capita income has the effect of reducing the fertility rate. As development is accelerated, the rate of population growth declines. Increased specialisation and social and economic mobility created by the sources of development lead to a constant rate of growth of population. As the economy tends to move along the path of sustained growth, the rate of growth of population declines. Therefore, Leibenstein argues that a critical minimum effort is necessary to overcome the Malthusian underemployment equilibrium.

The Critical Minimum Effort Thesis assumes the existence of certain favourable conditions, *i.e.* income-stimulating factors expand at a higher rate than the income-depressing factors. The favourable conditions are created in the path of development by what are called "the Growth Agents." These represent the quantum of capacities residing in the members of the population to carry out growth contributing activites. These agents may be the entrepreneurs, the investors, the savers and the innovators.

According to Leibenstein, "whether or not the growth agents expand will depend on the anticipated outcome of such activities, the actual result, and on the incentives for further expansion or contraction generated by the interaction of the anticipation, the activities and the results." They are :

1. The positive incentives which secure growth and national income.

2. Zero-sum incentives which do not raise national income but have only a distributive effort. The zero-sum activities are not real income creating activities, but simple transfers of liquidity from some holders to others.

According to Leibenstein, the Critical Minimum Effort will create a series of the following effects :

A. An expansion of growth agents ;

B. An increase in their contribution, per unit of capital due to a decline in the capital-output ratio ;

C. An ultimate decline in the effectiveness of factors inhibiting growth ;

D. The creation of social and environmental conditions that promote social and economic mobility;

E. Increased specialisation and expansion of secondary and tertiary sectors; and

F. The development of an atmosphere that leads to changes more conducive to economic and social changes and especially an environment that leads to eventual fertility decline and an eventual decline in the rate of population growth.

Criticisms: Leibenstein's Thesis is a logical and realistic analysis of the factors containing development process. It stresses the need for sustainded development in an underdeveloped country. The thesis suffers from certain inadequacies.

1. Critrics do not accept the relationship between per capita income and population growth, formulated by Leibenstein.

2. Secondly, the thesis does not take into consideration the influence of external factors, including foreign capital.

3. Thirdly, Leibenstein's thesis does not take into account the role of government in bringing down the fertility rate.

4. Finally, critics feel that the functional relationship between the level of per capita income and the rate of growth of total income is a complex process. They think that Leibenstein's approach is over-simplified.

G. Nelson's Low-Level Equilibrium Trap

R.P. Nelson developed the theory of Low-Level Equilibrium Trap for underdeveloped countries. Like Leibenstein's Critical Minimum Effort Thesis, Nelson's theory is also based on the Malthusian hypothesis that with the increase in the per capita income of a country above the 'minimum subsistence level', population tends to increase. Initially population grows rapidly with an increase in per capita income. But when the growth rate of population reaches "an upper physical limit," it starts declining with further increase in per capita income.

According to Nelson, "The malady of underdeveloped economy can be diagnosed as a stable equilibrium level of per capita income at or close to subsistence requirements." At a stable equilibrium level of per capita income, the rate of saving and consequently the rate of net investment are at a low level. Efforts made to raise the rate of saving and investment through an increase in the rate of growth of total national income are accompanied by a high rate of population growth which pushes back the per capita income to its stable equilibrium level. Thus,, underdeveloped economies are caught in a low-level equilibrium trap.

Nelson mentions four social and technological conditions which are conducive to trapping. They are :

(a) A high correlation between the level of per capita income and the rate of population growth.

(b) A low propensity to direct additional per capita income to increasing per capita investment.

(c) Scarcity of uncultivable arable land.

(d) Inefficient methods of production.

A study of the economic development of underdeveloped countries reveals that most of them are caught in the low-level equilibrium trap due to the presence of the above noted conditions.

Nelson uses three sets of relationships to show the trapping of an economy at a low level of income. *First,* income is a function of the capital stock, the level of technology and the size of the population. *Second,* net investment consists of capital created out of savings in the form of additions to the stock of tools and equipment in the industrial sector plus additions of new land to the amount of land under cultivaltion. Third, "with low per capita incomes, short run changes in the rate of population growth are causes by changes in the death rate, and change in the death rate are caused by changes in the level of per capita income. Yet once per capita income reaches a level well above subsistence requirements, further increases in per capita income have a negligible effect on the death rate."

Nelson point towards a number of factors to escape the low-level equilibrium trap. *First,* there should be a favourable socio-political environment in the country. *Second,* the social structure should be changed by laying greater emphasis on thrift and entrepreneurship. Greater incentives shoould be provided to produce more. And incentives should also be provided to limit the size of the family. *Third,* measures should be adopted to change the distribution of incomes at the same time enabling accumulation of wealth by investors. *Fourth,* there should be an all-pervading government investment programme. *Fifth,* income and capital should be increased by obtaining funds from abroad. *Sixth,* improved production techniques should be used to utilise existing resources more fully so that income is increased from given inputs.

To escape the low-level equilibrium trap in underdeveloped countries requires the simultaneous adoption of all these measures so that the growth rate of income is increased more than the growth rate of population. Once this is achieved above a certain minimum per capita income level, sustained growth will take place without further government action until a high level of per capita income is reached.

H. The "Big Push" Theory

The theory of the "big push" is associated with the name of *Professor Paul N. Rosenstein-Rodan.*The thesis is that a "big push" or a large comprehensive programme is needed in the form of a high minimum amount of investment to over-come the obstacles to development in an underdeveloped economy and to launch it on the path to progress.

The theory states that proceeding "bit by bit" will not launch the economy successfully on the development path; rather a minimum amount of investment is a necessary condition for this. It necessitates the obtaining of external economies that arise from the simultaneous establishment of technically interdependent industries. Thus,, indivisibilities and external economies flowing from a minimum quantum of investment are a prerequisite for launching economic development successfully.

Rosenstein-Rodan distinguishes between three different kinds of indivisibilities and external economies.

1. indivisibilities in the production function, especially the indivisibility of the supply of social overhead capital;
2. indivisibilities of demand;
3. indivisibilities in the supply of savings.

Given these three indivisibilities and the external economies to which they give rise, a "big push" or a minimum quantum of investment is required to over-come the obstacles to development in under-developed countries. "There may be finally a phenomenon of indivisibility in the vigour and drive required for a successful development policy," writes Rodan. But proceeding bit by bit in an isolated and small way does not lead to a sufficient impact on growth. A climate for development is only created when investment of a minimum speed or size is made with in an underdeveloped economy.

I. The Doctrine of Balanced Growth

The theory of balanced growth implies that there should be simultaneous investment in a variety of enterprises and there should be harmonious growth of the different parts of the economy. It implies balance between different consumer goods industries and capital goods industries. It also implies balance between agriculture and industry, between domestic and export sectors, between economic and social over heads and between vertical and horizontal external economies. The theory of balanced growth implies that the state must ensure simultaneous investments. It also implies controlled planning.

The theory of balanced growth has been developed by Rosenstein Rodan, Ragnar Nurkse, Arthur Lewis, Scitovsky and Harvey Leibenstein.

Main Versions of the Theory of Balanced Growth

Rosenstein Rodan's Version : *Rosenstein-Rodan* was the first economist who propounded the theory of balanced growth without using these words in his 1943 article. He realised the importance of pecuniary external economy. In underdeveloped economies, lack of market is a serious obstacle. No investor anticipates a market large enough to justify an investment, even though investment project is profitably based upon the availability of pecuniary external economies.

In addition to the lack of demand, Rodan mentions two difficulties on the supply side. Lack of infrastructure makes other investments uneconomic and huge capital required to build these infrastructures is not available. In addition, the absence of ability to save is another limitation.

To tackle these problems on the demand and supply sides, Rodan favours a comprehensive investment programme. This will cause an overall rise in demand which will make all projects profitable. At the same time, infrastructural facilities will be made available for the use of industries. This investment programme must of course be carried out by a central planning agency or a central authority.

Ragnar Nurkse's Version : Nurkse's Version given in his book "Problems of Capital Formation in Underdeveloped Countries" broadly follows the approach of Rodan. According to Nurkse "low real income is a reflection of low productivity, which in turn is due largely to lack of capital. The lack of capital is the result of the small capacity to save and so the circle is complete." On the other hand, inducement to invest is limited by the size of the market. This creates another vicious circle on the demand side.

To break the vicious circle, Nurkse favours a more or less synchronised application of capital to a wide range of different industries. This will lead to an overall enlargenmet of the market. Most of the industries producing mass consumption goods are complementary.

Nurkse's Version depends on the principle of complementarity in various directions between wants, between factors of production and between products at various stages of production. This kind of complementarity leads to the emergence of several external economies. Here, external economies refer to the economies which raise out of the establishment of a new industry, or from the expansion of an existing industry and those available to other industries. The scarcity of factor supply ensures that the relationship is mostly competitive. The supplies of skilled labour, capital and entrepreneur are comparatively inelastic.

J. The Concept of Unbalanced Growth

The theory of unbalanced growth is the opposite of the doctrine of balanced growth. According to this concept, investment should be made in selected sectors rather than simultaneously in all economy. No underdeveloped country possesses capital and other resources in such quantities as to invest simultaneously in all sectors. Therefore, investment should be made in a few selected sectors or industries for their rapid development and the economies accruing from them can be utilized for the development of other sectors. Thus, the economy gradually moves from the path of unbalanced growth to that of balanced growth. Economists like *Singer, Kindleberger, Streeten,* etc, have expressed their view in favour of the unbalanced growth doctrine which are in fact the criticisms of the theory of balanced growth. It is, however, *Hirschman* who has propounded the doctrine of unbalanced growth in a systematic manner.

Hirschman's View : The concept of 'unbalanced growth' has been popularized by Hirschman. It is his contention that deliberate unbalancing the economy, according to a predesigned strategy, is the best way to achieve economic growth in an underdeveloped country. According to *Hirschman,* investments in strategically selected industries or sectors of the economy will lead to new investment opportunities and so pave the way to further economic development. He maintains that "development has of course proceeded in this way, with growth being communicated from the leading sectors of the economy to the followers, from one industry to another, from one firm to another." He regards development as a "*chain of disequilibria*" that must keep alive rather than eliminate the disequilibria, of which profits and losses are symptoms in a competitive economy. If the economy is to be kept moving ahead, the task of development policy is to maintain tensions, disproportions and disequilibria. This "see-saw advance" is induced by one disequilibrium that in turn leads to a new disequilibrium and so on *ad infinitum.*

According to Hirschman, history show only unbalanced growth in many countries. Balanced growth was the result of the flow of innovations and changing factor combinations. It was not created by the simultaneous expansion of mutually supporting sectors as assumed by the authors of balanced growth. Hirschman considered that balanced growth was not a process but a goal to be achieved through a series of imbalances over a period of time.

Hirschman stresses three aspects of unbalanced growth :

A. A chain of unbalanced growth sequences initiated by private entrepreneurs and the state.
B. Unbalance in the direction of shortage of social overheads.
C. Development to be initiated in those sectors which are linked to the maximum extent with other sectors.

Development can only take place by unbalancing the economy. This is possible by investing either in Social Overhead Capital (SOC) or in Directly Productive Activities (DPA). The former creates external economies while the latter appropriates external economies.

Unbalancing the Economy with Social Overhead

Capital (SOC) : SOC has been defined as "comprising those basic services without which primary, secondary and tertiary productive activities cannot function." A large investment in SOC will encourage private investment later in direct productive activities (DPA). For example cheaper supply of electric power may encourage the establishment of small industries. Unless SOC investment provide cheap or improved services, private investments in DPA will not be encouraged. Thus,, the SOC approach to economic development is to 'unbalance' the economy so that subsequently investment in DPA are stimulated. As Hirschman puts it, "Investment in SOC is advocated not because of it permits and in fact invites DPA to come in. Some SOC investment is required as a prerequisite of DPA investment."

Unbalancing the Economy with DPA: An inbalance can also be created vice DPA. A government might directly or indirectly invest in DPA instead of investing in SOC. If DPA investment is undertaken first, the shortage of SOC facilities is likely to raise production costs substantially. In course of time, political pressures might stimulate investment in SOC also. Investment sequences are generated by profit expectations and political pressures. Profit expectations generate the sequence from SOC to DPA and political pressures from DPA to SOC.

Hirschman refers to two routes in the path of development. The first sequence is by expanding SOC. It is called by him the process of "development" via excess capacity of SOC." The second sequence is by expanding DPA. It is called by him the process to "development via shortage of SOC." According to Hirschman, "development via shortage is an instance of disorderly, compulsive sequence, while via excess SOC capacity is essentially permissive." It is pointed out that development via excess capacity is more continuous and smoother and Hirschman calls this self-propelling. But the process of development via shortage of SOC capacity is not so.

Linkage : Hirschman also analyses the problem of finding out what kind of imbalance is likely to be more effective. Any particular investment can have both effects called the '*forward linkage*' and '*backward linkage*'. The former will encourage investment in subsequent stages of production, while the latter will encourage investment in earlier stages of production. The problem is to choose projects which will have these greatest "total" linkage. The projects with greatest linkage vary from country to country and they can be found out only through empirical studies of input-output tables. Hirschman says, "*The industry with the highest combined linkage score is iron and steel.*

Hirschman points out that operations some where in the middle of the production process may have higher total linkage effects than operations at the beginning or end of the production process. This is because in underdeveloped countries the interdependence and linkage effects are weak. Primary production in underdeveloped countries has weak backward and forward linkage. According to Hirschman, a meaningful concept of linkage would be investment decisions up or down the line, which are prompted by creation of a particular industry.

In the case of underdeveloped countries, backward linkage is more reliable than forward linkage. In this connection, Hirschman is not in favour of too early encouragement of import-replacing industries. He regards forward linkage as "an important, powerful reinforcement to backward linkage" rather than as 'an independent inducement mechanism.'

K. Dualistic Development Theories

It is generally observed that poor countries exhibit some elements of modernisation in one sector and some element of backwardness in the other sector. In many countries, the modern money economy has developed along with the traditional indigenous economy, resulting in what is called "Dual Economy." Such an economy exhibits a contrast between economic and social organisation of the modern advanced sector and that of the indigenous backward sector. The existence of these two sectors creates a problem known as the "problem of dualism." Since the future development of any country requires the spread and expansion of the modern sector, any effort to accelerate the country's rate of development must deal with the problem of dualism.

Dualism is of two kinds :

A. Social Dualism

B. Technological Dualism

Dr. J.H. Boeke has been the leading exponent of the theory of social dualism. He was a civil servant in Netherlands and the concepts of social dualism is the result of his experience as a civil servant. Though his theory was largely based on Indonesian experience, Boeke thought that it had general application. He has given a formal definition of social dualism in the following words, "Social dualism is the clashing of an imported social system with an indigenous social system of another style. Most frequently the imported system is high capitalism. But it may be socialism or communism jush as well, or a blending of them." Social dualism, he further adds, is "a form of disintegration which came into existence with the appearance of capitalism in pre-capitalist countries." He believes that dualism arises from a clash between the social systems of East and West. To substantiate his view point Boeke quotes Rudyard Kipling's famous phrase "East is East and West is West and never the twin shall meet." This phrase makes the point very clear that "dualistic'" economies are a result of the clash between the Eastern and the Western social systems. This clash further results in social dualism arising in less developed countries.

Technological Dualism : As an alternative to Boeke's social dualism, *Professor Higgins* has developed the theory of technological dualism. Technological dualism implies the use of different production functions in the advanced sector and the traditional sector of an underdeveloped economy. The existence of such dualism has accentuated the problem of structural or technnological unemployment in the industrial sector and disguised unemployment in the rural sector. Higgin's theory of technological dualism is related to limited productive employment opportunities found in the two sectors of an underdeveloped economy because of market imperfections, different factor endowments and production function.

To explain the theory of technological dualism, Higgins takes two goods, two factors of production, two sectors with their factor endowments and production functions. Of the two sectors, one is the traditional sector and the other is the modern sector. The traditional or rural sector is engaged in the production of agricultural products, handicrafts and operates small industries. Production in this sector is carried on with a wide range of techniques and alternative combinations of two factors of production, *viz,* labour and capital. As such this sector has variable technical coefficients of production. The techniques of production are generally labour-intensive because of the excessive supply of labour and employment-oriented projects.

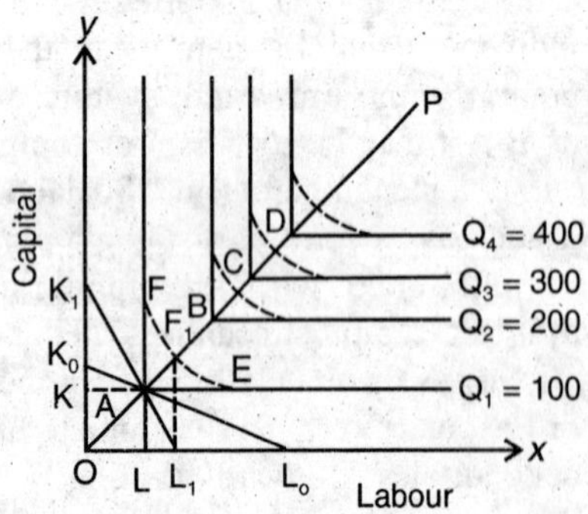

Fig. 11

On the other hand, the modern industrial sector is composed of heavy industries, plantations, mines, oil fields, etc. The production in this sector can be carried on with limited techniques because the technical coefficients are generally fixed. The production process are relatively capital-intensive in the sense that large amounts of capital are used with a small amount of labour. The situation of this sector can be explained with the help of the following Figure 11.

It represents the production function in the industrial sector. Units of labour are measured on the X-axis and units of capital are measured on the Y-axis. Q_1 is an isoquant representing a combination OK units of capital and OL units of labour, producing 100 units of output. Q_2, Q_3 and Q_4 represent higher levels of output, *viz,* 200, 300 and 400 units respectively. Higher level of output is possible by increasing the amounts of labour and capital in the same proportions. The points A, B, C and D show the fixed combinations of labour and capital to produce different levels of output. The line OP joining the points A, B, C and D is the expansion path and its slope represents the constant proportion in which labour and capital are combined. The production process is capital-intensive and it is shown by the line K_1 L_1. This line shows that OK units of capital are combined with OL units of labour, producing Q_1 (*i.e.,* 100 units) level of output. 'A' is the point of equilibrium because at this point the isocost line K_1 L_1 touches the isoquant curve Q_1 and as such the industrial sector will use OL units of labour and OK units of capital for producing an output Q_1, *i.e.,* 100 units. If OL_1 units of labour are available, the excess labour supply will have no effect on production techniques because the technical coefficients are fixed. LL_1 units of labour will remain unemployed. It is only through the incresase of capital stock to the extent of EF_1 that LL_1 units of labour can be absorbed in this sector; otherwise they must seek employment in the rural sector. However, the increase in employment will be relatively less than the increase in investment with the expansion of the industrial sector along the expansion path OP.

In actual working, the technical coefficients are not rigidly fixed; rather they are flexible. The dotted portion of the isoquant curves indicates a situation in which there is actually some flexibility in factor proportions. It can be easily seen that small changes in the factor endowments would not bring any marked change in the techniques of production by entrepreneurs. But if substantial changes in factor endowments take place as shown by $K_0 L_0$, a more labour-intensive technique would be useful.

Having discussed the production function in the industrial sector, Higgins explains the production function in the agricultural sector, where the technical coefficients are variable. This is explained in the following Figure 12 OX is labour and OY is capital : Q_1, Q_2 and Q_3 are the isoquant curves on the assumption that technical coefficients are available and a wide range of techniques and combination of labour and capital will be given the same output. The combination of labour and capital will actually depend on factor endowments and their relative prices. Here capital includes improved land.

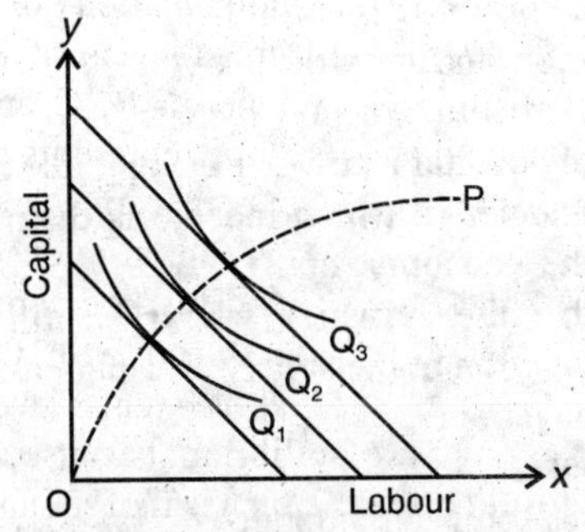

Fig. 12 : *The Agriculture Sector*

We begin with production at Q_1 in each sector. An increase in the output of the industrial sector, along OP results in a population explosion. Since the technical coefficients are fixed in that sector, the employment opportunities do not keep pace with the increase in population. Hence, the increased population will have to seek employment in agriculture or some other "variable coefficient" sector and the migration of labour from industry to agriculture starts.

At the beginning of production operations, no factor of production is abundant. But as migration continues, it may be possible to develop extensive cultivation in order to keep the labour-land ratio constant. Since land is fixed in supply the cultivation opportunities for each family is limited. Though for a short period the optimal combination of labour and capital (in this case improved land) may be possible as output rises from Q_1 to Q_2, eventually land becomes a scarce factor and labour an abundant factor. Since technical coefficients are available in this sector, production process would be more labour-intensive. Finally a point would be reached when all available land would be cultivated by these highly labour-intensive techniques. The marginal product of labour falls to zero and disguised unemployment emerges. Under these circumstances, there would be no incentives for the farmers either to make more investment or to introduce labour-saving innovations. As a result, the methods of production would be largely labour-intensive and levels of technique, man-hour productivity, and economic and social welfare would remain low in the rural sector.

Disguised unemployment is aggravated by technical progress in the long-run. The high wage rates put up by the trade unions or by goverment policies add further fuel. When industrial wage rates are high, relative to the productivity of the workers in the industrial sector, the entrepreneurs are left with no option but to introduce labour-saving devices. Such devices further diminish the capacity of the industrial sector to provide employment and absorb the growing population. Higgins argues that in the last two centuries there had been little or no technical progress in agriculture, while in the industrial sector rapid technological progress took place. Hence, it can be concluded that technological dualism accentuates the problem of unemployment in underdevelopment countries because of fixed factor proportions in the industrial sector and growing population in the rural sector.

Financial Dualism

Professor Myint has developed the theory of financial dualism. Financial dualism refers to the co-existence of different interest rates between the organised and unorganised money markets in the LDCs. The rate of interest in the unorganised money market in the traditional sector is much higher than the rate in the organised money market in the modern sector.

The unorganised money market consists of the non-institutional lenders, such as the village moneylenders, landlords, shopkeepers, traders or the combination of some of them. They charge very high interest rates on loans. On the other hand in the organised money market of the LDCs, the interest rates are low and credit facilities are abundant. The organised money market consists of the commercial banks and other financial institutions which lend short-term credit at low interest rates to the modern business sector consisting of the big foreign-owned enterprises in the export industries, the government and the larger-scale modern manufacturing enterprises.

L. Rostow's Growth Model

Professor W.W. Rostow has sought an historical approach to the process of economic development. He refers to five stages of economic growth. They are:

1. the traditional society which rests on static equilibrium until it is disturbed by some mechanism.
2. the pre-conditions for the take-off, which involve slow changes, especially in attitudes and organisation
3. the take-off it is a watershed in the life of a society. It involves a rapid increase in the rate of change as to involve discontinuity. The period of take-off is the interval when the old blocks to steady growth are finally overcome.The changes during this period are characterised by a wave-like expansion.
4. the drive to maturity it is a period of sustained growth extending over four decades after the end of take-off.
5. the age of mass consumption-during this period, the leading sectors of the economy shift towards the durable consumer goods and a large share of the population acquires a high level of living.

Criticism

1. Traditional Society not Essential For Developmet.
2. Overlapping in the Stages.
3. The Stage of Drive to Maturity Puzzling and Misleading.
4. The Stage of High Mass Consumption not Chronological

M. Mrs. Joan Robinson's Growth Model (Capital Accumulation Model)

In all the classical theories of economic growth, a good deal of attention was devoted to the analysis of the part played by population, savings, technology and social institutions in the growth of the capitalist economy. So modern economists have accepted these classical ideas of economic growth and presented then in the form of growth models by using the Keynesian and the Harrod-Domar technology. Such growth models are referred to as neo-classical growth models, and Mrs. Joan Robinson's model is one such. An important feature of the neo-classical models is that they invariably incorporate the population factor in the explanation of growth. Mrs. Joan Robinson's model, which deals with a developing economy, clearly brings out the effect of population on the rate of capital accumulation and growth of output. Her model is based on two fundamental factors :

(*i*) the capital formation is conditioned by the manner in which income is distributed in the economy, and

(*ii*) the rate at which labour is utilised is a function of the supply of capital and supply of labour.

Assumptions

Mrs. Robinson's model is based upon the following assumptions :

(*a*) There is a laissez-faire closed economy.

(*b*) In such an economy capital and labour are the only productive factors.

(*c*) In order to produce a given output, capital and labour are employed in fixed proportions.

(*d*) There is neutral technical progress.

(*e*) There is no shortage of labour and entrepreneurs can emply as much labour as they wish.

(*f*) There are only two classes—the workers and the entrepreneurs—between whom the national income is distributed.

(*g*) Workers save nothing and spend their wage income on consumption.

(*h*) Entrepreneurs consume nothing but save and invest their entire income (from profits) for capital formation.

(*i*) Total wage-bill is the real wage-rate multiplied by the number of workers.
(*j*) Total profit is the profit-rate multiplied by the amount of capital.
(*k*) Total national income is the sum of total wage-bill and total profit.

Symbolically, the total national income may be expressed as

$$Y = WN + PK$$

where Y = total income, net
W = wage-rate, real
P = profit rate
K = capital
N = the number of workers employed

The profit rate, according to Mrs. Joan Robinson, is the most strategic factor in the theory of capital accumulation. Symbolically, the rate of profit would be

$$P = \frac{Y - WN}{K}$$

Divided by N.

$$P = \frac{\frac{Y}{N} - \frac{WN}{N}}{\frac{K}{N}} = \frac{\frac{Y}{N} - W}{\frac{K}{N}}$$

by putting $\frac{Y}{N} = 1$ and θ (theta), we have

$$P = \frac{1 - W}{Q}$$

Thus,, the profit ratio is the ratio of labour productivity minus the total real wage bill to the amount of capital utilised per unit of labour. In other words, the profit rate (*p*) depends on income (*y*), labour productivity (*l*), the real wage rate (*w*) and the capital-labour ratio θ.

On the expenditure side, net national income (Y) equals consumption expenditure (C) plus investment expenditure (I),

$$Y = C + I$$

Since Joan Robinson assumes zero saving out of wages but attributes saving to entrepreneurs, profits are meant for investment only, we have

$$S = I$$

This saving-investment relation may be shown as :

$$S = PK$$

and I = ΔK[Δk is increase in real capital]

$$\therefore PK = \Delta K \quad [\because S = I] \text{ or } P = \frac{\Delta K}{K} = \frac{1 - W}{Q}$$

The growth rate of capital (Δk/k) being equal top, it depends on the ratio of the net return on capital relative to the given stock of capital. If income remains constant and the wage rate decreases or income increased and the wage-rate remains constant, the profit rate would tend to increase. The profit rate can also increase if the capital-labour ratio falls. In this way the entrepreneurs maximize profits.

Besides the growth rate of capital $\left(\frac{\Delta K}{K}\right)$, another factor which determines the growth rate of an economy is the growth rate of population $\left(\frac{\Delta N}{N}\right)$.

An increase in population and labour force unaccompanied by an increase in capital would reduce labour productivity. If real wages are hold constant, the reduction in labour productivity would lower the rate of profit. A lowering of the rate of profit would adversely affect the supply of capital and thus, widen the different between capital and labour supply.

An increase in labour supply without a proportionate increase in capital supply would cause unemployment in the economy. To maintain full employment of labour resources it is essential, according to this model, that the growth rate of population (labour supply) should be equal to the growth rate of capital,

i.e., $\frac{\Delta N}{N} = \frac{\Delta K}{K}$

if the growth rate of population is equal to the growth rate of capital, *i.e.*, $\frac{\Delta N}{N} = \frac{\Delta K}{K}$, there will be full employment of both labour and capital in the economy. Mrs. Joan Robinson calls this the *Golden Age*.

The Golden Age is explained diagrammatically in Figure 13. Capital-labour ratio $\frac{K}{N}$ or Q is measured along the horizontal axis and per capita output on the vertical axis. The growth rate of labour force is taken to the left of O along the horizontal axis. The curve OP shows the production function. Every point on this curve shows the ration of capital to labour. In order to find out the capital-labour ratio and the wage profit rerlation, we draw a tangent NT which touches the production function OP at point G and cuts the vertical axis at W. Point G shows the capital-labour raito for the golden age which is measured by OK. Per capita output is OA, out of this OW is paid as wages and WA or EG is the surplus which is the rate of profit on capital.

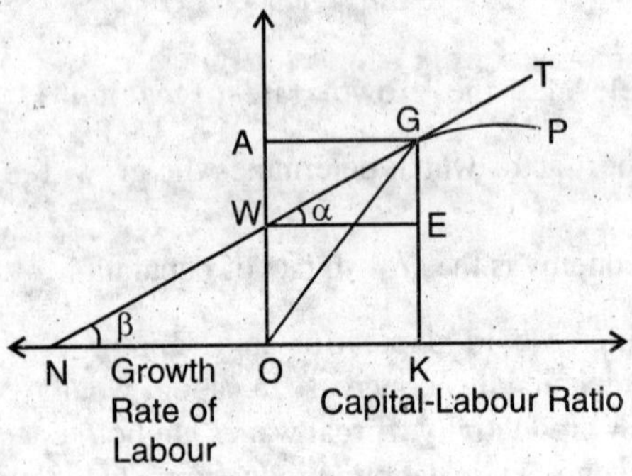

Fig. 13

This figure also proves that the growth rate of capital $\left(\frac{\Delta K}{K}\right)$ equals the growth rate of labour $\left(\frac{\Delta N}{N}\right)$. $\frac{EG}{EW}$ reflects $\frac{\Delta K}{K}$ and $\frac{OW}{ON}$ reflects $\frac{\Delta N}{N}$. Thus,

$$\frac{EG}{EW} = \frac{OW}{ON} \qquad [\because \tan\alpha = \tan\beta]$$

If an account of disequilibrium, the economy goes off the path of the Golden Age, there is every possibility of its returning to this path under certain conditions.

If $\frac{\Delta N}{N} > \frac{\Delta K}{K}$; *i.e.*, if the rate of growth of population exceeds the rate of growth of capital, a return to the Golden Age would be possible under certain conditions. The excess of labour supply would lower the money wage-rate, and assuming that prices do not change, the real wages would also be reduced. The reduction in real wages would increase the amount of profits which, in turn, would stimulate the rate of growth of capital, and would enable it to catch up with the increase in population. The parity between the two rates would be restored. Ultimately, the economy would come back to the position of the Golden Age. This return would be possible only if the real wages declines. If the real wages do not decline, either because the money wage-rate, are rigid, or because prices decline in the same proportion as the money wage-rate, the Golden Age would not be restored. On the contrary, than would be increasing unemployment in the economy. Generally speaking, a rise in prices helps to promote capital formation.

On the contrary, if the rate of growth of capital exceeds the rate of growth of populations, *i.e.*, $\frac{\Delta K}{K} > \frac{\Delta N}{N}$, there is a possibility of Golden Age equilibrium being restored through technological improvements leading to higher capital-output ratio. This would absorb the excess capital and restore the parity between the rate of growth of capital and the rate of growth of population. Any way parity between the growth rate of capital and growth rate of population is an essential prerequisite for the attainment of the Golden Age.

Mrs. Robinson makes a distinction between the desired rate of growth and the possible rate of growth. The desired growth rate is the rate of accumulation which makes the firm satisfied with the situation in which it finds itself. The desired growth rate is determined by the rate of profit caused by the rate of accumulation and the rate of accumulation induced by that rate of profit. She uses the following Figure 14 to explain it.

The curve ^ represents the expected rate of profit as a function of the rate of accumualation. The curve I represents the rate of accumulation as a function of the rate of profit. In a situation to the right of point D, the expected rate of profit is less than the rate of accumulation. Any further investment is not likely to be profitable and the rate of accumulation will fall. Between the points S and D the accumulation is less than the expected rate of profit. Therefore, there will be a tendency to increase investment and the rate of accumulation will rise to point D. This point D represents the desired growth rate.

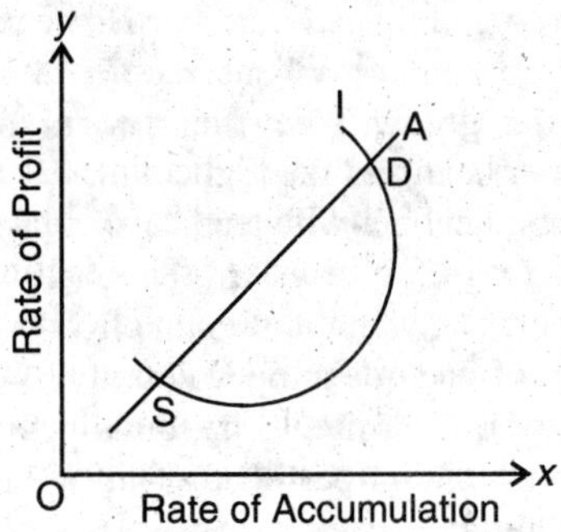

Fig. 14

On the other hand, the possible growth rate depends on the physical conditions resulting from the growth of population and technical knowledge.

When the desired growth rate equals the possible growth rate at near full employment, the economy is in a golden age.

The real wage rate is rising with increasing output per head due to technological progress. But the rate of profit on capital remains constant, and techniques of production appropriate to the rate of profit are chosen.

Mrs. Robinson's model with its stress on parity between the growth rate of capital and the growth rate of population, conforms closer to the realities of an underdeveloped economy. Mrs. Robinson's main contribution lies in the fact that she has integrated the classical value and distribution theory with the Keynesian saving investment theory.

Defects

1. The model is based on the assumption of a closed economy. This is an unrealistic assumption.
2. The role of institutional factors as one of the determinants of economic growth is neglected.
3. The model is based on the unrealistic assumption of constant prices.
4. Mrs. Robinson assumes that capital and labour are employed in fixed proportions; this is unrealistic because in a dynamic economy there are no fixed coefficients of production. Substitutability between factors takes place through times, the degree of substitutability being dependent upon the nature of technological changes.

Its Applicability to Underdeveloped Countries

Mrs. Robinson's model has a special attraction for underdeveloped countries for the following reason:

1. The theory studies the problem of population and its effect on the rate of capital accumulation. There is a "golden age" which any country can achieve through planned economic development.

2. An underdeveloped country faces the problem if $\frac{\Delta N}{N} > \frac{\Delta K}{K}$. It reveals the tendency of progressive underemployment in such economies.

3. In an underdeveloped economy, the rate of capital accumulation is always less than its potential growth ratio; that is why it is backward and possesses surplus labour force. It, therefore rests with the planning authority to increase the rate of accumulation to the level of the growth ratio of the economy. An underdeveloped country cannot, however, match the two by following the 'capitalist rules of the game.' On the contrary, it devolves on the planning authority to take the initiative in controlling and regulating not only private investment, but also public investment in such countries.

N. Investment Criteria in Economic Development

The problem of investment criteria involves the principles underlying the allocation of scarce investment resources in a rational manner so as to maximise the national income in an underdeveloped economy. It is a commonly known fact that private enterprise in such economies is motivated by profit maximisation. Very often private investment decisions are for projects that are not conducive to economic development. It is, therefore, felt that only a public authority can make decisions to allocate scarce investment resources and to influence the direction of private investment towards development oriented projects. For this, the choice before the public authorities is between techniques of a higher or lower capital intensity. Towards this end, economists have propounded a number of investment criteria which are discussed below.

The Capital-Turnover Criterion : The capital turnover criterion is known by various names *viz,* the rate of turnover criterion, the maximisation of output per unit of capital criterion or the ratio of output to capital criterion (minimum capital intensity or minimum capital-output ratio criterion). This criterion is attributed to **J.J. Polak and N.S. Buchanon.** The logic involved is that since capital is scarce in underdeveloped countries, that technique should be chosen which yields the maximum output per units of capital employed. In other words, for maximising output, investment projects with a high rate of capital turnover (*i.e.,* of a low capital output ratio) should be selected, Quick-yielding projects with a low capital intensity make it possible for scarce capital resources to be realized soon enough for reinvestment into other projects.

The Social Marginal Productivity Criterion : The social marginal productivity (SMP) criterion was first put forward by **A.E. Kahn** and later **Hollis B. Chenery** improved upon it, It is based on the conventional marginal productivity approach. As more and more capital is employed in any project in combination with given amounts of other inputs, its marginal product will after a time start falling, the marginal productivity of capital in different uses is equalised. The aim is to allocate limited investment resources in such a way as to maximise the national output. In other words, they should be utilised in the most productive projects. Kahn states that this criterion takes "in to account the total net contribution of the marginal unit to national product and not merely that portion of contribution (or of its costs) which may accrue to the private investor." Thus,, it is applicable to the economy as a whole and not to individual investment projects.

The Reinvestment Criterion : The reinvestment criterion is advanced by **Galenson** and **Leibenstein.** It is also known as the rate of surplus criterion or the marginal per capita investment quotient. The latter is defined as the "net productivity per worker minus consumption per worker." Galenson and Leibenstein emphasize the maximisation of per capita output in the future rather than in the present. This is possible when the rate of saving is maximised leading to the reinvestment of income. Assuming that national income is divided into wages and profits, the former are spent on consumption and the latter are saved for the purpose of investment. The larger the volume of profits, the higher will be rate of savings, as a result the larger will be the amount of capital available per head and the higher will be the growth rate of output which will lead to increased output per head in the future. In the early phase of development a "critical minimum effort" is required on the part of underdeveloped countries to increase the proportion of profits to national income and to restrict consumption per head. This would lead to larger savings and larger reinvestible surplus. Given the quality and quantity of labour force. It is the capital-labour ratio that determines per capita output. Galenson and Leibenstein use the following formula to determine the rate of investible surplus *(r)*

$$r = \frac{p - e.w}{c}$$

Where p = product per machine
e = number of men per machine
w = real wage rate
c = cost of machine

The Time Series Criterion : *A.K. Sen* has put forward the "time series" criterion. The criterion seeks to maximise output within a given period of time. Given the capital-output ratio and the rate of savings, the time path of two techniques (Capital intensive and labour-intensive) can be drawn and it can be found out which of the techniques yields the highest returns over the time-horizon.

Conclusion

The various investment criteria discussed above are not different in their ultimate objective, that of the maximisation of national output. Only the approach routes differ. The different components of national income (consumption, saving and investment) are used by economists to maximise the total output by giving more or less importance to one or the other. Some investment criteria aim at maximising total output at a point of time while others over a period of times. But all criteria are incomplete because they neglect the influence, of such factors as population growth, tastes, technical progress, market conditions, distribution of income, price changes, balance of payments and social and cultural conditions on the level of investment in one way or the other. Contrariwise, they also fail to study the impact of investment on these factors. But despite these apparent theoretical and practical limitations, the various investment criteria are being increasingly made use of in the programming of resource allocation in almost all the developing countries of world including India. It is, however, essential that they must be in keeping with the social and economic objectives of the developing country.

O. Two-Gap Model

Hollis Chenery and other writers have put forth the "two-grip" approach to economic development. The idea is that "saving gap" and "foreign exchange gap " are two separate and independent constraints, on the attainment of a target rate of growth in LDCs. Chenery sees foreign aid as a way of filling these two gaps in order to achieve the target growth rate of the economy.

To calculate the size of gaps, a target growth rate of the economy is postulated along with a given capital-output ratio. A savings gap arises when the domestic savings rate is less than the investment required to achieve the target. For example, if the growth target of national real income is 6 percent per annum and the capital-output ratio is 3:1, than the economy must save 18 percent of its national income to achieve this growth target. If only 12 percent of savings can be mobilised domestically, the savings gap is 6 percent of national income. The economy can achieve the target gowth rate by filling this savings gap with foreign aid. Similarly a fixed relationship is postulated between targeted foreign exchange requirements and net export earnings. If net export earnings fall short of foreign exchange requirements, a foreign exchange gap appears which can be filled by foreign aid. The two gaps are explained in terms of the national income accounting identities:

$$E - Y \equiv I - S \equiv MX \equiv F$$

Where E = national expenditure
Y = national income and output
I = investment
S = saving
M = imports
X = exports
F = net capital inflow
(I – S) = domestic saving gap
(M – X) = foreign exchange gap

Models of Technical Change

Neutral and Non-Neutral Technical Change

A technical change is said to be neutral when it is neither capital-saving nor labour-saving. On the contrary, non-neutral technical change is either capital-saving or labour-saving. In the literature on growth economies, the two important definitions, pertaining to neutral and non-neutral technical change are propounded by Hicks and Harrod.

Hicks Neutrality

According to *Hicks,* an invention is said to be neutral when it raises the marginal productivities of labour and capital in the same proportion. In other words, a technical change is neutral if the ratio of the marginal product of capital to that of labour remains unchanged at a constant capital-labour ratio. Hicks-neutral technical change is explained in Figure 15.

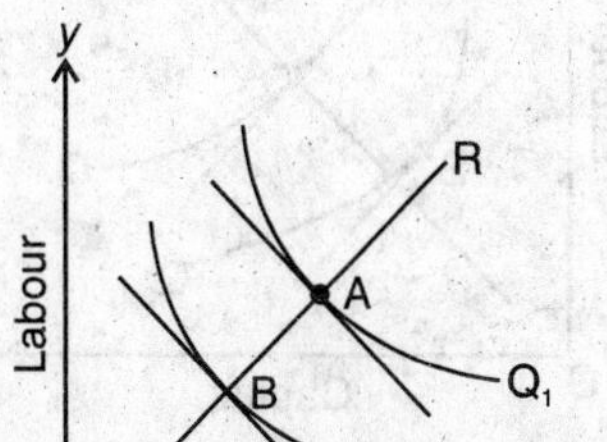

Fig. 15 : *Neutral Technical Change*

A technical change is *labour-saving* if it raises the marginal product of capital relative to that of labour, at a constant capital-labour ratio. The given output would now require less labour relatively to capital. Technical change implies that a given output can be produced with fewer inputs of labour and capital than before so that the isoquant after the change Q_2 shifts below the original isoquant Q_1 in Figures 15 and 16.

Figure 16 depicts the case of labour-saving technical change where Q_1 is the isoquant before the technical progress and Q_2 after the technical progress.

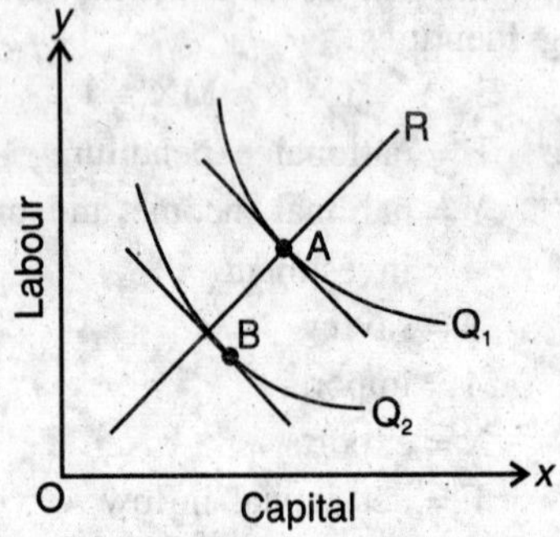

Fig. 16 : *Labour Saving Technical Change*

At the point B on the isoquant Q_2 less labour is required relatively to capital for a given capital-labour ratio. This type of technical change is relatively labour saving. If the amount of labour used is reduced absolutely and that of capital rises, then the technical change will be absolutely labour-saving and capital using.

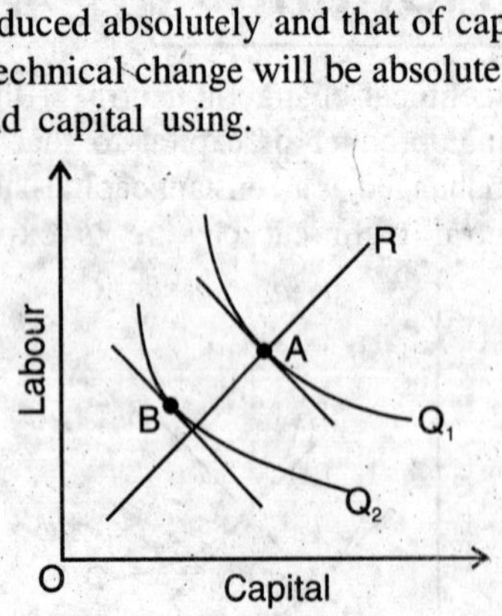

Fig. 17 : *Capital Saving Technical Change*

On the other hand, a technical change is *capital-saving* if it raises the marginal product of labour relatively to capital, at a constant capital-labour ratio. The given output will now require less capital relatively to labour. This is illustrated in Figure 17 where at the point B on the isoquant Q_2 less capital is required relatively to labour after the technical change for a given capital-labour ratio. This type of technical change is relatively capital-saving. If the amount of capital used reduced absolutely and that of labour rises, the techincal change is absolutely capital-saving and labour-using.

The precise manner in which the relative and absolute amounts of labour and capital used will change as the result of the technical change will depend upon the factor-elasticities of substitution and product elasticities of demand. It will depend on the elasticities of substitution between capital and labour in the economy, for these will help to determine what effects the technical change has on the prices of the two factors. It will also depend on the elasticities of demand for the products of the various industries that make up the economy."

Under Hicks-neutral technical progress, the factor shares remain constant if factor proportions and relative remunerations of labour and capital are constant.

Criticism

Hicks-neutrality has been criticised on the ground that it is a rigid type of definition even when a large number of factor of production are involved. Second, the dependence of Hicks-neutrality on demand elasticities, and substitution elasticities make it a cumbersome tool of analysis. Third, **Harrod** has criticised Hicks-neutrality because it is 'quite unrelated to the intrinsic character of the innovation itself' such as the elasticity of demand for products and factors. Lastly, the Hicksian neutrality is built within the framework of *static economic analysis.*

Harrod Neutrality

The alternative definition of neutral technical progress is given by *Harrod* in his *Towards a Dynamic Economics*. According to him, technical change is neutral if at a constant rate of profit (or interest) the capital-output ratio also remain constant. If the rate of profit remains constant after technical change but the capital-output ratio rises, then the technical change is labour-saving. On the other hand, if the capital-output ratio falls with technical change at a constant rate of profit, then the technical change is capital-saving.

Harrod neutrality is explained with the help of Figure 18 when capital per man *(k)* is measured along the x-axis and output per man *(q)* along the y-axis OP is the production function before the technical change and OP_1 is the production function after the technical change. The capital-output ratio at point A on the production function OP is $\frac{OK_1}{OY_1}$ and at point B on the production function OP_1 is $\frac{OK_2}{OY_2}$. Since the curve OR passes through both the point A and B, the capital- output ratios at these points are equal, *i.e.,* $\frac{OK_1}{OY_1} = \frac{OK_2}{OY_2}$.

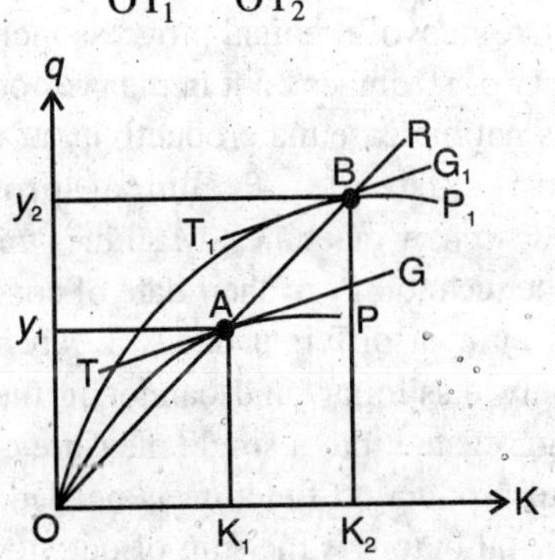

Fig. 18 : *Harrod Neutrality*

Harrod-neutrality also requires that the rate of profit must remain constant along with a constant capital-output ratio after technical progress. This means that the marginal productivity of capital (or rate of profit) must be the same at points A and B on the production functions OP and OP_1 respectively. This, in turn, requires that the slope of the production function OP at point A must equal the slope of the production function OP_1 at point B. In other words, it means that the tangents at A and B must be parallel to each other. In Figure 18, the tangent TG at point A is Parallel to the tangent $T_1 G_1$ at B. Thus,, Harrod-neutral technical change, as shown by the shifting of the production function OP upwards to OP_1, depicts the equality of the capital-output ratio at A and B as represented by the curve OR passing through them, and also the equality of the slopes of the tangents at A and B thereby showing a constant rate of profit.

Hence, Harrod's definition of neutral technical progress is superior to that of Hicks because it is applicable to a dynamic situation rather than to a static situation. As such, it forms an important part of the theory of economic growth because it uses the concept of the capital-output ratio which is indispensable in modern growth analysis. Assuming constant returns to scale, changes in the capital-output ratios can come about only through technical change.

Harrod neutrality can be shown in the form of a production function as

$$Q = F [K, A(t) L]$$

Here, Q is a function F of a K and A*(t)* L which means that the given constant returns to scale on equal proportionate rise in capital (K) and in effective labour units [A *(t)* L] must lead to an equal proportionate rise in national output (Q). With the rate of interest being constant, the efficiency of labour increase in the whole economy. "With population growth, there is an increase in the number of men at work, Harrod-neutral technical progress increases the amount of work each man can do. The result is that, both with population growth and with Harrod-neutral technical progress, the GNP rises at a given rate. The difference is that, with Harrod-neutral technical progress, income per head (real wage per head) increases; with population growth it remains the same. As Joan Robinson and Uzawa have shown, on the strict definition, Harrod-neutral technical progress raises income at the same rate whatever the (constant) level of capital-output ratio. It is this rate which measures technical progress. This formulation of Harrod neutrality has been described as 'pure labour augmenting technical progress.' Solow has, however, shown that Harrod-neutrality can be purely 'capital augmenting technical progress' with the production function

$$Q = F [A(t) K, L]$$

Here, A *(t)*, the index of technical progress, has been prefixed to K instead of L, unlike as in the labour augmentation case.

Economists have shown on the basis of Joan Robinson's analysis that technical progress is both Hicks-neutral and Harrod-neutral if the elasticity of substitution between labour and capital is unity and there is no change in the distribution of income. There is neutral technical change in Hick's sense if with given labour force capital remains unchanged and the distribution of income is the same. It is Harrod neutral if with given labour force, capital increases in the same proportion as national output and the distribution of income is the same.

Disembodied and Embodied Technical Change

Disembodied Technical Change : In 1956, *Abramkovitz* wrote the first paper followed by *Kendrick* and *Solow* in an attempt to measure the contribution of technical change to economic growth. They treated technical change as '*disembodied.' Disembodied technical change is purely organisational which permits more output to be produced from unchanged inputs, without any new investment.* Disembodied technical change refers to any kind of shift in the production function that leaves the balance between capital and labour undisturbed in the long run. The production function for such technical change is

$$Q = F(K, L, t) \qquad ...(1)$$

where Q = output
K = capital input
L = labour input
t = technical change

Taking Hicks-neutral technical change as the basis, Solow postulated the production function in the special form as

$$Q = A(t)\,F(K, L) \qquad ...(2)$$

Where $A(t)$ is an index of technical change or measures the cumulated effects of shifts over time. "Such a production function implies that technical progress is organisational in the sense that its effect on productivity does not require any change in the quantity of the inputs. Existing inputs are improved or used more effectively."

The growth rate of output (Q/Q) is equal to the rate of technical change (A/A) plus a weighted average of the growth rate of capital (K/K) and the growth rate of labour (L/L). Assuming linear homogeneous production function, these weights add to one and we have,

$$\frac{Q}{Q} = \frac{A}{A} + at\frac{K}{K} + (1-at)\frac{L}{L} \qquad ...(3)$$

where dots indicate time derivates and at is the capital elasticity of output.

Embodied Technical Change-Vintage Approach : In an alternative model entitled Investment and Technical Progress (1960), Solow himself modified the residual approach based on disembodied technical change in which capital stock is regarded as homogeneous and technical change floats down from the outside. "In this model new capital accumulation is regarded as the vehicle to technical progress. Technical progress increases the productivity of machines built in the previous period, but it does not increase the productivity of machines already in existence. Technical progress is 'embodied' in new machines. Machines unalterably embody the technology of their date of construction. Machines built at different dates...... are therefore qualitatively dissimilar, and cannot in the general case be aggregated into a single measure of capital. A separate production function is needed for each vintage. Total output is the sum of output of all the vintage in use."

Its Appraisal

Unlike the model of disembodied technical change in which the capital stock is assumed to be completely homogeneous, in the model of embodied technical change new machines are better than old machines and technological progress is embodied in the new machines. In the former approach, capital-labour ratios change at all times along the Cobb-Douglas production function. But in the latter approach, once a machine is constructed it has fixed labour requirements. In other words, each machine is designed to be worked with a given crew of men, and the size of the crew cannot thereafter be changed.'

Economic Planning

Meaning

Economic planning is the deliberate control and direction of the economy by a central authority for the purpose of achieving definite targets and objectives within a specified period of time.

Plan Formulation and Requisites for Successful Planning

The formulation and success of a plan require the following :

1. Planning Commission
2. Statistical Data
3. Objectives
4. Fixation of Targets and Priorities
5. Mobilisation of Resources
6. Balancing in the Plan
7. In Corrupt and Efficient Administration
8. Proper Development Policy
9. Economy in Administration
10. Public Cooperation

Various Types of Planning

1. Planning by Direction and Planning by Inducement

Planning by direction is an integral part of a socialist society. It entails complete absence of laissez-faire. There is one central authority which plans, directs and orders the execution of the plan in accordance with pre-determined targets and priorities. Such planning is comprehensive and encompasses the entire economy.

Planning by inducement is democratic planning. It means planning by manipulating the market. There is no compulsion but persuasion. There is freedom of enterprise, freedom of consumption and freedom of production. But these 'freedoms' are subject to state control and regulation. People are induced to act in a certain way through various monetary and fiscal measures. If the planning authority wishes to encourage the production of a commodity, it can give subsidy to the firms. And if it finds scarcity of goods in the market, it can introduce price control and rationing. In order to increase the rate of capital formation, the planning authority can then undertake public investment and/or encourage private investment. It can adopt a suitable monetary policy and at the same time a taxation policy which encourages investment and discourages consumption.

Thus, planning by inducement is able to achieve the same results as are likely to be achieved in planning by direction but with less sacrifice of individual liberty.

2. Financial and Physical Planning

Financial planning refers to the technique of planning in which resources are allocated in terms of money while physical planning pertains to the allocation of resources in terms of men, materials and machinery.

3. Perspective Planning and Annual Planning

The phrase 'perspective planning' refers to long-term planning in which long range targets are set in advance for a period of 15, 20 or 25 years. A perspective plan, according to the Indian Planning Commission, "is a blue print of developments to be under taken over a longer period." A perspective plan, however, does not imply one plan for the entire period of 15 or 20 years. In reality, the broader objectives and targets are to be achieved within the specified period of time by dividing the perspective plan into several short-period plans of four, five or six years.

4. Indicative Planning and Imperative Planning

Indicative planning prevails in *France*. This type of planning is not imperative but flexible. Planning in socialist countries is comprehensive in which the planning authority decides about the amount to be invested in each sector, in fixation of prices quantities of products and factors, and the types and quantities of products to be produced. There being rigidity in this type of planning if there is some distortion in one sector, it adversely affects the entire economy which cannot be remedied immediately. The French system of planning is free from all such troubles because it is based on the principle of decentralisation in the operation and execution of the national plans. It is known as indicative or soft planning, as distinct from comprehensive or imperative planning.

In indicative planning the private sector is neither rigidly controlled nor directed to fulfil the targets and priorities of the plan. Even then, the private sector is expected to fulfil the targets for the success of the plan. The state provides all types of facilities to the private sector but does not direct it, rather indicates the areas in which it can help in implementing the plan.

On the other hand, under imperative planning all economic activities and resources of the economy operate under the direction of the state. There is complete control over the factors of production by the state. The entire resources of the country are used to the maximum in order to fulfil the targets of the plan. There is no consumer's sovereignty in such planning. The consumers get commodities in fixed quantities at fixed prices. Often the commodities are rationed, production of commodities is in accordance with government policies. What and how much to produce—such decisions are taken by the managers of firms and factories on the direction of the planning commission or a central planning is in operation in China and Russia.

5. Rolling and Fixed Plans

Professor Myrdal was the first economist to advocate a rolling plan for developing countries in his book *India: Economic Planning in its Broader Setting*. It was introduced in Indian planning by the Janta Government on April 1, 1978 and was given up on April 1, 1980 with the coming to power of the Indira Government.

In a rolling plan, every year three new plans are made and acted upon. *First,* there is a plan for the current year which includes the annual budget and the foreign exchange budget. *Second*, there is a plan for a number of years, say three, four of five. It is changed every year in keeping with the requirements of the economy. It contains targets and techniques to be followed during the plan period, along with price relationships and price policies. *Third,* a perspective plan for 10, 15 or 20 or even more years is presented every year in which the broader goals are stated and the outlines of future development are forecast.

The concept of rolling plan is devised to overcome the rigidities encountered in the fixed five year plans. In the rolling plan there are plan targets, projections and allocations that are not fixed for the five-year period but are liable to revision every year in keeping with the changing conditions of the country. It not only provides greater flexibility but also a cleaner perspective and a better view of the priorities.

In contrast to the rolling plan, there is a fixed plan for four, five, six or seven years. A fixed plan lays down definite aims and objectives which are required to be achieved during the plan period. For this purpose, physical targets are fixed along with the total outlay. Physical targets and financial outlays are seldom changed except under emergencies.

6. Centralised and Decentralised Planning

Planning may be centralised or decentralised. This division is made from the view point of the execution of plans. Under centralised planning, the entire planning process in a country is under a central planning authority. This authority formulates a central plan, fixes objectives, targets and priorites for every sector of the economy. It takes all investment decisions in accordance with the goals and targets of the plan. The principal problems of the economy—what and how much is to be produced, how, when and where it is to be produced, and to whom it is to be allocated—are exclusively decided by this authority. The central planning authority controls every aspect of the economy.

On the other hand, decentralised planning refers to the execution of the plan from the grass roots. Under it, a plan is formulated by the central planning authority in consultation with the different administrative units of the country. The central plan incorporates plans under the central schemes and plans for the states under a federal set-up. The state plans incorporate district and village level plans. Similarly, plans for different industries are formulated in consultation with representatives of industries. But individual firms are free to take independent decisions about investment and output policies and so are individual farmers. Under decentralised planning, prices of goods and services are primarily determined by the market mechanism despite government control and regulation in certain fields of economic activity. There is freedom of consumption, production and enterprise under it. However the planning authority recommends to the central and state governments to provide certain incentives to the private sector. It also lays down areas of public sector activities.

Decentralised planning is superior to centralised planning in that it provides economic freedom and flexibility to the economy. But its dependence on the market mechanism leads to shortages or surpluses in the production of goods and services. They are likely to create problems for the government because adjustment are difficult to make.

Growth Models in Indian Planning

The five-year plans in India have been based on various growth models. We analyse below the main analytical features of the growth models used in India Planning. *The First Plan Model* : The model for the first five-year plan set out in 1952 was based on a simple application of *Harrod-Domar* growth model.

$$\frac{\Delta I}{I} = \sigma \alpha$$

where I = annual rate of investment

σ = potential social productivity of investment

α = marginal propensity to save

ΔI = increase investment

The Second Plan Model : The Second Five year plan was based on the *Mahalanobis Four-Sector Model.* This model divided the Indian economy into four sectors: the capital goods sector, the consumer goods sector, the small or household consumer goods producing sector including agriculture and the services producing sector. The basic strategy was "to increase investments in heavy industries and also expenditure on services, to increase purchasing power and create fresh demand, and on the other hand, to increase the supply of consumer goods by increasing investment and production as much as possible in the small and house hold industries to meet the new demand......Planning would be, thus, essentially a feed back process of matching a continuously increasing (planned) demand by a continuously increased (planned) production, giving rise to a steadily expanding economy." The implications of the model were to create larger employment opportunities, build a strong capital base capacity within the economy.

The Third Plan Model : The Third Plan was based almost on the same model as the second plan, but there was greater inter-industry consistency in its formulation. The Plan Model emphasized inter-dependence of agriculture and industry, of economic and social development of national and regional development, and of the mobilisation of domestic and external resources.

The Fourth Plan Model : A Consistency Model for India's Fourth Plan by *Alan S. Manne Ashok Rudra* and others was built in 1965 to provide a frame work for the setting of actual plan targets. With 1960 as the base year, and 1970 as the terminal year, it was a 30-sector consistency model based on the conventional *Leontif Inter-industry "open system.*

The Fifth Plan Model : The Fifth Five-year Plan model was based the document "Technical Note on the Approach to the Fifth Plan of India 1974-79," prepared by the perspective Planning Division of the India Planning Commission.

The Sixth Plan Model : The sixth plan model was based on the "Technical Note of the Sixth Plan" prepared by the perspective planning Division of the planning commissions. The macro-structure of the model had been prepared on 89-sector classifications of the input-output table.

MULTIPLE CHOICE QUESTIONS

1. Which one of the following is not true in case of Harrod Model ?
A. APC and MPC are different
B. Investment depends upon current increase in income
C. Capital and labour are not substitutable
D. It is a demand oriented model

2 In Solow's model of growth, the output per capita is a function of
A. labour-capital ratio
B. rate of change of capital-labour ratio
C. capital output ratio
D. technical progress

3. For Hick's technical progress, consider the following statements and choose the correct answer from the code given below :
Statements :
1. The capital-labour ratio is constant
2. It occurs in short period
3. It can be labour saving or labour using
4. It can only be neutral.

Code :
A. 1, 2 and 3 are true
B. 2 and 4 are true
C. only 2 is true
D. 2 and 4 are true

4. Which of the following is an obstacle to economic development ?
A. Low rate of capital formation
B. Vicious circles of poverty
C. Socio cultural barriers
D. All of the above

5. The classical model of economic development emphasises
A. Laissez-Fair policy
B. Capital accumulation
C. Both (A) and (B)
D. None of these

6. Harrod model does not talk about
A. Actual growth rate
B. Critical minimum growth rate
C. Warranted growth rate
D. Natural growth rate

7. Entrepreneurship is most closely associated with
A. Inventions
B. Innovations
C. Management
D. Public Administration

8. Lewis theory explains the process of development considering a—sector economy
A. One B. Two
C. Four D. None of these

9. "A country is poor because it is poor" are the words of
A. Singer B. Nurkse
C. Hicks D. Myrdal

10. According to Kuznets, during the process of development the income inequalities tend to
A. increase
B. decrease
C. increase first and then decrease
D. decrease first and then increase

11. A technical change which permits more output to be produced from unchanged inputs is considered to be
A. embodied
B. disembodied
C. both, embodied and disembodied
D. None of these

12 An underdeveloped economy is generally characterised by a
A. high ratio of commercial farming to subsistence farming
B. high ratio of industrial output to total output
C. high utilization of existing capital in the economy
D. coexistence of under-utilised labour will unexploited national and other resources

13. Which one of the following statements correctly defines the term Natural Rate of Growth ?
A. It is the minimum rate at which output can be advanced with full employ of labour
B. It is the natural rate at which output can be advanced with full employment of labour

C. It is the maximum rate at which output can be advanced with full employment of labour
D. It is the actual rate at which output can be advanced with full employment of labour

14. In the Lewis model of economic development, the capitalist sector generates and reinvests surplus and in turn, absorbs labour withdrawn from the subsistence sector. The process continues till
A. MP_L in the capitalist sector is greater than O
B. MP_L in the capitalist sector is less than MP_L in the subsistence sector
C. MP_L in the capitalist sector is greater than wage rate in that sector and MP_L in the subsistence sector is now positive
D. $MP_L = AP_L$ in the capitalist sector

15. Match List-I with List-II and select the correct answer using the codes given below the lists:

List-I
(Doctrine)
(a) Neo-classical theory of economic growth
(b) Big-push theory of economic development
(c) Critical minimum effort thesis
(d) Social Dualism

List-II
(Name of Economist)
1. Leibenstein
2. J.H. Boeke
3. Hirschman
4. Rosentein Rodan
5. Meade

Codes :	*(a)*	*(b)*	*(c)*	*(d)*
A.	2	3	4	5
B.	5	4	1	2
C.	3	5	2	1
D.	1	3	5	2

16. Consider the following statements :
According to Nurkse, disguised unemployment is a source of capital formation in an under-developed economy, if all unproductive workers are
1. maintained by productive workers
2. provided assets through loans
3. mobilised on works immediately raising productivity .

Of the above statements
A. 1, 2 and 3 are correct
B. 1 and 2 are correct
C. 1 and 3 are correct
D. 2 and 3 are correct

17. Consider the following statements regarding indicative planning :
1. It was followed in Russia.
2. It was used in France.
3. It has been used in all the Five year Plans of India
4. It is being used in India's Eight Five year Plan

Of these statements
A. 1 and 2 are correct
B. 1, 2 and 4 are correct
C. 2 and 4 are correct
D. 2, 3 and 4 are correct

18. Consider the following statements :
1. Disguised unemployment is present only in agriculture.
2. Disguised unemployment is a major cause of the low standard of living in the rural areas of India.
3. Disguised unemployment can be useful in India's developmental process as a source of potential saving.
4. Disguised unemployment occurs because people in village do not have motivation to work.

Of these statements
A. 1, 2 and 3 are correct
B. 2, 3 and 4 are correct
C. 2 and 3 are correct
D. 1 and 2 are correct

19. The concept of "economic growth" is:
A. uni-dimensional in nature measuring growth in national income
B. multi-dimensional in corporating non-economic aspects also
C. related to development but not to deprivation
D. related to resource development but not to human development

20. Nowadays we talk about "sustainable development" which relates to:

A. control of population to suit natural resources

B. development for sufficiency and efficiency which is bio-friendly

C. development which is within the central and state budgetary resources

D. development which takes into account the taxable capacity of people

21. The best indicator of economic development is

A. rising savings

B. rising investment

C. rising capital-output ratio

D. rising levels of living

22 Growth in developed countries is now mostly the result of

A. rising labour productivity

B. rising capital accumulation

C. innovation and technology

D. government assistance in exports

23. In Harrod-Domar models, "over production" is a condition where

A. all producers are producing too much

B. all producers are producing less than the warranted output

C. all producers are producing higher than the warranted output

D. where excess capacity has been created

24. In Domar's model

A. investment is needed to increase demand as well as supply

B. there is great emphasis on increasing the capital-output ratio

C. the classical economics is completely rejected

D. the keynesian economics is completely rejected

25. The development process under capitalism has been described as '*creative destruction*' by

A. Karl Marx

B. A.N. Hansen

C. R. Luxemburg

D. J. Schumpeter

26. In Harrod model :

A. if the actual growth rate is higher than the warranted growth rate, there will be inflation

B. if the actual growth rate is higher than the warranted growth rate, there will be deflation

C. the economy will be in equilibrium when actual and warranted growth rates are equal

D. higher growth is the consequence of economising on labour

27. In Domar's model

A. investment is the solution for both inflation and deflation

B. higher investment is solution only to control inflation

C. higher investment is solution only to control deflation

D. a high growth rate is preferable to a relatively lower compound growth rate

28. In Harrod model, investment demand is a function of which of the following

A. national income

B. rate of change in price level

C. rate of change in national income

D. interest rate

29. Who among the following Economists held the behaviour of population as an obstacle to economic growth in initiating the process of economic growth

A. P.N. Rosenstein Rodan

B. W.W. Rostow

C. R. Nurkse

D. H. Leibenstein

30. A number of indivisibilities hinder the process of economic growth in the initial stages. This view was enunciated by

A. R. Nurkse

B. H.W. Singer

C. P.N. Rosenstein Rodan

D. W.W. Rostow

31. Development process has been viewed as a 'chain of disequilibria' by

A. P.N. Rosenstein Rodan

B. R. E. Baldwin

C. H. Leibenstein

D. A.O. Hirschman

32 The growth of population has a bearing on the
A. natural rate of growth
B. actual rate of growth
C. warranted rate of growth
D. all the above

33. Nurkse was of the opinion that developing countries will have serious and adverse effect on their balance of payments due to
A. backwash effect
B. demonstration effect
C. multiplier effect
D. spread effect

34. Who among the following Economists held that a growing economy is essentially unstable
A. R.F. Harrod B. D. Ricardo
C. R. M. Solow D. T. Swau

35. In developing economies, investment is limited due to in sufficiency of demand. Who among the following Economists, has criticised this view
A. E. D. Domar B. R.F. Harrod
C. R. Nurkse D. J. Viner

36. In developing economies, surplus labour exists in the sense that each labour is working for hours less than the normal working hours. This view has been expressed by
A. J. Robinson B. M. Dobb
C. R. Nurkse D. A.K. Sen

37. In Harrod's model of economic growth, G_a is actual rate of growth G_w is warranted rate of growth and G_n is natural rate of growth. Steady rate of growth is ensured when
A. $G_a = G_n$ B. $G_w = G_n$
C. $G_a = G_w$ D. $G_w > G_n$

38. Who among the following Economists, developed the 'theory of circular causation
A. G. Myrdal
B. R. Nurkse
C. J. Robinson
D. J.R. Hicks

39. **Assertion (A) :** The neo-classical growth theory believes that there is substantial difference in the growth pattern of less developed countries and the developed countries.
Reason (R) : This is mostly due to the market failure in the less developed countries caused by a variety of imperfections existing in such economies.
Codes:
A. Both A and R are individually true and R is the correct explanation of A.
B. Both A and R are individually true but R is a *not* the correct explanation of A.
C. A is true but R is false.
D. A is false but R is true.

40. The process of economic development refers to
A. growth of national income over time
B. growth of per capita income and standards of living
C. full employment of the entire population
D. growth of national income with structural changes in the economy

41. Match List-I (concepts) with List-II (Economists) and select the correct answer using the codes given below the lists.
(List-I)
(Concepts)
(a) Critical minimum effort
(b) Unlimited supply of labour
(c) Theory of balanced growth
(d) Warranted growth rate
(List-II)
(Economists)
1. Rosenstein Rodan
2. Harrod-Domars
3. W.A. Lewis
4. H. Leibenstein

Codes :	*(a)*	*(b)*	*(c)*	*(d)*
A.	1	2	4	3
B.	4	3	1	2
C.	1	3	4	2
D.	4	2	1	3

42 Marx refers to the concept of organic composition of capital. Which one of the following ratios stands for this (where C is constant capital, V is variable capital and S is surplus value)?
A. $\frac{C}{V+S}$ B. $\frac{C}{V}$
C. $\left(\frac{C}{C+V}\right)$ D. $\left(\frac{C+V}{V}\right)$

43. The 'Big push' strategy of development was first advocated by

A. Rosenstein Rodan
B. Simon Kuznets
C. W.A. Lewis
D. A.O. Hirschman

44. Assertioin (A) : Non-economic factors play an important role in the process of economic development.

Reason (R) : Accumulation of capital takes the form of human capita formation also.

A. Both A and R are true and R is the correct explanation of A.
B. Both A and R are true but R is *NOT* a correct explanation of A.
C. A is true but R is false.
D. A is false but R is true.

45. Assertion (A) : Per capita income figures are poor tools of ordinal ranking of countries with respect to the real well being.

Reason (R) : A good portion of the national income in poor countries is unreported.

A. Both A and R are true and R is the correct explanation of A.
B. Both A and R are true but R is *NOT* a correct exlanation of A.
C. A is true but R is false.
D. A is false but R is true.

46. Human Development Index (HDI) is a composite index of

A. health, literacy and employment
B. national income, size of population and the general price level
C. national income, per capita income and per capita consumption
D. physical resources, monetary resources and population size

47. According to the Harrod-Domar model, the warranted rate of growth, given the incremental capital-output ratio, depends on the

A. rate of growth of labour force
B. marginal productivity of investment
C. marginal efficiency of capital
D. saving-income ratio

48. According to J.R. Hicks, technical progress is said to be neutral if it raises

A. the marginal physical productivity of labour and capital in the same proportion
B. the average productivity of labour and capital in the same proportion
C. the wage rate and the interest rate in the same proportion
D. the interest-rate and the profit-rate in the same proportion

49. According to Kuznets, during process of development the income inequalities tend to

A. decrease
B. increase
C. increase first and then decrease
D. decrease first and then increase

50. Perfectly elastic supplies of labour play a crucial role in

A. Malthus' model of growth
B. Kuznets' model of growth
C. The Prebisch hypothesis
D. Lewis model of growth

51. Consider the following statements : The correct order of specific stages of demographic transition associated with economic development is

1. low birth rate with low death rate.
2. high birth rate with high death rate.
3. high birth rate with low death rate.

Which of the above statements are correct ?

A. 1, 2, 3 B. 2, 1, 3
C. 2, 3, 1 D. 3, 2, 1

52 Consider the following statements for the Balanced Growth theory propounded by Ragnar Nurkse and select the correct answer from the code given below :

Statements :

(a) A package of industries be developed by private initiative
(b) A package of industries be developed by state initiative.
(c) If needed foreign capital be used to augment the capital supply
(d) Agriculture and industry be used together

Codes :

A. *(a)*, *(b)* and *(c)* are correct
B. *(a)* and *(c)* are correct
C. *(b)* and *(d)* are correct
D. *(b)*, *(c)* and *(d)* are correct

53. Assertion (A) : In the unbalanced theory of growth, different sectors grow at different rates.
Reasons (R) : This allows utilization of interdependence of economic sectors.
Codes :
A. Both A and R are true and R is correct explanation of A.
B. Both A and R are true but R is not the correct explanation of A.
C. A is true but R is false
D. A is false but R is true

54. "Development is a continuous and spontaneous change in the stationary state which forever alters and displaces the equilibrium state previously existing; while growth is a gradual and steady change in the long run which comes about by a gradual increase in the rate of savings and population", is the well-known definition of development and growth attributed to
A. C.P. Kindelberger
B. U. Hicks
C. J. A. Schumpeter
D. Ragner Nurkse

55. Consider the following statements :
According to Joan Robinson, "*golden age*" refers to a situation where
1. there is full employment at a high standard of living
2. there is full utilisation of capacity
3. the rate of growth of population is higher than the rate of growth of the economy
4. the per capita income increases at an increasing rate

Of these statements
A. 3 and 4 are correct
B. 1 and 4 are correct
C. 1 and 3 are correct
D. 1 and 2 are correct

56. Consider the following :
The process which enables
1. individuals of a country to accumulate more capital.
2. increasing the knowledge, skill and capacities of the people of the country.
3. accumulation of tangible wealth.
4. accumulation of intangible wealth.

Human capital formation as a concept is better explained in terms of
A. 1, 2 and 4 B. 1, 2 and 3
C. 3 and 4 D. 2 and 4

57. According to Hirschman, '*convergent*' series comprises investment projects that appropriate more external economies than they create and '*divergent*' series comprises investment projects that create more external economies than what they appropriate. In terms of this, investments in power and transport as
A. convergent series
B. divergent series
C. respectively convergent and divergent series
D. both (A) and (B)

58. Match List-I (Investment criteria) with List-II (Authors) and select the correct answer using the codes given below the lists :

List-I
(a) Capital turnover criterion
(b) Social marginal productivity criterion
(c) Time series criterion
(d) Ratio of reinvestment criterion

List-II
1. Galenson-Leibenstein
2. A.K. Sen
3. Kahn-Chenery
4. Buchanan-Polak

Codes :	*(a)*	*(b)*	*(c)*	*(d)*
A.	4	3	2	1
B.	4	2	3	1
C.	1	2	3	4
D.	1	3	2	4

59. The original interpretation of balanced growth relates to
A. large-scale expansion of activities to over come divergence between private and social benefits
B. all sectors growing at the same rate
C. equal amount to investment in all sectors
D. absence of shortages or excesses

60. The vicious circle of poverty can be broke with synchronised application of capital rather than investment in any single line production taken by itself. In this statement '*single line of production*' implies

A. investment in the production of particular type of commodity
B. specialising in a particular process of production
C. investment in a particular region of the economy
D. none of these

61. Match List-I with List-II and select the correct answer using the codes given below the lists :

List-I

(a) P.N. Rosenstein Rodan
(b) H. Leibenstein
(c) R. Nurkse
(d) W.W. Rostow

List-II

1. The critical minimum effort
2. The big push theory
3. Take-off into self-sustained growth
4. Vicious circle of poverty

Codes :	*(a)*	*(b)*	*(c)*	*(d)*
A.	2	1	4	3
B.	3	4	2	1
C.	3	1	4	2
D.	2	4	1	3

62. Consider the following statements :
'Economic Development' is a

1. continuous process
2. short-term process
3. long-term process

Of these statements

A. 2 alone is correct
B. 1 and 3 are correct
C. 3 alone is correct
D. 1 and 2 are correct

63. The index which combines social indicators of life expectancy and literacy with a measure of basic income adjusted to reflect purchasing power sufficient to raise the people above the poverty line is called

A. Basic Needs Index
B. Purchasing Power Index
C. Human Development Index
D. Welfare Index

64. A production possibility frontier (PPF) is shown in the given diagram. A less developed country (LDC) will be

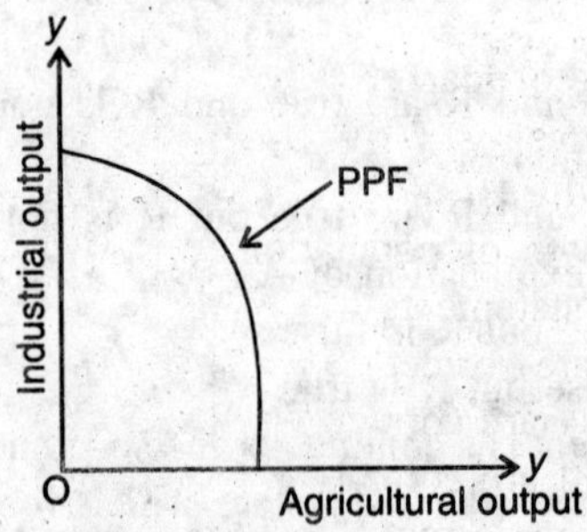

A. inside the PPF
B. on the PPF
C. above the PPF
D. at a point which coincides with the origin

65. In W.W. Rostow's 'Stages of Growth' the Drive to Maturity stage

A. follows take-off stage
B. starts development
C. completes development
D. follows High Mass Consumption stage

66. Capital deepening is a process in which

A. output remains constant
B. capital intensity remains constant
C. technology changes with an increase in output per worker
D. none of these

67. Match List-I with List-II and select the corrct answer using the codes given below the lists:

List-I

(a) Absorptive capacity of capital
(b) Technological dualism
(c) Permissive and compulsive sequences
(d) Physical Quality of Life Index

List-II

1. A.O. Hirschman
2. M. Kalecki
3. B. Higgins
4. D. Morris

Codes :	*(a)*	*(b)*	*(c)*	*(d)*
A.	2	3	4	1
B.	2	3	1	4
C.	3	2	1	4
D.	3	2	4	1

68. Consider the following statements :
On the supply side, the argument for a Big Push theory is tied up with assumed existence of
1. small size of market
2. externalities
3. indivisibilities
4. high growth of population

Of these statements
A. 1 and 2 are correct
B. 1, 3 and 4 are correct
C. 2, 3 and 4 are correct
D. 2 and 3 are correct

69. According to Friedrich List, the different stages of development follow the sequence
A. pastoral, agriculture, agricultural manufacturing
B. savage, agriculture, agricultural manufacturing
C. agriculture, agricultural manufacturing, industry
D. savage, pastoral, agriculture, agricultural manufacturing, commerce

70. Match List-I with List-II and select the correct answer using the codes given below the lists:

List-I
(a) Economic Growth and Structure
(b) Readings in the Theory of Income Distribution
(c) An Essay on Marxian Economics
(d) The Theory of Geographical Location of Economic Activity

List-II
1. Fellner
2. Kuznets
3. W.H. Dean
4. Joan Robinsons

Codes :	*(a)*	*(b)*	*(c)*	*(d)*
A.	2	1	4	3
B.	2	1	3	4
C.	1	2	3	4
D.	1	2	4	3

71. Generally speaking the optimum population of a country refers to the size of the population which
A. maximises output per head
B. maintains constant rate of growth of population
C. leads to an increase in the proportion of workers in the industry
D. provides gainful employment to the rural population

72 The most important objective of development planning is to
A. ensure a greater degree of economic equality
B. ensure a higher degree of economic growth and development
C. make available larger provisions for capital formation and investment
D. provide greater opportunities for full employment

73. Consider the following statements:
Mahalanobis model of planning can be described as a
1. sectoral planning model
2. bi-sector model
3. consistency model
4. growth model

Of these statements
A. 1 and 2 are correct
B. 2 and 3 are correct
C. 1 and 3 are correct
D. 3 and 4 are correct

74. **Assertion (A) :** According to Schumpeter, development is a spontaneous and discontinuous change in the channels of the circular flow.
Reason (R) : The entrepreneur is the agent of this change.
A. Both A and R are true and R is the correct explanation of A.
B. Both A and R are true but R is *not* a correct explanation of A.
C. A is true but R is false.
D. A is false but R is true.

75. Which one of the following pairs is *not* correctly matched ?

	Author	***Book***
A.	Siman Kuznets	Asian Drama
B.	J. Robinson	Essays on the Theory of Economic Growth

C. Karl Marx — Das Capital
D. Arthur W. Lewis — Theory of Economic Growth

76. The mercantilist theory of economic growth is primarily concerned with an increase in the
A. Volume of money in circulation through the import of gold
B. Size of population
C. State intervention for the creation of conditions for efficient entrepreneurial functions
D. Surplus in the balance of trade

77. Assuming capital-output ratio to be 3:1 and population grown to be 2.5% per annum, a 10.5% increase in investment will lead to an increase in per capita income to the extent of
A. 0%
B. 1.0%
C. 3.0%
D. 7.0%

78. Harrod's natural rate of growth is
A. the rate of growth which the increase of population and technical improvement allow
B. the rate of growth which will satisfy profit makers that they have done the right thing
C. the actual rate of growth
D. the increase in the rate of capital accumulation

79. "Economic Development with Unlimited Supplies of labour" is a model of development enunciated by
A. A. O. Hirschman B. W. W. Rostow
C. W. A. Lewis D. Holis Chenery

80. Leibenstein in his Critical Minimum Effort thesis treats population as a factor that is
A. income – generating
B. income– depressing
C. investment – inducing
D. market – expending

81. The First Five Year Plan of the Government of India was based on
A. Leontief input – output model
B. Harrod – Domar model
C. Mahalanobis two – sector model
D. Mahalanobis four – sector model

82 *'Economic Drain'* theory was popularised by
A. Dadabhai Naoroji
B. Vera Anstey
C. V. V. Bhatt
D. None of these

83. According to Fisher-Clark thesis which one of following is the correct sequence of shift of resources from one sector to the other for the continuity of development?
A. Agriculture → Services → Manufacturing
B. Agriculture → Manufacturing → services
C. Manufacturing → Services → Agriculture
D. Manufacturing → Agriculture → Services

84. Consider the following statements:
In the estimates of growth of the United States, 'residual growth' is attributed by Denison to
1. technological improvement
2. growth of capital
3. growth of labour
4. combined growth of labour and capital.
Of these statement
A. 1 alone is correct
B. 1 and 2 are corret
C. 1, 2, and 3 are correct
D. 1, 2, 3, and 4 are correct

85. **Assertion (A):** Technological change is regarded as an important factor in the process of economic growth.
Reason (R): Changes in the technology lead to increases in the productivity of labour, capital and other factors of production.
Codes:
A. Both A and R are true and R is the correct explanation of A
B. Both A and R are true but R is *not* the correct explanation of A
C. A is true but R is false
D. A is false but R is true

86. Which one of the following growth models was the basis of the planning strategy during the second and third Five-year plans of India?
A. Harrod-Domar Growth Model
B. The Mahalanobis Two-Sector model
C. Alan Manne and Ashok Rudra's 30-sector consistency model
D. Kaldor's model of growth

87. Which of the following was/were assumed in the neo-classical growth model as propounded by Solow?

1. A variable savings rate
2. A constant population growth rate
3. A variable capital-output ratio

Select the correct answer using the codes given below.

Codes:

A. 1 alone
B. 1 and 2
C. 3 alone
D. 2 and 3

88. Despite being a high saving economy, a developing country may still NOT grow fast primarily due to

A. week administrative machinery
B. illiteracy
C. high population density
D. high capital-output ratio

89. Hick's neutral technical change implies that

A. the unit isoquant undergoes a parallel sift upwards
B. the unit isoquant undergoes a parallel shift downwards
C. curvature of the unit isoquant changes
D. None of the above

90. Capital deepening means

A. using larger amount of labour as campared to capital
B. using more of the same type of capital due to increase number of workers
C. increase in capital per worker in already existing production
D. using more of human capital

91. Which one of the following pairs of Economists and doctrines they advocated, is correctly matched?

A. A. W. Lewis..."Big Push" theory
B. A. O. Hirschman...strategy of unbalanced growth
C. Rosenstein Rodan...stages of economic growth
D. W. W. Rostow... Theory of development with unlimited supplies of labour

92 If the marginal productivity of labour in agriculture is zero, then the labour supply curve for industry as assumed by Arthur Lewis will be

A. upward rising
B. perfectly inelastic
C. backward bending
D. perfectly elastic

93. Consider the following statements:

The Knife-edge problem in the Harrod-Domar growth model implies a constant

1. rate of population
2. output
3. rate of saving
4. capital-output ratio

Of these statements

A. 4 alone is correct
B. 1 and 2 are correct
C. 1, 2 and 3 are correct
D. 1, 3 and 4 are correct

94. In the analysis by Hirschman, the industry with the highest combined linkages turned out to be

A. Cement
B. Textiles
C. Iron and Steel
D. Food processing

95. The utilisation of disguised unemployment as a source of savings potential in under-developed countries was suggested by

A. R. Nurkse B. P. Baran
C. R. Harrod D. W.W. Rostow

96. Match list-I (Authors) with list-II (Concepts) and select the correct answer using the codes given below the lists

List I	*List II*
(a) Domar	1. Golden Age
(b) Rosenstein-Rodan	2. Big-Push
(c) Rostow	3. Stages of growth
(d) Joan Robinson	4. Required rate of growth

Codes :	*(a)*	*(b)*	*(c)*	*(d)*
A.	4	2	3	1
B.	2	4	3	1
C.	2	4	1	3
D.	4	2	1	3

97. Match List I (Authors) with List II (Theories) and select the correct answer using the codes given below the Lists.

List I	*List II*
(a) Solow	1. Neutral technological change, under which, despite the change in output, the capital labour ratio remains constant.
(b) Hicks	2. Neutral technological change, under which the labour output ratio remains constant, so that the factor proportions are baised in favours of saving capital
(c) Harrod	3. Neutral technological change, under which, the capital output ratio remains constant, so that the factor proportions are baised in favour of saving labour

Codes :	*(a)*	*(b)*	*(c)*
A.	2	1	3
B.	1	2	3
C.	3	2	1
D.	3	1	2

98. The two-gap theory as applied to development planning refers to

A. inflationary gap and investment gap
B. saving gap and deflationary gap
C. foreign exchange gap
D. saving constraint and foreign exchange constraint

99. Demographic transition refers to

A. migration of population from rural to urban areas
B. change in the male/female ratio of the population
C. shift from a stable population at high birth and death rates to one of low birth and death rates
D. shift from high birth and low death rates to low birth and low death rates

100. Which one of the following is NOT an assumption of the Harrod-Domar model?

A. Fixed capital-output ratio
B. Variable marginal and average propensity to save
C. Closed economy
D. Capital is the only factor of production

101. The 'Hindu Rate of Growth'

A. refers to growth of Hindu population
B. is the term used by Raj Krishna to represent the nature of the growth of Indian economy at around 3.5 per cent per year
C. is the term coined by Amartya Sen to represent the nature of the growth of the Indian economy at around 3.5 per cent per year.
D. is the term coined by V. K. R. V. Rao to decide the nature of the growth of the Indian economy at around 4 per cent

102. Disguised unemployment in the agricultural sector of India exists due to the

A. dependence of agriculture on the monsoons
B. abolition of Zamindari
C. heavy pressure of population on land
D. absence of trade unions in the agricultural sector

103. The concept of unbalanced growth has not been advocated by

A. H. W. Singer B. A. Lewis
C. A. O. Hirschman D. C. P. Kindleberger

104. The idea of balanced growth is related to the classical

A. idea of the nature of economic science
B. idea of full employment equilibrium
C. law of markets
D. school of thought

105. The difficulties of comparing growth of different countries are

A. Lack of empirical data
B. Choice of a common denominator
C. Assigning weights to the various items of output
D. All of these

106. Investment projects should be capital intensive because they would lead to greater saving and investment in future advocated by

A. H. Leibenstein
B. M. Leibenstein and W. Galenson
C. W. Galenson
D. W. Galenson and R. Nurkse

107. According to Lewis the subsistence sector is that part of the economy which

A. Makes use of reproducible capital

B. Does not make use of reproducible capital
C. Employs labour for wages in mines, factories, plantations for earning profits
D. None of the above

108. Myrdal builds his theory of economic development around the idea of
A. Regional inequalities on the national plane
B. Regional inequalities on the international plane
C. Both A and B
D. None of the above

109. If you like to increase the rate of economic development of a country, increase in which of the folllowing would you suggest
A. Government expenditure
B. Standard of living
C. Consumption
D. Saving

110. All underdeveloped countries are
A. Not developing at all
B. Developing but slowly
C. Developing at different rates
D. Receding backwards

111 To break the vicious circle on the demand side of capital, Nurkse has pleaded for
A. Balance growth
B. Unbalanced growth
C. Agricultural growth
D. Industrial growth

112. Incremental capital-output ratio (ICOR) is defined as

A. $\frac{\text{Increment in capital}}{\text{Increment in output}}$

B. $\frac{\text{Increment in output}}{\text{Increment in capital}}$

C. $\frac{\text{Increment in income}}{\text{Increment in consumption}}$

D. $\frac{\text{Increment in saving}}{\text{Increment in consumption}}$

113. The criticism of the balanced growth theory is mainly based on the considerations of
A. Market-size
B. External economies
C. Scarcity of resources
D. Large population

114. Unbalanced growth hypothesis is formulated on the assumption that
A. Expansion takes place simultaneously on several routes
B. Supplies of capital and labour are fixed
C. There are unlimited supplies of labour and capital
D. Underdeveloped countries impose ceiling on their rates of growth

115. Balanced growth, which is associated with Nurkse and Rosentein Rodan, means
A. Equal increase in resources allocated
B. Equal percentage growth in output
C. Different parts of the economic growth in harmonious manner
D. Different fields of growth at a natural rate

116. Who of the following supported the theory of balanced growth?
A. Ragnar Nurkse B. Hans Singer
C. Hirschman D. None of the above

117. Who has suggested that economic development of developing countries can be accelerated by weakening the '*back wash effects*' and strenghthening the '*Spread effects*'?
A. N. Kaldor B. J. Robinson
C. G. Myrdal D. J. H. Boeke

118. If the capital-output ratio is 3 per cent, the savings rate 5 per cent and the economy is growing at 4 per cent in simple terms and 1.5 per cent in per capita terms, what is the percentage of the rate of population growth?
A. 1.5 B. 2.5
C. 3.5 D. 4.5

119. Lewis means by an unlimited supply of labour
A. The supply of labour is more than the demand for labour
B. Infinite labour is available at whatever wage determined by the market
C. The supply of labour at the subsistence wage is greater than the demand for labour
D. The economy adopts only labour intensive techniques of production
E. None of the above

120. Which one of the following is not an assumption of Neoclassical's Growth theory?

A. Perfect competition in commodity and factor markets

B. Factor payment equal their marginal revenue productivity

C. A capital-output ratio

D. Full employment in the economy

121. Foreign aid is needed to

A. Supplement the domestic savings of developing nations

B. Assure the capital imports needed for development

C. Prevent the absolute gap between rich and poor nations from widening further

D. All of the above

122. "Under–developed countries are the slums of the world economy" is the statement given by

A. David Ricardo B. G. Myrdal

C. Cairncross D. Arthur Lewis

123. Dualistic economy is one where

A. Public and private sectors exist side by side

B. Modern industrial sector and traditional subsistence sector exist side by side

C. Agriculture and industrial sectors are equally developed

D. Indigeneous industries are developed in collaboration with foreign companies

124. Fei– Ranis theory of economic development is based on

A. Balanced growth during the take off process

B. Importance of agricultural product in capital accumulation in under developed countries

C. Dualistic approach to development

D. All of the above

125. According to Myrdal, the main cause of regional inequalities in the under developed countries has been

A. Weak backwash effects and strong spread effects

B. Weak back–wash and spread effects

C. Strong back–wash and spread effects

D. Strong back–wash and weak spread effects

126. The technique of input–output analysis has been popularised by

A. Nurkse B. Samuelson

C. Leontief D. Lange

127. According to Solow, the long–run rate of growth on an advanced economy equals Harrod's

A. Warranted rate of growth

B. Actual rate of growth

C. Natural rate of growth

D. None of the above

128. In terms of Harrod–Domar growth model, for achieving a postulated rate of growth an economy requires

A. Increase in the investment ratio

B. Reducing the capital–output ratio

C. Restricting the growth of population

D. All of the above

129. Harrod–Domar model of economic development presupposes—in the economy.

A. Low level of consumption

B. High level of consumption

C. Unemployment

D. Full employment

130. Who believed that the people in less developed countries are not economically motivated towards work and does not respond to normal monetary incentive?

A. A. Marshall B. D. Ricardo

C. J. H. Boeke D. R. Nurkse

131. With economic growth there is

A. A shift away from agriculture

B. A shift away from manufacturing

C. A shift in favour of agriculture

D. A shift away from services

132. The rate of growth of national income is equal to

A. $\frac{\text{National income}}{\text{growth of population}}$

B. $\frac{\text{Investment ratio}}{\text{Capital output ratio}}$

C. $\frac{\text{Capital output ratio}}{\text{Investment ratio}}$

D. None of these

133. An economy will face depression if the

A. Warranted rate of growth is higher than the actual rate of growth

B. Actual rate of growth is higher than the warranted rate of growth
C. Natural rate of growth is higher than the actual rate of growth
D. Actual rate of growth is higher than the natural rate growth

134. The condition of steady growth, in terms of rate of growth, in the Harrod growth model is
A. Actual growth rate = Warranted growth rate
B. Actual growth rate = "Take off" growth rate
C. actual gtowth rate = Natural grown rate
D. Warranted growth rate = Natural growth rate

135. According to the Hicksion theory, growth is checked when
A. Rate of growth of actual output exceeds rate of growth of ceiling output
B. Rate of growth of actual output is less than the rate of growth of ceiling output
C. Rate of growth of actual output is equal to the rate of growth of ceiling output
D. None of the above

136. According to Colin Clark the third and final stage of development is characterised by the predominance of
A. Manufacturing sector
B. Services sector
C. Agriculture sector
D. Exports sector

137. With economic growth the share of the secondary sector in National Product
A. Rises
B. Falls
C. Remains constant
D. Does not necessarily rise

138. The idea of a 'Big Push' is associated with which of the following theories?
A. Economic development with unlimited supply of labour
B. Theory of Balanced growth
C. Theory of Unbalanced growth
D. None of the above

139. Accumulation of capital involves:
A. Increase in real saving
B. Mobilisation of saving
C. Investment of saving
D. All of the above

140. Boeke, the originator of the theory of Sociological Dualism was
A. An English Civil Servant
B. A French Civil Servant
C. A Dutch Civil Servant
D. None of the above

141. In Harrod growth model, the rate of advance with the increase in population and technological change allow over the long period of time is called the
A. Warranted Growth Rate
B. Actual Growth Rate
C. Natural Growth Rate
D. "Take–off" Growth Rate

142. The 'Theory of Stages of Growth' is associated with the name
A. Simon Kuznets B. Colin Clark
C. Paul Samuelson D. W.W. Rostow

143. The concepts of 'forward linkage' and 'backward linkage' were used mainly in the developmental theory propounded by
A. Myrdal B. Hirschman
C. Boeke D. Leibenstein

144. The phrase 'demonstration effect', was coined by
A. J.K. Galbraith
B. J.M. Keynes
C. James Dussenberry
D. Joan Robinson

145. The stage of growth in which (1) basic needs are no longer a problem, and (2) there is popular consumption of durable goods is known as
A. The age of high mass consumption
B. The drive to maturity
C. The take–off
D. The pre–conditions for change

146. One of the conditions of take–off, as laid down by Rostow is
A. Rise in the rate of productive investment
B. One or more manufacturing sector with high rate of growth
C. Changes in social and institutional frame work
D. All of the above

147. In Rostow's theory, the drive to maturity
A. Starts the development process
B. Completes the development process
C. Comes before the take–off
D. Follows the take–off

148. Which one of the following is not an assumption of Harrod-Domar models?
A. MPS is greater than APs
B. MPS remains constant
C. There is no depreciation of capital goods
D. None of the above

149. The Harrod-Domar growth model suggests that growth is
A. Directly related to savings and inversely related to the capital-output ratio
B. Directly related to the capital-output ratio and inversely related to savings
C. Indirectly related to savings and the capital-output ratio
D. Directly related to savings and the capital-output ratio

150. The 'warranted growth' rates as defined by Harrod is the
A. Full capacity growth rate of income of an economy
B. Rates which producers will be content with what they are doing
C. Path on which the supply and demand for goods and services will remain in equilibrium given the propensity to save
D. All the above

151. The basic rationale of the theory of "big push" is based upon the idea of
A. Internal economics
B. External economics
C. Size of population
D. None of the above

152 In both the Laspayres and Paasche indices
A. The growth components are the same
B. The weighting factors are the same
C. Both growth and weight factors are the same
D. The growth component in the Laspayres index is larger for countries at the start of the industrialisation process

153. According to Domar's model, in order to maintain full employment the growth rate of net autonomous investment must be equal to
A. Growth rate of savings
B. Marginal propensity to save
C. Marginal propensity to save and productivity of capital
D. Growth rate of population

154. Rostow's condition for a country to achieve the take-off stage was a rise in the proportion of net investment to over
A. 7% B. 5 – 10%
C. 12% D. 14%

155. Nurkse says in the context of an under developed country inducement to invest is limited by
A. The size of the market
B. Lack of investment opportunities
C. Lack of savings
D. The policy of the government

156. The concept of technological dualism has been put forward by
A. B. Higgins B. J. H. Boeke
C. A. Lewis D. R. Rodan

157. Who put forward the theory of 'financial dualism'?
A. J.H. Beoke B. B. Higgins
C. A. Lewis D. H. Myint

158. Which one of the following countries was the first to reach the age of high mass consumption in 1920'S?
A. Japan B. U. S. A
C. Soviet Union D. Great Britain

159. Disguised unemployment generally means
A. Large number of people remaining unemployed
B. Alternative employment is not available
C. MP_L is zero
D. None of the above

160. In the Lewis' theory, capitalist surplus results because the marginal productivity of labour in the capitalist sector is
A. Higher than the capitalist wage
B. Higher than that in the subsistence sector
C. Positive
D. Ever increasing

161. Which one of the following is not the one of the indivisibilities as prescribed by Rodan for launching economic development?
A. Indivisibilities in the Production Function
B. Indivisibilities in the Consumption Function

C. Indivisibilities of Demand
D. Indivisibilities in the supply of savings

162 Which among the following has the highest forward linkage?
A. Foodgrains B. Guns
C. Iron Ore D. Machinery

163. The actual growth rate is defined by Harrod as the rate which is
A. Determined by the saving ratio and marginal capital-output ratio
B. The full capacity growth rate of income of an economy
C. The welfare optimum rate
D. None of the above

164. Who believed that a deliberate unbalancing of the economy according to a predesigned strategy is the best way to achieve economic growth
A. Rosenstein Rodan B. A. O. Hirschman
C. J. Schumpeter D. J.H. Boeke

165. In Lewis' Theory, capital formation dependes upon
A. Capitalist surplus
B. Bank credit
C. Both of (A) and (B)
D. None of the above

166. The 'critical minimum effort' theory is due to
A. H. Leibenstein B. Rosenstein Rodan
C. W. A. Lewis D. J. H. Boeke

167. The classical model of economic development considers:
A. Profits as incentive to investment
B. Tendency of profits to decline with larger capital accumulation
C. Both A and B
D. None of the above

168. "Golden age" corresponds to a situation where
A. Natural rate of growth exceeds warranted rate of growth
B. Actual rate of growth exceed warranted rate of growth
C. Warranted rate of growth exceeds natural rate of growth
D. Natural, warranted and the actual rate of growth of national income are all equal

169. The 'Financial dualism' refers to coexistence in the less developed countries of
A. Commercial banks and non-bank financial institutions
B. Scheduled and non-scheduled commercial banks
C. Stock exchange and new issue market
D. None of the above

170. Harrod-Domar models of economic growth are based on the experiences of
A. Underdeveloped economics
B. Developing economics
C. Advanced capitalist economics
D. Socialist economics

171. Which one of the following represents, at least in part, investment in human capital?
A. Formal education
B. On the Job training
C. Better health care
D. All of the above

172 Who was the first economist to advocate a Rolling plan for developing countries?
A. A. K. Sen
B. G. Myrdal
C. P. C. Mahalanobis
D. Rosenstein Rodan

173. Perspective planning refer to
A. Annual planning
B. Five-year planning
C. Long term planning
D. None of the above

174. Economist who first defined the concept of *Shadow Prices* is
A. Rosenstein-Rodan B. H. Leibenstein
C. J. Tinberger D. G. Myrdal

175. Solow's model or long run growth is a major improvement over that of
A. Harrod-Domar B. J. Robinson
C. J. E. Meade D. None of the above

176. Centralised planning refers to
A. Complete governmental control over the economy
B. Planning specific projects
C. The provision of the general frame work for the Five-year plans
D. The provision of economic projections and voluntary guidelines

177. The book entitled "The Accumulation of Capital" has been written by
A. J. Robinson B. N. Kaldor
C. J. E. Meade D. Rosenstein Rodan

178. A consistency Model for India's Fourth plan was designed by
A. P. C. Malhalanobis
B. K. N. Raj and A. K. Sen
C. A. S. Manne and A. Rudra
D. All of the above

179. Which one of the following is not included by J. E. Meade in the three principal means whereby an economy can grow
A. Capital accumulation
B. Foreign trade
C. Growth of working population
D. Technical progress

180. The term 'golden age' as used by Joan Robinson refers to
A. Primitive economics
B. The situation of smooth and steady growth with full employment
C. The economy which uses gold coins
D. All of the above

ANSWERS

1	2	3	4	5	6	7	8	9	10
A	A	A	D	C	B	B	B	B	A
11	12	13	14	15	16	17	18	19	20
B	D	C	C	B	A	B	A	B	B
21	22	23	24	25	26	27	28	29	30
D	C	C	A	D	A	A	A	D	C
31	32	33	34	35	36	37	38	39	40
D	A	B	D	C	D	B	A	A	D
41	42	43	44	45	46	47	48	49	50
B	B	A	B	A	A	D	A	B	D
51	52	53	54	55	56	57	58	59	60
C	C	A	C	D	D	B	B	C	A
61	62	63	64	65	66	67	68	69	70
A	B	C	A	A	C	B	D	D	B
71	72	73	74	75	76	77	78	79	80
A	B	A	A	A	D	B	A	C	A
81	82	83	84	85	86	87	88	89	90
B	A	B	A	A	B	D	D	B	C
91	92	93	94	95	96	97	98	99	100
B	D	D	C	A	A	A	D	D	B
101	102	103	104	105	106	107	108	109	110
B	C	B	B	D	B	B	C	A	C
111	112	113	114	115	116	117	118	119	120
A	A	C	B	C	A	C	B	C	C
121	122	123	124	125	126	127	128	129	130
D	C	B	D	D	C	C	D	D	C
131	132	133	134	135	136	137	138	139	140
A	B	A	A	A	B	A	B	D	C
141	142	143	144	145	146	147	148	149	150
C	D	B	C	B	D	D	A	A	D
151	152	153	154	155	156	157	158	159	160
B	A	C	B	B	A	D	B	C	A
161	162	163	164	165	166	167	168	169	170
B	C	A	B	C	A	C	D	A	C
171	172	173	174	175	176	177	178	179	180
D	B	C	C	A	A	A	C	B	B

❑❑❑

PUBLIC FINANCE

The Principle of Maximum Social Advantage

Public revenue and public expenditure are two important financial operations of a state. These two financial operations of the state must be governed by some fundamental principles, so that they may result in maximum social benefit. **Prof. Pigou** and **Prof. Dalton** were the two prominent economists, who were responsible for formulating and popularising this fundamental principle of public finance.

The principle says that the state should collect revenue and spent the money so as to maximum the welfare of the people. When the state imposes taxes, some disutility is created. On the other hand, when the state spends the money, there is some gain in utility. The state should so adjust the revenue and expenditure that the surplus of utility is maximised and disutility is minimised. It should be noted here that the individual welfare of all the people cannot be maximised, if the welfare of some may even decrease; but if the welfare of large majority of the people increases, the net welfare of the society as a whole would be greater. To state it in the words of Prof. Dalton—"As a result of these operations of public finance, changes take place in the amount and in the nature of wealth which is produced, and in the distribution of that wealth among individuals and classes". Are these changes in their aggregate effects socially advantageous? If so, the operations are justified, if not, not. The best system of public finance is that which secures the maximum social advantage from the operations, which it conducts." **Prof. Dalton** called this principle as the principle of **Maximum Social Advantage** and **Prof. Pigou** called it as the Principle of Maximum Aggregate Welfare.

How Maximum Social Advantage is Achieved

There are three fundamental principles of financial operations, which can help the state for achieving the objective of maximum social advantage.

1. Public expenditure should be carried on upto the point where the benefit derived from last unit of money spent by the state, is just equal to the sacrifice imposed in raising that unit of revenue.
2. The resources of the state should be so distributed on different heads of expenditure that the marginal return of satisfaction from each of them is the same.
3. The taxes should be so distributed that the marginal utility of the money pain in taxation is equal to all tax pagers.

The above proposition of maximum social advantage can be depicted graphically also. Through this graph the optimum tax and expenditure activity of the state can be determined. In the diagram let public expenditure and taxation be measured along the *x*-axis and let the social benefit and cost be measured along *y*-axis. The quantities measured along *y*-axis will be positive if measured above *x*-axis and negative if measured below *x*-axis. As a result, the curve showing the marginal social benefit from public expenditure will lie above the *x*-axis and the curve showing marginal disutility from taxation will lie below *x*-axis. In the diagram, the curve BB′ shows the marginal social benefit accruing to the society from different amounts of the public expenditure. The curve DD′ shows the marginal social cost to the society from the taxation levied by the state. The difference between BB′ and

DD′ indicates the net social benefit or advantage (that is the excess of the benefit over the cost to the society), and is depicted by the curve NN′. We find that when an amount OM is taxed and spent by the state, then the marginal social benefit and marginal social disutility are equated (MP being equal to MQ). Till then, the gain to the society is more than the loss. It is here that the state should stop expanding its activities. The net gain to the society (or the maximum possible social advantage) is equal to the shaded area ONM.

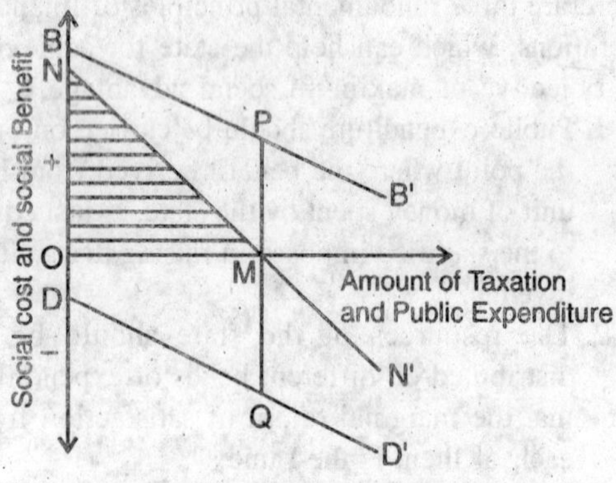

Fig. 1

If the state stops its public finance operations at a figure less than OM, the society will be foregoing a possible gain. If the operations are expanded beyond OM, the total net benefit will again start falling.

Limitations

The principle of maximum social advantage is the fundamental principle of public finance and it is supposed for granted to be the guiding principle of the state's financial activity, yet there are certain limitations and difficulties in the way of practical application of this principle.

In the first place it is very difficult for the state to balance the marginal disutilities caused by the imposition of a tax with the marginal utility of a public expenditure. Even an individual finds it difficult to do so often in his daily practical life, when the disutility of the sacrifice equals the utility of his income. And, this difficulty is much greater for the state, because actual government spending and taxing is done by a larger number of public employees at different places and in different departments. **Secondly**, the state can speculate about the future and try to see the coming event, but it is very difficult to estimate on the basis of there speculations, that expenditure made by the public authorities will yield higher utilities than the disutilities caused at present. Hence, it is very difficult, if not quite impossible for the state to balance marginal disutility of taxation with the marginal utility of expenditure. The success of the state in maximising the net social advantage lies in her ability to correctly foresee all these results of her financial activities. And it requires a sensitive and intelligent mind to be able to do so.

Public Expenditure

Public Expenditure is the expenditure incurred by public authorities—central, state and local governments—either for the satisfaction of collective needs of the citizens or for promoting their economic and social welfare. The volume of public expenditure has been increasing in almost all countries of the world, because of the continuous expansion in the activities of state and other public bodies on several fronts. A theory of public expenditure in the nineteenth century was not very necessary because the scope of the functions of government was restricted. In the twentieth century the development of the functions of the state in social matters, *e.g.*, in education, public health and in commercial and industrial undertakings, such as railways, irrigation and similar projects have increased public expenditure in a large degree.

Reasons For the Growth of Public Expenditure

1. Increase in the Activities of the state
2. Industrial Development
3. Social Security Measure
4. Nationalisation of Industries and Trade
5. Development of Agriculture
6. Rising Trend of Prices

7. Problems of Defence
8. Urbanisation
9. Economic Development

Wagner's Views on Public Expenditure

The German economist, Adolph Wagner, argued that a nation, as it experience economic development and growth, will experience an increase in the activities of the public sector. According to Wagner there are inherent tendencies for the activities of different layers of a government (such as central and state governments) to increase both intensively and extensively.

A number of early economists discussed the relationship between the level of development and public expenditure. However, Wagner was the first to butteress such remark with an extensive theoretical foundation.

To justify his generalisation that the share of public consumption expenditure would increase, Wagner divided public expenditure into two categories, expenditures for internal and external security and expenditures for "cultural and welfare" which should include education, health, transportation, banking and the like expenditures for external security would increase in a growing economy as the nature of the use of force by the state changes from simple aggression to prevention of attack and as armies use more capital equipment. For internal security Wagner foresaw greater expenditure because of greater friction between economic units and people as urbanisation progressed.

Canons of Public Expenditure

Like cannons of taxation, people have propounded canons of public expenditure also which should govern the public expenditure decision. Some of these canons are in the nature of administrative safeguards while others are expected to be of help to the economy and society in their diverse objectives. Some important cannons of public expenditure are—

1. Canon of Benefit
2. Canon of Economy
3. Canon of Sanction
4. Canon of Surplus
5. Canon of Elasticity
6. Canon of Equitable Distribution
7. Canon of Productivity

Wiseman-Peacock Hypothesis

The another thesis of the growth of public expenditure was put forth by **Wiseman and Peacock** in their study of public expenditure in UK for the period 1890-1955. The main thesis of the authors is that public expenditure does not increase in a smooth and continuous manner, but in jerks or steplike fashion. At times some social or other disturbance takes place which at once shows the need for increased public expenditure which the existing public revenue cannot meet. While earlier, due to an insufficient pressure for public expenditure, the revenue constraint was dominating and restraining an expansion in public expenditure, now under changed requirements such a restraint gives way. The public expenditure increases and makes the inadequacy of the present revenue quite clear to every one. The movement from the older level of expenditure and taxation to a new and higher level is the 'displacement effect.' The inadequacy of the revenue as compared with the 'required' public expenditure creates an 'inspection effect.' The government and the people review the revenue position and the need to find a solution of the important problems that have come up and agree to the required adjustments to finance the increased expenditure. They attain a new level of 'tax tolerance.' They are now ready to tolerate a greater burden of taxation and as a result the general level of expenditure and revenue goes up. In this way, the public expenditure and revenue get stabilized at a new level till another disturbance occurs to cause a 'displacement effect.' Since each major disturbance leads to the government assuming a larger proportion of the total national economic activity, the net result is the 'concentration effect.' The concentration effect also refers to the apparent tendency for central government economic activity to grow faster than that of the state and local level governments. British data are consistent with this finding, but its application to other countries needs verification.

The Public Budget

A budget is the statement of the financial plan of a government. It indicates the revenue and expenditure of the last completed financial year, the probable revenue and expenditure estimates for the current year, *i.e.*, not completed and the estimates of the anticipated revenue and proposed expenditure for the next financial year.

In the Constitution of India, a budget has been referred to as the annual financial statement of the estimated receipts and expenditure of the government of India or of a state government, in respect of a financial year. **Article 112** of the Constitution of India states that "an annual financial statement" will be placed before both Lok Sabha, and Rajya Sabha, while Article 202 of the Constitution states that a similar financial statement for each state will be placed before the Legislature of that state.

Revenue and Capital Budgets

In many countries, the budget is divided into revenue and capital accounts. Revenue account covers those items which are of recurring nature; while capital account covers those items which are in the nature of the acquiring and disposing of capital assets.

In India, the constitution demands that the budget must distinguish expenditure on Revenue Accounts from other expenditure. Accordingly, the budget is necessarily presented into two parts, namely, **Revenue Budget** and **Capital Budget**. Revenue Budget consists of the revenue receipts — both tax revenue and non-tax revenue — and the expenditure met out of revenue receipts. The non-tax-revenue receipts include revenue from currency, coinage and mint, interest receipts, dividends, profits revenue from general services (such as police, jails, public works etc.), revenue from social and community services (such as education, health, housing, broadcasting and so on), and revenue from economic services (such as agriculture and allied services, industry and mines, transport and communications, etc.)

Capital Account receipts, on the other hand, include market loans, borrowings from the RBI, etc., through the sale of Treasury Bills, loans from foreign governments and institutions, and repayment of loans by state governments and others to the central government. Capital disbursements would include expenditure on acquisition of various physical assets like land, buildings, machinery and equipment, investments in shares and debentures and loans to state governments and other bodies.

Zero-Base Budgeting

Zero-base budgeting (ZBB) is an innovative technique to guard against wastage in public expenditure. The technique works not through auditing which is a post — operative check, but through an examination of the very rational of an expenditure item under consideration. In a more practical way, ZBB means the evaluation and prioritisation of all programmes at different levels of efforts. To be more simple, each department is required to justify its budget requests from the bottom up, evaluating alternative programme packages and ranking programmes so as to select the best alternative and allocate resources accordingly. Thus, no consideration is given to the post or existing at present, any programme may be included or excluded. The Budget is considered as a whole and a fresh, *i.e.*, from zero-Base.

In the sphere of public budgeting, ZBB was first tried by **Mr. Jimmy Carter** in 1973 when he was the Governer of Georgia, with proper remoulding. Later on its was adopted by a number of states in the U.S.A.

Performance Budgeting

Performance Budgeting is generally understood as a system of presentation of public expenditure in terms of functions, programmes, performance units, viz., activities, projects, etc., reflecting primarily the government out-put and its cost.

The U.S. Bureau of the Budget defines a performance budget in these words, "As performance budget in one which presents the purpose and objectives for which funds are required, the cost of the programmes proposed for achieving those objective and quantitative data measuring the accomplishment and work performed under each programme."

Under Performance Budgeting System the over all budget is divided into functions based on the major purpose of government and then sub divided into programme and activities, funds are granted for doing a specific quantity of work. Performance budgeting implies that the budget statement should indicate the actual achievement expected by a Ministry over a period of time from certain amount of expenditure.

Thus, the process of performance budgeting is not merely a technique, it constitutes a new approach to budget formation and execution. Since the cost and benefits indicated side by side, this technique helps in the decision-making regarding allocations of funds.

Types of Deficits

1. Revenue Deficits. Revenue Deficit = Revenue Expenditure – Revenue Receipts

Current revenue expenditure of the central government is composed of plan and non-plan expenditure, and current-revenue receipts include net tax revenue and non-tax revenue of the central government.

2. Budget Deficit. Budget Deficit = Total Expenditure – Total Receipts

The total expenditure of the central governments always exceeded its total revenue which is known as budget deficit or overall budgetary deficit.

3. Fiscal Deficit. In simple terms, fiscal deficit is budgetary deficit plus market borrowings and other liabilities of the government of India.

∴ Fiscal Deficit = Revenue receipts (Net tax revenue + Non-tax revenue) + Capital receipts (only recoveries of loans and other receipts) – Total expenditure (Plan and non-plan)

4. Primary Deficit. The excess of fiscal deficit over payments of interest is called primary deficit.

5. Monetised Deficit. The increase in net RBI credit for central government is called monetised deficit. It includes: A. Net increase in holdings of treasury bills of RBI.

B. Contribution of RBI in market borrowings of the govt.

Public Revenue

Like any other economic unit, a government also needs funds to finance its activities. Such funds are raised from various sources. It is difficult to give a complete list of all the sources of public revenue, but the important and common sources of public revenue would include taxes, income from currency, market borrowings, sale of public assets, income from public undertakings, fees, fines, gifts and donations, etc.

What is a Tax?

A tax is a compulsory levy and those who are taxed have to pay the sums irrespective of any corresponding return of services or goods by the government. In other words, a tax-payer does not receive a definite and direct quid pro quo from the government. Note the word *direct* here. It is not a price paid by the tax-payer for any definite service rendered or a commodity supplied by the government. The tax-payers do get many benefits from the government but no tax-payer has a right to any benefit from the public expenditure on the ground that he is paying a tax.

The Base of Tax

The base of a tax is the legal description of the object with reference to which the tax applies. For example, the base of an excise duty is the production or packing or processing of a specific goods; the base of an income tax is the income of the assessee defined and estimated in terms of certain rules laid down for this purpose. Note that the base of each tax has to be defined legally and it is to be quantified for the purpose of determining the tax liability of an individual tax-payer. Each tax-payer is considered a legal entity for this purpose. It should be noted that a tax base may have a time dimension also. For example, income-tax is usually on an annual basis and the law has to decide whether income would be taxed on the basis of accrual or receipt. The authorities, while determining a tax base, are expected to give due consideration to various questions like those of cost of collection, administration and effects of that tax. With the passage of time, a tax base under consideration may grow or may shrink. For example, as production of excisable goods increases, the base of excise duties would be termed to have grown. Also, by law, new items may be brought under particular taxation, or the relevant provisions, definitions and rules etc. may be changed to extend the coverage or base of a tax. Thus, if new items are brought under excise duties, we shall say that the coverage of excise taxation has been extended and the base of excise taxation has been widened.

Buoyancy and Elasticity of a Tax

These terms denote the factors responsible for an increase in the yield of a tax over time. If a tax revenue increases with the growth of its base, but without an extension of the tax coverage or an upward revision of the tax rates, then the tax is said to be buoyant. It has an inherent tendency to yield more tax revenue with the growth of the base. Thus, for example, with given rates of income-tax and the definition of taxable income, if yield from income-tax increases as national income increases, it would be termed a buoyent tax. Similarly, excise duties are levied on production of specified goods. If new items are not brought under these duties and the rates of existing duties remain unchanged, but the revenue from excise duties increases with an increase in the production of excisable items, we have a case of buoyancy of excise duties. Numerically, the buoyancy of a tax is measured as a ratio of the proportionate increase in tax revenue to a proportionate increase in the tax base.

The yield of a tax may also go up on account of extension of its coverage or a revision of its rates. Such a characteristic of a tax is referred to as its elasticity. In other words, elasticity of a tax refers to its responsiveness to steps taken up authorities in increasing its yield through an extension of its coverage or revision of its rates. Numerically, the elasticity of a tax would be measured by as a ratio of the proportionate change in its yield to the proportionate change in its coverage or rates.

Principles of Taxation

A good tax system is one which is designed on the basis of an appropriate set of principles, such as equality and certainty. Adam Smith was probably the first economist, who stated the general principle of taxation or rules of taxation (which he called the canons of taxation).

The four canons of taxation as prescribed by **Adam Smith** are the following:

1. Canon of Equality
2. Cannon of Certainty
3. Cannon of Convenience
4. Cannon of Economy

Some writers, like Bastable, have added a few more canons of taxation to Adam Smith's four.

5. Canon of Productivity
6. Canon of Elasticity
7. Canon of Diversity
8. Canon of Simplicity
9. Canon of Co-ordination

Different Approaches to the Division of Tax Burden

Financial Approach : There are various theories with regard to the distribution of burden of taxation among the people. One of them is often called the financial theory, which embodied in principle attributed to collect, Pluck the goose with as little squealing as possible. It aims at obtaining maximum amount of revenue rather than on proper distribution of burden of taxation. The greatest danger of this theory is that the burden of taxation may fall mainly on weak and voiceless people rather than on rich and vocal.

Cost-of-Service Approach : This is one of the oldest principles advocated for the distribution of the tax burden. According to this thoery, the basis of taxation should be the cost incurred by government on different services for the benefit of the individual tax-payers. Each tax-payer has to pay the tax equal to the cost of service to him. It means, the higher the cost, the higher should be the tax rate and *vice versa*. The government acts like a producer of a commodity, who charges the price from his customers equal to the amount of cost of production of the commodity.

However, this principle cannot be accepted as the basis of taxation because of several reasons. In the first place, it is very difficult to estimate the cost of service to every individuals, *e.g.*, the government can estimate total expenditure on the defence of the country, but it is difficult to estimate the expenditure incurred by the government on the defence for a particular individual. Secondly, the basis of cost of service principle is not fair in a welfare state. If cost is taken as the basis of taxation, the government may not perform various functions which may be very much desirable for the welfare of the country as a whole, *e.g.*, relief in times of drought, flood and earthquake, free education and free medical facilities, etc. Hence, the cost of service principles cannot be accepted as the basis of taxation. Moreover, this principle is not in accordance with the character of a tax. A tax is a compulsory payment and there is no quid-pro-quo in return of the payment of a tax. But according to this theory, the payment of a tax is, in return of the cost of service.

The Benefits-Received Theory : According to this theory, the burden of taxation should be divided among the people in proporiton to the benefits received from the state. The persons receiving equal benefits from the state should pay equal amount as taxes and those who received greater benefits should pay more as taxes than those getting less benefit. The benefit principle is very much similar to the cost of service principle, the former looks at the problem from the side of demand while the latter looks at it from the side of supply.

Ability-to-Pay Approach : This approach considers the tax liability in its true form-a compulsory payment to the state without *quid pro quo*. It does not assume any commercial or semi-commercial relationship between the state and the citizens. According to this approach, a citizen is to pay taxes because he can, and his relative share in the total tax burden is to be determined by his relative paying capacity.

How to Measure Ability to Pay : The theory of ability of pay, however, involves the fundamental problem, as how to measure the ability to pay of a person. There are two approaches which have so far been advanced for this purpose — the subjective approach and the objective approach. In the **Subjective approach**, the sacrifice theory has been evolved to measure ability to pay. In the **objective approach**, the faculty theory has been evolved to measure ability to pay.

Objective Indices of Ability-to-Pay

1. Property as an Index of Ability-to-Pay.

2. Consumption Expenditure as the Index of Ability

3. Income as the Index of Ability-to-Pay.

Subjective Indices of Ability-to-Pay : The subjective approach is based on the psychological or mental reactions of the tax payers. In the subjective approach, we estimate the burden felt by the tax-payer or the sacrifice undergone by him. Each tax-payer should make equal sacrifice, if tax burden is to be justly distributed. In other words, the equal sacrifice approach maintains that each tax-payer should be subjected to the 'same' or 'equal' sacrifice. Equal sacrifice principle has three aspects:

A. Equal absolute sacrifice

B. Equal proportional sacrifice

C. Equal marginal sacrifice

A. Equal Absolute Sacrifice : This means that different tax-payers are made to sacrifice the same amount of utility by way of taxes. To put it differently, the difference between the aggregate utility from income before tax and the utility of income after tax is the same for every tax-payer. Symbolically, $U(y) - U(y - T)$ should be the same for all, where U is the total utility, y is the income before tax and $(y - T)$ is the income after tax.

Thus,

$[U(y) - U(y-T)]_A = [U(y) - U(y-T)]_B$ and so on.

B. Equal Proportional Sacrifice : In this case, each tax-payer is supposed to sacrifice the same percentage of the total satisfaction which he would have derived from his income. It means that the satisfaction lost in terms of tax payment bears the same proportion to the satisfaction from the pre-tax income in each case. It implies that the loss of utility, as a result of tax, should be proportional to the total income of the tax payers. Here an individual with higher incomes will pay more as a tax than those who have lower incomes. But the ratio of sacrifice to the income will be the same for all tax-payers. This can be expressed as—

$$\left[\frac{U(y)-U(y-T)}{U(y)}\right]_A = \left[\frac{U(y)-U(y-T)}{U(y)}\right]_B$$

and so on.

C. Equal Marginal Sacrifice or the Least Aggregate Sacrifice : According to this theory, the tax burden should be apportioned in such a way that the marginal utility of income left after tax with any tax payer would be the same. Symbolically, for each tax-payer.

$$\left[\frac{dU(y-T)}{d(y-T)}\right]_A = \left[\frac{dU(y-T)}{d(y-T)}\right]_B$$

should be the same.

Can	*Nature of Tax Structure*	*Burden of Higher Income Group*	*Taxation Lower Income Group*
1. Equal Absolute Sacrifice	Less Progressive	Lowest	Higher
2. Equal Proportional Sacrifice	More Progressive than absolute equal Sacrifice	Higher	Lower
3. Equal Marginal Sacrifice	Highly Progressive Taxation	Highest	Lowest

Incidence of Taxes

The burden of a tax does not always lie on the person from whom it is collected. In many cases it is borne by other people also. Thus, the person who initially pays the tax may not be actually bearing its money burden as such. Hence, it is necessary to know who bears the immediate burden of a tax and who bears the ultimate burden of the tax. The problem of determining the ultimate burden of a tax is the problem of determining the incidence of the tax.

Impact of a tax is its first point of contact with the tax-payers. It is upon those who bear the first responsibility of paying it to the authorities, that is those who have the statutory responsibility of paying it to the government. Incidence of a tax, on the other hand, is defined as its final resting place. To put it differently, the incidence of a tax is upon those economic units which finally bear the money burden of it and which are not able to pass it on to others. Incidence lies upon that final source from which the tax money comes.

Effects of a Tax

When a tax is imposed and collected, it involves certain responses from the tax-payers, and the economy. Such responses can be of great variety and can profoundly influence the working of the economy in terms of production, growth, saving, investment, choice of techniques of productions, regional in balances, in equalities of income and wealth, and so on. These responses and their results are collectively called the **effects of that tax**. The effects of a tax, therefore, stand apart, both conceptually, and analytically, from both the impact and the incidence of the tax. While the impact of a tax is its first point of contact with the tax-payers and while incidence is its final resting place, its effects will be the resultant responses and changes in the economy. These effects can be the result of the fact of tax imposition itself and they could also follow from the process of shifting its incidence.

Demand and Supply Theory of Tax Shifting

This is the most acceptable approach in explaining the incidence of a tax. Tax incidence can be shifted only through sale/purchase transactions and only through a revision of the prices. A price revision is possible and is determined by the relative values of demand and supply elasticities. A tax can, therefore, be shifted only through a shift in the demand and/or supply curves and the sharing of the incidence will be determined by the demand and supply elasticities. The general rule is that irrespectives of whether the statutory liability of a tax (the impact of the tax) rests upon the buyer or the seller, the share of the tax borne by the seller will be the larger according as the elasticity of demand is larger; and the share of the tax borne by the buyer will be the larger according as the elasticity of supply is larger. Actually, the tax burden will be shared between the buyer and the seller in the ratio of the elasticities of supply and demand.

Let us illustrate this statement by first taking the case of a single commodity which has been subjected to a specific (per unit) tax. Let us assume that the impact of the tax is upon the sellers. Let the original demand and supply curves for the commodity by DD′ and SS′. With the imposition of a tax SS_1 per unit upon the commodity, the supply curve shifts to S_1S_1' and the price of the commodity rise from PM to P′M′. However, out of this P′M′, the sellers get only AM′, the balance being collected by the government by way of tax. In other words, the incidence upon the sellers is equal to BA per unit. On the other hand, the buyers are paying now P′M′ instead of PM, an increase of P′B per unit which is the incidence upon them.

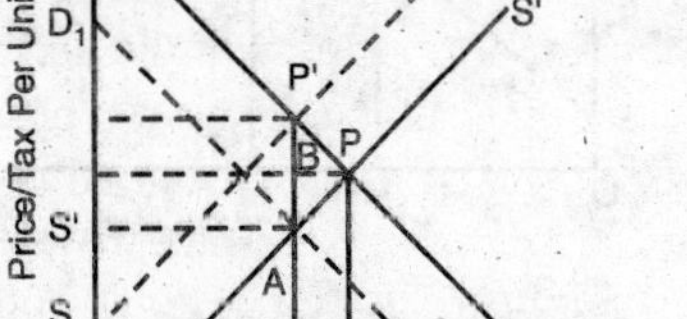

Fig. 2

It can be shown that this division of the tax P′A between the two shares P′B and BA is in the ratio of the elasticity of supply to the elasticity of demand. The elasticity of demand is given by proportionate change in demand divided by the proportionate change in the price to the buyers. That is to say, the elasticity of demand E_d is given by

$$E_d = \frac{\frac{MM'}{OM}}{\frac{P'B}{PM}}$$

Similarly, the elasticity of supply is given by the proportionate change in supply divided by the proportionate change in price to the sellers. That is to say the elasticity of supply, E_s is given by

$$E_s = \frac{\frac{MM'}{OM}}{\frac{BA}{PM}}$$

Therefore,

$$\frac{E_s}{E_d} = \left(\frac{MM'}{OM} \Big/ \frac{BA}{PM}\right) \Big/ \left(\frac{MM'}{OM} \Big/ \frac{P'B}{PM}\right)$$

$$= \frac{P'B}{BA}$$

$$= \frac{\text{Incidence on Buyers}}{\text{Incidence on Sellers}}$$

If the tax is imposed upon the buyer, the demand curve would shift left and down wards to D_1D_1'. The buyers would then pay a price of AM′ to the sellers and a tax P′A per unit to the authorities. The resultant incidence on the two parties will ramain unchanged. The formula

$$\frac{\text{Buyers's Share of Incidence}}{\text{Sellers's Share of Incidence}} = \frac{E_s}{E_d}$$

Shows that as the elasticity of supply increases in relation to elasticity of demands, the incidence will be more on the buyer and vice versa. Thus, if the commodity taxed is being produced under constant returns, it follows that the supply curve will run parallel to *x*-axis, and the elasticity of supply will tend to be infinity. In that case the incidence of the tax will lie wholly on the buyer. This will happen even when the tax is imposed upon the buyer (in which case the demand curve will shift downwards). Figure 3-A illustrates this phenomenon and it is seen that here the points A and B coincide, so that P′B = P′A.

The tax will be fully borne by the buyers if the demand elasticity is zero (in the ratio E_s / E_d, the denominator becomes zero, see Fig. 3-B). Here the demand curve will run parallel to *y*-axis and an upward shift in the supply curve will automatically mean an equivalent increase in the price being paid

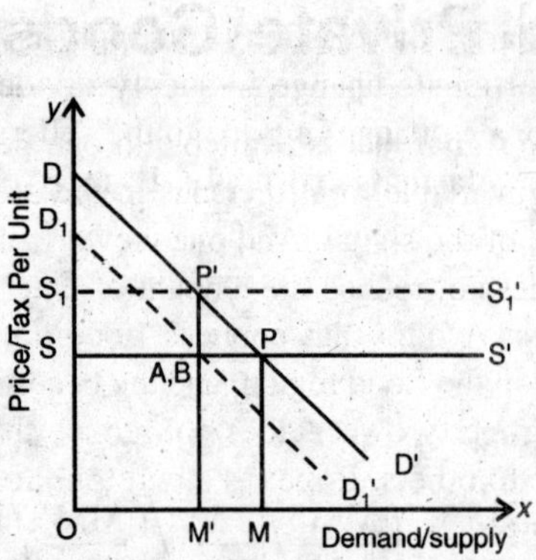

Fig. 3-A

by the buyer. If the tax is ad valorem, say *t* per cent, the price will increase by exactly *t* per cent because the quantity demanded and supplied remains unchanged.

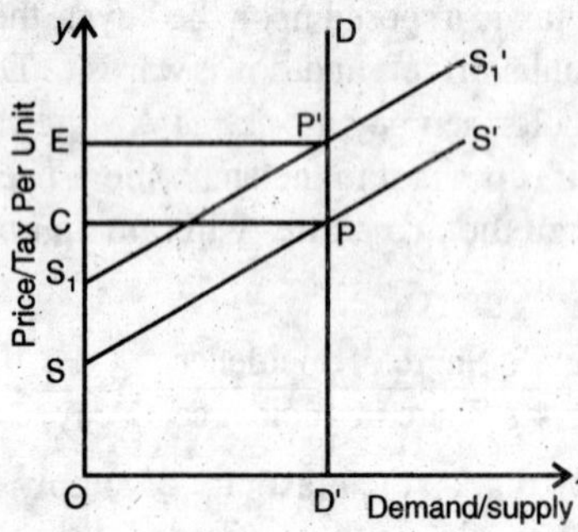

Fig. 3-B

It can be shown in the same way that if the elasticity of supply is zero, or if the elasticity of demand is perfect, the sellers will bear the full incidence of the tax (see Figures 3-C and 3-D).

Conclusion

1. If the elasticity of supply is equal to the elasticity of demand, *i.e.*, $E_s = E_d$; the burden of the tax is equally divided between buyers and sellers, and the price of the commodity will rise by half the amount of tax.
2. When the degree of elasticity of supply is greater than the elasticity of demand, *i.e.*, $E_s > E_d$, the burden of tax will fall upon the buyers in higher proportion than the sellers, and the rise in price will be more than fifty per cent of the amount of the tax per unit.
3. When the degree of elasticity of supply is less than the elasticity of demand, *i.e.*, $E_s < E_d$, the burden of the tax will fall upon the seller in higher proportion than the buyers, and the rise in price will be less than fifty per cent of the tax per unit.

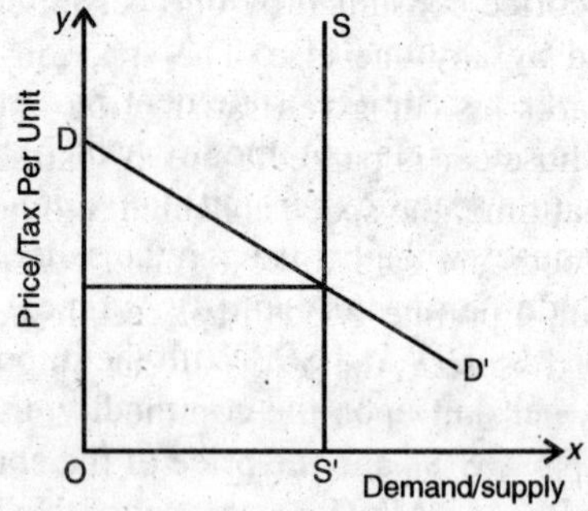

Fig. 3-C

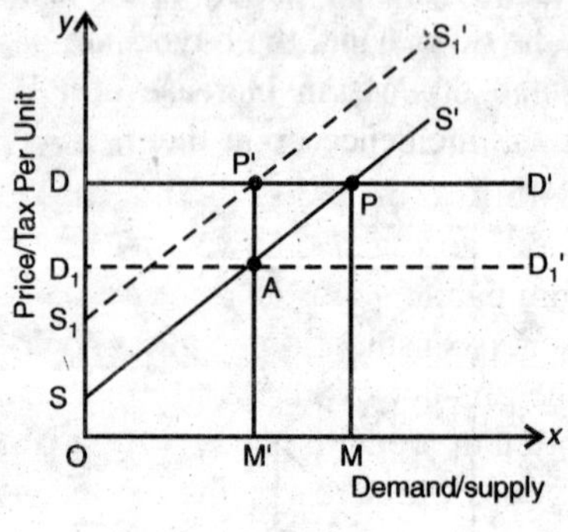

Fig. 3-D

4. If the demand for a commodity is perfectly elastic and its supply is inelastic, the entire burden of the tax will be upon the seller.
5. If the demand for commodity is perfectly inelastic and its supply is elastic, the entire burden of the tax will be upon the buyer.
6. If the supply of a commodity is perfectly elastic and the demand is relatively inelastic the entire burden of the tax will be upon the buyer.
7. If the supply of a commodity is perfectly inelastic and the demand is elastic, the entire burden will be upon the seller.

The Theory of Social and Private Goods

Private Goods have been defined as "Private goods yield utility (satisfaction) only to the person consuming the good, it is denied to others, only the person who drinks a cup of coffee, for example, benefits from the consumption of that cup of coffee. And the coffee consumed by one person cannot be consumed by any one else. The space in which a person parks his car given satisfaction only to the person whose car is parked there at that time. And during that time, the space is denied to other. Thus, private goods are said to be rival in consumption.

Again, a private goods is priced in the market and only those may be allowed the use of it who pay its stipulated price. Thus, those who do not agree to pay its market price, or those who cannot pay for it, are excluded from the use of this good. It means the principle of **exclusion** is applicable in case of private goods. The good becomes divisible so far at its use is concerned. Suppose an individual does not voluntarily agree to pay the market price for milk, the market would refuse to supply him the required quantity. Thus the ability to price a goods, the divisibility of a good and the exclusion principle, all go together in case of private goods.

A pure public goods is defined as a goods that one person's consumption of the goods does not reduce the amount available to other; that is, the consumption of a public goods is non-rival. That is they are goods where A's partaking of consumption benefits does not reduce the benefits derived by all othes. The same benefits are available to all and without mutual interference. So the total supply available to the community can be made available to each person in community. For example, a television signal that is available to one person can be made available to all persons in the area within the range of the signal. And one viewer's use of the signal does not reduce the amount of entertainment for others. A dam that controls flooding, benefits everyone in the flood region, and the benefit enjoyed by one property owner does not reduce the benefit available to others. It means a pure public goods is **indivisible**.

Merit Goods : Some goods are considered 'meritorious' while other are held undesirable. For instance, low cost housing is subsidised because decent housing is held to be desirable, while some taxes are imposed on liquor because drinking is held undesirable. Note, however, that the consumption choices which are supported or penalised may involve goods which are private (rival in consumption) as well as goods which are social (non rival). Thus, goods for which it is thought that consumption should be encouraged are called merit goods; goods having the opposite characteristic may be called non-merit goods or demerit goods. They (merit goods) become public goods if considered so meritorious that their satisfaction is provided for through the public budget, over and above what is provided for through the market and paid for by private buyers.

Difference Between Public Goods and Merit Goods

The Public goods satisfy the conditions of non-excludability, indivisibility and non-rival nature of consumption of goods while these are not the necessary conditions for merit goods, *i.e.*, they may apply or may not apply.

Public Debt

Public debt arises due to borrowing by the government. The government may borrow from banks, business organisations, business houses and individuals. The borrowings of the government may be within the country or from outside the country or both. The public debt is generally in the form of bonds (or treasury bills, if the loans are required for a short period), which carries with them the promises of the government to pay interests, to the holders of these bonds at stipulated rate of interest at regular intervals, or lump sum at the end, in addition to the principal which has to be repaid at the stated time.

Objectives of Public Debt

1. To Cover Budget Deficits
2. Rapid Expansion in the States Functions
3. In Times of Depression
4. To Curb Inflation
5. To Finance Development Plan
6. To Finance Public Enterprises
7. Creation of Social Overhead Capital
8. Expansion of Education of Health Services
9. To Finance War

Internal and External Debts

Internal debt refers to the public loans floated within the country, while external debt refers to the obligations of country to foreign governments or foreign nationals or international institution. The payment of interest on foreign debt reduces the net income of the debtor country by transferring a part of its income abroad, the payment of interest on internal debt has no such effect. The country's national income is the same whether the interest on internal debt is left with the tax-payers or is taken from them as taxes and paid out as interest on internal loan.

Factors on which the Effects of Public Debt Depend

The effects of public debt depend upon such factors as the sources of borrowing, the purpose for which borrowing is done, the terms and conditions under which the debt is floated, the volume of the existing public debt, the interest rates, the types of loan employed and the general economic condition of the community.

Effects of the Public Debt Upon the Economy

1. Effects on Consumption
2. Effects on Production
3. Effects on Distribution
4. Effects on Private Sector
5. Effects on the Cost of Production
6. Effects of Public Debt on Investment
7. Effects of Public Debt on Working of the Money Market
8. Effects of Public Debt on Resource Allocation and National Income

Public Debt Management

The objective of the management of public debt refers to the aim that the method of borrowing funds and the repayment of loans by the government should not have any adverse effect upon the economic situation of the country. Moreover, the methods of borrowing funds and repayment of loans should help to maintain economic stability, *i.e.*, It should reduce inflationary or deflationary effects upon the economy, and should make available the needed funds to the government. Therefore, all those methods which are adopted by the government to achieve these obejectives, through the process of borrowing funds and repayment of loans, come under public debt management.

Principles of Public Debt Management

1. The Interest Cost of Servicing Public Debts must be Minimised
2. Satisfaction of the Needs of Investors
3. Public Debt Policy must be co-ordinated with Fiscal and Monetary Policy

Redemption of Public Debt

Redemption means repayment of a loans. All government loans, excepting permanent investment in self supporting industries, should be repaid promptly.

Advantages of Debt Redemption

1. It saves the government from bankruptcy.
2. It discourages extravagant expenditure of the government.
3. It maintains the confidence of the lenders.
4. It would be easy for the government to float loan in future.
5. It reduces the cost of debt management.

Fiscal Policy

Fiscal Policy relates to the governmental decision-making with respect to (1) taxation (2) government spending (3) government borrowing and (4) the management of the government debt.

Classical Concept of Fiscal Policy

Classical economists believed in the policy of *laissez faire*. They believed that supply creates its own demand and, therefore, general over production or involuntary unemployment is well nigh impossible. They believed that a free operation of market forces would achieve full employment and ensure an optimum allocation of resources in an economy. Thus, according to classical economists, full employment is supposed to reach automatically and there is no necessity of any interference.

Modern Concept of Fiscal Policy

The classical concept of fiscal policy has not been accepted by the modern economists like Keynes and Lerner. They believed that the government has to pay a positive role so as to regulate and control the economy by means of taxes and expenditure, which they called as the principle of functional finance.

Modern economists rejected the concept of classical economists, that supply creates it own demand and, therefore, there is no possibility of unemployment, and the equilibrium in the economy is automatically achieved due to the market forces. Contrary to this, Keynes believed that in an advanced economy, the propensity to consume tends to diminish as income increases, in other words, propensity to save increases with the increase in income. Hence, a larger proportion of the additional incomes is saved and not spent. The tendency of less consumption and larger savings results in lowering the demand for goods and services produced at that time; hence dis-equilibrium occurs in the economy. Thus, to maintain income and employment at the present level, it is necessary to offset the effects of decrease in demand for output due to decrease in consumption by a corresponding increase in public expenditure. Hence, if unemployment is to be avoided, the gap between the income and expenditure must be filled either by government expenditure or by increasing the propensity to consume. For instance, during the period of depression, the effective demand is not enough to absorb the available supply of goods and services, resulting in unemployment and under-employment. Therefore, according to modern economists, to maintain full employment and income, it is the duty of the government to increase public expenditure directly by under taking public works programmes on large scale and thereby inducing people to spend more.

Thus, modern fiscal policy is the policy of government under which the government uses its expenditure and revenue programmes to produce desirable of the increase in aggregate production and employment. In other words, the modern fiscal policy is a technique to attain and maintain full employment by manipulating public expenditure and revenue in such a way so as to keep an equilibrium between effective demand and supply of goods and services at that time. Thus, modern fiscal policy is nothing but the application of the principle of functional finance.

Functional Finance

The concept of functional finance was first stated by Keynes and was developed by **Prof. AP. Lerner. Prof. Lerner** believed that Fiscal measures should be judged only by their effects. The way is which the fiscal measures work in the economy is called as functional finance by Prof. Lerner. The central idea is that the government's Fiscal policy involves government spending, and taxing, spending and borrowing of loans, issue of new money and withdrawl of money from circulation should all be viewed with the consideration of their impact upon the national economy as a whole and not to any established doctrine of finance, just as the doctrine of sound finance was established by classical economists. **Hence, Judging a Fiscal policy by its effects or the way in which it functions in an economy is called as functional finance.**

Balanced Budget

The budget is the most important instrument of fiscal policy, since the necessary finance is obtained and the public expenditure is made through budget. A government budget is said to be balanced when its tax revenues and expenditures are equal. When the budget is not balanced, there is either a deficit or surplus budget and it is said to be an unbalanced budget in either case. The value of multiplier is more than 1 in case of unbalanced budget, it is 1 in case of balanced budget and less than 1 in case of surplus budget.

MULTIPLE CHOICE QUESTIONS

1. Cannon of equity in taxation is generally considered to be satisfied by
   A. Proportional taxation
   B. Progressive taxation
   C. Regressive taxation
   D. Lump sum tax
2. Which one of the following is **NOT** a source of the state tax revenue?
   A. Land revenue B. Motor vehicles tax
   C. Entertainment tax D. Corporate tax
3. The receipts from disinvestment of public sector undertakings are shown under which one of the following sub-heads in the budget of the Government of India?
   A. Revenue receipts
   B. Non-tax revenue receipts
   C. Non-debt capital receipts
   D. Debt capital receipts
4. The Principle of Maximum Social Advantage is concerned with
   A. Taxation only
   B. Expenditure only
   C. Public debt only
   D. Both taxation and public expenditure
5. Justice in taxation is best exsured by applying the principle of
   A. equal absolute sacrifice
   B. equal proportional sacrifice
   C. equal marginal sacrifice
   D. quid pro quo
6. Tobin tax is a tax on
   A. exports
   B. imports
   C. transactions in foreign exchange
   D. sales
7. Budgetary deficit does NOT take into account
   A. revenue deficit
   B. capital budget deficit
   C. balance of payment deficit
   D. interest payment on public debt
8. **Assertion (A) :** In developing countries, government borrowing is preferred over taxation in financing public expenditure.
   Reason (R) : Taxation would require a curtailment in current consumption.
   A. Both A and R are true and R is the correct explanation of A
   B. Both A and R are true but R is not a correct explanation of A
   C. A is true but R is false
   D. A is false but R is true
9. Which of the following taxes is an exclusive source of revenue for the state governments?
   A. Excise duties B. Customs duties
   C. Land revenue D. Wealth tax
10. Which one of the following is **NOT** a source of the 'Union Tax revenue'?
    A. Property taxes B. Wealth tax
    C. Corporate taxes D. Customs duties
11. Given a proportional income tax structure and balanced budget, an autonomous increase in investment will increase the level of equilibrium income and the budget will
    A. still be in balance
    B. have a surplus
    C. have a deficit
    D. the outcome is uncertain
12. Provision of social goods possess problem because
    A. Such goods tend to be non-rival in consumption
    B. Consumption preferences with respect to such goods are not revealed
    C. Market mechanism is not well suited for the provision of such goods
    D. All the above
13. The imposition of a Selective Sales Tax will raise the price of the taxed product by equal amount if it is produced under
    A. constant cost
    B. increasing cost
    C. decreasing cost
    D. imperfect competition
14. Fiscal and Monetary Policies are intended to combat
    A. Structural unemployment
    B. Frictional unemployment
    C. Cyclical unemployment
    D. Both A and B

15. Assuming a declining marginal utility of money schedule, which one of the following principles will call for "maximum progression"?

A. Principle of equal absolute sacrifice
B. Principle of equal proportional sacrifice
C. Principle of equal marginal sacrifice
D. None of the above

16. In a many person economy with a public and a private goods, revenue allocation will be optimal at the point where

A. the marginal rate of substitution (MRS) is equal to the marginal rate of transformation (MRT) for each individual considered separately
B. the summation of the MRS is equal to the MRT
C. the MRS is not equal to the MRT since we are dealing with a public goods
D. none of the above conditions obtain

17. If supply is perfectly inelastic, then the short run impact of a specific sales tax would be to shift the tax burden

A. entirely on to the consumers
B. entirely on to the producers
C. equally between the producers and the consumers
D. on the other goods where the supply condition may be more elastic

18. Consider the following statements:

1. In the context of the classical model loan finance may be a means of transferring the burden to the future generation.
2. Foreign borrowing permits financing public programmes without placing a burden on the persent generation.
3. Foreign borrowing is not burden some to the future generations even if the funds are used unproductively.

Of the above statements

A. 1 alone is correct
B. 1 and 2 are correct
C. 2 and 3 are correct
D. 1 and 3 are correct

19. **Octrio** is levied and collected by:

A. Centre B. State Government
C. Local bodies D. All the above

20. The One Rupee currency note bears the signature of the

A. Governor, Reserve Bank of India
B. The Minister for Finance
C. Chairman, State Bank of India
D. None of the above

21. Stagflation means

A. Inflation with recession
B. Recession and stagnation
C. Inflation galloping like a stag
D. Inflation and increasing output

22. The effect of deficit financing is

A. Always inflationary
B. Never inflationary
C. Sometimes inflationary and sometimes not so depending on the response of output and the dose of deficit financing
D. Always inflationary unless acompanied by effective counteracting measures

23. The Economist on whose suggestions the Wealth Tax, Gift Tax and Expenditure Tax were introduced in India is

A. V.K.R.V. Rao B. Kaldor
C. Galbraith D. None of the above

24. Agricultural Income Tax is

A. Levied and appropriated by the respective states
B. Levied and collected by the Union, but given over to the respective states
C. Levied by the Union, but collected and appropriated by the respective states
D. None of the above

25. The MODVAT scheme of taxation benefits

A. Those manufacturers who import components
B. Those manufacturers who depend on indigenous material
C. It is neutral between the above two
D. Those manufacturers who are importing technology

26. Indirect tax are objectionable because they

A. Are hard to collect
B. Are regressive
C. Do not raise enough revenue
D. Are particularly hard on the rich

27. All the revenues received, loans raised and money received in repayment of loans by the Union government go into
A. Consolidated Fund of India
B. Contingency Fund of India
C. Public Account of India
D. Prime Minister's Relief Fund

28. Loans of Public enterprises is a part of
A. Capital expenditure
B. Revenue expenditure
C. Both revenue and capital expenditure
D. None of the above

29. Interest payment is an item of
A. Revenue expenditure
B. Capital expenditure
C. Plan expenditure
D. None of the above

30. In India, the states get maximum income from
A. Sales Tax
B. Land Revenue
C. Agricultures income tax
D. State excise duties

31. In order to reduce inequalities, the government should adopt
A. Proportional system of taxation
B. Progressive system of taxation
C. Regressive system of taxation
D. None of the above

32. Market borrowings of the Central Government are included in
A. Capital receipts
B. Non-tax revenue
C. Tax revenue
D. None of the above

33. MODVAT means
A. Modified Value Added Tax
B. Moderate Value Added Tax
C. Modest Value Added Tax
D. Modern Value added Tax

34. Which one of the following taxes is not levied by the State Governments
A. Agricultural Income Tax
B. Profession Tax
C. Excise on Liquor
D. Corporation Tax

35. Who appoints the Finance Commission
A. President of India
B. Prime Minister of India
C. Chairman of the Rajya Sabha
D. Speaker of the Lok Sabha

36. Excise duties, which are the biggest source of revenue of the Union Government, are levied on
A. Sale of goods
B. Production of goods
C. Consumption of goods
D. Resale of goods

37. Which of the following is not a direct tax?
A. Income Tax B. Wealth Tax
C. Expenditure Tax D. Entertainment Tax

38. The incidence of which of the following will entirely be on the monopolist—
A. lump-sum tax
B. specific tax
C. regulated monopoly pricing
D. none of the above

39. If supply is perfectly inelastic and demand is highly elastic, then in the short run the incidence of a specific sales tax will be—
A. entirely on the consumers
B. entirely on the sellers
C. equally distributed between the consumers and the sellers
D. more on the consumers than on the sellers

40. Provision of social goods poses problems because
A. such goods tend to be non-rival in consumption
B. individual consumer preferences with respect to these goods is not revealed.
C. market mechanism is not well suited for the provision of such goods
D. all the above

41. Which one of the following is not an objective of fiscal policy:
A. economic growth
B. economic stability
C. maximisation of emloyment level
D. regulating of financial institutions

42. The concept of Zero-Based-Budget (ZBB) was given by
A. R.A. Musgrave B. J.M. Keynes
C. Peter A. Pyhr D. A.H. Hansen

43. Which of the following concepts of Budget deficit has become practically redundant in India
A. Fiscal Deficit B. Budgetary Deficit
C. Primary Deficit D. Revenue Deficit

44. The tax-multiplier is generally—
A. greater than the government expenditure multiplier
B. equal to the government expenditure multiplier
C. less than the government expenditure multiplier
D. equal to the investment multiplier

45. Which of the following statements regarding incidence of tax is true:
A. the incidence of a tax on imports is totally borne by the consumers in the importing country.
B. the incidence of a tax on exports is totally on the producer
C. the incidence of taxes on imports and exports is shared equally by the producer and users in the importing country
D. the incidence of taxes on imports and exports is shared by producers and users in the inverse proportion to the elasticities of their respective demand

46. The difference between Total Public Revenue and Total Public Expenditure in a particular year is termed as
A. Primary deficit B. Revenue deficit
C. Budgetary deficitD. Fiscal deficit

47. The tax which is not shared by states is—
A. Sales tax B. Income tax
C. Corporation tax D. Central Excise duty

48. Which one of the following is not an objective of fiscal policy?
A. Economic growth
B. Price stability
C. Maximization of employment level
D. Regulating of financial institutions

49. Which of the following does not measure income inequality?
A. Lorenz curve
B. Per capita income
C. Ginni's coefficient
D. Percentage of population in different income groups

50. Black money in India—
A. Raises prices alone
B. Encourage lavish consumption alone
C. Causes only loss of revenue to government
D. Effects all the above three

51. Agricultural income tax is a source of revenue to—
A. Central Government
B. State Government
C. Local Administration
D. Central and State Government

52. The chairman of the 12th Finance Commission is—
A. Dr. C. Rangarajan
B. Raja J. Chalia
C. T.S. Papola
D. Y.K. Alagha

53. It is generally believed that a rise in the tax rate would normally lead to a rise in the revenue. But there is also a view the reduced rates on income tax would lead to a significant rise in income tax revenue. This later view has been attributed to
A. Arthur Laffer
B. Robert Lucas
C. Herbert Simon
D. J.B. Say

54. After allowing for state's share of taxation which one of the following tax revenues brings in the largest amount of revenue to the Central Government?
A. Corporation tax B. Income tax
C. Custom duties D. Union Excise duties

55. Match list I with list II and select the correct answer using the codes given below the lists—

List I	List II
(*a*) Service tax	1. Central government
(*b*) Stamp duty	2. State government
(*c*) Property tax	
(*d*) Sales tax	

Codes:	(*a*)	(*b*)	(*c*)	(*d*)
A.	1	2	2	–
B.	1	2	–	2
C.	–	1	2	–
D.	–	1	–	2

56. As per the recommendations of the Finance Commission, besides income tax, the net proceeds of which of the following tax (es) is/ are to be shared between the centre and the states?

1. Additional duties of excise

2. Wealth tax on agricultural properties

3. Union Excise Duties

Select the correct answer using the codes given below—

Codes :

A. 1, 2 and 3 B. 3 only

C. 1 and 2 D. 2 and 3

57. Assertion (A) : The burden of Union taxation is borne mainly by the lower and middle income groups in India.

Reason (R) : The tax structure is such that taxes on commodities is predominant.

A. Both A and R are true and R is the correct explanation of A

B. Both A and R are true but R is NOT a correct explanation of A

C. A is true but R is false

D. A is false but R is true

58. Match list-I (Nature of deficit) with list-II (How it is calculated) and select the correct answer by using the codes given below the lists:

List-I	List-II
(*a*) Fiscal deficit	1. (Revenue and interest receipts) minus (Revenue expenditure)
(*b*) Revenue deficit	2. (Revenue receipts + Recovery of loans and other receipts) minus (Total expenditure)
(*c*) Budgetary deficit	3. Receipts minus disbursements in capital account
(*d*) Capital deficit	4. (Total receipts) – (Total disbursements)

Codes:	(*a*)	(*b*)	(*c*)	(*d*)
A.	1	2	4	3
B.	2	1	4	3
C.	2	1	3	4
D.	1	2	3	4

59. Consider the following statements—

The incidence of corporate income tax under competition depends upon

1. the elasticity of substitution between factors in the non-corporate sector industries.

2. the income elasticity of demand for the output of the corporate sector industries.

3. the elasticity of substitution in demand between the outputs of the corporate sector and non-corporate sector industries.

4. the difference between the factor proportions in the corporate and non-corporate sectors.

Of these statements

A. 1 and 4 are correct

B. 1, 3 and 4 are correct

C. 2, 3 and 4 are correct

D. 1, 2 and 3 are correct

60. Which of the following is/are included in the capital budget of the Government of India?

1. Borrowings from the RBI

2. Loans received from foreign governments

3. Expenditure on acquisition of assets like roads, buildings, machinery etc.

4. Loans and advances granted to the states and Union Territories.

Select the correct answer using the codes given below:

Codes:

A. 1, 2 and 4 B. 2 and 3

C. 1 alone D. 1, 2, 3 and 4

61. Assertion (A) : A progressive income tax is based on equimarginal sacrifice.

Reason (R) : Higher the income, lower will be the marginal utility of money for the tax payer.

A. Both A and R are true and R is the corrrect explanation of A

B. Both A and R are true but R is **NOT** a correct explanation of A

C. A is true but R is false

D. A is false but R is true

62. Consider the following statements—

The two main objectives of fiscal policy in developing countries are

1. rapid economic growth

2. price stability

3. full employment

4. equitable distribution

Of these statements

A. 1 and 2 are correct

B. 2 and 3 are correct

C. 2 and 4 are correct

D. 1 and 4 are correct

63. The whole burden of a tax will be borne by the sellers, if
- A. the demand for a commodity is inelastic and supply is perfectly elastic
- B. the elasticity of demand for a commodity is same as the elasticity of supply of the commodity
- C. the demand for a commodity is perfectly elastic and supply is inelastic
- D. the elasticity of demand for a commodity is less than the elasticity of supply of that commodity

64. Which one of the following pairs is correctly matched?
- A. Fiscal deficit — G.D.P
- B. Primary deficit — Money supply
- C. Monetised deficit -- Interest payments
- D. Budget deficit — Revenue expenditure and receipts on Revenue Account

65. Which one of the following dealt exclusively with taxation of agricultural wealth and income in India?
- A. John Mathai Committee 1953
- B. Kaldor's Report 1956
- C. Wanchoo Committee 1971
- D. Raj Committee 1972

66. Which one of the following is not the reason for rising debt over the last two decades in India?
- A. The failure to generate adequate resources from internal sectors for financing development plans
- B. The need for foreign aid in the form of technologial assistance to carry out different development projects
- C. Failure to increase exports sufficiently
- D. Decrease in the cost of foreign debt

67. Which one of the following types of revenues is not shared by the Central Government with the State Governments?
- A. Central Sales Tax
- B. Income Tax
- C. Excise Duty
- D. Customs Duty

68. Which one of the following sources is not considered as a source of government revenue?
- A. Taxes
- B. Surplus of public enterprises
- C. Transfer payments
- D. Mobilisation of internal loans and deposits

69. **Assertion (A) :** Public Finance is a normative science.

Reason (R) : The objective of Fiscal operation implies proper allocation of resources, distribution of income, full employment and stability with grown.
- A. Both A and R are true and R is the correct explanation of A
- B. Both A and R are true but R is not correct explanation of A
- C. A is true but R is false
- D. A is false but R is true

70. Zero-Based Budgeting (ZBB) lays emphasis on
1. Unlimited deficit financing
2. Preparing new budget right from the scratch
3. Preparing the budget neglecting history of expenditure

- A. 1, 2 and 3
- B. 1 and 3
- C. 2 and 3
- D. 1 and 2

71. Which one of the following taxes is levied by the states and shared with the Union Government?
- A. Irrigation tax
- B. Agriculture income tax
- C. Entertainment tax
- D. None of the above

72. Which of the following taxes is levied by the State Government only
- A. Entertainment tax
- B. Wealth tax
- C. Income tax
- D. Corporation tax

73. In the Indian context deficit financing means
- A. An excess of government's revenue over expenditure
- B. An excess of government's current expenditure over its current revenue
- C. An excess of government's total expenditure over its total revenue
- D. None of these

74. Food and Fertilizer subsidies are included in
- A. Capital expenditure
- B. Revenue expenditure
- C. Plan expenditure
- D. All of the above

75. Which one of the following taxes is levied by the centre but wholly assigned to the states
   A. Personal Income tax
   B. Excise on drugs and narcotics
   C. Railway passenger tax
   D. Gift tax

76. Expenditure on 'general services' is
   A. Revenue Expenditure
   B. Capital Expenditure
   C. Plan Expenditure
   D. None of the above

77. The basis of corporate tax is
   A. Total turnover of the company
   B. Profit after distribution of dividend
   C. Profit before distribution of dividend
   D. Capital employed in the company

78. If external debt of country rises faster than its interest obligations, it is a case of
   A. Liquidity trap   B. Debt trap
   C. Poverty trap   D. Export led growth

79. Central assistance for State and UT Plan is a part of
   A. Plan expenditure
   B. Non-Plan expenditure
   C. Revenue expenditure
   D. None of the above

80. Loans of foreign governments is
   A. Revenue expenditure
   B. Capital expenditure
   C. Both revenue and capital expenditure
   D. Neither revenue nor capital expenditure

81. India's Fiscal policy since independence has centered around
   A. More borrowings B. Higher taxation
   C. Deficit financing D. All the three

82. Fiscal policy in a developing country like India aims at
   A. Widening the tax base
   B. Mopping up most of the surpluses through taxation
   C. Achieving socio-economic objectives of the state
   D. All of these

83. The revenue of the state governments are raised from the following sources except one, which is that
   A. Land revenue
   B. Agricultural income tax
   C. Entertainment tax
   D. Expenditure tax

84. As a source of revenue, a tax on a commodity will be more successful if
   A. the higher the percentage of the tax
   B. the lower the percentage of the tax
   C. the more elastic the supply and demand for the commodity
   D. the more inelastic the supply and demand for the commodity

85. The long term Fiscal Policy formulated in the context of the Seventh Five Year Plan lays emphasis on
   A. Tackling problem of poverty and unemployment
   B. Reforming tax system
   C. Capital formation by increasing money income and reducing consumption
   D. Making taxes easily comprehensible to the tax payers

86. The Agricultural Holding Tax (AHT) was recommended by a committee headed by
   A. C.H. Hanumantha Rao
   B. M.L. Dantewala
   C. R.J. Chelliah
   D. K.N. Raj

87. **Assertion (A) :** Indirect taxes contribute a major part of the total Taxation Revenue in India.
Reason (R) : These taxes cannot be evaded.
   A. Both A and R are true and R explains A
   B. Both A and R are true but R does not explains A
   C. A is true but R is false
   D. A is false but R is true

88. Debt-Service Ratio is a ratio of—
   A. GDP which is to be paid as debt
   B. Total debt which is to be paid in the form of interest burden
   C. Export earnings which are to be paid by way of interest and principal
   D. None of these

89. The relationship between tax collections and tax rates has been expressed by
   A. Lorenz Curve   B. Engel's Law
   C. Laffer Curve   D. Indifference Curve

90. Fiscal deficit in the Union Budget means—
A. the sum of budgetary deficit and net increase in internal and external borrowings
B. the difference between current expenditure and current revenue
C. the sum of monetised deficit and budgetary deficit
D. net increase in Government's borrowing from the RBI

91. Since the introduction of '**Ways and Means Advances**' mechanism by the Union government vis-a-vis the RBI, one of the following has become redundant—
A. Monetised deficit B. Revenue deficit
C. Budgetary deficit D. Primary deficit

92. MODVAT is different from VAT in the sense that—
1. under MODVAT, tax is levied only on value addition while under VAT, excise is imposed on final value and then rebate is given on inputs
2. MODVAT is only at the production stage while VAT extends both to production and distribution stage
3. Under MODVAT, excise is levied on final value and then rebate is given on inputs while under VAT, tax is levied only on value addition
4. MODVAT implies rationalization of excise duty only while VAT implies rationalization of excise, sales and turn over taxes etc. also

Choose correct answer from—
A. 1, 2 and 4 B. 1, 3 and 4
C. 2, 3 and 4 D. 1, 2, 3 and 4

93. Which of the following does not help to broaden the Tax Base—
A. MAT
B. VAT
C. Zero-Based-Budgeting
D. Tax on Agricultural Income

94. All Taxes come under—
A. capital receipts B. revenue receipts
C. public debt D. public expenditure

95. The merit of zero-based budgeting is that—
A. Tax liability is reduced
B. Profits go up
C. Deficit Financing becomes zero
D. Expenditure is rationalized

96. When the rate of tax goes up with increase in income is called—
A. Proportional tax B. Regressive tax
C. Progressive tax D. Presumptive tax

97. A budgetary deficit means—
A. Total expenditure is more than total revenue
B. Current expenditure is more than current revenue
C. Capital expenditure is more than capital revenue
D. Total expenditure is more than current revenue

98. The main source of revenue of the Union Government in ascending order of importance are—
1. Income Tax 2. Corporate Tax
3. Customs Duties 4. Excise Duties
A. 3, 2, 4, 1 B. 2, 4, 3, 1
C. 2, 1, 3, 4 D. 1, 2, 3, 4

99. When the ratio of indirect taxes to total taxation revenue is very high, it leads to—
1. rise in the price level
2. higher taxation burden on the rich
3. higher taxation burden on the poor
4. fall in tax revenues
A. 1 and 2 B. 1 and 3
C. 1, 2 and 4 D. 1, 3 and 4

100. Which of the following is not a part of Fiscal Policy?
A. Subsidy under the Public Distribution System
B. Control of population
C. Imposition of taxation
D. Issue of bonds by Government

101. Ad Valorom means—
A. According to value
B. According to weight
C. According to size
D. According to advertisement costs

102. Which of the following come under Non-Plan expenditure—
1. Subsidies
2. Interest Payments
3. Defence Expenditure
4. Maintenance expenditure for the infra-structure created in previous plans

Choose the correct answer using the codes given below—

A. 1 and 2 B. 1 and 3
C. 2 and 4 D. 1, 2, 3 and 4

103. When the ratio of direct taxes to GDP goes on increasing, the economy is said to be moving more and more towards—

1. Unequal distribution of income
2. Progressive tax structure
3. Equal distribution of income
4. Proportional tax structure

Select your answer from the following—

A. 1, 2, 3, 4 B. 1, 4
C. 2, 3 D. 1, 2

104. Which of the following is not an indirect tax?

A. Land Revenue B. Sales Tax
C. Custom Duties D. Entertainment Tax

105. In India, federal financial assistance to states is given on the basis of

A. the tax effort of the states
B. the revenue collection of the states
C. population, tax effort and special problems of the states
D. the demands of the states

106. Which one of the following sources of central revenue belongs to the category of indirect taxes?

A. Corporation Tax B. Customs
C. Wealth Tax D. Interest Receipts

107. Exemption from the entertainment tax is granted if the entire proceeds are devoted to

1. postal savings
2. shares in new industrial undertakings
3. charitable purposes
4. redemption of debt

Select the correct answer using the codes given below—

Codes:

A. 1 and 2 B. 1 and 3
C. 2 and 3 D. 3 and 4

108. The most expensive head under public revenue expenditure in the Union Budgets of India of the last decade has been—

A. defence B. interest payments
C. subsidies D. social services

109. Which of the following effects of deficit financing of the central Government effects the common man most adversely?

A. Forced savings
B. Credit creation by banks
C. Inflationary rise in prices
D. Changes in the pattern of social investment

110. The rapid increase of public debt of the Central Government of India since 1950-51 has been due to

A. uncontrolled inflation
B. mounting shares of state governments from revenues raised by the central government
C. mounting costs of financing public expenditure
D. rising population

111. "Maximum Social Welfare" in public finance is attained when—

A. marginal disutility of taxation is greater than the marginal utility of public expenditure
B. marginal disutility of taxation is less than the marginal utility of public expenditure
C. marginal disutility of taxation is equal to marginal utility of public expenditure
D. taxation and public expenditure are at the lowest level

112. Which of the following pairs are examples of direct tax?

1. Income tax and wealth tax
2. Sales tax and Excise duty
3. Capital gains tax and Corporation tax

Select the correct answer using the codes given below—

Codes:

A. 1 and 3 B. 1 and 2
C. 2 and 4 D. 2 and 3

113. Consider the following statements Non-Plan Revenue Expenditure includes expenditure incurred on

1. interest payments
2. maintenance of capital assets
3. flood control

Of these statements

A. 2 and 3 are correct
B. 1 and 2 are correct
C. 1 and 3 are correct
D. 1, 2 and 3 are correct

114. Consider the following statements—
The division of incidence of a tax between buyers and sellers is governed by
1. elasticity of demand and supply
2. cost conditions
3. market structure
Of these statements
A. 1 and 2 are correct
B. 2 and 3 are correct
C. 1 and 3 are correct
D. 1, 2 and 3 are correct

115. Capital gains mean
A. increase in the sales on which capital is invested
B. increase in the value of the property owned
C. gross profit earnings on a capital asset
D. marginal efficiency of capital

116. Consider the following statements
A government may cover up the deficit by—
1. withdrawing its cash balances from the central bank of the country.
2. borrowing from the central bank and commercial banks
3. printing new money
Of these statements
A. 1 and 2 are correct
B. 1 and 3 are correct
C. 2 and 3 are correct
D. 1, 2 and 3 are correct

117. Which one of the following is the most important source of revenue of state governments in India?
A. Land revenue
B. State excise duties
C. Sales tax
D. Stamps and registration fees

118. Assertion (A) : More reliance should be placed on progressive income taxes.
Reason (R) : It is in accordance with the principles of equity.
A. Both A and R are true and R is the correct explanation of A
B. Both A and R are true but R is NOT a correct explanation of A
C. A is true but R is false
D. A is false but R is true

119. The burden of a tax on monopoly profit will be
A. entirely on the producer
B. entirely on the consumer
C. equally distributed among the producer and the consumer
D. more on the consumer than on the producer

120. The incidence of a sales tax will be on the sellers when
A. the demand for the commodity is perfectly elastic
B. the demand for the commodity is perfectly inelastic
C. the demand curve is a rectangular hyperbola
D. the demand for the commodity is moderately elastic

121. Match list-I (Tax) with list-II (Imposed and collected by) and select the correct answer using the codes given below the list—

List-I	**List-II**
(*a*) Corporation Tax	1. State
(*b*) Sales Tax	2. Municipal corportation
(*c*) House Tax	
(*d*) Wealth Tax	3. Government of India

Codes:	(*a*)	(*b*)	(*c*)	(*d*)
A.	3	1	2	3
B.	2	1	1	3
C.	2	3	3	2
D.	3	2	2	1

122. Assertion (A): Indirect taxes are generally regressive in character.
Reason (R): They are imposed uniformly on all tax payers irrespective of their incomes.
A. Both A and R are individually true and R is the correct explanation of A
B. Both A and R are individually true but R is not the correct explanation of A
C. A is true but R is false
D. A is false but R is true

123. Which one of the following pairs is not correctly matched in the Indian context?
A. Cash Reserve Ratio — Monetary Policy
B. Non-performing Assets — Profitability of Commercial banks

C. Market-determined rate of interest — Post Office deposits
D. Administered rate of interest — Public Provident Fund

124. Assertion (A): In developing countries, government borrowing is preferred over taxation in financing public expenditure.

Reason (R): Taxation would require a curtailment in current consumption.

A. Both A and R are true and R is the correct explanation of A
B. Both A and R are true but R is not a correct explanation of A
C. A is true but R is false
D. A is false but R is true

125. Match list-I with list-II and select the correct answer using the codes given below the lists:

List-I	List-II
(*a*) New Economic Policy	1. Controlling bank credit
(*b*) Monetary Policy	2. Deficits and debt management
(*c*) Trade Policy	3. Globalisation
(*d*) Fiscal Policy	4. Liberalisation

Codes:

	(*a*)	(*b*)	(*c*)	(*d*)
A.	4	1	3	2
B.	3	2	4	1
C.	4	2	3	1
D.	3	1	4	2

ANSWERS

1	2	3	4	5	6	7	8	9	10
B	D	B	D	C	C	C	A	C	A
11	**12**	**13**	**14**	**15**	**16**	**17**	**18**	**19**	**20**
A	D	A	D	B	A	B	B	C	D
21	**22**	**23**	**24**	**25**	**26**	**27**	**28**	**29**	**30**
A	C	B	A	B	B	A	A	A	A
31	**32**	**33**	**34**	**35**	**36**	**37**	**38**	**39**	**40**
B	A	A	D	A	B	D	A	B	D
41	**42**	**43**	**44**	**45**	**46**	**47**	**48**	**49**	**50**
D	C	B	C	D	B	C	D	B	D
51	**52**	**53**	**54**	**55**	**56**	**57**	**58**	**59**	**60**
B	A	A	D	B	B	A	B	D	D
61	**62**	**63**	**64**	**65**	**66**	**67**	**68**	**69**	**70**
A	C	C	A	D	D	D	C	A	C
71	**72**	**73**	**74**	**75**	**76**	**77**	**78**	**79**	**80**
D	A	C	B	C	A	A	B	B	B
81	**82**	**83**	**84**	**85**	**86**	**87**	**88**	**89**	**90**
C	D	D	D	B	D	C	B	C	A
91	**92**	**93**	**94**	**95**	**96**	**97**	**98**	**99**	**100**
A	A	C	B	D	C	A	D	B	B
101	**102**	**103**	**104**	**105**	**106**	**107**	**108**	**109**	**110**
A	D	C	A	C	B	D	B	C	C
111	**112**	**113**	**114**	**115**	**116**	**117**	**118**	**119**	**120**
C	A	D	C	B	D	C	A	A	A
121	**122**	**123**	**124**	**125**					
A	A	C	A	A					

❑❑❑

INTERNATIONAL ECONOMICS

Theories of International Trade

International trade deals with business transactions that take place between citizens of different nations and with considerations of commercial diplomacy that spring from such business transactions. Consequently, international trade may be defined as the exchange of goods and services among the citizens of independent or sovereign states or countries. It consists of the exchange by each country of its low-priced goods and services for those goods and services which can be secured at lower prices from abroad than the prices at home.

A. Absolute Cost Advantage Theory of Adam Smith

In Smith's model of international trade, every one will be better off without making any one worse off. As such each country will gain by trading. Taking the case of two individual producers, a tailor and a shoe-maker, tailor does not make his own shoes; he exchanges a suit with shoes. Thereby both the shoe-maker and the tailor gain. In the same manner, Smith argued, a whole country can gain by trading with other countries.

If it takes 10 labour units to manufacture 1 unit of good A in country I but 20 labour units in country II, and if it takes 20 units of labour to manufacture 1 unit of good B in country I but only 10 labour units in country II, then both countries can gain by trading.

If the two countries exchanged the 2 goods at a ratio of 1 to 1, so that 1 unit of good A is exchanged for 1 unit of good B, country I could get 1 unit of good B by sacrificing only 10 units of labour, whereas it would have to give up 20 units of labour if it produced the good itself. Likewise, country II would have to sacrifice only 10 units of labour to get 1 unit of good A, whereas it would have to give up 20 units of labour if it produced it itself. The implication of this is clearly that both countries could have more of both goods, with a given effort, by trading.

This was a simple and powerful illustration of the benefits of trade, and on it Adam Smith rested his plea for non-interference for free trade as the best policy for trade between nations. Smith's argument seems convincing, but it is not very deep. It was left to Torrens and Ricardo to produce the stronger and more subtle argument for the benefits of trade contained in the theory of comparative advantage.

B. David Ricardo and the Theory of Comparative Cost Advantage

While it is true that a large part of world trade rests upon absolute differences in costs, such differences in costs cannot explain trade that takes place between two such countries one of which can produce both commodities at a cheaper cost than the other country but she can produce one commodity more cheaply. To express the same idea differently : Why does trade take place when one country produces both goods at an absolutely lower unit cost than the other but her cost is comparatively lower in the production of one good, *i.e.*, the country commands comparative cost advantage in the production of only one good although she possess absolute cost advantage in the production of both the goods? It was David Ricardo who first explained the basis of trade under such situations. According to Ricardo, "Each country will specialise in the production of those commodities in which it has greater comparative advantage or least comparative disadvantage. Thus a country will export those commodities in which its comparative advantage is the greatest, and import those commodities in which its comparative disadvantage is the least."

Assumptions of the Theory

The Ricardian theory is based on the following assumptions :

1. Labour is the only factor of production.
2. All labour units are homogeneous.
3. Labour is perfectly mobile within the country but is perfectly immobile between different countries.
4. Production of two goods takes place under constant cost conditions so that the unit cost ratios of the two goods are constant.
5. Trade takes place between only two countries and in two commodities produced by labour alone. In other words, Ricardian theory is a 2 × 2 × 1 trade model.
6. Prices of the two commodities are determined by labour cost, *i.e.*, the number of labour units employed to produce each.
7. Technological knowledge is unchanged.
8. There is free trade between the two countries, there being no trade barriers or restrictions in the movement of commodities.
9. No transport costs are involved in carrying trade between the two countries.
10. All factors of production are fully employed in both the countries.

Given these asssumptions, Ricardo enunciated the "principle of comparative costs", also called the "principle of comparative cost advantage" by taking the example of two countries England and Portugal and of two commodities wine and cloth. In his celebrated example, Portugal produces both wine and cloth at an absolutely lower cost than does England, *i.e.*, she possesses absolute advantage over England in the production of the both goods. Her comparative advantage is, however, greater in the production of wine than in the production of cloth. Conversely, England is inefficient in the production of both wine and cloth as her absolute real cost of production of both wine and cloth is higher compared with that of Portugal. However, her inefficiency is less marked in the production of cloth than in the production of wine. Under such a situation, it would be mutually advantageous for both the countries if Portugal concentrated only on the production of wine and exchanged her surplus wine against England's surplus cloth and England concentrated only on the manufacture of cloth exchanging her surplus production of cloth for the Portuguese wine. We may now reproduce Ricardo's celebrated example of Portugal and England by means of the following table:

	Per Unit Cost (in labour hours) of	
Country	*Wine*	*Cloth*
Portugal	80	90
England	120	100

According to the above cost data, one unit of wine costs 80 labour hours and one unit of cloth costs 90 hours of labour in Portugal. The corresponding cost of producing 1 unit of wine and 1 unit of cloth in England is 120 and 100 hours of labour. It is, therefore, obvious that Portugal commands absolute superiority over England in the production of both the goods. This absolute superiority of Portugal is, however, more marked (greater) in the production of wine than in the production of cloth. She has, therefore, a comparative cost advantage in the production of wine because here her cost ratio difference (or productivity) is relatively higher than it is in the case of cloth, *i.e.*, 80/120 < 90/100 < 1. It means that Portuguese labour's productivity in wine is 1.5 times (120/80) that of the productivity of English labour while her labour's productivity in cloth is only 1.1 times (100/90) that of the English labour. Since both 1.5 and 1.1 are greater than 1, it follows that Portugal's labour is more efficient or productive than England's labour in both the branches of production. It is, however, equally true that, since 1.5 is greater than 1.1, Portuguese labour is relatively more efficient or productive in wine than in cloth. In other words, Portugal possesses a comparative advantage over England in the production of wine relative to the production of cloth. Conversely, England suffers from a greater disadvantage in wine than in cloth.

But how can it be said that in the situation envisaged by Ricardo both countries will gain from trade? Returning to Ricardo's example, in the absence of trade 1 unit of wine will exchange for 0.88 unit of cloth in Portugal while in England 1 unit of wine will exchange for 1.2 units of cloth. If trade between the two countries begins, it is to the advantage of Portugal to export wine to England where 1 unit of it is exchanged for 1.2 units of cloth. Assuming perfect interindustry labour mobility within the country, Portugal will produce wine instead of cloth. Conversely, it will be to the advantage of England to specialise in the manufacture of cloth because she can obtain wine at a cheaper cost from Portugal by exchanging cloth against wine. There exists sufficient inducement for both the countries to engage in trade. Portugal would gain by trading off her surplus wine against English cloth so long as she can get more than 0.88 unit of cloth for 1 unit of wine while England would gain so long as she is asked to give less than 1.2 units of cloth for 1 unit of wine. Consequently, any exchange ratio between 0.88 and 1.2 units of cloth for 1 unit of wine will be acceptable to both the countries making trade possible between them. The theory of comparative cost advantage leads to the conclusion that each country will specialise in the production of that good in which it enjoys comparative cost advantages as by doing so it will be able to obtain a greater total product-mix from its given endowment of factors of production. Ricardo did not, however, explain where the actual exchange ratio between 0.88 and 1.2 units of cloth for 1 unit of wine will be fixed. In fact, there are possible a vast myriad of exchange ratios between the range of 0.88 and 1.2.

Its Criticism

The principle of comparative advantage has been criticised on the following grounds.

1. Unrealistic Assumption of Labour Theory of Value
2. Static Assumption of Fixed Proportions
3. Unrealistic Assumption of Constant Costs
4. Two-country Two-commodity Model is Unrealistic
5. Unrealistic Assumption of Free Trade
6. Neglects the Role of Technology
7. Unrealistic Assumption of Full Employment
8. Consider only Supply Side of International Trade

C. Modern Theory : Heckscher-Ohlin Theory

Bertin Ohlin in his famous book "Interregional and International Trade" criticised the classical theory of international trade and formulated the General Equilibrium or Factor Endowment Theory of International Trade. It is also known as the *Modern Theory of International Trade* or the Heckscher-Ohlin Theorem. In fact, it was Eli Heckscher, Ohlin's teacher, who first propounded the idea in 1919 that trade results from differences in factor endowments in different countries, and Ohlin carried it forward to build the modern theory of international trade.

Assumptions of the Theory

1. It is a 2 × 2 × 2 model, *i.e.*, there are two countries (A and B), two commodities (X and Y) and two factors of production (capital and labour).
2. There is perfect competition in commodity as well as factor markets.
3. There is full employment of resources.
4. There are quantitative differences in factor endowments in different regions, but qualitatively they are homogeneous.
5. The production function of the two commodities have different factor intensities, *i.e.*, labour-intensive and capital-intensive.
6. The production functions are different for different commodities, but are the same for each good in both countries. It means that the production function of commodity X is different from commodity Y. But the technique used to produce commodity X in both countries is the same, and the technique used to produce commodity Y in both countries is the same.
7. There is perfect mobility of factors within each region but internationally they are immobile.
8. There are no transport costs.
9. There is free trade between the two countries.
10. There are constant returns to scale in the production of each commodity in each region.

11. There is no change in technological knowledge.

Given these assumptions, Ohlin contends that the immediate cause of international trade is the difference in relative commodity prices caused by differences in relative demand and supply of factors (factor prices) as a result of differences in factor endowments between two countries. Fundamentally the relative scarcity of factors—the shortage of supply in relation to demand—is essential for trade between two regions. Commodities which use large quantities of scarce factors are imported because their prices are high, while those using abundant factors are exported because their prices are low.

Factor Abundance in Terms of Factor Prices

Ohlin explains richness in factor endowment in terms of factor prices. According to his definition, country A is abundant in capital if $\left(\frac{P_C}{P_L}\right)_A < \left(\frac{P_C}{P_L}\right)_B$, where P_C and P_L refer to prices of capital and labour and the subscripts A and B denote the two countries. In other words, if capital is relatively cheap in country A, the country is abundant in capital, and if labour is cheap in country B, the country is abundant in labour. Thus country A will export the capital-intensive good and country B will export the labour-intensive good.

Factor Abundance in Physical Terms

Another way to explain the Ohlin theorem is in physical terms of factor abundance. If country A is relatively capital-abundant and country B is relatively labour abundant, then measured in physical amounts $\left(\frac{C_A}{L_A}\right) > \frac{C_B}{L_B}$, where C_A and L_A are the total amounts of capital and labour respectively in country A and C_B and L_B are the total amounts of capital and labour respectively in country B.

Its Superiority Over the Classical Theory

Ohlin's theory is an improvement over the classical theory of international trade in many respects.

1. Ohlin's theory is superior to the classical theory in that it regards international trade as a special case of interregional or inter-local trade as distinct from the classical theory which considers international trade totally different from domestic trade.
2. The Ohlin model takes two factors–labour and capital–as against the one factor (labour) classical model, and is thus superior to the latter.
3. Again, the Ohlin theory is superior to the Ricardian theory in that it regards differences in factor supplies as basic for determining the pattern of international trade while the latter theory takes no notice of it.
4. The Ohlin model is more realistic because it is based on the relative prices of factors which in turn influence the relative prices of goods, while the Ricardian theory considers the relative prices of goods only.

Its Criticism

Ohlin's theory has been criticised on the following grounds.

1. Two-by-two-by-two Model is Unrealistic.
2. Static Theory
3. Factors not Homogeneous
4. Production Techniques not Homogeneous
5. Leontief Paradox has Falsified the Theory

Leontief Paradox

The most interesting empirical test of the Heckscher-Ohlin theorem that has been made so far is the study undertaken by Wassily Leontief in the early 1950s. Leontief tests his hypothesis with the help of an input-output table for the United States for 1947. He attempted to verify the empirical validity of the Heckscher-Ohlin theorem that a capital abundant country would export relatively capital intensive goods and in turn import more labour intensive goods. In context of U.S.A. economy, the Heckscher-Ohlin model tells that this country specialised in export of those good which use more capital than labour and import relatively labour intensive goods. But by Leontief's practical test, it was found that U.S.A. exported more of labour intensive goods and imported more of capital intensive goods, a situation that was in direct contrast to its relative factor endowment position. As such Leontief's result came as a great surprise to many economists of the world. Some economists criticised Leontief's findings on the ground that 1947 was not the right year for testing the theory as during this year the economy was beset with the post war disorganisation of production. In defence to criticisms Leontief stated that America's participation in international division of labour was based on its specialisation in labour intensive rather than capital intensive lines of production. In other words the country resorts to foreign trade in order to economise its capital and dispose of its surplus labour, rather than the reverse. It was also argued that the U.S. export industries employed more skilled labour and are thus human capital intensive rather than physical capital intensive. Abundance of human capital in the U.S. economy explains its exports of labour intensive goods.

Haberler's Theory of Opportunity Cost

The Opportunity Cost Theory, propounded by *Prof. Gottfried Haberler* in 1883, has been applied to the theory of international trade as a substitute for the doctrine of comparative cost expressed in terms of labour cost or real cost. Haberler's theory explains that if a country can produce either commodity X or Y, the opportunity cost of commodity X is the amount of the other commodity Y that must be given up in order to get one additional unit of commodity X. To explain this theory let us take examples of two countries say England and Russia. Suppose with the given resources England can produce 30 kgs. of wheat and no cloth or 90 metres of cloth and no wheat. Russia on the other hand with its resources can produce 60 kgs. of wheat and no cloth or 90 metres of cloth and no wheat. The opportunity cost of wheat is the production of cloth foregone, *i.e.*, it is the amount of one commodity given up to get the other commodity. Thus in England opportunity cost is

$$30W = 90C$$

$$\Rightarrow \quad 1W = 3C$$

and in Russia opportunity cost is

$$60W = 90C$$

$$\Rightarrow \quad 1W = 1.5C$$

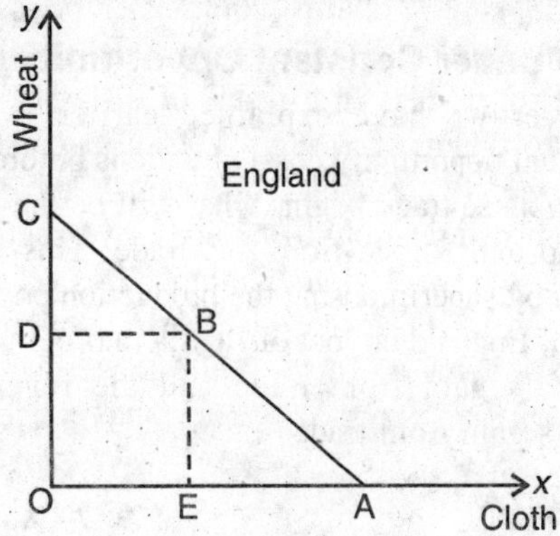

Fig. 1

The production possibilities of wheat and cloth in England and Russia and their opportunity cost can be shown in the following figures.

Since, with all its resources England can produce either OC of wheat or OA of cloth, the line CA is the production possibility curve in Figure 1. The point B on production possibility line CA, shows that England can produce OD of wheat and OE of cloth. Hence CD of wheat is the opportunity cost of OE of cloth in England, in the same way as OC of wheat is the opportunity cost of OA of cloth. Since the production possibility curve AC is a straight line. It bears a constant slope. It shows the constant opportunity cost of wheat in terms of cloth and cloth in terms of wheat.

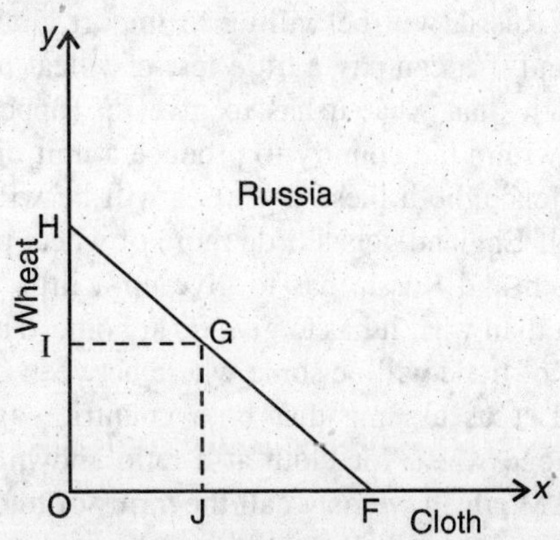

Fig. 2

In the same way FH is the production possibility curve of Russia. At point G Russia can produce OI of wheat and OJ of cloth. Hence IH of wheat is the opportunity cost of OJ of cloth in the same way as OH of wheat is the opportunity cost of OF of cloth.

Trade under Constant Opportunity Costs

Whatever we have explained earlier, was the individual opportunity costs of nations before trade. Now suppose trade begins what will be the gain to England and Russia from this trade. This we can explain by superimposing the production possibility curve of England on that of Russia in order to know England's gain from trade and the reverse for Russia's gain from trade.

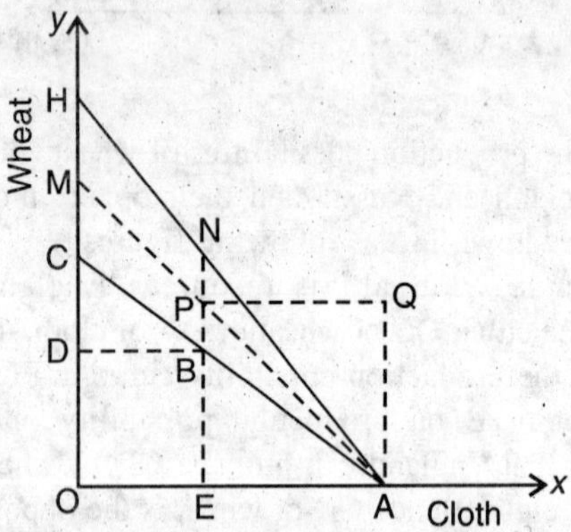

Fig. 3

From the above Figure 3, it is clear that the production possibility curve of Russia (AH) is higher than that of England. It reveals that Russia has to sacrifice more of wheat per unit of cloth within the country than England has to do within her country. Thus, Russia will be willing to import cloth from England if it can pay a little less of wheat per unit of cloth than what it has to give up (opportunity cost) within the country to produce a unit of cloth.

Hence, both these countries will be willing to trade if England gets a little more of wheat per unit of cloth and Russia has to give up a little less of wheat than what it has to give up at home. Thus, the terms of trade will be some where between CA and HA. Let us assume that both countries agree to exchange wheat for cloth at a ratio shown by the line AM which we may call the terms of trade line. Now England will specialise in production of cloth and Russia will specialise in production of wheat. Now England will produce OA of cloth from which OE amount will be kept for domestic consumption and will export EA of cloth for PB amount of wheat which it imports from Russia. Thus England gets an additional amount of wheat PB through specialisation and trade. Hence after trade PQ = EA are England's export and PE = QA are its imports. In the similar process Russia too gains from specialisation and trade through its exports of wheat sacrificing the units of production of cloth.

Trade Under Increasing and Decreasing Opportunity Cost Conditions

The implicit assumption behind the straight line production possibility curve is that all the factors used in production process and equally efficient both in production of wheat and cloth. But the fact is that all factors are not equally efficient in production of both these goods. So the slope of the production possibility curve cannot be a straight line. It is also not possible that both the commodities may be produced either under decreasing opportunity costs or under increasing opportunity costs. Rather the situation may be where wheat is being produced under decreasing opportunity costs and cloth under increasing opportunity costs. This can be shown with the following Figure 4.

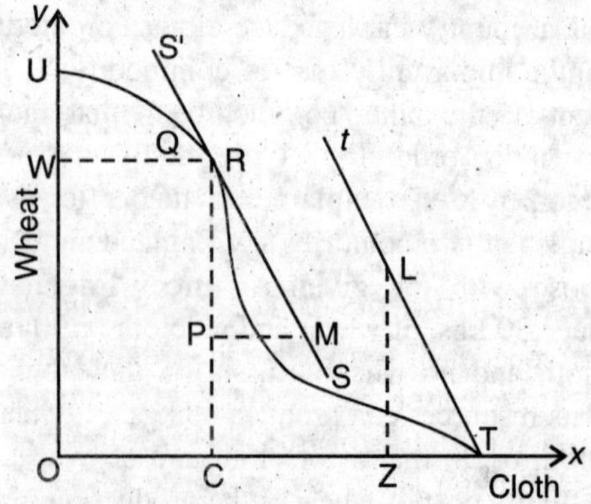

Fig. 4

In Figure 4 UT is the PPC of England. This curve is concave in the portion UQ showing increasing opportunity costs and convex in region QT showing decreasing opportunity cost. The point dividing the curve UT into these segments is called the point of inflection. In region UQ international terms of trade line is tangent to point R where both wheat and cloth are being produced under increasing opportunity cost. Russia is producing OC of cloth and OW of wheat. Its consumption point is at M whereby it imports PM of cloth and exports PR of wheat. Since point M is outside the production possibility curve, the country is better off trading with the other country. When the production of cloth starts under decreasing opportunity costs due to internal economics and the PPC becomes convex in the region QT of the UT curve. Consequently as more and more of cloth is produced costs of production diminishes. Now the country (England) reaches point T when it completely specialises in production of cloth. Assuming that the international terms of trade remain the same as before we draw Tt parallel to SS′ so that the new consumption point is T. The country will now export ZT of cloth and import LZ of wheat. The country gains more from trade at L than point M. This is possible so long as the terms of trade line Tt is to the right of SS′.

Assumptions

Haberler makes the following assumptions for his theory:

1. There are only two countries, two factors of production, labour and capital and two commodities, say X and Y.
2. There is perfect competition in both the factor and commodity markets.
3. The price of each commodity equals its marginal money costs.
4. The supply of each factor is fixed.
5. No change in technology.
6. Free Trade
7. Full employment
8. Factors are mobile within and immobile between the countries.

Terms of Trade

The terms of trade is one of the measurements of the gains from international trade to a particular country.

In international economics, the phrase terms of trade refers to the ratio index of export prices to import prices. In other words, it is the rate at which a country's exports are exchanged for imports. John Stuart Mill, one of the great classical economists has shown that the terms of trade between two commodities depend upon the strength of the world supply and demand for each of the two commodities. In other words, the terms of trade are determined by reciprocal demand.

Different Concepts of Terms of Trade

Several concept of terms of trade, such as the net barter, gross barter, income, single factoral, and double factoral terms of trade have been given by different writers. These several concepts have been put by **Meier** under the following three broad groups.

1. Those terms of trade that relate to the real ratio of international exchange between the commodities. In this group we have the
   - A. Net barter terms of trade
   - B. Gross barter terms of trade
   - C. Income terms of trade
2. Those terms of trade that relate to their interchange between the productive resources. In this group we have the
   - A. Single factoral terms of trade
   - B. Double factoral terms of trade
3. Those terms of trade that interpret the gains from trade in terms of the utility analysis. In this group we have the
   - A. Real cost terms of trade
   - B. Utility terms of trade

Net Barter or Commodity Terms of Trade

While discussing the terms of trade, **Frank William Taussing** introduced the concept of the net barter or commodity terms of trade. His net barter terms of trade, popularly called 'the commodity terms of trade', is the ratio between import prices and export-prices and can be written as

$$T_C = \frac{P_x}{P_m}$$

where

T_C = net barter terms of trade

P_x = price of export commodity

P_m = price of import commodity

When this concept of net barter terms of trade is applied to more than one export and import commodity we use the export price and the import price indices instead of using the prices of particular export and import goods. Consequently, a change in the net barter terms of trade would be written as

$$T_C = \frac{P_{x_1}/P_{x_0}}{P_{M_1}/P_{M_0}}$$

$$= \frac{P_{x_1}}{P_{M_1}} \cdot \frac{P_{M_0}}{P_{x_0}}$$

where

T_C = net barter terms of trade

= price index of exports for any given year

= price index of imports for any given year

= price index of exports for base year

= price index of imports for base year

As the price index of imports and exports for the base year will always be equal to 100, the term in the formula will be equal to 100/100 = 1. Consequently, the net barter terms of trade will, therefore, move in accordance with the movement of any given year's price indices of imports and exports. Let us suppose that the price index of imports and exports in India in the base year 1960 is 100 and in 1988 the price indices of imports and exports are 120 and 160 respectively. Consequently, the net barter terms of trade will be

$$T_C = \frac{160}{120} \cdot \frac{100}{100}$$

$$= 1.33$$

This means that in 1988 the net barter terms of trade show an improvement of 33 per cent over the base year.

Gross Barter Terms of Trade

Introduced by **Taussing**, the gross barter terms of trade is the ratio of the total physical quantity of imports to the total physical quantity of exports of a country, greater this ratio the more favourable being the gross barter terms of trade. Taussing introduced this concept to correct the commodity or net barter terms of trade for unilateral transactions, or unrequited exports or imports such as tributes, gifts, immigrant's remittance etc. The gross barter terms of trade can be expressed as

$$T_G = \frac{Q_M}{Q_x}$$

where

T_G = gross barter terms of trade

Q_M = total quantity of imports

Q_x = total quantity of exports

For comparing changes in the gross barter terms of trade between two time periods we use the index numbers of the quantities of exports and imports in the two time periods instead of the quantities alone. The ratio is expressed as

$$T_G = \frac{Q_{M_1}}{Q_{x_1}} \cdot \frac{Q_{x_0}}{Q_{M_0}}$$

where the terms Q_x and Q_M stand for the index of quantity of exports and imports of the country and the subscripts 0 to 1 stand for the base year and the given year respectively.

Income Terms of Trade

Dorrance and Staehle refined the concept of the commodity terms of trade and developed a new concept known as the 'income terms of trade'. The income terms of trade is the ratio of the value of exports divided by the price index of imports and can be written as

$$T_I = \frac{P_x Q_M}{P_M}$$

where T_I = income terms of trade

P_x = price of exports

P_M = price of imports

Q_M = quantity of exports

It is obvious from the formula that given the import prices, if the export prices rise and the volume of country's exports fall equally, the net barter terms of trade will improve while the income terms of trade will show no change.

Unilateral or Single Factoral Terms of Trade

With changing factor productivity, the concept of the net barter terms of trade is distinctly misleading as a measure of the gains for a country from trade without keeping in view the improvement in factor productivity which results from trading. The concepts which used the commodity technical coefficient index were developed by **Jacob Viner**. The concepts developed by him are known as the 'single factoral' terms of trade.

The single factoral terms of trade is the ratio of the export price index and the import price index adjusted for changes in the productivity of a country's factors of production engaged in the production of export commodities. If the commodity terms of trade index is multiplied by the reciprocal of the export commodity technical coefficients index, the resultant index is known as the 'single factoral terms of trade' which can be expressed as

$$T_S = \frac{P_x}{P_M}.Z_x$$

where T_S = single factoral terms of trade
= net barter terms of trade
Z_x = index of factor productivity in exports

Bilateral or Double Factoral Terms of Trade

The concept of the double factoral terms of trade takes account of the productivity of factors of production entering into the production of country's exports as well as of the productivity of foreign factors of production producing country's imports. The concept of double factoral terms of trade can be expressed as

$$T_D = \frac{P_x}{P_M}.\frac{Z_x}{Z_M}$$

where T_D = double factoral terms of trade
Z_M = index of factor productivity in imports
Z_x = index of factor productivity in exports
P_x = price index of exports
P_M = price index of imports

Real Cost Terms of Trade

The real cost terms of trade are obtained by multiplying the single factoral terms of trade with the index of the amount of disutility per unit of the productive resources employed in producing the exports. The real cost terms of trade can be symbolically expressed as

$$T_R = T_S.R_x$$
$$= \frac{P_x}{P_M}.Z_x.R_x.$$

where T_R denotes the real cost terms of trade and R_x stands for the index of the amount of disutility suffered per unit of productive resources employed in producing exports. The terms R_x, P_M and Z_x have the same meaning as they have in the formula of the single factoral terms of trade.

Utility Terms of Trade

The utility terms of trade are obtained by multiplying the real cost terms of trade with the index of the relative desirability or utility of imports as compared to the goods that could have been produced for home consumption with those factors of production which are now used in the production of export goods (U_M). The utility terms of trade may be written as

$$T_U = T_R.U_M$$
$$= \frac{P_x}{P_M}.Z_x.R_x.U_x$$

Factors Affecting the Terms of Trade

The major factors which affect the terms of the trade of a country are:

1. Economic growth
2. Shifts in the demand for exports and/or import
3. Tariff
4. Devaluation
5. Availability of Substitutes

Economic Growth and Terms of Trade

Economic growth of a country causes an outward shift in the production possibilities curve allowing the larger aggregate output. The upward shift in the production possibilities curve may have occurred due to increase in the availability of factors of production and technological improvements allowing the production of larger aggregate output with the given quantity of resources. The influence of economic growth in the terms of trade will depend upon the pattern of country's economic growth. If growth is neutral, the terms of the trade will remain unaffected. If growth is ultra-export biased the country will produce more quantity of the export goods and positively less quantity of the import goods. This condition will necessarily worsen the terms of trade of the country. On the other hand, if growth is ultra-import-biased, the production of import commodities will increase so much that the production of the export commodities will decrease in absolute terms and the terms of trade will be favourable for the country.

If the country is significantly large to influence the international terms of trade by her action, then even with the neutral trade biased growth there exists the possibility that the terms of trade may turn so strongly against the growing country that she will actually wind up on a lower indifference curve than she could attain without economic growth. **Jagdish Bhagwati** has described it as a case of "**immiserizing growth**".

Devaluation and Terms of Trade

Devaluation lowers the value of the home currency expressed in terms of the currency of foreign country. After the foreign exchange value of the home currency has been lowered as a result of devaluation, it is natural to think that the terms of trade of the currency devaluing country will deteriorate because the prices of country's exports fall in terms of the foreign currency while prices of her imports rise in terms of the local currency. But this is not a bare fact. As a matter of fact, the effects of devaluation depend upon the elasticities of demand and supply of imports and exports of the country. The tendency of devaluation is to improve the terms of trade if the product of the demand elasticities for the country's imports and exports is greater than the product of the supply elasticities of her imports and exports.

In general, if the elasticities of supply of exports and imports are large in proportion to the elasticities of demand for exports and imports, devaluation of a country's currency will worsen its terms of trade and revaluation will improve its terms of trade. Expressed differently, if the product of the supply elasticities is greater than the product of the demand elasticities, devaluation will cause deterioration in the country's terms of trade and vice-versa. If the elasticities of supply of exports and imports are equal to the elasticities of demand for exports and imports so that the product of the supply elasticities equals the product of the demand elasticities, the country's terms of the trade will remain unchanged consequent upon devaluation. This relationship between the terms of trade and devaluation can be stated thus:

A. Terms of trade will improve due to currency devaluation if $\mathbf{D_x.D_M > S_x.S_M}$

B. Terms of trade will deteriorate due to currency devaluation if $\mathbf{D_x.D_M < S_x.S_M}$

C. Terms of trade will remain unchanged due to currency devaluation if $\mathbf{D_x.D_M = S_x.S_M}$

Underdeveloped Countries and Terms of Trade

For world's most underdeveloped countries which are caught in the vicious trap of low income, low employment and low technical know-how, foreign trade is life and blood of the economy. Consequently, '*Trade or Perish*' is an appropriate slogan in the context of the need of their rapid economic development. It is, however, argued by the spokesmen of the underdeveloped countries that international trade which had served as an engine of economic growth for the open lands in the nineteenth century is no more an engine of economic growth for them today. According to the less developed countries, today they face unfavourable conditions which are very different from the favourable ones faced by the open lands in the nineteenth century. **Raul Prebisch insists that the terms of trade of the less developed countries have been secularly deteriorating.**

In his well-known work '*Towards a New Trade Policy for Development*' Raul Prebisch maintains that there is a long-run tendency for the prices of the primary products to deteriorate relative to the prices of manufactured goods. Prebisch's argument is based on the fact that the underdeveloped countries are net producers of primary products such as coffee, copper, tea, rice, sugar, fats, etc. These products are roughly the same goods today that these were 50 years ago. On the other hand, the quality of manufactured goods produced by the developed countries such as the automobiles, radios, petroleum refinery, equipments, trucks, etc., has improved tremendously. Consequently, in the world markets these goods fetch higher prices relative to those fetched by the primary products.

Singer gives a different explanation for the deteriorating terms of the trade of the primary products producing countries. According to him, the fruits of technical progress can either be retained by the producers in terms of the high incomes or passed on to the consumers in the form of low prices. The fruits of technical progress in the underdeveloped countries have been passed on to the consumers in the developed countries in the form of lower prices of primary products whereas these have been retained by the producers in the developed countries in the form of higher incomes of producers. Singer does not give any explanation in support of his argument. A.M. McLeod, however, states that it has happened due to the presence of greater degree of monopolistic control prevalent in the production of finished goods in the developed countries. The less developed countries more or less produce the same (identical) goods and search the markets for these goods abroad. As these countries are less organised they compete among themselves for the export markets for their products and in the process give away a substantial part of their gains in productivity to the developed countries in the form of fall in the prices of their exports.

Balance of Payments

The balance of payments of a country is a statistical record kept in the form of a balance sheet comprising of all her foreign economic transactions during any given period of time. It presents a summary account of all international transactions of a country during a certain given period of time.

Since the balance of payments is a systematic record of a country's total money receipts from and payments to abroad, the difference between receipts and payments is the surplus or deficit. A country's total money receipts are the receipts or payments that accrue to its residents while the total payments refer to the payments made by the residents of a country. Dividing resident's total receipts, R, and their total payments, P, into their domestic and foreign components and if the domestic receipts and domestic payments are identical, then the international balance of payments, B, of a country can be expressed as

$$B = R - P$$
$$= (R_d + R_f) - (P_d + P_f)$$
$$= R_f - P_f \quad (\text{since } R_d = P_d)$$

For an open economy, the total receipts may differ from the total payments and their difference represents the difference between foreign receipts (R_f) and foreign payments (P_f). The positive difference is termed as a surplus while the negative difference is termed as a deficit in the balance of payments of a country.

The balance of payments of a country is not a balance sheet showing a country's foreign assets and liabilities at any given point of time. It shows for any given period of time the flow of a nation's total receipts from abroad and its total payments made to abroad. Following the conventional rules of double entry accounting, a nation's total payments and total receipts for any given period of time must be in balance. Further more, one nation's receipts are payments for others while the receipts of other nations are payments for the nation.

Usually, a country's balance of payments distinguishes between items on the current and capital accounts. In the current account are included all kinds of exports and imports of goods and services, interest and dividend payments, private gifts and so on. The capital account, sub-divided into short term capital transfers, lists the imports and exports of all kinds of debt instruments and corporate stocks as well as imports and exports of monetary gold. The following table explains the different items included under various subheads in the balance of payments of a country.

Components of Balance of Payments

Receipts (Credits)	*Payments (Debits)*
1. Exports of goods	1. Imports of goods
2. Exports of services	2. Imports of services
3. Unrequited receipts (gifts, indemnities, etc.,) from foreigners)	3. Unrequited payments (gifts, indemnities, etc. to foreigners)
4. Capital receipts (borrowings from, capital repayments by, or sale of assets to, foreigners)	4. Capital payments (lending to, capital repayments to, or purchase of assets from, foreigners)

Balance of Payments and Balance of Trade

The concepts of balance of trade and balance of payments are often misunderstood. Economists frequently say that while the balance of payments includes the balance of trade, the balance of trade does not include the balance of payments. A country exports and imports many **visible** goods and **invisible** services. **Invisible services** include tourism, shipping and other transport services, banking and insurance services for whose exports and imports payments are made and received by the country in international trade. A country's balance of trade refers to the value of imports and exports of commodities only. The balance of payments is, however, more comprehensive including as it does the total debits and credits relating to all the items on account of which a country makes payments to and receives payments from rest of the world. In short, the balance of trade is only a part of the balance of payments.

Equilibrium and Disequilibrium

The balance of payments of a country is said to be in equilibrium when the demand for foreign exchange is exactly equivalent to the supply of it. The balance of payments is in disequilibrium when there is either a surplus or deficit in the balance of payments. When there is a deficit in the balance of payments, the demand for foreign exchange exceeds the supply for it.

Correction of Disequilibrium

A country may not be bothered about a surplus in the balance of payments; but every country strives to remove, or at least to reduce a balance of payments deficit. A number of measures are available for correcting the balance of payments disequilibrium. We outline below the important measures for correcting the disequilibrium caused by a deficit in the balance of payments.

A. Monetary measures
B. Trade measures
C. Miscellaneous

A. Monetary Measures

The important monetary measures are outlined below:

Monetary Contraction : The level of aggregate domestic demand, the domestic price level and the demand for imports and exports may be influenced by a contraction or expansion in money supply and correct the balance of payments disequilibrium. The measure required is a contraction in money supply. A contraction in money supply is likely to reduce the purchasing power and there by the aggregate demand. It is also likely to bring about a fall in domestic prices. The fall in the domestic aggregate demand and domestic prices reduce the demand for imports. The fall in domestic prices is likely to increase exports. Thus, the fall in imports and the rise in exports would help to correct the disequilibrium.

Devaluation : Devaluation means a reduction in the official rate at which one currency is exchanged for another currency. A country with a fundamental disequilibrium in the balance of payments may devalue its currency in order to stimulate its exports and discourage imports to correct the disequilibrium.

The balance of payments deficit of a country will be eliminated as a consequence of devaluation, *i.e.*, the position of the country's balance of payments will improve if the price elasticities of demand for the currency devaluing country's imports and exports are high and at any rate in order to effect improvement in the country's balance of payments the combined absolute value of the two demand elasticities must be greater than one, *i.e.*,

$$e_x + e_m > 1$$

Where the terms e_x and e_m respectively represent the price elasticity of demand for exports, and imports, of the currency devaluing country.

Exchange Control : Exchange control is a popular method employed to influence the balance of payments position of a country. Under exchange control, the government or central bank assumes complete control of the foreign exchange reserves and earnings of the country. The recipients of foreign exchange such as exporters, are required to surrender foreign exchange to the government/ central bank in exchange for domestic currency. By the virtue of its control over the use of foreign exchange the government can control the imports.

B. Trade Measures

Trade measures include export promotion measures and import control measures.

Exports may be encouraged by reducing or abolishing export duties, providing an export subsidy and encouraging export production and export marketing by offering monetary, fiscal, physical and institutional incentives and facilities.

Imports may be controlled by imposing or enhancing import duties, restricting imports through import quotas and licensing and even by prohibiting altogether the import of certain non-essential items.

C. Miscellaneous Measures

Apart from the measures mentioned above, there are a number of other measures that can help to make the Balance of Payments position more favourable, such as obtaining foreign loans, encouraging foreign investment in the home country, development of tourism to attract foreign tourists, providing incentives to enhance inward remittances, developing import substituting industries, etc.

The Import Function

Imports are an increasing function of income. This functional relationship can be expressed in the following way

$$M = M(y)$$

A country's average propensity to import is defined as the total imports divided by the total national income, *i.e.*,

$$API = \frac{M}{Y}$$

The marginal propensity to import measures how much of a change in the national income is spent on imports. Using algebraic terms it is defined as.

Devaluation

By devaluation of a country's currency unit is meant the decrease in the external value of a unit of that currency expressed in terms of gold, SDR or foreign currency by government edict. A country may reduce the foreign exchange value of her currency unit for more than one reason, *e.g.*, to create surplus in her balance of payments by means of dumping her goods abroad, or to remove deficit in her external balance of payments. In short, devaluation means an act of officially reducing the external value of the currency unit of the country and appreciation to the extent of devaluation in the external value of the currency unit of the country in whose relationship the country has devalued her currency.

Methods of Removing Balance of Payments Deficit

The conditions under which devaluation would cause an improvement in the balance of payments position of the currency devaluing country have been discussed by Lerner, Robinson, Meade and others. The extent to which deficit of the external balance of payments of the currency devaluing country can be corrected through devaluation depends upon the price elasticities of demand and the price elasticities of supply of her exports and imports. Considering first the price elasticity of demand for the exports of the country, if the price elasticity of demand for the exports of the currency-devaluing country is less than unity in absolute value, devaluation will not reduce deficit of the balance of payments of the country; rather the balance of payments deficit of the country would increase as a consequence of devaluation.

If the price elasticity of demand for the exports of the country is less than unity, a given percentage fall in the rate of exchange, say of 20 per cent, will cause less than 20 per cent (say only 10 per cent) increase in the total quantity of exports of the country. This is the positive quantity effect of devaluation. But while the total quantity of exports increases by 10 per cent the total foreign exchange earnings or total value of exports of the country will be less than the pre-devaluation total value of exports because while the total quantity of exports has increased by 10 per cent, the foreign currency price per unit of export goods has fallen by 20 per cent. The negative price factor more than offsets the positive quantity factor reflected in the increase of the total quantity of exports, making the net effect on the total foreign exchange earnings of the country through exports negative. It has been illustrated in Figure 5 where the two countries taken are India and America with India devaluing her currency rupee in order to correct her external balance of payments deficit. In this figure, the demand and supply of India's exports have been shown on the *x*-axis and price expressed in the US dollars has been shown on the Y-axis. D_xD_x is inelastic demand curve for India's exports while AS_x is perfectly elastic supply curve of Indian exports.

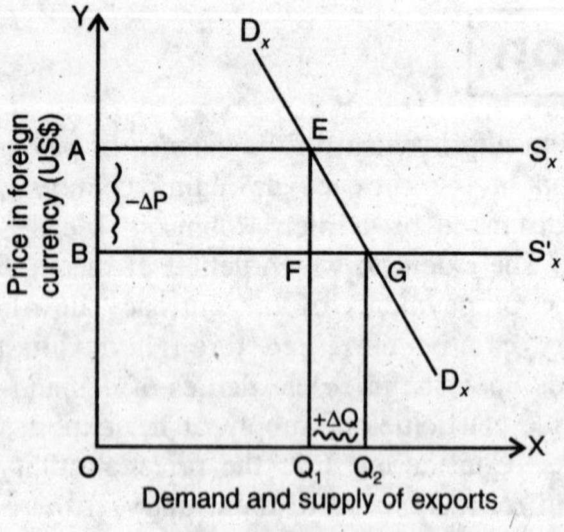

Fig. 5

Before devaluation of the Indian rupee, the dollar price of export was OA, the total quantity exported was OQ_1 and the total foreign exchange (dollars) earned by the country through the exports was $OQ_1 \times OA$ (= rectangle AOQ_1E). Consequent on devaluation of the rupee, the dollar (foreign currency) price of Indian exports falls by AB from OA to OB showing that the dollar price in percentage terms has fallen by the full extent of devaluation. Consequently, the supply curve of India's exports AS_x shifts downward to the position of BS'_x while the total quantity of exports increases by Q_1Q_2 (= ΔQ) from OQ_1 to OQ_2. The new total foreign exchange revenue (total dollar earnings) is $OQ_2 \times OB$ (= rectangle BOQ_2G). The net change in the total foreign exchange earnings of the country due to devaluation will be positive (increase) or negative (decrease) according as ABFE is smaller or greater than rectangle Q_1Q_2GF. In this case, the demand for India's exports being inelastic, rectangle ABFE > rectangle Q_1Q_2GF. Consequently, devaluation increases rather than decrease the deficit of India's balance of payments. It, therefore, follows that although currency devaluation will always lead to an increase in the total quantity of exports of the currency-devaluing country (unless the price elasticity of demand for her exports is zero), it does not, however, necessarily follow from this that it will always also lead to an increase in the total foreign exchange earnings of the country from exports.

Figure 6 shows the position of total export earnings in terms of rupees (domestic currency). It is obvious that the total rupee-earnings will always increase as result of devaluation even when the foreign demand for country's exports is inelastic. In this case, instead of the country's perfectly elastic supply curve shifting downward the demand curve shifts upward from D_xD_x to $D'_xD'_x$, showing higher demand for exports at each different rupee-price since the same rupee-price now means lower dollar-price for the Americans inducing them to buy Q_1Q_2 amount more. However, although the total rupee earnings from exports increase by EQ_1Q_2F amount but it does not necessarily follow from this that the total dollar-earnings also increase.

Coming to imports, devaluation will help in reducing the deficit of external balance of payments only if the price elasticity of domestic demand for imports is greater than unity ($e_m > 1$) because in that situation a given percentage increase in the price of imports measured in terms of the domestic currency would cause more than proportionate fall in the quantity of imports as shown in Figure 7 when the demand for and supply of imports have been shown on the X-axis and the price of imports expressed in domestic currency has been shown on the Y-axis. D_MD_M is the demand curve for imports while AS_M is the perfectly elastic supply curve for imports. Before devaluation, the rupee-price of imports was OA and the total imports were OQ_1 giving the total rupee value of imports represented by rectangle OQ_1EA (= OA × OQ_1). As a consequence of devaluation, although the price of imports in foreign currency (dollars) remains unchanged, since the supply curve for imports is expressed in terms of the domestic currency, it shifts upward by the full amount of the difference between the pre-devaluation and post-devaluation rupee-price. The new supply curve is now BS'_M. Consequently, the total amount of imports decreases by Q_1Q_2 from OQ_1 to OQ_2. However, after devaluation India pays higher price OB for her imports. The total rupee-cost of imports is now OQ_2GB. The improvement in the balance of payments resulting from decrease in total imports consequent on devaluation of the rupee would depend on the relative sizes of rectangle Q_2Q_1EF and ABGF. If the elasticity of demand for imports is greater than unity, then rectangle Q_2Q_1EF will be larger than rectangle ABGF. Consequently, the balance of payments position of the country, in so far as imports are concerned, will improve due to devaluation.

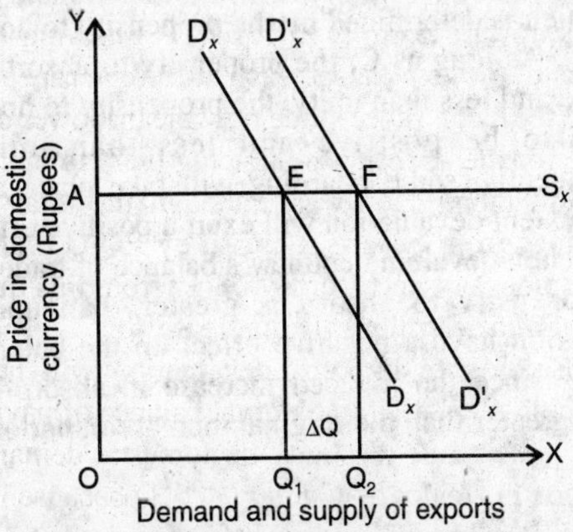

Fig. 6

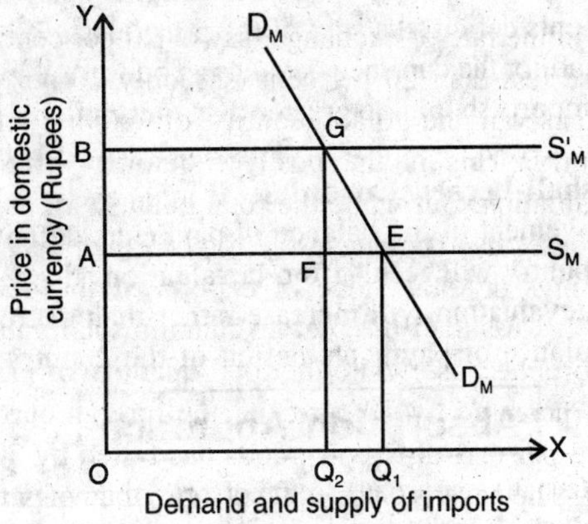

Fig. 7

Figure 8 shows the effect of devaluation on the total imports and total foreign exchange bill which must fall unless the demand for imports is perfectly inelastic. However, although the total dollar payments obligation is reduced from OQ_1EA to OQ_2FA but it does not necessarily follow from this that the total rupee-payments burden of the country will also fall. It will fall only if the demand for imports is elastic, *i.e.*, if the elasticity of demand for imports is greater than unity. There will be no change in the total-rupee payments burden if the elasticity of demand for imports is unity and the burden will increase in the event of the elasticity of demand for imports being less than unity.

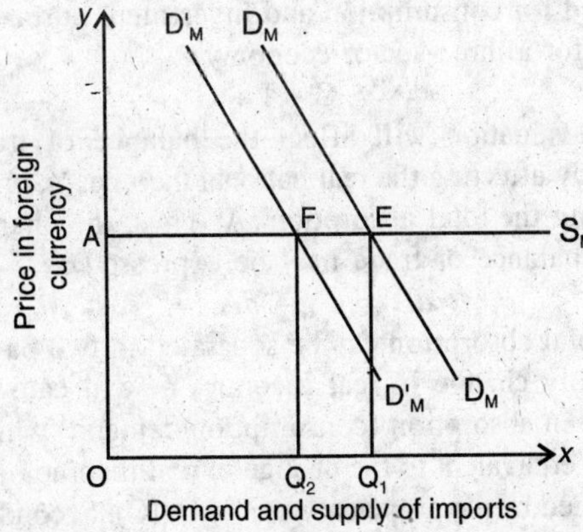

Fig. 8

It can be proved by means of a formula that under conditions of perfectly elastic supply of imports and exports, if a country devalues her currency in order to remove her external balance of payments deficit, the sum of the price elasticities of demand for the currency devaluing country's exports and imports should be greater than unity in absolute value, *i.e.*, $e_x + e_m > 1$. This is the well-known **Marshall-Lerner Condition**. If $e_x + e_m = 1$, no improvement in the balance of payments deficit of the country will result from devaluation. If $e_x + e_m < 1$, devaluation will increase rather than decrease the balance of payments deficit of the country.

Absorption Approach

An alternative approach to the effects of devaluation formulated in macro terms, as against the elasticity approach formulated in micro terms, is the absorption approach. This approach as first developed by **Sidney Alexander** in his famous paper published in 1952. According to the absorption approach, the balance of trade can be treated as the difference between national income (Y) and total expenditure (E) or absorption so that

$$B = Y - E \qquad ...(1)$$

where B = balance of trade

E = total expenditure

Designating total expenditure (E) or total demand as total absorption (A), the above equation can be rewritten as

$$B = Y - A \qquad ...(2)$$

Since total absorption is composed of the demand created for all purposes, it includes the demand for consumption and investment purposes. Thus, for a three-sector economy

$$A = C + I + G \qquad ...(3)$$

Devaluation will affect the balance of trade either by affecting the real national income, Y, or by affecting the total absorption, A. Thus, the change in the balance of trade may be expressed as

$$dB = dY - dA \qquad ...(4)$$

Total absorption can be separated in two parts. First, any change in real income (Y) will cause a change in absorption (consumption demand) which will be equivalent to the change in real income (dY) multiplied by the propensity to absorb (C). Secondly, devaluation will directly affect absorption which will depend, among other things, on the level of real income at which devaluation takes place. Let us call this direct effect on absorption as D. Consequently

$$dA = CdY + dD \qquad ...(5)$$

By substituting equation (5) for the term dA in equation (4) we obtain

$$dB = (1 - C)\, dY - dD \qquad ...(6)$$

Equation (6) states that the effects of a devaluation on the balance of trade depend on first, the effect of devaluation on real income (Y), second, the propensity to absorb (C), and third, the effect on direct absorption (D).

If there are enough unemployed resources in the currency-devaluing country (as is generally true of most developing countries) production can increase in the short period following the devaluation. The process of expansion will start from expansion in exports which will raise real national income through the multiplier process. The increase in exports will, however, depend on the extent to which export's prices in the currency-devaluing country rise and the extent to which rest of the world is willing to absorb the exports from the currency-devaluing country.

The net effect of the increase in real national income on the balance of trade does not, however, comprise the total increase in real income or production; it comprises the difference between the increase in real income and the induced increase in total absorption. This difference between increase in real production and real absorption may be called real hoarding (saving). The effect of devaluation on the balance of trade is, therefore, equal to the amount of real hoarding which takes place in the economy and which is determined by the propensity to hoard (1 – C). As long as C, the propensity to absorb, is positive and less than unity, the propensity to hoard will also be positive and less than unity. Consequently, some hoarding will take place and to this extent devaluation will exert a positive effect on currency-devaluing country's balance of trade. If the propensity to absorb is greater than unity, devaluation have a negative effect on the balance of trade since the induced increase in absorption will be greater than the original increase in national income.

MULTIPLE CHOICE QUESTIONS

1. In which of the following year, the Articles of Agreement of IMF were changed for the first time?
   A. 1969 B. 1975
   C. 1980 D. 1985
2. The value of the foreign trade multiplier is equal to
   A. $\frac{1}{mpm + mps}$ B. $\frac{1}{mpm - mps}$
   C. $mpm + mps$ D. $\frac{1}{mpm}$
3. The devaluation according to Marshall and Learner conditions will not be helpful, if the sum of the elasticities of exports and imports is
   A. equal to unity B. greater than unity
   C. less than unity D. zero
4. Under the system of fluctuating exchange rates regime, the adjustment in the balance of payments is brought about by the changes in
   A. Prices
   B. Exchange rate
   C. Income
   D. Prices and income
5. The members of the NAFTA are
   A. USA, Canada, Mexico
   B. USA, Canada, India
   C. USA, Canada, Japan
   D. USA, UK, India
6. Consider a Ricardian economy that is endowed with 45 units of labour. It can produce two goods: Gajar-Halwa and Kulfi. One unit of labour can produce 4 kilos of Gajar-Halwa or 6 kilos of Kulfi. The international price of Gajar-Halwa in terms of Kulfi is 2. In free trade, this country will produce
   A. 15 kilos of Kulfis
   B. 130 kilos of Kulfis
   C. 180 kilos of Gajar-Halwa
   D. 270 kilos of Gajar-Halwa
7. If protection is given to a small import competing industry, consumer surplus and domestic profits will, respectively.
   A. rise, rise B. fall, fall
   C. rise, fall D. fall, rise
8. Which one of the following conditions is **not** assumed by the factor price equalisation theorem?
   A. The countries are characterised by different factor endowments
   B. The countries are characterised by different production functions
   C. The industries are characterised by different factor intensities
   D. Each country will export the commodity which uses its abundent factor relatively intensively
9. India is large exporter of tea and a small exporter of bicycles. In this context, which one of the following is true?
   A. An export subsidy to tea would improve India's terms of trade in the world tea market.
   B. An export subsidy to tea would worsen India's terms of trade in the world tea market.
   C. An export subsidy to bicycles would improve India's terms of trade in the world bicycle market.
   D. An export subsidy to bicycles would worsen India's terms of trade in the world bicycle market.
10. There are two countries. Sugarland and Saltland. Each country produces sugar and salt. The former exports sugar and the latter, salt. Starting from a free trade equilibrium, a tariff on salt by Sugarland would affect the offer curves and the relative price of sugar from Sugarland's perspective in which one of the following ways?
    A. Shift the offer curve of Saltland, increase the price of sugar.
    B. Shift the offer curve of Saltland, decrease the price of sugar.
    C. Shift the offer curve of Sugarland, increase the price of sugar.
    D. Shift the offer curve of Sugarland, decrease the price of sugar.

11. Consider the following diagram in the context of India importing edible oil:

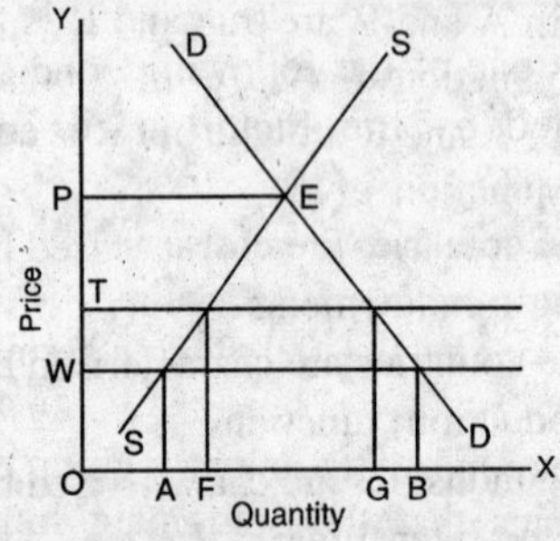

Before trade, demand curve DD and supply curve SS intersect at E to give domestic price OP, which is higher than world price OW. At world price OW:
demand for edible oil = OB
domestic supply of edible oil = OA
import of edible oil = AB
Assume that a tariff is levied on import of edible oil. Price rises to OT.
The following inferences may be drawn from the diagram regarding the effect of tariff. The import tariff.
1. reduces consumption
2. increases production
3. decreases the volume of trade
Select the correct answer using the codes given below:
Code :
A. 1, 2 and 3 B. 1 and 2
C. 2 and 3 D. 1 and 3

12. The country can improve its balance of payments by devaluation when the sum of elasticities of demand for exports and imports is
A. greater than unity B. equal to unity
C. less than unity D. zero

13. The Purchasing Power Parity (PPP) theory of the exchange-rate implies that the currency of a counrty A would depreciate against that of country B if
A. the inflation rate in A exceeds that in B
B. the normal interest-rate in A exceeds that in B
C. the growth rate of GDP in B exceeds that in A
D. foreign direct investment moves from B to A

14. In a freely floating exchange rate system.
A. the current account and capital account add to zero.
B. each account can individually be equal to zero.
C. exchange rate is determined by market forces.
D. all the above statements are correct.

15. In the diagram showing the demand and supply curves for dollars, the Central Authority wants to maintain the exchange rate (rupees per dollar) at E_2.

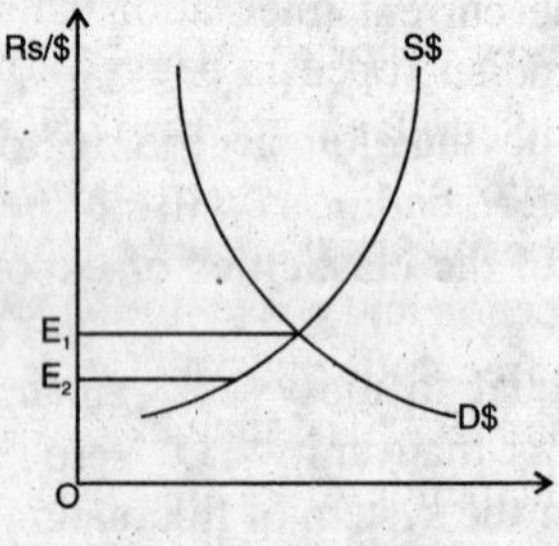

Demand/Supply of Dollars

Then the Central Authority will need to
A. buy dollars and sell rupees
B. sell dollars and buy rupees
C. reduce tariff on imports
D. impose a tax on exports

16. Which one of the following is **not** permissible under India's current account convertibility?
A. Residents holding foreign exchange accounts.
B. Foreigners holding accounts in Indian banks.
C. Exporters holding foreign currency accounts.
D. Free movement of short-term capital.

17. During the last visit to India, Bill Gates travelled by the government owned airline. He also watched cricket at Bangalore and for the growth of the game, donated one million dollars to the Karnataka Fund for Cricket (KFC). The amount he paid for the air ticket and his donation to KFC would be classified as
A. service exports and unilateral transfers to India respectively.
B. unilateral transfers to India in both the cases respectively.

C. service imports and service exports respectively.
D. merchandise imports and service imports respectively.

18. In a flexible exchange-rate system, an increase in the domestic interest rate would tend to
A. improve the current account and worsen the capital account.
B. improve both the current and capital accounts.
C. worsen both the accounts.
D. worsen the current account and improve the capital account.

19. In the current international monetary system the Indian rupee is pegged to
A. U.S. dollar B. U.K. pound
C. Euro D. A basket of currencies

20. **Assertion (A) :** Compared to no trade, there are production and consumption gains to a country from free trade.
Reason (R) : The magnitude of gain from trade is independent of the magnitude of price change from no trade.
A. Both A and R are true and R is the correct explanation of A.
B. Both A and R are true but R is ***not*** a correct explanation of A.
C. A is true but R is false.
D. A is false but R is true.

21. **Assertion (A) :** Suppose, Pakistan forms a FTA (Free Trade Area) with its neighbouring countries including India, and before the formation of this FTA, Pakistan used to import a certain kind of jewellery from South Africa but now imports this from India. This is called trade diversion.
Reason (R) : Now there is a lot of FDI (Foreign Direct Investment) by India in Pakistan, which was non-existent before. This is called trade creation.
A. Both A and R are true and R is the correct explanation of A.
B. Both A and R are true but R is ***not*** a correct explanation of A.
C. A is true but R is false.
D. A is false but R is true.

22. **Assertion (A) :** A country's balance of Payments is always equal to zero.
Reason (R) : If a country has a deficit in the balance of payments account, this must be financed by change in reserve, long term capital movements or long term borrowing.
A. Both A and R are true and R is the correct explanation of A.
B. Both A and R are true but R is ***not*** a correct explanation of A.
C. A is true but R is false.
D. A is false but R is true.

23. Which one of the following statements is ***not*** correct?
A. Free Trade Area among a group of countries means that they eliminate import tariffs against one another but maintain their original tariff levels against the rest of the world.
B. Customs Union among a group of countries means that they eliminate import tariffs against one another, coordinate their macro-policies and impose a common tariff wall against the rest of the world.
C. In a common market the member countries eliminate import tariffs against one another, allow free mobility of factors between them and maintain a common tariff wall against the rest of the world.
D. In an Economic Union, the member countries eliminate import tariffs against one another, allow free mobility of factors between them, coordinate their macro-policies and maintain a common tariff wall against the rest of the world.

24. For a large trading country, the optional tariff argument is based on the proposition that a tariff on imports
A. lowers the country's terms of trade.
B. improves the country's terms of trade.
C. leaves the country's terms of trade unchanged.
D. fails to protect the import competing industries.

25. Suppose, a country has adopted a freely floating exchange rate system. Then, ceteris paribus, if the price level in the country rises, it leads to a
A. rise in the demand for the country's currency and the currency depreciates.
B. rise in the demand for the country's currency and the currency appreciates.

C. fall in the demand for the country's currency and the currency appreciates.
D. fall in the demand for the country's currency and the currency depreciates.

26. Which one of the following pairs is correctly matched?

A. MFA : Agricultural Free Trade
B. UNCTAD : Free Trade Area
C. IMF : Balance of Payments Difficulties
D. MFN : Direct Foreign Investment

27. The terms of trade refer to—

A. the excess of import expenditures over export earnings.
B. trade agreements.
C. the ratio between export prices and import prices.
D. the terms and conditions on which a country is offered loan in the event of balance of payments difficulties.

28. The Government of India announces a new NRI deposit scheme. This offers a very high interest rate, compared to the interest rates abroad, on foreign currency deposits by NRIs in Indian Commercial Banks. Many NRIs in the US do invest under this scheme. Under a flexible exchange rate system, this would tend to

A. depreciate the value of Indian rupee against US dollar.
B. appreciate the value of Indian rupee against US dollar.
C. deplete the foreign exchange reserve of India.
D. leave the value of rupee against US dollar unchanged.

29. India is a net exporter of hand-made carpets and an importer of high-tech products like computer memory chips and printers. This pattern of Indian trade is explained by the

A. Ricardian theory
B. Heckscher-Ohlin theory
C. Labour theory of value
D. Purchasing power parity theory

30. Presently, India's exchange rate policy towards current account and capital account transactions is that the rupee is

A. fully convertible for current account transactions, but not for capital account transactions.
B. fully convertible for capital account transactions, but not for current account transactions.
C. fully convertible for both capital and current account transactions.
D. not convertible for either type of transactions.

31. Mr. Ramprakash travelled to England for medical operation. He had to bear the cost of his air travel by Air India as well as the cost of hospitalisation. In this context, which one of the following is true in terms of entry in India's balance of payments transactions?

A. The cost of hospitalisation is included in service imports but the cost of air travel is not.
B. The cost of air travel is included in service imports but the cost of hospitalisation is not.
C. Both expenditures are included in the category of service imports.
D. Both expenditures are included in service exports.

32. Suppose that the world economy consists of two countries, 'Home' and 'Foreign'. A tariff imposed by the Home on its imports from the Foreign shifts.

A. Home's offer curve to the right
B. Foreign's offer curve to the right
C. Home's offer curve to the left
D. Foreign's offer curve to the left

33. In the context of a small, competitive currency, an increase in import tariff causes

A. a consumption dead weight loss in terms of welfare since consumers now pay a higher price for the product.
B. a production dead weight gain in terms of welfare since domestic producers gain from tariff protection.
C. an overall welfare gain.
D. a trade gain since the amount imported decreases.

34. In the two-good Ricardian trade model, complete specialisation in production occurs in free trade equilibrium because

A. the production possibility frontier satisfies increasing opportunity cost.

B. there are diminishing returns to the factor of production.
C. there are increasing returns to the factor of production.
D. the production possibility frontier satisfies constant opportunity cost.

35. Special Drawing Rights (SDRs) is the currency of IMF. This is in the form of
A. paper currency
B. gold
C. silver and gold both
D. book-keeping entry only

36. Consider the following statements :
The Brettonwoods conference led to the establishment of
1. IMF 2. IBRD
3. United Nations
Which of the above statements are correct?
A. 1 and 2 B. 2 and 3
C. 1 and 3 D. 1, 2 and 3

37. A deficit in a country's balance of payments refers to the difference between
A. autonomous receipts and autonomous payments.
B. accommodating receipts and autonomous payment.
C. accommodating receipts and accommodating payments.
D. autonomous receipts and accommodating payments.

38. What is the correct sequence of the following?
1. Uruguay Round Talks
2. WTO's Seattle Meet
3. Establishment of GATT
Select the correct answer using the codes given below:
Codes:
A. 1, 2, 3 B. 3, 1, 2
C. 3, 2, 1 D. 2, 3, 1

39. Which one of the following treaties was covered by the Uruguay Round Negotiations:
A. General agreement on trade in services.
B. Trade-related intellectual property rights.
C. Trade-related investment measures.
D. All of the above.

40. The Heckscher-Ohlin theory of trade pattern assumes
A. perfect competition in the product markets but not in the factor markets.
B. perfect competition in the factor markets but not in the product markets.
C. perfect competition in both product and factor markets.
D. unemployment in the labour market.

41. **Assertion (A) :** The open-economy Keynesian multiplier is less than the closed economy Keynesian multiplier.
Reason (R) : The marginal propensity to import is always greater than the marginal propensity to consume.
A. Both A and R are true and R is the correct explanation of A.
B. Both A and R are true but R is ***not*** a correct explanation of A.
C. A is true but R is false.
D. A is false but R is true.

42. **Assertion (A) :** Intellectual property rights were brought into the Uruguay Round Trade Negotiations.
Reason (R) : International trade restrictions can be used to discourage the violation of intellectual property rights.
A. Both A and R are true and R is the correct explanation of A.
B. Both A and R are true but R is ***not*** a correct explanation of A.
C. A is true but R is false.
D. A is false but R is true.

43. Which of the following does ***not*** form a part of the foreign exchange reserves of India?
A. Gold
B. SDRs
C. Foreign currency assets
D. Foreign currency and securities held by the banks and corporate bodies.

44. Match List-I (Institution) with List-II (Main objective) and select the correct answer using the codes given below the lists:

List-I *(Institution)*	**List-II** *(Main objective)*
(*a*) IMF	1. To promote viable and durable multilateral trading system.
(*b*) UNCTAD	2. To promote harmony between developed and developing countries on trade-related developmental issues.

(c) World Bank	3. To promote socio-economic development of the member-countries.
(d) WTO	4. To reduce the degree of balance of payments dis-equilibrium of the member countries.

Codes :	(a)	(b)	(c)	(d)
A.	4	3	2	1
B.	1	2	3	4
C.	4	2	3	1
D.	1	3	2	4

45. Which one of the following is a possible compromise between the fixed and the flexible exchange rate systems?

A. Adjustable peg system
B. Crawling peg system
C. Managed floating system
D. All the above three

46. Consider the following statements:
Under the Gold Standard System, represented

1. common unit value.
2. international means of payment.
3. a store of value.

which of these statements are correct?

A. 1 and 2 B. 1 and 3
C. 2 and 3 D. 1, 2 and 3

47. Match List-I with List-II and select the correct answer using the codes given below the lists:

List-I	List-II
(a) Forward exchange	1. A device of covering exchange risk against the price rise of foreign currency.
(b) Hedging	2. A contract to buy and sell foreign exchange against another currency at some fixed rate in the future at a price agreed upon now.
(c) Arbitrage	3. The movement of exchange rate between two limits set by the cost of moving gold from one country to another.
(d) Specie points	4. A mechanism which makes two markets that are physically separate, into a single market in the economic sense.

Codes :	(a)	(b)	(c)	(d)
A.	4	3	2	1
B.	2	1	4	3
C.	4	1	2	3
D.	2	3	4	1

48. Which one of the following is non-debt flow of capital between countries?

A. Commercial borrowings
B. Portfolio investment
C. Short-term borrowings from IMF
D. Sale and purchase of bonds in the capital markets

49. In respect of the production possibility curve under increasing opportunity costs given above, consider the following statements:

1. The production possibility curve is not identical with price curve as in the case of constant costs.
2. There would be complete specialisation of a country in a single commodity in a two-commodities and two-countries model.

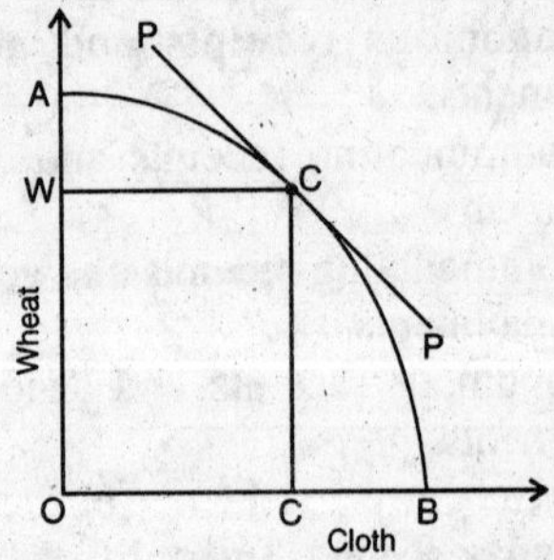

Which of the statements is/are correct?

A. 1 only B. 2 only
C. Both 1 and 2 D. Neither 1 nor 2

50. The diagram shows the demand and supply, DD and SS, curves respectively, for fertilizers in India.
OP = price of fertilisers in India, before trade.
OW = price of fertilizers in world market.

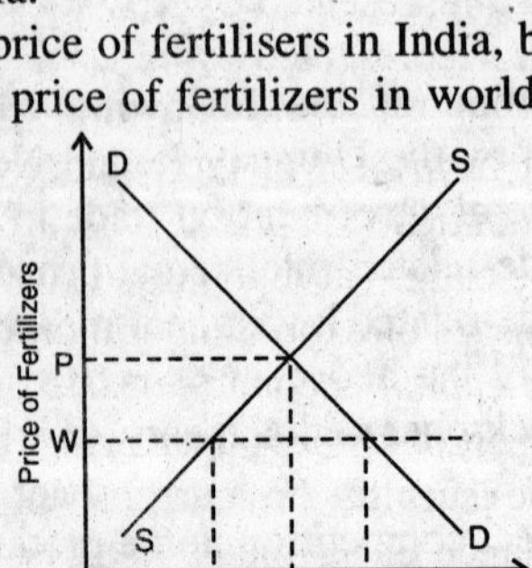

Consider the following statements:
Under free trade
1. prices of fertilizers will be lowered compared to world prices.
2. consumption of fertilizers will increase.
3. imports of fertilizers will be zero.

Which of these statements are correct?
A. 1 and 2 B. 1 and 3
C. 2 and 3 D. 1, 2 and 3

51. Gains in trade results from
A. exporting as much as possible and receiving gold.
B. reallocation of existing goods between the two countries.
C. the fact that exchange brings both specialisation and reallocation of greater output and the increased welfare in each country.
D. one country receiving both imports and gold.

52.

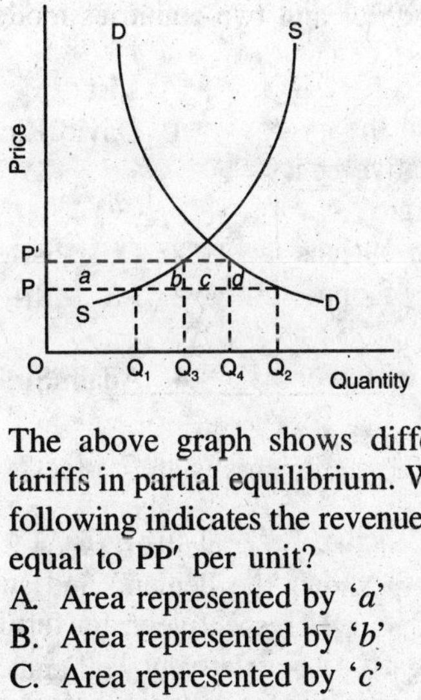

The above graph shows different effects of tariffs in partial equilibrium. Which one of the following indicates the revenue effect of a tariff equal to PP′ per unit?
A. Area represented by '*a*'
B. Area represented by '*b*'
C. Area represented by '*c*'
D. Area represented by '*d*'

53. Which of the following statements is not correct in respect of the balance of payments of a country?
A. The current account of balance of payments consists of export and import of goods and the capital account consists of export and import of services, borrowings and lendings.
B. The surplus on current account in the balance of payments must be equal to the deficit on capital account and vice versa.
C. If in the actual balance of payments, the credit and debit do not balance, the balance is usually achieved by adding one item "errors and omissions".
D. The balance of payments of a country must always balance in the accounting sense.

54. The flexible exchange rate has a number of advantages. Which one of the following is not to be considered as such an advantage?
A. The exchange rate moves in a free market to equate demand and supply so that the market does not face the problem of scarcity or surplus of foreign currency.
B. It permits a continued existence of free trade and convertible currencies.
C. It permits a country to follow independent monetary and fiscal policies.
D. There is no need for keeping official foreign exchange reserves.

55. Which one of the following pairs is not correctly matched?

A.	Exchange depreciation	Market mechanism
B.	Devaluation	Policy action of the government
C.	Deflation	Cheap money policy
D.	Exchange control	Foreign exchange rationing

56. Which one of the following pairs is not correctly matched?

A.	Gross barter terms of trade	— Taussing
B.	Purchasing power parity theory	— J.S. Mill
C.	Offer curves	— A. Marshall
D.	Factor-endowment model	— Heckscher-Ohlin

57. **Assertion (A) :** Devaluation leads to expenditure switching.
Reason (R) : Devaluation makes imports relatively costhier than domestic goods.
A. Both A and R are individually true and R is the correct explanation of A
B. Both A and R are individually true but R is ***not*** the correct explanation of A.
C. A is true but R is false.
D. A is false but R is true.

58. **Assertion (A) :** Special Drawing Rights (SDRs) have the characteristics of an international currency.

Reason (R) : SDRs were introduced to increase international liquidity.

A. Both A and R are individually true and R is the correct explanation of A.
B. Both A and R are individually true but R is *not* the correct explanation of A.
C. A is true but R is false.
D. A is false but R is true.

59. **Assertion (A) :** The gains from trade are determined by the terms of trade.

Reason (R) : The gains from trade depend on the differences in comparative cost ratios.

A. Both A and R are individually true and R is the correct explanation of A.
B. Both A and R are individually true but R is *not* the correct explanation of A.
C. A is true but R is false.
D. A is false but R is true.

60. In Heckscher-Ohlin theory of international trade, the most important source of difference in relative commodity prices between nations is a difference in

A. factor endowments
B. technology
C. tastes
D. demand conditions

61. The scope of international trade and division of labour is limited by

A. availability of technology
B. size of the international market
C. availability of capital
D. surplus production for exports

62. Match List-I with List-II and select the correct answer using the codes given below the lists:

List-I *(Assumption)*	**List-II** *(Implication)*
(*a*) No transport costs in trade	1. Commodity prices same in the two countries
(*b*) Perfect competition in factor markets	2. Optimal allocation of factors
(*c*) Factor intensities differ between goods	3. Techniques of production different for the two goods
(*d*) Production functions same in both countries	4. Techniques of production same in the two countries
	5. Techniques of production different in the two countries

Codes :	(*a*)	(*b*)	(*c*)	(*d*)
A.	2	1	5	4
B.	3	4	2	5
C.	3	2	4	1
D.	1	2	3	4

63. The tariff which maximises a country's economic welfare is called

A. protective tariff
B. discriminatory tariff
C. non-discriminatory tariff
D. optimum tariff

64. Match List-I with List-II and select the correct answer using the codes given below the lists:

List-I	**List-II**
(*a*) Classical theory of comparative cost advantage	1. David Ricardo
(*b*) Vent for surplus theory	2. G. Haberler
(*c*) Theory of opportunity cost	3. J.S. Mill
(*d*) Theory of reciprocal demand	4. Adam Smith

Codes:	(*a*)	(*b*)	(*c*)	(*d*)
A.	1	4	2	3
B.	1	2	3	4
C.	4	1	2	3
D.	3	1	2	4

65. A country is said to be relatively well-endowed with capital if the

A. aggregate value of capital in the country is greater than that of labour and land.
B. the wage-rental ratio in that country is higher in relation to that in its trading partners.
C. the interest rate on capital is lower in that country relatively to the interest rate in its trading partners.
D. the per capita amount of investment in the country had shown a rising trend.

66. Which one of the following transactions represents a credit entry in the current account of a country's balance of payments?
A. Merchandise imports.
B. Transportation services rendered by foreign companies.
C. Expenditure of foreign tourists in a country.
D. Fees paid to foreign contractors and engineers.

67. Match List-I with List-II and select the correct answer using the codes given below the lists:

List-I	List-II
(*a*) Buying and selling of home currency in the foreign exchange market by government or its authorised agency	1. Pegging operation
(*b*) Charging different prices in different markets for an internationally traded commodity	2. Dumping operation
(*c*) The price of imports paid by local purchasers, which is more than their normal value	3. Free on board (*f.o.b.*)
(*d*) Local producers of an export good receiving only the price of the good as it leaves the country	4. Cost, insurance and freight (*c.i.f.*)

Codes:	(*a*)	(*b*)	(*c*)	(*d*)
A.	2	1	3	4
B.	1	2	4	3
C.	3	1	2	4
D.	1	4	3	2

68. Which one of the following pairs is correctly matched?

A. Change in imports associated with a given change in income	Average propensity to import
B. Value of imports as a percentage of total national income	Marginal propensity to import
C. Change in nation's income caused by a change in its exports	Foreign trade multiplier
D. When some products contribute much more to growth than others	Balanced growth

69. According to the elasticity approach, for a devaluation to have a positive effect on a country's trade balance, the sum of the elasticities of demand for a country's exports and of its demand for imports has to be equal to
A. unity
B. less than unity
C. zero
D. greater than unity

70. Consider the following statements:
Under the gold-standard inflow of gold from the deficit to the surplus nation results in
1. a fall in the interest rate in the surplus nation.
2. a fall in the interest rate in the deficit nation.
3. an outflow of capital from surplus to deficit nation.
4. an outflow of capital from deficit to surplus nation.

Of the above statements
A. 1 and 4 are correct B. 1 and 3 are correct
C. 2 and 3 are correct D. 2 and 4 are correct

71. Direct control refers to
A. interference with the operation of the market forces
B. price and wage control
C. trade and exchange control
D. all of the above

72. Which of the following items were responsible for most of the increase in international liquidity since World War II?
1. Gold
2. Dollars
3. Other convertible currencies
4. SDRs

Select the correct answer using the codes given below:
A. 1, 2 and 4 B. 1 and 3
C. 2 and 3 D. 2 and 4

73. 'Most Favoured National Clause' under GATT requires
A. Preferential treatment to particular identified countries.
B. preferential treatment only to developing countries.
C. preferential treatment to countries with a balance of payments deficit.
D. preferential treatment to all member countries of GATT.

74. Assertion (A) : Factor price equalisation theorem deals with the effect of trade on factor prices.

Reason (R) : Trade in goods has no effect on factor prices.

A. Both A and R are true and R is the correct explanation of A.
B. Both A and R are true but R is ***not*** a correct explanation of A.
C. A is true but R is false.
D. A is false but R is true.

75. Assertion (A) : Heckscher-Ohlin theory in validates the classical theory of comparative costs.

Reason (R) : Heckscher-Ohlin theory goes behind the comparative cost theory.

A. Both A and R are true and R is the correct explanation of A.
B. Both A and R are true but R is ***not*** a correct explanation of A.
C. A is true but R is false.
D. A is false but R is true.

76. Given the usual shapes of LM and IS curves and BOP curve, if there is a shift in the LM curve to the right, the economy will face

A. surplus in the balance of payment and a fall in the rate of interest.
B. Deficit in the balance of payment and an increase in the rate of interest.
C. Surplus in the balance of payment and an increase in the rate of interest.
D. Deficit in the balance of payment and a fall in the rate of interest.

77. If the sum of the elasticities of the exports and imports is less than one, any devaluation will further aggravate the deficit in the BOP. Who has given this view?

A. Marshall and Lerner
B. Harrod and Domar
C. Solow and Swan
D. Hickscher and Ohlin

78. Where the foreign offer curves has an elasticity of one, the optimum tariff will be

A. infinity
B. unity
C. less than unity
D. zero

79. The Ricardian theory of comparative advantage relates to

A. short-run outcome
B. long-run outcome
C. intermediate outcome
D. all the above

80. Which one of the following assumptions is the most important assumption in the Heckscher-Ohlin theorem of international trade?

A. Two factor model
B. Two commodities
C. No tariff
D. Constant tastes

81. The country is likely to be better off after export-led growth provided that

A. gains from export-led-growth exceed the losses from worsening terms of trade.
B. gains from growth off-set the losses from worsening terms of trade.
C. the long-run terms of trade are favourable.
D. the elasticity of demand for imports is less than unity.

82. In a three-country two-commodity model, countries being of unequal sizes, the domestic exchange ratios are as under:

Country	*Domestic Exchange Ratio*
1	$2a : 1b$
2	$1a : 1b$
3	$1a : 2b$

As per this model, the stability in international trade is most likely at the international terms of trade of

A. $2a : 1b$
B. $1a : 1b$
C. $1a : 2b$
D. $0.5a : 1b$

83. Assume that the nominal rate of tariff on imports of final commodity is 30%. The nominal rate of tariff on the imported inputs is 10% and the ratio of imported inputs to the value of the final commodity is 50%. Then the effective rate of tariff will be

A. 50%
B. 40%
C. 30%
D. 10%

84. The balance of payments of a country is in equilibrium when the
A. demand for the domestic currency is equal to its supply.
B. demand for the domestic currency is the highest.
C. demand for the domestic currency is the lowest.
D. demand as well as supply of the domestic currency are the highest.

85. Dusenberry was of the opinion that less developed countries will have serious and adverse effect on their balance of payments due to
A. backwash effect
B. spread effect
C. demonstration effect
D. multiplier effect

86. **Assertion (A)** : A change in the income terms of trade is an indicator of welfare.
Reason (R) : Income terms of trade measure the quantity of imports bought by exports.
A. Both A and R are true and R is the correct explanation of A.
B. Both A and R are true but R is ***not*** a correct explanation of A.
C. A is true but R is false.
D. A is false but R is true.

87. Match List-I with List-II and select the correct answer using the codes given below the lists:

List-I	List-II
(*a*) Hamilton-List	1. Trade creation and Trade diversion effects
(*b*) Marshall-Lerner	2. Infant-industry argument
(*c*) F.Y. Edgeworth	3. Elasticity approach
(*d*) Jacob Viner	4. Impoverishing growth

Codes:	(*a*)	(*b*)	(*c*)	(*d*)
A.	2	3	1	4
B.	2	3	4	1
C.	3	2	4	1
D.	3	2	1	4

88. In the given diagram, curves *aa* and *bb* represent the isoquants for good A and good B. P_0P_0 represents relative factor prices in country I. P_1P_1 and P_2P_2 represent relative factor prices in country II. Which of the following inferences can be drawn from the data presented in the diagram?

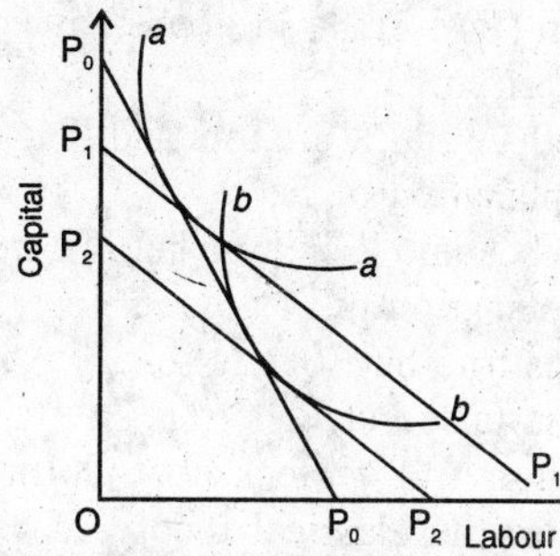

1. Good A is the capital intensive good.
2. Good B is a labour intensive good.
3. Capital is cheap in country I.

Select the correct answer using the codes given below:
A. 1, 2 and 3 B. 1 and 2
C. 2 and 3 D. 1 and 3

89. Match List-I with List-II and select the correct answer using the codes given below the lists:

List-I	List-II
(*a*) Supply side of International Trade	1. David Ricardo
(*b*) Demand side of International Trade	2. Bastable and Alfred Marshall
(*c*) Opportunity cost of International Trade	3. G. Haberler
(*d*) Real cost theory of International Trade	4. Alfred Marshall and Edgeworth

Codes:	(*a*)	(*b*)	(*c*)	(*d*)
A.	1	4	2	3
B.	1	4	3	2
C.	4	1	2	3
D.	4	1	3	2

90. The main objective of the World Trade Organization is to secure among others
A. a general agreement among Common Market countries on technical training and mutual prices of traded goods.
B. the maintenance of intellectual property rights and patent rights of member countries.
C. an improvement in the USA's terms of trade in the next decade.
D. a reduction in tariffs through negotiation, elimination of import quotas and globalization of international trade.

ANSWERS

1	2	3	4	5	6	7	8	9	10
A	A	C	D	A	C	D	B	C	C
11	**12**	**13**	**14**	**15**	**16**	**17**	**18**	**19**	**20**
A	A	A	C	A	D	A	D	D	B
21	**22**	**23**	**24**	**25**	**26**	**27**	**28**	**29**	**30**
C	D	B	B	D	C	C	B	B	A
31	**32**	**33**	**34**	**35**	**36**	**37**	**38**	**39**	**40**
A	C	D	D	D	A	A	B	D	C
41	**42**	**43**	**44**	**45**	**46**	**47**	**48**	**49**	**50**
A	B	D	C	D	D	B	B	A	A
51	**52**	**53**	**54**	**55**	**56**	**57**	**58**	**59**	**60**
C	C	A	C	C	B	A	A	A	A
61	**62**	**63**	**64**	**65**	**66**	**67**	**68**	**69**	**70**
B	D	A	A	D	C	B	C	D	C
71	**72**	**73**	**74**	**75**	**76**	**77**	**78**	**79**	**80**
D	A	D	B	A	A	A	A	B	A
81	**82**	**83**	**84**	**85**	**86**	**87**	**88**	**89**	**90**
A	D	A	A	C	A	B	A	B	D

❑❑❑

STATISTICS

Statistics

Measures of Central Tendency or Statistical Averages

There are five alternative measures of central tendency. They are:

1. Arithmetic Mean (A.M.)
2. Median
3. Mode
4. Geometric Mean (G.M.)
5. Harmonic Mean (H.M.)

Arithmetic Mean

Arithmetic mean of given set of observations is their sum divided by the number of observations. For example, the arithmetic mean of 5, 8, 10, 15, 24, and 28 is

$$\frac{5+8+10+15+24+28}{6}=\frac{90}{6}=15$$

Calculation : Arithmetic mean can be calculated in the following manner:

A. Arithmetic Average in Individual Series

(i) Direct method

$$\overline{X} = \frac{\Sigma X}{N}$$

where

$\overline{X}$ = Arithmetic Average or Mean

Σ = Sum of values and read as summation

X = Values of variable X

N = Number of items

(ii) Short cut method

$$\overline{X} = A+\frac{\Sigma dx}{N}$$

where

$\overline{X}$ = Arithmetic mean

A = Assumed Mean

Σdx = Total of deviations of the values of variables from an assumed mean

N = Number of is observations

B. Arithmetic Average in Discrete Series

(i) Direct Method $\overline{X} = \frac{\Sigma fx}{N}$

where

Σfx = Total of products of the frequencies (*f*) and the variable X

N = Total of frequencies, *i.e.,* N = Σf.

(ii) Shortcut Method

$$\overline{X} = A+\frac{\Sigma fdx}{N}$$

Σfdx = Total of products of the frequencies (*f*) and the deviations of the values of variables from an assumed mean (*dx*)

N = Total of frequencies

C. Arithmetic Average in Continuous Series

(i) Direct Method

$$\overline{X} = A+\frac{\Sigma fm}{N}$$

where

M = Mid-point

Σfm – Total of products of frequencies (*f*) and the mid-point (*m*)

(ii) Short-cut Method

$$\overline{X} = A+\frac{\Sigma fdx}{N}$$

where

Σfdx = Total of products of frequencies (*f*) and the deviations of the values of mid-points from an assumed mean (*dx*)

(iii) Step-Deviation Method

$$\overline{X} - A+\frac{\Sigma fdx}{N}\times i$$

where Σfdx = Total of products of frequencies and the deviation from assumed mean by step-deviation

i = Magnitude of class-intervals

D. Charliers Accuracy Check

$$\Sigma[f(dx+1)] = \Sigma fdx + \Sigma f$$

E. Combined Mean

$$\overline{X}_{12} = \frac{N_1\overline{X}_1 + N_2\overline{X}_2}{N_1 + N_2}$$

where

$\overline{X}_{12}$ = Combined Mean

N_1 = Number of items of the first group

N_2 = Number of items of the second group

$\overline{X}_1$ = Arithmetic Average of the first group

$\overline{X}_2$ = Arithmetic Average of the second group

F. Weighted Mean

$$\overline{X}_w = \frac{\Sigma WX}{\Sigma W}$$

where X_w = Weighted mean

ΣWX = Total of products of weights and the variables X

ΣW = Total of weights

Mathematical Properties of Arithmetic Mean

Arithmetic mean possesses some very interesting and important mathematical properities as given below:

Property-1

The algebraic sum of the deviations of the given set of observations from their arithmetic mean is zero.

Mathematically, $\Sigma(X - \overline{X}) = 0$

or for a frequency distribution

$$\Sigma f(X - \overline{X}) = 0$$

Property–2

If n_1 and n_2 are the sizes and $\overline{X}_1$, $\overline{X}_2$ are the respective means of two series then the mean $\overline{X}$ of the combined series of size $n_1 + n_2$ is given by :

$$\overline{X} = \frac{n_1\overline{X}_1 + n_2\overline{X}_2}{n_1 + n_2}$$

The above result can be generalised to the case of more than two series. If we have k series with respective sizes $n_1, n_2, \ldots n_k$ and means $\overline{X}_1, \overline{X}_2, \ldots\ldots \overline{X}_k$ respectively, then the mean $\overline{X}$ of the combined series of size $n_1 + n_2 + \ldots. + n_k$ is given by:

$$\overline{X} = \frac{n_1\overline{X}_1 + n_2\overline{X}_2 + n_3\overline{X}_3 + \ldots\ldots + n_k\overline{X}_k}{n_1 + n_2 + \ldots.. + n_k}$$

Property–3

The sum of the squares of deviations of the given set of observations is minimum when taken from the arithmetic mean.

Mathematically, for a given frequency distribution, the sum

$$S = \Sigma f(X - A)^2$$

which represents the sum f the squares of deviations of given observations from any arbitary value 'A' is minimum when

$$A = \overline{X}$$

Property–4

If all the observations of a series are added, subtracted, multiplied or divided by a constant, the mean is also added, subtracted, multiplied or divided by the same constant.

Property–5

The weighted arithmetic mean of first n natural numbers whose weights are equal to the corresponding numbers is equal to

$$\left(\frac{2n+1}{3}\right)$$

Property–6

The arithmetic mean of first n natural numbers is equal to the arithmetic mean of its first and last term.

$$\overline{X} = \frac{1+2+3+\ldots..+n}{n}$$

$$= \frac{n(n+1)}{2} \cdot \frac{1}{n} = \frac{n+1}{2}$$

Merits and Demerits of Arithmetic Mean

Merits

1. It is rigidly defined.
2. It is easy to understand and calculate.

3. It is based on all the observations.
4. It is least affected by the fluctuations of sampling.
5. It does not require the arranging the data.

Demerits

1. The strongest draw back of arithmetic mean is that it is very much affected by extreme observations. Two or three very large values of the variable may unduly affect the value of the arithmetic mean.
2. Arithmetic mean can not be used in the case of open end classes such as less than 10, more than 70 etc.
3. It cannot be determined by inspection nor can it be located graphically.
4. Arithmetic mean cannot be used if we are dealing with qualitative characteristics which can not be measured quantitatively such as intelligence, honesty, bequty etc. In such cases median is the only average to be used.
5. Arithmetic mean can not be obtained if a single observation is missing or last or is illegible unless we drop it out and compute the arithmetic mean of the remaining values.
6. In extremely asymmetrical (skewed) distribution, usually arithmetic mean is not representative of the distribution and hence is not a suitable measure of location.

Median

Median is the central value of the variable when the values are arranged in ***ascending*** or ***descending*** order of magnitude.

According to Connor—"The median is that value of the variable which divides the groups into two equal parts, one part comprising all the values greater and the other all values less than median."

Calculation—Median may be, calculated in the following manner :

A. Calculation of Median in Individual Series

$$M = \text{Size of} \left(\frac{N+1}{2}\right) \text{th item}$$

where

M = Median
N = Number of items

2. Calculation of Median in Discrete Series

$$M = \text{Size of} \left(\frac{N+1}{2}\right) \text{the item}$$

where

M = Median
N = Total of frequencies

3. Calculation of Median in Continuous Series

$$M = \text{Size of} \left(\frac{N}{2}\right) \text{th item}$$

$$M = L_1 + \frac{i}{f}(m-c)$$

where

L = Lower limit of median group
i = Difference of lower and upper limit of median group
f = Frequency of median group
m = Median number = $\left(\frac{N}{2}\right)$ th item
c = Cumulative frequency of the group preceding the median group

If data are arranged in descending order then we apply the following formula—

$$M = L_2 - \frac{i}{f}\left(\frac{N}{2} - c\right)$$

where

L_2 = Upper limit of the median group

Merits and Demerits of Median

Merits

1. It is rigidly defined.
2. Median is easy to understand and easy to calculate for a non–mathematical person.
3. Since median is a positional average, it is not affected at all by extreme observations and as such is very useful in the case of Skewed distributions, J–Shaped or inverted J–Shaped distribution such as the distribution of wages, incomes and wealth. So in case of extreme observations, median is a better average to use than the arithmetic mean since the latter gives a distorted picture of the distribution.
4. Median can be computed while dealing with a distribution with open end classes.

5. Median can sometimes be located by simple inspection and can also be computed graphically.
6. Median is the only average to be used while dealing with qualitative characteristics which cannot be measured quantitatively but can still be arranged in ascending or descending order of magnitude, *e.g.*, to find the average intelligence, average beauty, average honesty etc., among a group of people.

Demerits

1. In case of even number of observations for an ungrouped data, median cannot be determined exactly. We merely estimate it as the arithmetic mean of the two middle terms.
2. Median, being a positional average, is not based on each and every item of the distribution. It depends on all the observations only to the extent whether they are smaller than or greater than it; the exact magnitude of the observations being immoterial.
3. It does not lead itself to algebric treatment.
4. It is affected by fluctuations of items.
5. It is less stable measure of central tendency than the mean.
6. In the case of continuous series, it cannot be calculated exactly.

Mode

Mode is the value which occurs frequently in a set of observations and around which the other items of the set cluster densely. In other words, mode is the value of a series which is predominant in it. In the words of Croxton and Cowden, "The mode of a distribution is value at the point around which the items tend to be most heavily concentrated. It may be regarded as too most typical of a series of values."

Computation of Mode

The value of mode is obtained by the following formula:

$$\text{Mode} = L_1 + \frac{f_1 - f_0}{2f_1 - f_0 - f_2} \times i$$

where L = lower limit of the modal class

f_1 = frequency of the modal class

f_0 = frequency of the class preceding the modal class

f_2 = frequency of the class succeeding the modal class

i = class interval of modal class

When mode is ill–defined, the value of mode may be caluculated with the help of following formula:

$$\boxed{\text{Mode} = 3\ \text{Median} - 2\ \text{Mean}}$$

Merits and Demerits of Mode

Merits

1. Mode is easy to calculate and understand. In some cases it can be located merely by inspection. It can also be estimated graphically from a histogram.
2. Mode is not all affected by extreme observations and as such is preferred to arithmetic mean while dealing with extreme observations.
3. It can be conveniently obtained in the case of open end classes which do not pose any problems here.

Demerits

1. Mode is not rigidly defined.
2. Since mode is the value of X corresponding to the maximum frequency, it is not based on all the observations of the series.
3. Mode is not suitable for further mathematical treatment.
4. As compared with mean, mode is affected to a greater extent by the fluctuations of sampling.

Empirical Relation Between Mean (M), Median (M_d) and Mode (M_0)

In case of a *symmetrical distribution* mean, median and mode, coincide. Thus

$$\text{Mean} = \text{Median} = \text{Mode}$$

However, for a *moderately asymmetrical (non–symmetrical or Skewed)* distribution, mean and mode usually lie on the two ends and median lies in between them and they obey the following important empirical relationships given by Prof. Karl Pearson.

$$\text{Mode} = \text{Mean} - 3(\text{Mean} - \text{Median}) \qquad ...(1)$$

$$\Rightarrow \text{Mean} - \text{Mode} = 3(\text{Mean} - \text{Median})$$

$$\Rightarrow \text{Mean} - \text{Median} = \frac{1}{3}(\text{Mean} - \text{Mode})$$

Thus we see that the difference between mean and mode is three times the difference between mean and median. In other words, median is closer to mean than Mode. The above relation between mean (M), median (M*d*) and mode (M*o*) can be exhibited diagrammatically as follows:

Relationship Between Arithmetic Mean, Median and Mode

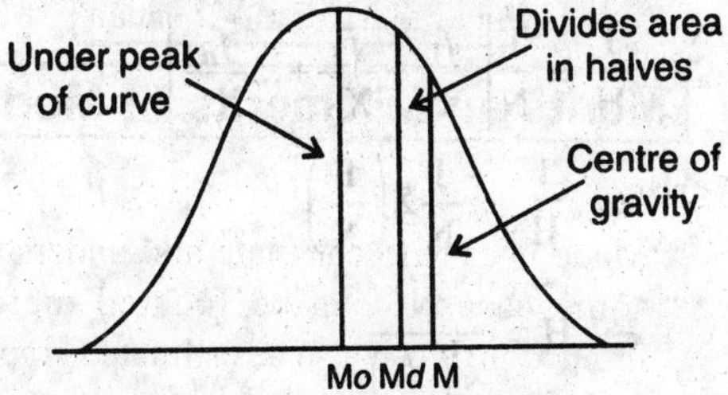

Remarks

1. Equation (1) may be rewritten to give:
Mode = Mean − 3 Mean + 3 Median
Mode = 3 Median − 2 Mean . . . (2)
This formula is specially useful to determine the value of mode in case of bimodal or multimodal distributions.

2. If we know any two of the three values M, M*d* and M0 the third can be estimated by using the formula (2).

3. For a positively Skewed distribution, mean will be greater than median and median will be greater than mode *i.e.*

$$M > Md > Mo \Rightarrow Mo < Md < M$$

However, in a negatively Skewed distribution the order of the magnitudes of the three averages will be reversed, *i.e.*, for negatively Skewed distribution we have

$$Mo > Md > M \Rightarrow M < Md < Mo$$

GEOMETRIC MEAN

The geometric mean (usually abbreviated as G.M.) of a set of *n* observations is the *n*th root of their product. Thus if $X_1, X_2, ..., X_n$ are the given *n* observations then their G.M. is given by

$$\text{G.M.} = \sqrt[n]{X_1.X_2.X_3.........X_n}$$

$$= (X_1.X_2.X_3.........X_n)^{1/n} \quad ...(3)$$

If $n = 2$, *i.e.*, if we are dealing with two observations only then G.M. can be computed by taking the square root of their product. For example G.M. of 4 and 16 is

$$\text{G.M.} = \sqrt{4 \times 16} = \sqrt{64} = 8$$

But if the number of observations is greater than 2, then the computation of the *n*th root is very tedious. In such a case the calculations are facilitated by making use of the logarithms. Taking logarithm of both sides in (3), we get

$$\log(\text{G.M.}) = \frac{1}{n}\log(X_1.X_2......X_3)$$

$$= \frac{1}{n}(\log X_1 + \log X_2 + ...\log X_n)$$

$$= \frac{1}{n}\Sigma \log X \quad ...(4)$$

Thus, we see that the logarithm of the G.M. of a set observations is the arithmetic mean of their logarithms.

Taking Antilog of both sides in (4) we finally obtain,

$$\text{G.M.} = \text{Antilog}\left[\frac{1}{n}\Sigma \log X\right]$$

Calculation of Geometric Mean in Case of Discrete Series

$$\text{G.M.} = \text{Antilog}\left[\frac{1}{n}\Sigma f \log X\right]$$

where

$\Sigma f \log X$ = Sum of the products of frequencies (*f*) with logarithms of variable log X

n=Total of frequencies (Σf)

Calculation of Geometric Mean in Case of grouped or continuous frequency distributions

$$\text{G.M.} = \text{Antilog}\left[\frac{\Sigma f \log m}{n}\right]$$

where

$\Sigma f \log m$ = Sum of the products of frequencies (*f*) with logarithms of mid–points (log *m*)

n = Total of frequencies (Σf)

$$\textbf{Weighted G.M.} = \text{Antilog}\left[\frac{\Sigma w \log x}{\Sigma w}\right]$$

where $\Sigma w \log x$ = Sum of the products of weights (w) with logarithms of variable log X

Σw = Total of weights

Merits and Demerits of Geometric Mean

Mersits

1. Geometric mean is rigidly defined.
2. It is based on all the observations.
3. It is suitable for further mathematical treatment. If G_1 and G_2 are the geometric means of two series of sizes n_1 and n_2 respectively, then the geometric means G of the combined series of size $n_1 + n_2$ is given by

$$\log G = \frac{n_1 \log_1 + n_2 \log G_2}{n_1 + n_2}$$

4. Unlike arithmetic mean which has a bias for higher values, geometric mean has bias for smaller observations
5. As compared with mean, G.M. is affected to a lesser extent by extreme observations.
6. It is not affected much by fluctuations of sampling.

Demerits

1. Because of its abstract mathematical character, geometric mean is not easy to understand and to calculate for a non–mathematical person.
2. If any one of the observations is zero geometric mean becomes zero and if any one of the observations is negative, geometric mean becomes imaginary regardless of the magnitude of other items.
3. It cannot be calculated if some of values in a series are not known.

Harmonic Mean

If $X_1, X_2, \ldots\ldots X_n$ is a given set of n observations, then their harmonic mean abbreviated as H.M. or simply it is given by:

$$H = \frac{1}{\frac{1}{n}\left[\frac{1}{X_1} + \frac{1}{X_2} + \ldots. + \frac{1}{X_n}\right]}$$

$$= \frac{1}{\frac{1}{n}\left[\Sigma\left(\frac{1}{X}\right)\right]} = \frac{n}{\Sigma\left(\frac{1}{X}\right)}$$

In other words, Harmonic Mean is the reciprocal of the arithmetic mean of the reciprocals of the given observations.

In case of frequency distribution, we have

$$\frac{1}{H} = \frac{1}{N}\left[\frac{f_1}{X_1} + \frac{f_2}{X_2} + \ldots \frac{f_n}{X_n}\right]$$

$$\Rightarrow \frac{1}{H} = \frac{1}{N}\Sigma\left(\frac{F}{X}\right)$$

$$\Rightarrow H = \frac{N}{\Sigma\left(\frac{f}{X}\right)}$$

where N = total frequency (Σf)

X = value of the variable or the mid value of the class

(In case of grouped or continuous frequency distribution)

f = corresponding frequency of X

Merits and Demerits of Harmonic Mean

Merits

1. Harmonic mean is rigidly defined.
2. It is based on all the observations.
3. It is suitable for further mathematical treatment.
   If H_1 and H_2 are the harmonic means of two series of sizes N_1 and N_2 respectively, then the harmonic mean H of the combined series of size $N_1 + N_2$ is given by

$$\frac{1}{H} = \frac{1}{N_1 + N_2}\left[\frac{N_1}{H_1} + \frac{N_2}{H_2}\right]$$

4. It is not affected very much by fluctuations of sampling.
5. It is the most suitable average for measuring the time, speed, etc.

Demerits

1. It is not easy to understand and calculate.
2. Its value cannot be obtained if any one of the observations is zero.
3. It is less popular.

4. It cannot be calculated if some of the values in a series are not known.

Relation Between Arithmetic Mean, Geometric Mean and Harmonic Mean

The arithmetic mean (A.M.), the geometric mean (G.M.) and the harmonic mean (H.M.) of a series of n observations are connected by the relation

$$A.M. \geq G.M. \geq H.M. \quad \ldots (1)$$

the sign of equality holding if and only if all the n observations are equal.

Dispersion

Averages or the measures of central tendency give us an idea of the concentration of the observations about the central part of the distribution. In spite of their great utility in statistical analysis, they have their own limitations. If we are given only the average of a series of observations, we cannot form complete idea about the distribution since there may exist a number of distributions whose averages are same but which may differ widely from each other in a number of ways. The following example will illustrate this view point.

Consider the following ten observations on a certain variable: 5, 5, 5, 5, 5, 5, 5, 5, 5, 5.

Clearly A.M. = 5, and all deviations from A.M. are zero. Therefore, there is no dispersion at all.

Another example has following observations on the variable:

4, 3, 6, 5, 7, 4, 8, 8, 2, 3.

The A.M. is again equal to 5, but the nature of distribution of values is quite different in this case.

Therefore, knowledge of the central value alone is not enough to appreciate the nature of distribution of values. In one case the values may have wide disparity whereas in the other case they may be close to the central value. The frequency curves shown in the Figure 1 may help to illustrate this point graphically.

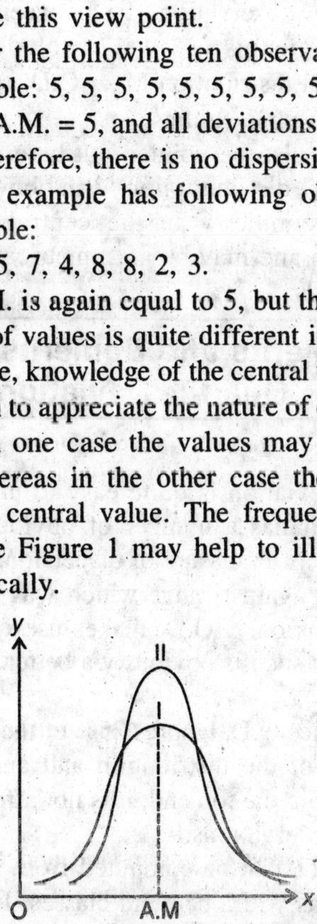

Fig. 1

Both in case of I and II the distributions have the same A.M. but in case I there is larger dispersion of values than in II.

From the above illustration it is obvious that the measures of central tendency are in adequate to describe the distribution completely. Thus, the measures of central tendency must be supported and supplemented by some other measures. One such measure (v) Dispersion.

According to Connor "Dispersion is the measure of the extent to which the individual items vary."

Measures of Dispersion

The various measures of dispersion are

1. Range
2. Quartile deviation or Semi-interquartile range
3. Mean deviation
4. Standard deviation
5. Lorenz curve

Range

The range is defined as the difference between the highest and lowest values in the series. This is the simplest method of measuring dispersion. Thus

$$\text{Range} = L - S$$

where L = Largest value, S = Smallest value

Absolute and Relative Measures of Range

Range as defined above is an absolute measure of dispersion and depends upon the units of measurement. Thus if want to compare the variability of two or more distributions with the same units of measurement, we may use the above formula. However, to compare the variability of the distributions given in difference units of measurement we cannot use the above formula but we need a relative measure which is independent of the units of measurement. This relative measure, called the *coefficient of range*, is defined as follows:

$$\text{Coefficient of Range} = \frac{L-S}{L+S}$$

In other words, coefficient of range is the ratio of the difference between two extreme observations (biggest and smallest) of the distribution to their sum.

Merits and Demerits of Range

Merits

1. It is easy to understand.
2. It is easy to calculate.
3. It can be used in Open-end frequency distribution.

Demerits

1. Range is not based on the entire set of data.
2. Range is very much affected by fluctuations of smapling. Its value varies very widely from sample to sample.
3. It is not possible to find out the range in open-end frequency distribution.
4. It does not present the very accurate picture of the series.
5. It is affected by extreme values.

Quartile Deviation or Semi Inter Quartile Range

Quartile deviation is obtained by dividing the difference of third quartile and first quartile ($Q_3 - Q_2$) by 2. Thus

$$\text{Quartile Deviation (Q.D.)} = \frac{Q_3 - Q_1}{2}$$

where Q_3 = Third Quartile or Upper Quartile
Q_1 = First Quartile or Lower Quartile

Q.D. as defined obove is only an absolute measure of dispersion. For comparative studies of variability of two distributions we need a relative measure which is known as coefficient of Quartile Deviation and is given by

$$\text{Coefficient of Q.D.} = \frac{Q_3 - Q_1}{Q_3 + Q_1}$$

Remark

The quartile deviation gives the average amount by which the two quartiles differ from median. For a *symmetrical distribution,* we have

$$Q_3 - Q_d = M_d - Q_1$$

$$\Rightarrow \quad M_d = \frac{Q_3 + Q_1}{2} \quad \text{... (1)}$$

i.e., median lies half way on the scale from Q_1 to Q_3. Thus, for a symmetrical distribution we have

$$\text{Q.D.} + Q_1 = \frac{Q_3 - Q_1}{2} + Q_1$$

$$= \frac{Q_3 + Q_1}{2} = M_d \text{ [From (1)]}$$

$$\text{and } Q_3 - \text{Q.D.} = Q_3 - \frac{Q_3 - Q_1}{2}$$

$$= \frac{Q_3 + Q_1}{2} = M_d \text{ [From(1)]}$$

In other words, for a symmetrical distribution we have $Q_1 = M_d - \text{Q.D.}$

and $Q_3 = M_d + \text{Q.D.}$ ... (2)

Since in a distribution 25% of the observations lie below Q_1 and 25% observations lie above Q_3, 50% of the observations lie between Q_1 and Q_3. Therefore, using (2) we conclude that for a symmetrical distribution $M_d \pm \text{Q.D.}$ covers exactly 50% of the observations.

It may also be pointed out here that the word symmetrical distribution used in above connection refers to symmetry in the central 50% of the distribution and may be asymmetrical (Skewed) at the tail ends.

Merits and Demerits of Quartile Deviation

Mertis

Quartile deviation is quite easy to understand and calculate. It has a number of obvious advantages over range as a measure of dispersion. For example

(a) As against range which was based on two observations only, Q.D. makes use of 50% of the data and as such is obviously a better measure than range.

(b) Since Q.D. ignores 25% of the data from the beginning of the distribution and another 25% of the data from the top end, it is not affected at all by extreme observations.

(c) Q.D. can be computed from the frequency distributions with open end classes. In fact Q.D. is the only measure of dispersion which can be

obtained while dealing a distribution having open end classes.

Demerits

1. Q.D. is not based on all the observations since it ignores 25% of the data at the lower end and 25% of the data at the upper end of the distribution, it cannot be regarded as a reliable measure of variability.
2. Q.D. is affected considerably by fluctuations of sampling.
3. Q.D. is not suitable for further mathematical treatment.

Thus quartile deviation is not a reliable measure of variability, particularly for distribution in which the variation is considerable.

Percentile Range

This is a measure of dispersion based on the difference between certain percentiles. It P_i is the *i*th percentile and P_j is the *j*th percentile then the so-called *i–j* percentile range is given by

i–j Percentile Range = $P_j - P_i \; (i < j)$

and *i –j* Semi Percentile Range = $\dfrac{P_j - P_i}{2} \; (i < j)$

The above measures are absolute measures only. The relative measure of variability based on percentiles is given by

$$\text{Coefficient of } i - j \text{ percentile} = \frac{P_j - P_i}{P_j + P_i}$$

Mean Deviation

Mean deviation is defined as the arithmetic average of the deviations of various items from a measure of central tendency, may it be, mean, median or mode. Generally mean deviations is calculated either from mean or from median. Mode is usually not considered as its value and is indeterminate. Between mean and median, the median is supposed to be better than the mean because the sum of the deviations from the median is less than the sum of the deviations from the mean. It is also known as first moment of dispersion.

Computation of Mean Deviation

If $X_1, X_2, \ldots\ldots, X_n$ are *n* given observations then the mean deviation (M.D.) about an average A, say, is given by M.D. = $\dfrac{1}{n}\Sigma|X-A| = \dfrac{1}{n}\Sigma|D|$

where $|D| = |X-A|$ read as mod (X – A) is the modulus value or absolute value of the deviation (after ignoring the negative sign) d = X – A and $\Sigma|d|$ is the sum of these absolute deviations and A is any one of the averages mean (M), median (M_d) and mode (M_0).

In the case of frequency distribution or grouped or continuous frequency distribution, mean deviation about an average A is given by

$$\text{M.D.} = \frac{1}{N}\Sigma f\,|X-A|$$

where

X = value of the variable or mid–value of the class interval

N = Σf

A = Mean/Median/Mode

Remarks

1. Usually, we obtain the mean deviation (M.D.) about any one of the three averages mean (M), median (M_d) or mode (M_0). Thus

$$\text{M.D. (about mean)} = \frac{1}{N}\Sigma f|X-M|$$

$$\text{M.D. (about median)} = \frac{1}{N}\Sigma f|M-D_d|$$

$$\text{M.D. (about mode)} = \frac{1}{N}\Sigma f|X-M_0|$$

2. The sum of the absolute deviations (after ignoring the signs) of a given set of observations is minimum when taken about median. Hence *mean deviation is minimum when it is calculated from median.* In other words, mean deviation calculated about median will be less than mean deviation about mean or mode.

3. For a symmetrical distribution the range Mean $\pm$ M.D. (about mean) or $M_d \pm$ M.D. (about median), [$\because M = M_d$ for a symmetrical distribution] covers 57.5% of the observations of the distribution. If the distribution is moderately (Skewed) the range will cover approximately 57.5% of the observations. Thus, a small value of mean deviation would imply that the distribution is uniform since in this case a small interval around the average will contain more than 50% of the observations of the series.

Relative Measures of Mean

The relative measure of dispersion, called the coefficient of mean deviation is given by

Co-efficient of M.D.

$$= \frac{\text{Mean Deviation}}{\text{Average about which it is calculated}}$$

Thus

$$\text{Co-efficient of M.D. about mean} = \frac{\text{M.D.}}{\text{Mean}}$$

$$\text{Co-efficient of M.D. about median} = \frac{\text{M.D.}}{\text{Median}}$$

The co-efficients of mean deviation defined above are pure numbers independent of the units of measurement and are useful for comparing the variability of different distributions.

Merits and Demerits of Mean Deviation

Merits

1. Mean deviation is rigidly defined and is easy to understand and calculate.
2. Mean deviation is based on all the observations and is thus definitely a better measure of dispersion than the range and quartile deviation.
3. As compared with standard deviation it is less affected by extreme observations.
4. Since mean deviation is based on the deviations about an average, it provides a better measure for comparison about the formation of different distributions.

Demerits

1. The strongest objection against mean deviation is that while computing its value we take the absolute value of the deviations about an average and ignore the signs of the deviations.
2. It is not a satisfactory measure when taken about mode or while dealing with a fairly Skewed distribution. As already pointed out, theoretically mean deviation gives the best result when it is calculated about median. But median is not a satisfactory measure when the distribution has great variations.
3. It is rarely used in Sociological studies.
4. It cannot be computed for distributions with open end classes.
5. Mean deviation tends to increase with the size of the sample though not proportionately and not so rapidly as range.

Standard Deviation

Standard deviation, usually denoted by the letter σ (sigma) of the Greek alphabet was first suggested by *Karl Pearson* as a measure of dispersion in 1893. It is defined as the positive square root of the arithmetic mean of the squares of the deviations of the given observations from their arithmetic mean. Thus, if $X_1, X_2, ..., X_n$ is a set of *n* observations then its standard deviation is given by

$$\sigma = \sqrt{\frac{1}{n}\Sigma(X-\overline{X})^2}$$

where

$$\overline{X} = \frac{\Sigma X}{n} = \text{arithmetic mean of the given values}$$

Computation of Standard Deviation in Case of Frequency Distribution : In case of frequency distribution, the standard deviation is given by

$$\sigma = \frac{1}{N}\sqrt{\Sigma f(X-\overline{X})^2}$$

where X is the value of the variable or the mid-value of the class (in case of grouped or continuous frequency distribution); *f* is the corresponding frequency of the value X; $N = \Sigma f$, is the total frequency and

$$\overline{X} = \frac{1}{N}\Sigma fX$$

is the arithmetic mean of the distribution.

Remarks

1. It may be pointed out that although mean deviation could be calculated about any one of the averages (M, M_d or M_0), standard deviation is always computed about arithmetic mean.

2. The value of the *s.d.* depends on the numerical value of the deviations $(X_1-\overline{X}), (X_2-\overline{X})..., (X_n-\overline{X})$. Thus the value of σ will be greater if the values of X are scattered widely away from the mean. Thus, a small value of σ will imply that the distribution is *homogeneous* and a large value of σ will imply that it is heterogeneous. In particular

s.d. is zero if each of the deviations is zero, *i.e.*, $\sigma = 0$ if and only if,

$$X_1 - \overline{X} = 0,\ X_2 - \overline{X} = 0, \ldots\ldots X_n - \overline{X} = 0$$

$$\Rightarrow X_1 = X_2 = X_3 + \ldots X_n = \overline{X}$$

which is the case if the variable assumes the constant value, *i.e.*, $\sigma = 0$

if $X_1 = X_2 = X_3 = \ldots\ldots\ldots X_n = K$ (constant)

Merits and Demerits of Standard Deviation

Merits

1. It is rigidly defined.
2. Its value is very precise.
3. Its calculation is based on all the items of the series.
4. It is least affected by fluctuations in sampling.
5. It tends itself to further algebric treatment.

Demerits

1. It is difficult to calculate.
2. It gives more weight to extreme items.

Variance

Variance is the square of the a standard deviation and is denoted by σ^2. For a frequency distribution variance is given by

$$\text{variance} = \sigma^2 = \frac{1}{N}\Sigma f(X - \overline{X})^2$$

Remark

Variance or standard deviation is independent of the change of origin but not of the scale.

Example 1. Find the mean and standard deviation of the first *n* natural numbers.

Solution–If the variable X denotes the natural number, then the first *n* natural numbers are 1, 2, 3..., *n*

$$\therefore \text{Mean} = \frac{\Sigma X}{n}$$

$$= \frac{1+2+3+\ldots\ldots+n}{n} = \frac{n(n+1)}{2}\cdot\frac{1}{n}$$

$$= \frac{n+1}{2}$$

and $\quad \text{Variance} = \dfrac{\Sigma X^2}{n} - \overline{X}^2$

$$= \frac{1^2+2^2+3^2+\ldots.n^2}{n} - \left(\frac{n+1}{2}\right)^2$$

$$= \frac{n(n+1)(2n+1)}{6}\cdot\frac{1}{n} - \frac{(n+1)^2}{4}$$

$$= \frac{(n+1)}{12}[2(2n+1) - 3(n+1)]$$

$$= \frac{(n+1)}{12}[4n+2-3n-3]$$

$$= \frac{(n+1)(n-1)}{12} = \frac{(n^2-1)}{12}$$

$$\Rightarrow \quad s.d. = \sqrt{\frac{n^2-1}{12}}$$

Remark: *For any discrete distribution standard deviation is not less than mean deviation from mean.*

Co-efficient of Variation

Standard deviation is only an absolute measure of dispersion, depending upon the units of measurement. The relative measure of dispersion based on standard deviation is called the coefficient of standard deviation and is given by

$$\text{Coefficient of Standard Deviation} = \frac{\sigma}{\overline{X}}$$

This is a pure number independent of the units of measurement and thus, is suitable for comparing the variability, homogeneity or uniformity of two or more distributions.

We have already discussed the relative measures of dispersion based on range, quartile deviation and mean deviation. Since standard deviation is by for the best measure of dispersion, for comparing the homogeneity or heterogeneity of two or more distributions we generally compute the coefficient of standard deviation asked otherwise.

100 times the coefficient of dispersion based on standard deviation is called the *coefficient of variation,* abbreviated as C.V. Thus,

$$\text{C.V.} = 100 \times \frac{\sigma}{\overline{X}}$$

For comparing the variability of two distribution we compute the 'coefficient of variation' for each distribution. A distribution with smaller C.V. is said to be more homogeneous or uniform or less variable than the other and the series with greater C.V. is said to be more heterogeneous or more variable than the other.

Lorenz Curve

This is the graphic method of measuring dispersion between two series. It was designed by Dr. Lorenz for measuring inequalities in the distribution of wealth. It is a cumulative percentage curve.

A very distinctive feature of the Lorenz curve consists in dealing with the cumulative values of the variable and the cumulative frequencies rather than its absolute values and the given frequencies. The technique of drawing the curve is fairly simple and consists of the following steps:

(a) The size of the item (variable value) and the frequencies are both cumulated. Taking grand total for each as 100, express these cumulated totals for the variable and the frequencies as percentage of their corresponding grand totals.

(b) Now take coordinate axes, X-axis representing the percentages of the cumulated frequencies (x) and Y-axis representing the percentages of the cummulated values of the variable (y). Both x and y take the value from 0 to 100 as shown in the Figure 2.

(c) Draw the diagonal line $y = x$, joining the origin O (0, 0) with the point P (100, 100) as shown in the Figure 2. The line OP will make an angle of 45° with the X–axis and is called the *line of equal distribution.*

(d) Plot the percentages of the cumulative values of the variable (y) against the percentages of the corresponding cumulated frequencies (x) for the given distribution and join these points with a smooth free hand curve. Obviously, for any given distribution this curve will never cross the line of equal distribution OP. It will always lie below OP unless the distribution is uniform (equal) in which case it will coincide with OP.

Thus when the distribution of items is not proportionately equal, the variability (dispersion) is indicated and the curve is farther from the line of equal distribution OP. The greater the variability the greater is the distance of the curve from OP.

Let us consider the following Lorenz curve (Figure 2) for the distribution of income. In this Figure, OP is the line of equal distribution of income. If the plotted cumulative percentages lie on this line, there is no variability in the distribution of income of persons. The points lying on the curve OAP indicate a less degree of variability as compared to the points lying on the curve OBP. Variability is still greater, when the points lie on the curve OCP. Thus a measure of variability of the distribution is provided by the distance of the curve of the cumulated percentages of the given distribution from the line of equal distribution.

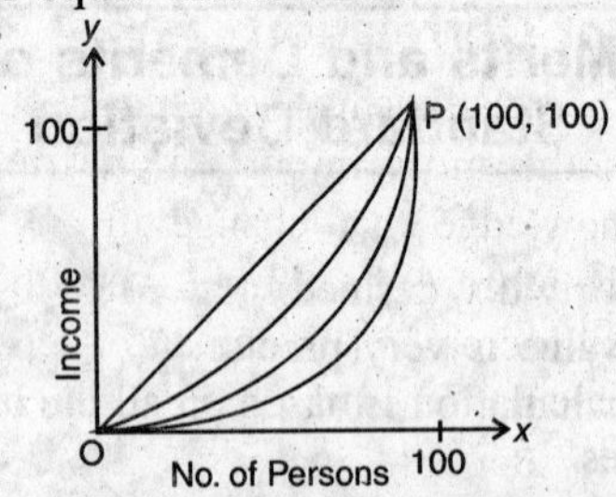

Fig. 2 : *Lorenz Curve*

Remarks

1. An obvious disadvantage of the Lorenz curve is that it gives us only a relative idea of the dispersion as compared with the line of equal distribution. It does not provide us any numerical value of the variability for the given distribution. Accordingly it should be used together with some numerical measure of dispersion. However, this should not undermine the utility of Lorenz curve in studying the variability of the distributions particularly relating to income wealth, wages, profits, lands and capital etc.

2. From the Lorenz curve we can immediately find out as to what percentage of persons (frequencies) correspond to a given percentage of the item (variable value).

Ginni's Coefficient of Concentration

Ginni's coefficient of concentration, also known as concentration Ratio is based on his coefficient of mean difference and is defined as:

$$G = \frac{\Delta_1}{2\overline{X}}$$

where

G = Ginni's coefficient of concentration

Δ_1 = Ginni's coefficient of mean difference

$\overline{X}$ = Mean of the given distribution

Ginni's Coefficiennt of concentration G is a pure

number independent of units of measurement and lies between 0 and 1. G is equal to 0 in *equal distribution* and its value goes up with increase in the inequality.

In fact, Ginni's coefficient is the ratio of area of concentration to the total area of lower triangle below the line of equal distribution.

Correlation

Meaning of Correlation

The study of relationship between two or more variables is the most important in life. It is a common knowledge that change in any variable will affect the other. For example, when the price of a commodity increases, its demand decreases and on the other hand, when the price of a commodity decreases, its demand increases. The statistical device with the help of which relationships between two or more than two variables are studied is called correlation.

According to L.R. Connor, "If two or more quantities vary in sympathy so that movement in the one tend to be accompanied by corresponding movements in the others, then they are said to be correlated."

Utility of the Study of Correlation

1. With the help of correlation we can measure the degree of relationship existing between the variables.
2. Correlation analysis contribute to the economic behaviour, aids in locating the critically important variable and on which other depend.

Positive and Negative Correlation

A. Positive Correlation—If both the variables move in the same direction, correlation is said to be positive.

Some examples of series of positive correlation are:

(*a*) Heights and weights.

(*b*) The family income and expenditure on luxury items.

(*c*) Price and supply of a commodity and so on.

B. Nagative Correlation—If both the variables move in opposite direction, the correlations is said to be negative.

Some examples of negative correlation are—

(*a*) Price and demand of a commodity.

(*b*) Volume and pressure of a perfect goes.

(*c*) Sale of woollen garments and the day temperature, and so on.

Linear and Non-linear Correlation

The correlation between two variables is said to be linear if corresponding to a unit change in one variable, there is a constant change in the other variable over the entire range of the values. For example, let us consider the following data:

X	1	2	3	4	5
Y	5	7	9	11	13

Thus for a unit change in the value of X, there is a constant change in the corresponding values of Y (2 Units). Mathematically, above data can be expressed by the equation.

$$Y = 2X + 3$$

In general two variables X and Y are said to be linearly related, if these exists a relationship of the form

$$Y = a + bX \quad \ldots (1)$$

between them. But we know that (1) is the equation of a straight line with slope '*b*' and which an intercept '*a*' on the Y-axis. Hence, if the values of the two variables are plotted as points in XY-plane, we shall get a straight line.

The relationship between two variables is said to be *Non-linear or curvilinear* if corresponding to a unit change in one variable, the other variable does not change at a constant rate but at fluctuating rate. In such cases if the data are plotted on the XY-plane we do not get a straight line curve mathematically speaking, the correlation is said to be non-linear if the slope of the plotted curve is not constant. Such phenomena are common in the data relating to economics and social sciences.

Degree of Correlation

Degree	*Positive*	*Negative*
Perfect	+1	–1
High	Between + .75 and +1	Between – .75 and – 1
Moderate	Between + .50 and + .75	Between – .50 and –.75
Low	Between 0 and + .50	Between 0 and – .50
Absence	0	0

Methods of Studying Correlation

The commonly used methods for studying the correlation between two variables are:

1. Scatter Diagram Method
2. Karl Pearson's coefficient of correlation
3. Ran King Method
4. Concurrent Deviations Method

Scatter Diagram Method : The scatter diagram implies the plotting of values of two variables on graph paper and then observe the movements. The following points may be borne in mind in interpreting the scatter diagram regarding the correlation between the two variables:

(i) If the points are very dense, *i.e.,* very close to each other, a fairly good amount of correlation may be expected between the two variables. On the other hand, if the points are widely scattered, a poor correlation may be expected between them.

(ii) If the points on the scatter diagram reveal any trend (either upward or downward), the variables are said to be correlated and if no trend is revealed, the variables are uncorrelated.

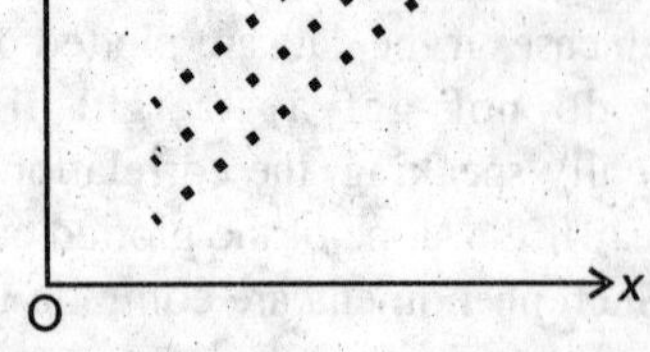

Fig. 3 : *High Degree of Positive Correlation*

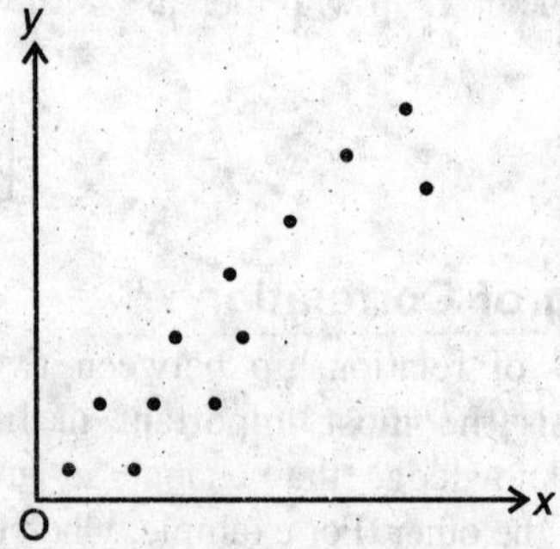

Fig. 4 : *Low Degree of Positive Correlation*

(iii) If there is an upward trend rising from lower left hand corner and going upward to the upper right hand corner, the correlation is positive since this reveals that the values of the two variables move in the same direction. If, on the other hands, the points depict a downward trend from the upper left hand corner to the lower right hand corner, the correlation is negative since in this case the values of the two variables move in the opposite directions.

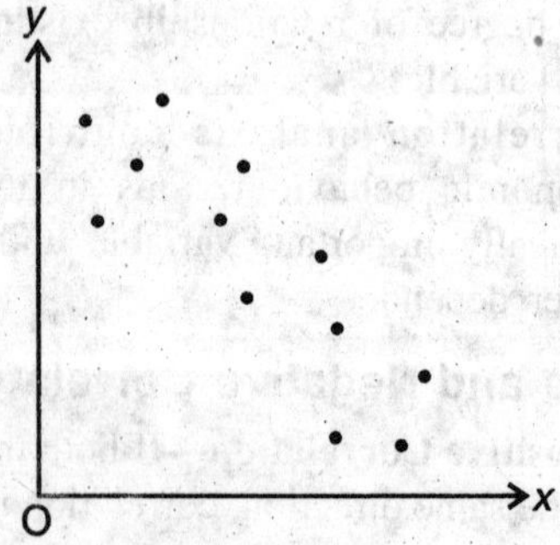

Fig. 5 : *Low Degree of Negative Correlation*

(iv) In particulars if all the points lie on a straight line starting from the left bottom and going up towards the right top, the correlation is perfect all positive, and if all the points lie on a straight line starting from left top and coming down to right bottom, the correlation is perfect and negative.

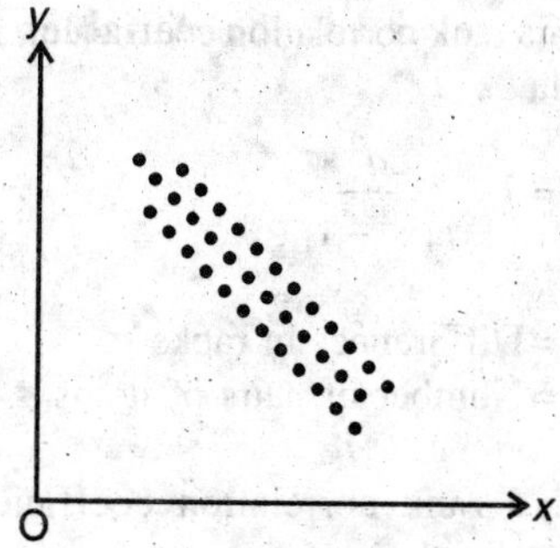

Fig. 6 : *High Degree of Negative Correlation*

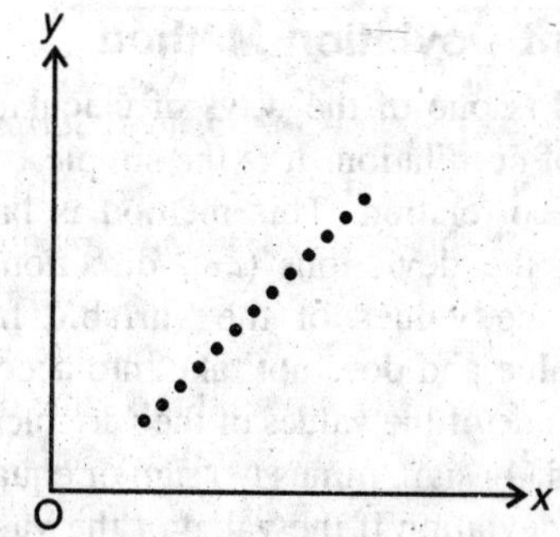

Fig. 7 : *Perfect Positive Correlation*

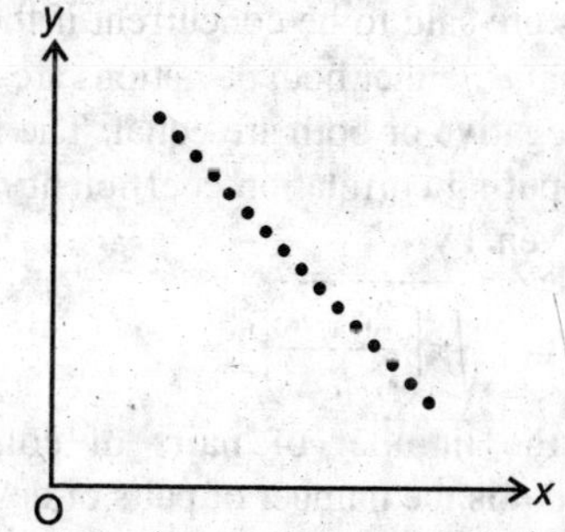

Fig. 8 : *Perfect Negative Correlation*

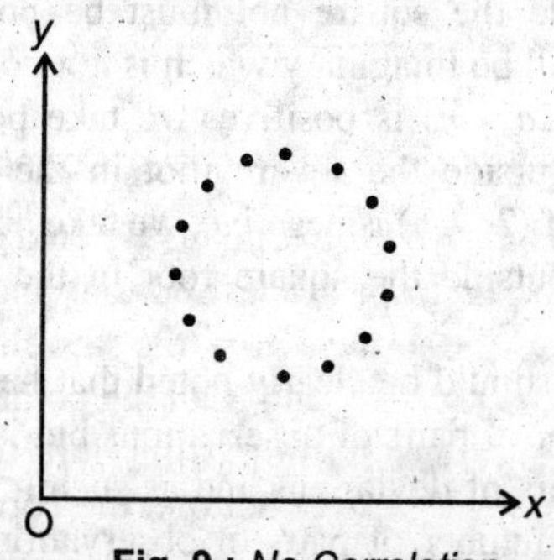

Fig. 9 : *No Correlation*

Karl Pearson's Coefficient of Correlation

A mathematical method for measuring the intensity or the magnitude of linear relationship between two variables was suggested by *Karl Pearson,* a great British Bio-metriciam and statistician and is by for the most widely used method in practice.

Karl Pearson's coefficient of correlation is calculated by applying the following formula:

Ungrouped Data

When deviations are taken from an actual mean

$$r = \frac{\Sigma xy}{N.\sigma x\, \sigma y}$$

where

r = Karl Pearson's Coefficient of Correlation

$x = (X - \bar{x})$

$y = (y - \bar{y})$

σx = Standard Deviation of x-series

σy = Standard Deviation of y-series

N = Number of pairs of item

An alternate formula of the above is:

$$r = \frac{\Sigma xy}{\sqrt{\Sigma x^2 . \Sigma y^2}}$$

where

Σx^2 = Total of squares of deviations taken from an actual mean of X-series

Σy^2 = Total of squares of deviations taken from an actual mean of Y-series

When deviations are taken from an assumed mean

$$r = \frac{N\Sigma dx.dy - (\Sigma dx)(\Sigma dy)}{\sqrt{[N\Sigma dx^2 - (\Sigma dx)^2][N\Sigma dy^2 - (\Sigma dy)^2]}}$$

where

dx = Deviations taken from an assumed mean of X variable (X – A)

dy = Deviations taken from an assumed mean of Y variable (Y – A)

Grouped Data

$$r = \frac{N.\Sigma dxdy - (\Sigma fdx)(\Sigma fdy)}{\sqrt{[N\Sigma fdx^2 - (\Sigma fdx)^2][N\Sigma fdy^2 - (\Sigma fdx)^2]}}$$

Properties of Correlation Coefficient

Property–1

Pearsonian correlation coefficient can not exceed 1 numerically. In other words it lies between –1 and + 1. Symbolically,

$$-1 \leq r \leq 1$$

In other words, $r = +1$ implies perfect positive correlation between the variables and $r = -1$ implies perfect negative correlation between the variables.

Property–2

Correlation coefficient is independent of the change of origin and scale.

Property–3

Two independent variables are uncorrelated but the converse is not true.

Rank Correlation Method

Sometimes we come across statistical series in which the variables under consideration are not capable of quantitative measurement but can be arranged in serial order. This happens when we are dealing with qualitative characteristics such as honesty, beauty, character, morality, etc., which cannot be measured quantitatively but can be arranged serially. In such situations Karl Pearson's coefficient of correlation cannot be used as such. *Charles Edward Spearman*, a British Psychologist, developed a formula in 1904 which consists in obtaining the correlation coefficient between the ranks of n individuals in the two attributes under study.

Suppose we want to find if two characteristics A, say, intelligence and B, say, beauty are related or not. Both the characteristics are incapable of quantitative measurement, but we can arrange a group of n individuals in order of merit (ranks) *w. r. t.* proficiency in the two characteristics. Let the random variables X Y denote the ranks of the individuals in the characteristics A and B respectively. If we assume that there is no tie, *i.e.*, if no two individuals get the same rank in a characteristic then, obviously, X and Y assume numerical values ranging from 1 to n.

Spearman's rank correlation coefficient, is given by the formula

$$rk = 1 - \frac{\Sigma d^2}{n(n^2 - 1)}$$

where

d = Differences in ranks

n = Number of pairs of items

Remark

Spearman's rank correlation coefficient lies between – 1 and + 1, *i.e.*,

$$-1 \leq rk \leq 1$$

Concurrent Deviation Method

This method is one of the ways of calculating the coefficient of correlation. It is the simplest method of studying correlation. This method is based on the signs of the deviations (*i.e.*, direction of the change) of the values of the variable from its preceding value and does not take into account the exact magnitude of the values of the variables. Thus, we put a plus (+) sign, minus (–) sign or equality (=) sign for the deviation if the value of the variable is greater than, less than or equal to the preceding value respectively. The deviations in the values of two variables are said to be concurrent if they have the same sign, *i.e.*, either both deviations are positive or both are negative or both are equal. The formula used for computing correlation coefficient r by this method is given by

$$r = \pm\sqrt{\pm\left(\frac{2c - n}{n}\right)}$$

where c is the number of pairs of concurrent deviations and n is the number of pairs of deviations. In the above formula plus/minus $-1 \leq r \leq 1$, the quantity inside the square not must be positive, otherwise r will be imaginary which is not possible.

Thus if $(2c - n)$ is positive, we take positive sign in and outside the square root in the above equation and if $(2c - n)$ is negative, we take negative sign in and outside the square root in the above equation.

Note—It should be clearly noted that here n is not the number of pairs of observations but it is the number of pairs of deviations and as such it is one less than the number of pairs of observations.

Assumptions Underlying Karl Pearson's Correlation Coefficient

Pearsonian correlation coefficient r is based on the following assumptions:—

(i) The variables X and Y under study are linearly related. In other words, the scatter diagram of the data will give a straight line curve.

(ii) Each of the variables is being affected by a large number of independent contributory causes of such a nature as to produce normal distribution.

(iii) The forces so operating on each of the variable series are not independent of each other but are related in a causal fashion.

Probable Error

After computing the value of the correlation coefficient the next step is to fina the extent to which it is dependable. Probable error of correlation coefficient, usually denoted by P.E. *(r)* is an old measure of testing the reliability of an observed value of correlation coefficient in so far as it depends upon the conditions of random sampling.

If r is the observed correlation coefficient in a sample of n pairs of observations then its standard error, usually denoted by

S.E. *(r)* is given by

$$\text{S.E. }(r) = \frac{1-r^2}{\sqrt{n}}$$

Probable error of the correlation coefficient is given by

$$\text{P.E. }(r) = 0.6745 \times \text{S.E. }(r)$$

$$= 0.6745 \; \frac{1-r^2}{\sqrt{n}}$$

Reason for taking the factor 0.6745 is that in a normal distribution 50% of the observations lie in the range $M \pm 0.6745\sigma$, where M is the mean and σ is the S.d.

Use of Probable Error

1. The probable error of correlation coefficient may be used to determine the limits within which the population correlation coefficient may be expected to lie.

Limits for population correlation coefficient are

$$r \pm \text{P.E.}(r) \qquad \ldots (1)$$

This implies that if we take another random sample of the same size n from the same population from which the first sample was taken, then the observed value of the correlation coefficient, say, r_1 in the second sample can be expected to lie within the limits given in (1).

2. P.E. *(r)* may be used to test if an observed value of sample correlation coefficient is significant of any correlation in the population. The following guidelines may be used.

(a) If $r <$ P.E. (r), *i.e.,* if the observed value of r is less than its P.E then correlation is not at all significant.

(b) If $r < \sigma$ P.E. (r), *i.e.,* if observed value of r is greater than σ times its P.E. then r is definitely significant.

(c) In other situations, nothing can be concluded with certainty.

Remarks

P.E. can be used only under the following conditions:

(i) The data must have been drawn from a normal population.

(ii) The conditions of random sampling should prevail in selecting sampled observations.

Coefficient of Determination

Coefficient of correlation between two variable series is a measure of linear relationship between them and indicates the amount of variation of one variable which is associated with or is accounted for by another variable. A more useful and readily comprehensible measure for this purpose is the coefficient of determination which gives the percentage variation in the dependent variable that is accounted for by the independent variable. In other words, the coefficient of determination gives the ratio of the explainea variance to the determination is given by the square of the correlation coefficient, *i.e.,* r^2. Thus,

Coefficient of determination

$$= r^2 = \frac{\text{Explained Variance}}{\text{Total Variance}}$$

The coefficient of determination is a much useful and better measure for interpreting the value of r.

For example, if the value of $r = 0.8$, we cannot conclude that 80% of the variation in the relative series (dependent variable) is due to the variation in the subject series (independent variable). But the coefficient of determination in this case is $r^2 = 0.64$ which implies that only 64% of the variation in the relative series has been explained by the subject series and the remaining 36% of the variation is due to other factors.

By the same argument while comparing two correlation coefficient, one of which is 0.4 and the other is 0.8 it is misleading to conclude that the correlation in the second case is twice as high as correlation is the first case. The coefficient of determination clearly explains this view point, since in the case $r = 0.4$, the coefficient of determination is 0.16 and in the case $r = 0.8$, the coefficient of determination is 0.64, from which we conclude that correlation in the second case is four times as high as correlation in the first case.

Remarks

1. The above discussion implies that—

"The closeness of the relationship between two variables as determined by correlation coefficient r is not proportional".

2. The following table gives the values of the coefficient of determination (r^2) for different values of r.

r	r^2
0.1	0.01
0.2	0.04
0.3	0.09
0.4	0.16
0.5	0.25
0.6	0.36
0.7	0.49
0.8	0.64
0.9	0.81
1.0	1.00

It may be seen from the above table that as the value of r decreases, r^2 decreases very rapidly except in two particular cases $r = 0$ and $r = 1$ when we get $r = r^2$.

3. Coefficient of determination—It is always non-negative and as such it does not tell us about the direction of the relationship (whether it is positive or negative) between the two series.

4. Coefficient of Non-determination—The ratio of the unexplained variation to the total variation is called the coefficient of non-determination. It is usually denoted by K^2 and is given by the formula:

$$K^2 = \frac{\text{Un-explained Variance}}{\text{Total Variance}}$$

$$= 1 - \frac{\text{Explained Variance}}{\text{Total Variance}}$$

$$= 1 - r^2$$

5. Coefficient of Alienation—The coefficient of alienation is given by the square root of the coefficient of non-determination, *i.e.*, by K as given below $K = \pm\sqrt{1-r^2}$

Regression

Regression analysis, in the general sense, means the estimation or prediction of the unknown value of the variable from the known value of the other variable. It is one of the very important statistical tools which is extensively used in almost all sciences–natural; social and physical. It is specially used in business and economics to study the relationship between two or more variables that are related casually and for estimation of demand and supply curves, cost functions, production and consumption functions, etc.

Prediction or estimation is one of the major problems in almost all spheres of human activity. The estimation or prediction of future production, consumption, prices, investments, sales, profits, income, etc, are of paramount importance to a businessman or economist. Regression analysis is one of the very scientific techniques for making such predictions. In the words of M.M.Blair "Regression analysis is a mathematical measure of the average relationship between two or more variables in terms of the original units of data."

In regression analysis there are two types of variables. The variable whose value is influenced or is to be predicted is called dependent variable and the variable which influences the values or is used for prediction, is called independent variable. In regression analysis independent variable is also known as regresser or predictor or explanator while the dependent variable is also known as regressed or explained variable.

Lines of Regression

Line of regression is the line which gives the best estimate of one variable for any given value of the other variable. In case of two variables x and y, we shall have two lines of regression, one of y on x and the other of x on y.

1. Line of Regression of *y* on *x*

Line of regression of y on x is the line which gives the best estimate for the value of y for any specified value of x. Hence, the equation of line of regression of y on x is

$$y = a + bx \text{ or } y - \bar{y} = r.\frac{\sigma y}{\sigma x}(x - \bar{x})$$

where

$\bar{x}$ = Arithmetic Mean of x-series

y = Arithmetic Mean of y-series

σx = Standard Deviation of x-series

σy = Standard Deviation of y-series

r = Coefficient of Correlation between two Variables x and y.

2. Line of Regression of *x* on *y*

Line of regression of x on y is the line which gives the best estimate for the value of x for any specified value of y.

Mathematically

$$x = A + By \text{ or } x - \bar{x} = r.\frac{\sigma x}{\sigma y}(y - \bar{y})$$

Remarks

1. Both the lines of regression passes through the point $(\bar{x}, \bar{y})$. In other words, the mean values $(\bar{x}, \bar{y})$ can be obtained as the point of intersection of the two regression lines.

2. There are always two lines of regression. In a particular case of perfect correlation, positive or negative *i.e.*, $r = \pm 1$, the equation of line of regression of y on x becomes

$$y - \bar{y} = \pm\frac{\sigma y}{\sigma x}(x - \bar{x})$$

$$\Rightarrow \quad \frac{y - \bar{y}}{\sigma y} = \pm\left(\frac{x - \bar{x}}{\sigma x}\right) \quad \ldots (1)$$

Similarly, the equation of the line of regression of x on y becomes:

$$x - \bar{x} = \pm\frac{\sigma x}{\sigma y}(y - \bar{y})$$

$$\Rightarrow \quad \frac{y - \bar{y}}{\sigma y} = \pm\left(\frac{x - \bar{x}}{\sigma x}\right) \quad \ldots (2)$$

Both the equations are same.

Hence in case of perfect correlation ($r = \pm 1$) both the lines of regression coincide. Therefore, in general we always have two lines of regression except in the particular case of perfect correlation when both the lines coincide and we get only one line.

Angle Between the Regression Lines

The equations of the lines of regression of y on x and x on y are respectively:

$$y - \bar{y} = r.\frac{\sigma y}{\sigma x}(x - \bar{x}) \quad \ldots (1)$$

and $$x - \bar{x} = r.\frac{\sigma x}{\sigma y}(y - \bar{y})$$

$$\Rightarrow \quad y - \bar{y} = \frac{\sigma y}{r.\sigma x}(x - \bar{x}) \quad \ldots (2)$$

This slopes of lines (1) and (2), are respectively:

$$M_1 = \frac{r\sigma y}{\sigma x} \text{ and } M_2 = \frac{\sigma y}{r\sigma x}$$

If Q is the angle between the two lines of regression, then

$$\tan\theta = \frac{m_1 - m_2}{1 + m_1 m_2}$$

$$= \frac{\frac{r\sigma y}{\sigma x} - \frac{\sigma y}{r\sigma x}}{1 + r.\frac{\sigma y}{\sigma x}.\frac{\sigma y}{r.\sigma x}}$$

$$= \frac{\frac{\sigma y}{\sigma x}\left(r - \frac{1}{r}\right)}{\left(\frac{\sigma x^2 + \sigma y^2}{\sigma x^2}\right)}$$

$$= \frac{\sigma x \sigma y}{\sigma x^2 + \sigma y^2} \cdot \left(\frac{r^2 - 1}{r}\right)$$

$$\Rightarrow \qquad \theta = \tan^{-1}\left\{\frac{\sigma x \sigma y}{\sigma x^2 + \sigma y^2}\left(\frac{r^2 - 1}{r}\right)\right\}$$

If $\quad r = \pm 1$, then

$\theta = \tan^{-1}(0)$

$\Rightarrow \quad \theta = 0$ or π

i.e., the two lines are either coincident ($\theta = 0$) or they are paralled ($\theta = \pi$). But since both the lines of regression intersect at the point $(\bar{x}, \bar{y})$, they cannot be parallel. Hence in case of perfect correlation, positive or negative, the two lines of regression coincide.

If $\quad r = 0$, then

$\theta = (\infty) = \pi/2 = 90°$

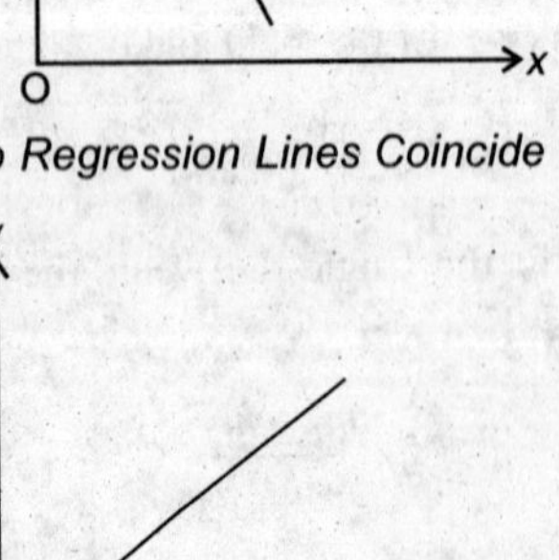

Fig. 10 : *Two Regression Lines Coincide (If r = –1)*

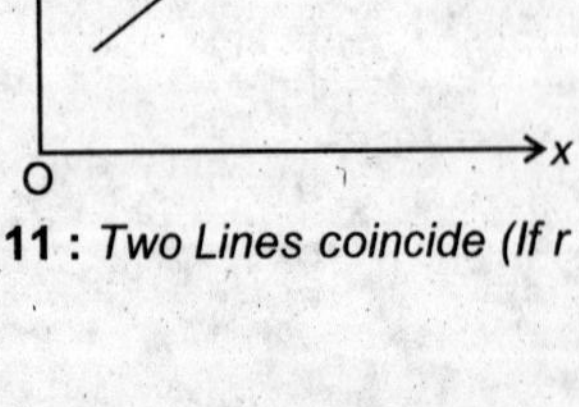

Fig. 11 : *Two Lines coincide (If r = +1)*

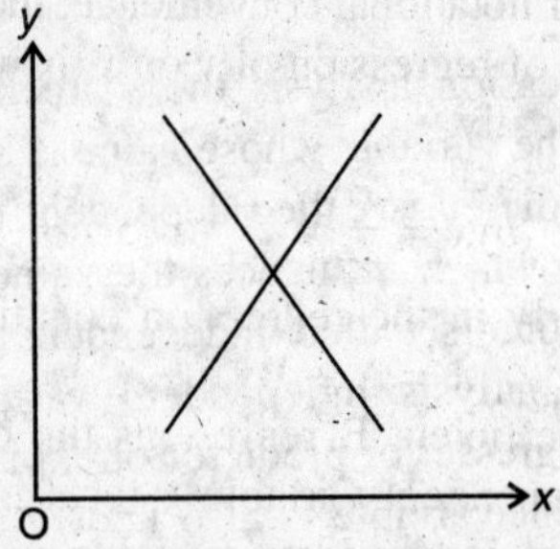

Fig. 12 : *Two Lines Perpendicular (If r = 0)*

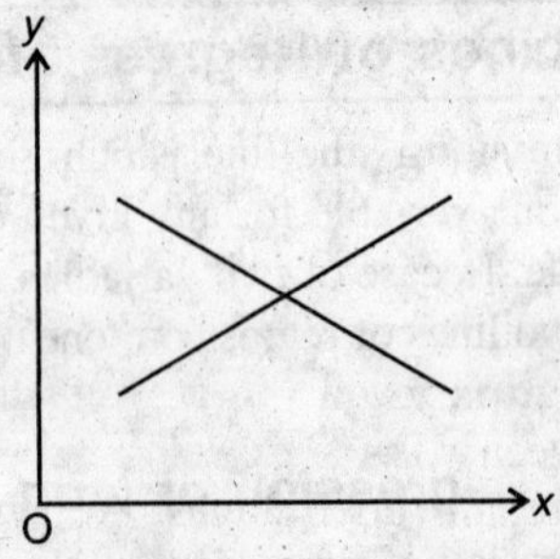

Fig. 13 : *Two lines Apart (Low Degree of Correlation)*

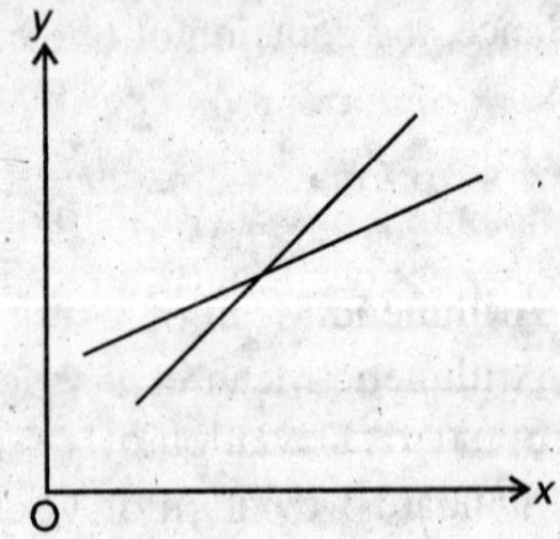

Fig. 14 : *Two Line Closer (High Degree of Correlation)*

i.e., if the variables are uncorrelated, the two lines of regression become perpendicular to each other.

Coefficients of Regression

Let us consider the line of regression of y on x,

$$y = a + bc$$

The coefficient *'b'* which is the slope of the line of regression of y on x is called the coefficient of regression of y on x. ***It represents the increment in the value of the dependent variable y*** for a unit change in the value of the independent variable x. In other words, it represents the rate of change of y

w.r.t. x. For notational convenience, the slope *b, i.e.,* coefficient of regression of *y* on *x* is written as *byx.* Mathematically

$$byx = \frac{r\sigma y}{\sigma x}$$

similarly in the regression equation of *x* on *y*

$$x = A + By$$

the coefficient B represents the change in the value of dependent variable *x* for a unit change in the value of independent variable *y* and is called the coefficient of regression of *x* on *y*. For convenience, it is written as *bxy*.

$$bxy = \frac{r\sigma x}{\sigma y}$$

Remarks

1. **Correlation coefficient between two variables** *x* and *y* is a symmetrical function between *x* is *y, i.e., rxy = ryx*. However, the regression coefficients are not symmetric functions of *x* and *y, i.e., byx ≠ bxy.*
2. Both the regression coefficients must have the same sign.
3. The sign of correlation coefficient is same as that of the regression coefficients. If regression coefficients are positive, *r* is positive and if regression coefficients are negative, *r* is negative.

Theorems on Regression Coefficients

Theorem–1

The correlation coefficient is the geometric mean of the regression.

Coefficients, *i.e.,*

$$r = \sqrt{byx.bxy}$$

Proof. We have

$$bxy = r.\frac{\sigma x}{\sigma y} \quad \text{. . . (i)}$$

and $$byx = r.\frac{\sigma y}{\sigma x} \quad \text{. . . (ii)}$$

Multiplying *(i)* and *(ii),* we get

$$r^2 = byx.\ bxy$$

$$\Rightarrow \quad r = \pm\sqrt{byx.bxy}$$

which establishes the result.

Theorem–2

If one of the regression coefficients is greater than unity, the other must be less than unity.

Proof: Let $byx > 1$

$$\Rightarrow \quad \frac{1}{bxy < 1} \quad \text{... (i)}$$

we have

$$byx\ .\ bxy = r^2 \leq 1 \Rightarrow bxy \leq \frac{1}{byx} < 1 \text{ From } (i)$$

Hence, if one of the regression coefficients is greater than one, the other must be less than one.

Theorem–3

The arithmetic mean of the regression coefficients is greater than the correlation coefficient.

Proof. We know that for any two real distinct positive numbers *a* and *b*:

$$\text{A.M.} > \text{G.M.} \Rightarrow \frac{a+b}{2} > \sqrt{ab} \quad \text{. . . (i)}$$

Taking $a = byx$ and $b = bxy$ in *(i),* we get

$$\frac{1}{2}(byx + bxy) > \sqrt{byx.bxy} \Rightarrow \frac{(byx + bxy)}{2} > r$$

$$\because \quad r = \sqrt{byx - bxy}$$

Theorem–4

Regression coefficients are independent of change of origin but not of scale.

Correlation Analysis *Vs.* Regression Analysis

1. Correlation coefficient *rxy* is a relative measure of the linear relationship between *x* and *y* and is independent of the units of measurement. On the other hand, the regression coefficients are absolute measures representing the change in the value of the variable *y(x),* for a unit change in the value of the variable *x(y).*
2. Correlation analysis is confined only to the study of linear relationship between the variables and, therefore, has limited applications. Regression analysis has much wider applications as it studies linear as well as non-linear relationship between the variables.
3. Correlation need not imply cause and effect relationship between the variables under study. However, regression analysis clearly indicates the cause and effect relationship between the variables.

Index Numbers

Meaning

An index number is as its name suggests, an indicator of the general trend of a set of figures. Index numbers are devices for measuring the net amount of change in a group of related variables over a certain period of time. Index numbers are used to measure changes in industrial output, fluctuations in the level of business or variations in the size of agricultural output etc. The important definitions of index numbers are given below:

According to Croxton and Cowden, "Index numbers are devices for measuring differences in the magnitude of a group of related variables."

According to Blair, "Index numbers are a specialised type of averages."

Uses of Index Numbers

Following are the main uses of Index Numbers:

1. Index numbers are used to measure the changes in the price level over a period of time.
2. Index numbers are used to reduce complex forms of measurement to simple numbers.
3. Index numbers are also used for the purpose of forecasting.
4. Index numbers are also compelled to compare physical changes over a period of time. Such changes relate to industrial production, sales, volume of imports or exports, etc.
5. Since the index numbers study the relative changes in the level of a phenomenon at different periods of time, they are specially useful for the study of the general trend for a group phenomena in a time series data.

Types of Index Numbers

1. Price Index Numbers
2. Quantity Index Numbers
3. Value Index Numbers

Methods of Constructing Index Numbers

The various methods for constructing index numbers are given below:

1. *Fixed Base Method*

$$\text{Price Relatives (R)} = \frac{P_1}{P_0} \times 100$$

where

P_1 = Price of the current year

P_0 = Price of the base year

2. *Simple Aggregative Method*

$$P_{01} = \frac{\Sigma P_1}{\Sigma P_0} \times 100$$

where

P_{01} = Price index of the current year

ΣP_1 = Total of current year prices

ΣP_0 = Total of base year prices

Remark

Based on this method, the quantity index is given by the formula

$$Q_{01} = \frac{\Sigma q_1}{\Sigma q_0} \times 100$$

where Σq_0 and Σq_1 are the quantities of all the selected commodities consumed in the base year and the current year respectively.

3. *Simple Average of Price Relatives Methods*

$$P_{01} = \frac{\Sigma\left(\frac{P_1}{P_0} \times 100\right)}{N}$$

where N stands for number of items or commodities.

4. *Weighted Aggregate Method*

$$P_{01} = \frac{\Sigma WP_1}{\Sigma WP_0} \times 100$$

where W is the weight attached to a commodity.

By using different systems of weighting we get a number of formulas. Some of the important formulas are given below:

Laspeyre's Price Index or Base Year Method

Taking base year quantities as weights, *i.e.*, $w = q_0$

we get Laspeyre's Price Index given by:

$$P_{01} = \frac{\Sigma P_1 q_0}{\Sigma P_0 q_0} \times 100$$

where

P_1 = Current Year Price
q_0 = Base Year Quantity
P_0 = Base Year Price
q_1 = Current Year Quantity

This formula was devised by French Economist Laspeyre in 1871.

Paasche's Price Index

If we take current year quantities as weights we obtain Paasche's Price Index which is given by:

$$P_{01} = \frac{\Sigma P_1 q_1}{\Sigma P_0 q_0} \times 100$$

This formula was given by German statistician Paasche in 1874.

Dorbish – Bowley Price Index

This index is given by the arithmetic mean of Laspeyre's and Paasche's price index numbers and we have:

$$P_{01} = \frac{1}{2}\left[\frac{\Sigma P_1 q_0}{\Sigma P_0 q_0} + \frac{\Sigma P_1 q_1}{\Sigma P_0 q_1}\right] \times 100$$

This is also sometimes known as L – P formula.

Fisher's Price Index

Irving Fisher advocated the geometric mean of Laspeyre's and Paasche's price index numbers and is given by:

$$P_{0-1}\left[\frac{\Sigma P_1 q_0}{\Sigma P_0 q_0} \times \frac{\Sigma P_1 q_1}{\Sigma P_0 q_1}\right] \times 100$$

Fisher's index is termed as an Ideal index since it satisfies time reversal and factor reversal tests for the consistency of index numbers.

Marshall Edgeworth Price Index

Taking the arithmetic cross of the quantities in the base year and the current year as weights, *i.e.*, $w = \frac{(q_1 + q_1)}{2}$, we obtain the Marshall – Edgeworth formula given by

$$P_{01} = \frac{\Sigma P_1 . \frac{(q_0 + q_1)}{2}}{\Sigma P_0 . \frac{(q_0 + q_1)}{2}} \times 100$$

$$= \frac{\Sigma P_1 (q_0 + q_1)}{\Sigma P_0 (q_0 + q_1)} \times 100$$

$$= \left[\frac{\Sigma P_1 q_0 + \Sigma P_1 q_1}{\Sigma P_0 q_0 + \Sigma P_0 q_1} \times 100\right]$$

Walsch Price Index

Instead of taking the arithmetic mean of base year and current year quantities as weights, if we take their geometric mean, *i.e.*, $w = \sqrt{q_0 q_1}$, then we obtain Walsch Index given by the formula:

$$P_{01} = \frac{\Sigma P_1 \sqrt{q_0 q_1}}{\Sigma P_0 \sqrt{q_0 q_1}} \times 100$$

Kelly's Price Index or Fixed Weights Index

This formula, named after L. Kelly, requires the weights to be fixed for all periods and is also sometimes known as aggregative index with fixed weights and is given by the formula:

$$P_{01} = \frac{\Sigma P_1 q}{\Sigma P_0 q} \times 100$$

where the weights are the quantities *(q)* which may refer to some period (not necessarily the base year or the current year) and are kept constant for all periods.

Value Indices

Value index numbers are obtained on expressing the total value (or expenditure) in any given year as a percentage of the same in the base year symbolically, we write

$$V_{01} = \frac{\text{Total value in current year}}{\text{Total value in base year}} \times 100$$

$$\Rightarrow \quad V_{01} = \frac{\Sigma P_1 q_1}{\Sigma P_0 q_0} \times 100$$

Remarks

1. In general, Laspeyre's price index is greater than Paasche's price index. In other words, Laspeyre's price index has an upward bias in general, with rise in price.
   But if the correlation coefficients between the price relatives and quantity relatives is positive (a phenomenon which is rarely observed in economics), then Laspeyre's price index is less than Paasche's price index.
2. Fisher's ideal index number lies between Laspeyre's and Paasche's index numbers.

Tests of Consistency of Index Number Formula

1. Unit Test—This test requires that the index number formula should be independent of the units in which the prices or quantities of various commodities are quoted. All the formulae discussed above except the index number based on simple Aggregate of prices (Quantities) satisfy this test.

2. Time Reversal Test—The time reversal tests proposed by *Prof. Irving Fisher* requires the index number formula to possess time consistency by working both forward and backward *w.r.t.* time.

In other words, if the index numbers are computed for the same data relating to two periods by the same formula but with the bases reversed, then the two index numbers so obtained should be the reciprocals of each other. Mathematically, we should have (omitting the factor 100),

$$P_{01} \times P_{10} = 1$$

or more generally

$$P_{ab} \times P_{ba} = 1$$

where

P_{ab} = Price index (without factor 100) for year '*b*' with year '*a*' as base

P_{ba} = Price index (without factor 100) for year '*a*' with year '*b*' as base

Time reversal test is satisfied by the following index number formulae:

(i) Marshall – Edgeworth formula
(ii) Fisher's ideal formula
(iii) Walsch formula
(iv) Kelly's fixed weight formula
(v) Simple aggregate index
(vi) Simple Geometric mean of Price Relatives formula
(vii) Weighted Geometric mean of Price Relatives formula with fixed weights

Remark

Laspeyre's and Paasche's index numbers do not satisfy this test.

Let us verify this test for Kelly's fixed weight formula. We have (without factor 100)

$$P_{10}^{k} = \frac{\Sigma WP_1}{\Sigma WP_0}$$

and $$P_{10}^{k} = \frac{\Sigma WP_0}{\Sigma WP_1}$$

$$\therefore P_{01}^{k} \times P_{10}^{k} = \frac{\Sigma WP_1}{\Sigma WP_0} \times \frac{\Sigma WP_0}{\Sigma WP_1} = 1$$

Hence, Kelly's fixed weight formula satisfies time reversal test.

3. Factor Reversal Test—This is the second of the two important tests of consistency proposed by Prof. Irving Fisher. This implies that if the price and quantity indices are obtained for the same data, same base and current periods and using the same formula, then their product (without the factor 100) should give the true value ratio, since price multiplied by quantity gives total value. Symbolically, we should have (without factor 100),

$$P_{01} \times Q_{01} = \frac{\Sigma P_1 q_1}{\Sigma P_0 q_0}$$

where

$\Sigma P_1 q_1$ and $\Sigma P_0 q_0$ denote the total value in the current and base year respectively.

Fisher's formula satisfies the factor reversal test. In fact Fisher's index is the only index satisfying this test and none of the formulae discussed above satisfies this test.

Remark—Since Fisher's index is the only index which satisfies both the time reversal and factor reversal tests, it is sometimes termed as Fisher's Ideal Index.

4. Circular Test— Circular test, first suggested by Westergaard, is an extension of time reversal test for more than two periods and is based on the shiftability of the base period. This requires the index to work in a circular manner add this property enables us to find the index numbers from period to period without referring back to the original base each time. For, three periods *a, b, c,* the test requires:

$$P_{ab} \times P_{bc} \times P_{ca} = 1,\ a \neq b \neq c$$

or, $P_{01} \times P_{12} \times P_{20} = 1$

For instance

$$P_{01}^{La} \times P_{12}^{La} \times P_{20}^{La} = \frac{\Sigma p_1 q_0}{\Sigma p_0 q_0} \times \frac{\Sigma p_2 q_1}{\Sigma p_1 q_1} \times \frac{\Sigma p_0 q_2}{\Sigma p_2 q_2} \neq 1$$

Hence, Laspeyre's index does not satisfy the circular test. Similarly, it can be verified that none of Paasche's, M – E's, Walsch's, and Fisher's indices satisfies this test. In fact, circular test is not satisfied by any of the weighted aggregative formula with changing weights, *i.e.,* if the weights used in the construction of index numbers P_{01}, P_{12} and P_{20} change. This test is satisfied only by the index number formulae based on:

(i) Simple geometric mean of the price relatives

(ii) Kelly's fixed base method.

Remark— The circular test can be generalised to the case of more than three periods to give:

$$P_{01} \times P_{12} \times P_{23} \times \ldots \times P_{n,o} = 1$$

where the indices are considered without the factor 400.

(i) Conversion of Fixed Base to Chain Base

Chain Index No.

$$= \frac{\text{Current year fixed base index No.}}{\text{Previous year fixed base index No.}} \times 100$$

(ii) Conversion of Chain Base to Fixed Base

Fixed Base Index No.

$$= \frac{\text{Current year's chain base index No.} \times \text{Previous year's fixed base index No.}}{100}$$

Theory of Probability

Meaning of Probability

In every day life we talk about probability of occurrence of various events. Whenever there is an element of uncertainty about the occurrence of some event one makes a probability statement. For example, the probability that India will win a cricket match against West Indies is 30% or 0.30; the probability that it will rain tonight is 80% or 0.80, etc.

The concept of probability originally developed in the 17th century with the games of chance, line games of cards, tossing of coins and dies etc.

Let us illustrate the concept of probability with the help of the classical example of coin tossing experiment. Suppose a coin is tossed, what is the probability that it will turn up head? Perhaps the immediate answer it, provided it is an ideal coin and it is not worn out or biased in any way. The argument will be that there are only two possible ways in which the coin can be tossed (either head or tail will turn up), and the coin being an ideal one both head and tail are equally likely. Therefore, the odds are fifty – fifty, *i.e.*, the probability of getting head is and so is the probability of getting tail. This is, in fact, the classical approach to obtaining the probability of occurrence of an event.

According to La Place—"Probability is the ratio of favourable events to the total number of equally likely events."

Symbolically,

$$P = \frac{\text{Number of favourable cases}}{\text{Total number of equally likely cases}}$$

where P = Probability that the event will take place.

Similarly,

$$q = \frac{\text{Number of cases not favourable}}{\text{Total number of equally likely cases}}$$

In simple words, probability can be defined in the following manner.

The probability of the happening of any one of the several equally likely events is the ratio of the number of cases favourable to it to the total number of possible cases.

Mathematical Definition

If there are n mutually exclusive and equally likely cases and of these n cases, there are p cases favourable and q cases unfavourable to some event, then the probability of occurance of the event is denoted by

$$P = \frac{p}{n}$$

The probability of non–occurance of the event is denoted by

$$Q = \frac{q}{n}$$

where P = Chance of success
Q = Chance of failure

Examples 1. A uniform die is thrown at random. Find the probability that the number on it is 5.

Solution. As we know a die has six sides with 1, 2, 3, 4, 5 and 6 written on them. Since it is an ideal die all the six sides are equally likely to turn up. Also, only one of the sides will turn up at a time and thus the six possible ways are mutually exclusive. The number 5 can turn up in only one possible way. Therefore, the required probability is 1/6.

2. Suppose an ideal die is tossed twice. What is the probability that 6 will appear on both occasions?

Solution. There are 36 (= 6 × 6) possible ways in which the die can be thrown twice we may get 1 in the first toss and also 1 in the second, or, 1 in the first and 2 in the second, or, 1 in the first and 3 in the second and so on. Let us list the number of possible outcomes as follows:

(1, 1) (1, 2) (1, 3) (1, 4) (1, 5) (1, 6)
(2, 1) (2, 2) (2, 3) (2, 4) (2, 5) (2, 6)
(3, 1) (3, 2) (3, 3) (3, 4) (3, 5) (3, 6)
(4, 1) (4, 2) (4, 3) (4, 4) (4, 5) (4, 6)
(5, 1) (5, 2) (5, 3) (5, 4) (5, 5) (5, 6)
(6, 1) (6, 2) (6, 3) (6, 4) (6, 5) (6, 6)

All these ways are equally likely and mutually exclusive. There is only one possible way in which we get 6 in both the first and the second toss.

Therefore, the required probability is $\frac{1}{36}$.

3. In the above example, what is the probability of getting a sum of 10?

Solution. What is required is that the sum of the two numbers shown on the die in two tosses should be 10. This is possible in only three ways:

Either we get 5 in the 1st toss and 5 in the 2nd. or, we get 4 in the 1st toss and 6 in the 2nd. or, we get 6 in the 1st toss and 4 in the second.

Thus the required probability is

$$= \frac{3}{36} = 1/12$$

4. If a coin is tossed two times, what is the probability of getting head at least once?

Solution. The total number of equally likely and mutually exclusive ways is, now, 4:

(H, H) (H, T) (T, H) (T, T)

and the number of favourable way (*i.e.*, the number of ways in which head appears at least once) is 3.

Therefore, the required probability is $\frac{3}{4}$.

5. What is the chance of drawing a queen in a draw from a pack of 52 cards?

Solution. Total number of cases = 52
Total number of queen = 4
The probability of drawing a queen is

$$= \frac{4}{52} = \frac{1}{13}$$

6. A bag contains 10 black and 20 white balls. What is the probability of drawing:

(*a*) a black ball, and
(*b*) a white ball.

Solution. Total number of balls = 10 + 20 =30

(*a*) Probability of drawing a black ball is

$$P = \frac{\text{Number of Black Balls}}{\text{Total Numbers of Balls}}$$

$$= \frac{10}{30} = \frac{1}{3}$$

(*b*) Probability of drawing a white ball is

$$P = \frac{\text{Number of White Balls}}{\text{Total Number of Balls}}$$

$$= \frac{20}{30} = \frac{2}{3}$$

Mutually Exclusive Events

Two or more events are said to be mutually exclusive if the hoppening of any one of them excludes the happening of all others in the same experiment.

For example, in toss of a coin the events 'head' and 'tail' are mutually exclusive because if head comes, we cannot get tail and if tail comes we cannot get head.

Equally Likely Cases

The outcomes are said to be equally likely or equally probable if none of them is expected to occur in preference to other. Thus, in tossing of a coin, all the outcomes, namely, H and T are equally likely if the coin is unbiased.

Independent Events

Events are said to be independent of each other if happening of any one of them is not affected by and does not affect the happening of any one of others.

For example, in tossing of a die repeatedly the event of getting '5' in 1st throw is independent of getting '5' in second, third or supsequent throws.

Remark

The two events A and B are said to be disjoint or mutually exclusive if they cannot happen simultaneously, *i.e.,* if their intersection is a null set. Thus if A and B are disjoint events, then

$$A \cap B = \phi \Rightarrow P(A \cap B) = P(\Phi) = 0$$

Thus $P(A \cap B) = 0$, provides us with a criterion for finding if A and B are mutually exclusive.

Addition Rule of Probability

The probability of occurrence of at least one of the two events A and B is given by:

$$P(A \cup B) = P(A) + P(B) - P(A \cap B)$$

where

P (A) = Probability of occurrence of an event A

P (B) = Probability of occurrence of an event B

$P(A \cap B)$ = Probability of simultaneous occurrence of A and B

$P(A \cup B)$ = Probability of occurrence of at least one of the two events A and B

Addition Rule of Probability for Mutually Exclusive Events

If two events A and B are mutually exclusive (*i.e.,* only one of them can occur at a time) and P (A) and P (B) are the probabilities of occurrence of A and B, respectively; then

$$P(A \cup B) = P(A) + P(B)$$

Multiplication Rule of Probability

The probability of simultaneous happening of two events A and B is given by :

$$P(A \cap B) = P(A) \,.\, P(B/A) \;;\; P(A)\ 0$$

or $$P(B \cap A) = P(B) \,.\, P(A/B) \;;\; P(B)\ 0$$

where P (B/A) is the conditional probability of happening of B under the condition that A has happened and P (A/B) is the conditional probability of happening of A under the condition that B has happened.

Remark—*Multiplicative Rule for Independent Events.*

If A and B are independent so that the probability of occurrence or non-occurrence of A is not affected by the occurrence or non-occurrence of B, we have

$$P(A/B) = P(A) \text{ and } P(B/A) = P(B)$$

Hence

$$P(A \cap B) = P(A) \,.\, P(B)$$

Thus, the probability of simultaneous happening of two independent events is equal to the product of their individual probabilities.

Generalisation

The multiplication law of probability can be extended to more than two events. Thus, for these events A, B and C we have

$$P(A \cap B \cap C) = P(A).\ P(B/A)\ P(C/A \cap B)$$

In particular, if A, B and C are *independent events* then

$$P(A \cap B \cap C) = P(A) \,.\, P(B) \,.\, P(C)$$

i.e., the probability of the simultaneous happening of n independent events is equal to the product of their individual probabilities.

Theorem:

$$P(\overline{A}) = 1 - P(A)$$

where

$P(\overline{A})$ = Probability of event A does not happen
P (A) = Probability of event A happens

Theorem:

(i) $P(\overline{A} \cap B) = P(B) - P(A \cap B)$

where $P(\overline{A} \cap B)$ = Probability of A does not happen but B happens

(ii) $P(A \cap \overline{B}) = P(A) - P(A \cap B)$

(iii) $P(\overline{A} \cap \overline{B}) = 1 - P(A \cup B)$

$= 1 - [P(A) + P(B) - P(A \cap B)]$

$= 1 - P(A) - P(B) + P(A \cap B)]$

where A and B are independent event.

$P(A \cap B) = P(A) . P(B)$

$P(\overline{A} \cap \overline{B}) = 1 - P(A) - P(B) + P(A) .P(B)$

$= 1 - P(A) - P(B) [1 - P(A)]$

$= [1 - P(A)] [1 - P(B)]$

$= P(\overline{A}).P(\overline{B})$

Examples 1. A card is drawn from a well shuffled pack of playing cards. Find the probability that it is either a diamond or a king.

Solution. Let A denote the event of drawing a diamond and B denote the event of drawing a king from a pack of cards.

Then we have

$$P(A) = \frac{13}{52} = \frac{1}{4}$$

and $$P(B) = \frac{4}{52} = \frac{1}{13}$$

and we want $P(A \cup B)$

Now $P(A \cup B) = P(A) + P(B) - P(A \cap B)$

$$= \frac{1}{4} + \frac{1}{3} - P(A \cap B) \quad ...(i)$$

There is only one case favourable to the event $A \cap B$, namely, king of diamond. Hence

$$P(A \cap B) = \frac{1}{52}$$

Substituting in *(i)*, we get

$$= \frac{1}{4} + \frac{1}{13} - \frac{1}{52} = \frac{13+4-1}{52} = \frac{16}{52} = \frac{4}{13}$$

2. In a certain college, the students engage in various sports in the following proportions:

Football (F) : 60% of all students

Basket ball (B) : 50% of all students

Both Football and Basketball : 30% of all students.

If a student is selected at random, what is the probability that he will:

(i) play football or basketball?

(ii) play neither sports?

Solution: Let A denote the event that the student is engaged in Football and B denote the event that he is engaged in Basketball. Then we are given;

$$P(A) = 0.60$$
$$P(B) = 0.50$$

and $$P(A \cap B) = 0.30$$

(i) The probability that a student selected at random plays Football or Basketball is given by:

$$P(A \cup B) = P(A) + P(B) - P(A \cap B)$$
$$= 0.60 + 0.50 - 0.30 = 0.80$$

(ii) The probability that the student plays neither Football nor Basketball is given by:

$P(\overline{A} \cap \overline{B}) = 1 - P$ [the plays at least one of the two games]

$= 1 - 0.80 = 0.20$

3. Probability that a man will be alive 25 years hence is 0.3 and the probability that his wife will be alive 25 years hence is 0.4. Find the probability that 25 years hence.

(i) both will be alive

(ii) only the man will be alive

(iii) only the woman will be alive

(iv) at least one of them will be alive

Solution. Let us define the following events:

A: The man will be alive 25 years hence,

B: His wife will be alive 25 years hence,

we are given

$P(A) = 0.3$

and $P(B) = 0.4$

(i) The probability that 25 years hence both man and his wife will be alive is

$$P(A \cap B) = P(A) . P(B)$$

(A and B are independent)

$= 0.3 \times 0.4 = 0.12$

(ii) The probability that 25 years hence only the man will be alive is

$$P(A \cap \overline{B}) = P(A) \cdot P(\overline{B})$$
$$= P(A) \cdot [1 - P(B)]$$
$$= 0.3 \times (1 - 0.4) = 0.3 \times 0.6 = 0.18$$

(iii) The probability that only the woman will be alive 25 years hence is

$$P(\overline{A} \cap \overline{B}) = P(\overline{A}) \times P(\overline{B})$$
$$= [1 - P(A)] \times P(B)$$
$$= (1 - 0.3) \times 0.4 = 0.7 \times 0.4 = 0.28$$

(iv) The probability 'p' that 25 years hence at least one of them will be alive is

$$p = 1 - P \text{ (None will be alive)}$$
$$= 1 - P(\overline{A} \cap \overline{B})$$
$$= 1 - P(\overline{A}) \times P(\overline{B})$$
$$= 1 - (1 - 0.3) \times (1 - 0.4)$$
$$= 1 - 0.7 \times 0.6 = 1 - 0.42 = 0.58$$

4. The probability that a person stopping at a petrol pump will get his tyres checked is 0.12, the probability that he will get his oil checked is 0.29, and the probability that he will get both checked is 0.07.

(i) What is the probability that a person stopping at this pump will have neither his tyres nor oil checked?

(ii) Find the probability that a person who has his oil checked will also have his tyres checked.

Solution. Let A denote the event that a person stopping at a petrol pump will have his tyres checked, and B denote the event that he will get his oil checked. Then we are given:

$$P(A) = 0.12$$
$$P(B) = 0.29$$
$$P(A \cap B) = 0.07$$

(i) The probability that a person stopping at this pump will have neither his tyres nor oil checked is given by:

$$P(\overline{A} \cap \overline{B}) = 1 - P(A \cup B)$$
$$= 1 - [P(A) + P(B) - P(A \cap B)]$$
$$= 1 - (0.12 + 0.29 - 0.07)$$
$$= 1 - 0.34 = 0.66$$

(ii) Required probability = P (A/B)

$$= \frac{P(A \cap B)}{P(B)} = \frac{0.07}{o.29} = 0.24$$

5. There are 5 white and 7 red balls in a bag. A ball is drawn and then replaced. What is the probability that a white and a red ball are drawn in that order?

What would be the probability if the balls drawn were not put back into the bag?

Solution: Let A denote the event of drawing a white ball and B denote the event of drawing a red ball.

Balls drawn with replacement—If the drawn ball is replaced before the 2nd draw is not affected by the result of the 2nd draw. In other words, A and B are independent events and hence the probability of drawing a white ball and then a red ball in that order is given by:

$$P(A \cap B) = P(A) \cdot P(B)$$
$$= \frac{5}{12} \times \frac{7}{12} = \frac{35}{144}$$

Balls drawn without replacement—If the drawn ball is not replaced before the 2nd draw, then the events A and B are not independent.

$$P(A \cap B) = P(A) \cdot P(B/A) \quad ...(i)$$

For the 2nd draw, the total number of balls left in the bag is 12 – 1 = 11 and

∴ P (B/A) = P (drawing a red ball when there are 4 white and 7 red balls)

$$= \frac{7}{11}$$

Hence from *(i)*

$$P(A \cap B) = P(A) \cdot P(B/A)$$
$$= \frac{5}{12} \cdot \frac{7}{11} = \frac{35}{132}$$

Mathematical Expectation

If x is a random variable which can assume any one of the values $x_1, x_2, ... x_n$ with respective probabilities $p_1, p_2 .... p_n$ there the mathematical expectation of x usuall called the expected value of x and denoted by E (x) is defined as:

$$E(x) = p_1 x_1 + p_2 x_2 + ... + p_n x_n = \Sigma p.x$$

where

$$\Sigma p_i = p_1 + p_2 + ... p_n = 1$$

More precisely, if x is a random variable with probability distribution $\{x, p(x)\}$, Hence

$$E(x) = \Sigma x \cdot p(x)$$

Remark.

Mathematical expectation of a random variable is nothing but its arithmetic mean.

Theorems on Expectation

Theorem-1

$$E(c) = C$$

where c is a constant

Proof: —we have

$$E(c) = \text{Mean of } c$$

$$= \frac{c+c+c+....+c}{n} = \frac{nc}{n} = c$$

Theorem-2

$$E(cx) = C\,E(x)$$

where c is a constant

Theorem-3

$$E(ax \times b) = a\,E(x) + b$$

where a and b are constants.

***Theorem-4.* Addition Rule of Expectation**

If X and Y are random variables, then

$$E(X + Y) = E(X) + E(Y)$$

i.e., Expected value of the sum of two random variables is equal to the sum of their expected values.

Corollary

$$E(ax - by) = AE(X) + bE(Y)$$

when a and b are constants.

Theorem—5 (Multiplication Rule of Expectation)

If X and Y are independent random variables, then

$$E(XY) = E(X)\,.\,E(Y)$$

i.e., the expected value of the product of two independent random variables is equal to the product of their expected values.

Binomial Distribution

Suppose the variable under study is measured in such a way that each observation can be classified into two categories. For example, if a coin is tossed, the result of each throw can be either a head or a tail. Similarly, if a die is thrown we may call getting 5 or 6 a 'success' and getting 1, 2, 3 or 4 a 'failure'. If data on income of households are collected, we may classify each household as 'poor' or 'Not – Poor' on the basis of its income. For example, if the household monthly income is less than or equal to Rs. 500/– it may be classified as 'Poor' and if it is more than Rs.500/– we may call it 'Not – Poor.'

In Binomial Distribution it is necessary that each observation is classified into only two categories.

For the sake of convenience we name them two categories as *'success'* and 'failure'.

In Binomial distribution it is necessary that the probability of success (failure) remains the same for each observation or in each trial. Thus the probability of getting head (or tail) must remain the same in each toss; similarly, in case of the die throwing experiment the probability of success (*i.e.,* getting 5 or 6) must remain the same in each throw.

If the probability of success (or failure) changes from trial to trial or if the results of each trial are classified into more than two categories, then the Binomial distribution cannot be used.

Another condition underlying the Binomial distribution is that the trials (or individual observations) should be independent of each other

If n independent observations (or n independent trials) are made, the result of each trial is classified into two categories called 'success' and 'failure' and the probability of success is the same for each observation or in each trial, then the probability of getting x successes in n trials is equal to

$$\frac{n!}{x!(n-x)!}p^x q^{n-x}$$

where

p = probability of success in a single trial

q = probability of failure in a single trial.

and $p + q = 1$

Remark

Putting $x = 0, 1, 2,.......n$ in above equation we get the probabilities of 0, 1, 2, 3,......n successes respectively in n trials, which are tabulated below:

The Binomial Distribution

Numbers of Successes x	*Probability*
0	q^n
1	$n\,q^{n-1}$
2	$\frac{n(n-1)}{2-1}q^{n-2}p^2$
⋮	⋮

x	$\frac{n(n-1)...(n-x+1)}{x(x-1)...3.2.1} q^{n-x} p^x$
$\vdots$	$\vdots$
n	p^n
Total	1

It should be noted that

1. The variable x (number of success) is discrete it can take only the integral values 0, 1, 2, ..., n.
2. The probabilities specified above
$$q^n, nq^{n-1} p, ... p^n$$
are in fact successive terms in the Binomial Expansion of $(q+p)^n$.
3. The sum of binomial coefficient is 2^n.
4. For n trials the binomial probability distribution consists of $(n+1)$ terms.

For Binomial Distribution

1. *Mean* $= n\,p$
2. *Variance* $= (\text{s.d.})^2 = npq$
3. *Third moments* $\mu_3 = npq\,(q-p)$
4. *Fourth moments* $\mu_4 = npq\,[1 + 3pq\,(n-2)]$
5. *Moment coefficient of Skewness is*
$$\beta_1 = \frac{(q-p)^2}{npq}$$
6. *Coefficient of Kurtosis is*
$$\beta_2 = 3 + \frac{1-6pq}{npq}$$

Remarks

1. Since q is the probability (of failure), we always have $0 < q < 1$.
Variance $= np \times q < np \qquad (\because 0 < q < 1)$
$\Rightarrow \qquad$ Variance < Mean
Hence for the Binomial distribution variance is less than mean.
2. Binomial distribution is symmetrical if $p = q$ $0.5 = \frac{1}{2}$. It is positively Skewed if $p < 0.5$ and negatively Skewed if $p > 0.5$.

Examples 1. comment on the following:

For a binomial distribution, mean = 7 and variance = 11

Solution: For a binomial distribution with parameters n and p,

$$\text{Mean} = np = 7 \qquad ... (1)$$
$$\text{and variance} = npq = 11 \qquad ... (2)$$

Dividing (2) by (1), we get

$$q = \frac{11}{7} = 1.6$$

which is impossible, since q being the propability must lie between 0 and 1. Hence, the given statement is wrong.

2. If the probability of a defective bolt is 1/10, find (*i*) the mean; (*ii*) variance; (*iii*) moment coefficient of Skewness; (*iv*) Kurtosis, for the distribution of defective bolts in a total of 400.

Solution: In the usual notations, we have

$$n = 400,\ p = \frac{1}{10} = 0.1,$$
$$q = 1 - p = 0.9$$

According to Binomial Probability law:

(*i*) Mean $= np$
$= 400 \times 0.1 = 40$

(*ii*) Variance $= npq$
$= 400 \times 0.1 \times 0.9$

(*iii*) The moment coefficient of Skewness

$$\beta_1 = \frac{(q-p)^2}{npq}$$

$$= \frac{(0.8)^2}{36} = \frac{0.64}{36} = 0.1777 = 0.018$$

$$\gamma_1 = \pm\sqrt{\beta_1} = \sqrt{0.018} = 0.134$$

(*iv*) Coefficient of Kurtosis is given by:

$$\beta_2 = 3 + \frac{1-6pq}{npq}$$

$$= 3 + \frac{1 - 6 \times 0.1 \times 0.9}{36}$$

$$= 3 + \frac{0.46}{36} = 3 + 0.013 = 3.013$$

Remarks

Since, the distribution is not symmetrical. But since it is nearly zero, it is moderately symmetrical. $\beta_2 > 3$ implies that the distribution is platy Kurtic.

Poisson Distribution (As a Limiting Case of Binomial Distribution)

Poisson distribution was derived in1837 by *Simon D. Poisson.* Poisson distribution may be obtained as a limiting case of Binomial probability distribution under the following conditions:

(i) n, the number of trials is indefinitely large

(ii) p, the constant probability of success for each trial is indefinitely small, *i.e.,* $p \to 0$.

(iii) $np = m$ is finite

Under the conditions given above the probability of getting x successes is

$$\frac{e^{-n}.m^x}{x!} \qquad ...(i)$$

where $x = 0, 1, 2, 3.........$

m = mean = np

$e = 2.71828$

and $x! = x(x-1)(x-2) ... \times 3 \times 2 \times 1$.

Remarks

1. Poisson distribution is a discrete probability distribution, since the variable can take only integral values 0, 1, 2,... ∞
2. Putting $x = 0, 1, 2, 3$....in *(i)* we obtain the probabilities of 0, 1, 2, 3..., successes respectively, which are tabulated below:

Poisson Distribution

No. of Successes (x)	Probability $p(x)$
0	e^{-m}
1	$\frac{e^{-m}.m}{1!}$
2	$\frac{e^{-m}.m^2}{2!}$
3	$\frac{e^{-m}.m^3}{3!}$
⋮	⋮
x	$\frac{e^{-m}.m^x}{x!}$
⋮	⋮
Total	1

3. If we know m, all the probabilities of the Poisson distribution can be obtained. m is, therefore, called the parameter of the Poisson distribution.

Constants of Poisson Distribution

The mean of Poisson distribution

Mean = $m = np$

and the Variance = m = mean

Hence for the Poisson distribution with parameter m, we have

Mean = Variance = m

i.e., mean and variance are equal, each being equal to the parameter m.

Other Constants : The moments (about mean) of the Poisson distribution are:

$\mu_1 = 0$

μ_2 = Variance = m

$\mu_3 = m$

$\mu_4 = m + 3m^2$

Hence, $$\beta_1 = \frac{(\mu_3)^2}{(\mu_2)^3} = \frac{m^2}{m^3} = \frac{1}{m}$$

and $$\beta_2 = \frac{\mu_4}{\mu_2^2} = \frac{m+3m^2}{m^2} = 3+\frac{1}{m}$$

Remarks

1. As $m \to \infty$, $\beta_1 \to 0$ and $\beta_2 \to 3$
2. Since $\mu_3 = m > 0$, from above equation we observe that $\beta_1 > 0$. This means that Poisson distribution is a positively Skewed distribution. As the value of the parameter m increases, β_1 decreases and thus Skewness is reduced for increasing values of m. In particular as $m \to \infty$ (large values of m), $\beta_1 \to 0$ and consequently the distribution tendes to be symmetrical for large m.

Mode of Poisson Distribution

The Poisson distribution has mode at X = x, if P (x) > P $(x-1)$ and P (x) > P $(x+1)$.

Case 1. ***When m is an integer.*** If m is an integer, equal to K, (say), then the Poisson distribution is bi-modal, the two modes being at the points X = k and X = k –1.

Case 2. ***When m is not an integer.*** If m is not an integer than the distribution is unimodal, the unique modal value being the integral part of m. For example, if m = 5.6, then mode is 5, the integral part of 5.6.

Utility or Importance of Poisson Distribution

The conditions under which Poisson distribution is obtained as a limiting case of the Binomial distribution and also the conditions for the general model underlying. Poisson distribution suggest that Poisson distribution can be used to explain the behaviour of the discrete random variables where the probability of occurrence of the event is very small and the total number of possible cases is sufficiently large. We give below some practical situations where Poisson distribution can be used:

(i) Number of accidents taking place per day on a busy road.

(ii) The number of suicides reported in a particular day or the number of casualties due to a rare disease such as heart attack or cancer or snake bite in a year.

(iii) The number of defective material in a packing manufactured by a good concern.

(iv) To count the number of radio-active disintegrations of a radio-active element per unit of time.

Example 1. Comment on the following:

For a Poisson distribution,

Mean = 8 and Variance = 7

Solution. The given statement is wrong, since for a Poisson distribution mean and variance are equal.

Normal Distribution

Normal distribution is one of the most important continuous theoretical distributions in statistics. Most of the data relating to economic and business statistics or even in social and physical sciences conform to this distribution.

Normal Curve

The $$y = \frac{1}{\sigma\sqrt{2\pi}} e^{-\frac{1}{2}\frac{(x-m)^2}{\sigma^2}}$$

is called the Normal Curve.

where

m = Mean

σ^2 = Standard deviation

As a special case, we may write $m = 0$ and $\sigma^2 = 1$ then

$$y = \frac{1}{\sqrt{2\pi}} e^{-\frac{1}{2}x^2}$$

is the standard Normal Curve (S.N.C.).

Remark

If X is a random variable following normal distribution with mean m and standard deviation σ, then the random variable Z defined as follows:

$$Z = \frac{X - E(X)}{\sigma_x} = \frac{X - m}{\sigma}$$

is called the standard normal variate (S.N.V.), we have

$$E(Z) = E\left(\frac{X-m}{\sigma}\right)$$

$$= \frac{1}{\sigma}E(X-m) \quad \because E(cx) = CE(x)$$

$$[E(x) = E(x)]$$

$$= \frac{1}{\sigma}E(x) - E(m)$$

$$= \frac{1}{\sigma}[m-m] = 0$$

$$Var(Z) = Var\left(\frac{x-m}{\sigma}\right)$$

$$= \frac{1}{\sigma^2}Var(x-m)$$

$$[Var(cx) = c^2\ Var(x)]$$

$$= \frac{1}{\sigma^2}.Var(x)$$

because variance is independent of the change of origin.

$$\therefore \quad Var(Z) = \frac{1}{\sigma^2}\sigma^2 = 1$$

Therefore, *the standard normal variate (S.N.V.) Z has mean 0 and standard deviation* 1.

Properties of Normal Distribution

1. If the parameters m and σ^2 of the normal curve are specified, the normal curve is fully determined and we can draw it by obtaining the value of (y) corresponding to different values of x – the abscissa.

we note that the normal curve

$$y = \frac{1}{\sigma\sqrt{2\pi}} e^{-\frac{1}{2}\frac{(x-m)^2}{\sigma^2}}$$

is bell-shaped and it is symmetric about the Straight line $x = m$.

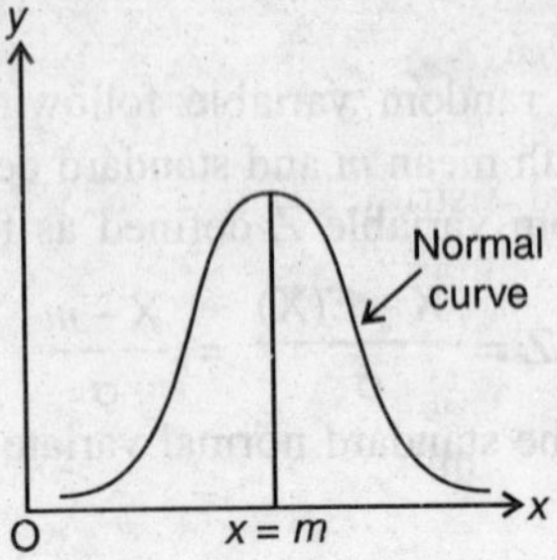

Fig. 15

2. The normal curve tends to touch the x-axis only at infinity, *i.e.*, the x-axis is an 'asymptote' to the normal curve. It is a continuous curve stretching from $-\infty$ to $+\infty$.
3. Since the distribution is symmetrical, mean, median and mode coincide. Thus,
Mean = Median = Mode = m
4. Since Mean = Median = m, the ordinate at $x = m$, divides the whole area into two equal parts. Further, since total area under normal curve is 1, the area to the right of the ordinate as well as to the left of the ordinate at $x = m$ is 0.5.
5. Also, by virtue of symmetry the quartiles are equidistant from median (m) *i.e.*,
$Q_3 - M_d = M_d - Q_1 \Rightarrow Q_1 + Q_3 = 2M_d = 2M$
6. Since the distribution is symmetrical, the moment coefficient of Skewness is given by:
$$\beta_1 = 0$$
7. The coefficient of Kurtosis is given by:
$$\beta_2 = 3$$
8. No portion of the curve lies below the x-axis.
9. Theoretically, the range of the distribution is from $-\infty$ to ∞. But practically, Range = σ_σ.
10. Since the distribution is symmetrical, all moments of odd order about the mean are zero. Thus
$$\mu_1 = \mu_3 = \mu_5 = \ldots = 0$$
11. X-axis is an asymptote to the curve, *i.e.*, for numerically large value of x (on either side of the point $x = m$), the curve becomes parallel, to the x-axis and is supposed to meet it at infinity.
12. Points of inflexion of the normal curve are at $x = m\ \sigma$ and $x = m - \sigma$.
At the point of inflexion the tangent changes its sign.
13. **Area Property**—One of the most fundamental properties of the normal probability curve is the area property. The area under the normal curve between the ordinates at $x = m - \sigma$ and $x = m + \sigma$ is 0.6826. In other words, the range covers 68.26% of the observations.

The area under the normal probability curve between the ordinates at $x = m - 3\sigma$ and $x = m + 3\sigma$ is 0.9973, *i.e.*, the range $m \pm 3\sigma$ covers 99.73% of the observations. Hence, for practical purposes, the range $m \pm 3\sigma$ covers the entire area, which is 1.

Areas Under Normal Curve

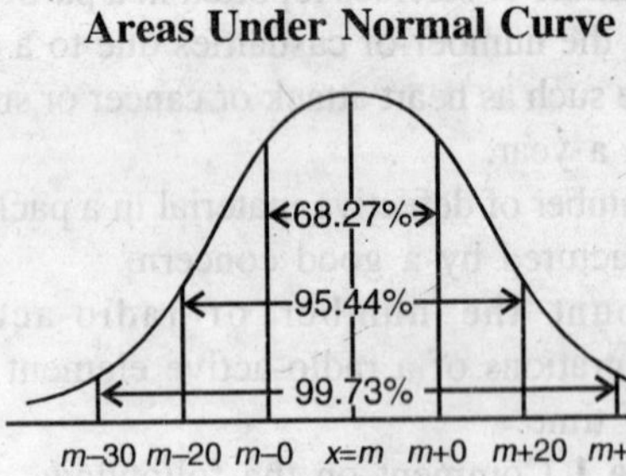

Fig. 16

Importance of Normal Distribution

Normal distribution has occupied a very important role in statistics. We enumerate below some of its important applications.

1. Most of the discrete probability distributions (*e.g.*, Binomial distribution, Poisson distribution) tend to normal distribution as n the number of trials increases. For large values of n, computation of probability for discrete distributions becomes quite tedious and time consuming. In such cases, normal distribution can be used with great ease and convenience.
2. Almost all the exact sampling distributions *e.g.*, student's t – distribution, Snedecor's F-distribution, Fisher's Z-distribution and the Chi square distribution conform to normal distribution for large degrees of freedom (*i.e.*, as).
3. The whole theory of exact sample (small sample) tests, namely, t, F, ϕ^2 tests, etc., is

based on the fundamental assumption that the parent population from which the samples have been drawn follows Normal distribution.

4. Perhaps, one of the most important applications of the Normal distribution is inherent in one of the most fundamental theorems in the theory of statistics, namely, the Central Limit Theorem.
5. If X is a normal variate with mean m and variance σ^2, then we have proved that $P(m - 3\sigma < X < m + 3\sigma) = P(-3 < z < 3) = 0.9973$

$\Rightarrow P[|z| > 3] = 1 - 0.9973 = 0.0027$

Thus, the probability of standard normal variate going outside the limits 3 is practically zero. In other words, in all probability we should expect a standard normal variate to lie between the limits 3. This property of the normal distribution forms the basis of entire large sample theory.

6. Normal distribution is used in Statistical Quality Control in Industry for the setting of control limits.

MULTIPLE CHOICE QUESTIONS

1. X measures Wages in Rupees
- A. Unit of its average is Rs. and unit of variance is Rs.
- B. Unit of its average is Rs. and unit of variance is Rs. square
- C. Unit of its average is Rs. but variance does not have any unit
- D. Unit of its average is Rs. but unit of variance is square not of Rs.

2. In order to apply correctly the χ^2-test for goodness of fit, which of the following assumption is correct?
- A. The observed and theoretical distribution contain the same number of elements
- B. No expected frequency be less than five
- C. The observed values are taken from a random sample
- D. All of the above

3. If a boy cycles 8 km at the speed of 8 km per hour, and walks another 8 km at the speed of 2 km per hour. His average speed per hour is
- A. 5 km B. $\frac{16}{5}$ km
- C. 4 km D. 6 km

4. Two events are said to be independent, as per the theory of probability, if the occurrence of one
- A. affects the probability of another
- B. does not affect the probability of another
- C. prevents the occurrence of another
- D. makes the probability of occurrence of other as zero.

5. The Fisher index number is
- A. GM of Laspeyres and Paasche index numbers
- B. AM of Laspeyres and Paasche index numbers
- C. HM of Laspeyres and Paasche index numbers
- D. GM of Laspeyres and Marshall-Edgeworth index numbers

6. Given the following numbers
2, 8, 6, 5, 0, 9, 7, 11.
The product of their arithmetic and geometric means is
- A. 64 B. 16
- C. 0 D. 6

7. Given the following two regression equations
$y - 0.5 = \beta_1 x$
$x + 10 = \beta_2 y$
then the coefficient of correlation between x and y is
- A. $\sqrt{\beta_1 \beta_2}$ B. $\sqrt{\beta_1 \beta_2} + 0.5$
- C. $\sqrt{\beta_1 \beta_2} + 10.0$ D. $\sqrt{\beta_1 \beta_2}$

8. A commuter drives 10 miles on first day at a speed of 60 km/hour, the second day at 15 km/hour and third day 10 km/hour. The mean speed of the commuter is
- A. 16.32 B. 42.50
- C. 36.35 D. 22.10

9. The sum of squares of deviation of 20 observations from their mean is 720 and the mean is 60. The coefficient of vatriation is

A. 5% B. 10%
C. 15% D. 20%

10. If x is a random variable and 'a' and 'b' are constants, then Var $(ax + b)$ is

A. $(a + b)$ Var (x) B. $(a^2 + b^2)$ Var (x)
C. ab Var (x) D. a^2 Var (x)

11. The probability of drawing a 'spade' from a well shuffled pack of cards is

A. $\frac{1}{52}$ B. $\frac{4}{52}$
C. $\frac{1}{4}$ D. $\frac{2}{3}$

12. The coefficient of correlation between two series x and y is found to be 0.80. If all the values of x and y are reduced by 50 per cent, the correlation coefficient will be

A. 0.80 B. 0.40
C. 0.60 D. 0.20

13. For a Poisson's distribution with $n = 200$, $p = 0.02$, the mean is

A. 20 B. 40
C. 4 D. 10

14. The value of χ^2 in a 2 × 4 contingency table is computed as 4.0. The Null hypothesis that then no associationship will be accepted at 5% level of significance, if this computed value is less than or equal to the value of χ^2 from the table at ..... degrees of freedom.

A. 8 B. 6
C. 4 D. 3

15. The significance of the difference between two means of the populations, when σ^2 values are known and equal, is tested by

A. Z-test B. t-test
C. F-test D. χ^2-test

16. The portion of the total area covered in a normal curve under $\bar{x} \pm 2.54\,\sigma$ is

A. 85% B. 95%
C. 99% D. 90%

17. If A and B are dependent events, then

A. $P(A/B) = \frac{P(A).P(B/A)}{P(A)}$

B. $P(A/B) = P(A).P(B/A)$

C. $P(A/B) = P(B).P(A/B)$

D. $P(A/B) = \frac{P(A).P(B/A)}{P(B)}$

18. Arithmetic mean of earning of 42 workers in a factory is Rs. 1200 per month. On account of price rise, the workers managed to get 10% hike in their earnings. In addition to this, the management paid Rs. 100 per month to each employee as bonus. The arithmetic mean of total earning of the workers after these changes will be

A. Rs. 1300 B. Rs. 1320
C. Rs. 1420 D. Rs. 1510

19. If the Karl Pearson coefficient of correlation between x and y is 0.3, then the coefficient of correlation between—x and $2y$ is

A. –0.6 B. –0.3
C. 0.3 D. 0.5

20. The arithmetic mean of series 'A' is twice that of series 'B' and the standard deviation of series 'B' is twice that of series 'A'. The coefficient of variation of series 'A' in relation to that of series 'B' will be

A. 1/4 B. 1/2
C. same D. twice

21. The sum of squared deviation is the least when taken from

A. mode B. median
C. arithmetic mean D. geometric mean

22. Suppose the average weight of 9 persons is 50 kg. Average weight of the first 5 persons is 45 kg, whereas average weight of the last 5 persons is 55 kg. Then the weight of the 5th member will be

A. 45. 0 kg B. 47.5 kg
C. 50.0 kg D. 52.5 kg

23. Which one of the following statistical measures is NOT affected by extremely large or small values?

A. Median
B. Harmonic mean
C. Standard deviation
D. Coefficient of variation

24. Given is the following distribution of two variables x and y:

x :	1	2	3	4	5
y :	3	4	5	6	7

The standard deviation of y is
A. Same as standard deviation of x
B. (the standard deviation of x) × 2
C. (the standard deviation of x) + 2
D. (the standard deviation of x) – 2

25. The standard deviation of six numbers 3, 3, 3, 5, 5, 5 is
A. 1
B. 4
C. 0
D. Cannot be obtained since the unit of measurement is not given

26. If for a sample data: Mean < Median < Mode, then the distribution is
A. skewed to the right
B. symmetric
C. skewed to the left
D. neither symmetric nor skewed

27. Let $x = \frac{9-U}{3}$ and $y = V - 4$ and the correlation coefficient between U and V is – 0.93. Then the correlation coefficient between x and y will be
A. 0.093 B. –0.093
C. –0.93 D. cannot be derived

28. Which one of the following statements is NOT correct?
Fisher's index
A. lies between Laspeyres's index (L) and Paasche's index (P)
B. is the arithmetic mean of L and P
C. is the geometric mean of L and P
D. is equal to L or P if L = P

29. Consider the following statements:
1. Quartile deviation is more instructive range as it discards the dispersion of extreme items
2. Coefficient of quartile deviation cannot be used to compare the degree of variations in different distributions
3. There are 10 deciles for a series

Which of the above statements is/are correct?
A. 1, 2 and 3 B. 2 alone
C. 3 alone D. 1 alone

30. Which one of the following indices satisfies both time reversal and factor reversal tests?
A. Laspeyres' index B. Fisher's index
C. Paasche's index D. Keely's index

31. Given the following data – 1, 2, 3, 4 and 100; the best measure of central tendency is the
A. arithmetic mean B. median
C. mode D. geometric mean

32. If for a given data, mode = 5, median = 15 and mean = 20, it means that the sample data is
A. skewed to the right
B. skewed to the left
C. symmetric
D. neither symmetric nor skewed

33. Consider the following statements:
1. Correlation analysis helps in determining the relationship between two or more variables—it does not tell us anything about the cause and effect relationship
2. The ratio of explained variation to the total variation is called the coefficient of correlation
3. Pearsonian coefficient always assumes linear relationship and is unduly effected by the extreme items

Which of the above statements is/are correct?
A. 2 alone B. 1 and 2
C. 1 and 3 D. 2 and 3

34. The right-hand tail of a frequency distribution is found to the mirror image of the left-hand tail. The distribution is
A. positively skewed B. negatively skewed
C. asymmetric D. symmetric

35. From the cumulative frequency diagram which one of the following types of average can be estimated?
A. Geometric Mean B. Harmonic Mean
C. Median D. Mode

36. During one year the ratio of prices of two commodities is 3, whereas during the next year it is 2. For averaging these ratios
A. arithmetic mean is most appropriate
B. harmonic mean is most appropriate
C. geometric mean is most appropriate
D. all the three, arithmetic, harmonic and geometric means are equally appropriate

37. Consider the following statements:

1. Median is not useful while dealing with skewed distribution such as income distribution or price distribution

2. Median can be determined graphically by drawing only one ogive

3. Mode can be used to describe qualitative phenomenon

Which of the above statements are correct?

A. 1 and 2 B. 1 and 3
C. 2 and 3 D. 1, 2 and 3

38. The following equation indicates the relationship among average median and mode:

A. Mode = 3 Median – 2 Mean
B. Mean = 2 Mode – 3 Median
C. Median = 3 Mean – 2 Mode
D. None of these

39. What is the median of 36, 72, 49, 45, 60, 33, 61, 72, 52?

A. 33 B. 52
C. 61 D. 60

40. In a moderately asymmetrical distribution.

A. A.M. > G.M > H.M
B. A.M. < G.M < H.M
C. A.M < G.M > H.M
D. None of these

41. The geometric mean of 8,64 and 512 is

A. 194 B. 64
C. 16 D. None of these

42. The points of intersection of the 'less than' and the 'more than' ogives correspond to

A. mean B. median
C. geometric mean D. None of these

43. Histogram is useful to determine graphically the value of:

A. arithmetic mean B. median
C. mode D. None of these

44. In a series of values if one value is zero, G.M. is

A. positive B. zero
C. indeterminate D. None of these

45. The sum of squared deviations is minimum when taken from

A. mean B. median
C. mode D. None of these

46. Coefficient of quartile deviation is calculated by the formula

A. $\frac{Q_3 + Q_1}{4}$ B. $\frac{Q_3 + Q_1}{2}$

C. $\frac{Q_3 - Q_1}{Q_3 + Q_1}$ D. $\frac{Q_3 + Q_1}{Q_3 - Q_1}$

47. Mean ± 3 σ covers

A. 99.37% items B. 90% items
C. 99.9% items D. 99.73% items

48. Quartile deviation is

A. $\frac{4}{5}\sigma$ B. $\frac{3}{2}\sigma$

C. $\frac{2}{3}\sigma$ D. $\frac{5}{4}\sigma$

49. Coefficient of variation is calculated by the formula:

A. $\frac{\bar{x}}{\sigma} \times 100$ B. $\frac{\sigma}{\bar{x}} \times 100$

C. $\frac{\bar{x}}{\sigma}$ D. $\frac{\sigma}{\bar{x}}$

50. The measure of variation that is least effected by extreme observations is

A. Range B. Mean deviation
C. Standard deviation D. Quartile deviation

51. When coefficient of skewness is zero the distribution is

A. J-shaped B. U-shaped
C. Symmetrical D. L-shaped

52. When $\beta_2 < 3$ the distribution is

A. Leptokurtic B. Platykurtic
C. Mesokurtic D. None of these

53. The second moment about mean is

A. $\frac{\Sigma(x-\bar{x})^2}{N}$ B. $\frac{(x-\bar{x})^3}{N}$

C. $\frac{(x-\bar{x})^2}{N}$ D. None of these

54. In a negatively skewed distribution

A. Mode > Median > Mean
B. Median > Mode > Mean
C. Mode < Median < Mean
D. None of these

55. Karl Pearson's coefficient of skewness is... Bowley's coefficient of skewness for any skewed distribution.

A. equal to B. less than
C. greater than D. not related to

56. If a frequency distribution is positively skewed, the mean of the distribution is:

A. greater than the mode
B. less than the mode
C. equal to the mode
D. none of these

57. When coefficient of skewness is negative
A. $Q_2 + Q_3 = 2Q_1$ B. $Q_3 + Q_1 < 2Q_2$
C. $Q_3 + Q_1 > 2Q_2$ D. $Q_3 + Q_2 < 2Q_1$

58. The coeficient of correlation is independent of change of
A. Origin B. Scale
C. Both A and B D. None of these

59. The coefficient of correlation
A. has no limits
B. can be less than one
C. can be more than one
D. varies between ± 1

60. Probable error is
A. 0.6745 S.E. B. 0.6457 S.E.
C. 0.6753 S.E. D. 0.7645 S.E.

61. Coefficient of determination is defined as
A. r^3 B. $1 - r^2$
C. $1 + r^2$ D. r^2

62. If sum of the product of deviations of x and y series from their means, *i.e.*, Σxy is zero, the coefficient of correlation shall be
A. +1 B. 0
C. –1 D. none of these

63. Mention the correct answers.
The ranks according to two attributes in a sample are given below:
R_1 1 2 3 4 5
R_2 5 4 3 2 1
The rank correlation between them is
A. 0 B. +1
C. –1 D. None of these

64. If both the regression coefficients are negative, the correlation coefficient would be...
A. negative B. positive
C. zero D. none of these

65. The under root of two... coefficients gives us the value of correlation coefficient.
A. regression B. S.E
C. S.D D. None of these

66. Both the regression coefficients cannot be
A. less than one B. greater than one
C. equal to one D. none of these

67. The regression lines cut each other at the point of
A. average of x and y B. average of x only
C. average of y only D. none of them

68. Regression coefficient is independent of change of
A. origin but not of scale
B. both origin and scale
C. scale but not of origin
D. none of these

69. There will be only one regression line in case of two variables if
A. $r = 0$ B. $r = \pm 1$
C. $r = 0.5$ D. none of them

70. When one regression coefficient is negative the other would be
A. negative B. positive
C. zero D. none of them

71. Where r is zero the regression lines but each other making an angle of
A. 45° B. 60°
C. 90° D. none of them

72. The farther the two regression lines cut each other
A. the greater will be the degree of correlation
B. the lesser will be degree of correlation
C. does not really matter
D. none of them

73. If with a rise of 10% in prices the wages are increased by 20%, the real wage increase is by
A. 10% B. more than 10%
C. less than 10% D. 20%

74. The circular test is satisfied when
A. $P_{12} \times P_{23} \times P_{31} = 0$ B. $P_{12} \times P_{32} \times P_{31} = 1$
C. $P_{12} \times P_{23} \times P_{31} = 1$ D. $P_{12} \times P_{23} \times P_{13} = 1$

75. Time reversal test is satisfied when
A. $P_{01} \times P_{10} = 0$ B. $P_{01} \times P_{10} = 1$
C. $P_{02} \times P_{10} > 1$ D. $P_{01} \times P_{10} < 1$

76. Fisher's ideal index is
A. arithmetic mean of Laspeyre's and Paasche's index
B. median of Laspeyre's and Paasche's index
C. geometric mean of Laspeyre's and Paasche's index
D. none of these

77. Laspeyre's index is based on
A. base year quantities

B. current year quantities
C. average of current and base year
D. none of these

78. A good index number is one that satisfies
A. Unit test
B. Time test
C. Time Reversal Test and Factor Reversal Test
D. None of these

79. Theoretically the best average in the construction of index number is
A. median B. geometric mean
C. mode D. arithmetic mean

80. Hostorically the first index was constructed in...
A. 1764 B. 1844
C. 1850 D. 1744

81. ... is known as the 'ideal' formula for constructing index numbers.
A. Fisher's Ideal Index
B. Laspeyre's Index
C. Paasche's Index
D. None of these

82. The most important factors causing seasonal variations are
A. growth of population
B. technological improvements
C. weather and social customs
D. change in fashions

83. The most widely used method of measuring seasonal variations is
A. Ratio-to-moving average method
B. Ratio-to-trend method
C. Link relative method
D. None of these

84. Cyclical fluctuations are caused by
A. Wars B. Earth quakes
C. Floods D. None of these

85. If E(X) is the mathematical expectation of the variable X and C is constant, then E(CX) = ?
A. EC. + E(x) B. EC. × E(x)
C. CE(x) D. None of these

86. E(x + y) = ?
A. E(x) + E(y) B. E(x) × E(y)
C. E($x.y$) D. None of these

87. If A and B are mutually exclusive events, P(AB) = ?
A. Zero B. P(A) + P(B)
C. P(A) D. None of these

88. The probability that the throw of two dice yields a total of 5 or 8 is...
A. 1/4 B. 1/5
C. 2/5 D. None of these

89. In case of conditional probability (A and B) =?
A. P(B) × P(A/B) B. P(B) × P(A)
C. P(A) + P(B) D. None of these

90. If a card is drawn from a pack of cards the probability of getting either a king or a queen is...
A. 2/13 B. 5/15
C. 1/4 D. None of these

91. If an event cannot take place, probability will be
A. +1 B. –1
C. 0 D. None of these

92. Addition theorem states that if two events A and B are mutually exclusive the probability of occurrence of either A or B is given by:
A. P(A) + P(B) B. P(A) × P(B)
C. P(A) – P(B) D. None of these

93. If two events A and B are independent, the probability that they will both occur is given by:
A. P(A) + P(B) B. P(A) × P(B)
C. P(A) – P(B) D. P(A) + P(B) – P(AB)

94. If two events A and B are dependent, the conditional probability of B given A, *i.e.*, P(A/B) is calculated as:
A. P(AB)/P(B) B. P(A) / P(B)
C. P(AB) / P(A) D. P(A) / P(AB)

95. If two events A and B are dependent, the conditinal probability of A given B, *i.e.*, P(A/B) is calculated as:
A. P(B/A)/P(AB) B. P(B)/P(A)
C. P(AB)/P(A) D. P(AB)/P(B)

96. $^5C_2$ is equal to
A. 20 B. 10
C. 30 D. 100

97. Two cards are drawn from a well-shuffled pack of 52 cards. Find the probability that they are both aces if the first is replaced.
A. $\frac{1}{169}$ B. $\frac{2}{52}$
C. $\frac{1}{221}$ D. None of these

98. The standard deviation of Binomial distribution is:

A. $\sqrt{npq}$ B. npq

C. $n^2p^2q^2$ D. np

99. The standard deviation of Poisson distribution is : (m = mean)

A. m B. $\sqrt{m}$

C. m^2 D. $1/\sqrt{m}$

100. In case of normal distribution $\bar{x} \pm 2\sigma$ covers

A. 95.45% B. 95.54%

C. 94.45% D. 99.73%

101. If in Binomial distribution mean is 10 and standard deviation 2, q will be

A. 0 B. 1

C. 0.4 D. 0.8

102. The normal distribution is an approximation to...

A. Binomial distribution

B. Poisson distribution

C. Both A and B

D. None of these

103. In a normal distribution the points of inflexion occur at...

A. $\overline{X} + \sigma$ B. $\overline{X} + 2\sigma$

C. $\overline{X} + 3\sigma$ D. None of these

104. The normal distribution with $x = 0$ and $\sigma = 1$ is known as.....

A. Standard normal distribution

B. Poisson distribution

C. Both A and B

D. None of these

105. The mean plus and minus 1.96 standard deviation includes... per cent of the items of normal distribution.

A. 75 B. 47.5

C. 74.5 D. None of these

106. ..... asserts that there is no true difference in the sample and the population in the particular matter under consideration

A. Null hypothesis B. Alternate hypothesis

C. Both A and B D. None of these

107. ..... error is committed when the hypothesis is true but out test rejects it.

A. Type I B. Type II

C. Both A and B D. None of these

108. ..... errors are made when we accept a null hypothesis which is not true.

A. Type I B. Type II

C. Both A and B D. None of these

109. The standard deviation of sampling distribution is called...

A. Standard error B. Probable error

C. Both A and B D. None of these

110. Standard error of number of successes is given by:

A. $\sqrt{\frac{pq}{n}}$ B. $\sqrt{npq}$

C. npq D. n^2p^2

111. Large sample theory is applicable when:

A. N is > 30 B. N is < 30

C. N = 30 D. None of these

112. Student's 't' Distribution was discovered by:

A. Karl Pearson B. Laplace

C. Fisher D. Gosset

113. The difference of two means in case of small samples is tested by the formula:

A. $t = \frac{\bar{x}_1 - \bar{x}_2}{s}$

B. $t = \frac{\bar{x}_1 - \bar{x}_2}{s}\sqrt{\frac{n_1 + n_2}{n_1 - n_2}}$

C. $t = \frac{\bar{x}_1 - \bar{x}_2}{s}\sqrt{\frac{n_1\, n_2}{n_1 + n_2}}$

D. None of these

114. While testing the significance of the difference of two sample means in case of small samples, the degrees of freedom is calculated by:

A. $\nu = n_1 + n_2 - 2$ B. $\nu = n_1 + n_2 - 1$

C. $\nu = n_1 - n_2 - 2$ D. $\nu = n_1 - n_2 + 2$

115. Which one of the following average can be computed from a cumulative frequency curve?

A. Geometric Mean B. Harmonic Mean

C. Mode D. Median

116. If the standard deviation of a variable x is s and if $y = a + bs$, where a and b are constants, the standard deviation of y would be

A. $a + bs$ B. bs

C. $\sqrt{b}.s$ D. b^2s

117. Which one of the following statistical measures is based on all observations?

A. Quartile Deviation B. Harmonic Mean
C. Range D. Mode

118. Consider the following measures:

1. Correlation coefficient
2. Covariance
3. Coefficient of variation
4. Index number

Which of these are unit-free?

A. 1 and 2 B. 1 and 3
C. 2 and 4 D. 1, 3 and 4

119. If r is the correlation coefficients between the two variables, then

A. $0 \le r \le 1$ B. $-1 \le r \le 0$
C. $-1 \le r \le 1$ D. $1 \le r \le 2$

120. If all values of a variable are multiplied by a given number, which one of the following will NOT be affected?

A. Mean
B. Median
C. Range
D. Coefficient of variation

121. Dispersions are NOT calculated about

A. Mean B. Median
C. Mode D. Geometric Mean

122. The price index that uses base year quantities as weights is called

A. Paasche's index
B. Laspeyere's index
C. Fisher's ideal index
D. Wholesale price index

ANSWERS

1	2	3	4	5	6	7	8	9	10
C	D	C	B	A	C	A	A	B	A
11	**12**	**13**	**14**	**15**	**16**	**17**	**18**	**19**	**20**
B	A	C	D	D	C	C	C	C	A
21	**22**	**23**	**24**	**25**	**26**	**27**	**28**	**29**	**30**
C	C	A	A	C	C	C	B	C	A
31	**32**	**33**	**34**	**35**	**36**	**37**	**38**	**39**	**40**
D	A	C	B	C	C	B	A	B	A
41	**42**	**43**	**44**	**45**	**46**	**47**	**48**	**49**	**50**
B	B	C	B	A	C	D	C	B	B
51	**52**	**53**	**54**	**55**	**56**	**57**	**58**	**59**	**60**
C	B	A	A	D	A	A	C	D	A
61	**62**	**63**	**64**	**65**	**66**	**67**	**68**	**69**	**70**
D	B	C	A	A	B	A	A	B	A
71	**72**	**73**	**74**	**75**	**76**	**77**	**78**	**79**	**80**
D	B	C	C	B	C	A	C	B	A
81	**82**	**83**	**84**	**85**	**86**	**87**	**88**	**89**	**90**
A	C	A	D	C	A	A	A	A	A
91	**92**	**93**	**94**	**95**	**96**	**97**	**98**	**99**	**100**
C	A	B	C	D	B	A	A	B	A
101	**102**	**103**	**104**	**105**	**106**	**107**	**108**	**109**	**110**
C	A	A	A	B	A	A	B	A	B
111	**112**	**113**	**114**	**115**	**116**	**117**	**118**	**119**	**120**
A	D	C	A	D	B	B	D	C	D
121	**122**								
D	B								

□□□

INDIAN ECONOMY

1. NATIONAL INCOME

- According to the National Income Committee (1949), "A national income estimate measures the volume of commodities and service turned out during a given period counted without duplication". Thus, national income measures the net value of goods and services produced in a country during a year and it also includes net earned foreign income. In other words, a total of national income measures the flow of goods and services in an economy.
- National income is a flow concept not a stock concept.
- In India, National income estimates are related with the financial year (April 1 to 31st March).
- The various concepts of national income are as follows:
  - *(i)* **GNP (Gross National Product):** GNP refers to the money value of total output or production of final goods and services produced by the nationals of a country during a given period of time, generally a year.
  - *(ii)* **NNP (Net National Product):** NNP is obtained by subtracting depreciation value from GNP. NNP can be calculated in two ways: (*a*) at market prices of goods and services and (*b*) at factor cost.
  - *(iii)* **National Income:** When NNP is obtained at factor cost, it is known as National Income. National Income is calculated by subtracting net indirect taxes from NNP at market prices. The obtained value is known as NNP at factor cost or National income.
  - *(iv)* **Personal Income:** Personal income is that income which is actually obtained by nationals. Personal income is obtained by subtracting corporate taxes and payments made for social securities provisions from national income and adding to it government transfer payments, business transfer payments and net interest paid by the government.

Methods of Measuring National Income

- According to Simon Kuznets, national income of a country is calculated by following mentioned three methods:
  - *(i)* **Product Method:** S. Kuznets gave a new name to this method, *i.e.*, product service method. In this method, net value of final goods and services produced in a country during a year is obtained and the total obtained value is called total final product.
  - *(ii)* **Income Method:** In this method, a total of net incomes earned by working people in different sectors and commercial enterprises is obtained.
  - *(iii)* **Consumption Method:** It is also called expenditure method. Income is either spent on consumption or saved. Hence, national income is the addition of total consumption and total savings.
- In India, a combination of production method and income method is used for measuring estimating national income.
- For measuring national income in India, in 1868, the first attempt was made by *Dada Bhai Naoroji.* He, in his book, *"Poverty and Un-British Rule in*

India", estimated Indian per capita annual income at a level of ₹ 20.

- After independence, the Government of India appointed the National Income Committee in August, 1949, under the Chairmanship of Prof. P.C. Mahalanobis, to compile authoritative estimates of national income.
- Estimation and publishing of National Income data by CSO (Central Statistical Organization) is done every year.
- National income includes the contribution of three sectors—primary sector, secondary sector, Tertiary sector.
- Under Primary Sector—Agriculture, Forest, Fisheries and allied sector are included.
- Under Secondary Sector—Manufacturing, Construction, Electricity, Gas and Water Supply are included.
- Under Teritiary Sector—Trade, Transport, Communication, Banking, Insurance, Real Estate, Community and Personal Services are included.
- The contribution of primary sector in GDP was 55.4% in 1950-1951. But now the share of primary sector in national income has come down. In 2024-2025, the contribution of primary sector in GDP was 19.7%.
- The contribution of secondary sector has shown a steady increase from 15% in 1950-51 to 25.3% in 2024-25.
- The contribution of tertiary sector indicated a sharp improvement from 29.6% in 1950-51 to about 55% in 2024-25.
- At present estimation of national income is based on the base year of 2011-2012.
- The structural change in the composition of national income by industrial origin is the consequence of the process of economic growth initiated during the plans. Since the growth process involved a rapid expansion of manufacturing in the organised sector, the share of manufacturing was bound to indicate a relatively sharp increase. However, agriculture did not indicate a fast rate of growth.

Annual Average of Growth Rate in Various Plans

Five Year Plan	*NNI at Constant Price*	*Per Capita NNI*
First Plan (1951-56)	4.6	2.7
Second Plan (1956-61)	4.1	2.1
Third Plan (1961-66)	3.3	1.0
Three Annual Plans (1966-69)	3.5	1.3
Fourth Plan (1969-74)	3.0	0.7
Fifth Plan (1974-79)	5.0	2.7
Annual Plan (1979-80)	–5.9	–8.2
Sixth Plan (1980-85)	5.3	3.1
Seventh Plan (1985-90)	5.8	3.6
Two Annual Plan (1990-92)	2.8	0.8
Eighth Plan (1992-97)	6.5	4.4
Ninth Plan (1997-2002)	5.4	3.4
Tenth Plan (2002-07)	7.6	5.9
Eleventh Plan (2007-12)	7.5	6.0
Twelfth Plan (2012-17)	—	—

Source: CSO

2. POPULATION

- Every year 11th July is celebrated as the World Population Day.
- The first census of India was done in 1872 during the reign of Viceroy Lord Mayo. But a series of census (After every ten years) was adopted in 1881 during the reign of Viceroy Lord Ripon.
- 2011 census is the 15th census of India, and the 7th census of free India.
- The entire census of 2011 exercise has been completed by March 15, 2011.
- The term density of population implies the average number of persons living per sq. km. It is denoted in the following way:

The density of population

$$= \frac{\text{Total population of a certain place}}{\text{Total area of the certain place}}$$

- No. of females in comparison to per 1000 males is known as sex ratio. It is denoted in the following way:

$$\text{Sex Ratio} = \frac{\text{No. of Females}}{\text{No. of Males}} \times 1000$$

- No. of females in age group between 0-6 year, in comparison of per 1000 males of same age group is known as child sex ratio. It is denoted in the following way:

Child Sex Ratio (0-6 year)

$$= \frac{\text{No. of Females Children (0-6)}}{\text{No. of Males Children (0-6)}} \times 1000$$

- Birth Rate (or crude Birth Rate) is number of the birth per thousand of the population during a period, usually a year. Only live births are included in the calculation of birth rate.
- Death rate signifies the number of deaths in a year per thousand of the population. It is mostly known as crude death rate. Life expectancy is important determinant of death rate. A country having high life expectancy will have a high crude death rate.
- The term fertility refers to the actual bearing of children or 'occurrence of births'. Fertility rate measures the average number of the live births per 1000 women. This rate is one of the most important and useful aids to population projection. It helps in assessing population trends in the economy.
- Percentage of literates between the age of 7 and above of total population is called 'Literacy Rate'.
- The people between the age of 7 and above, who can understand, write and read any language are known as 'literate'.
- An urban area having population of 1,00,000 or above persons is known as a city.
- In the 2011 census, an urban area was defined as follows:
  - (a) All places with a municipality, corporation, cantonment board or notified towns area committee, etc.
  - (b) All other places which satisfied the following criteria:
    - (i) A minimum population of 5,000;
    - (ii) At least 75 per cent of male main working population engaged in non-agricultural pursuits; and
    - (iii) A density of population of at least 400 persons per sq. km (1,000 persons per sq. mile).
- From the 1920s onwards, the rate of growth of population picked up. The year 1921 is termed as year of 'great divide'.
- High birth rate supplemented with improved health and medical facilities (which makes death rate fall) pushes the economy towards the state of "population explosion". India faces the same situation at present.
- An increasing difference between birth rate and death rate has created a scene of population explosion in India. This problem in India is not the result of declining death rate alone, which is actually an indicator of social development. But a simultaneous effort for reducing birth rate should have been made, where we have totally failed.
- The framework of the new population policy, 2000 was derived from recommendations of M.S. Swaminathan Committee. Three main objectives of this policy are:
  - (i) The immediate objective of this policy is to address the unmet needs of contraception, health infrastructure, health personnel and to provide integrated service delivery for basic reproductive and child healthcare.
  - (ii) The medium term objective is to bring the total fertility rates to replacement level by 2010.
  - (iii) The long-term objective is to achieve a stable population by 2045.
- The National Commission on Population (NCP) was constituted in May 2000 to review, monitor and give direction for the implementation of the National Population Policy (NPP), 2000.
- The National Commission of Population was reconstituted on 11th April, 2005 with 40 members under the chairmanship of the Prime Minister. Minister of Health and Family Welfare and the Deputy Chairman of the Planning Commission are Vice Chairmen of the Commission. The present membership also includes the Chief Ministers of the states of Uttar Pradesh, Madhya Pradesh, Rajasthan, Bihar, Jharkhand, Kerala and Tamil Nadu.

- According to the census 2011, total population of India is 1,21,08,54,977. Census 2011 makes India the second most populated country in the world.
- The growth rate of the population between 2001 and 2011 is 17.7 per cent. Meghalaya recorded the highest growth rate of 27.9 per cent while Nagaland the lowest –0.6 per cent.
- There were 623.27 million males and 587.58 million females according to Census 2011, making a ratio of 943 males per 1000 females. Kerala is the only state where females outnumber males. The sex-ratio these was 1084 females per 1000 males.
- According to census 2011, five most populous states (in descending order) are: Uttar Pradesh (19.9 crore), Maharashtra (11.2 crore), Bihar (10.4 crore), W. Bengal (9.12 crore) and Andhra Pradesh (8.4 crore).
- According to census 2011, three least populous states (in ascending order) are: Sikkim (6.10 lakh), Mizoram (10.9 lakh) and Arunachal Pradesh (13.8 lakh).
- According to census 2011, three most populous Union Territories (in descending order) are: Delhi, Puducherry and Chandigarh.
- According to census 2011, three least populo Union Territories (in ascending order) ar Lakshadweep, Daman and Diu, Dadra and Nag Haveli.
- **Population Density:** In 2011, 382 persons we living in per square km area. Bihar was mc densely populated state with a population densi of 1,106 followed by West Bengal (1,028). Amo the Union Territories, Delhi had the density 11,320 and Chandigarh of 9,258. In Arunach Pradesh, only 17 people were living in per s km area while in Mizoram 52.
- According to census-2011, 73.0 per cent of t country's population are literate. The ma literacy rate (80.9%) is far more than the fema literacy rate (64.6%). Kerala retains the top sp with 94.0 per cent literacy rate. Bihar is at t bottom with a literacy rate of 61.8 per cent.
- According to census 2011, five states with lea sex ratio (in ascending order) are: Haryana (87 Jammu & Kashmir (889), Sikkim (890), Punj (895), and Uttar Pradesh (912).
- According to census 2011, five states with mc decadal growth rate (in descending order) a Meghalaya (27.9%), Arunachal Pradesh (26% Bihar (25.4), Jammu & Kashmir (23.6%), a Mizoram (23.5%).

Occupational Pattern 2011 (per cent)

Category	*Total Population*	*Rural Population*	*Urban Population*
Main Worker			
Cultivators	26.44	37.74	2.66
Agricultural Labourers	23.77	32.94	4.46
Household Industry Workers	3.4	2.95	4.36
Other Workers	46.38	26.37	88.52
Marginal Workers			
Cultivators	19.15	21.62	3.77
Agricultural Labourers	48.75	54.48	12.93
Household Industry Workers	5.03	4.58	7.91
Other Work	27.06	19.33	75.38

Census-2011: Area, Population, Density, Decadal Growth Rate

S.N.	State/UTs	Area (sq. km.)	*Population* 2001	*Population* 2011	*Density* 2001	*Density* 2011	*Decadal G. (%)* 2001–2011
1.	J&K	222,236.00	10,143,700	1,25,41,302	100	124	23.6
2.	Himachal Pradesh	55,673.00	6,077,900	68,64,602	109	123	12.9
3.	Punjab	50,362.00	24,358,999	2,77,43,338	484	551	13.9
4.	Chandigarh	114.00	900,635	10,55,450	7,900	9258	17.2
5.	Uttarakhand	53483.00	8,489,349	1,00,86,292	159	189	18.8
6.	Haryana	44212.00	21,144,564	2,53,51,462	478	573	19.9
7.	Delhi	1483.00	13,850,507	1,67,87,941	9,340	11320	21.2
8.	Rajasthan	342,239.00	56,507,188	6,85,48,437	165	200	21.3
9.	Uttar Pradesh	240,928.00	166,197,921	19,98,12,341	690	829	20.2
10.	Bihar	94,163.00	82,998,509	10,40,99,452	881	1106	25.4
11.	Sikkim	7,096.00	540,851	6,10,577	76	86	12.9
12.	Arunachal Pradesh	83,743.00	1,097,968	13,83,727	13	17	26.0
13.	Nagaland	16,579.00	1,990,036	19,78,502	120	119	–0.6
14.	Manipur	22,327.00	2,293,896	28,55,794	103	128	31.79
15.	Mizoram	21,081.00	888,573	10,97,206	42	52	23.5
16.	Tripura	10,486.00	3,199,203	36,73,917	305	350	14.8
17.	Meghalaya	22,429.00	2,318,822	29,66,889	103	132	27.9
18.	Assam	78,438.00	26,655,528	3,12,05,576	340	398	17.1
19.	West Bengal	88752.00	80,176,197	9,12,76,115	903	1028	13.8
20.	Jharkhand	79714.00	26,945,829	3,29,88,134	338	414	22.4
21.	Odisha	155,707.00	36,804,660	4,19,74,218	236	270	14.0
22.	Chhattisgarh	135,191.00	20,833,803	2,55,45,198	154	189	22.6
23.	Madhya Pradesh	308,245.00	60,348,023	7,26,26,809	196	236	20.3
24.	Gujarat	196,024.00	50,671,017	6,04,39,692	258	308	19.3
25.	Daman & Diu	112.00	158,204	2,43,247	1,413	2191	53.8
26.	Dadra & N. Haveli	491.00	220,490	3,43,709	449	700	55.9
27	Maharashtra	307,713.00	96,878,627	11,23,74,333	315	365	16.0
28.	Andhra Pradesh	160,205.00	76,210,007	4,93,86,799	277	308	11.0
29.	Karnataka	191,791.00	52,850,562	6,10,95,297	276	319	15.6
30.	Goa	3,702.00	1,347,668	14,58,545	364	394	8.2
31.	Lakshadweep	32.00	60,650	64,473	1,895	2149	6.3
32.	Kerala	38863.00	31,841,374	3,34,06,061	819	860	4.9
33.	Tamil Nadu	130,058.00	62,405,679	7,21,47,030	480	555	15.6
34.	Puducherry	479.00	974,345	12,47,953	2,030	2546	28.1
35.	Andaman & Nicobar Islands	8249.00	356,152	3,80,581	43	46	6.9
36.	Telangana	112,077.00	—	3,51,93,978	—	307	13.58
	India	**3,287,240.00**	**1,028,737,436**	**1,21,08,54,977**	**325**	**382**	**17.7**

Census-2011: Population and Sex-Ratio

S.N.	State/UTs	Census 2011			Sex-Ratio	
		Population	*Male*	*Female*	*2001*	*2011*
1.	J&K	1,25,41,302	66,40,662	59,00,640	892	889
2.	Himachal Pradesh	68,64,602	34,81,873	33,82,729	968	972
3.	Punjab	2,77,43,338	1,46,39,465	1,31,03,873	876	895
4.	Chandigarh	10,55,450	5,80,663	4,74,784	777	818
5.	Uttarakhand	1,00,86,292	51,37,773	49,48,519	962	963
6.	Haryana	2,53,51,462	1,34,94,734	1,18,56,728	861	879
7.	Delhi	1,67,87,941	89,87,326	78,00,615	821	868
8.	Rajasthan	6,85,48,437	3,55,50,997	3,29,97,440	921	928
9.	Uttar Pradesh	19,98,12,341	10,44,80,510	9,53,31,831	898	912
10.	Bihar	10,40,99,452	5,42,78,157	4,98,21,295	919	918
11.	Sikkim	6,10,577	3,23,070	2,87,507	875	890
12.	Arunachal Pradesh	13,83,727	7,13,912	6,69,815	893	938
13.	Nagaland	19,78,502	10,24,649	9,53,853	900	931
14.	Manipur	28,55,794	14,38,586	·14,17,208	974	985
15.	Mizoram	10,97,206	5,55,339	5,41,867	935	976
16.	Tripura	36,73,917	18,74,376	17,99,541	948	960
17.	Meghalaya	29,66,889	14,91,832	14,75,057	972	989
18.	Assam	3,12,05,576	1,59,39,443	1,52,66,133	935	958
19.	West Bengal	9,12,76,115	4,68,09,027	4,44,67,088	934	950
20.	Jharkhand	3,29,88,134	1,69,30,315	1,60,57,819	941	949
21.	Odisha	4,19,74,218	2,12,12,136	2,07,62,082	972	979
22.	Chhattisgarh	2,55,45,198	1,28,32,895	1,27,12,303	989	991
23.	Madhya Pradesh	7,26,26,809	3,76,12,306	3,50,14,503	919	931
24.	Gujarat	6,04,39,692	3,14,91,260	2,89,48,432	920	919
25.	Daman & Diu	2,43,247	1,50,301	92,946	710	618
26.	Dadra & N. Haveli	3,43,709	1,93,760	1,49,949	812	774
27.	Maharashtra	11,23,74,333	5,82,43,056	5,41,31,277	922	929
28.	Andhra Pradesh	4,93,86,799	2,47,38,068	2,46,48,731	978	993
29.	Karnataka	6,10,95,297	3,09,66,657	3,01,28,640	965	973
30.	Goa	14,58,545	7,39,140	7,19,405	961	973
31.	Lakshadweep	64,473	33,123	31,350	948	947
32.	Kerala	3,34,06,061	1,60,27,412	1,73,78,649	1,058	1084
33.	Tamil Nadu	7,21,47,030	3,61,37,975	3,60,09,055	987	996
34.	Puducherry	12,47,953	6,12,511	6,35,442	1,001	1037
35.	Andman & Nicobar Islands	3,80,581	2,02,871	1,77,710	846	876
36.	Telangana	3,51,93,978	1,77,04,078	1,74,89,900	—	988
	India	**1,21,08,54,977**	**62,32,70,258**	**58,75,84,719**	**933**	**943**

Census 2011: Literacy

S. No.	State/Union Territories	Total Population	Total Literacy	Male Literacy	Female Literacy	Literacy (%)		
						Total	*Male*	*Female*
1.	J&K	1,25,41,302	70,67,233	42,64,671	28,02,562	67.2	76.8	56.4
2.	Himachal Pradesh	68,64,602	50,39,736	27,52,590	22,87,146	82.8	89.5	75.9
3.	Punjab	2,77,43,338	1,87,07,137	1,04,36,056	82,71,081	75.8	80.4	70.7
4.	Chandigarh	10,55,450	8,05,438	4,65,346	3,40,092	86.0	90.0	81.2
5.	Uttarakhand	1,00,86,292	68,80,953	38,63,708	30,17,245	78.8	87.4	70.0
6.	Haryana	2,53,51,462	1,65,98,988	97,94,067	68,04,921	75.6	84.1	65.9
7.	Delhi	1,67,87,941	1,27,37,767	71,94,856	55,42,911	86.2	90.9	80.8
8.	Rajasthan	6,85,48,437	3,82,75,282	2,36,88,412	1,45,86,870	66.1	79.2	52.1
9.	Uttar Pradesh	19,98,12,341	1,43,97,555	6,82,34,964	4,61,62,591	67.7	77.3	57.2
10.	Bihar	10,40,99,452	5,25,04,553	3,16,08,023	2,08,96,530	61.8	71.2	51.5
11.	Sikkim	6,10,577	4,44,952	2,51,269	1,93,683	81.4	86.6	75.6
12.	Arunachal Pradesh	13,83,727	7,66,005	4,39,868	3,26,137	65.4	72.6	57.7
13.	Nagaland	19,78,502	13,42,434	7,23,957	6,18,477	79.6	82.8	76.1
14.	Manipur	28,55,794	17,68,181	9,60,015	8,08,166	79.2	86.1	72.4
15.	Mizoram	10,97,206	8,48,175	4,38,529	4,09,646	91.3	93.3	89.3
16.	Tripura	36,73,917	28,04,783	15,01,369	13,03,414	87.2	91.5	82.7
17.	Meghalaya	29,66,889	17,85,005	9,13,879	8,71,126	74.4	76.0	72.9
18.	Assam	3,12,05,576	1,91,77,977	1,05,68,639	86,09,338	72.2	77.8	66.3
19.	West Bengal	9,12,76,115	6,15,38,281	3,38,18,810	2,77,19,471	76.3	81.7	70.5
20.	Jharkhand	3,29,88,134	1,83,28,069	1,08,82,519	74,45,550	66.4	76.8	55.4
21.	Odisha	4,19,74,218	2,67,42,595	1,50,89,681	1,16,52,914	72.9	81.6	64.0
22.	Chhattisgarh	2,55,45,198	1,53,79,922	88,07,893	65,72,029	70.3	80.3	60.2
23.	Madhya Pradesh	7,26,26,809	4,28,51,169	2,51,74,328	1,76,76,841	69.3	78.7	59.2
24.	Gujarat	6,04,39,692	4,10,93,358	2,34,74,873	1,76,18,485	78.0	85.8	69.7
25.	Daman & Diu	2,43,247	1,88,406	1,24,643	63,763	87.1	91.5	79.5
26.	Dadra & N. Haveli	3,43,709	2,23,230	1,42,521	80,709	76.2	85.2	64.3
27.	Maharashtra	11,23,74,333	8,15,54,290	4,52,57,584	3,62,96,706	82.3	88.4	75.9
28.	Andhra Pradesh	4,93,86,799	2,97,72,532	1,65,01,990	1,32,70,542	67.0	74.9	59.1
29.	Karnataka	6,10,95,297	4,06,47,322	2,25,08,471	1,81,38,851	75.4	82.5	68.1
30.	Goa	14,58,545	11,65,487	6,15,823	5,49,664	88.7	92.6	84.7
31.	Lakshadweep	64,473	52,553	28,023	24,530	91.8	95.6	87.9
32.	Kerala	3,34,06,061	2,81,35,824	1,37,04,903	1,44,30,921	94.0	96.1	92.1
33.	Tamil Nadu	7,21,47,030	5,18,37,507	2,80,40,491	2,37,97,016	80.1	86.8	73.4
34.	Puducherry	12,47,953	9,57,309	4,97,378	4,59,931	85.8	91.3	80.7
35.	Andaman & Nicboar Islands	3,80,581	2,94,281	1,64,377	1,29,904	86.6	90.3	82.4
36.	Telangana	3,51,93,978	2,07,84,228	1,17,49,253	90,34,975	66.4	74.9	57.9
	India	**1,21,08,54,977**	**76,34,98,517**	**43,46,83,779**	**32,88,14,738**	**73.0**	**80.9**	**64.6**

State & UTs Rankings (in descending order) based on Decadal Growth (2001-2011)

Rank	*State/UTs*	*Decadal Growth*
1.	Dadra & Nagar Haveli	55.9
2.	Daman and Diu	53.8
3.	Manipur	31.79
4.	Puducherry	28.1
5.	Meghalaya	27.9
6.	Arunachal Pradesh	26.0
7.	Bihar	25.4
8.	Jammu and Kashmir	23.6
9.	Mizoram	23.5
10.	Chhattisgarh	22.6
11.	Jharkhand	22.4
12.	Rajasthan	21.3
13.	NCR Delhi	21.2
14.	Madhya Pradesh	20.3
15.	Uttar Pradesh	20.2
16.	Haryana	19.9
17.	Gujarat	19.3
18.	Uttarakhand	18.8
19.	Chandigarh	17.2
20.	Assam	17.1
21.	Maharashtra	16.0
22.	Karnataka	15.6
23.	Tamil Nadu	15.6
24.	Tripura	14.8
25.	Odisha	14.0
26.	Punjab	13.9
27.	West Bengal	13.8
28.	Telangana	13.5
29.	Himachal Pradesh	12.9
30.	Sikkim	12.9
31.	Andhra Pradesh	11.0
32.	Goa	8.2
33.	A & N Islands	6.9
34.	Lakshadweep	6.3
35.	Kerala	4.9
36.	Nagaland	–0.6
	India	**17.7**

Child Sex-Ratio in State/UTs based on 2011

Rank	*State/UTs*	*Decadal Growth*
1.	Arunachal Pradesh	972
2.	Mizoram	970
3.	Meghalaya	970
4.	Chhattisgarh	969
5.	A & N Islands	968
6.	Puducherry	967
7.	Kerala	964
8.	Assam	962
9.	Tripura	957
10.	Sikkim	957
11.	West Bengal	956
12.	Jharkhand	948
13.	Karnataka	948
14.	Goa	942
15.	Odisha	941
16.	Tamil Nadu	943
17.	Nagaland	943
18.	Andhra Pradesh	939
19.	Bihar	935
20.	Telangana	933
21.	Manipur	930
22.	Dadra & Nagar Haveli	926
23.	Lakshadweep	911
24.	Madhya Pradesh	918
25.	Himachal Pradesh	909
26.	Daman & Diu	904
27.	Uttar Pradesh	902
28.	Maharashtra	894
29.	Uttarakhand	890
30.	Gujarat	890
31.	Rajasthan	888
32.	Chandigarh	880
33.	Delhi	871
34.	Jammu & Kashmir	862
35.	Punjab	846
36.	Haryana	834
	India	**918**

State/UTs Rankings based on Sex-ratio (in descending order) as per Census-2011

Rank	State/UTs	Sex Ratio
1.	Kerala	1,084
2.	Puducherry	1,037
3.	Tamil Nadu	996
4.	Andhra Pradesh	993
5.	Chhattisgarh	991
6.	Meghalaya	989
7.	Telangana	988
8.	Manipur	985
9.	Odisha	979
10.	Mizoram	976
11.	Karnataka	973
12.	Goa	973
13.	Himachal Pradesh	972
14.	Uttarakhand	963
15.	Tripura	960
16.	Assam	958
17.	West Bengal	950
18.	Jharkhand	948
19.	Lakshadweep	946
20.	Arunachal Pradesh	938
21.	Nagaland	931
22.	Madhya Pradesh	931
23.	Maharashtra	929
24.	Rajasthan	928
25.	Gujarat	919
26.	Bihar	918
27.	Uttar Pradesh	912
28.	Punjab	895
29.	Sikkim	890
30.	Jammu and Kashmir	889
31.	Haryana	879
32.	A & N Islands	876
33.	Delhi	868
34.	Chandigarh	818
35.	Dadra & Nagar Haveli	774
36.	Daman and Diu	618
	India	**943**

State/UTs Rankings based on Literacy as per Census 2011

Rank	State/UTs	Literacy Rate
1.	Kerala	94.0
2.	Lakshadweep	91.8
3.	Mizoram	91.3
4.	Goa	88.7
5.	Tripura	87.2
6.	Daman and Diu	87.1
7.	A & N Islands	86.6
8.	NCR Delhi	86.2
9.	Chandigarh	86.0
10.	Puducherry	85.8
11.	Himachal Pradesh	82.8
12.	Maharashtra	82.3
13.	Sikkim	81.4
14.	Tamil Nadu	80.1
15.	Nagaland	79.6
16.	Manipur	79.2
17.	Uttarakhand	78.8
18.	Gujarat	78.0
19.	West Bengal	76.3
20.	Dadra & Nagar Haveli	76.2
21.	Punjab	75.8
22.	Haryana	75.6
23.	Karnataka	75.4
24.	Meghalaya	74.4
25.	Odisha	72.9
26.	Assam	72.2
27.	Chhattisgarh	70.3
28.	Madhya Pradesh	69.3
29.	Uttar Pradesh	67.7
30.	Jammu & Kashmir	67.2
31.	Andhra Pradesh	67.0
32.	Jharkhand	66.4
33.	Telangana	66.4
34.	Rajasthan	66.1
35.	Arunachal Pradesh	65.4
36.	Bihar	61.8
	India	**73.0**

State/UTs Rankings based on Male Literacy as per Census 2011

Rank	State/UTs	Literacy Rate
1.	Kerala	96.1
2.	Lakshadweep	95.6
3.	Mizoram	93.3
4.	Goa	92.6
5.	Tripura	91.5
6.	Daman and Diu	91.5
7.	Puducherry	91.3
8.	NCR Delhi	90.9
9.	A & N Islands	90.3
10.	Chandigarh	90.0
11.	Himachal Pradesh	89.5
12.	Maharashtra	88.4
13.	Uttarakhand	87.4
14.	Tamil Nadu	86.8
15.	Sikkim	86.6
16.	Manipur	86.1
17.	Gujarat	85.8
18.	Dadra & Nagar Haveli	85.2
19.	Haryana	84.1
20.	Nagaland	82.8
21.	Karnataka	82.5
22.	West Bengal	81.7
23.	Odisha	81.6
24.	Punjab	80.4
25.	Chhattisgarh	80.3
26.	Rajasthan	79.2
27.	Madhya Pradesh	78.7
28.	Assam	77.8
29.	Uttar Pradesh	77.3
30.	Jharkhand	76.8
31.	Jammu and Kashmir	76.8
32.	Meghalaya	76.0
33.	Andhra Pradesh	74.9
34.	Telangana	74.9
35.	Arunachal Pradesh	72.6
36.	Bihar	71.2
	India	**80.9**

State/UTs Rankings based on Female Literacy as per Census 2011

Rank	State/UTs	Literacy Rate
1.	Kerala	92.1
2.	Lakshadweep	89.3
3.	Mizoram	89.3
4.	Goa	84.7
5.	Tripura	82.7
6.	A & N Islands	82.4
7.	Chandigarh	81.2
8.	NCR Delhi	80.8
9.	Puducherry	80.7
10.	Daman and Diu	79.5
11.	Nagaland	76.1
12.	Himachal Pradesh	75.9
13.	Maharashtra	75.9
14.	Sikkim	75.6
15.	Tamil Nadu	73.4
16.	Meghalaya	72.9
17.	Manipur	72.4
18.	Punjab	70.7
19.	West Bengal	70.5
20.	Uttarakhand	70.0
21.	Gujarat	69.7
22.	Karnataka	68.1
23.	Assam	66.3
24.	Haryana	65.9
25.	Dadra & Nagar Haveli	64.3
26.	Odisha	64.0
27.	Chhattisgarh	60.2
28.	Madhya Pradesh	59.2
29.	Andhra Pradesh	59.1
30.	Telangana	57.9
31.	Arunachal Pradesh	57.7
32.	Uttar Pradesh	57.2
33.	Jammu & Kashmir	56.4
34.	Jharkhand	55.4
35.	Rajasthan	52.1
36.	Bihar	51.5
	India	**64.6**

Census-2011: Rural and Urban Population

S. No.	State/UTs	Rural Population	Urban Population	Percentage of Rural Population	Percentage of Urban Population
1.	J&K	91,08,060	34,33,242	72.6	27.4
2.	Himachal Pradesh	61,76,050	6,88,552	90.0	10.0
3.	Punjab	1,73,44,192	1,03,99,146	62.5	37.5
4.	Chandigarh	28,991	10,26,459	2.7	97.3
5.	Uttarakhand	70,36,954	30,49,338	69.8	30.2
6.	Haryana	1,65,09,359	88,42,103	65.1	34.9
7.	Delhi	4,19,042	1,63,68,899	2.5	97.5
8.	Rajasthan	5,15,00,352	1,70,48,085	75.1	24.9
9.	Uttar Pradesh	15,53,17,278	4,44,95,063	77.7	22.3
10.	Bihar	9,23,41,436	1,17,58,016	88.7	11.3
11.	Sikkim	4,56,999	1,53,578	74.8	25.2
12.	Arunachal Pradesh	10,66,358	3,17,369	77.1	22.9
13.	Nagaland	14,07,536	5,70,966	71.1	28.9
14.	Manipur	20,21,640	8,34,154	70.8	29.2
15.	Mizoram	5,25,435	5,71,771	47.9	52.1
16.	Tripura	27,12,464	9,61,453	73.8	26.2
17.	Meghalaya	23,71,439	5,95,450	79.9	20.1
18.	Assam	2,68,07,034	43,98,542	85.9	14.1
19.	West Bengal	6,21,83,113	2,90,93,002	68.1	31.9
20.	Jharkhand	2,50,55,073	79,33,061	76.0	24.0
21.	Odisha	3,49,70,562	70,03,656	83.3	16.7
22.	Chhattisgarh	1,96,07,961	59,37,237	76.8	23.2
23.	Madhya Pradesh	5,25,57,404	2,00,69,405	72.4	27.6
24.	Gujarat	3,46,94,609	2,57,45,083	57.4	42.6
25.	Daman & Diu	60,396	1,82,851	24.8	75.2
26.	Dadra & N. Haveli	1,83,114	1,60,595	53.3	46.7
27.	Maharashtra	6,15,56,074	5,08,18,259	54.8	45.2
28.	Andhra Pradesh	3,99,70,761	1,46,10,410	66.6	33.4
29.	Karnataka	3,74,69,335	2,36,25,962	61.3	38.7
30.	Goa	5,51,731	9,06,814	37.8	62.2
31.	Lakshadweep	14,141	50,332	21.9	78.1
32.	Kerala	1,74,71,135	1,59,34,926	52.3	47.7
33.	Tamil Nadu	3,72,29,590	3,49,17,440	51.6	48.4
34.	Puducherry	3,95,200	8,52,753	31.7	68.3
35.	Andman & Nicobar Islands	2,37,093	1,43,488	62.3	37.7
36.	Telangana	2,15,85,313	1,36,08,665	61.33	38.64
	India	**83,37,48,852**	**37,71,06,125**	**68.9**	**31.1**

3. POVERTY

- Poverty can be defined as a social phenomenon in which a section of society is unable to fulfil even the basic necessities of life.
- The term 'poverty' has been defined in different societies in a different ways but all of them are conditioned by the vision of minimum or good life living in society.
- The concept of poverty in the U.S.A. would be significantly different from that in India because the average person is able to afford a much higher level of living in the United States.
- There is an effort in all definitions of poverty to approach the average level of living in a society and as such these definitions reflect the existence of inequalities in a society and the extent to which different societies are prepared to tolerate them.
- In India, the generally accepted definition of poverty emphasises minimum level of living rather than a reasonable level of living.
- Several economists and organisations have given different estimates of poverty. Most of them estimated poverty line on the basis of an average number of persons below the calories intake of 2250 per capita per day, according to the report of 'Task Force on Minimum Needs and Effective Consumption Demand'.
- An expert group of planning commission, defined poverty line on a nutritional norm of per capita daily intake of 2400 calories in rural areas and 2100 calories for urban areas. A person who fails to obtain this minimum level of calories is treated as being below the poverty line.
- There are two types of common standards in economic literature for the measurement of poverty:
  1. **Absolute Poverty:** In the absolute standard, minimum physical quantities of cereals, pulses, milk, butter, etc. are determined for a subsistence level and then the price quotations converted into monetary terms the physical quantities. Aggregating all of the quantities included, a figure expressing per capita consumer expenditure is determined. The population whose level of income or expenditure below the figure, is considered to be below the poverty line.
  2. **Relative Standard:** According to the relative standard, income distribution of the population in different fractile groups is estimated and a comparison of the levels of living of the top 5 to 10 per cent with the bottom 5 to 10 per cent of the population reflects the relative standards of poverty.
- The defect of the relative standard approach is that it indicates the relative position of different segments of the population in the income hierarchy. Even in affluent societies, such pockets of poverty exist. But for underdeveloped countries, it is the existence of mass poverty that is the cause for concern.
- The Planning Commission, the nodal agency for estimating the number and proportion of people living below the poverty line at national and state levels, separately for rural and urban areas, makes poverty estimates based on a large sample survey of household consumption expenditure carried out by the National Sample Survey Office (NSSO) approximately every five years.
- For estimation and review of poverty, the Planning Commission constituted an expert group under the chairmanship of Prof. Suresh D. Tendulkar in December 2005, which submitted its report in December 2009.
- The recomputed poverty estimates for the years 1993-94 and 2004-05 as recommended by the Tendulkar Committee have been accepted by the Planning Commission.
- As per the Tendulkar Committee Report, the national poverty line at 2004-05 prices was a monthly per capita consumption expenditure of ₹ 446.68 in rural and ₹ 578.80 in urban areas.

Poverty Line

Committee	Year	Per capita Expenditure per day (₹)		Per capita Average Montly Expenditure (₹)		All India Poverty Line (Average Monthly Expenditure per Family of 5)	
		Rural	*Urban*	*Rural*	*Urban*	*Rural*	*Urban*
Rangarajan	2011-12	32.4	46.9	972	1407	4760	7035
	2009-10	26.7	39.9	801	1198	4005	5990
Tendulkar	2011-12	27.2	33.3	816	1000	4080	5000
	2009-10	22.4	28.7	673	860	3365	4300

Development, Poverty Alleviation and Employment Generation Programmes

Programme	Year of beginning	Objective
☛ Community Development Programme (CDP)	1952	Overall development of rural areas with people's participation.
☛ Green Revolution	1966-67	To increase the foodgrains, specially wheat production.
☛ Drought-Prone Area Programme (DPAP)	1973	To try an expedient for protection from drought by achieving environmental balance and by developing the ground water.
☛ Command Area Development Programme (CADP)	1974-75	To ensure better and rapid utilisation of irrigation capacities of medium and large projects.
☛ Twenty Point Programme (TPP)	1975	Poverty eradication and raising the standard of living.
☛ Antyodaya Yojana	1977-78	To make the poorest families of the village economically independent (only in Rajasthan State).
☛ Training Rural Youth for Self-Employment (TRYSEM)	Aug., 15, 1979	Programme of training rural youth for self-employment.
☛ Integrated Rural Development Programme (IRDP)	Oct., 2, 1980	All-round development of the rural poor through a programme of asset endowment for self-employment.
☛ National Rural Employment Programme (NREP)	1980	To provide profitable employment opportunities to the rural poor.
☛ Development of Women and Children in Rural Areas (DWCRA)	Sept. 1982	To provide suitable opportunities of self-employment to the women belonging to the rural families who are living below the poverty line.
☛ Council for Advancement of People's Action and Rural Technology (CAPART)	Sept. 1, 1986	To provide assistance for rural prosperity.
☛ Jawahar Rozgar Yojana	April 1989	For providing employment to rural unemployed.
☛ Nehru Rozgar Yojana	Oct. 1989	For providing employment to urban unemployed.
☛ District Rural Development Agency (DRDA)	1993	To provide financial assistance for rural development.
☛ Mahila Samridhi Yojana	2 Oct., 1993	To encourage the rural women to deposit in Post-office Saving Account.

Programme	Year of beginning	Objective
☛ Ganga Kalyan Yojana	1997-98	To provide financial assistance to farmers for exploring and developing ground and surface water resources.
☛ Kasturba Gandhi Education Scheme	Aug., 15, 1997	To establish girls schools in districts having low female literacy rate.
☛ Swarna Jayanti Shahari Rozgar Yojana (SJSRY)	Dec., 1997	To provide gainful employment to urban unemployed and under-employed poor through self-employment or wage-employment.
☛ Swarna Jayanti Gram Swarozgar Yojana	April 1999	For eliminating Rural poverty and unemployment and promoting self-employment.
☛ Jan Shree Bima Yojana	Aug., 10, 2000	Providing Insurance Security to people living below poverty line.
☛ Antyodaya Anna Yojana	Dec., 25, 2000	To provide food security to poor.
☛ Ashraya Bima Yojana	June 2001	To provide compensation to labourers who have lost their employment.
☛ Pradhan Mantri Gram Sadak Yojana (PMGSY)	Dec., 25, 2000	To line all villages with Pacca Road.
☛ Mahatma Gandhi National Rural Employment Guarantee Act (MNREGA)	Feb., 2, 2006	To provide at least 100 days wage-employment in rural areas.
☛ Pradhan Mantri Kaushal Vikas Yojana	March 2015	To Provide skill training to youth.
☛ Pradhan Mantri Jeevan Jyoti Bima Yojana	2015-16	Renewable one year life cover of ₹ 2 lakh to all savings bank account holders in the age group of 18-50 years covering death due to any reason for a premium of ₹ 330 per annum per sub-scriber.
☛ Pradhan Mantri Suraksha Bima Yojana	2015-16	Renewable one year accidental death cum disability to all savings bank account holders in the age group of 18-70 years for a premium of ₹ 12 per annum per subscriber.
☛ Atal Pension Yojana	2015-16	Pension to the labourers of unorganized sector
☛ Deen Dayal Upadhyay Grameen Kaushlya Yojana	Sep. 24, 2015	Skill development of rural youth.
☛ Atal Innovation Mission	2015-16	Atal Innovation Mission and Self Employement and Talent Utilisation.
☛ Swachh Bharat Mission	Oct. 2, 2014	Providing access to clean toilet to all rural households and initiating solid and liquid waste management activities in all gram panchayats.
☛ Pandit Deen Dayal Upadhyay Shramev Jayate Scheme	Oct. 16, 2014	To improve employability, skill development and other conveniences for labour.
☛ Shyama Prasad Mukherjee Rurban Mission	Sept. 16, 2015	Setting up 300 village clusters by 2019-20 across the country with all possible urban amenities.

Programme	Year of beginning	Objective
☛ HriDay	2015-16	Heritage City Development and Augmentation Yojana to preserve and rejuvenate the rich cultural heritage of the country through the identified 12 cities.
☛ PRASAD	2015-16	National Mission on Pilgrimage Rejuvenation and Spiritual Augmentation Drive (PRASAD).
☛ Pradhan Mantri Awas Yojana	June 25, 2015	Providing housing facilities in rural areas.
☛ Startup India, Standup India	16 Jan., 2016	To provide Support to all start-up businesses in al! aspects of doing business in India.
☛ Pradhan Mantri Ujjwala Yojana	May 1, 2016	Launched to Provide free LPG connection to women from below poverty line families.
☛ Urja Ganga Yojana (UGY)	Oct. 24, 2016	To provide the accessibility of approx, 5 Lakh LPG gas cylinders within next 5 years.
☛ Pradhan Mantri Vittiya Saksharta Abhiyan (PMVSA)	Dec. 1, 2016	To go for cashless transaction and payment modes like using credit or debit cards or the payment wallets to reduce the malpractice in the country.
☛ Digi Dhan Vyapar Yojana (DDVY)	Dec. 15, 2016	To increase the "Cashless Transactions".
☛ Pradhan Mantri Garib Kalyan Yojana (PMGKY)	Dec. 2016	To improve the financial position of the poor people.
☛ Atal Amrit Abhiyan (AAA)	Dec. 25, 2016	To provide health insurance against 437 illnesses including 5 critical diseases.
☛ Pradhan Mantri Sahaj Bijli Har Ghar Yojana "Saubhagya"	Sep. 25, 2017	The objective of the 'Saubhagya' is to Provide energy access to all by last mile connectivity and electricity connections to all remaining un-electrified households in rural as well as urban areas to achieve universal household electrification in the country.
☛ PM Jan Vikas Karyakram	2018	Development of Minority Concentration areas.
☛ Ayushman Bharat Yojana	2018	To provide free access to healthcare for 50 crore people.
☛ PM Shram Yogi Mandhan	2019	For Security to unorganized sector.
☛ Garib Kalyan Rojgar Abhiyaan	2020	Employment campaign for the poor.
☛ PM Poshan Shakti Nirman Abhiyaan	2021	Reducing undernutrition, anemia and low birth weight.
☛ Mahila Samman Savings Certificate (MSSC)	2023	MSSC scheme was launched for woman and girls in India.
☛ PM-SURAJ	March 13, 2024	The Ministry of Social Justice and Empowerment launched a nationwide initiative aimed at offering credit support to the marginalized segments.
☛ VB-G RAM G Act	2025	This act replaces MGNAREGA to modernize rural employment, providing 125 days of guaranteed work per household to boost income and create infrastructure.

4. AGRICULTURE

- Agriculture is an important sector of the economy. Though the share of agriculture in national income has come down since the inception of planning era in the economy but still it has substantial share in GDP.
- In terms of composition, out of the total share of 16.1 per cent that agriculture and allied sector had in GDP in 2024-25.
- Agriculture in our country provides livelihood to about 46.1% of the population.
- Gross Capital Formation (GCF) in Agriculture and Allied sector relative to GVA in this sector has been showing a fluctuating trend from 19.04 per cent in 2011-12 to 20.2 per cent in 2022-23.
- Agriculture provides raw materials to various industries and other agro-based industries. Cotton and Jute textile industries, Sugar, Vanaspati industry etc. are directly dependent on agriculture.
- India's foreign trade is deeply associated with Agriculture Sector. Value of agriculture exports to total exports of the country was 13.8 per cent in 2013. But the share of agriculture has come down in foreign trade at present. Share of agriculture in foreign trade was 16.16 per cent in 2023-24.

Land Reform Programmes

- Land reform programme in India include:
  - (i) Elimination of intermediaries.
  - (ii) Tenancy Reform.
  - (iii) Determination of ceiling of holding per family and to distribute surplus land among landless people.
  - (iv) Consolidation of holdings.
- The legislation for abolition of intermediaries was aimed at providing land to the tiller.
- Measures of tenancy reform pertain to—
  - (*i*) Regulation of rent
  - (*ii*) Security of tenure
  - (*iii*) Confirment of ownership on tenants.
- Land ceiling laws were first enacted in the 50s and 60s. It was further revised in 1972. Family ceiling were lowered to 5 hectares for irrigated land with two crops, 7.5 hectares for irrigated land with one crops and 12 hectares for other lands.

Irrigation

- The planning commission has introduced a new classification of irrigation schemes:
  1. **Major Irrigation Schemes—**Those with culturable command areas (CCA) more than 10,000 hectares.
  2. **Medium Irrigation Schemes—**Those with culturable command areas (CCA) between 2,000 to 10,000 hectares.
  3. **Minor Irrigation Scheme—**Those with culturable command area (CCA) upto 2,000 hectares.
- **Accelerated Irrigation Benefits Programme (AIBP):** The Central Government initiated the Accelerated Irrigation Benefit Programme (AIBP) from 1996-97 for extending assistance for the completion of incomplete irrigation schemes. Under this programme, projects approved by the Planning Commission are eligible for assistance.
- **Micro Irrigation:** A centrally sponsored scheme on Micro Irrigation (MI) was launched in Tenth Plan for promoting water use efficiency by adopting drip and sprinkler irrigation. All states and Union Territories and all horticulture as well as agricultural crops are covered under the scheme. The National Committee on Plasticulture Applications in horticulture (NCPAH) provides the required technical guidance in association with Precision Farming Development Centers (PDFCs) at 22 locations. The PRI's are involved in selecting the beneficiaries. Since its inception, about 10 lakh hactares has been covered under drip and sprinkler irrigation.
- **Sprinkler/Drip Irrigation:** Under Sprinkler/Drip Irrigation System water is sprinkled evenly on total agriculture ground through a pipe network cropped area. Empircal studies show that this system of drip irrigation saves 30% to 40% water as compared to irrigation with traditional method

i.e., surface irrigation. This new system of irrigation also ensures 20-25% more productivity per hectare.

- **Source of Irrigation:** There are three main sources of irrigation in India:

  Canals: Canals water apporoximately 26% of irrigation in India. This include large areas in Punjab, Haryana, Uttar Pradesh, Bihar and some parts of the Southern States.

  Well & Tubewells: Wells and Tubewell irrigate around 64% of the irrigated land in India. Wells and Tubewells are now spread over large area of Punjab, Uttar Pradesh, Bihar, Rajasthan, Tamil Nadu and Haryana.

  Tanks: Tank irrigation is resorted to mostly in Tamil Nadu, Andhra Pradesh, and some parts of West Bengal and Bihar. Tanks irragate arround 8% of the irrigated land.

- In agriculture, new technology was tried in 1960-61 as a pilot project in seven districts and was called Intensive Agricultural District Programme (IADP). Later, the high-yielding varieties programme (HYVP) was also added and the strategy was extended to cover the entire country. This strategy has been called by various names—modern agricultural technology, seed-fertilizer-water technology or simply Green revolution.

Achievements of the New Agricultural Strategy

(*i*) Increase in the production of cereals.
(*ii*) Increase in the production of commercial crops.
(*iii*) Significant changes in the crop pattern.
(*iv*) Boost to agricultural production and employment.

Agricultural Prices

- **Minimum Support Prices (MSP):** Keeping in view the interests of the farmers as also the need of self reliance, Govt. has been announcing minimum support price. The main objectives of announcing MSP are:
  1. To prevent fall in price in the situation of over production.
  2. To protect the interest of farmers by ensuring them a minimum price for their crops in the situation of a price fall in the market.
- **Procurement Prices:** The price at which government buys surplus from the farming coming in the market. The minimum support price and the procurement price may be the same.
- **Issue Prices:** The prices at which fair price shops sell cereals like wheat rice etc.

New Agricultural Policy (2000)

Union Government has announced new Agricultural Policy in the parliament on July 28, 2000. This policy has been planned under the povisions of WTO so as to face the challenges of agriculture sector. This policy gives emphasis on promoting agricultural exports after fulfilling domestic demand.

The sailent features of this policy are:

- To achieve 4% growth rate per annum for the next two decades.
- To do Land reforms to provide land to poor farmers.
- Consolidation of holding in all states of the nation.
- Promoting private investment in agriculture.
- To provide insurance umbrella for crops to farmers.
- To promote biotechnology.
- Promoting research for developing new varieties and ensuring protection to the developed varieties.
- New Agriculture policy has been described as 'Rainbow Revolution' which includes the following revolutions:

(*i*) Green	– Food Grain Production
(*ii*) White	– Milk
(*iii*) Yellow	– Oil Seeds
(*iv*) Blue	– Fisheries
(*v*) Red	– Meat/Tomato
(*vi*) Golden	– Fruits-Apple
(*vii*) Grey	– Fertiliser
(*viii*) Black/Brown	– Non-conventional Energy Sources
(*ix*) Silver	– Eggs
(*x*) Round	– Potato
(*xi*) Sweet	– Honey
(*xii*) Purple/Lavender	– Aromatic Crops

Major Crops and Their Seasons

The Indian crops can be devided into two major groups:

1. **Kharif Crops:** This crop is sown in the month of July and harvested in October every year. Kharif

crop includes—Rice (Paddy), Jowar, Bajra, Maize, Cotton, Sugarcane, Seasamum, Soyabean, and Groundnut etc.

2. **Rabi Crop:** This crop is sown in October end and harvested in March/April every year. Rabi crop includes—Wheat, Jowar, Barley, Gram, Tur, Rapseed, and Mustard etc.
3. **Zayad Crop:** In some parts of the country a crop, known as Zayad crop is sown during March to June every year. Zayad crops include—Melon, Watermelon, Vegetables, Cucumber, Moong, and Urad etc.

Commercial Crops

Commercial crops are those crops which are produced for trade purpose and earning money and not for self-consumption by the farmers. These commercial crops include:

(i) **Oilseeds crops:** Groundnut, Mustard, Sesamum, Rapeseed, Linseed, Castor, Sunflower, Nigenseed and Soyabean etc.

(ii) **Sugar Crops:** Sugarcane and Beat.

(iii) **Fibre Crops:** Jute, Mesta, Sunhemp and Cotton.

(iv) **Narcotic Crop:** Tobacco.

(v) **Beverage Crops:** Tea, Coffee.

National Mission on Oilseeds and Oil Palm: National Mission on Oilseeds and Oil Palm (NMOOP) envisages increase in production of vegetable oils sourced from oilseeds, oil palm and tree borne oilseeds from 7.06 million tonnes to 9.51 million tonnes by the end of 12th Plan (2016-17). The Mission is being implemented through three mini missions with specific target.

The strategy to implement the proposed mission will include increasing seed replacement ratio with focus on varietal replacement; increasing irrigation coverage under oilseeds from 26 per cent to 36 per cent; diversification of area from low yielding cereals crops to oilseeds crops; inter-cropping of oilseeds with cereals/pulses/sugarcane; use of fallow land after paddy potato cultivation; expansion of cultivation of oil palm in watersheds and wastelands; increasing availability of quality planting materials of oil palm.

National Mission for Sustainable Agriculture: (NMSA) as a programmatic intervention made operational from the year 2014-15 aims at making agriculture more productive, sustainable and remunerative and climate resilient by promoting location specific integrated / composite farming systems; soil and moisture conservation measures; comprehensive soil health management; efficient water management practices and mainstreaming rainfed technologies.

Various Crops and their producing states

Crops/Groups of Crops	*Producing State (In Descending Order)*
I. Foodgrains	
Rice	Uttar Pradesh, Telangana, West Bengal
Wheat	Uttar Pradesh, Madhya Pradesh, Punjab
Maize	Bihar, Madhya Pradesh, Karnataka
Total Coarse	Rajasthan, Karnataka
Cereals	Madhya Pradesh
Gram	Maharashtra, Madhya Pradesh, Rajasthan
Tur	Maharashtra, Karnataka, Jharkhand
Total Pulses	Madhya Pradesh, Maharashtra, Rajasthan
Total Food-grains	Uttar Pradesh, Madhya Pradesh, Punjab
II. Oilseeds	
Groundnut	Gujarat, Rajasthan, Madhya Pradesh
Rapeseed & Mustard	Rajasthan, Uttar Pradesh, Haryana,
Soyabean	Maharashtra, Madhya Pradesh, Rajasthan
Sunflower	Karnataka, Haryana, Odisha
Total Oilseeds	Rajasthan, Madhya Pradesh, Maharashtra
III. Other Cash Crops	
Sugarcane	Uttar Pradesh, Maharashtra, Karnataka
Cotton	Maharashtra, Gujarat, Telangana
Jute & Mesta	West Bengal, Bihar, Assam

Source: Directorate of Economics & Statistics, 2024-25

Paramparagat Krishi Vikas Yojana: Government is implementing a cluster based programme to encourage the farmers for promoting organic farming called Paramparagat Krishi Vikas Yojana (PKVY). Under this programme, group of farmers would be motivated to take up organic farming. Fifty or more farmers will form a cluster having 50 acre land to take up organic farming under the scheme. In this way during three years (2015-16 to 2017-18) 10,000 clusters will be formed covering 5.0 lakh acre area under organic farming. There will be no liability on the farmers for expenditure on certification. Every farmer will be provided ₹ 20,000 per acre over three years to meet end to end expenditure— seed to harvesting of crops to transport of produce to the market. Organic farming will be promoted by using traditional resources and the organic products will be linked with the market. It will increase domestic production and certification of organic produce by involving farmers.

MAJOR SCHEMES/PROGRAMMES IN THE AGRICULTURE SECTOR

1. National Food Security Mission (NFSM)

National Food Security Mission (NFSM) was launched in 2007-08 to increase the production of rice, wheat and pulses by 10, 8 and 2 million tonnes, respectively by the end of 11th Plan through area expansion and productivity enhancement; restoring soil fertility and productivity; creating employment opportunities; and enhancing farm level economy. The Mission is being continued during 12th Five Year Plan with new target of additional production of 25 million tonnes of foodgrains comprising 10 million tonnes of rice, 8 million tonnes of wheat, 4 million tonnes of pulses and 3 million tonnes of coarse cereals by the end of the 12th Plan.

The major interventions/activities covered under NFSM include cluster demonstrations of rice, wheat, pulses and coarse cereals, distribution of improved varieties/hybrid seeds, need based plant and soil management, farm mechanization, resource conservation techniques/energy management, efficient water/application tools, cropping system based trainings and local initiatives, etc. NFSM-coarse cereals and NFSM-commercial crops are included under revamped NFSM. From 2016-17, NFSM is being implemented in 644 districts of 28 states and 2 UTs. From the year 2015-16, the programme is being implemented on a fund sharing ratio of 50 : 50 between Government of India and states.

2. Macro Management of Agriculture (MMA)

The Macro Management of Agriculture (MMA) scheme was revised in 2008 to improve its efficacy in supplementing/complementing the efforts of the States towards enhancement of agricultural production and productivity and provide opportunity to draw upon their agricultural development programmes relating to crop production and natural resource management, with the flexibility to use 20 per cent of resources for innovative components. The revised MMA Scheme has formula-based allocation criteria and provides assistance in the form of grants to the states/UTs on 90 : 10 basis except in case of the north-eastern States and Union Territories where the Central share is 100 per cent. Out of the total outlay for the 11th Plan *i.e.*, ₹ 5500 crore, funds amounting ₹ 3845 crore have been utilised/relesed to the States/UTs during the first four years of the plan period.

Main features of the revised MMA scheme are as follows:

- The practice of allocating funds to States/UTs on a historical basis has been replaced by a new allocation criteria based on gross cropped area and area under small and marginal holdings. The assistance would be provided to the states/UTs as 100% grant.
- The subsidy structure has been rationalized to make the pattern of subsidy uniform under all the schemes implemented by the Department of Agriculture and permissible limit of assistance.
- Two new components have been added namely, (a) Integrated Scheme of Oilseeds, Pulses, (b) 'Reclamation of Acidic Soil'.
- The permissible ceiling for new initiatives has been increased from the existing 10% to 20% of the allocation.

- At least 33% of the funds have to be earmarked for small, marginal and women farmers.
- Active participation of the Panchayati Raj Institutions (PRIs) of all tiers would have to be ensured in the implementation of the Revised MMA scheme including review, monitoring and evaluation at district and sub-district level.

3. Rashtriya Krishi Vikas Yojana (RKVY)

The RKVY was launched in 2007-08 with an outlay of of ₹25,000 crore for the 11th five year plan. The RKVY aims at achieving the 4% annual growth in the agriculture sector during the 11th five year plan period by ensuring a holistic development of agriculture and allied sectors. The funds under the RKVY is provided to the states as 100 per cent grant by the Central Government. The main objective of the schemes were:

- To incentivise the states to increase public investment to achieve 4% growth in agriculture and allied sector during 11th plan.
- To provide flexibility and autonomy to the states in planning and exceuting agriculture and allied sector schemes.
- To ensure the preparation of plans for the district and the states based on agro-climatic conditions, availability of technology and natural resources.
- To ensure that the local needs/crops priorities are better reflected.
- To achieve the goal of reducing the yield gaps in important crops, through focused interventions.
- To maximize returns to farmers.

4. Integrated Scheme of Oilseeds, Pulses, Oil palm, and Maize (ISOPOM)

The ministry of agriculture has restructured oilseeds, pulses, oil palm and maize development programmes into one centrally sponsored ISOPOM which is being implemented in 14 major states for oilseeds and pulses, 15 for maize, and 9 for oil palm. The pulses component has been merged with the NFSM with effect from 1 April, 2010.

5. National Mission for Sustainable Agriculture (NMSA)

NMSA as a programmatic intervention made operational from the year 2014-15 aims at making agriculture more productive, sustainable and remunerative and climate resilient by promoting location specific integrated/composite farming systems; soil and moisture conservation measures; comprehensive soil health management; efficient water management practices and mainstreaming rainfed technologies.

6. Pradhan Mantri Krishi Sinchai Yojana

To Boost irrigation facilities, Pradhan Mantri Krishi Sinchai Yojana (PMKSY) has been formulated to provide end-to-end solutions in irrigation supply chain, viz. water sources, and distribution network and farm level applications. A budget provision of ₹ 6,587 crore for 2026-27 has been made for implementation of PMKSY. The PMKSY programme will focus on : (*i*) ensuring access to water to every agriculture farm (*Har Khet Ko Pani*); (*ii*) increasing agricultural production and productivity by increasing availability and efficient use of water; (*iii*) providing flexibility and autonomy to states in the progress of planning and executing programmes; and (*iv*) ensuring a holistic approach by way of preparation of comprehensive district and state irrigation plans.

7. Mission for Integrated Development of Horticulture

The Mission for Integrated Development of Horticulture (MIDH), was launched during the Twelfth Plan with effect from 2014-15, for the holistic development of the horticulture sector covering fruits, vegetables, mushrooms, spices, flowers, aromatic plants, coconut, cashew, cocoa and bamboo. The MIDH subsumes the National Horticulture Mission (NHM), the Horticulture Mission for North East & Himalayan States (HMNEH), the National Bamboo Mission (NBM), the National Horticulture Board (NHB), the Coconut Development Board (CDB) and the Central Institute for Horticulture (CIH), Nagaland. The Government of India (GOI) contributes 85 per cent of the total outlay for developmental programmes in all the states. From 2015-16, the pattern of assistance is 60 : 40 between the Government of India and NHM states and 90 : 10 for HMNEH states. All states are covered under the MIDH. During 2014-15, a budget provision of ₹ 2,263.00 crore had been made for the MIDH, out of which, an amount of ₹ 1,584.84 crore was released for the NHM and HMNEH components.

Since the inception of the NHM, an area of 24.63 lakh ha has been covered under various horticulture crops. In addition, an area of 5.25 lakh ha of old orchards, has been rejuvenated. 12.04 lakh farmers have been trained under various horticulture activities. 2,923 nurseries have been established for supply of quality planting material to beneficiaries. Under protected cultivation practices, and area of 1.54 lakh ha has been covered. An area of 11.96 lakh ha has been covered under Integrated Pest Management (IPM)/ Integrated Nutrient Management (INM). 816 IPM infrastructures have been established. A total of 45,858 water harvesting structures have been created. To promote apiculture, 6,10,048 bee colonies, with hives have been distributed. Under Horticulture Mechanization, 82,771 mechanical equipments including Plant Protection equipments have been distributed.

8. Pradhan Mantri Fasal Bima Yojana (PMFBY)

The erstwhile crop insurance schemes have recently been reviewed in consultation with various stakeholders including States/UTs. As a result of the review, a new scheme "Pradhan Mantri Fasal Bima Yojana (PMFBY) has been approved for implementation from Kharif 2016 along with pilot Unified Package Insurance Scheme (UPIS) and restructured Weather Based Crop Insurance Scheme (WBCIS). Under the PMFBY, a uniform maximum premium of only 2% will be paid by farmers for all Kharif crops and 1.5% for all Rabi crops. In case of annual commercial and horticultural crops, the maximum premium to be paid by farmers will be only 5%. The premium rates to be paid by farmers are very low and balance premium will be paid by the Government, to be shared equally by State & Central Government, to provide full insured amount to the farmers against crop loss on account of natural calamities. There is no upper limit on Government subsidy.

The Salient features of PMFBY are as under :

- PMFBY provides a comprehensive insurance cover against failure of the crop thus helping in stabilising the income of the farmers and encouraging them to adopt innovative practices.
- The Scheme envisages coverage of all Food & Oilseeds crops and Annual Commercial/ Horticultural Crops for which past yield data is available and for which requisite number of Crop Cutting Experiments (CCEs) will be conducted being a part of the General Crop Estimation Survey (GCES).
- The scheme is compulsory for loanee farmer obtaining Crop Loan /KCC account for notified crops. However, voluntary for Other/non loanee farmers who have insurable interest in the insured crop(s).
- The difference between premium and the rate of Insurance charges payable by farmers is shared equally by the Centre and State.
- The scheme is implemented by AIC, all companies of General Insurers' (Public Sector) Association (GIPSA) and other empanelled private general insurance companies. Selection of Implementing Agency (IA) will be done by the concerned State Government through bidding.
- The existing State Level Co-ordination Committee on Crop Insurance (SLCCCI), Sub-Committee to SLCCCI, District Level Monitoring Committee (DLMC) is responsible for proper management of the Scheme.
- The Scheme is implemented on an 'Area Approach basis'. The unit of insurance shall be Village/Village Panchayat level for major crops and for other crops it may be a unit of size above the level of Village/Village Panchayat.
- The Threshold Yield (TY) shall be the benchmark yield level at which Insurance protection shall be given to all the insured farmers in an Insurance Unit Threshold of the notified crop will be moving average of yield of last seven years excluding yield upto two notified calamity years multiplied by Indemnity level.
- Three levels of Indemnity, viz., 70%, 80% and 90% corresponding to crop Risk in the areas is available for all crops.
- The Loss assessment for crop losses due to non-preventable natural risks will be on Area approach.

- However losses due to localised perils (Hailstorm, landslide & inundation) and Post-Harvest losses due to specified perils, (Cyclone/Cyclonic rain & Unseasonal rains) shall be assessed at the affected insured field of the individual insured farmer.
- In case of majority of insured crops of a notified area are prevented from sowing/planting the insured crops due to adverse weather conditions that will be eligible for indemnity claims upto maximum of 25% of the sum-insured.
- The designated / empanelled companies participating in bidding have to bid the premium rates for all the crops notified / to be notified by the State Govt. and non-compliance will lead to rejection of company's bid
- Crop Cutting Experiments (CCE) shall be undertaken per unit area /per crop, on a sliding scale, as prescribed under the scheme outline and operational guidelines. Improved Technology like Remote Sensing. Drone etc will be utilised for estimation of yield losses.
- The cost of using technology etc. for conduct of CCEs etc will be shared between Central Government and State/U.T. Governments on 50:50 basis.
- The claim amount will be credited electronically to the individual Insured Bank Account.
- Adequate publicity needs to be given in all the villages of the notified districts/areas
- A crop insurance Portal www.agriinsurance.gov.in has been developed for better administration, coordination amongst Stakeholders, transmission/ dissemination of information and transparency.

During first season i.e. Kharif 2016 about 374 lakh farmers for a sum insured of Rs. 141487 crore have been covered under PMFBY & WBCIS.

9. Agricultural Credit

The Government has taken many policy initiatives for strengthening of farm credit delivery system for providing credit at affordable rate of interest to support the resource requirments of the agricultural sector. Some sources of agricultural credit are as follows:

- Agricultural credit is disbursed through a Multi Agency network comprising of Commercial Banks (CBs), Regional Rural Bank (RRBs) and Cooperative with their vast network covering allmost all the villages in the country and outreach extending to the remotest part of the country. In addition, on the lines of the Business Correspondent and Business Facilitator model, Banks are using the services of NGOs, SHGs, Joint Liability Groups (JLGs), Micro Finance Institutions and other civil society organisation as intermediates in providing financial and banking services in the rural areas.
- Kisan Credit Card (KCC) scheme was introduced in August, 1998 with major share of crop loans being routed through it. Banks were advised that the credit card should normally be valid for 3 years subject to an annual review.
- The scheme was revised in October 2004. The revised scheme aims at providing adequate and timely credit for the comprehensive credit requirements of farmers under single window, with flexible and simplified procedure, adopting whole farm approach including the short term credit needs, term loan and a reasonable component for consumption needs, through Kisan Credit Card.
- There is coverage of risk of KCC holder against accidental death or permanent disability upto a maximum of ₹ 50,000 and ₹ 25,000 respectively. It has been decided to convert KCCs into Smart Cards to facilitate its operation through ATMs.

Agricultural Insurance

There are various major crop insurance schemes under implementation in the country. Some Insurance schemes are as follows:

1. **National Agricultural Insurance Scheme (NAIS):** With a view to provide insurance coverage and financial support to the farmers in the event of failure of any of the notified crop in the notified areas as a result of natural calamities,

pest and diseases; to encourage the farmers to adopt progressive farming practices, high value inputs and higher technology in agriculture and to stabilise farm incomes, particularly in disaster years, NAIS is being implemented in the country from Rabi 1999-2000 season. At present, the scheme is being implemented by 25 states and 2 UTs.

2. **Modified NAIS (MNAIS):** With the aim of further improving crop insurance scheme, the MNAIS is under implementation on pilot basis in 50 districts in the country from the Rabi 2010-11 season. The Salient features of MNAIS are as under:
   - only upfront premium is shared by the Central and State Governments on 50:50 basis and all chains liability would be on the insurance companies.
   - Actuarial premium with subsidy in premium ranging 40% to 75% to all farmers.
   - Unit area of insurance reduced to village/ village panchayat level for major crops.
   - Indemnity for prevented sowing/planting risk and for post harvest losses due to cyclone.
   - One account payment up to 25% advance of likely claims as immediate relief.
   - Minimum indemnity level of 70% instead of 60%.
   - Scheme is available to all the farmers—loanee and non-loanee—irrespective of their size of holding.
   - Loanee farmers are covered on compulsory basis in a notified area for notified crops whereas for non-loanee farmers scheme is voluntary.
   - Uniform seasonality disciplines both for loanee and non-loanee farmers.
   - Participation of private sector insurers for creation of competitive environment for crop insurance.

3. **Weather Based Crop Insurance Scheme (WBCIS):** The WBCIS is being implemented as a central-sector scheme from Kharif 2007 season. The scheme is intended to provide insurance protection to farmers against adverse weather incidence, such as deficit and excess rainfall, high or low temperature and humidity that are deemed to adversely impact crop production. The WBCIS is based on actuarial rates of premium but to make the scheme attractive, premium actually charged from farmers has been restricted to be on a par with NAIS.

4. **Coconut Palm Insurance Scheme (CPIS):** The Department of Agriculture and Cooperation is implementing CPIs on pilot basis during years 2009-10 and 2010-11 in the selected areas of Andhra Pradesh, Goa, Karnataka, Kerala, Maharashtra, Odisha, Tamilnadu and West Bengal. The scheme is being administered by the Coconut Development Board (CDB) through AIC. The scheme propose to cover entire palms in the region selected for implementation, according to eligibility criteria. The Sum Insured (SI) is based on average input cost of the plantation and the age of the specific plant.

Agricultural Marketing

Organised marketing of agricultural commodities has been promoted of regulated markets. Most of the state governments and Union Territories have enacted legislations (APMC Act) to provide for regulation of agricultural produce market. According to the provision of the APMC Acts of the state every APMC is authorised to collect market fees from the buyers/ traders in the prescribed manner on the sale of notified agricultural produce.

The Government of India has circulated model legislation titled "The State Agricultural Produce Marketing (Development and Regulation) Act 2003 to bring about reform in agricultural marketing. Contract farming, direct marketing and public-private partnership in management and development of agricultural markets are the major instruments of change among others.

Infrastructure Requirement

Investment requirement for the development of marketing, storage and cold storage infrastructure in the country has been estimated to be huge and with a view to induce investment in the development of marketing infrastructure as envisaged above, the Ministry has implemented the following plan schemes:

(*i*) ***Grameen Bhandaran Yojana:*** The Government of India, Ministry of Agriculture has launched 'Grameen Bhandaran Yojana' w.e.f. 1st April, 2011. The main objectives of the scheme include creation of scientific storage capacity with allied facilities in rural areas to meet out various requirements of farmers for storing farm produce, processed farm produce, agricultural inputs, etc, and prevention of distress sale by creating the facility of pledge loan and marketing credit.

(*ii*) ***Marketing Research and Information Network:*** The Ministry of Agriculture has launched an ICT based Central Sector Scheme of Marketing Research and Information Network in March 2000 to provide electronic connectivity to important wholesale agricultural markets in the country for collection and dissemination of wholesale prices and other market related information to the farmers and other users through AGMARKNET portal (www.agmarknet.nic.in). As on date, 3026 markets have been linked with AGMARKNET portal from all over the country. These markets are reporting daily prices and arrival in respect of more than 300 commodities and 2000 varieties from more than 1800 market covering all major agricultural and horticultural produce.

(*iii*) ***Development/Strengthening of Agricultural Marketing Infrastructure, Grading and Standardization:*** The Ministry of Agriculture is implementing another Central Sector Scheme for 'Development Strengthening of Agricultural Marketing Infrastructure, Grading and Standardisation' under which, investment subsidy is provided @ 25 per cent on the capital cost of the marketing infrastructure development subject to a maximum of ₹ 60 lakh for each project in case of North-Eastern States, Jammu and Kashmir, Uttarakhand, Himachal Pradesh, hilly area and to SC/ST and their cooperatives.

(*iv*) ***Terminal Market Complex:*** The Department has taken the initiative to promote modern terminal markets for fruits, vegetables and other perishables in important urban centres of the country. These markets would provide state of art infrastructure facilities for electronic auction, cold chain and logistics and operate through primary collection centres conveniently locate in producing areas to allow easy access to farmers.

Food Management

Food Management in India has three basic objectives:

- Procurement of foodgrains from farmers at remunerative prices.
- Distribution of foodgrains to the consumers particularly, the vulnerable sections of the society at affordable prices.
- Maintenance of food buffers for food security and price stability. The instruments for food management are—the Minimum Support Price (MSP) and Central Issue Price (CIP).
- Food Stock are maintained by the Central Government for three purposes:
  (*i*) Meeting the prescribed minimum buffer stock norms for food security.
  (*ii*) For monthly release of foodgrains for supply through Public Distribution System (PDS).
  (*iii*) For market intervention to augment supply so as to help moderate the open market prices.

Miscellaneous

- ***Krishi Shramik Suraksha Yojana:*** The multi-benefit scheme for the agricultural workers, commenced on 1 July, 2001 provides life insurance protection, perodical lumpsum survival benefit and pension to those who were between the age of 18-50 years.
- ***Pradhan Mantri Kisan Samman Nidhi Scheme:*** The Pradhan Mantri Kisan Samman Nidhi (PM-KISAN), a Central Sector Scheme, aims at providing financial assistance to all cultivable landholding farmer families across the country, subject to certain exclusion criteria. Under the Scheme, an amount of ₹ 6000 is transferred annually in three equal installments of ₹ 2000 directly into the Aadhaar Seeded bank accounts of the farmers. A farmer-centric digital infrastructure has ensured the benefits of the scheme reach all the farmers across the country without any involvement of the middlemen,

maintaining absolute transparency in registering and verifying beneficiaries. The Government of India has disbursed over ₹ 2.60 Lakhs Crores to more than 11 Cr farmers. The PM-KISAN Scheme was launched in Feb. 2019. The state of West Bengal joined the Scheme from 8th installment (April-July, 2021) as initially the State desired that the funds under PM-KISAN Scheme be transferred to the State Government for onward disbursement to the farmers through the State Government.

- ***Command Area Development & Water Management Programme (CADWMP):*** The centrally-sponsored Command Area Development (CAD) programme was launched in 1974-75, with the main objectives of improving the utilisation of created irrigation potential and optimising agriculture production and productivity from irrigated lands on sustainable basis, by integrating all functions related with irrigated agriculture through a multi-disciplinary team under an area Development Authority. The CAD Programme was initiated with 60 major and medium irrigation projects.

  The CAD Programme has been restructured and renamed as Command Area Development and Water Management Programme (CADWMP) w.e.f. 1st April, 2004.

5. INDUSTRY

- After independence, the first industrial policy was declared on April 6, 1948 by then Union Industry Minister Mr. Shyama Prasad Mukherjee.
- Under this first industrial policy established a base for Mixed and Controlled Economy in India and clearly divided the industrial sector into private and public sectors.
- Second Industrial Policy Resolution declared on April 30, 1956 with the basic objective of establishing 'Socialistic Pattern of Society' in the country.
- The 1956 Resolution laid down the following objectives for the industrial policy:
  1. To accelerate the rate of growth and to speed up industrialisation;
  2. To develop heavy industries and machine making industries;
  3. To expand public sector;
  4. To reduce disparities in income and wealth;
  5. To build up a large and growing cooperative sector; and
  6. To prevent monopolies and the concentration of wealth and income in the hands of a small number of individuals.
- To control and regulate the process of industrial development in the country, an Act was passed by the parliament in October 1951. Known as the Industries (Development and Regulation) Act, 1951, the Act came into force on May 8, 1952. Though it aimed at both, development and regulation of private sector, its main task over the year has been to concentrate more on the 'regulation aspect'.
- Because of the criticisms indicating the failure of the industrial licensing policy in achieving its objectives, the Government of India announced a number of liberalisation measures in the industrial Licensing Policy announced in 1970, 1973 and 1978. In 1980, the government came forward with an Industrial Policy statement which served as a guideline to various liberalisation measures undertaken all through the 1980s.
- In line with the liberalisation measures announced during the 1980s, the government announced a New Industrial Policy on July 24, 1991. This new policy de-regulates the industrial economy in a substantial manner. The major objectives of the new policy are "to build on the gains already made, correct the distortions or

weaknesses that might have crept in, maintain a sustained growth in productivity and gainful employment, and attain international competitiveness." In pursuit of these objectives, the government announced a series of initiatives in respect of the policies relating to the following areas:

1. **Abolition of Industrial Licencing:** Industrial licensing policy in India has been governed by the Industries (Development and Regulation) Act, 1951. Industrial licensing policy and procedures have been liberalised considerably from time to time. Yet, the industrial licensing policy has all along been resented to by the entrepreneurs as it led to unnecessary governmental interference, delays in investment decisions and bureaucratic red-tapism, corruption etc. Not only this, the industrial licensing policy was also unable to achieve the objectives laid down for it by the government. On account of these considerations, and in order to liberalise the economy and to enable the entrepreneurs to make investment decisions on the basis of their own commercial judgement, the 1991 industrial policy abolished industrial licensing for all but 18. The 18 industries for which licensing was kept necessary, with the passage of time, most of these industries have also been delicensed. As of now, licensing is compulsory for only 5 industries. These are:
   (*a*) Distillation and brewing of alcoholic drinks.
   (*b*) Cigar, Cigarettes and other substitutes of prepared tobacco.
   (*c*) Electronic, Aerospace and all types of defence equipment.
   (*d*) Industrial Explosive including match boxes.
   (*e*) Hazardous chemicals.
2. **Public Sector's Role Diluted:** The 1956 Resolution had reserved 17 industries for the public sector. The 1991 industrial policy reduced this number to 8. The policy has been liberalised progressively and presently only 3 industries are reserved for the public sector. These are:
   (*a*) atomic energy,
   (*b*) the substances specified in the schedule to the notification of the Government of India in the Department of Atomic Energy dated the 15 March, 1995 and
   (*c*) railway transport.
3. **MRTP Limit Goes:** Under the MRTP Act, all firm with assets above a certain size were classified as MRTP firms. Such firms were permitted to enter selected industries only and this also on a case by case approval basis. In addition to control through industrial licensing, separate approvals were required by such large firms for any investment proposals. The new industrial policy therefore scrapped the threshold limit of assets in respect of MRTP and dominant undertakings. These firms will now be at par with others, and not require prior approval from the government for investment in the delicensed industries. The MRTP Act was accordingly amended. The amended Act gave more emphasis to prevention and control monopolistic, restrictive and unfair trade practices so that consumers are adequately protected from such practices.
4. **Industrial location policy liberalised:** In a departure from the earlier locational policy for industries, the new industrial policy provided that in locations other than cities of more than 1 million population, there will be requirement of obtaining industrial approvals from the centre, except for industries subject to compulsory licensing. In cities with a population of more than 1 million, industries other than those of a polluting nature, were required to be located outside 25 kms. of the periphery.
5. **Free Entry to Foreign Investment and Technology:** Presently FDI (Foreign Direct

Investment) is permitted upto 100 per cent on the automatic route in most sectors subject to sectorial rules/regulations applicable. FDI is prohibited only in the following sectors:

(*a*) retail trading except single brand product retailing,

(*b*) atomic energy,

(*c*) lottery business, and

(*d*) gambling and betting.

- The new Index of industrial production (IIP) series with 2011-12 as base years was released in 12 May, 2017, replacing the earlier IIP series with base year 1993-94.
- The new IIP series not only has a more recent base, it has larger and more representative product basket and weights that appropriately reflect the relative importance of the sectors, products and product group.
- The government released the National Manufacturing policy (NMP) on 4 November 2011 for bringing about a quantitative and qualitative change with objectives to (*i*) increase manufacturing sector growth to 12-14 per cent over the medium term; (*ii*) enable manufacturing to contribute at least 25 per cent of GDP by 2022; (*iii*) create 100 million additional jobs in the manufacturing sector by 2022; (*iv*) create appropriate skill sets among the rural migrant and urban poor for their easy absorption in manufacturing; (*v*) increase domesting value addition and technological depth in manufacturing; and (*vi*) enhance global competitiveness of Indian manufacturing.
- With a view to delegating enhanced financial and operational powers to CPSEs (Central Public Sector Enterprises), the government introduced the Navratna Scheme in July 1997.
- In December 2009, the Government introduced the Maharatna Scheme enhancing financial delegation to CPSEs.
- In December 2004, the government established a Board for Reconstruction of Public Sector Enterprises (BRPSE) to advice on revival/ restructuring of sick and loss-making CPSEs.
- Some of the recent reforms are: reducing the list of industries that can be considered defence industries requiring industrial licence; and amendments in FDI policy which include allowing FDI in defence up to 74 per cent, in railway infrastructure up to 100 per cent and in the insurance and pension sector up to 100 per cent.
- The government has launched several programmes/initiatives such as ease of doing business, Make in India, Invest India, and e-biz Mission Mode Project under the National e-Governance Plan.
- With the objective of making India a global hub of manufacturing, design and innovation, the Make in India initiative, which is based on four pillars — new processes, new infrastructure, new sectors and new mindset — has been taken by the government. The initiative is set to boost entrepreneurship, not only in manufacturing but in relevant infrastructure and service sectors as well.
- The 1991 industrial policy brought the public sector units at par with the private sector units. As a result, the public sector units were also brought within the jurisdiction of Board of Industrial and Financial Reconstruction (BIFR). Thus BIFR was given the responsibility to decide whether a sick public sector unit can be effectively restructured or whether it has to be closed down.
- One of the major initiatives towards the public sector as outlined in the new industrial policy of July 1991 was to bring all public sector enterprises under the system of Memorandum of Understanding (MoU). The system of MoU envisages an arm's length relationship between the PSU and the administrative ministries. It gives clear targets to PSUs and ensures operational autonomy to them for achieving those targets. The MoU system was started in 1987-88.
- The first unit in the public sector, now known as the Visvesvaraya Iron and Steel Works Ltd., started functioning at Bhadravati in 1923.

- During the second five year plan (1956-61) a major task in industry was building up of three steel plants in the public sector—Rourkela Steel Plant in Odisha (then Orissa), Bhilai Steel Plant in Chhattisgarh (then Madhya Pradesh) and Durgapur Steel Plant in West Bengal. The three steel plants came into operation in stage between 1959 and 1962.
- Bokaro steel plant was established in third five year plan.
- Increased production capacity of iron and steel was planned by establishing new steel plants at Salem (Tamil Nadu), Vijai Nagar (Karnataka) and Vishakhapatanam (Andhra Pradesh), during the fourth-five year plan.
- In 1974, the Steel Authority of India Limited (SAIL) was created and was made responsible for the development of steel industry.
- SAIL is also responsible for management of Bhilai, Durgapur, Rourkela, Bokaro and Burnpur steel plants. Besides SAIL has been given responsibility of managing Alloy Steel Plant, Durgapur and Salem Steel Plant.
- On July 14, 1976, the Government took over the ownership of IISCO plant and as a result IISCO also came under the control of SAIL.
- The National Steel Policy (NSP) 2005 has already been approved by Government. The long-term goal of NSP is to ensure that India has a modern and efficient steel industry, capable of standing up to international competition and catering to the growing domestic demand for steel.
- Globally, India is the largest producer and second largest exporter of jute goods. There are 119 jute mills in the country which are located in West Bengal, Bihar, Odisha, Uttar Pradesh, Andhra Pradesh, Assam, Chhattisgarh and Tripura.
- The government has formulated first ever National Jute policy in 2005 with an objective of increasing production, improving quality, ensuring remunerative prices to the jute farmers and per hectare yield.
- Sugar industry occupies an important place among agriculture based industries. This industry took a shape of a large industry in the beginning of 20th century. Sugar industry is the second largest industry after cotton textile industry among agriculture based industries of the country.
- India is the second largest producer of cement in the world after China. The cement industry was delicensed in 1991.
- The small and medium sector has been defined as micro, small and medium enterprises with effect from October 2, 2006 (the Act defined the medium enterprises for the first time). Further, separate investment limits have been prescribed for manufacturing and service enterprises. The new definition is as follows:

MSMEs Criteria for Manufacturing and Services:

- ❑ A micro enterprise, where the investment in plant and machinery does not exceed ₹ 2.5 crore;
- ❑ A small enterprise, where the investment in plant and machinery is more than ₹ 2.5 crore but does not exceed ₹ 25 crore; and
- ❑ A medium enterprise, where the investment in plant and machinery is more than ₹ 25 crore but does not exceed ₹ 125 crore.

- As of March, 2026, there were more than 7.8 crores MSMEs in the country, which provide employment to about 28 crores people. Of the total, 33 per cent were in the manufacturing sector and 67 per cent in the other sectors.
- Manufacturing enterprises constitute 31.8 per cent of the micro, small, and medium enterprises (MSME) sector and service enterprises account for the remaining 68.2 per cent. About 51 per cent of these enterprises are located in rural areas.
- A Cottage Industries Board was set up in 1947 itself. This was split into the following three board during the First Five Year Plan—All India

Handloom Board, All India Handicrafts Board, and All India Khadi and Village Industries Board. In addition, three more boards were set up. These were the small scale Industries Board, Coir Board and Central Silk Board. Thus at the end of First Five Year Plan, there were a total of six boards covering the entire field of small-scale and cottage industries.

- Small Industries Development Organisation (SIDO) was set up in 1954. It functions as an apex body in the formulation of policies and co-ordination of institutional activities for sustained and organised growth of small-scale industries. It has a large network of small industries services institutes, branch institutes, toolrooms etc. SIDO has now been renamed as the Micro, Small and Medium Enterprises Development Organisation.
- National Small Industries Corporation Ltd. (NSIC) was set up in 1955 to provide machinery to small-scale units an hire-purchase basis and to assist these units in procuring orders from government departments and offices.
- The programme of District Industries Centre (DICs) was introduced in May 1979. The idea was to establish on agency in each district called the District Industries Centre to provide and arrange a package of assistance and facilities for credit guidance, raw materials, training, marketing etc. including the necessary help to unemployed educated young entrepreneurs in general and custom services.
- Several Schemes were introduced to provide financial assistance to small scale industries. These include—

  (*i*) **SIDF :** The Small Industries Development Fund (SIDF) was set up in 1986. It provides refinance assistance for development, expansion, diversification and rehabilitation of small scale, cottage and village industries and tiny sector in rural areas.

  (*ii*) **NEF :** National Equity Fund (NEF) was set up in 1987. It provides equity type support to small entrepreneurs for setting up new projects in tiny/small scale sector and also assistance for rehabilitation of viable sick units in the small-scale sector.

  (*iii*) **SWS :** Single Window Scheme (SWS) was set up in 1988. It provides working capital loans alongwith term loans for fixed capital to new tiny and small scale units.
- Small Industries Development Bank of India (SIDBI) was set up in 1990. It is a Separate Apex Bank, to provide financial assistance to the small-scale industries.
- Due to the policy of de-reservation, the number of items reserved for the SSI Sector (Small Scale Industry Sector) came down from 836 in July 1969 to 114 in March 2007. At present, only 20 items are reserved for the small-scale sector.
- Since the adoption of the economic reforms programme in 1991, the argument is that the MRTP Act has lost its relevance in the new liberalised and global competitive scenario. In view of this, the government appointed an expert committee headed by SVS Raghavan to examine the whole issue. The Raghavan Committee submitted its Report to the government on May 22, 2000 wherein it proposed the adoption of a new competition law and doing away with the MRTP Act, 1969. Accordingly, the government decided to enact a law on competition. Competition Bill, 2001 was introduced in parliament and passed in December 2002. The Act is called Competition Act, 2002. The Act was amended in September 2007.
- The definition of a sick industrial company was changed by the companies (Second Amendment) Act, 2002. According to this Act, "sick industrial company" means an industrial company which has—

  (*i*) the accumulated losses in any financial year which are equal to 50 per cent or more of its average network during four years immediately preceding such financial year; or (*ii*) failed to repay its debt within any three consecutive quarters on demand made in writing for its repayment by a creditor or creditors of such company.

- By a notification issued on March 20, 1985, the government converted the IRCI (which was a company registered under the companies Act, 1956) into a statutory corporation and it was given the name Industrial Reconstruction Bank of India (IRBI). The authorised capital and paid-up capital of IRBI are ₹ 200 crore and ₹ 50 crore respectively.
- IRBI was reconstituted into a full-fledged all purpose development financial institution with effect from March 27, 1997 and its new name is Industrial Investment Bank of India Ltd. (IIBIL). The head office of IIBIL is situated at Kolkata.

6. LABOUR

- Labour policy in India has evolved in response to sepcific needs of the situation to suit the requirements of a planned economic development and social justice and has a two fold objective—(*i*) Maintaining Industrial peace and (*ii*) promoting the welfare of labour.
- The Factories Act, 1948 is the principal legislation for regulating various aspects relating to safety, health and welfare of workers employed in factories. This Act is a Central Enactment, which aims at protecting workers employed in factories from industrial and occupational hazards.
- The Factories Act, 1948 prescribes a 48 hours week for adult workers and forbids employment of children below the age of 14 years in any factory.
- The Minimum Wages Act, 1948 was enacted primarily to safeguard the interests of the workers engaged in an unorganised sector who are vulnerable to exploitation due to illiteracy and lack of bargaining power. The Act binds the employers to pay the minimum wages to the workers as fixed under the statute and workers get protected against exploitation.
- Under the provisions of the Minimum Wages Act, 1948 both the Central and State Governments are appropriate Governments to fix, review, revise and enforce the minimum rates of wages for workers employed in the scheduled employments under their respective jurisdictions. All the provisions of the Act equally apply to both male and female.
- The Payment of Wages Act, 1936, which is labour-friendly legislation, ensures primarly timely payment of wages and that no unauthorized deductions are made from the wages of the workers.
- The Central Government, on the basis of figures of the Consumer Expenditure Survey published by National Sample Survey Organization, has enhanced the wage ceiling from ₹ 10,000 to ₹ 21,000 per month from September 2014.
- The payment of Bonus Act, 1965 provides for payment of bonus to employees of the factories and other establishments employing 20 or more persons. The minimum bonus of 8.33% is payable by every industry and establishment under the section 10 of the Act. The maximum bonus including productivity linked bonus that can be paid in any accounting year shall not exceed 20% of the salary/wage of an employee under the Sections 11 and 31A of the Act.
- The Working Journalist and other Newspaper Employees (conditions of service) and Miscellaneous Provisions Act, 1955 regulates conditions of service of working journalists and other persons employed in newspaper

establishments. The Act provides for setting up of Wage Board for fixation and revision of rates of wages in respect of working journalists and non-journalists newspaper/news agency employees.

- Child Labour (Prohibition & Regulation) Act, 1986, employment of children below the age of 14 years are prohibited in notified hazardous occupations and processes. The Act also regulates employment of children in non-hazardous occupations and processes. There are at present 16 hazardous occupations and 65 processes, where employment of children is prohibited.
- The issue of 'Bonded Labour came in force first in national politics, when it was included in the old 20-point programme in 1975. To implement this Bonded Labour System (Abolition) ordinance was promulgated. This was later replaced by the Bonded Labour System (Abolition) Act, 1976. The district and sub-district magistrates have been entrusted with certain duties and responsibilities towards implementation of statutory provisions.
- The Social Security Act, 2008, provides the social security of unorganised sector workers. The 'unorganised sector' means an enterprise owned by individuals or self-employed workers and engaged in the production or sale of goods or providing service of any kind whatsoever, and where the enterprise employs workers, the number of such workers is less than ten.
- V.V. Giri National Labour Institute is a premier institution involved with research, training, education, publication, and consultancy on labour and related issues. The institute, established in 1974, at Noida (Uttar Pradesh), is an autonomous body of the Ministry of Labour and Employment, Government of India. The Institute engages in research pertaining to labour and training of labour, administrators concerned with labour. Seminar, workshops and lectures are organised on specific issues from time to time.
- The Central Board for Workers Education (CBWE) was established in 1958 by the Ministry of Labour & Employment, Government of India to implement the workers education scheme at national, regional and unit/village levels for the workers from organized, unorganized and rural sectors. The Board has its headquarters at Nagpur with a network of 50 Regional and Subregional Directorates spread throughout the country. The six Zonal Directorates at Delhi, Guwahati, Kolkata, Chennai, Mumbai and Bhopal monitor the activities of the Regional Directorates within respective zone. The Board has an apex training institute at Mumbai called IIWE.

WORKER'S SAFETY ACT

- The Factories Act, 1948 is the principal legislation for regulating various aspects relating to safety, health and welfare of workers employed in factories. This Act is a Central Enactment, which aims at protecting workers employed in factories from industrial and occupational hazards. The factories employing one thousand workers or more and five hundred workers or more, are required to employ safety officer/s and welfare officer/s respectively.
- Provisions relating to safety, health and welfare of workers employed in docks are contained in the Dock Workers (Safty, Health and Welfare) Act, 1986 and rules and regulations framed there under. The Act came into force on 15th April, 1987.
- Provisions for safety, health and welfare of workers employed in mines are contained in the Mines Act, 1952 and rules and regulations framed there under. These provisions are enforced by the Ministry of Labour and Employment through the Directorate General of Mines Safety. The Directorate General, has its headquarters at Dhanbad.
- The National Safety Council was set up in 1966 to promote safety consciousness among workers to prevent accidents, minimize dangers and mitigate human suffering, arrange programmes, lectures and conferences on safety, conduct educational compaign to increase consciousness among employers and workers and collect educational and information datas, etc.

INDUSTRIAL RELATIONS

- The Industrial Disputes Act, 1947 provides the machinery and procedure for the investigation and settlement of industrial disputes. The Act has been amended vide the Industrial Disputes (Amendment) Act, 2010 and enforced w.e.f. 15th September, 2010.
- The Trade Unions Act, 1926 provides for registration of trade unions of employers and workers, and in certain respects, it defined the law relating to registered trade union. It confers legal and corporate status on registered trade unions. The Trade Unions Act, 1926 is administered by the concerned State Governments. The act has been amended and enforced from 9th January, 2002.
- The Plantations Labour Act, 1951 provides for welfare of plantation labourers and regulates their conditions of work. The Plantations Labour Act, 1951 has been amended and the Plantation Labour (Amendement) Act, 2010 has been enforced w.e.f. 7th June, 2010.
- The 'Rashtriya Swasthya Bima Yojana' for BPL families (a unit of five) in Unorganised Sector was launched on 1st October, 2007 and became operational w.e.f. 1st April, 2008. Under the scheme, smart card based cashless health insurance cover of ₹ 30,000 per annum on a family is provided. The premium is shared on 75:25 basis by centre and state Government. In case of states of North East region and Jammu & Kashmir, the premium is shared in the ratio of 90:10.

SOCIAL SECURITY

- A beginning in social security in India was made in 1923 when Workmen's Compensation Act was passed. The Act is very wide in coverage and covers many diverse industries including mines, factories, transport, plantations, construction activities, electricity generation etc.
- The Workmen's Compensation Act, 1923, does not apply to those industries or factories where Employee's State Insurance Act, 1948, is in operation.
- The Workmen's Compensation Act was amended in 2000. Under this amendment, the workmen or their family members will get the compensation money at the enhanced rate if they die or get disabled. As a result of the death in the working capacity, the compensation money will be minimum 1,20,000. The maximum limit can be ₹ 9.14 lakhs. In the case of disability, the minimum limit is increased from 90,000 to 1,40,000 rupees. The maximum limit in this case, can go upto 10.97 lakh rupees.
- The Maternity Benefit Act, 1961, regulates the employment of women in certain establishments for certain period before and after child birth (six week before and six weeks after confinement) and provides for maternity and other benefits.
- The Materity Benefit Act, 1961 applies to mines, factories, circus, industry, plantations, shops and establishments employing 10 or more persons except the employees who are covered under the ESI Act, 1948. There is no wage limit coverage under the Act.
- The most important step in the field of social security was taken in 1948 when the Employee's State Insurance (ESI) Act was passed. The Act is applicable to non-seasonal factories using power and employing 10 or more persons and non-power using factories employing 20 or more persons. The Employees' State Insurance Corporation (ESIC) raised the monthly wage limit to ₹ 21,000 from the existing ₹ 15,000 for coverage with effect from 1st January, 2017.
- The Employees Provident Funds and Miscellaneous Provision Act, 1952 seeks to provide the financial social security to the employees in the form of provident fund, pension and deposit-linked insurance. It extends to the whole of India except the State of Jammu and Kashmir. It applies to every establishment specified in the schedule and in which 20 or more persons are employed. The object of this Act is to make:
    - (*i*) Some provisions for the future of the industrial workers after the retirement.

(*ii*) to provide for the dependants in the case of the employee's death, and

(*iii*) to cultivate the spirit of saving among the employees.

- Other important social security schemes are:

(*a*) The payment of Gratuity Act, 1972.

(*b*) Employee's Deposit Linked Insurance Scheme, 1976.

(*c*) Employee's Pension Scheme, 1995.

TRADE UNION

- Trade unions are voluntary organisations of workers formed to protect the interest of workers through collective action.
- In India, the first trade union was formed in 1918.
- There are number of trade unions in India, which are associated with main political parties. Some important trade unions are as follows:

(*i*) Bharatiya Mazdoor Sangh (BMS), associated with the Bharatiya Janta Party.

(*ii*) Indian National Trade Union Congress (INTUC), associated with the Congress Party.

(*iii*) All-India Trade Union Congress (AITUC), associated with the Communist Party of India.

(*iv*) Centre of Indian Trade Unions (CITU), associated with the CPI (M).

- The First National Labour Commission was formed on December 24, 1966.
- The Second National Labour Commission was formed on October 15, 1999 under the Chairmanship of Ravindra Verma.
- Trade Union (Amendment) Act, 2001 was introduced with the following objectives:

(*i*) To control multiplicity of trade unions.

(*ii*) Establishing industrial democracy.

(*iii*) Encourage well managed expansion of trade unions.

- The amended Act was introduced after incorporating the recommendations of Ramanujan Committee. The Act has following important provisions:

(*i*) Minimum 10% of the total labour force or 100 labourers in an organization (whichever is less) must be required to form trade union.

(*ii*) No. of members should not be less than of in any condition.

(*iii*) At least 5 members or one-third (whichever is less) should be the employees of the concern.

(*iv*) Annual contribution for trade union should not be less than ₹ 12.00

7. ECONOMIC PLANNING

- Economic Planning refers to any directing or planning of economic activity outside the mechanisms of the market. Planning is an economic mechanism for resources allocation and decision-making held in contrast with the market mechanism. Economic Planning can be applied to production, investment, distribution or all three of these functions.
- In the year 1934, Sir M. Visheshvraya wrote a book named 'Planned Economy for India', which was the first attempt in this direction.
- In 1938, the Indian National Congress, under the leadership of Pt. Jawaharlal Nehru, made a National Planning Committee.
- In 1944, eight industrialists of Bombay (Now Mumbai) presented a well-organised plan called 'The Bombay Plan'.
- Inspired by the economic views of Mahatma Gandhi, Shri Sriman Narayan Constructed a plan in 1944 which is known as 'Gandhian Plan'.
- Mr. M.N. Rai, chairman of post-war Reconstruction Committee of Indian Trade Union, introduced a 'People's Plan' in April 1945.
- In January 1950, Shri Jaiprakash Narayan published a plan called 'Sarvodaya Plan'.
- The Planning Commission was constituted on 15th March, 1950, by the Government of India.

- There is no account of Planning Commission in the Indian Constitution. Therefore, it was constituted in the form of an advisory and specialised institution by means of a document of the Government. Consequently, the Government has been changing its nature and organisation from time to time.
- Pt. Jawaharlal Nehru was appointed as the first Chairman of Planning Commission.
- The Prime Minister is the ex-officio chairman of Planning Commission.
- National Development Council (NDC) is a non-statutory body which was constituted to build co-operation between the States and the Planning Commission for economic planning.
- The National Development Council (NDC) was constituted on 6th August, 1952. The Prime Minister is the chairman and the secretary of the Planning Commission remains its secretary.

Niti Aayog

- The government on January 1, 2015 replaced the 65-year-old Planning Commission—a relic of the Socialist era—with a Niti Aayog or National Institution for Transforming India, marking a major shift in policy making by involving states. The Aayog will recommend a national agenda, including strategic and technical advice on elements of policy and economic matters. It will also develop mechanisms for village-level plans and aggregate these progressively at higher levels of government. To be headed by PM Narendra Modi, the new body will have a governing council comprising CMs of all states and Lt Governors of Union Territories and will work towards fostering co-operative federalism for providing a national agenda to the Centre and states. The membership of states has rendered the National Development Council, a body of CMs that approves five-year Plans, defunct. Former secretary of Defence Research and Development Organisation (DRDO) VK Saraswat, Ramesh Chand, V.K. Paul and Arvind Virmani are appointed as full-time members. The Aayog will have Amit Shah, Rajnath Singh, Nirmala Sitharaman and Narendra Singh Tomar as ex-officio members. Union ministers Nitin Gadkari, Piyush Goyal, Virendra Kumar, Ashwini Vaishnaw and Rao Inderjit Singh are special invitees to the panel.

First Five Year Plan (1951-1956)

- The First Five Year Plan began on April 1, 1951 and ended on March 31, 1956.
- The plan was based on the model of Harrod-Domer.
- The plan has given highest priority to agriculture, irrigation and power projects.
- The achievements of this plan were more than its targets. The annual compound growth rate of national income was 3.6% (target 2.1%) during the planning period.
- The per capita income growth rate was 1.8% and ICOR was 2.95 during this plan.

Second Five Year Plan (1956-1961)

- Based on the model prepared by Prof. P.C. Mahalanobis, the Second Five Year Plan was started on April 1, 1956 and ended on March 31, 1961.
- The fundamental objective of this plan was to initiate and accelerate the process of industrialisation so that the development of Indian economy takes a firm base.
- The Industrial policy, 1956 (During Second Five Year Plan), was based on the objective of establishing the socialistic pattern of society.
- Large industries including steel plants (Durgapur, Bhilai and Rourkela) were set up. The Locomotive factory at Chittaranjan and Coach factory at Perambur were other major projects of this period.

Third Five Year Plan (1961-1966)

- This plan started on April 1, 1961 and ended on March 31, 1966.
- The basic aim of this plan was to push the economy upto the take-off stage development.
- This plan set as its goal the establishment of a self-reliant and self-generating economy.
- In this plan top priority was given to agriculture but it also laid adequate emphasis on the

development of basic industries, which were vitally necessary for rapid economic development of the country.

Annual Plans (1966-1969)

- The Fourth Plan was scheduled to begin from April 1, 1966, but due to the unfortunate failure of third plan, the production in various sector of the economy became stagnant.
- In 1966, the Government of India declared the devaluation of rupee, with a view to increase the exports of the country. However, favourable results couldnot be obtained. Under these circumstances the fourth plan was postponed for sometime and Three Annual Plans were implemented during this period.
- Some of the economists called this period, *i.e.* from 1966 to 1969 as 'Plan Holiday' because no regular planning was done during this period.

Fourth Five Year Plan (1969-1974)

- The Fourth Plan started on April 1, 1969 and ended on March 31, 1974.
- Growth with stability and progress towards self-reliance were the prime objective of the plan.
- The plan aimed at 5.5 per cent average rate of growth in the national income.

Fifth Five Year Plan (1974-1979)

- The Fifth Five Year Plan began on April 1, 1974 which was scheduled to end on March 31, 1979.
- The final draft of the Fifth Plan was prepared and launched by D.P. Dhar proposed to achieve the two main objectives—removal of poverty and attainment of self-reliance.
- The plan objective, 'removal of poverty is also known as the slogan 'Garibi Hatao'.
- This plan also gave high priority to bring inflation under control and to achieve stability in economic situation.

Sixth Five Year Plan (1980-1985)

- The Janta Government ended the Fifth Five Year Plan, one year to its term, *i.e.*, only within four years span (1974-78) and introduced a new plan since April 1, 1978. This plan was named as the "Rolling Plan".
- In 1980, the Sixth Plan (Rolling Plan) prepared by Janta Government was abandoned by the Congress Government and a new Sixth Plan was introduced for the period 1980-85.
- The focus of Janta Government's Sixth Plan (Rolling Plan) was enlargement of the employment potential in agriculture and allied activities, whereas the focus of Congress Sixth Plan was to solve the problem of poverty by creating conditions of an expanding economy.

Seventh Five Year Plan (1985-1990)

- The 7th plan began on April 1, 1985 and ended on March 31, 1990.
- This plan emphasised policies and programmes which aimed at rapid growth in foodgrains production, increased employment opportunities and productivity within the framework of basic tenents of planning, *i.e.*, growth, modernisation, self-reliance and social justice.

Eighth Five Year Plan (1992-1997)

- The 8th Five Year Plan which was supposed to start from April 1, 1990 could not be started on scheduled time because of some political changes at the Centre during 1990-92.
- NDC ratified the format of the Plan in one of its meeting held on May 23, 1992. This Plan began on April 1, 1992 which ended on March 31, 1997.
- The Plan has initiated the process of fiscal reforms as also of economic reforms with a view to provide a new dynamism to economy.
- Fundamental objective of this Plan was human development.
- Pradhanmantri Rojgar Yojana (1993) was started during this Plan.

Ninth Five Year Plan (1997-2002)

- The 9th Plan began on April 1, 1997 and ended on March 31, 2007.
- 'Growth with Equity and Distributive Justice' was determined as the main focus of the Ninth

Plan. In order to achieve this focus, four fields were identified which are as follows:

(i) Quality of life

(ii) Employment promotion

(iii) Regional imbalance

(iv) Self-dependence

Tenth Five Year Plan (2002-2007)

- The 10th Plan began on April 1, 2002 and ended on March 31, 2007.
- The Plan has not been able to achieve its target of 8 per cent growth of GDP, but has taken the economy to a higher trajectory of growth rate at 7.8 per cent as against 5.5 per cent in the 9th Plan.
- Gross domestic savings averaged 28.2 per cent in 10th Plan as against 23.1 per cent in the 9th plan.
- The economy has been able to reduce its ICOR from a level of 4.3 during the 9th Plan to a level of 4.2 during the 10th Plan.
- Our foreign exchange reserve reached a level of US $ 185 billion in February 2007. This is another indication of the strength of the economy.

Eleventh Five Year Plan (2007-12)

- The 11th Plan began on April 1, 2007 and ended on March 31, 2012.
- The 11th Plan visualises "Faster and more inclusive growth" as its objective.
- 11th Plan has fixed a target of pushing up overall GDP growth to an average rate of 9.0 per cent.

Twelfth Five Year Plan (2012-17)

- The 12th Plan began on April 1, 2012 and will end on March 31, 2017.
- Real GDP Growth Rate of 8.0 per cent.
- Agriculture Growth Rate of 4.0 per cent.
- Manufacturing Growth Rate of 7.1 per cent.
- Industrial Sector Growth Rate of 7.6 per cent.
- Service Sector Growth Rate of 9.0 per cent.
- Generate 50 million new work opportunities.
- Eliminate gender and social gap in school enrolment.
- Reduce Total Fertility Rate to 2.1 by the end of Twelfth Five Year Plan.

8. MONEY AND BANKING

- A money market is not a market for money but it is the market for lending and borrowing of short term funds. It is the market where the short-terms surplus investible funds for bank and other financial institutions are demanded by borrowers comprising of individuals, companies and the Government.
- Capital market is the market for long-term funds. It refers to all the facilities and the institutional arrangements for borrowing and lending term funds (medium-term and long-term funds). It does not deal in capital for purposes of investment.
- In monetary economics, control of money supply usually refers to control of the supply of currency and deposit money.
- The RBI now calculates on four concepts of money supply in India. These are known as money stock measures or measures of monetary aggregate. The four concepts of money supply are:

M_1 = Currency with the public, i.e. coins and currency notes + demand deposits of the public; also known as narrow money.

M_2 = M_1 + Post office saving deposits

M_3 = M_1 + Time deposits of the public with banks; also known as broad money

M_4 = M_3 + Total post office deposits

- The monetary policy referes to a regulatory policy whereby the central bank (RBI) maintains its control over the supply of monetary for the realisation of general economic goals.
- Among the functions of RBI, one main function is to control and regulate the credit in the country. In India, this function is performed by the Reserve Bank of India (RBI). The measures of credit control can be divided into two types:

(*i*) Quantitative Credit Control

(*ii*) Selective Credit Control

- The main objective of quantitative credit control is to establish control over the total quantity of credit in the country. For quantitative credit control, the central bank (RBI) takes the help of bank rate, open market operations, SLR and CRR, whereas publicity, rationing of credit, regulation of consumer credit, moral suasion, variation in margin requirements are the selective credit (qualitative) control methods.
- Reserve Bank of India (RBI) is the central bank of the country.
- Reserve Bank of India was established on April 1, 1935 under Reserve Bank of India Act, 1934 with a authorised capital of ₹ 5 crore.
- The Reserve Bank of India was nationalised on January 1, 1949.
- The general administration and direction of RBI is managed by a Central Board of Directors consisting of 20 members which includes 1 Governor and 4 Deputy Governors.
- The head office of the Reserve Bank of India is in Mumbai.
- SBI functions as an agent of RBI, where there are not any branches of RBI.

Governors of RBI

S.N.	*Governors*	*Period*
1.	Sir Osborne Smith	1-4-35 to 30-6-37
2.	Sir James Braid Taylor	1-7-37 to 17-2-43
3.	Sir C. D. Deshmukh	11-8-43 to 30-6-49
4.	Sir Benegal Rama Rau	1-7-49 to 14-1-57
5.	K. G. Ambegaonkar	14-1-57 to 28-2-57
6.	H. V. R. Iyengar	1-3-57 to 28-2-62
7.	P. C. Bhattacharya	1-3-62 to 30-6-67
8.	L. K. Jha	1-7-67 to 3-5-70
9.	B. N. Adarkar	4-5-70 to 15-6-70
10.	S. Jagannathan	16-6-70 to 19-5-75
11.	N. C. Sen Gupta	19-5-75 to 19-8-75
12.	K. R. Puri	20-8-75 to 2-5-77
13.	M. Narasimham	2-5-77 to 30-11-77
14.	Dr. I. G. Patel	1-12-77 to 15-9-82
15.	Dr. Manmohan Singh	16-9-82 to 14-1-85
16.	A. Ghosh	15-1-85 to 4-2-85
17.	R. N. Malhotra	4-2-85 to 22-12-90
18.	S. Venkataramanan	22-12-90 to 21-12-92
19.	Dr. C. Rangarajan	22-12-92 to 21-11-97
20.	Dr. Bimal Jalan	22-12-97 to 6-9-03
21.	Dr. Y. V. Reddy	6-9-03 to 5-9-08
22.	Dr. Duvvuri Subbarao	5-9-08 to 4-9-13
23.	Raghuram Rajan	4-9-13 to 4-9-16
24.	Urjit Patel	4-9-16 to 10-12-2018
25.	Shaktikanta Das	12-12-18 to 12-12-24
26.	Sanjay Malhotra	12-12-24 to till date

- Functions of Reserve Bank of India:
  - ❖ Issue of Notes.
  - ❖ Bankers to the Government.
  - ❖ Banker's Bank.
  - ❖ Controller of Credit.
  - ❖ Custodian of Foreign Reserves.
  - ❖ Other Functions (function of clearing house arranging credit for agriculture, collecting and publishing the economic data, buying and selling of government securities and trade bills etc.)

Foundation Years of Main Indian Banks

Reserve Bank of India	1935
Nationalisation of RBI	1949
State Bank of India	1955
Nationalisation of 14 Commercial Banks	1969
Nationalisation of 6 other Banks	1980
Regional Rural Bank	1975
Bharatiya Mahila Bank	2013

- **Bank Rate:** Bank Rate is the rate of discount at which the central bank of the country discounts first class bills. It is the rate of interest at which the central bank lends money to the lower banking institutions. Bank rate is a direct quantitative method of credit control in the economy.
- **Cash Reserve Ratio (CRR):** Commercial banks are required to keep a certain amount of cash reserves at the central bank. This percentage amount is called CRR. It influences the commercial bank's volume of credit because variation in CRR affects the liquidity position of the banks and hence their ability to lend.
- **Prime Lending Rate (PLR):** Prime Lending Rate (PLR) is that rate of interest at which bank gives

loan to its most reliable customer. This reliability means 'zero risk'. Thus, PLR provides the role of a basic interest rate at which loan is provided to other customers.

- **Repo Rate:** Repo (Repurchase option) rate is a instrument under the Liquidity Adjustment Facility (LAF) at which RBI lends to commercial banks. In case of inflationary tendencies RBI perceived need to inject liquidity into the system, RBI can reduce the Repo rate which will lead to release of money into the market.
- **Reverse Repo Rate:** Reverse Repo Rate is the rate at which RBI borrows from commercial banks. In case of inflationary tendencies, RBI can hike the Reverse Repo rate to absorb the excess liquidity in the market. It is also a Liquidity Adjustment facility instrument.
- **Statutory Liquidity Ratio (SLR):** Commercial banks are also required to keep (in additon to CRR) a certain percentage of their net demand and time liabilities (NDTL) as liquid assets in the shape of cash, gold or approved securities. As most of the SLR money is kept in treasury bills, government had, in the past, been using SLR as a means to mobilise low cost resources.
- The Reserve Bank Act, 1934 and the Banking Regulation Act, 1949 have given the RBI wide powers of supervision and control over commercial and co-operative banks, relating to licensing and establishments, branch expansion, liquidity of their assets, management and method of working, amalgmation, reconstruction and liquidation.
- On the recommendation of the Rural Credit Survey Committee the Imperial Bank of India was converted into the State Bank of India on July 1, 1955.
- On 1st April, 2017, State Bank of India, which is India's largest Bank merged with five of its Associate Banks (State Bank of Bikaner & Jaipur, State Bank of Hyderabad, State Bank of Mysore, State Bank of Patiala and State Bank of Travancore) and Bharatiya Mahila Bank with itself. This is the first ever large scale consolidation in the Indian Banking Industry.

Reasons for Nationalisation of Banks

(*i*) Removal of control by a few.

(*ii*) Provision of adequate credit for agriculture and small industry and export.

(*iii*) Giving a professional bent to management.

(*iv*) Encouragement of a new class of entrepreneurs; and

(*v*) The provision of adequate training as well as terms of service for bank staff.

- In order to have more control over the banks, 14 large commercial banks whose reserves were more than ₹ 50 crore each were nationalised on 19th July, 1969. These banks are as follows:
  1. The Central Bank of India
  2. Bank of India
  3. Punjab National Bank
  4. Canara Bank
  5. United Commercial Bank
  6. Syndicate Bank
  7. Bank of Baroda
  8. United Bank of India
  9. Union Bank of India
  10. Dena Bank
  11. Allahabad Bank
  12. Indian Bank
  13. Indian Overseas Bank
  14. Bank of Maharashtra
- After one decade, on April 15, 1980 another 6 private sector banks whose reserves were more than ₹ 200 crore each were nationalised. These banks are as:
  1. Andhra Bank
  2. Punjab and Sindh Bank
  3. New Bank of India
  4. Vijaya Bank
  5. Corporation Bank
  6. Oriental Bank of Commerce.

- On 4th September, 1993 the Government merged the New Bank of India with Punjab National Bank and as a result of this the total number of nationalised bank got reduced from 20 to 19. But after the transformation of IDBI into Scheduled Bank in October 2004, and establishment of Bharatiya Mahila Bank, the number of nationalise banks has increased to 21.

10 PUBLIC SECTOR BANKS MERGED INTO FOUR

The Union Cabinet has approved the merger of 10 public sector banks into four, paving the way for the largest consolidation among the state-owned lenders.

According to the Plan:

- Punjab National Bank has taken over Oriental Bank of Commerce and United Bank.
- Canara Bank has taken over Syndicate Bank.
- Union Bank of India has taken over Andhra bank and Corporation Bank.
- Indian Bank has been merged with Allahabad Bank.

The merger has become effective from April 1, 2020. In 2017, State Bank of India was merged with five of its associate banks and Bharatiya Mahila Bank. In 2018, it decided to merge Bank of Baroda with Vijaya Bank and Dena Bank. The government also allowed Life Insurance Corporation of India to take over IDBI Bank.

After the merger of these banks total number of public sector banks is now 12:

1. State Bank of India
2. Punjab National Bank
3. Bank of Baroda
4. Canara Bank
5. Union Bank of India
6. Indian Bank
7. Bank of Maharashtra
8. Punjab and Sindh Bank
9. Indian Overseas bank
10. United Commercial Bank
11. Central Bank of India
12. Bank of India.

TYPES OF BANKS

On the basis of functions, the banking institutions in India may be divided into the following types:

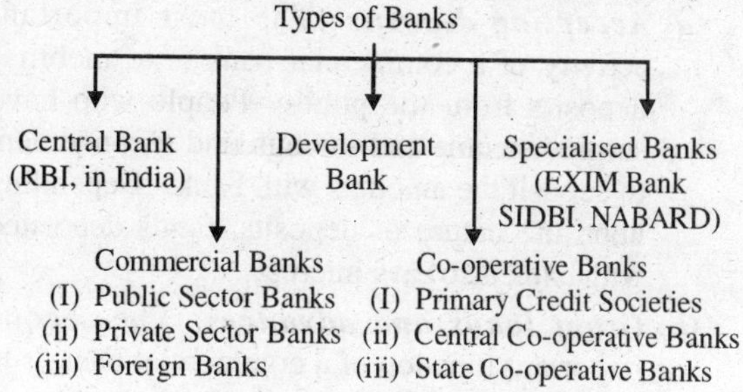

CLASSIFICATION OF COMMERCIAL BANKS

The commercial banking institutions of the country can be divided into two groups:

A. Scheduled Banks: Those banks are scheduled banks which have been included in the Schedule (Second) of Reserve Bank Act, 1934. The banks included in this scheduled list should fulfil two conditions:

1. The paid up capital and collected funds of bank should not be less than ₹ 5 lakh.
2. Any activity of the bank should not adversely affect the interest of depositors.

Every scheduled bank enjoys following facilities:

1. Such bank becomes eligible for obtaining debts/loans on bank rate from RBI.
2. Such bank automatically acquires the membership of clearing house.
3. Such banks also get the facility of rediscount of first class exchange bills from RBI.

B. Non-scheduled Banks: Those banks which are not included in the list of scheduled banks are called non-scheduled banks. These non-scheduled banks are not eligible for having loans from RBI for meeting their day-to-day general activities but under emergency conditions these banks can be granted loans by RBI.

FUNCTIONS OF COMMERCIAL BANKS

The functions of commercial banks are of **two** types.

(A) Primary functions; and

(B) Secondary functions.

Primary functions

There are two primary functions of a commercial bank. These are:

(*a*) ***Accepting deposits:*** The most important activity of a commercial bank is to mobilise deposits from the public. People who have surplus income and savings find it convenient to deposit the amounts with banks. Depending upon the nature of deposits, funds deposited with bank also earn interest.

(*b*) ***Grant loans and advances:*** The second important function of a commercial bank is to grant loans and advances. Such loans and advances are given to members of the public and to the business community at a higher rate of interest than allowed by banks on various deposit accounts.

Secondary functions

In addition to the primary functions of accepting deposits and lending money, banks perform a number of other functions, which are called secondary functions. These are as follows:

(a) Issuing letters of credit, travellers cheque, etc.

(b) Undertaking safe custody of valuables, important document and securities by providing safe deposit vaults or lockers.

(c) Providing customers with facilities of foreign exchange dealings.

(d) Transferring money from one account to another; and from one branch to another branch of the bank through cheque, pay order, demand draft.

(e) Standing guarantee on behalf of its customers, for making payment for purchase of goods, machinery, vehicles etc.

(f) Collecting and supplying business information.

(g) Providing reports on the credit-worthiness of customers.

(i) Providing consumer finance for individuals by way of loans on easy terms for purchase of consumer durables like televisions, refrigerators, etc.

(j) Educational loans to students at reasonable rate of interest for higher studies, especially for professional courses.

NON-BANKING FINANCIAL COMPANIES (NBFCS)

Introduction

Non-banking financial companies (NBFCs) are fast emerging as an important segment of Indian financial system. It is an heterogeneous group of institutions (other than commercial and co-operative banks) performing financial intermediation in a variety of ways, like accepting deposits, making loans and advances, leasing, hire purchase, etc.

Differences Between Banks & NBFCs

NBFCs are doing functions akin to that of banks, however there are a few differences:

(*i*) An NBFC cannot accept demand deposits (demand deposits are funds deposited at a depository institution that are payable on demand—immediately or within a very short period—like your current or savings accounts.)

(*ii*) It is not a part of the payment and settlement system and as such cannot issue cheque books to its customers; and

(*iii*) Deposit insurance facility of DICGC is not available for NBFC depositors unlike in case of banks.

Types of NBFCs

The types of NBFCs registered with the RBI are:

1. **Equipment leasing companies:** It is any financial institution whose principal business is that of leasing equipments or financing of such an activity.
2. **Hire-purchase companies:** It is any financial intermediary whose principal business relates to hire purchase transactions or financing of such transactions.
3. **Loan companies:** It means any financial institution whose principal business is that of providing finance, whether by making loans or advances or otherwise for any activity other than its own (excluding any equipment leasing or hire-purchase finance activity).
4. **Investment companies:** It is any financial intermediary whose principal business is that of buying and selling of securities.

NBFCs by their Principal Business

Non-Banking Financial Companies (NBFCs)	Principal Business
Equipment Leasing Companies (EL)	Equipment leasing or financing of such activity
Hire Purchase Finance Companies (HP)	Hire purchase transaction or purchasing or such transactions
Investment Companies (IC)	Acquisition of securities and trading in such securities to earn a profit
Loan Companies (LC)	Making loans or advances for any activity other than its own; EL/HP/ Housing Finance
Residuary Non-Banking Companies (RNBCs)	Receives deposits under any scheme or arrangement, by whatever name called, in one lump-sum or in instalments by way of contributions or subsriptions or by sale of units or certificates or other instruments, or in any manner
Mutual Benefit Financial Companies (MBFC) *i.e.* Nidhi Companies	Any company which is notified by the Central Government as a Nidhi Company under section 620A of the Companies Act, 1956. It is an NBFC doing the business of lending and borrowing with its members or shareholders.
Miscellaneous Non-Banking Company (MNBC) *i.e.* Chit Fund Companies	Managing, conducting or supervising as a promoter, foreman or agent of any transaction or arrangement by which the company enters into an agreement with a specified number of subscribers that every one of them shall subscribe a certain amount in instalments over a definite period and that every one of such subscribers shall in turn, as determined by lot or by auction or by tender or in such manner as may be provided for in the arrangement, be entitled to the prize amount.

Salient Features of RBI Amendment Act, 1997 Regarding NBFSc

RBI has taken a series of measures to enhance the regulatory and supervisory standards of the NBFCs and to bring them at par with commercial banks over a period of time. These include:

1. Secure a certificate of registration from RBI, the net owned funds (NoF) should be ₹ 2 crores (initially) only ₹ 25 lakhs).
2. There is a quantum of public deposits which can be received by an NBFC, depending upon whether it is a loan and investment company or whether it is a leasing and hire-purchase company, and so on—fixed between 1.5 times to 4 times NoF.
3. NBFCs have to invest at least 5 per cent of their assets in unencumbered approved securities.
4. Every NBFC has to create a reserve fund and transfer at least 20 per cent of its net profit every year to the reserve fund.
5. Prudential norms are fixed for those NBFCs which are raising public deposits. For instance, such NBFCs should maintain Capital to Risks Asset Ratio (CRAR) comprising TIER I and II Capital:

   12% for leasing hire-purchase finance companies.

   15% for loan and investment companies, and

   12% for RNBCs (Residuary Non-Banking Companies).

   Certain norms were prescribed for all NBFCs whether they hold or receive public deposits or not.
6. Under RBI regulations, RNBCs are required to invest not less than 80 per cent of aggregate liabilities with the depositors in Government securities, Government-guaranteed bonds, debentures, etc. RBI has reviewed these regulations.

7. All registered NBFCs should submit half yearly returns to RBI at the end of March and September every year. As non-submission of periodic returns to RBI was a common feature, RBI has now decided to impose penalties besides cancellation of certificates of registration and permission to receive deposits from the public.

   The RBI is now entrusted with the following powers:

   (a) specify from time to time a minimum percentage of investment for NBFCs in unencumbered "approved" securities;

   (b) determine their policies and give directions to any or all NBFCs on capital adequacy, provisioning and other prudential norms, as also on the deployment of funds (similar to those applicable to banks).

   (c) direct them on balance sheet, profit and loss accounts and disclosure of liabilities,

   (d) levy fines and penalty on an NBFC for contravention and default, as also cancel its registration,

   (e) prohibit an NBFC from accepting deposits and alienate its assets; and

   (f) file a winding up petition for continued violation of the provisions of the Act and /or failure to comply with any direction or orders of the RBI.

- Liquidity Adjustment Facility (LAF) is started by RBI in June 2000.
- Liquidity Adjustment Facility (LAF) refers to RBI's policy of Using Repos and Reverse Repos to adjust liquidity on a day to day basis.
- Regional Rural Banks (RRBs) were established since 1975 under the provisions of the RRB Act 1976 with a view to developing the rural economy as well as to creating an alternative channel to 'Co-operatives'.
- With a view to consolidating and strengthening RRBs, the Government of India initiated in September 2005, the process of amalgamation of RRBs in a phased manner.
- RBI introduced a Banking ombudsman scheme in the country on June 14, 1995, for giving a solution for customer's complaints.
- The IDBI which was established as Development Finance Institution under IDBI Act, 1964 has been converted as a banking company (on October 11, 2004)
- Small Industries Development Bank of India (SIDBI) was established as wholly-owned subsidiary of IDBI under the Small Industries Development Bank of India Act, 1989 as the principal financial institution for promotion, financing and development of industries in the Small Scale Sector. Its headquarter is situated at Lucknow.
- ICICI was established in 1955 as public limited company under Indian Companies Act for developing medium and small industries of private sector.
- With effect from May 3, 2002, erstwhile ICICI limited and two of its wholly-owned subsidiaries were merged with ICICI Bank. The appointed date for merger was March 30, 2002.
- In 1987, a National Equity Fund Scheme was started for providing equity assistance to Tiny Small Scale units having capital investment of less than ₹ 10 lakh and working in areas having population less than 5 lakh (15 lakh for hill areas and north-east areas). SIDBI and Central Government contribute 50:50 share in this scheme of SIDBI.
- IRBI was established on March 20, 1985 under Indian Industrial Reconstruction Bank Act, 1984 as a Result of reconstituting Indian Industrial Reconstruction Corporation Ltd. The basic aim of establishing IRBI was to revive sick and closed industrial units and to act as a prime loan and reconstruction agency.
- But now under the new arrangements, IRBI is functioning with the new name IIBIL (Industrial Investment Bank of India Ltd.). IIBIL's head office is situated at Kolkata.
- State Governments have established State Industrial Development Corporations (SIDCs) under their sole ownerships. The objectives of SIDCs include:

Establishment Years of Major Financial Institutions in India

Imperial Bank of India	1921
Reserve Bank of India (Nationalisation of RBI took place on January 1, 1949)	April 1, 1935
Industrial Finance Corporation of India (IFCI)	1948
State Bank of India (SBI)	July 1, 1955
Unit Trust of India (UTI)	Feb. 1, 1964
IDBI	July 1964
NABARD	July 12, 1982
IRBI (Now it has been renamed as IIBIL since March 6, 1997)	March 20, 1985
SIDBI	1990
EXIM Bank	January 1, 1982
National Housing Bank (NHB)	July 1988
Life Insurance Corporation (LIC)	September 1956
General Insurance Corporation (GIC)	November 1972
Regional Rural Banks (RRBs)	Oct. 2, 1975
Risk Capital and Technology Finance Corporation Ltd.	March 1975
Technology Development & Information Co. of India Ltd.	1989
Infrastructure Leasing & Financial Services Ltd.	1988
Housing Development Finance Corporation Ltd. (HDFC)	1977

(*i*) To develop industrial areas

(*ii*) To esnure market facilities

(*iii*) To establish new development centres.

- EXIM bank in India was established on January 1, 1982 for financing, facilitaing and promoting foreign trade in India. Besides, EXIM Bank also discharge duties of coordinating the activities of various financial invititutions, providing finances for export-imports of goods and services. Besides India, this bank also manages finances to third world countries for export-import of goods and services.
- National Housing Bank (NHB) was established in July 1988 as wholly owned subsidiary of RBI. A major activity of NHB includes extending financial assistance to eligible institutions in the housing sector by way of refinance and direct finance.
- National Bank for Agriculture and Rural Development (NABARD) is the apex banking institution providing finance for agriculture and rural development. It was established on July 12, 1982 with the paid-up capital of ₹ 100 crore having 50:50 contribution of Indian Government and RBI. NABARD's head office is situated at Mumbai.
- IDFC (Infrastructure Development Finance Company) was proposed to be established on January 31, 1997, Under Companies Act, 1956, for financing infrastructure sector for the country. The mission of IDFC is to:

  (*i*) Lead private capital to commercially viable intrastructural projects in India.

  (*ii*) Provide a strong policy advisory role to government to meet this objective.

  (*iii*) Develop and strengthen the connectivity of infrastructure projects to markets and institutions.
- Agriculture and Rural Development Banks basically known as Land Mortgage Banks/Land Development Banks have now been redesignated

as Agricultural and Rural Development. These banks provide long term credit to agriculture and rural sector. A two-tier structure is in operation:

⇒ State Co-operative and Rural Development Banks (SCARDBs).

⇒ Primary Co-operative Agriculture and Rural Development Banks (PCARDBs).

- Under an Act passed by the parliament, on September 1, 1956 Life Insurance Corporation (LIC) of India was established with the capital of ₹ 5 crore given by the Government of India. LIC head office is situated at Mumbai.
- General Insurance Company (GIC) was established in November, 1972.
- The insurance sector was opened for private participation with the enactment of Insurance Regulatory and Development Authority Act (IRDA Act), 1999.
- On the recommendation of Malhotra committee, government has permitted privatization of Insurance sector. The committee was constituted in April 1993.
- The Wholesale Price Index (WPI) is the price of a representative basket of wholesale goods. It also influences stock and fixed price markets. The WPI is published by the Economic Adviser in the Ministry of Commerce and Industry. The Wholesale Price Index focuses on the price of goods traded between corporations, rather than goods bought by consumers, which is measured by the Consumer Price Index.
- The wholesale price index (WPI) is based on the wholesale price of a few relevant commodities of over 240 commodities available. The commodities chosen for the calculation are based on their importance in the region and the point of time the WPI is employed. For example in India about 435 items were used for calculating the WPI in base year 1993-94 while the advanced base year 2004-05 uses 676 items. Currently the base year has been revised from 2004-05 to 2011-12 by the Office of Economic Advisor (OEA), Department of Industrial Policy and Promotion, Ministry of Commerce and Industry.

Non-Performing Assets (NPA)

In simple words the assets of the Banks which don't perform (means don't bring any return) are called Non-Performing Assets. In more general sense they are 'bad loans'. Any asset, including a based asset, becomes non-performing when it ceases to generate income for the bank.

However, there is a prescribed definition by the RBI which defines the NPAs as—

- Terms loans on which interest and/or instalment of principal remain overdue for a particular quarter for a period of more than 90 days from the end of that particular quarter.
- The Bills those remain overdue for a period of more than 90 days from the end of a quarter.
- Any amount to be received remains overdue for a period of more than 90 days.
- The Cash Credit Account remains out of order for a period of more than 90 days. Out of order means over the sanctioned limit.

Printing of Securities and Minting in India

- ***India Security Press (Nasik Road) :*** Postal Material, Postal Stamps, Non-postal Stamps, Judicial and Non-judicial Stamps, Cheques, Bonds, NSCs, Kisan Vikas Patras, Securities of State Governments, Public Sector Enterprise and Financial Corporations.
- ***Security Printing Press (Hyderabad) :*** Established in 1982 for meeting the demand for postal material by Southern States. It also fulfils the demand for Union Excise Duty Stamps of the Country.
- ***Currency Notes Press (Nasik Road):*** Since 1991, this press prints currency notes of ₹ 1, ₹ 2, ₹ 5, ₹ 10, ₹ 50, and ₹ 100. (Earlier printing of ₹ 50 and ₹ 100 currency notes was not done here).
- ***Bank Notes Press (Dewas):*** Currency notes of ₹ 20, ₹ 50, ₹ 100 and ₹ 500 are printed here.
- ***Modernised Currency Notes Press:*** Two new modernised currency notes press are established at Mysore (Karnataka) and Salboni (West Bengal).
- ***Coins are minted at four places:*** Mumbai, Kolkata, Hyderabad and Noida.

- ***Security Paper Hoshangabad*** (Established in 1967-68) makes production of Bank and Currency notes paper.
- ***Bhartiya Reserve Bank Note Mudran Private Limited Mysore:*** Currency notes of ₹ 200 and ₹ 500 are printed here.

9. CAPITAL MARKET

- Capital Market may be defined as a market dealing in medium and long-term funds. It is an institutional arrangement for borrowing medium and long term funds and which provides facilities for marketing and trading of securities.
- Capital Market Constitutes all long term borrowings from banks and financial institutions, borrowings from foreign markets and raising of capital by issue various securities such as share debentures, bonds etc.
- For trading of securities there are two different segments in capital market. They are:

  1. Primary Market, 2. Secondary Market.

Primary Market

- The primary market deals with new/fresh issue of securities and is, therefore known as new issue market.
- The new issue market primarily consists of the arrangements, which facilitates the procurement of long-term finance by the companies in the form of shares, debentures and bonds. The companies usually issue those securities at the initial stages of their formation and so also later on for expansion and/or modernization of their activities.
- However, the selling of securities is not an easy task, as the companies have to fulfil various legal requirements and decide upon the appropriate timing and the method of issue.
- The new issues seek assistance of various inter-median'es such as merchant bankers, underwriters, stock brokers etc. All these inter-mediaries form an integral part of the primary market.

Secondary Market

- The secondary market is an association or organisation or a body of individuals established for the purpose of assisting, regulating and controlling the business of buying selling and dealing in securities.
- It may noted that it is called a secondary market because only the securities already issued can be traded on the floor of the stock exchange.
- Secondary market is open only to its members, most of whom are brokers acting as agents of the buyers and sellers of securities.
- The main functions of this market lie in providing liquidity to securities and safety in dealing. It is because of the availability of such facilities that people are ready to invest in securities.

Distinction Between Capital Market and Money Market

Capital Market	*Money Market*
1. The capital market is related to long term funds.	1. Money market is related to short term fund.
2. The capital market deals in shares, debentures, bonds and government securities.	2. Money market deals in securities like treasury bills, commercial papers, trade bills, deposit certificates etc.
3. The participants in capital market are stockbrokers, under-writers, mutual funds, financial institutions and individual investors.	3. The participants in money market are RBI, commercial banks, NBFCs etc.
4. The capital market is regulated by Securities Exchange Board of India (SEBI).	4. Money market is regulated by RBI.

- Discount Bill Market is one that deals in short-term loans. Treasury Bills and Commercial Bills of Exchange also fall in this category.
- Dividend is the amount which the company distributes to shareholders when the profits of the company are calculated by the board of directors.
- The debenture is a written acknowledgement of money borrowed. It specifies the terms and conditions, such as rate of interest, time of repayment, security offered, etc. These are offered to the public to subscribe in the same manner as is done in the case of shares.
- Share is the smallest unit into which the total capital of the company is divided. For example, when a company decides to raise ₹ 50 crores of capital from the public by issuing shares, then it can divide its capital into units of a definite value, say ₹ 10/or ₹ 100/- each, these individual units are called as its share. In order to tap the savings of different types of people, a company can issue two type of Shares—(*a*) Equity Shares, and (*b*) Preference Shares.

  (*a*) ***Equity Shares:*** Equity shares are shares, which do not enjoy any preferential right in the matter of claim of dividend or repayment of capital. The equity shareholders get dividend only after making the payment of dividends on preference shares. There is no fixed rate of dividend for equity shareholders.

  (*b*) ***Preference Shares:*** Preference Shares are those shares, which carry preferential rights in respect of dividend and return of capital. Before any dividend is paid to the equity shares, the dividend at a fixed rate must be paid on the preference shares. However, this dividend is payable only if there are profits.
- Financial institutions which are engaged in borrowing and lending money are called financial intermediaries. It also includes commercial banks. Financial intermediary is a middle man between manufacturer and whole-seller and retailer and between a retailer and consumer.
- Business in the country's oldest stock exchange, namely the Bombay Stock Exchange (BSE) dating back to 1875, which is also one of the oldest stock exchanges in the world, continued to operate.
- The National Stock Exchange (NSE), which emerged in the mid-1990 and catalysed improvements in trading system to provide the necessary depth and choice to investors, made sustained progress.

Difference between Shares and Debenture

S.No.	Basis	Shares	Debentures
1.	Status	Shareholders are the owners of the company. They provide ownership capital which is not refundable unless the company is liquidated.	Debentureholders are the creditors of the company. They provide loans generally for a fixed period, which are to be paid back.
2.	Nature of return on investment	Shareholders get dividends. Its amount is not fixed as it depends on the profit of the company.	Interest is paid on debentures at a fixed rate. Interest is payable even if the company is running at a loss.
3.	Rights	Shareholders are the real owners of the company. They have the right to vote and determine the policies of the company.	Debentureholders do not have the right to attend meetings of the company. So they have no say in the management of the company.
4.	Security	No security is required to issue shares.	Generally debentures are secured. So, sufficient fixed assets are required when debentures are to be issued.
5.	Order of repayment	Share capital is paid back only after paying the debentureholders and creditors.	Debentureholders have the priority of repayment over shareholders.
6.	Risk	Risk is high due to uncertainty of returns.	Little risk due to certainty of return.

Difference between Equity Shares and Preference Shares

S.No.	Basis of difference	Equity shares	Preference Shares
1.	Choice	It is compulsory to issue these shares.	It is not compulsory to issue these shares.
2.	Payment of dividend	Dividend is paid on these shares only after paying dividend on preference shares.	Dividend is paid on these shares in preference to the equity shares.
3.	Return of capital	In case of winding up of the company the equity share capital is refunded only after the refund of preference share capital.	In case of winding up of the company the capital is refunded in preference over the equity shares.
4.	Voting Right	The equity shareholders enjoy voting rights.	The preference shareholders do not have voting rights.
5.	Accumulation of Dividend	The dividends on equity shares are not accumulated and therefore cannot be carried forward.	The unpaid dividends are accumulated and are carried forward to the future years in case of cumulative preference shares.

- On June 15, 1998 National Stock Exchange has launched two new Reference Rates for the loans of Inter-Bank Call Money Market. These rates are MIBOR (Mumbai Inter Bank Offer Rate) and MIBID (Mumbai Inter-Bank Bide Rate)
- MIBOR will be the indicator of Lending Rate for loans while MIBID will be the lending rate for receipts.

Securities and Exchange Board of India (SEBI)

- Securities and Exchange Board of India (SEBI) is an independent statutory regulatory authority.
- SEBI was initially constituted on April 12, 1988 as a non-statutory body through a resolution of the Government for dealing with all matters relating to development and regulation of securities market and investor protection and to advise the Government of all these matters.
- SEBI was given statutory status and powers through an ordinance promulgated on January 30, 1992.
- SEBI is managed by six members—one chairman (nominated by Central Government), two members (officers of Central Ministries), one member (from RBI) and remaining two members are nominated by Central Government.
- The office of SEBI is situated at Mumbai with its regional office at Kolkata, Delhi and Chennai.

Functions of SEBI

- To safeguard the interests of investors and to regulate capital market with suitable measures.
- To regulate the business of stock exchanges and other securities market.
- To regulate the working of Stock Brokers. Sub-brokers, Share Transfer Agents, Trustees, Merchant Bankers, Underwriters, Portfolio Managers etc. and also to make their registration.
- To register and regulate collective investment plans of mutual funds.
- To encourage self-regulatory organisations.
- To eliminate malpractices of security markets.
- To train the persons associated with security markets and also to encourage investors' education.
- To check insider trading of securities.
- To supervise the working of various organisations trading in security market and also to ensure systematic dealings.
- To promote research and investigations for ensuring the attainment of above objectives.

	Recognised Stock Exchanges in India
1.	Ahmedabad Stock Exchange Ltd.
2.	Bangalore Stock Exchange Ltd.
3.	Calcutta Stock Exchange Ltd.
4.	India International Exchange (India INX)
5.	Magadh Stock Exchange Ltd.
6.	Metropolitan Stock Exchange of India Ltd.
7.	National Stock Exchange of India Ltd.
8.	NSE IFSC Ltd.
9.	Ace Derivatives and Commodity Exchange Limited
10.	Hapur Commodity Exchange Ltd
11.	India Pepper & Spice Trade Association
12.	Indian Commodity Exchange Limited
13.	Multi Commodity Exchange of India Ltd.
14.	National Commodity & Derivatives Exchange Ltd.
15.	National Multi Commodity Exchange of India Ltd.
16.	Rajkot Commodity Exchange Ltd.
17.	Universal Commodity Exchange Ltd.

Concept of Depository System

Depository system is that system in which ownership of security is changed by an electronic account entry and physical transaction of securities does not take place. The main functions of depository are as follows:

- To accept deposits for ensuring safe custody of securities.
- To make computerised account entry for ensuring evidence of ownership transfer.
- To keep record of mortgaged securities.

Different countries possess generally two types of depositories:

(*a*) Securities immobilisation system of depositories.

(*b*) Securities dematerialisation system of depositories.

Main Share Price Index in Famous Share Market of the World

BSE (Mumbai)	SENSEX
NSE (Mumbai)	S & P CNX Nifty
New York	DOW JONES
Tokyo	NIKKEI
Frankfurt (Germany)	MID DAX
Hong Kong	HANG SENG
Singapore	SIMEX STRAITS TIMES

10. PUBLIC FINANCE

- Direct Taxes are—Income Tax, Corporation Tax, Wealth Tax, Estate Duty, Gift Tax, Expenditure Tax and Interest Tax.
- Indirect Taxes are—Custom Duties, Union Excise Duties, Sale/Purchase Tax, Advertisements Tax.
- India possesses a federal structure in which a clear distinction is made between the Union and the State functions and sources of revenue.
- Our constitution provides residual powers of the centre. Article 264 and 293 explain the financial relations between the Union and State Government.

A. The List I of Seventh Schedule of Indian Constitution enlists the Union taxes which are as follows:

- Taxes on income other than agriculture income
- Corporation tax
- Custom duties
- Excise duties except on alcoholic liquors and narcotics not contained in medical or toilet preparation
- Estate and succession duties other than on agricultural land
- Taxes on the capital value of assets except agricultural land of individuals and companies

- Rates of stamp duties on financial documents
- Taxes other than stamp duties on transactions in stock exchanges and future markets
- Taxes on sales or purchases of newspapers and on advertisements therein
- Taxes on railway freight and fares
- Terminal taxes on goods or passengers carried by railways, sea or air
- Taxes on the sale or purchase of goods in the course of inter state trade

B. List II of Seventh Schedule enlists the taxes which are within the jurisdiction of the states:

- Land revenue
- Taxes on the sale and purchase of goods, except newspapers
- Taxes on agricultural income
- Taxes on land buildings
- Succession and estate duties on agricultural land
- Excise on alcoholic liquors and narcotics
- Taxes on the entry of goods into a local area
- Taxes on the consumption and sale of electricity
- Taxes on mineral rights (subject to any limitations imposed by the Parliament)
- Taxes on vehicles, animals and boats
- Stamp duties except those on financial documents
- Taxes on luxuries including entertainments, betting and gambling
- Tolls
- Taxes on professions, trades, callings and employment
- Capitation taxation
- Taxes on advertisements other than those contained in newspapers

C. Apart from taxes levied and collected by the states, the constitution has provided for the revenues for certain taxes on the union list to be alloted, partly or wholly to the states. These provisions fall into various categories:

- Duties which are levied by the Union Government but are collected and appropriated by the States. These include stamp duties, excise duties on medical preparations containing alcohol or narcotics.
- Taxes which are levied and collected by the union, but the entire proceeds of which are assigned to the states, in proportion determined by the Parliament.

  These taxes include:

  (*i*) Succession and Estate duty

  (*ii*) Taxes on railway freight and fares

  (*iii*) Terminal taxes on goods and passengers

  (*iv*) Taxes on transactions in stock exchanges and future markets

  (*v*) Taxes on sale and purchase of newspapers and advertisements therein
- Central taxes on income and union excise duties are levied and collected by the union but are shared by it with the states in a prescribed manner.
- Proceeds of additional excise duty on mill made textiles, sugar and tobacco which are levied by the union since 1957 in replacement of state sales taxes on these commodities, are wholly distributed among the states in a manner as to guarantee their former incomes from the displaced sales taxes.
- The central government levies four main taxes, viz; taxes on income (personal income tax and corporation tax), customs duties. Union excise duties and service tax. These taxes account for almost total tax proceeds of the central government.
- The principal tax revenue sources of the state government are the share of the state in the central taxes and duties, commercial taxes land revenue, stamp duties and registration fees and the state excise duties on alcohol and other narcotics, of all commercial taxes, sales tax has been the most important. However, this tax has been now replaced by Value Added Tax (VAT).
- Corporation Tax is the major source of central government revenue.

- Like all other countries, tendency of income tax is progressive in India.
- The Laffer Effect which implies that a reduction in the rate of taxation leads to more than proportionate increase in tax yield.
- In India, the base of income tax is very narrow.
- Minimum Alternative Tax—MAT has been levying on companies.
- Estate Duty was first introduced in India in 1953. It was levied on total property passing on the death of a person. The whole property of the deceased constituted the estate and was considered liable to pay estate duty. Hence, the central government decided to abolish it with effect from April 1, 1985.
- An Annual Tax on wealth was first introduced in May 1957 on the recommendations of Kaldor. It is levied on the excess of net wealth over exemption of individuals, joint Hindu families and companies.
- Excise duties on commodities other than alcoholic liquors and narcotics are levied by the central government.
- The state have exclusive jurisdiction over the excise duties on alcohol and narcotics.
- Service tax was introduced in 1994-95 in a small way to operationalise the principle of neutrality of the tax system to different forms of production and in recognition of the fact that value additions whether in manufacturing or service should form the basis of taxation.
- VAT (Value Added Tax) seeks to tax the value added at every stage of manufacturing and sale, with a provision of refunding the amount of VAT already paid at earlier stages to avoid double taxation. In other words, the tax already paid can be claimed at the next stage of value addition.
- Following the June 18, 2004 decision of the Empowered Committee of State Finance Ministers to implement state-level VAT from April 1, 2005, all states/UTs had introduced VAT to replace the sales tax by December 31, 2005.
- Haryana was the first state to introduce VAT in 2003.
- MODVAT, was introduced in budget of 1986-87.
- Nobel Prize recipient Prof. James Tobin had suggested in 1978 to impose a tax on all transactions in Foreign Money Markets. Tobin was of the opinion that most of transactions of foreign currencies are for speculation and arbitrage benefits which can be used for mobilising enough resources by imposing a tax. This suggested tax was given a name of 'Tobin Tax'.
- CENVAT, was introduced at first in budget of 2000-01.
- Performance Budgetting is generally understood as a system of presentation of public expenditure in terms of functions, programmes, performance units, viz; activities, projects, etc., reflecting primarily the government output and its cost. At first it adopted by USA federal government in 1951.
- Zero-base budgeting (ZBB) is an innovative technique to guard against wastage in public expenditure. The technique works not through auditing which is a post-operative check, but through an examination of the very rational of ar expenditure item under consideration.
- In the sphere of public budgeting, ZBB was first tried by Mr. Jimmy Carter in 1973 when he was the Governor of Georgia, Later on it was adopted by a number of states in the USA.
- GST full form is Good and Services Tax in India. GST applies throughout India and is indirect tax. Moreover from now on GST replaces many taxes. Generally state and central Governments levy taxes. But after may meetings, Finance Minister of India and Indian Government Introduced GST on July 1, 2017. Government of India introduced Goods and Services Tax as the Costitution Act 2017.
- Finance Commission is constituted to define financial relations between the Centre and the States. Under the provision of Article 280(1) of the constitution, the President appoints a Finance Commission for the specific purpose of devolution of non-plan revenue resources.

Finance Commission: At a Glance

Finance Commission	*Chairman*	*Operational Duration*
I	K.C. Niyogi	1952-57
II	K. Santhanam	1957-62
III	A.K. Chanda	1962-66
IV	P.V. Rajamannar	1966-69
V	Mahaveer Tyagi	1969-74
VI	Brahma Nand Reddy	1974-79
VII	J.M. Shellet	1979-84
VIII	Y.B. Chawan	1984-89
IX	N.K.P. Salve	1989-95
X	K.C. Pant	1995-00
XI	A.M. Khusro	2000-05
XII	Dr. C. Rangrajan	2005-10
XIII	V.L. Kelkar	2010-15
XIV	Y.V. Reddy	2015-20
XV	N.K. Singh	2020-26
XVI	Arvind Panagariya	2026-31

Various Types of Deficits of the Central Government

- Budget may take a shape of deficit when the public revenue falls short to public expenditure. Budget deficit is the difference between the estimated public expenditure and public revenue. The government meets this deficit by way of printing new currency or by borrowing. Some types of deficits are as follows:
- **Revenue Deficits:** Revenue Deficit = Revenue Expenditure – Revenue Receipts

  Current revenue expenditure of the central government is composed of plan and non-plan expenditure, and current-revenue receipts include net tax revenue and non-tax revenue of the central government.
- **Budget Deficit:** Budget Deficit = Total Expenditure – Total Receipts

  The total expenditure of the central governments always exceeded its total revenue which is known as budget deficit or overall budgetary deficit.
- **Fiscal Deficit:** In simple terms, fiscal deficit is budgetary deficit plus market borrowings and other liabilities of the government of India.

  ∴ Fiscal Deficit = Revenue receipts (Net tax revenue + Non-tax revenue) + Capital receipts (only recoveries of loans and other receipts)– Total expenditure (Plan and non-plan)
- **Primary Deficit:** The excess of fiscal deficit over payments of interest is called primary deficit.
- **Monetised Deficit:** The increase in net RBI credit for central government is called monetised deficit. It includes:

  A. Net increase in holdings of treasury bills of RBI.

  B. Contribution of RBI in market borrowings of the govt.

Important Committees: At a Glance

Committees	Constituted Year	Related Area
• Hanumant Rao Committee	*28 January, 1997*	Fertilisers
• Mahajan Committee	*March 1997*	Sugar Industry
• R.V. Gupta Committee	*December 1997*	Agriculture Credit
• Narsimham Committee (Second)	*1997*	Banking Reforms
• Khan Working Group	*1998*	Development Finance Institutions
• Chandrate Committee	*Feb. 1997*	Delisting in Share Market
• UK Sharma Committee	*January 1998*	NABARD's role in RRB
• Ajit Kumar Committee	*December 1997*	Army Pay Scales
• CB Bhave Committee	*October 27, 1997*	Company Information
• NN Vohra Committee	*September 8, 1997*	Relations of Politicians with Criminals
• Bimal Julka Committee	—	Working Conditions ATCOS
• Dhanuka Committee	—	Simplification of Transfer Rules in Securities Market
• C. Babu Rajeev Committee	—	Reforming Ship Act, 1908 and Ship Trust Act, 1963.

Committees	Constituted Year	Related Area
• S.L. Kapoor Committee	December 1997	Credit & Flow Problems of SSIs
• Dave Committee	2000	Pension Scheme for Unorganised Sector
• Mashelkar Committee	Jan. 2002	Auto Fuel Policy
• S.N. Verma Committee	1999	Restructuring the Commercial Banks
• Y.B. Reddy Committee	Oct. 2001	Review of Income Tax Rebates
• Bhurelal Committee	—	Increase in Motor Vehicle Tax
• Sapta Rishi Committee	July 2002	Development of Domestic Tea Industry
• Abhijit Sen Committee	July 2002	Long Term Food Policy
• Kelkar Committee	—	Tax Structure Reforms
• J.J. Irani Committee	—	Company Law Reforms
• Parekh Committee	—	Infrastructure Financing

International Organisation: At a Glance

Organisation	Establishment Year	Head quarter	Important Features
1. IMF and IBRD	1945	Washington D.C.	IBRD, IFC, IDA, MIGA are associate institutions of World Bank. Initially IBRD was constituted in 1945. IFC and IDA were established in 1956 and 1960 respectively
2. European Union	Changed form of EEC Established in 1958	Brussels	18 nations have accepted to circulate a common 'EURO' currency since January 1, 1999 (10 nations joined the EU since May 1, 2004)
3. OPEC	1960	Vienna (Austria)	—
4. OECD	1961	Paris	Changed name of OEEC established in 1948
5. ADB	1966	Manila	—
6. ASEAN	1967	Jakarta	Indonesia, Philippines, Malaysia, Singapore, Thailand, Brunei, Vietnam, Laos, Myanmar and Combodia.
7. ACU	1975	Tehran	India, Pakistan, Bangladesh, Nepal, Sri Lanka, Iran, Myanmar, Bhutan and Maldives
8. SAARC	1985	Kathmandu	India, Pakistan, Bhutan, Bangladesh, Sri Lanka, Nepal, Maldives and Afghanistan. SAARC nations started SAPTA since December 7, 1995, but since January 1, 2006 SAPTA has been replaced by SAFTA.
9. G-15	1989	Geneva	A group of 17 developing countries
10. APEC	1989	—	APEC declared to convert Asia pacific region into free trade zone by 2020 A.D. which will be the largest free trade area of the world.
11. NAFTA	1992	—	USA, Canada and Mexico
12. WTO	1995	Geneva	
13. Mercosur	1995	—	Brazil, Argentina, Paraguay, Uruguay & Venezuela (Free trade zone of south American region)
14. ASEM	1996	—	27 countries of EU, 10 from ASEAN, and 8 other countries including Japan, South Korea and China
15. BRICS	2014	Shanghai China	Brazil, Russia, India, China, South Africa, Argentina, Egypt, Ethiopia, Iran, Saudi Arabia and UAE.

EXERCISE

1. Which state has maximum branches of public sector commercial banks?
A. U.P. B. Maharashtra
C. Karnataka D. Gujarat

2. In which plan phase of industrialisation was initiated?
A. Fourth B. Third
C. Second D. First

3. Which is the first Export Processing Zone declared as Free Trade Zone in India?
A. Santacruz B. Kandla
C. Falta D. Noida

4. Which institution is known as 'soft loan window' of World Bank?
A. IFC
B. IDA
C. IMF
D. Indian Development Forum

5. 'Backwash Effect' was firstly introduced by—
A. Gunnar Myrdal B. Peter Suderland
C. Arthur Dunkel D. Kindelberger

6. Meera Seth Committee was related to—
A. Development of Handlooms
B. Sex-differentiation in employment
C. Abolition of Child Labour
D. Welfare of working women

7. Finance Commission is appointed by the President under Article—
A. 256 of constitution
B. 280 of constitution
C. 293 of constitution
D. 356 of constitution

8. 'SAPTA' is related to—
A. Education B. Trade
C. Security D. Environment

9. National Income estimates in India is prepared by—
A. Planning Commission
B. RBI
C. Finance Ministry
D. C.S.O.

10. Scheduled bank is that bank which is—
A. Nationalised
B. Not–nationalised
C. Based at foreign country
D. Included in the second schedule of R.B.F

11. The definition of small scale industry in India is based on—
A. Sales of a unit
B. Investment in machines and equipment
C. Market coverage
D. Export capacity

12. Which one of the following committees was set up to review the concept of poverty line?
A. S. Chakravarty Committee
B. K.N. Wanchoo Committee
C. D.T. Lakdawala Committee
D. R.C. Dutt Committee

13. Which one of the folloiwng is not the canon of taxation as stated by Adam Smith?
A. Canon of productivity
B. Canon of convenience
C. Canon of certainty
D. None of these

14. According to 2011 census the state having highest urban population is—
A. U.P. B. Maharashtra
C. Tamil Nadu D. Kerala

15. Which place India holds in milk production?
A. Fourth B. Third
C. Second D. First

16. Who is the chairman of Island Development Authority?
A. President B. Prime Minister
C. Home Minister D. Planning Minister

17. The book 'Politics with Charkha' is written by—
A. Ashok Mehta B. J.B. Kriplani
C. K.G. Mashruwala D. Morarji Desai

18. The base year of the present Wholesale Price Index (WPI) is—
A. 2011-12 B. 1971-72
C. 1980-81 D. 1981-82

19. The base year of present Consumer Price Index (CPI) for industrial labourers is—
A. 2016 B. 2014
C. 2015 D. 2012

20. CAPART is related with—
A. Assisting and evaluating rural welfare programmes
B. Computer hardware
C. Consultant service of export promotion
D. Controlling pollution in big industries

21. Note issuing deptt. of RBI should always possess the minimum gold stock of worth—
A. ₹ 85 crores B. ₹ 115 crores
C. ₹ 200 crores D. None of these

22. Which of the following does not grant any tax rebate?
A. National Saving Certificate
B. Indira Vikas Patra
C. National Saving Scheme
D. Public Provident Fund

23. 13th Finance Commission was constituted under the chairmanship of—
A. C. Rangrajan
B. V.L. Kelkar
C. K.C. Pant
D. None of these

24. SEBI was established in—
A. 1993 B. 1992
C. 1988 D. 1990

25. The working of SEBI includes—
A. To regulate the dealings of share market
B. To check the foul dealings in share market
C. To control the inside trading of shares
D. All of these

26. The "Ad hoc Treasury Bill System" of meeting budget deficit in India was replaced by 'Ways and means Advances System' which has come into force on—
A. March 31, 1997 B. April 1, 1996
C. April 1, 1997 D. None of these

27. Asian Development Bank has opened its Residential Office in—
A. New Delhi B. Kolkata
C. Mumbai D. Bangalore

28. Which statement of the following is true for IMF?
A. It is not an agency of UNO
B. It can grant loan to any country of the world
C. It can grant loan to state Govt. of a country
D. It grants loan only to member nations

29. Chairman of Tax Reform Committee was—
A. Pranab Mukherjee B. K.P. Narsimham
C. S. Janakiraman D. Raja Chelliah

30. Which of the following is public sector organisation?
1. FCI Food Corporation of India
2. FCI Fertilizer Corporation of India
3. Cotton Corporation of India
4. Jute Corporation of India
A. only 1 and 2 B. only 2, 3
C. only 3, 4 D. All of these

31. Find the odd one out—
A. SAIL B. BHEL
C. ONGC D. ESSAR OIL

32. SAIL was established in—
A. 1974 B. 1984
C. 1990 D. 1964

33. Rural women can avail the benefit of Mahila Samriddhi Yojana if they open their account in–
A. Rural Post Offices
B. Commercial Banks
C. Rural Development Bank
D. Any of the above

34. Pradhan Mantri Gram Sadak Yojana (PMGSY) was launched in—
A. 2000 B. 1999
C. 2001 D. 2004

35. The Headquarter of CAPART is situated at—
A. Mumbai B. Kolkata
C. New Delhi D. Bangalore

36. The main security guard of International Trade is–
A. IMF B. World Bank
C. WTO D. IFC

37. Which is true for existing Economic and Industrial Policies of Indian Govt?
1. FERA was abolished
2. MRTP was abolished

3. Cash compensatory support for exports was abolished
4. Industrial licensing (except a few goods) was abolished

A. 1, 2, 3 and 4 B. 1, 3 and 4
C. only 3 and 4 D. only 2 and 3

38. Cheque which is crossed can be encashed only—
A. Through SBI B. Through the payee
C. Through any bank D. None of these

39. Post office funds will now be managed in capital market by—
A. Unit Trust of India Mutual Fund
B. SBI Mutual Fund
C. LIC Mutual Fund
D. Both (A) and (B)

40. One major proposal of New Industrial Policy (1991) was—
A. NRIs will not be allowed for capital investment in India
B. All types of industries have been made licence free
C. Import restrictions of technical know-how for one year
D. Facility of direct foreign investment upto 51% in high priority industries.

41. 'Closed Economy' is that economy in which—
A. Only export takes place
B. Money supply is fully controlled
C. Deficit financing takes place
D. Neither export nor import takes place

42. Which one of the following method is not used by N.S.S.O. for the measurement of unemployment in India?
A. Current Monthly Status
B. Current Weekly Status
C. Current Daily Status
D. Usual Principal Status

43. National Rural Development Institute is situated at—
A. Shimla B. Hyderabad
C. Patna D. New Delhi

44. Which of the following have/has not been included in wealth of a nation?
A. Mines B. Dams
C. Money Supply D. Animals

45. Which statement of the following is false (according to literacy data of 2011 census)?
A. Literacy rate was calculated among people having age 6 years or above
B. During 2001-2011, the number of literate population increased
C. Indian literacy rate was estimated to be 73%
D. Kerala was cent-per cent literate state

46. The Headquarter of World Bank is situated at—
A. Manila B. Washington D.C.
C. New York D. Geneva

47. Which state has a lower literacy rate than country's literacy rate according to 2011 census?
A. Maharashtra B. Gujarat
C. Orissa D. West Bengal

48. According to 2011 census, Indian Population was—
A. 98.7 crore B. 100.0 crore
C. 121.08 crore D. 105.7 crore

49. Which pair is not correct?
A. EXIM Bank—Financing for export-import
B. RBI—Banker's bank
C. IDBI—Industrial finance
D. FCI—Financial assistance to commercial institutions

50. Which of the rate is not determined by RBI?
A. Bank Rate B. CRR
C. SLR D. PLR

51. Which of the following controls the working of share market in India?
A. MRTP Act B. FERA
C. BIFR D. SEBI

52. The main foodgrains of India is—
A. Rice B. Wheat
C. Sugarcane D. Maize

53. Which rank India attains in tobacco production in the world?
A. First B. Sixth
C. Second D. Fourth

54. Which district of Hindi speaking belt has firstly been declared as fully literate?
A. Narsinghpur (M.P.)
B. Palampur (H.P.)

C. Jhunjhanu (Rajasthan)
D. Palamu (Jharkhand)

55. Which sector has the maximum quantum of disguised unemployment in India?
A. Agriculture B. Industry
C. Trade D. Transport

56. 'Food for work programme' was renamed as—
A. RLEGP B. IRDP
C. NREP D. MNP

57. The proportion of rainfed agriculture to the net sown area in India is about—
A. 45% B. 75%
C. 50% D. 60%

58. India has emerged in the world as the
A. Second Largest Steel Producer
B. Fourth Largest Steel Producer
C. Third Largest Steel Producer
D. None of these

59. Who is the ex-officio chairman of 'National Child Labour Abolition Authority'?
A. Prime Minister
B. Industry Minister
C. Social Welfare Minister
D. Labour Minister

60. Employees State Insurance Scheme in India was introduced in—
A. 1947 B. 1952
C. 1955 D. 1972

61. The goods can be taxed heavily to earn additional revenue if they are—
A. Highly elastic B. Unit elastic
C. Perfectly elastic D. Inelastic

62. Scheduled Bank is that bank which is—
A. Nationalised
B. Not nationalised
C. Based at foreign country
D. Included in the second schedule of RBI

63. For which type of fertilizer India is fully dependent on imports?
A. Nitrogen Fertilizer
B. Phosphetic Fertilizer
C. Potash Fertilizer
D. None of these

64. Which Union Territory ensured Lowest Population in 2011 census?
A. Delhi B. Chandigarh
C. Puducherry D. Lakshadweep

65. The Headquarter of Asian Development Bank (ADB) is at—
A. Singapore B. Manila
C. Hong Kong D. Tokyo

66. Match the following—

List-I	List-II
(*a*) Aquaculture	1. Silk
(*b*) Floriculture	2. Grapes
(*c*) Sericulture	3. Flower
(*d*) Viticulture	4. Fisheries

	A	B	C	D
A.	4	3	2	1
B.	3	4	1	2
C.	3	4	2	1
D.	4	3	1	2

67. The CSO has changed the base year for national income estimates. The new base year is—
A. 1990-91 B. 2011-2012
C. 1994-95 D. 1995-96

68. The Ex-officio Secretary of NDC is—
A. Secretary of Finance Ministry
B. General Secretary of Lok Sabha
C. Secretary of Planning Commission
D. Vice-Chairman of Planning Commission

69. India's National Hydroelectric Power corporation is establishing 'Tamarthi Power Project' in—
A. Bangladesh B. Bhutan
C. Myanmar D. Nepal

70. 'Hydro carbon Vision-2025' is associated with—
A. Storage of petroleum products
B. Euro-I & Euro II
C. Green house effect
D. None of these

71. Which state possesses the maximum percentage of SC population?
A. U.P. B. M.P.
C. Kerala D. Punjab

72. Which country is not the member of IMF?
A. Russia B. Uzbekistan
C. India D. None of these

73. What is 'NIKKEI'?
A. Share Price Index of Tokyo Share Market
B. Name of Japanese Central Bank
C. Japanese name of Country's Planning Commission
D. Foreign Exchange Market of Japan

74. Which statement is correct for Indian Planning Commission?
A. It is not defined in Indian Constitution
B. Members and Vice-Chairman of it do not have fixed working duration
C. Members do not require any minimum education
D. All of these

75. The GST council has decided to fix GST rate structure of ....
A. Two tier B. Three tier
C. Five tier D. Four tier

76. Who is the Chairman of NDC?
A. Finance Minister B. Prime Minister
C. Planning Minister D. Lok Sabha Speaker

77. NABARD was established on the recommendation of—
A. Public Account Committee
B. Shivaraman Committee
C. Narsimham Committee
D. None of these

78. The Chairman of 10th Finance Commission was–
A. Pranab Mukherjee B. K.C. Pant
C. Mohan Dharia D. Man Mohan Singh

79. The field given to Rangarajan Committee was—
A. Modernisation of Cloth Industry
B. To probe Share scam
C. To probe Sugar scam
D. To suggest measures for controlling BOP deficit

80. VAT is imposed—
A. Directly on consumer
B. On final stage of production
C. On first stage of production
D. On all stages between production and final sale

81. Kutir Jyoti scheme is associated with—
A. Promoting cottage industry in villages
B. Promoting employment among rural unemployed youth
C. Providing electricity to rural families living below the poverty line
D. All of these

82. The Headquarter of 'Economic and Social Commission for Asia and Pacific' is at—
A. Singapore B. Bangkok
C. Manila D. Hong Kong

83. OTCEI is—
A. Atomic submarine of China
B. Economic policy of USA
C. An Indian Share Market
D. A defence research organisation

84. Which is the most liquid measure of money supply?
A. M_1 B. M_2
C. M_3 D. M_4

85. M_3 measure of money supply does not include—
A. Cash with public
B. Demand deposits with Post offices
C. Demand deposits with Banks
D. Time deposits with Banks

86. Which public sector enterprise has become the largest from annual sales point of view?
A. BHEL B. SAIL
C. IOCL D. Coal India Ltd

87. NITI Aayog was constituted in—
A. 1948 B. 1949
C. 2015 D. 1951

88. Which of the following represents the correct combination of sex-ratio in India in 1951 and 2011?
A. 941, 933 B. 946, 943
C. 946, 927 D. 972, 933

89. Gresham's Law is related to—
A. Consumption and Demand
B. Supply and Demand
C. Circulation of Money
D. Deficit Financing

90. TRYSEM was—
A. a modern technique of agriculture produc-tion
B. a code used in space science
C. a programme to train rural youth for self employment
D. none of these

91. Kelkar committee report is related on—
A. Tax Reforms
B. Financial Sector Reforms
C. Trade Reforms
D. Administrative Reforms

92. The process of budget making after re-evaluating every item of expenditure in every financial year is known as—
A. Performance Budgeting
B. Deficit Budgeting
C. Zero Based Budgeting
D. Fresh Budgeting

93. Which place India holds in milk production?
A. Fourth B. Third
C. Second D. First

94. In which production India has attained self-sufficiency?
A. Fertilizers B. Foodgrains
C. Edible oil D. Petroleum

95. What is 'Super 301'?
A. A name of modern computer
B. A new variety of Rice
C. American trade law
D. American treatment name for Aids

96. If the capital stock is always stable, its depreciation will be—
A. High B. Low
C. Zero D. Infinite

97. The proportion of labour in GNP becomes low, due to the following reason—
A. Wages lag behind prices
B. Prices lag behind wages
C. Profit lags behind prices
D. Prices lag behind profit

98. When development in economy takes place the share of tertiary sector in National Income?
A. Declines
B. Increases
C. Remains constant
D. First rises and then falls

99. Which country among following is relatively more industrialised?
A. Bangladesh B. Thailand
C. India D. Pakistan

100. Plan expenditure in India is met by—
A. Internal debt and other resources
B. Assistance from Aid India Club
C. Assistance from IMF
D. Assistance from OECD countries

101. National Income in India is estimated by—
A. NITI Aayog
B. Finance Commission
C. Indian Statistical Institute
D. Central Statistical Organisation

102. Population Density means—
A. No. of persons living per sq. km.
B. No. of persons living per kilometre
C. Ratio of population living below poverty line to total population
D. No. of persons in a village

103. Which tax is collected by Panchayat?
A. Sales Tax B. Custom Duty
C. Land Revenue D. Tax on local fairs

104. Centralised planning was first adopted in the economy of—
A. Russia B. Poland
C. China D. India

105. Which Indian plan ensured high growth rate as compared with targetted growth rate?
A. Fifth Plan B. Fourth Plan
C. Second Plan D. Eighth Plan

106. Which among the following states is a leading industrialised state?
A. West Bengal B. Orissa
C. Maharashtra D. Madhya Pradesh

107. The first fully literate district outside the Kerala State is—
A. Wardhaman (West Bengal)
B. Chingelpattu (Tamil Nadu)
C. Nasik (Maharashtra)
D. Merkata (Karnataka)

108. The Headquarter of IMF is in—
A. New York B. Washington D.C.
C. London D. Manila

109. Which committee recommended tax on Agriculture Holdings?
A. Bhootlingam Committee
B. Wanchoo Committee
C. Raj Committee
D. None of these

110. Which bank in India performs duties of Central Bank?
A. Central Bank of India
B. State Bank of India
C. Reserve Bank of India
D. Both (A) and (B)

111. Which part of separated UTI is under SEBI's regulation?
A. UTI-I B. UTI-II
C. Both the above D. None of these

112. Mixed Economy means—
A. Co-existence of small and large industries
B. Promoting both Agriculture and Industries in the economy
C. Co-existence of public and private sectors
D. Co-existence of rich and poor

113. Which statement of the following is true regarding India's foreign trade over past three years?
A. Imports declined
B. Exports declined
C. Imports declined but exports increased
D. Both import and export increased

114. Foreign currency which has a tendency of quick migration is called—
A. Scarce currency B. Soft currency
C. Gold currency D. Hot currency

115. Indian State having the lowest Infant Mortality Rate is—
A. Maharashtra B. Goa
C. Gujarat D. Kerala

116. Which state in India has largest area under production of food grains?
A. Punjab B. Uttar Pradesh
C. West Bengal D. Andhra Pradesh

117. The main objective of TRYSEM was—
A. To train rural youth for self employment
B. To train urban youth for self employment
C. Both of the above
D. None of these

118. Inside Trading is related to—
A. Share Market B. Horse racing
C. Taxation D. Public Expenditure

119. The largest source of National Income in India is:
A. Service Sector B. Agriculture
C. Industrial Sector D. Trade Sector

120. 'Public Sector' means—
A. Government ownership on commerce and trade
B. Capitalist ownership on commerce and trade
C. Private ownership on trade
D. None of these

121. NABARD is—
A. A bank B. A board
C. A block D. A department

122. Indian Green Revolution is the most successful in—
A. Wheat and Potato B. Jwar and Oil Seeds
C. Wheat and Rice D. Tea and Coffee

123. The period of 12th plan in India is—
A. 2000-2005 B. 2001-2006
C. 2012-2017 D. 2003-2008

124. Economic Planning is in—
A. Union list B. State list
C. Concurrent list D. Not any specified list

125. Indian Banks have the maximum foreign branches in—
A. Bangladesh B. U.K.
C. USA D. Sri Lanka

126. Which types of tax helps in reducing disparities of income?
A. Proportionate tax B. Progressive tax
C. Regressive tax D. All of these

127. Which Bank is limited to the needs of agriculture and rural finance?
A. SBI B. IFC
C. NABARD D. RBI

128. 'Golden Handshake Scheme' is associated with—
A. Inviting foreign companies
B. Private investment in public enterprises
C. Establishing joint enterprises
D. Voluntary retirement

129. Which state has the lowest women literary rate in India (2011 census)?
A. Bihar B. Jharkhand
C. U.P. D. Rajasthan

130. Which country is the largest oil producing country of the world?
A. America B. Russia
C. Saudi Arabia D. None of these

131. Which is an indicator of economic under-development and backwardness?
A. High birth rate
B. High illeteracy
C. High pressure of population on agriculture
D. All of these

132. Which of the following took the decision of establishing 'South Asian Development Fund'?
A. ADB B. World Bank
C. SAARC D. IMF

133. MRTP Act was implemented since—
A. 1970 B. 1968
C. 1969 D. 1967

134. TRIPS-'Trade Related Intellectual Property Rights' and TRIMS-'Trade Related Investment Measures' are associated with—
A. Preston Proposal B. Dunkel Proposal
C. Chelliah Committee D. None of these

135. Which is true for Finance Commission?
A. It is a statutory body
B. It is constituted under article 280 of the constitution
C. Mr. K.C. Pant was Chairman of 10th Finance Commission
D. All of these

136. Which committee was constituted for reforms in tax-structure?
A. Narsimham Committee
B. Chelliah Committee
C. Gadgil Committee
D. Kelkar Committee

137. What is the CRR minimum limit for a commercial bank to be deposited with RBI?
A. 3% B. 10%
C. 5% D. 6%

138. Which is not a part of new economic reforms in India?
A. Globalisation B. Centralisation
C. Privatisation D. Liberalisation

139. The official exchange rate of Indian rupee is associated with
A. Pound Sterling
B. Dollar
C. SDR
D. A basket of selected currencies

140. As a result of Green Revolution which foodgrains had a reduced percentage in total foodgrain production?
A. Wheat B. Rice
C. Cereals and Pulses D. None of these

141. Which sector constitutes the maximum share in National Income of India?
A. Primary
B. Secondary
C. Tertiary
D. All the above have equal share

142. Corporate Tax is imposed by—
A. State Government
B. Local Government
C. Central Government
D. Both Centre and State Government

143. The First Finance Commission was constituted in the year—
A. 1947 B. 1950
C. 1951 D. 1952

144. Who has not yet been appointed Chairman of Finance Commission among the following?
A. Amrish Baghchi B. Mahaveer Tyagi
C. N.K.P. Salve D. Brahmanand Reddy

145. MRTP is related to—
A. Monopoly and trade restrictions
B. Inflation control
C. Transport control
D. Foreign Exchange Regulations

146. The basis of determining dearness allowance to employee in India is—
A. National Income
B. Consumer Price Index
C. Standard of Living
D. Per Capita Income

147. The State having the highest literacy rate among woman in India is—
A. Tamil Nadu B. Kerala
C. West Bengal D. Maharashtra

148. IRDP was introduced in the year—
A. 1978-79 B. 1979-80
C. 1980-81 D. 1981-82

149. The industry having the largest investment in Indian Economy is—

A. Tea B. Cement
C. Steel D. Jute

150. The maximum outlay was proposed in 9th plan (among public sectors) in—
A. Agriculture Sector
B. Transport Sector
C. Energy Sector
D. Communications Sector

151. The outlines of second five year plan was made by—
A. B.N. Gadgil B. VKRV Rao
C. P.C. Mahalanobis D. C.N. Vakil

152. The main aim of fifth five year plan was—
A. Poverty elimination B. Self dependence
C. Both the above D. None of these

153. NABARD was established in—
A. Fourth Plan B. Fifth Plan
C. Sixth Plan D. Eighth Plan

154. The first type of co-operative societies established in India was—
A. Credit Societies B. Marketing Societies
C. Agriculture Societies D. Housing Societies

155. Which currency has got the highest value when compared with Indian Rupee?
A. Marc B. Yen
C. Rial D. Pound sterling

156. The State with the second largest population in India is—
A. Uttar Pradesh B. Bihar
C. West Bengal D. Maharashtra

157. Dalal street is situated at—
A. London B. Paris
C. Mumbai D. New Delhi

158. RBI was nationalised in—
A. 1959 B. 1947
C. 1945 D. 1949

159. R.N. Malhotra committee gave recommendations on the field of—
A. Sick Industries B. Tax Reforms
C. Insurance Sector D. Banking Sector

160. India is not a member of—
A. G-15 B. UNO
C. ASEAN D. Commonwealth

161. Which states have not yet established any RRB?
A. Sikkim and Goa
B. Bihar and Rajasthan
C. Sikkim and Arunachal Pradesh
D. Nagaland

162. On the recommendations of Kelkar committee, no new RRB was established since—
A. April 1987 B. April 1988
C. April 1989 D. April 1990

163. IRBI—Industrial Reconstruction Bank of India was established in—
A. 1975 B. 1985
C. 1990 D. 1992

164. The headquarter of SIDBI is in—
A. Lucknow B. New Delhi
C. Mumbai D. Bangalore

165. LIC of India was established in—
A. 1897 B. 1950
C. 1956 D. 1965

166. Consumer Protection Act (COPRA) was implemended in—
A. 1985 B. 1986
C. 1987 D. 1988

167. Narsimham committee recommended to make banking structure of the country—
A. Two tier B. Three tier
C. Four tier D. Five tier

168. 'Canfina' is associated with—
A. Canara Bank
B. SBI
C. National Housing Bank
D. Standard Chartered Bank

169. Inside Trading is related to—
A. Share Market B. Horse Market
C. Taxation D. Public Expenditure

170. Grameen Bank and Micro Credit are associated with—
A. Manmohan Singh B. Bill Gates
C. Md. Yunus D. Aung San Su Ki

171. 20 rupee and above value notes are printed in—
A. Currency Note Press, Nasik Road
B. Bank Note Press, Dewas
C. Security Printing Press, Hyderabad
D. All of these

172. Central Revenue Board was divided into 'Central Excise and Custom Duty Board' and 'Central Direct Tax Board' in—

A. 1950 B. 1958

C. 1963 D. 1975

173. Which direct tax gives maximum net revenue to the Government—

A. Corporate Tax B. Income Tax

C. Wealth Tax D. Gift Tax

174. The view that 'Planning in India should, in future, pay more attention to the people than to commodities' was given by—

A. Amartya Sen B. Yashwant Sinha

C. A.B. Vajpayee D. None of these

175. Operation Flood programme was introduced in—

A. 1951 B. 1970

C. 1975 D. 1985

ANSWERS

1	**2**	**3**	**4**	**5**	**6**	**7**	**8**	**9**	**10**
A	C	A	B	A	A	B	B	D	D
11	**12**	**13**	**14**	**15**	**16**	**17**	**18**	**19**	**20**
B	C	A	B	D	B	B	A	A	A
21	**22**	**23**	**24**	**25**	**26**	**27**	**28**	**29**	**30**
B	B	B	C	D	C	A	D	D	D
31	**32**	**33**	**34**	**35**	**36**	**37**	**38**	**39**	**40**
D	A	A	A	C	C	C	C	D	D
41	**42**	**43**	**44**	**45**	**46**	**47**	**48**	**49**	**50**
D	D	B	C	D	B	C	C	D	D
51	**52**	**53**	**54**	**55**	**56**	**57**	**58**	**59**	**60**
D	A	C	A	A	C	D	B	D	B
61	**62**	**63**	**64**	**65**	**66**	**67**	**68**	**69**	**70**
D	D	C	D	B	D	B	C	B	A
71	**72**	**73**	**74**	**75**	**76**	**77**	**78**	**79**	**80**
D	D	A	D	D	B	B	B	D	D
81	**82**	**83**	**84**	**85**	**86**	**87**	**88**	**89**	**90**
C	B	C	A	B	C	C	B	C	C
91	**92**	**93**	**94**	**95**	**96**	**97**	**98**	**99**	**100**
A	C	D	B	C	C	A	B	B	A
101	**102**	**103**	**104**	**105**	**106**	**107**	**108**	**109**	**110**
D	A	D	A	D	C	A	B	C	C
111	**112**	**113**	**114**	**115**	**116**	**117**	**118**	**119**	**120**
B	C	D	D	D	B	A	A	A	A
121	**122**	**123**	**124**	**125**	**126**	**127**	**128**	**129**	**130**
A	C	C	C	B	B	C	D	A	C
131	**132**	**133**	**134**	**135**	**136**	**137**	**138**	**139**	**140**
D	C	A	B	D	B	A	B	D	C
141	**142**	**143**	**144**	**145**	**146**	**147**	**148**	**149**	**150**
C	C	C	A	A	B	B	A	C	C
151	**152**	**153**	**154**	**155**	**156**	**157**	**158**	**159**	**160**
C	C	C	A	D	D	C	D	C	C
161	**162**	**163**	**164**	**165**	**166**	**167**	**168**	**169**	**170**
A	A	B	A	C	B	C	A	A	C
171	**172**	**173**	**174**	**175**					
B	C	A	A	B					